Lecture Notes in Computer Science 3089

Commenced Publication in 1973
Founding and Former Series Editors:
Gerhard Goos, Juris Hartmanis, and Jan van Leeuwen

Springer
Berlin
Heidelberg
New York
Hong Kong
London
Milan
Paris
Tokyo

Markus Jakobsson   Moti Yung
Jianying Zhou (Eds.)

Applied Cryptography and Network Security

Second International Conference, ACNS 2004
Yellow Mountain, China, June 8-11, 2004
Proceedings

 Springer

Volume Editors

Markus Jakobsson
RSA Laboratories
1203 Garden Street, Hoboken, NJ 07030, USA
E-mail: mjakobsson@rsasecurity.com

Moti Yung
Columbia University, Computer Science Department
New York, NY 10027, USA
E-mail: moti@cs.columbia.edu

Jianying Zhou
Institute for Infocomm Research
21 Heng Mui Keng Terrace, Singapore 119613
E-mail: jyzhou@i2r.a-star.edu.sg

Library of Congress Control Number: 2004106759

CR Subject Classification (1998): E.3, C.2, D.4.6, H.3-4, K.4.4, K.6.5

ISSN 0302-9743
ISBN 3-540-22217-0 Springer-Verlag Berlin Heidelberg New York

Springer-Verlag is a part of Springer Science+Business Media

springeronline.com

© Springer-Verlag Berlin Heidelberg 2004
Printed in Germany

Typesetting: Camera-ready by author, data conversion by PTP-Berlin, Protago-TeX-Production GmbH
Printed on acid-free paper   SPIN: 11014096   06/3142   5 4 3 2 1 0

Preface

The second International Conference on Applied Cryptography and Network Security (ACNS 2004) was sponsored and organized by ICISA (the International Communications and Information Security Association). It was held in Yellow Mountain, China, June 8–11, 2004. The conference proceedings, representing papers from the academic track, are published in this volume of the Lecture Notes in Computer Science (LNCS) of Springer-Verlag.

The area of research that ACNS covers has been gaining importance in recent years due to the development of the Internet, which, in turn, implies global exposure of computing resources. Many fields of research were covered by the program of this track, presented in this proceedings volume. We feel that the papers herein indeed reflect the state of the art in security and cryptography research, worldwide.

The program committee of the conference received a total of 297 submissions from all over the world, of which 36 submissions were selected for presentation during the academic track. In addition to this track, the conference also hosted a technical/industrial track of presentations that were carefully selected as well. All submissions were reviewed by experts in the relevant areas.

Starting from the first ACNS conference last year, ACNS has given best paper awards. Last year the best student paper award went to a paper that turned out to be the only paper written by a single student for ACNS 2003. It was Kwong H. Yung who got the award for his paper entitled "Using Feedback to Improve Masquerade Detection." Continuing the "best paper tradition" this year, the committee decided to select two student papers among the many high-quality papers that were accepted for this conference, and to give them best student paper awards. These papers are: "Security Measurements of Steganographic Systems" by Weiming Zhang and Shiqu Li, and "Evaluating Security of Voting Schemes in the Universal Composability Framework" by Jens Groth. Both papers appear in this proceedings volume, and we would like to congratulate the recipients for their achievements.

Many people and organizations helped in making the conference a reality. We would like to take this opportunity to thank the program committee members and the external experts for their invaluable help in producing the conference's program. We also wish to thank Thomas Herlea of KU Leuven for his extraordinary efforts in helping us to manage the submissions and for taking care of all the technical aspects of the review process. Thomas, single-handedly, served as the technical support committee of this conference! We extend our thanks also to the general chair Jianying Zhou (who also served as publication chair and helped in many other ways), the chairs of the technical/industrial track (Yongfei Han and Peter Landrock), the local organizers, who worked hard to assure that the conference took place, and the publicity chairs. We also thank the various sponsoring companies and government bodies. Finally, we would like to thank all the authors who submitted papers to the conference.

April 2004   Markus Jakobsson and Moti Yung

ACNS 2004

Second International Conference on Applied Cryptography and Network Security

Yellow Mountain, China
June 8–11, 2004

Sponsored and organized by the

International Communications and Information Security Association (ICISA)

In co-operation with

MiAn Pte Ltd (ONETS), China
RSA Security Inc., USA
Ministry of Science and Technology, China
Yellow Mountain City Government, China

General Chair

Jianying Zhou .... Institute for Infocomm Research, Singapore

Program Chairs

Markus Jakobsson .... RSA Labs, USA
Moti Yung ....Columbia University, USA

Program Committee

Masayuki Abe ....NTT, Japan
N. Asokan .... Nokia, Finland
Feng Bao .... I2R, Singapore
Kijoon Chae .... Ewha Women's Univ., Korea
Ed Dawson ....QUT, Australia
Xiaotie Deng .... City Univ. of HK, China
Philippe Golle .... PARC, USA
Dieter Gollmann .... TU Hamburg, Germany
Goichiro Hanaoka ....Univ. of Tokyo, Japan
Els van Herreweghen ....IBM, Zurich
Chi-Sung Laih ....NCKU, Taiwan
Kwok-Yan Lam .... Tsinghua Univ., China
Heejo Lee .... Korea Univ., Korea

Pil Joong Lee .... Postech, Korea
Helger Lipmaa .... Helsinki Univ. of Tech., Finland
Javier Lopez .... Univ. of Malaga, Spain
Charanjit Jutla .... IBM T.J. Watson, USA
Hiroaki Kikuchi .... Univ. of Tokai, Japan
Kwangjo Kim .... Info. & Communication Univ., Korea
Wenbo Mao .... HP Labs, UK
David Naccache .... Gemplus, France
Chanathip Namprempre .... Thammasat U., Thailand
Phong Nguyen .... ENS, France
Adrian Perrig .... Carnegie Mellon Univ., USA
Josef Pieprzyk .... Macquarie University, Australia
Radha Poovendran .... Univ. of Washington, USA
Tomas Sander .... HP Labs, USA
Dawn Song .... Carnegie Mellon Univ., USA
Julien Stern .... Cryptolog International, France
Sal Stolfo .... Columbia Univ., USA
Michael Szydlo .... RSA Labs, USA
Wen-Guey Tzeng .... NCTU, Taiwan
Shouhuai Xu .... Univ. of Texas at San Antonio, USA
Bennet Yee .... Google, USA
Yuliang Zheng .... UNC Charlotte, USA

Chairs of Technical/Industrial Track
Yongfei Han .... ONETS, China
Peter Landrock .... Cryptomathic, Denmark

Publicity Chairs
Michael Szydlo .... RSA Labs, USA
Guilin Wang .... I2R, Singapore

Technical and Administrative Support
Thomas Herlea .... KU Leuven, Belgium
Li Xue .... ONETS, China

External Reviewers
Michel Abdalla, Nuttapong Attrapadung, Dan Bailey, Dirk Balfanz, Endre-
Felix Bangerter, Alexandra Boldyreva, Colin Boyd, Eric Brier, Julien Brou-
chier, Sonja Buchegger, Christian Cachin, Jan Camenisch, Cedric Cardon-
nel, Haowen Chan, Xiaofeng Chen, Benoît Chevallier-Mames, Hung Chim,
Jung-Hui Chiu, Jae-Gwi Choi, Chen-Kang Chu, Siu-Leung Chung, Andrew Clark, Scott Contini, Jean-Sébastien Coron, Yang Cui, Matthew Dailey,

Table of Contents

Security and Storage

Provably Secure Constructions

Internet Security

Digital Signature

CamouflageFS: Increasing the Effective Key Length in Cryptographic Filesystems on the Cheap

Michael E. Locasto and Angelos D. Keromytis

Department of Computer Science
Columbia University in the City of New York
{locasto,angelos}@cs.columbia.edu

Abstract. One of the few quantitative metrics used to evaluate the security of a cryptographic file system is the key length of the encryption algorithm; larger key lengths correspond to higher resistance to brute force and other types of attacks. Since accepted cryptographic design principles dictate that larger key lengths also impose higher processing costs, increasing the security of a cryptographic file system also increases the overhead of the underlying cipher.
We present a general approach to effectively extend the key length without imposing the concomitant processing overhead. Our scheme is to spread the ciphertext inside an artificially large file that is seemingly filled with random bits according to a key-driven spreading sequence. Our prototype implementation, *CamouflageFS*, offers improved performance relative to a cipher with a larger key-schedule, while providing the same security properties. We discuss our implementation (based on the Linux Ext2 file system) and present some preliminary performance results. While CamouflageFS is implemented as a stand-alone file system, its primary mechanisms can easily be integrated into existing cryptographic file systems.

*"Why couldn't I fill my hard drive with random bytes, so that individual files would not be discernible? Their very existence would be hidden in the noise, like a striped tiger in tall grass." –*Cryptonomicon, by Neal Stephenson [17]

1   Introduction

Cryptographic file systems provide data confidentiality by employing encryption to protect files against unauthorized access. Since encryption is an expensive operation, there is a trade-off between performance and security that a system designer must take into consideration. One factor that affects this balance is the key length of the underlying cipher: larger key lengths imply higher resistance against specific types of attacks, while at the same time requiring more rounds of processing to spread the influence of the key across all plaintext bit ("avalanche effect"). This is by no means a clear-cut comparison, however: different ciphers can exhibit radically different performance characteristics (*e.g.,* AES with 128 bit keys is faster than DES with 56 bit keys), and the security of a cipher is not simply encapsulated by its key length. However, given a well designed variable-key length cryptographic cipher, such as AES, the system designer or administrator is faced with the balance of performance *vs.* key length.

M. Jakobsson, M. Yung, J. Zhou (Eds.): ACNS 2004, LNCS 3089, pp. 1–15, 2004.

We are interested in reducing the performance penalty associated with using larger key sizes without decreasing the level of security. This goal is accomplished with a technique that is steganographic in nature; we camouflage the parts of the file that contain the encrypted data. Specifically, we use a spread-spectrum code to distribute the pointers in the file index block. We alter the operating system to intercept file requests made without an appropriate key and return data that is consistently random (*i.e.*, reading the same block will return the same "garbage"), without requiring that such data be stored on disk. This random data is indistinguishable from encrypted data. In this way, each file appears to be an opaque block of bits on the order of a terabyte. There is no need to actually fill the disk with random data, as done in [13], because the OS is responsible for generating this fake data on the fly. An attacker must mount a brute force attack not only against the underlying cipher, but also against the spreading sequence. In our prototype, this can increase an attacker's work factor by 2^{28} without noticeable performance loss for legitimate users.

1.1 Paper Organization

The remainder of this paper is organized as follows. In Section 2, we discuss our approach to the problem, examine the threat model, and provide a security analysis. In Section 3 we discuss in detail the implementation of CamouflageFS as a variant of the Linux Ext2fs, and Section 4 presents some preliminary performance measurements of the system. We give an overview of the related work on cryptographic and steganographic file systems in Section 5. We discuss our plans for future work in Section 6, and conclude the paper in Section 7.

2 Our Approach

Our primary insight is that a user may decrease the performance penalty they pay for employing a cryptographic file system by using only part of the key for cryptographic operations. The rest of the key may be used to unpredictably spread the data into the file's address space. Note that we are not necessarily fragmenting the placement of the data on disk, but rather mixing the placement of the data within the file.

2.1 Key Composition: Maintaining Confidentiality

While our goal is to mitigate the performance penalty paid for using a cryptographic file system, it is not advisable to trade confidentiality for performance. Instead, we argue that keys can be made effectively longer *without* incurring the usual performance penalty. One obvious method of reducing the performance penalty for encrypting files is to utilize a cipher with a shorter key length; however, there is a corresponding loss of confidentiality with a shorter key length. We address the tradeoff between key length and performance by extending the key with "spreading bits," and exploiting the properties of an indexed allocation file system.

A file system employing indexed allocation can efficiently address disk blocks for files approaching terabyte size. In practice, most files are much smaller than this and do

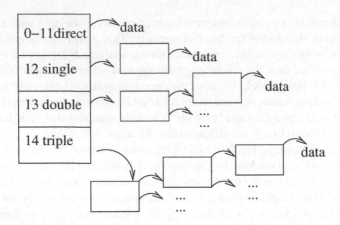

Fig. 1. Outline of a multi-level index scheme with triple-indirect addressing. The first 12 index entries point directly to 12 data blocks. The next three index entries are single, double, and triple indirect. Each indirect block contains 1024 entries: the first level can point to 1024 data blocks, the second level can point to 1024^*, and the third level points to 1024^* data blocks.

not use their full "address space." The Linux Ext2fs on 32-bit architectures commonly provides an address range of a few gigabytes to just short of two terabytes, depending on the block size, although accessing files larger than two gigabytes requires setting a flag when opening the file [4].

We use the extra bits of the cryptographic key to spread the file data throughout its address space and use the primary key material to encrypt that data. By combining this spreading function with random data for unallocated blocks, we prevent an attacker from knowing which blocks to perform a brute force search on. To maintain this illusion of a larger file without actually allocating it on disk, we return consistently random data on *read()* operations that are not accompanied by the proper cryptographic key.

2.2   Indexed Allocation

In a multi-level indexed allocation scheme, the operating system maintains an index of entries per file that can quickly address any given block of that file. In the Ext2 file system, this index contains fifteen entries (see Figure 1). The first twelve entries point directly to the first twelve blocks of the file. Assuming a block size of 4096 bytes, the first twelve entries of this index map to the first 48Kb of a file. The next three entries are all indirect pointers to sub-indices, with one layer of indirection, two layers of indirection, and three layers of indirection, respectively [4].

Figure 2 shows a somewhat simplified example of a single-level direct-mapped index. The file index points directly to blocks with plaintext data. Holes in the file may exist; reading data from such holes returns zeroed-out blocks, while writing in the holes causes a physical disk block to be allocated. Cryptographic file systems encrypt the stored data, which leaves the index structure identical but protects the contents of the data blocks, as shown in Figure 3.

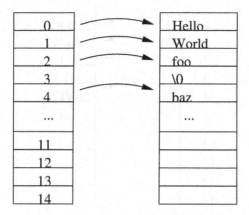

Fig. 2. File index for a normal data file. Pointers to plaintext data blocks are stored sequentially at the beginning of the index. Files may already contain *file holes* – this index has a hole at the third block position.

Usually, most files are small and do not need to expand beyond the first twelve direct mapped entries. This design allows the data in a small file to be retrieved in two disk accesses. However, retrieving data pointed to by entries of the sub-indices is not prohibitively expensive, especially in the presence of disk caches [4].

Therefore, instead of clustering the pointers to file data in the beginning entries of the index, we can distribute them throughout the index. In order for the operating system to reliably access the data in the file, we need some sequence of numbers to provide the *spreading schedule*, or which index entries point to the different blocks of the file. Figure 4 shows encrypted data that has been spread throughout the file's address space.

2.3   Spreading Schedule

The purpose of the *spreading schedule* is to randomly distribute the real file data throughout a large address space so that an attacker would have to first guess the spreading schedule before he attempts a brute force search on the rest of the key.

Normally, the number of the index entry is calculated by taking the floor of the current file position "pos" divided by the block size.

$$index = pos/blocksize$$

This index number is then used to derive the *logical block number* (the block on disk) where the data at "pos" resides.

$$lbn = get\_from\_index(index)$$

This procedure is altered to employ the spreading schedule. The initial calculation of the index is performed, but before the logical block number is derived, a pseudo-random permutation (PRP) function takes the calculated index and the bits of the spreading seed

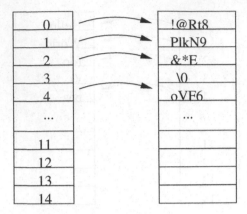

Fig. 3. Index for an encrypted file. The indexing has not changed, merely the contents of the data blocks. Again, the file hole at block three is present.

to return a new index value, without producing collisions. The logical block number is then derived from this new index.

$$index = pos/blocksize$$

$$index = map(index, spread\_seed)$$
$$lbn = get\_from\_index(index)$$

Note that the actual disk block is irrelevant; we are only interested in calculating a new entry in the file index, rather than using the strictly sequential ordering. Given the secret spreading seed bits of the key, this procedure will return consistent results. Therefore, using the same key will produce a consistent spreading schedule, and a legitimate user can easily retrieve and decrypt their data.

2.4   Consistent Garbage

The spreading schedule is useless without some mechanism to make the real encrypted data appear indistinguishable from unallocated data blocks. To accomplish this blending, camouflage data is generated by the operating system whenever a request is made on an index entry that points to unallocated disk space (essentially a file hole). Each CamouflageFS file will contain a number of file holes. Without the key, a request on any index entry will return random data. There is no way to determine if this data is encrypted without knowing the spreading schedule, because data encrypted by a strong cipher should appear to be random in its ciphertext form. We employ a linear congruential generator [11] (LCG) to provide pseudo-random data based on a secret random quantity known only to the operating system. This final touch camouflages the actual encrypted data, and the file index is logically similar to Figure 5. Note that camouflage data is only needed (and created on the fly) when the system is under attack; it has no impact on performance or disk capacity under regular system operation.

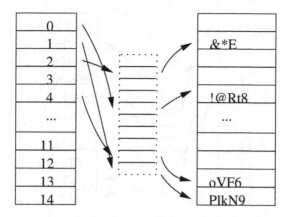

Fig. 4. Index where the entries for the data blocks have been spread. We have created an implicit *virtual index* to spread the file data blocks throughout the file's address space. The file address space is now replete with file holes. Note that it is simple to distinguish the encrypted data from the file holes because the operating system will happily return zeroed data in place of a hole.

2.5 Security Analysis

Threat Model. The threat model is based on two classes of attacker. The first has physical access to the disk (*e.g.*, by stealing the user's laptop). The second has read and write access to the file, perhaps because they have usurped the privileges of the file owner or because the file owner inadvertently provided a set of permission bits that was too liberal. The attacker does not know the secret key (including the spreading bits).

The attacker can observe the entire file, asking the operating system to provide every block. The attacker has access to the full range of Unix user-level tools, as well as the CamouflageFS tool set. The attacker could potentially corrupt the contents of the file, but our primary concern is maintaining the data's confidentiality. Integrity protection can be accomplished via other means.

Mechanism. For the purposes of this analysis, we assume that data would normally be enciphered with a 128 bit key. We also assume that 32 "spreading bits" are logically appended to the key, making an effective key of length 160 bits. Finally, we assume that the cipher used does not have any weakness that can be exploited to allow the attacker a less-than-brute-force search of the key space. Since only the operating system and the user know the 160 bits of the key, anyone trying to guess the spreading schedule would have to generate and test 2^{32} runs of the schedule generator even before they attempt any decryption. Note that if the operating system did not generate camouflage data, the attacker could easily ignore the spreading schedule function and simply grab disk blocks in the file that did not return null data. At this point, the attacker would still have to perform a 2^{128} brute force search on the key space.

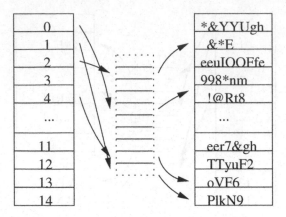

Fig. 5. Index where the data has been spread and camouflaged. Instructing the operating system to return consistent random data instead of zero-filled blocks for file holes effectively camouflages the encrypted data.

Camouflage Synchronization. There are some important issues that must be resolved in order for the generated camouflage data to actually protect the encrypted data. Most importantly, we do not want the attacker to be able to distinguish between the generated camouflage and the real encrypted data. Both sets should appear uniformly random. We assume that the attacker is free to make requests to the operating system to read the entire file. There are two instances of the problem of the camouflage data being "out of sync" with the real file data.

The first instance is that if the same camouflage data is returned consistently over a long period of time, the attacker could surmise that only the parts of the file that actually *do* change are being encrypted and thus correspond to the actual data in the file. This kind of de-synchronization could happen with a frequently edited file.

On the other hand, if the file data remains stable for a long period of time, and we repeatedly update the camouflage data, the attacker could conjecture that the parts of the file that *do not* change are the real data. This type of file could be a configuration file for a stable or long–running service.

These kinds of de-synchronization eliminate most of the benefits of the spreading schedule, because the attacker only has to rearrange a much smaller number of blocks and then move on to performing a search of the key space. In some cases, it may be reasonable to assume that these blocks are only a subset of the file data, but as a general rule, these "hotspots" (or "deadspots") of data (in)activity will stick out from the camouflage.

A mechanism should be provided for updating the composition of the camouflage data at a rate that approximates the change of the real file data. Since we do not actually store the camouflage data on disk, this requirement amounts to providing a mechanism for altering the generation of the camouflage data in some unpredictable manner.

Attacks. First, note that most attacks on the system still leave the attacker with a significant brute force search. Second, we are primarily concerned (as per the threat

model described above) with data confidentiality, including attacks where an intruder
has access to the raw disk.

1. An attacker could request the entire file contents and perform a brute force search
   for the key. This attack is the least rewarding.
2. An attacker may discover the camouflage magic value by reading the i-node information. This would allow the attacker to identify camouflage data. The solution is
   to encrypt the index portion of the i-nodes with the user's full key, or with a file
   system-wide key. In either case, the performance penalty would be minimal, due to
   the small size of the encrypted data.

   Alternatively, we can use a smart card during a user session to allow the OS to decrypt
   the i-nodes. Recent work on disk encryption techniques [9] discusses various ways
   to accomplish this goal.
3. An attacker could use a bad key to write into the file, corrupting the data. Two possible
   solutions are to use an integrity protection mechanism or to store some redundancy in
   the i-node to check if the provided key correctly decrypts the redundancy. However,
   these measures act like an oracle to the attacker; failing writes indicate that the
   provided key was not correct.
4. The attacker could observe the file over a period of time and conjecture that certain
   parts of the file are camouflage because they do not change or change too often. A
   mechanism would need to be implemented to change the camouflage seed at the
   same rate other file data changes.

3   Implementation

CamouflageFS is a rather straightforward extension to the standard Ext2 file system
for the Linux 2.4.19 kernel. The current implementation can coexist with normal file
operations and does not require any extra work to use regular Ext2 files.

CamouflageFS consists of two major components. The first is a set of *ioctl()*'s through
which the user can provide a key that controls how the kernel locates and decrypts
camouflaged files. The second component is the set of read and write operations that
implement the basic functionality of the system. In addition, a set of user-level tools
was developed for simple file read and write operations (similar to *cat* and *cp*) that
encapsulate the key handling and *ioctl()* mechanisms.

3.1   LFS: Large File Support

Employing the entire available address range for files is implied in the operation of
CamouflageFS. Large File Support [8] for Linux is available in the kernel version of our
implementation and requires that our user level utilities be compiled with this support.

The thirty-two bit architecture implementation of Ext2 with LFS and a block size of
4096 bytes imposes a twenty-eight bit limit on our "extension" of a key. This limitation
exists because of the structure of the multi-level index (see Figure 1) and the blocksize
of 4096 bytes. Since the index works at the block, rather than byte, granularity, the 2^{40}
bytes in the file are addressed by blocks of 4096 (2^{12}) bytes, with 4 bytes per index entry.

This relationship dictates a selection of roughly 2^{28} index blocks (so that we do not run into the Ext2 file size limitation of just under 2 terabytes).

The O_LARGEFILE flag is needed when opening a file greater than two gigabytes; this flag and the 64-bit versions of various file handling functions are made available by defining _LARGEFILE_SOURCE and _LARGEFILE64_SOURCE in the source code of the utilities. The utilities are then compiled with the _LARGEFILE_SOURCE and _FILE_OFFSET_BITS flags.

3.2 Data Structures

The first changes to be made were the addition of the data structures that would support the CamouflageFS operations. In order to simplify the implementation, no changes were made to the structure of the Ext2 i-node on disk, so CamouflageFS can peacefully co-exist with and operate on Ext2 formatted partitions.

An unsigned thirty-two bit quantity (i_camouflaged) was added to the in-memory structure for an Ext2 i-node. This quantity served as a flag, where a zero value indicated that the file was not a CamouflageFS file. Any non-zero value indicated otherwise. Once a file was marked as a CamouflageFS file, a secret random value was stored in this field for use in producing the camouflage for the file holes. This field is initialized to zero when the i-node is allocated. A structure was defined for the cryptographic key and added to the file handle structure.

Other changes include the addition of various header files for the encryption and hash algorithms, our LCG operations, additional *ioctl()* commands, and our index entry spreading functions. The actual operation and implementation of these functions are described below.

3.3 Cryptographic Support

CamouflageFS uses the Blowfish encryption algorithm [15] to encrypt each block of data, and can use either SHA-1 or an adaptation of RC6 during the calculation of the spread index entries. Code for these algorithms is publicly available and most was adapted for use from the versions found in the Linux 2.5.49 kernel.

3.4 Command and Control

The *ioctl()* implementation for Ext2 was altered to interpret five new commands for controlling files that belong to CamouflageFS. The two most important commands are:

1. EXT2_IOC_ENABLE_CAMOUFLAGE is a command that marks a file as being used by CamouflageFS. When a file is marked as part of the CamouflageFS, a random number is extracted from the kernel entropy pool and stored in the i_camouflaged field of the i-node. This has the dual effect of marking the file and preparing the system to return random camouflage data in place of file holes.
2. EXT2_IOC_SHOW_KEY_MATERIAL is the primary command for interacting with the file once it has been marked as a CamouflageFS file. This command is accompanied by a key structure matching the one described above and is used during subsequent read or write operations on the file handle. Note that the supplied key could be incorrect; at no time is the genuine key stored on disk.

3.5 User Tools and Cryptographic Support

Several user-level tools were developed to aid in the use of the system. These tools primarily wrap the ioctl() commands and other routine work of supplying a key and reading from or writing to a file. A userland header file (*cmgfs.h*) is provided to define the *ioctl()* commands and the file key structure.

The *read()* and *write()* operations for Ext2 were augmented to use the provided key if necessary to decrypt or encrypt the file data, respectively. Each page was encrypted or decrypted as a whole. Before a write could succeed, the page needed to be decrypted, the plaintext added at the appropriate position, and then the altered page data encrypted and written to disk.

3.6 Index Mapping

A variable length block cipher is utilized as a pseudo-random permutation (PRP) to map sequential block indices to ostensibly random indices. The underlying concept and justification for the variable length block cipher construction of which the implementation in CamouflageFS is a particular instance is beyond the scope of this paper. While only the 28-bit PRP implemented for CamouflageFS is briefly described here, it should be noted the variable length block cipher can be built upon any existing block cipher and stream cipher. RC6 was chosen for this implementation because its construction makes it applicable to small block sizes and RC4 was utilized due to its simplicity.

The PRP is an unbalanced Feistel network consisting of the RC6 round function combined with initial and end of round whitening. RC4 is used to create the expanded key. The PRP operates on a 28-bit block split into left and right segments consisting of 16 bits and 12 bits, respectively. The RC6 round function is applied to the 16-bit segment using a word size of 4 bits. The number of rounds and specific words swapped after each round were chosen such that each word was active in 20 rounds, equally in each of the first four word positions.

While the current mapping of block indices cannot be considered pseudo-random in theory, because the maximum length of an index is restricted to 28 bits in the file system and thus an exhaustive search is feasible, the use of a variable length block cipher will allow support for longer indices when needed.

3.7 Producing Camouflage Data

Camouflage data is produced whenever an unallocated data block is pointed to by the file index. If the block is part of a hole and the file is camouflaged, then our LCG is invoked to provide the appropriate data.

In order to avoid timing attacks, whereby an attacker can determine whether a block contains real (encrypted) or camouflaged data based on the time it took for a request to be completed, we read a block from the disk before we generate the camouflage data. The disk block is placed on the file cache, so subsequent reads for the same block will simulate the effect of a cache, even though the data returned is camouflage and independent of the contents of the block that was read from disk.

Finally, notice that camouflage data is only produced when an attacker (or curious user) is probing the protected file — under regular use, no camouflaged data would be produced.

4 Performance Evaluation

To test the performance of the system, we compared three implementations of Ext2. The first implementation was the standard Ext2. The second implementation modified Ext2 to use the Blowfish algorithm to encrypt data inside the kernel. The third implementation was CamouflageFS and incorporated our techniques along with encryption under Blowfish. In all cases, performance (measured by the amount of time to read or write a file) is largely dependent on file size. Execution time was measured with the Unix *time(1)* utility; all file sizes were measured for ten runs and the average is recorded in the presented tables.

The primary goal of our performance measurements on the CamouflageFS prototype is to show that the work necessary for a brute force attack can be exponentially increased without a legitimate user having to significantly increase the amount of time it takes to read and write data files, which is shown in Figure 6.

file size (kb)	ext2 R	ext2 W	BF R	BF W	cmgfs R	cmgfs W
1	0.002	0.001	0.003	0.001	0.003	0.001
21	0.01	0.001	0.010	0.002	0.010	0.002
42	0.02	0.001	0.020	0.003	0.003	0.004
63	0.03	0.001	0.030	0.004	0.004	0.005
210	0.09	0.002	0.094	0.012	0.206	0.148
2107	0.8395	0.008	0.930	1.096	1.319	1.105
21070	8.371	0.071	9.305	11.019	9.851	11.047
84280	33.5	55.17	37.180	65.416	37.756	67.493

Fig. 6. Time to read and write various size files in our various ext2 file system implementations. All times are in seconds (s).

Using a longer key contributes to the performance penalty. Most notably, a longer key length is achieved in 3DES by performing multiple encrypt and decrypt operations on the input. This approach is understandably quite costly. A second approach, used in AES-128, simply uses a number of extra rounds (based on the keysize choice) and not entire re-runs of the algorithm, as with 3DES. Blowfish takes another approach, by effectively expanding its key material to 448 bits, regardless of the original key length. The performance impact of encryption (using Blowfish) on ext2fs is shown in the second set of columns in Figure 6.

Therefore, we want to show that CamouflageFS performs nearly as well as ext2 *read()* and *write()* operations that use Blowfish alone. Using our prototype implementation, the performance is very close to that of a simple encrypting file system, as shown in

Figure 6. However, we have increased the effective cryptographic key length by 28 bits, correspondingly increasing an attacker's work factor by 2^{28}.

The CamouflageFS numbers closely match the performance numbers for a pure kernel-level Blowfish encryption mechanism, suggesting that the calculation of a new index has a negligible impact on performance. For example, the performance overhead (calculated as an average over time from Figure 7) of Blowfish is 11% for *read()* operations and 17% for *write()* operations. CamouflageFS exhibits essentially the same performance for these operations: 12% for *read()*'s and 22% for *write()*'s.

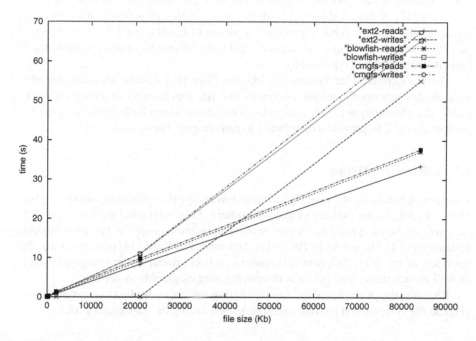

Fig. 7. Comparison of ext2 reads and writes versus CamouflageFS. CamouflageFS closely matches a file system that only performs encryption.

5 Related Work

The work presented in this paper draws on a number of research areas. Most notably, the recent work in information hiding and steganographic file systems serves the similar goal of hiding sensitive data. Our technique, on the other hand, combines steganography with the encryption mechanisms used by traditional cryptographic file systems to improve performance without the related cost.

5.1   Cryptographic File Systems

Most related efforts on secure file systems have concentrated on providing strong data integrity and confidentiality. Further work concentrates on making the process transparent or adjusting it for network and distributed environments. The original Cryptographic File System (CFS) [3] pointed out the need to embed file crypto services in the file system because it was too easy to misuse at the user or application layers.

Cryptfs [18] is an attempt to address the shortcomings of both CFS and TCFS [5] by providing greater transparency and performance. GBDE [9] discusses practical encryption at the disk level to provide long-term cryptographic protection to sensitive data.

FSFS [12] is designed to deal with the complexities of access control in a cryptographic file system. While the primary concern of CamouflageFS is the speedup of data file encryption, file system access control mechanisms are another related area that benefits from applied cryptography.

The Cooperative File System [6], like the Eliot [16] system are examples of file systems that attempt to provide anonymity and file survivability in a large network of peers. The Mnemosyne [7] file system takes this cause a step further, based on the work presented in [1], to provide a distributed steganographic file system.

5.2   Information Hiding

Information hiding, or steganography, has a broad range of application and a long history of use, mainly in the military or political sphere. Steganographic methods and tactics are currently being applied to a host of problems, including copyright and watermarking technology [14]. The survey by Petitcolas, Anderson, and Kuhn [14] presents an excellent overview of the field. Anderson [2] constructs a background for steganographic theory as well as examining core issues in developing steganographic systems.

Recently, the principles of information hiding have been applied to creating steganographic file systems that provide mechanisms for hiding the existence of data.

5.3   Steganographic File Systems

Steganographic file systems aim to hide the presence of sensitive data. While some implementations merely hide the data inside other files (like the low–order bits of images), other systems use encryption to not only hide the data, but protect it from access attempts even if discovered. This hybrid approach is similar to CamouflageFS.

StegFS [13,1] is one such steganographic file system. The primary goal of StegFS is to provide (and in some sense define) legal plausible deniability of sensitive data on the protected disk, as proposed and outlined by Anderson *et al* [1]. Unfortunately, using StegFS's strong security results in a major performance hit [13]. StegFS is concerned with concealing the location of the disk blocks that contain sensitive data. In short, StegFS acts as if two file systems were present: one file system for allocating disk blocks for normal files, and one file system for allocating blocks to hidden files using a 15 level access scheme. The multiple levels allow lower or less-sensitive levels to be revealed under duress without compromising the existence of more sensitive files.

Each of these two file systems uses the same collection of disk blocks. Normal files are allowed to overwrite the blocks used for hidden file data; in order to protect the hidden files, each block of a hidden file is mapped to a semi-random set of physical blocks. Since each disk block is initialized with random data, the replication makes the sensitive data appear no different than a normal unallocated disk block while ensuring that the hidden data will survive allocation for normal files.

6   Future Work

The work presented here can be extended to other operating systems and file systems. For example, OpenBSD provides a wide array of cryptographic support [10]. Further work includes performing standard file system benchmarks and implementing AES as a choice of cipher.

Beyond this work, there are two primary issues to be addressed: preventing both collisions in the spreading schedule and an attacker's discernment of camouflage data.

The use of a variable length block cipher to calculate the virtual index should address the possibility of collisions; however, as noted previously, the length should be increased to lessen the possibility of a brute force attack. The length of 28 bits in our implementation is an architecture and operating system limitation.

To prevent an attacker from knowing which data was actually camouflage, we would have to create some mechanism whereby the i_camouflaged field is updated at some rate to "stir" the entropy source of the camouflage data.

Further work includes both examining the feasibility of various attack strategies against the system and discovering what effect (if any) the spreading schedule has on the placement of data on disk. There should be little impact on performance here; the virtual index is relatively independent of what disk blocks contain the data.

7   Conclusions

CamouflageFS is a simple, portable, and effective approach to improving data confidentiality in cryptographic file systems. The approach taken is to hide the encrypted data in an artificially large file, using a key-driven spread-spectrum sequence. Attackers must guess both the cryptographic key and the spreading key, effectively increasing their work factor. Appropriate measures are taken to prevent an attacker from determining which disk blocks contains encrypted data. The performance impact of the technique to legitimate users is negligible.

We intend to investigate further applications of this *practical* combination of steganographic and cryptographic techniques for improving security in other areas.

References

1. R. Anderson, R. Needham, and A. Shamir. The Steganographic File System. In *Information Hiding, Second International Workshop IH '98*, pages 73–82, 1998.
2. R. J. Anderson. Stretching The Limits of Steganography. In *Information Hiding, Springer Lecture Notes in Computer Science*, volume 1174, pages 39–48, 1996.

3. M. Blaze. A Cryptographic File System for Unix. In *Proceedings of the 1st ACM Conference on Computer and Communications Security*, November 1993.
4. D. P. Bovet and M. Cesati. *Understanding the Linux Kernel: From I/O Ports to Process Management*. O'Reilly, second edition, 2003.
5. G. Cattaneo and G. Persiano. Design and Implementation of a Transparent Cryptographic File System For Unix. Technical report, July 1997.
6. F. Dabek, F. Kaashoek, R. Morris, D. Karger, and I. Stoica. Wide-Area Cooperative Storage with CFS. In *Proceedings of ACM SOSP*, Banff, Canada, October 2001.
7. S. Hand and T. Roscoe. Mnemosyne: Peer-to-Peer Steganographic Storage. In *Proceedings of the 1st International Workshop on Peer-to-Peer Systems*, March 2002.
8. A. Jaeger. Large File Support in Linux, July 2003.
9. P.-H. Kamp. GBDE - GEOM Based Disk Encryption. In *BSDCon 2003*, September 2003.
10. A. D. Keromytis, J. L. Wright, and T. de Raadt. The Design of the OpenBSD Cryptographic Framework. In *Proceedings of the USENIX Annual Technical Conference*, June 2003.
11. D. Lehmer. Mathematical Methods in Large-scale Computing Units. In *Proc. 2nd Sympos. on Large-Scale Digital Calculating Machinery*, pages 141–146. Harvard University Press, 1949.
12. S. Ludwig and W. Kalfa. File System Encryption with Integrated User Management. In *Operating Systems Review*, volume 35, October 2001.
13. A. D. McDonald and M. G. Kuhn. Stegfs: A Stegonographic File System for Linux. In *Information Hiding, Third International Workshop IH '99*, pages 463–477, 2000.
14. F. A. Petitcolas, R. Anderson, and M. G. Kuhn. Information Hiding–A Survey. In *Proceedings of the IEEE, special issue on protection of multimedia content*, volume 87, pages 1062–1078, July 1999.
15. B. Schneier. Description of a New Variable-Length Key, 64-Bit Block Cipher (Blowfish). In *Fast Software Encryption, Cambridge Security Workshop Proceedings*, pages 191–204. Springer-Verlag, December 1993.
16. C. Stein, M. Tucker, and M. Seltzer. Building a Reliable Mutable File System on Peer-to-peer Storage.
17. N. Stephenson. *Cryptonomicon*. Avon Books, 1999.
18. E. Zadok, I. Badulescu, and A. Shender. Cryptfs: A Stackable Vnode Level Encryption File System. In *Proceedings of the USENIX Annual Technical Conference*, June 2003.

Private Keyword-Based Push and Pull with Applications to Anonymous Communication

Extended Abstract

Lea Kissner[1], Alina Oprea[1], Michael K. Reiter[1,2], Dawn Song[1,2], and Ke Yang[1]

Dept. of Computer Science, Carnegie Mellon University
{leak,alina,yangke}@cs.cmu.edu
Dept, of Electrical and Computer Engineering, Carnegie Mellon University
{reiter,dawnsong}@cmu.edu

Abstract. We propose a new keyword-based Private Information Retrieval (PIR) model that allows private modification of the database from which information is requested. In our model, the database is distributed over n servers, any one of which can act as a transparent interface for clients. We present protocols that support operations for accessing data, focusing on privately appending labelled records to the database (**push**) and privately retrieving the next unseen record appended under a given label (**pull**). The communication complexity between the client and servers is independent of the number of records in the database (or more generally, the number of previous **push** and **pull** operations) and of the number of servers. Our scheme also supports access control oblivious to the database servers by implicitly including a public key in each **push**, so that only the party holding the private key can retrieve the record via **pull**. To our knowledge, this is the first system that achieves the following properties: private database modification, private retrieval of multiple records with the same keyword, and oblivious access control. We also provide a number of extensions to our protocols and, as a demonstrative application, an unlinkable anonymous communication service using them.

1 Introduction

Techniques by which a client can retrieve information from a database without exposing its query or the response to the database was initiated with the study of oblivious transfer [17]. In the past decade, this goal has been augmented with that of minimizing communication complexity between clients and servers, a problem labelled Private Information Retrieval (PIR) [8]. To date, PIR has received significant attention in the literature, but a number of practically important limitations remain: queries are limited to returning small items (typically single bits), data must be retrieved by address as opposed to by keyword search, and there is limited support for modifications to the database. Each of these limitations has received attention (e.g., [9,8,14,6]), but we are aware of no solution that fully addresses these simultaneously.

In this extended abstract we present novel protocols by which a client can privately access a distributed database. Our protocols address the above limitations while retaining privacy of queries (provided that at most a fixed threshold t of servers is compromised)

M. Jakobsson, M. Yung, J. Zhou (Eds.): ACNS 2004, LNCS 3089, pp. 16–30, 2004.

and while improving client-server communication efficiency over PIR solutions at the cost of server-server communication. Specifically, the operations we highlight here include:

- push   In order to insert a new record into the database, the client performs a push operation that takes a label, the record data, and a public key as arguments.
- pull   To retrieve a record, a client performs a pull operation with a label and a private key as arguments. The response to a pull indicates the number of records previously pushed with that label and a corresponding public key, and if any, returns the first such record that was not previously returned in a pull (or no record if they all were previously returned).

Intuitively, the pull operation functions as a type of "dequeue" operation or list iterator: each successive pull with the same label and private key will return a new record pushed with that label and corresponding public key, until these records are exhausted. We emphasize that the above operations are private, and thus we call this paradigm Private Push and Pull (P^3).

As an example application of these protocols, suppose we would like to construct a private bulletin board application. In this scenario, clients can deposit messages which are retrieved asynchronously by other clients. An important requirement is that the communication between senders and receivers remains hidden to the database servers, a property called *unlinkability*. Clients encrypt messages for privacy, and label them with a keyword, the mailbox address of the recipient. If multiple clients send messages to the same recipient, there exist multiple records in the database with the same keyword. We would like to provide the receiver with a mechansim to retrieve some or all the messages from his mailbox. Thus, the system should allow insertion and retrieval of multiple records with the same keyword. Another desirable property would be to provide *oblivious access control*, such that a receiver can retrieve from its mailbox only if he knows a certain private key. In addition, the database enforces the access control obliviously, i.e., the servers do not know the identity of the intended recipient. All these properties are achieved by our P^3 protocols and the construction of such a private bulletin board is an immediate application of these protocols.

Our protocols have additional properties. Labels in the database, arguments to push and pull requests, and responses to pull requests are computationally hidden from up to t maliciously corrupted servers and any number of corrupted clients. The communication complexity incurred by the client during a push or pull operation is independent of both the number of servers and the number of records in the database, and requires only a constant number of ciphertexts. While communication complexity between the servers is linearly dependent on both the number of servers and the number of records in the database, we believe that this tradeoff—i.e., minimizing client-server communication at the cost of server-server communication—is justified in scenarios involving bandwidth-limited or geographically distant clients.

Beyond our basic push and pull protocols, we will additionally provide a number of enhancements to our framework, such as: a peek protocol that, given a label and private key, privately retrieves the i-th record pushed with that label and corresponding public key; a modification to pull to permit the retrieval of arbitrary-length records; and the ability to perform a pull based not only on identical label matching, but based on any predicate on labels (with additional cost in server-server communication complexity).

We define security of the P^3 protocols in the malicious and honest-but-curious adversary models. The definition of security that we employ is very similar to the definition of secure multi-party computation [11]. Proofs that P^3 satisfies the definition of security in the malicious adversary model will be given in the full version of the paper. We also propose a more efficient P^3 protocol that is secure in the honest-but-curious model. We thus achieve a tradeoff between the level of security guaranteed by our protocols and their computational complexity.

To summarize, the contributions of our paper are:

- The definition of a new keyword-based Private Information Retrieval model
  Our model extends previous work on PIR in several ways. Firstly, we enable private modification of the database, where the database servers do not learn the modified content. Secondly, we allow retrieval of a subset or all records matching a given keyword. And, finally, we provide *oblivious access control*, such that only the intended recipients can retrieve messages and the servers do not know the identity of message recipients.
- The construction of secure and efficient protocols in this model
  We design P^3 protocols, that achieve a constant communication complexity (in number of ciphertexts) between the clients and the servers and that are provably secure in the malicious adversary model.
- The design of an unlinkable [16] anonymous messaging service using the new proposed protocols
  The anonymous messaging service we design is analogous to a bulletin board, where clients deposit messages for other clients, to retrieve them at their convenience. The security properties of the P^3 protocols provide the system with unlinkability.

2 Related Work

As already mentioned, our P^3 primitive is related to other protocols for hiding what a client retrieves from a database. In this section we differentiate P^3 from these other protocols.

Private information retrieval (PIR) [9,8,3] enables a client holding an index $i, 1 \le i \le d$, to retrieve data item i from a d-item database without revealing i to the database. This can be trivially achieved by sending the entire database to the client, so PIR mandates sublinear (and ideally polylogarithmic) communication complexity as a function of d. Our approach relaxes this requirement for server-to-server communication (which is not typically employed in PIR solutions), and retains this requirement for communication with clients; our approach ensures client communication complexity that is *independent* of d. In addition, classic PIR does not address database changes and does not support labelled data on which clients can search.

Support for modifying the database was introduced in *private information storage* [14]. This supports both reads and writes, without revealing the address read or written. However, it requires the client to know the address it wants to read or write. P^3

eliminates the need for a client to know the address to read from, by allowing retrieval of data as selected by a predicate on labels. P^3 does not allow overwriting of values, but allows clients to retrieve all records matching a given query.

The problem of determining whether a keyword is present in a database without revealing the keyword (and again with communication sublinear in d) is addressed in [6]. The P^3 framework permits richer searches on keywords beyond identical matching—with commensurate additional expense in server complexity —though P^3 using identical keyword matching is a particularly efficient example. Another significant difference is that P^3 returns the data associated with the selected label, rather than merely testing for the existence of a label.

Also related to P^3 is work on *oblivious keyword search* [13], which enables a client to retrieve data for which the label identically matches a keyword. Like work on oblivious transfer that preceded it, this problem introduces the security requirement that the client learn nothing about the database other than the record retrieved. It also imposes weaker constraints on communication complexity. Specifically, communication complexity between a client and servers is permitted to be linear in d.

3   Preliminaries

A public-key cryptosystem is a triplet of probabilistic algorithms (G, E, D) running in expected polynomial time. $G(1^\kappa_{\mathcal{TE}})$ is a probabilistic algorithm that outputs a pair of keys (pk, sk), given as input a security parameter $\kappa_{\mathcal{TE}}$. Encryption, denoted as $E_{pk}(m)$, is a probabilistic algorithm that outputs a ciphertext c for a given plaintext m. The deterministic algorithm for decryption, denoted as $D_{sk}(c)$, outputs a decryption m of c. Correctness requires that for any message m, $D_{sk}(E_{pk}(m)) = m$.

The cryptosystems used in our protocols require some of the following properties:

- message indistinguishability under chosen plaintext attack (IND-CPA security) [12]: an adversary is given a public key pk, and chooses two messages m_0, m_1 from the plaintext space of the encryption scheme. These are given as input to a test oracle. The test oracle chooses $b \leftarrow_R \{0, 1\}$ and gives the adversary $E_{pk}(m_b)$. The adversary must not be able to guess b with probability more than negligibly different from $\frac{1}{2}$.
- (t, n) threshold decryption: a probabilistic polynomial-time (PPT) share-generation algorithm S, given pk, sk, t, n, outputs private shares $sk_1, \ldots, sk_n$ such that parties who possess at least $t + 1$ shares and a ciphertext c can interact to compute $D_{sk}(c)$. Specifically we require $(n - 1, n)$ threshold decryption, where the private shares are additive over the integers, such that $sk = \sum_{i=1}^{n} sk_i$.
- threshold IND-CPA security [10]: the definition for threshold IND-CPA security is the same as for normal IND-CPA security, with minor changes. Firstly, the adversary is allowed to choose up to t servers to corrupt, and observes all of their secret information, as well as controlling their behaviour. Secondly, the adversary has access to a partial decryption oracle, which takes a message m and outputs all n shares (constructed just as decryption proceeds) of the decryption of an encryption of m.
- partial homomorphism: there must be PPT algorithms $+_{pk}$, $-_{pk}$, $\cdot_{pk}$ for addition and subtraction of ciphertexts, and for the multiplication of a known constant by

a ciphertext such that for all a, b, in the plaintext domain of the encryption scheme, $c \in Z$, such that the result of the desired operation is also in the plaintext domain of the encryption scheme:

$$D_{sk}(E_{pk}(a) +_{pk} E_{pk}(b)) = a + b$$
$$D_{sk}(E_{pk}(a) -_{pk} E_{pk}(b)) = a - b$$
$$D_{sk}(c \cdot_{pk} E_{pk}(a)) = ca$$

– blinding: there must be a PPT algorithm Blind_{pk} which, given a ciphertext c which encrypts message m, produces an encryption of m, pulled from a distribution which is uniform over all possible encryptions of m.
– indistinguishability of ciphertexts under different keys (key privacy) [1]: the adversary is given two different public keys pk_0, pk_1 and it chooses a message from the plaintext range of the encryption scheme considered. Given an encryption of the message under one of the two keys, chosen at random, the adversary is not able to distinguish which key was used for encryption with probability non-negligibly higher than $\frac{1}{2}$.

3.1 Notation

– $a||b$ denotes the concatenation of a and b;
– $x \leftarrow D$ denotes that x is sampled from the distribution D;
– $\bar{x}$ denotes an encryption of x under an encryption scheme, that can be inferred from the context;
– $\mathcal{E} = (G, E, D)$, an IND-CPA secure, partially homomorphic encryption scheme, for which we can construct proofs of plaintext knowledge and blind ciphertexts. For the construction in Sec. 5, we also require the key privacy property. The security parameter for $\mathcal{E}$ is denoted as $\kappa_{\mathcal{E}}$.
– $\mathcal{TE} = (G^h, E^h, \text{threshDecrypt})$, a threshold decryption scheme, which is threshold IND-CPA secure. threshDecrypt is a distributed algorithm, in which each party uses its share of the secret key to compute a share of the decryption. In addition, it should have the partial homomorphic property and we should be able to construct proofs of plaintext knowledge. The security parameter for $\mathcal{TE}$ is denoted as $\kappa_{\mathcal{TE}}$.
– $M_{pk}^{\mathcal{E}}$ denotes the plaintext space of the encryption scheme $\mathcal{E}$ for public key pk.
– $\Pi = \text{zkp}[p]$ denotes the zero-knowledge proof of predicate p, $\Pi = \text{zkpk}[p]$ denotes the zero-knowledge proof of knowledge of p

3.2 Paillier

The Paillier encryption scheme defined in [13] satisfies the first six defined properties. In the Paillier cryptosystem, the public key is an RSA-modulus N and a generator g that has an order a multiple of N in $\mathbb{Z}_{N^2}^*$. In order to encrypt a message $m \in \mathbb{Z}_N$, a random r is chosen in $\mathbb{Z}_N$, and the ciphertext is $c = g^m r^N \bmod N^2$. In this paper, we will consider the plaintext space for the public key (N, g) to be $M_{(N,g)} = (-\frac{N}{2}, \frac{N}{2})$ so that we can safely compute $-x$, given x in the plaintext space.

For the construction in Sec. 5, we need key privacy of the encryption scheme used. In order to achieve that, we slightly modify the Paillier scheme so that the ciphertext is $c + \mu N^2$, where μ is a random number less than a threshold $T = \frac{2^{4\kappa_{T\mathcal{E}}}}{N^2}$ ($\kappa_{T\mathcal{E}}$ is the security parameter).

The threshold Paillier scheme defined in [10] can be easily modified to use additive shares of the secret key over integers (as this implies shares over $N\lambda(N)$), and thus with the modification given above, satisfies the properties required for $\mathcal{TE}$.

The unmodified Pailler cryptosystem satisfies the requirements for $\mathcal{E}$. Zero-knowledge proofs of plaintext knowledge are given in [7].

3.3   System Model

We denote by n the number of servers, and t the maximum number that may be corrupted. Privacy of the protocols is preserved if $t < n$.

Assuming the servers may use a broadcast channel to communicate, every answer returned to a client will be correct if $t < n$ or all servers are honest-but-curious. This does not, however, guarantee that an answer will be given in response to every query. If every server may act arbitrarily maliciously (Byzantine failures), a broadcast channel may be simulated if $t < \frac{n}{3}$.

We do not address this issue in this paper, but liveness (answering every query) can be guaranteed with $t < \frac{n}{3}$ if every misbehaving server is identified and isolated, and the protocol is restarted without them. Note that this may take multiple restarts, as not every corrupted server must misbehave at the beginning.

In the malicious model, our protocols are simulatable [11], and thus the privacy of client queries, responses to those queries (including the presence or absence of information), and database records is preserved. In the honest-but-curious model, we may achieve this privacy property more efficiently. For lack of space, we defer the proofs to the full version of this paper.

The database supports two types of operations. In a push operation, a client provides a public key pk, a label ℓ, and data δ. In a pull operation, the client provides a secret key sk and a label x, and receives an integer and a data item in response. The integer should be equal to the number of previous push operations for which the label $\ell = x$ and for which the public key pk is the corresponding public key for sk. The returned data item should be that provided to the first such push operation that has not already been returned in a previous pull. If no such data item exists, then **none** is returned in its place.

4   The P· Protocol

We start the description of P^3 with the push protocol. Before going into the details of the pull protocol, we construct several building block protocols. We give several extensions to the basic protocols. We then analyze the communication complexity of the proposed protocols. At the end of the section, we suggest a more efficient implementation of our protocols in the honest-but-curious model.

In the protocols given in this paper, the selection predicate is equality of the given label x to the ith record label ℓ_i, under a given secret key sk. This selection predicate is evaluated using the protocol testRecord. The P^3 system can be modified by replacing testRecord with a protocol that evaluates an arbitrary predicate, e.g., using [7].

4.1   Initial Service-Key Setup

During the initial setup of a P^3 system, the servers collectively generate a public/private key pair $(\mathsf{PK}, \mathsf{SK})$ for the threshold encryption scheme $\mathcal{TE}$, where PK is the public key, and the servers additively share the corresponding private key SK. We call the public/private key pair the system's *service key*. We require that $d < q$, $n \cdot d \cdot q^2 < 2^{\kappa_{\mathcal{TE}}-1}$, $\frac{2^{2\kappa_{\mathcal{E}}+3}n}{n-t} < 2^{\kappa_{\mathcal{TE}}-1}$, and $2^{\kappa_{\mathcal{E}}+1} + 3 \cdot 2^{2\kappa_{\mathcal{E}}+2} < 2^{\kappa_{\mathcal{TE}}-1}$ so that the operations (presented next) over the message space $M_{pk}^{\mathcal{TE}}$ (which is an integer interval of length about $2^{\kappa_{\mathcal{TE}}}$, centered around 0) will not "overflow". Here d denotes the number of records in the database, and q is a prime.

For notational clarity, the protocols are given under the assumption that the data sent to the server in a push operation can be represented as an element of $\mathbb{Z}_q$. This can be trivially extended to arbitrary length records (see 4.5).

4.2   The Private Push Protocol

When a client $\mathcal{C}$ wants to insert a new record in the distributed database, it first generates a public key/secret key pair (pk, sk) for the encryption scheme $\mathcal{TE}$ and then invokes a push operation $\text{push}_{PK}(pk, \ell, \delta)$. Here PK is the service key, ℓ is the label and δ is the data to be inserted. The protocol is a very simple one and is given in Fig. 1. $\mathsf{H}(\cdot)$ is a cryptographically secure hash function, e.g., MD5.

Note that the data is sent directly to the server, and thus if privacy of the contents of the data is desired, the data should be encrypted beforehand.

$\text{push}_{PK}(pk, \ell, \delta)$
Client $\mathcal{C}$ computes $y \leftarrow E_{pk}^h(\ell)$ and sends $\langle y, \mathsf{H}(\delta) \| \delta \rangle$ together with a zero knowledge proof of knowledge $\Pi = \mathsf{zkpk}[l : l \in \mathbb{Z}_q, D_{sk}(y) = l]$.
This server adds the tuple $\langle y, \langle \mathsf{H}(\delta), \delta \rangle, E_{PK}^h(1) \rangle$ to the shared database.

Fig. 1. The push protocol

4.3   Building Block Protocols

The Decrypt Share Protocol. When the decryptShare protocol starts, one of the servers receives a ciphertext c encrypted using the public key pk of the threshold homomorphic encryption scheme $\mathcal{TE}$. It also receives an integer R representing a randomness range large enough to statistically hide the plaintext corresponding to c. We assume that the servers additively share the secret key sk corresponding to pk, such that each server knows a share sk_i. After the protocol, the servers additively share the corresponding plaintext m. Each server will know a share m_i such that $\sum_{i=1}^{n} m_i = m$ and it will output a commitment of this share $(\bar{m}_i = E_{pk}^{h}(m_i))$. The protocol is given in Fig. 2 and is similar to the Additive Secret Sharing protocol in [7].

---

decryptShare$_{sk_1,\ldots,sk_n}(c, R)$
We assume that an arbitrary server holds c — assume it is $\mathcal{S}_j$.

1. For $1 \leq i \leq n$, $\mathcal{S}_i$ chooses $a_i \leftarrow [0, \ldots, R]$, computes $c_i \leftarrow E_{pk}^{h}(a_i)$.
2. For $i = 1, \ldots, n$, $\mathcal{S}_i$ broadcasts c_i together with a zero knowledge proof of plaintext knowledge of c_i: $\Pi_i = \mathsf{zkpk}[a_i : a_i \in [0, \ldots, R], D_{sk}(c_i) = a_i]$.
3. All the servers check the zero knowledge proofs received from the other servers. If some proofs do not verify, then the servers that sent them are excluded from the protocol.
4. $\mathcal{S}_j$ computes $c' \leftarrow c +_{pk} c_{\bullet} +_{pk} c_{\bullet} +_{pk} \cdots +_{pk} c_n$.
5. All servers participate in $m' = \mathsf{threshDecrypt}_{sk_1,\ldots,sk_n}(c')$.
6. The additive share of m for $\mathcal{S}_j$ is $m_j = -a_j + m'$ and the commitment $\bar{m}_j$ can be computed as $\bar{m}_j = c' -_{pk} c_j$;
   The additive share of m for $\mathcal{S}_i$, $i \neq j$ is $m_i = -a_i$ and the commitment $\bar{m}_i$ can be computed as $\bar{m}_i = -_{pk} c_i$.

Fig. 2. The decryptShare protocol

The Multiplication Protocol. The mult protocol receives as input two encrypted values $\bar{x}$ and $\bar{y}$ under a public key pk of the threshold homomorphic encryption scheme $\mathcal{TE}$, and an integer R, used as a parameter to decryptShare. We assume that the servers additively share the secret key sk corresponding to pk, such that each server knows a share sk_i. The output of the protocol is a value $\bar{z}$ such that $D_{sk}(\bar{z}) = xy$. The protocol is given in Fig. 3 and is similar to the Mult protocol in [7].

---

mult$_{pk}(\bar{x}, \bar{y}, R)$

1. All the servers participate in decryptShare$_{sk_1,\ldots,sk_n}(\bar{y}, R)$, ending with additive shares of y: $y_{\bullet}, \ldots, y_n$ and commitments of these shares $\bar{y}_{\bullet}, \ldots, \bar{y}_n$.
2. For $1 \leq i \leq n$, $\mathcal{S}_i$ computes $\bar{t}_i = \bar{x} \cdot_{pk} y_i$ and broadcasts $\bar{t}_i$ together with a zero knowledge proof of knowledge $\Pi_i = \mathsf{zkpk}[y_i : D_{sk}(\bar{y}_i) = y_i, \bar{t}_i = \bar{x} \cdot_{pk} y_i]$.
3. All the servers check the zero knowledge proofs received from the other servers. If some proofs do not verify, then the servers that sent them are excluded from the protocol.
4. The output of the protocol is $\bar{z} = \bar{t}_{\bullet} +_{pk} \cdots +_{pk} \bar{t}_n$.

Fig. 3. The mult protocol

The Share Reduction Protocol. The shareModQ protocol receives as input a prime q, an encrypted value $\bar{x}$ under a public key pk of the threshold homomorphic encryption scheme $\mathcal{TE}$, and an integer R, used as a parameter to decryptShare. We assume that the servers additively share the secret key sk corresponding to pk, such that each server knows a share sk_i. The output of the protocol is $\bar{y}$ st $D_{sk}(\bar{y}) = D_{sk}(\bar{x})$, $\bar{y} = y_1 + \cdots + y_n$, $y_i \in \mathbb{Z}_q$. The protocol is given in Fig. 4.

---

shareModQ$_{pk}(\bar{x}, q, R)$

1. All the servers participate in decryptShare$_{sk_1,\ldots,sk_n}(\bar{x}, R)$, ending with additive shares of x: $x., \ldots, x_n$ and commitments of these shares $\bar{x}., \ldots, \bar{x}_n$.
2. For $1 \leq i \leq n$, $\mathcal{S}_i$ computes $y_i = x_i \bmod q$ and broadcasts $\bar{y}_i = E_{pk}^h(y_i)$ together with a zero knowledge proof of knowledge $\Pi_i = \mathsf{zkpk}[x_i, y_i : y_i \in \mathbb{Z}_q, D_{sk}(\bar{y}_i) = y_i, D_{sk}(\bar{x}_i) = x_i, y_i = x_i \bmod q]$.
3. All the servers check the zero knowledge proofs received from the other servers. If some proofs do not verify, then the servers that sent them are excluded from the protocol.
4. All the servers compute $\bar{y} = \bar{y}. +_{pk} \cdots +_{pk} \bar{y}_n$, which is the output of the protocol.

Fig. 4. The shareModQ protocol

The Modular Exponentiation Protocol. The expModQ protocol receives as input an encrypted value $\bar{x}$ under a public key pk of the threshold homomorphic encryption scheme $\mathcal{TE}$, an integer exponent k and a prime modulus q, and and an integer R, used as a parameter to decryptShare. The output of the protocol is $\bar{y}$ such that $D_{sk}(\bar{y}) = D_{sk}(\bar{x})^k$. In addition, the decryption of $\bar{y}$, y, can be written as $y = y_1 + \cdots + y_n$ with $y_i \in \mathbb{Z}_q$. We have thus the guarantee that $0 \leq y \leq (q-1)n$. The protocol is simply done by repeated squaring using the mult protocol. After each invocation of the mult protocol, a shareModQ protocol is executed.

4.4   The Private Pull Protocol

We have now all the necessary tools to proceed to the construction of the pull protocol. To retrieve the record associated with the label x encrypted under public key pk, the client $\mathcal{C}$ must know both x and the secret key sk corresponding pk. $\mathcal{C}$ encrypts both the label x and the secret key sk under the public service key PK and picks a public/secret key pair (pk', sk') for the encryption scheme $\mathcal{E}$. It then sends $\bar{x}$, $\bar{sk}$ and pk' to an arbitrary server.

Overview of the Pull Protocol. The servers will jointly compute a *template* $T = (T_1, \ldots, T_d)$, where d is the number of records in the database. The template is a series of indicators encrypted under pk', where T_i indicates whether x matches the label ℓ_i under sk (threshDecrypt$_{sk}(\ell_i) = x$) and whether i is the first record that matches ℓ_i not previously read. This determines whether it should be returned as a response to the query ($D_{sk'}(T_i) = 1$) or not ($D_{sk'}(T_i) = 0 \bmod q$). The protocol returns to the client the template T and an encrypted counter, $\bar{m}$ that denotes the total number of records matching a given label.

The protocol starts in step 2 (Figure 5) with the servers getting additive shares of the secret key sk, sent encrypted by the client. In step 3, several flags are initialized, the meaning of which will be explained in Sec. 4.4. Then, in step 4, it performs an iteration on all the records in the database, calculating the template entry for each record. In steps 4(a)-4(e), for each record j in the database with the label encrypted under public key pk_j, a decryption under the supplied key sk and re-encryption of the label is calculated under the service public key PK. In order to construct the template, the additive homomorphic properties of the encryption scheme $\mathcal{TE}$ are used. For record j in the database, the servers jointly determine the correct template value (as explained above), using the building block testRecord.

The return result is constructed by first multiplying each entry in the template with the contents of the corresponding record, and then adding the resulting ciphertexts using the additive homomorphic operation $+_{pk'}$. At most one template value will hold an encryption of 1, so an encryption of the corresponding record will be returned. All other records will be multiplied by a multiple of q, and will thus be suppressed when the client performs $D_{sk'}(T) \bmod q$. The bounds on the size of the plaintext range ensure that the encrypted value does not leave the plaintext range.

An interesting observation is that our approach is very general and we could easily change the specification of the pull protocol, by just modifying the testRecord protocol. An example of this is given in Sec. 4.5, when we describe the peek protocol.

Flags for Repeated Keywords. In this section we address the situation in which multiple records are associated with the same keyword under a single key. The protocol employs a flag $\bar{f}$, which is set at the beginning of each pull invocation to an encryption of 1 under the public service key. $\bar{f}$ is obliviously set to an encryption of 0 mod q after processing the first record which both matches the label and has not been previously read. It will retain this value through the rest of the pull invocation. In addition, each record i in the database has an associated flag, $\bar{r}_i$. The decryption of $\bar{r}_i$ is 1 if record i has not yet been pulled and 0 mod q afterwards. Initially, during the push protocol, $\bar{r}_i$ is set to an encryption of 1.

The testRecord Protocol. The equality test protocol, testRecord, first computes $\bar{w}$ (steps 1-2), such that $\bar{1} -_{PK} \bar{w}$ is an encryption of 1 if $x = y \bmod q$ and an encryption of 0 mod q otherwise. In step 3, a flag $\bar{s}$ is computed as an encryption of 1 if the record matches the label, $f = 1$ (this is the first matching record), and $r = 1$ (this record has not been previously retrieved). We then convert $\bar{s}$ from an encryption under the service key PK to an encryption under the client's key pk of the same plaintext indicator (0 mod q or 1). This is performed in steps 4-7 with result u. We then update the flags $\bar{f}$ and $\bar{r}$, as well as the counter $\bar{m}$. Both $\bar{r}$ and $\bar{f}$ are changed to encryptions of 0 mod q if the record will be returned in the pull protocol. The new value of $\bar{m}$ is obtained by homomorphically adding the match indicator $\bar{1} -_{PK} \bar{w}$ to the old value.

The detailed pull and testRecord protocols are given in Figs. 5 and 6.

$\mathsf{pull}(sk, x, pk', sk')$

The database, is a collection of d tuples $\{\mathcal{D}_j = \langle E^h_{pk_j}(\ell_j), e_j, \bar{r}_j = E^h_{PK}(r_j)\rangle\}^d_j$. .

Here $\ell_j \in Z_q$ and $e_j \in M_{pk'}$ can be parsed as $e_j = \mathsf{H}(\delta_j) \| \delta_j$

1. $\mathcal{C}$ sends $(pk', \bar{x} = E^h_{PK}(x), \bar{sk} = E^h_{PK}(sk))$ to an arbitrary server $\mathcal{S}_j$, who broadcasts pk'.

2. All the servers participate in $\mathsf{decryptShare}_{SK_1, \ldots, SK_n}\left(\bar{sk}, \frac{\cdot^{2\kappa_{\mathcal{E}}+3}}{n-t}\right)$ and end with additive shares of sk: $sk\cdot, \ldots, sk_n$ and commitments $\bar{sk}\cdot, \ldots, \bar{sk}_n$.

3. An arbitrary sever computes $\bar{f} \leftarrow E^h_{PK}(1), \bar{m} \leftarrow E_{pk'}(0)$ and broadcasts them to all the servers.

4. For $1 \leq j \leq d$, do:
    a) The server that holds $\mathcal{D}_j = \langle E^h_{pk_j}(\ell_j), e_j\rangle$ broadcasts it;

    b) All the servers participate in $\mathsf{decryptShare}_{sk_1, \ldots, sk_n}\left(E^h_{pk_j}(\ell_j), \frac{\cdot q^2}{n-t}\right)$ and end with additive shares of ℓ'_j: $\ell'_j\cdot, \ldots, \ell'_{jn}$ and commitments of these shares: $\bar{\ell}'_j\cdot, \ldots, \bar{\ell}'_{jn}$ ($\ell'_j = \ell_j \Leftrightarrow sk = sk_j$);

    c) Each server $\mathcal{S}_i$ broadcasts $\bar{y}_{ji} \leftarrow E^h_{PK}(\ell'_{ji})$, together with a zero knowledge proof of plaintext equality $\Pi_i = \mathsf{zkp}[y_{ji} : D_{SK}(\bar{y}_{ji}) = y_{ji}, D_{sk}(\bar{\ell}'_{ji}) = y_{ji}]$;

    d) All the servers check the zero knowledge proofs received from the other servers. If some proofs do not verify, then the servers that sent them are excluded from the protocol;

    e) All the servers compute $\bar{y}_j = \bar{y}_j\cdot +_{PK} \cdots +_{PK} \bar{y}_{jn}$;

    f) All the servers participate in $\mathsf{testRecord}_{pk'}(\mathsf{PK}, \bar{x}, \bar{y}_j, \bar{f}, \bar{r}_j, \bar{m})$ to obtain $(T_j, \bar{f}, \bar{r}'_j, \bar{m})$.

    g) Set the database tuple $\mathcal{D}_j$ to be $\langle E^h_{pk_j}(\ell_j), e_j, \bar{r}'_j\rangle$.
    (the template is $(T\cdot, T\cdot, \ldots, T_d)$)

5. An arbitrary server computes $T = (T\cdot \ _{pk'} e\cdot) +_{pk'} \cdots +_{pk'} (T_d \cdot_{pk'} e_d)$ and sends T and $\bar{m}$ to $\mathcal{C}$.

6. $\mathcal{C}$ computes $e \leftarrow D_{sk'}(T) \bmod q, m \leftarrow D_{sk'}(\bar{m}) \bmod q$ and parses e as $e = (r, \delta)$.
    - if $m = 0$, output none;
    - otherwise, check $r = \mathsf{H}(\delta)$ and if this holds, output data δ and m number of matches;
    - if consistency check does not hold, output error.

Fig. 5. The pull protocol

4.5 Extensions

Data of Arbitrary Length. The protocols given above can be extended to record data of arbitrary length as follows. First, the push operation can be naturally extended to include multiple data items, e.g., $\mathsf{push}(E_{pk}(\ell), \delta_1, \ldots, \delta_k)$. Next, step 4 in the pull protocol (Fig. 5) can be performed for each of the k data items, using the same template $(T_1, \ldots, T_d)$. Note that this does not increase the communication complexity among the servers. This is particularly efficient for large data records. For example, if the Paillier system is used, then the client/server communication complexity is asymptotically twice the actual data size transmitted.

$\text{testRecord}_{pk}(\text{PK}, \bar{x}, \bar{y}, \bar{f}, \bar{r}, \bar{m})$

1. All the servers participate in $\bar{z} \leftarrow \text{shareModQ}_{PK}\left(\bar{x} -_{PK} \bar{y}, q, \frac{\cdot q^2}{n-t}\right)$.

2. All the servers participate in $\bar{w} \leftarrow \text{expModQ}_{PK}\left(\bar{z}, q-1, q, \frac{\cdot q^2}{n-t}\right)$.

3. All the servers participate in $\bar{g} \leftarrow \text{mult}_{PK}\left(\bar{1} -_{PK} \bar{w}, \bar{r}, \frac{\cdot q^2}{n-t}\right)$
   and $\bar{s} \leftarrow \text{mult}_{PK}\left(\bar{g}, \bar{f}, \frac{\cdot q^2}{n-t}\right)$.

4. All the servers participate in $\text{decryptShare}_{SK_1, \ldots, SK_n}\left(\bar{s}, \frac{\cdot\cdot n - \cdot\cdot^2 q^2}{n-t}\right)$ and end up with shares $s_\cdot, \ldots, s_n$ and commitments $\bar{s}_\cdot, \ldots, \bar{s}_n$.

5. S_i computes $u_i \leftarrow E_{pk}(s_i), i = 1, \ldots, n$. Then, S_i broadcasts u_i together with a zero knowledge proof $\Pi_i = \text{zkp}[t_i : D_{sk}(u_i) = s_i, D_{SK}(\bar{s}_i) = s_i]$.

6. All the servers check the zero knowledge proofs received from the other servers. If some proofs do not verify, then the servers that sent them are excluded from the protocol.

7. All the servers compute $u = u_\cdot +_{pk} u_\cdot +_{pk} \cdots +_{pk} u_n$.

8. $\bar{r}' \leftarrow \text{mult}_{PK}\left(\bar{r}, \bar{1} -_{PK} \bar{s}, \frac{\cdot\cdot n - \cdot\cdot^2 q^2}{n-t}\right)$,
   $\bar{f}' \leftarrow \text{mult}_{PK}\left(\bar{f}, \bar{1} -_{PK} \bar{g}, \frac{\cdot\cdot n - \cdot\cdot^2 q^2}{n-t}\right)$.

9. The servers get a re-encryption of $1 - w$ under public key pk', analogously to steps 4-6 above. Denote the additive shares by $h_\cdot, \ldots, h_n$ and the encryption of $1 - w$ under pk' by h. Then, the servers update $\bar{m}' \leftarrow \bar{m} +_{pk} h$.

10. The output of the protocol is the tuple $(u, \bar{f}', \bar{r}', \bar{m}')$.

Fig. 6. The testRecord protocol

The Peek Protocol. In order to retrieve a matching record by index, here we sketch a peek protocol, which can be easily derived from the pull protocol.

In addition to the parameters to the pull protocol, the peek protocol includes a flag $\bar{i}$, which is an encryption of the desired index i under the public service key. The database will return the ith record matching label i or 0, if this does not exist, as well as the number of records matching the label. The flags $\bar{r}_j$ for each record and the flag $\bar{f}$ are not used in this version of the protocol. In step 4(f) the parameters passed to the testRecord protocol are $PK, \bar{x}, \bar{y}_j$, and $\bar{i}$. These are the only changes to the pull protocol.

The servers obliviously decrement $\bar{i}$ at each match found in the database, and return the record at which $\bar{i}$ becomes an encryption of 0. After steps 1-2 in testRecord, we test if $\bar{i}$ is an encryption of 0. We insert a step 2' after step 2, in which $\bar{e} \leftarrow \text{expModQ}_{PK}\left(\bar{i}, q-1, q, \frac{2q^2}{n-t}\right)$ is computed. $\bar{1} -_{PK} \bar{e}$ is an encryption of 1 if $i = 0$. Step 3 changes to $\bar{t} \leftarrow \text{mult}_{PK}\left(\bar{1} -_{PK} \bar{w}, \bar{1} -_{PK} \bar{e}, \frac{2(n-1)^2 q^2}{n-t}\right)$. Steps 4-7 remain the same. In step 8, we update the value of the index to $\bar{i} -_{PK} (\bar{1} -_{PK} \bar{w})$.

Beyond Exact Label Matching. We have described our push and pull protocols in terms of exact label matching, though this can be generalized to support retrieval based on other predicates on labels. Specifically, given a common predicate Π, on a pull request with label x the servers could use secure multiparty computation (the techniques in [7] are particularly suited in our setting) to compute the template $(T_1, \ldots, T_d)$ indicating the records for which the labels match x under predicate Π.

4.6 Efficiency

Our push, pull and peek protocols achieve a constant communication complexity in ciphertexts between the client and the servers. The communication among the servers in the pull protocol is proportional to the number of records in the distributed database and the number of servers.

We achieve a tradeoff between the level of security obtained by our protocols and their computational and communication complexity. If complexity is a concern, then more efficient protocols can be constructed by removing the zero-knowledge proofs and the value commitments generated in the protocols. Using standard techniques, we could show that the protocols constructed this way are secure in the honest-but-curious model. However, due to space limitations, we do not address this further in the paper.

5 Asynchronous Anonymous Communication

P^3 potentially has many uses in applications where privacy is important. As an example, in this section we outline the design of a simple anonymous message service using P^3 as a primitive. This message service enables a client to deposit a message for another client to retrieve at its convenience.

The messaging scheme is as follows:

- A sender uses the push protocol to add a label, encrypted under the receiver's public key, and a message to the database. In this context we call the label a *mailbox address*.
  - The message should be encrypted for privacy from the servers.
  - The mailbox address can either be a default address or one established by agreement between the sender and receiver. This agreement is necessary so that the receiver may retrieve the message.
- A receiver uses the pull or peek protocol to retrieve messages sent to a known mailbox address under his public key.

Because messages will accumulate at the servers, they may wish to determine some schedule on which to delete messages. Reasonable options include deleting all messages at set intervals, or deleting all messages of a certain set age.

Privacy. We achieve the content privacy and unlinkability anonymity properties as described in [9]. If the sender encrypts the message submitted to the servers, the servers cannot read the message, and thus achieves content privacy. Unlinkability concerns the ability for the servers to determine which pairs of users (if any) are communicating. As the P^3 servers can not determine the public key under which a label was encrypted, the label itself, or the text of the message, it has no advantage in determining the intended recipient of a message. Nor can they determine which message a client retrieved, if any, or even if a message has been retrieved by any client at any past time. Thus the servers have no advantage in determining which client was the actual recipient of any given message.

As well as these properties, we achieve anonymity between senders and receivers. Any party may either retain this anonymity, or identify himself to other parties.

Senders are by default anonymous to receivers if they address their message to the default mailbox address. Note that the key with which they addressed their message is invisible to the recipient, and so a recipient cannot give a certain public key to a certain sender to abridge their anonymity. A sender may construct an anonymous return address, for use in addressing return messages, by encrypting an appropriate label under the sender's own public key. As we require key privacy of the cryptosystem used, the receiver cannot link the public key used to the identity of the sending party. A sender may sign their messages using a key to which they have attached an identity, if they do not wish to be anonymous.

Asynchronous Communication. Our system also benefits from the property of asynchrony, meaning that the senders and receivers do not have to be on-line simultaneously to communicate. The system is analogous to a bulletin board, where senders deposit messages and from which receivers retrieve them in a given interval of time. From this perspective, our system offers a different type of service than most prior approaches to anonymous communication (e.g., [4,16,5,19,18]) which anticipate the receiver being available when the sender sends. A notable exception is [9], which bears similarity to our approach. However, our use of P^3 permits better communication complexity between the clients and servers than does the use of PIR in [9].

6   Conclusion

We defined the Private Push and Pull (P^3) architecture. This allows clients to privately add (through the push protocol) and retrieve (through the pull or peek protocols) records in the database through transparent interaction with any of the distributed database servers. Under the protocols given, the servers identify which record is to be returned through keyword matching under a particular secret key. If at most t of n servers are actively corrupted, the keyword, key, and return result of a pull or peek protocol is computationally hidden from the servers, and any number of colluding clients.

Client communication in P^3 is independent of both the size of the database and the number of database servers, and requires only the number of ciphertexts corresponding to encryption of the data. Communication between the servers is linear in both the number of records in the database and the number of servers.

Using these protocols, we suggest an implementation of an anonymous messaging system. It achieves unlinkability, but both sender and receiver anonymity can be achieved through slight modifications.

References

1. M. Bellare, A. Boldyreva, A. Desai, D. Pointcheval. *Key-Privacy in Public Key Encryption.* In *Advances in Cryptology — Asiacrypt'01*, LNCS 2248.

2. M. Blum, A. De-Santis, S. Micali, G. Persiano. *Noninteractive Zero-Knowledge*. In *SIAM Journal on Computation*, vol. 20, pp. 1084-1118, 1991.
3. C. Cachin, S. Micali, M. Stadler. *Computational Private Information Retrieval with Polylogarithmic Communication*. In *Advances in Cryptology — Eurocrypt '97*, pp. 455-469, 1997.
4. D. Chaum. *Untraceable electronic mail, return addresses, and digital pseudonyms*. In *Communications of the ACM* 24(2):84–88, February 1981.
5. D. Chaum. *The Dining Cryptographers Problem: Unconditional Sender and Recipient Untraceability*. In *Journal of Cryptology*, 1(1), pp 65-75, 1988.
6. B. Chor, N. Gilboa, M. Naor. *Private Information Retrieval by Keywords* Technical Report TR CS0917, Department of Computer Science, Technion, 1997
7. R. Cramer, I. Damgård, J. Buus Nielsen. *Multiparty Computation from Threshold Homomorphic Encryption*. In *Advances in Cryptology – Eurocrypt 2001*, pp. 280-299, 2001.
8. B. Chor, O. Goldreich, E. Kushilevitz, M. Sudan. *Private information retrieval*. In *Proc. 36th IEEE Symposium on Foundations of Computer Science*, 1995.
9. D. A. Cooper, K. P. Birman. *Preserving privacy in a network of mobile computers*. In *Proceedings of the 1995 IEEE Symposium on Security and Privacy*, pages 26–38, May 1995.
10. P. Fouque, G. Poupard, J. Stern. *Sharing Decryption in the Context of Voting of Lotteries*. In *Financial Crypto 2000*, 2000.
11. O. Goldreich. *Secure Multi-Party Computation*. Working draft available at `http://theory.lcs.mit.edu/~oded/gmw.html`.
12. S. Goldwasser, S. Micali. *Probabilistic Encryption*. In *Journal of Computer and Systems Sciencee*, vol. 28, pp 270-299, 1984.
13. W. Ogata, K. Kurosawa. *Oblivious keyword search*. Available at `http://eprint.iacr.org/2002/182/`.
14. R. Ostrovsky, V. Shoup. *Private information storage*. In *Proceedings of the 29th ACM Symposium on Theory of Computing*, 1997.
15. P. Paillier. *Public-key cryptosystems based on composite degree residue classes*. In *Advances in Cryptology – EUROCRYPT '99* (LNCS 1592), pp. 223–238, 1999.
16. A. Pfitzmann, M. Waidner. *Networks without user observability*. *Computers & Security* 2(6):158–166, 1987.
17. M. Rabin. *How to exchange secrets by oblivious transfer*. Technical Report, Tech. Memo. TR-81, Aiken Computation Laboratory, Harvard University, 1981.
18. M G. Reed, P. F. Syverson, D. M. Goldschlag. *Anonymous connections and onion routing*. *IEEE Journal on Selected Areas in Communication*, Special Issue on Copyright and Privacy Protection, 1998.
19. M. K. Reiter, A. D. Rubin. *Crowds: Anonymity for web transactions*. *ACM Transactions on Information and System Security* 1(1):66–92, November 1998.

Secure Conjunctive Keyword Search
over Encrypted Data

Philippe Golle[1], Jessica Staddon[1], and Brent Waters[2*]

[.] Palo Alto Research Center
3333 Coyote Hill Road
Palo Alto, CA 94304, USA
{pgolle,staddon}@parc.com
[.] Princeton University
Princeton, NJ 08544, USA
bwaters@cs.princeton.edu

Abstract. We study the setting in which a user stores encrypted documents (e.g. e-mails) on an untrusted server. In order to retrieve documents satisfying a certain search criterion, the user gives the server a *capability* that allows the server to identify exactly those documents. Work in this area has largely focused on search criteria consisting of a single keyword. If the user is actually interested in documents containing each of several keywords (*conjunctive* keyword search) the user must either give the server capabilities for each of the keywords individually and rely on an intersection calculation (by either the server or the user) to determine the correct set of documents, or alternatively, the user may store additional information on the server to facilitate such searches. Neither solution is desirable; the former enables the server to learn which documents match each individual keyword of the conjunctive search and the latter results in exponential storage if the user allows for searches on every set of keywords.

We define a security model for conjunctive keyword search over encrypted data and present the first schemes for conducting such searches securely. We propose first a scheme for which the communication cost is linear in the number of documents, but that cost can be incurred "offline" before the conjunctive query is asked. The security of this scheme relies on the Decisional Diffie-Hellman (DDH) assumption. We propose a second scheme whose communication cost is on the order of the number of keyword fields and whose security relies on a new hardness assumption.

Keywords: Searching on encrypted data.

1 Introduction

The proliferation of small hand-held devices and wireless networking enables mobile users to access their data at any time and from anywhere. For reasons

---

* Much of this work was completed while this author was an intern at PARC.

M. Jakobsson, M. Yung, J. Zhou (Eds.): ACNS 2004, LNCS 3089, pp. 31–45, 2004.
© Springer-Verlag Berlin Heidelberg 2004

of cost and convenience, users often store their data not on their own machine, but on remote servers that may also offer better connectivity. When the server is untrusted, users ensure the confidentiality of their data by storing it encrypted.

Document encryption, however, makes it hard to retrieve data selectively from the server. Consider, for example, a server that stores a collection of encrypted emails belonging to a user. The server is unable to determine the subset of encrypted emails defined by a search criteria such as "urgent e-mail" or "e-mail from Bob".

The first practical solution to the problem of searching encrypted data by keyword is given in [15]. Documents and keywords are encrypted in a way that allows the server to determine which documents contain a certain keyword W after receiving from the user a piece of information called a *capability for keyword* W. The capability for W reveals only which documents contain keyword W and no other information. Without a capability, the server learns nothing about encrypted documents. Recent improvements and extensions to this scheme are given in [3,9,17].

A limitation common to all these schemes is that they only allow the server to identify the subset of documents that match a certain keyword, but do not allow for boolean combinations of such queries. Yet boolean combinations of queries appear essential to make effective use of a document repository, since simple keyword search often yields far too coarse results. For example, rather than retrieving *all* emails from "Bob", a user might only want those emails from Bob that are marked urgent and pertain to finance, in which case what is needed is the ability to search on the conjunction of the keywords, "Bob", "urgent" and "finance".

In this paper, we propose protocols that allow for *conjunctive* keyword queries on encrypted data. Although such conjunctive searches certainly do not encompass all possible search criteria, we believe that they are a crucial building block as indicated by the reliance of today's web search engines on conjunctive search (see, for example [10]). To motivate the problem of conjunctive search further, and illustrate the difficulties it raises, we briefly review two simple solutions and explain why they are unsatisfactory:

- **Set intersection.** A first approach to the problem of conjunctive keyword search is to build upon the simple keyword search techniques of [15]. Given a conjunction of keywords, we may provide the server with a search capability for every individual keyword in the conjunction. For every keyword, the server finds the set of documents that match that keyword, then returns the intersection of all those sets. This approach is flawed because it allows the server to learn a lot of extra information in addition to the results of the conjunctive query. Indeed, the server can observe which documents contain each individual keyword. Over time, the server may combine this information with knowledge of statistically likely searches to infer information about the user's documents.
- **Meta-keywords.** Another approach is to define a meta-keyword for every possible conjunction of keywords. Like regular keywords, these meta-keywords can be associated with documents. For example, a document that

contains the keywords "Bob", "urgent" and "finance" may be augmented with the meta-keyword "Bob: urgent: finance". With the techniques of [15], meta-keywords allow for conjunctive keyword search. The obvious drawback of this approach is that a document that contains m keywords requires an additional 2^m meta-keywords to allow for all possible conjunctive queries. This leads to an exponential (in m) blow-up in the amount of data that must be stored on the server.

These two failed approaches illustrate the twin requirements of conjunctive search protocols: security and efficiency. The first contribution of this paper is to formalize these goals. Specifically, we define a formal security model for conjunctive keyword search on encrypted data. This security model states, essentially, that the server should learn nothing other than the result of the conjunctive query. In particular, the server should not be able to generate new capabilities from existing capabilities, other than logical extensions, such as using a capability for W_1 and a capability for W_2 to generate a capability for $W_1 \wedge W_2$. Recall that security is only considered in the context of single keyword search in [3,15, 9], and so our definitions present a significant extension to prior security models.

We present two schemes that provably meet our definition of security. Both of our schemes come with a moderate storage cost. Our first scheme incurs a communication cost per query that is linear in the number of documents stored. However, the linear portion of this cost may be pre-transmitted and a constant size cost can then be paid when the user decides which query is of interest. Our second scheme works in groups for which there exists an admissible bilinear map [13,2] and relies on a new hardness assumption for its security. This scheme has the desirable attribute of requiring only constant communication with no need for pre-transmissions.

OVERVIEW. This paper is organized as follows. In Section 1.1 we discuss related work. Section 2 covers our notation, security definitions and hardness assumptions. We present a scheme for conjunctive search with amortized linear cost in Section 3 and a scheme with constant cost in Section 4. We conclude in Section 5.

1.1   Related Work

In [15], Song, Wagner and Perrig study a model of secure search over encrypted data that is similar to ours in that they consider a bandwidth constrained user who stores documents on an untrusted server. When the user needs all documents containing a certain keyword he provides the server with a small piece of information (called a *capability*) that enables the server to identify the desired (encrypted) documents. They propose an efficient, secret key method for enabling single keyword search that is provably secure. However, they do not provide a method for secure conjunctive search and it is hard to see how their techniques might be extended to accomplish this because their capabilities are deterministic and thus can potentially be combined to generate new capabilities. In our schemes we use modular exponentiation (hence, we incur more computational cost than [15]) and randomization of the capabilities to ensure that a capability to search for documents containing both keyword W_1 and keyword W_2 is incompatible with a capability for W_1, and thus can't be used to generate a capability for W_2.

The use of search over encrypted data in file-sharing networks is investigated in [4], where a secret key system enabling sharing of, and searching for, encrypted data is described.

In [9], Goh presents an efficient scheme for keyword search over encrypted data using Bloom filters. Determining whether a document contains a keyword can be done securely in constant time, however, the scheme does not support secure conjunctive search.

The first public key schemes for keyword search over encrypted data are presented in [3]. The authors consider a setting in which the sender of an email encrypts keywords under the public key of the recipient in such a way that the recipient is able to give capabilities for any particular keyword to their mail gateway for routing purposes. Conjunctive keyword search is not supported in [3]. An efficient implementation of a public key scheme for keyword search tailored for documents that are the audit trails of users querying a database is in [17].

The related notion of negotiated privacy is introduced in [12]. A negotiated privacy scheme differs from the problem of encrypted search as studied here and in [15,3,9] in that the goal is to provide data collectors with the guaranteed ability to conduct specific searches.

Finally, we note that there are existing techniques for searching over encrypted data with increased security but with far less efficiency than our schemes and those described above. For example, private information retrieval (PIR) schemes (see, for example [6,7,5]) can potentially be used to solve this problem. A PIR scheme allows a user to retrieve information from a database server privately, that is without the server learning what information was retrieved. Hence, with a PIR scheme a user can search the documents stored on the database, and thus recover the documents of interest on their own. However, PIR schemes are designed in order to achieve higher security than we require (in a computational sense, the server in a PIR scheme has *no* information about what documents are retrieved) and thus come with far higher communication cost. Similarly, the notion of an oblivious RAM [11] can be leveraged to achieve heightened security, but with a significant efficiency cost. By accepting a weaker security guarantee that seems quite reasonable for our applications we are able to achieve a moderate communication cost.

2   Model

We consider a user that stores encrypted documents on an untrusted server. Let n be the total number of documents. We assume there are m keyword fields associated with each document. If documents were emails for example, we might define the following 4 keyword fields: "From", "To", "Date" and "Subject". For simplicity, we make the following assumptions:

- We assume that the same keyword never appears in two different keyword fields. The easiest way to satisfy this requirement is to prepend keywords with the name of the field they belong to. Thus for example, the keyword "From:Bob" belongs to the "From" field and can not be confused with the keyword "To:Bob" that belongs to the "To" field.

- We assume that every keyword field is defined for every document. This requirement is easily satisfied. In our email example, we may assign the keyword "Subject:NULL" in the "Subject" field to emails that have no subject.

From here onwards, we identify documents with the vector of m keywords that characterize them. For $i = 1, \ldots, n$, we denote the ith document by $D_i = (W_{i,1}, \ldots, W_{i,m})$, where $W_{i,j}$ is the keyword of document D_i in the jth keyword field. The body of the ith document can be encrypted with a standard symmetric key cipher and stored on the server next to the vector of keywords D_i. For ease of presentation we ignore the body of the document and concern ourselves only with the encryption of the keyword vector, D_i.

When discussing a capability that enables the server to verify that a document contains a specific keyword in field j, we denote the keyword by W_j. A scheme for conjunctive keyword search consists of five algorithms, the first four of which are randomized:

- A parameter generation algorithm $\mathsf{Param}(1^k)$ that takes as input a security parameter k and outputs public system parameters ρ.
- A key generation algorithm $\mathsf{KeyGen}(\rho)$ that outputs a set K of secret keys for the user.
- An encryption algorithm $\mathsf{Enc}(\rho, K, D_i)$ that takes as input ρ, K and a document $D_i = (W_{i,1}, \ldots, W_{i,m})$ and outputs an encryption of the vector of keywords.
- An algorithm to generate capabilities $\mathsf{GenCap}(\rho, K, j_1, \ldots, j_\ell, W_{j_1}, \ldots, W_{j_\ell})$ that takes as input ρ, K as well as $1 \leq \ell \leq m$ keyword field indices $j_1, \ldots, j_\ell$ and ℓ keyword values $W_{j_1}, \ldots, W_{j_\ell}$ and outputs a value Cap, the *capability to search for keywords* $W_{j_1}, \ldots, W_{j_\ell}$. We call the portion of the capability that consists of the fields being searched over, $\{j_1, \ldots, j_\ell\}$, the support of the capability and denote it $\mathsf{Sup}(\mathsf{Cap})$.
- A verification algorithm: $\mathsf{Ver}(\rho, \mathsf{Cap}, \mathsf{Enc}(\rho, K, D_i))$ that takes as input ρ, a capability $\mathsf{Cap} = \mathsf{GenCap}(\rho, K, j_1, \ldots, j_\ell, W_{j_1}, \ldots, W_{j_\ell})$ and an encrypted document $\mathsf{Enc}(\rho, K, D_i)$ where $D_i = (W_{i,1}, \ldots, W_{i,m})$ and returns true if the expression $((W_{i,j_1} = W_{j_1}) \wedge (W_{i,j_2} = W_{j_2}) \wedge \ldots \wedge (W_{i,j_\ell} = W_{j_\ell}))$ holds and false otherwise.

Finally, throughout this paper we use the term *negligible function* to refer to a function $\eta : \mathbb{N} \to \mathbb{R}$ such that for any $c \in \mathbb{N}$, there exists $n_c \in \mathbb{N}$, such that $\eta(n) < 1/n^c$ for all $n \geq n_c$.

2.1   Security Definitions

A capability Cap enables the server to divide documents into two groups: those that satisfy the capability, and those that do not. Intuitively, a conjunctive keyword search scheme is secure if the server learns no other information from a set of encrypted documents and capabilities. In this section, we formalize this notion of security. To facilitate the security definitions we define a randomized document $\mathrm{Rand}(D,T)$, for any set of indices $T \subseteq \{1,\ldots,m\}$ and document $D = (W_1,\ldots,W_m)$. $\mathrm{Rand}(D,T)$ is formed from D by replacing the keywords of D that are indexed by T (i.e., the set $\{W_i | i \in T\}$) by random values. Now we define *distinguishing capabilities*:

Definition 1. *A capability* Cap *is distinguishing for documents* D_i *and* D_j *if*

$$\mathsf{Ver}(\rho, \mathsf{Cap}, \mathsf{Enc}(\rho, K, D_i)) \neq \mathsf{Ver}(\rho, \mathsf{Cap}, \mathsf{Enc}(\rho, K, D_j))$$

Given a set of indices, $T \subseteq \{1,\ldots,m\}$, *a capability* Cap *distinguishes a document* D *from* $\mathrm{Rand}(D,T)$ *if*

$$\mathsf{Ver}(\rho, \mathsf{Cap}, \mathsf{Enc}(\rho, K, D)) = \text{true} \quad \text{and} \quad T \cap \mathsf{Sup}(\mathsf{Cap}) \neq \emptyset$$

Note that with high probability the capabilities defined in part 2 of Definition 1 are distinguishing for D and $\mathrm{Rand}(D,T)$ as defined in part 1 of the definition. We provide the second part of the definition largely to introduce some convenient terminology.

We define security for a conjunctive keyword search scheme in terms of a game between a polynomially bounded adversary $\mathcal{A}$ (the server) and a challenger (the user). The goal of $\mathcal{A}$ is to distinguish between the encryptions of two documents, D_0 and D_1 chosen by $\mathcal{A}$. Observe that $\mathcal{A}$ succeeds trivially if it is given a distinguishing capability for D_0 and D_1. We say that the scheme is secure if $\mathcal{A}$ cannot distinguish D_0 and D_1 with non-negligible advantage without the help of a distinguishing capability for D_0 and D_1. Formally:

Security Game ICC (indistinguishability of ciphertext from ciphertext)

1. The adversary, $\mathcal{A}$, adaptively requests the encryption, $\mathsf{Enc}(\rho, K, D)$, of documents, D, and search capabilities, Cap.
2. $\mathcal{A}$ picks two documents, D_0, D_1 such that none of the capabilities Cap given in step 1 is distinguishing for D_0 and D_1. The challenger then chooses b randomly from $\{0,1\}$ and gives $\mathcal{A}$ an encryption of D_b.
3. $\mathcal{A}$ may again ask for encrypted documents and capabilities, with the restriction that $\mathcal{A}$ may not ask for a capability that is distinguishing for D_0 and D_1. The total number of all ciphertext and capability requests is polynomial in k.
4. $\mathcal{A}$ outputs $b_\mathcal{A} \in \{0,1\}$ and is successful if $b_\mathcal{A} = b$. We define the adversary's advantage as: $Adv_\mathcal{A}(1^k) = |\Pr[b_\mathcal{A} = b] - 1/2|$, and the adversary is said to have an ϵ-advantage if $Adv_\mathcal{A}(1^k) > \epsilon$.

Definition 2. *We say a conjunctive search scheme is secure according to the game ICC if for any polynomial time adversary* $\mathcal{A}$, $Adv_\mathcal{A}(1^k)$ *is a negligible function of the security parameter* k.

We next define two variants of this security game that will simplify our proofs. In the first variant, the adversary chooses only one document D_0 as well as a subset T of the keywords of D_0. The challenger creates a document $D_1 = \text{Rand}(D_0, T)$. The goal of $\mathcal{A}$ is to distinguish between an encryption of D_0 and an encryption of D_1. As before, to make the game non-trivial, we need to place restrictions on the capabilities that $\mathcal{A}$ is allowed to ask for. Specifically, $\mathcal{A}$ may not ask for a capability that is distinguishing for D_0 and D_1.

Security Game ICR (indistinguishability of ciphertexts from random)

1. $\mathcal{A}$ may request the encryption $\text{Enc}(\rho, K, D)$ of any documents D, and any search capabilities Cap.
2. $\mathcal{A}$ chooses a document D_0 and a subset $T \subseteq \{1, \ldots, m\}$ such that none of the capabilities Cap given in step 1 distinguishes D_0 from $D_1 = \text{Rand}(D_0, T)$. The challenger then chooses a random bit b and gives $\text{Enc}(\rho, K, D_b)$ to $\mathcal{A}$.
3. $\mathcal{A}$ again asks for encrypted documents and capabilities, with the restriction that $\mathcal{A}$ may not ask for a capability that distinguishes D_0 from D_1. The total number of ciphertext and capability requests is polynomial in k.
4. $\mathcal{A}$ outputs $b_{\mathcal{A}} \in \{0, 1\}$ and is successful if $b_{\mathcal{A}} = b$. As in game ICC, we define the adversary's advantage as $Adv_{\mathcal{A}}(1^k) = |\Pr[b_{\mathcal{A}} = b] - 1/2|$.

Proposition 1. *If there is an adversary $\mathcal{A}$ that wins Game ICC with advantage ϵ, then there exists an adversary $\mathcal{A}'$ that wins Game ICR with advantage $\epsilon/2$.*

Proof. The proof of this proposition is standard and is left to the extended version of this paper.

Our final security game is quite similar to ICR except that we now consider an adversary who is able to distinguish between $\text{Rand}(D, T)$ and $\text{Rand}(D, T - \{t\})$, for some document D and set of indices T, $t \in T$. Again, this game enables simpler security proofs.

Security Game ICLR (indistinguishability of ciphertexts from limited random)

1. $\mathcal{A}$ may request the encryption $\text{Enc}(\rho, K, D)$ of any documents D and any search capabilities Cap.
2. $\mathcal{A}$ chooses a document D, a subset $T \subseteq \{1, \ldots, m\}$ and a value $t \in T$ such that none of the capabilities Cap given in step 1 are distinguishing for $\text{Rand}(D, T)$ and $\text{Rand}(D, T - \{t\})$. The challenger then chooses a random bit b. If $b = 0$, the adversary is given $\text{Enc}(\rho, K, D_0)$, where $D_0 = \text{Rand}(D, T - \{t\})$. If $b = 1$, the adversary is given $\text{Enc}(\rho, K, D_1)$, where $D_1 = \text{Rand}(D, T)$.
3. $\mathcal{A}$ again asks for encrypted documents and capabilities, with the restriction that $\mathcal{A}$ may not ask for a capability that is distinguishing for D_0 and D_1. The total number of ciphertext and capability requests is polynomial in k.
4. $\mathcal{A}$ outputs $b_{\mathcal{A}} \in \{0, 1\}$ and is successful if $b_{\mathcal{A}} = b$. As in game ICC, we define the adversary's advantage as $Adv_{\mathcal{A}}(1^k) = |\Pr[b_{\mathcal{A}} = b] - 1/2|$.

Proposition 2. *If there is an adversary $\mathcal{A}$ that wins Game ICR with advantage ϵ, then there exists an adversary $\mathcal{A}'$ that wins Game ICLR with advantage ϵ/m^2.*

Proof. The proof of this proposition is standard and is left to the extended version of this paper.

2.2 Hardness Assumptions

The proofs of security of our conjunctive search schemes are based on two well-known hardness assumptions, Decisional Diffie-Hellman (DDH) and Bilinear Decisional Diffie-Hellman (BDDH). We briefly describe each of them here, referring the reader to [1] for additional information on DDH and to [2,13] for additional information on BDDH.

DECISIONAL DIFFIE-HELLMAN. Let G be a group of prime order q and g a generator of G. The DDH problem is to distinguish between triplets of the form (g^a, g^b, g^{ab}) and (g^a, g^b, g^c), where a, b, c are random elements of $\{1, \ldots, q - 1\}$. We say a polynomial time adversary $\mathcal{A}$ has advantage ϵ in solving DDH if $|Pr[\mathcal{A}(g^a, g^b, g^{ab}) = \text{true}] - Pr[\mathcal{A}(g^a, g^b, g^c) = \text{true}]| > \epsilon$.

BILINEAR DECISIONAL DIFFIE-HELLMAN[1] Let G_1 and G_2 be groups of prime order q, with an admissible bilinear map (see [2]) $\hat{e} : G_1 \times G_1 \to G_2$, and let g be a generator of G_1. The BDDH problem is to distinguish 4-tuples of the form (g^a, g^b, g^c, g^{abc}) and (g^a, g^b, g^c, g^d), where a, b, c, d are random elements of $\{1, \ldots, q-1\}$. We say a polynomial time adversary $\mathcal{A}$ has advantage ϵ in solving BDDH if $|Pr[\mathcal{A}(g^a, g^b, g^c, g^{abc}) = \text{true}] - Pr[\mathcal{A}(g^a, g^b, g^c, g^d) = \text{true}]| > \epsilon$.

3   A Conjunctive Search Scheme with Constant Online Communication Cost

In the following protocol, the size of the capabilities for conjunctive queries is linear in the total number of documents stored on the server, but the majority of the communication cost between the user and the server can be done *offline*. More precisely, each capability consists of 2 parts:

- **A "proto-capability" part,** that consists of an amount of data that is linear in n, the total number of encrypted documents stored on the server. This data is *independent* of the conjunctive query that the capability allows, and may therefore be transmitted *offline*, possibly long before the user even knows the actual query that the proto-capability will be used for.
- **A "query" part:** a constant amount of data that depends on the conjunctive query that the capability allows. This data must be sent online at the time the query is made. Note that we call this amount of data *constant* because it does not depend on the number of documents stored on the server, but only on the number, m, of keyword fields per documents.

[·] BDDH has appeared in two forms, one in which the last element of the challenge 4-tuple is in the range of bilinear map and a stronger version that we present here and which is used in [16].

The following scenario illustrates how this search protocol might work in practice. An untrusted server with high storage capacity and reliable network connectivity stores encrypted documents on behalf of a user. Whenever the user has access to a machine with a high bandwidth connection (say a home PC), they precompute a lot of proto-capabilities and send them to the server. The server stores these proto-capabilities alongside the encrypted documents until they are used (proto-capabilities are discarded after being used once). If the user has only access to a low-bandwidth connection (a hand-held device for example) at the time they want to query their document repository, the user only need send the constant-size query part of the capability. The server combines that second part with one proto-capability received earlier to reconstitute a full capability that allows it to reply to the user's query. In this manner the high cost portion of the communication complexity can be pre-transmitted by the higher performance desktop and only a small burden is placed on the hand-held device.

Note that this scenario assumes the user does not store their documents directly on their own machine but on an untrusted server. We justify this assumption with the observation that the untrusted server likely offers more reliable and more available network connectivity than a machine belonging to the user.

System parameters and key generation. The function $\mathsf{Param}(1^k)$ returns parameters $\rho = (G, g, f(\cdot, \cdot), h(\cdot))$, where G is a group of order q in which DDH is hard, g is a generator of G, $f : \{0,1\}^k \times \{0,1\}^* \to \mathbb{Z}_q^*$ is a keyed function and h is a hash function. We use h as a random oracle. The security parameter k is used implicitly in the choice of the group G and the functions f and h. The key generation algorithm KeyGen returns a secret key $K \in \{0,1\}^k$ for the function f, and we denote $f(K, \cdot)$ by $f_K(\cdot)$. The family $\{f_K(\cdot)\}_K$ is a pseudorandom function family.

Encryption algorithm. We show how to compute $\mathsf{Enc}(\rho, K, D_i)$ where $D_i = (W_{i,1}, \dots, W_{i,m})$. Let $V_{i,j} = f_K(W_{i,j})$ for $j = 1, \dots, m$. Let a_i be a value chosen uniformly at random from $\mathbb{Z}_q^*$. The output is:

$$\mathsf{Enc}(\rho, K, D_i) = (g^{a_i}, g^{a_i V_{i,1}}, g^{a_i V_{i,2}}, \dots, g^{a_i V_{i,m}})$$

Generating a capability $\mathsf{Cap} = \mathsf{GenCap}(\rho, K, j_1, \dots, j_t, W_{j_1}, \dots, W_{j_t})$.
The capability Cap consists of a vector Q of size linear in the number of documents (the proto-capability that can be sent offline), and of an additional value of constant size (the query part). Let s be chosen uniformly at random from $\mathbb{Z}_q^*$. The vector Q is defined as:

$$Q = \left(h(g^{a_1 s}), h(g^{a_2 s}), \dots, h(g^{a_n s}) \right)$$

In addition, we define the value $C = s + (\Sigma_{w=1}^t f_K(W_{j_w}))$. The capability is the $(t+2)$-tuple, $\mathsf{Cap} = \{Q, C, j_1, \dots, j_t\}$.

Verification. The server computes $R_i = g^{a_i C} \cdot g^{-a_i(\Sigma_{w=1}^t (V_{i,j_w}))}$ and returns true if $h(R_i) = h(g^{a_i s})$ and false otherwise.

3.1 Security Analysis

Proposition 3. *The scheme of Section 3 is secure according to game ICC in the random oracle model if DDH is hard in G.*

Proof. By Propositions 1 and 2, we know that the existence of an adversary that wins game ICC with non-negligible probability implies the existence of an adversary that wins game ICLR with non-negligible probability. Let $\mathcal{A}$ be an adversary that wins game ICLR with advantage ϵ. We build an adversary $\mathcal{A}'$ that uses $\mathcal{A}$ as a subroutine and breaks DDH with non-negligible advantage.

The algorithm $\mathcal{A}'$ first calls the function Param to generate the parameters $\rho = (G, g, f, h)$. Let g^a, g^b, g^c be a Diffie-Hellman challenge (the challenge is to determine whether $c = ab$). $\mathcal{A}'$ guesses a value z for the position t that $\mathcal{A}$ will choose in step 2 of the game ICLR, by picking z uniformly independently at random in $\{1, \dots, m\}$.

The algorithm $\mathcal{A}'$ simulates the function Enc as follows. $\mathcal{A}'$ associates with every keyword W_i a random value x_i. When asked to compute $\mathsf{Enc}(\rho, k, D)$ where $D = (W_1, \dots, W_m)$, $\mathcal{A}'$ chooses a random value a_i and outputs:

$$\mathsf{Enc}(\rho, k, D) = (g^{a_i}, g^{a_i x_1}, \dots, (g^b)^{a_i x_z}, \dots, g^{a_i x_m})$$

When asked to compute $\mathsf{Cap} = \mathsf{GenCap}(\rho, K, j_1, \dots, j_t, W_{j_1}, \dots, W_{j_t})$, $\mathcal{A}'$ outputs a vector $Q = (T_1, \dots, T_n)$ of random values and a random value for C. To evaluate $\mathsf{Ver}(\rho, \mathsf{Cap}, \mathsf{Enc}(\rho, K, D_i))$, $\mathcal{A}$ must compute R_i and then ask $\mathcal{A}'$ for the value $h(R_i)$. $\mathcal{A}'$ knows whether D_i satisfies Cap or not. If it does, $\mathcal{A}'$ defines $h(R_i) = T_i$. Otherwise $\mathcal{A}'$ returns a random value for $h(R_i)$.

Finally, $\mathcal{A}$ submits a challenge document $D = (W_1, \dots, W_m)$ for encryption along with a set $T \subseteq \{1, \dots, m\}$ and a value $t \in T$. If $z \neq t$, $\mathcal{A}'$ returns a random guess in reply to the DDH challenge. With probability $1/m$, we have $z = t$ and in that case $\mathcal{A}'$ proceeds as follows. Let $E_t = (g^c)^{x_t}$. For $j \in T$, $j \neq t$, let $E_j = R_j$ for a random value R_j. For $j \notin T$, let $E_j = (g^a)^{x_j}$. $\mathcal{A}'$ returns to $\mathcal{A}$ the following ciphertext:

$$(g^a, E_1, \dots, E_m)$$

Observe that this ciphertext is an encryption of D in every position $j \notin T$. If $c = ab$, this ciphertext is also an encryption of D in position t; otherwise it is not.

Now $\mathcal{A}$ is again allowed to ask for encryption of documents and for capabilities, with the restriction that $\mathcal{A}$ may not ask for capabilities that are distinguishing for $\mathrm{Rand}(D, T - \{t\})$ and $\mathrm{Rand}(D, T)$. This restriction ensures that $\mathcal{A}'$ can reply to all the queries of $\mathcal{A}$ as before.

Finally $\mathcal{A}$ outputs a bit $b_\mathcal{A}$. If $b_\mathcal{A} = 0$, $\mathcal{A}'$ guesses that g^a, g^b, g^c is not a DDH triplet. If $b_\mathcal{A} = 1$, $\mathcal{A}'$ guesses that g^a, g^b, g^c is a DDH triplet. Since the encryption will be random at position i if and only if the challenge is not a DDH tuple $\mathcal{A}'$ solves the DDH challenge with the same advantage that $\mathcal{A}$ has in winning game ICLR. □

4   A Conjunctive Search Scheme with Constant Communication Cost

In this section, we describe a protocol for which the total communication cost of sending a capability to the server is constant in the number of documents (but linear in the number of keyword fields). With this protocol, a low-bandwidth hand-held device will be able to construct capabilities on its own and the overall communication overhead will be low.

System parameters and key generation. The function $\mathsf{Param}(1^k)$ returns parameters $\rho = (G_1, G_2, \hat{e}, g, f(\cdot, \cdot))$, where G_1 and G_2 are two groups of order q, g is a generator of G_1, $\hat{e} : G_1 \times G_1 \to G_2$ is an admissible bilinear map and a keyed function $f : \{0,1\}^k \times \{0,1\}^* \to \mathbb{Z}_q^*$. The security parameter k is used implicitly in the choice of the groups G_1 and G_2. The key generation algorithm KeyGen returns a secret value α and K. Again, we denote $f(K, \cdot)$ by $f_K(\cdot)$, and $\{f_K(\cdot)\}_K$ forms a pseudorandom function family.

Encryption algorithm. We show how to compute $\mathsf{Enc}(\rho, K, D_i)$ where $D_i = (W_{i,1}, \ldots, W_{i,m})$. Let $V_{i,j} = f_K(W_{i,j})$ for $j = 1, \ldots, m$. Let $R_{i,j}$ for $j = 1, \ldots, m$ be m values drawn uniformly independently at random from $\mathbb{Z}_q^*$. Let a_i be a value chosen uniformly at random from $\mathbb{Z}_q^*$. The function Enc returns:

$$g^{a_i}, \left(g^{a_i(V_{i,1}+R_{i,1})}, \ldots, g^{a_i(V_{i,m}+R_{i,m})} \right), \left(g^{a_i \alpha R_{i,1}}, \ldots, g^{a_i \alpha R_{i,m}} \right)$$

Generating a capability $\mathsf{Cap} = \mathsf{GenCap}(\rho, K, j_1, \ldots, j_t, W_{j_1}, \ldots, W_{j_t})$.
Let r be a value chosen uniformly at random from $\mathbb{Z}_q^*$. The capability Cap is:

$$\mathsf{Cap} = (g^{\alpha r}, g^{\alpha r (\sum_{w=1}^{t} f_K(W_{j_w}))}, g^r, j_1, \ldots, j_t)$$

Verification. We show how to compute $\mathsf{Ver}(\rho, \mathsf{Cap}, \mathsf{Enc}(\rho, K, D_i))$ where $\mathsf{Cap} = (g^{\alpha r}, g^{\alpha r (\sum_{w=1}^{t} f_K(W_{j_w}))}, g^r, j_1, \ldots, j_t)$ and $D_i = (W_{i,1}, \ldots, W_{i,m})$. The algorithm checks whether the following equality holds:

$$\hat{e}(g^{\alpha r (\sum_{w=1}^{t} f_K(W_{j_w}))}, g^{a_i}) = \prod_{k=1}^{t} \left(\frac{\hat{e}(g^{\alpha r}, g^{a_i(V_{i,j_k} + R_{i,j_k})})}{\hat{e}(g^r, g^{a_i \alpha R_{i,j_k}})} \right)$$

and returns true if the equality holds, and false otherwise.

4.1   Security Analysis without Capabilities

We first demonstrate a partial security result; namely, that when no capabilities are generated ciphertexts are indistinguishable provided BDDH is hard. To that end, we define a game ICC' which is identical to security game ICC of Section 2 except that *no* capabilities are generated (i.e. steps 1 and 3 are modified). Hence, the adversary who engages in Security Game ICC', renders an adaptive, chosen-plaintext attack.

Proposition 4. *If the Bilinear Decisional Diffie-Hellman (BDDH) problem is hard in G_1, then no adversary can win game ICC' with non-negligible advantage.*

Proof. Let A be an adversary who wins Security Game ICC' with advantage ϵ. We build an adversary A' which uses A as a subroutine and solves the BDDH problem. Let g^α, g^A, g^a, g^d be a BDDH challenge (the challenge is to decide whether $d = \alpha A a$).

When A asks for a document to be encrypted, A' does the following. For each keyword W_i it chooses a random value x_i. A' keeps track of the correspondence between keywords W_i and values x_i so that if a keyword appears multiple times (possibly in different documents), the same x_i is used consistently for that keyword. A' then chooses a random value a_i and random values $R_{i,1}, \ldots, R_{i,m}$. Finally, A' outputs

$$g^{a_i}, \left(g^{a_i(Ax_1 + R_{i,1})}, \ldots, g^{a_i(Ax_m + R_{i,m})} \right) \left(g^{a_i \alpha R_{i,1}}, \ldots, g^{a_i \alpha R_{i,m}} \right)$$

Note that A' can compute all of these values since it knows a_i, x_j and the $R_{i,j}$. Note also that the above is a valid encryption of the document requested by A. Now for its challenge, A asks for one more document D to be encrypted. The problem is for A to determine whether the encryption it receives from A' is an encryption of D or of a random document. A' chooses random values $b_1, \ldots, b_m$ and outputs

$$g^a, \left(g^{b_1}, \ldots, g^{b_m} \right), \left(g^{\alpha b_1 - dx_1}, \ldots, g^{\alpha b_m - dx_m} \right)$$

Note that A' can compute the value above and that if $d = \alpha A a$, the encryption above is an encryption of D. Otherwise it is an encryption of a random document. A outputs a guess as to whether it's been given an encryption of D or an encryption of a random document, and A' outputs the same guess as to whether $d = \alpha A a$ or not. Hence, just as in Proposition 3, if A's advantage in Security Game ICC' is ϵ, then the advantage of A' in solving BDDH is ϵ. □

4.2   Security Analysis with Capabilities

We present here a complete security analysis of the protocol of Section 4, including capabilities. Unfortunately, in a security model that includes capabilities (Game ICC), we do not know how to reduce the security of the protocol to a standard security assumption. Indeed, the breadth of applications for bilinear maps often necessitates new, nonstandard, hardness assumptions (see, for example [8]). We rely on the following new assumption:

Hardness Assumption (Game HA):
We define the following game. Let $\mathcal{G}$ be a group of order q, and let $g \in \mathcal{G}$ be a generator of $\mathcal{G}$. We assume the existence of an admissible bilinear map $\hat{e} : \mathcal{G} \times \mathcal{G} \to \mathcal{G}_2$. The game proceeds as follows:

1. We choose two random values $a, \alpha \in \mathbb{Z}_q^*$ and give $\mathcal{A}$, the adversary g^a and g^α.
2. $\mathcal{A}$ can request as many times as it wants and in any order the following:
   - **A variable.** Whenever $\mathcal{A}$ requests a new variable, we pick a random value $x_i \in \mathbb{Z}_q^*$ and give the adversary g^{x_i}.
   - **A product.** $\mathcal{A}$ specifies a subset $S = \{i_1, \dots, i_k\}$ of variables. We pick a random value $r \in \mathbb{Z}_q^*$ and return to the adversary g^r, $g^{\alpha r}$ and $g^{\alpha r(x_{i_1} + \dots + x_{i_k})}$.
3. $\mathcal{A}$ chooses two subsets T and T' of indices such that $T \cap T' = \emptyset$.
4. We give $\mathcal{A}$ the value $g^{a \alpha x_i}$ for all $i \in T'$. Next, we flip a bit b. If $b = 0$, we give the adversary the value $g^{a \alpha x_i}$ for all $i \in T$. If $b = 1$, we give the adversary g^{r_i} for a randomly chosen value $r_i \in \mathbb{Z}_q^*$ for all $i \in T$.
5. $\mathcal{A}$ outputs a bit $b_{\mathcal{A}}$.

We say that $\mathcal{A}$ wins game HA if the following two conditions hold:

- The adversary's guess is correct, i.e. $b_{\mathcal{A}} = b$.
- Let $S_1, \dots, S_n$ be the list of sets requested by $\mathcal{A}$ in step 2 of the game HA. For any $i = 1, \dots, n$, if $S_i \subseteq (T \cup T')$ then $S_i \cap T = \emptyset$.

Proposition 5. *If game HA is hard for $\mathcal{G}_1$, then no adversary can win the game ICC with non-negligible advantage.*

Proof. By Proposition 1, we know that the existence of an adversary who wins game ICC with non-negligible advantage implies the existence of an adversary who wins game ICR with non-negligible advantage. Let $\mathcal{A}$ be an adversary who wins game ICR with non-negligible advantage. We show how to construct an algorithm $\mathcal{A}'$ that uses $\mathcal{A}$ as a subroutine and wins game HA with non-negligible probability. The algorithm $\mathcal{A}'$ begins by asking for two values g^a and g^α (step 1 of game HA).

Next, we show how $\mathcal{A}'$ simulates the encryption function Enc for $\mathcal{A}$. When $\mathcal{A}$ wants a document encrypted, $\mathcal{A}'$ asks for a variable g^{x_i} for every new keyword W_i. The algorithm $\mathcal{A}'$ keeps track of the correspondence between keywords and values in $\mathcal{G}$ such that it can reuse values consistently if a keywords appears several times. To compute $\mathsf{Enc}(\rho, K, D)$ where $D = (W_1, \dots, W_m)$, the algorithm $\mathcal{A}'$ chooses a random value a_i and m random values $R_1, \dots, R_m$ and gives to $\mathcal{A}$:

$$g^{a_i}, \left((g^{x_1})^{a_i} g^{R_1}, \dots, (g^{x_m})^{a_i} g^{R_m} \right), \left((g^\alpha)^{a_i R_1}, \dots, (g^\alpha)^{a_i R_m} \right)$$

We show now how $\mathcal{A}'$ simulates capabilities for $\mathcal{A}$. Suppose that $\mathcal{A}$ asks for the following capability: $\mathsf{Cap} = \mathsf{GenCap}(\rho, K, j_1, \dots, j_t, W_{j_1}, \dots, W_{j_t})$. The algorithm $\mathcal{A}'$ asks for the values g^r, $g^{\alpha r}$ and $g^{\alpha r(x_{j_1} + \dots + x_{j_t})}$ and outputs:

$$\mathsf{Cap} = \left(g^r, g^{\alpha r}, g^{\alpha r(x_{j_1} + \dots + x_{j_t})} \right)$$

It is easy to verify that $\mathsf{Cap} = \mathsf{GenCap}(\rho, K, j_1, \dots, j_t, W_{j_1}, \dots, W_{j_t})$.

At some point, $\mathcal{A}$ chooses a challenge document $D = (W_1, \ldots, W_m)$ and a subset $T \subseteq \{1, \ldots, m\}$ (step 2 of game ICR). Without loss of generality, we assume that every keyword W_i has already appeared, i.e. $\mathcal{A}'$ already has a corresponding value g^{x_i}. If not, $\mathcal{A}'$ simply asks for the missing values g^{x_i}. The adversary $\mathcal{A}'$ defines $T' = \{1, \ldots, m\} \setminus T$.

Now $\mathcal{A}'$ chooses m new random values $y_1, \ldots, y_m$ and computes $g^{\alpha y_1}, \ldots, g^{\alpha y_m}$. Next, $\mathcal{A}'$ submits the sets T and T' as in step 3 of game HA. In return, $\mathcal{A}'$ gets values $g^{\delta_1}, \ldots, g^{\delta_m}$, where $\delta_j = a\alpha x_j$ for every $j \in T'$ and for $j \in T$, either $\delta_j = a\alpha x_j$ or δ_j is random (recall that the goal of $\mathcal{A}'$ is to distinguish between these two cases). Finally, $\mathcal{A}'$ gives to $\mathcal{A}$ the following value as the encryption of the challenge document D chosen by $\mathcal{A}$:

$$g^a, \left(g^{y_1}, \ldots, g^{y_m}\right), \left((g^{\alpha y_1}/g^{\delta_1}), \ldots, (g^{\alpha y_m}/g^{\delta_m})\right)$$

It is easy to verify that this is a correct encryption of the challenge document D in every position $j \notin T$, and in every position $j \in T$, it is either an encryption of W_j or an encryption of random. In such positions, it is up to the adversary $\mathcal{A}$ to guess which.

In step 3 of game ICR, $\mathcal{A}$ is again allowed to ask for encryption of documents and capabilities. We simulate these exactly as above.

In step 4 of game ICR, $\mathcal{A}$ outputs a bit $b_{\mathcal{A}}$. The adversary $\mathcal{A}'$ then outputs the same bit $b_{\mathcal{A}'} = b_{\mathcal{A}}$. Clearly, if $\mathcal{A}$ wins game ICR with non-negligible advantage, then $\mathcal{A}'$ guesses the bit correctly in game HA with the same non-negligible advantage. What remains to be shown is that the second condition for winning the game holds. That holds since whenever $\mathsf{Ver}(\rho, \mathsf{Cap}, \mathsf{Enc}(\rho, K, D)) = \mathsf{true}$ we must have that the set T was not queried on and therefore for any S that $\mathcal{A}'$ requests to construct a capability $S \cap T = \emptyset$. $\qquad\square$

5   Conclusion and Open Problems

We have presented two protocols for conjunctive search for which it is provably hard for the server to distinguish between the encrypted keywords of documents of its own choosing. Our protocols allow secure conjunctive search with small capabilities. Our work only partially solves the problem of secure Boolean search on encrypted data. In particular, a complete solution requires the ability to do *disjunctive* keyword search securely, both across and within keyword fields.

An important issue that isn't addressed by our security games is the information leaked by the capabilities. In both of our protocols, the server learns the keyword fields that the capability enables the server to search. This alone may be enough to allow the server to infer unintended information about the documents. It would be interesting to explore solutions for the secure search problem that also protect keyword fields.

References

1. D. Boneh. *The decision Diffie-Hellman problem.* In Proceedings of the Third Algorithmic Number Theory Symposium, Lecture Notes in Computer Science, Vol. 1423, Springer-Verlag, pp. 48–63, 1998.
2. D. Boneh and M. Franklin. *Identity based encryption from the Weil pairing.* In *SIAM J. of Computing*, Vol. 32, No. 3, pp. 586-615, 2003.
3. D. Boneh, G. Di Crescenzo, R. Ostrovsky and G. Persiano. *Searchable public key encryption.* To appear in Adances in Cryptology – Eurocrypt '04. Cryptology ePrint Archive, Report 2003/195, September 2003. http://eprint.iacr.org/2003/195/
4. K. Bennett, C. Grothoff, T. Horozov and I. Patrascu. *Efficient sharing of encrypted data.* In proceedings of ACISP 2002.
5. C. Cachin, S. Micali and M. Stadler. *Computationally private information retrieval with polylogarithmic communication.* In Advances in Cryptology – Eurocrypt '99.
6. B. Chor, O. Goldreich, E. Kushilevitz and M. Sudan. *Private information retrieval.* In proceedings of FOCS '95.
7. B. Chor,N. Gilboa and M. Naor. *Private Information Retrieval by Keywords.* Technical report, TR CS0917, Department of Computer Science, Technion, 1997
8. Y. Dodis. *Efficient construction of (distributed) random functions.* In proceedings of the Workshop on Public Key Cryptography (PKC), 2003.
9. E. Goh. *Secure Indexes.* In the Cryptology ePrint Archive, Report 2003/216, March 16, 2004. http://eprint.iacr.org/2003/216/
10. Google, Inc. The basics of Google search. http://www.google.com/help/basics.html
11. O. Goldreich and R. Ostrovsky. *Software protection and simulation on oblivious RAMs.* In J. ACM, pp.431-473, 1996.
12. S. Jarecki, P. Lincoln and V. Shmatikov. *Negotiated privacy.* In the International Symposium on Software Security, 2002.
13. A. Joux. *The Weil and Tate pairings as building blocks for public key cryptosystems.* In Proceedings Fifth Algorithmic Number Theory Symposium, 2002.
14. A. Joux and K. Nguyen. *Separating decision Diffie-Hellman from Diffie-Hellman in cryptographic groups.* In IACR ePrint Archive: http://eprint.iacr.org/2001/003/
15. D. Song, D. Wagner and A. Perrig. *Practical Techniques for Searches on Encrypted Data.* In Proc. of the 2000 IEEE Security and Privacy Symposium, May 2000.
16. V. Tô, R. Safavi-Naini and F. Zhang. *New Traitor Tracing Schemes Using Bilinear Map.* In 2003 ACM Workshop on Digital Rights Management (DRM 2003), October 27, 2003, The Wyndham City Center Washington DC, USA.
17. B. Waters, D. Balfanz, G. Durfee and D. Smetters. *Building an Encrypted and Searchable Audit Log.* In proceedings of NDSS 2004.

Evaluating Security of Voting Schemes in the Universal Composability Framework

Jens Groth[1,2]

• BRICS[***], University of Aarhus, IT-parken Åbogade 34, 8000 Århus C, Denmark
• Cryptomathic A/S[†], Jægergårdsgade 118, 8000 Århus C, Denmark
jg@brics.dk

Abstract. In the literature, voting protocols are considered secure if they satisfy requirements such as privacy, accuracy, robustness, etc. It can be time consuming to evaluate a voting protocol with respect to all these requirements and it is not clear that the list of known requirements is complete. Perhaps because of this many papers on electronic voting do not offer any security proof at all.

As a solution to this, we suggest evaluating voting schemes in the universal composability framework. We investigate the popular class of voting schemes based on homomorphic threshold encryption. It turns out that schemes in this class realize an ideal voting functionality that takes the votes as input and outputs the result. This ideal functionality corresponds closely to the well-known ballot box model used today in manual voting. Security properties such as privacy, accuracy and robustness now follow as easy corollaries. We note that some security requirements, for instance incoercibility, are not addressed by our solution.

Security holds in the random oracle model against a non-adaptive adversary. We show with a concrete example that the schemes are not secure against adaptive adversaries. We proceed to sketch how to make them secure against adaptive adversaries in the erasure model with virtually no loss of efficiency. We also briefly hint at how to achieve security against adaptive adversaries in the erasure-free model.

Keywords: Voting, homomorphic threshold encryption, universal composability.

1 Introduction

We consider the security of voting protocols. As time has progressed, more and more security requirements have been published in the literature. Examples of such requirements are privacy, accuracy, fairness, robustness, universal verifiability, incoercibility and receipt-freeness [1,2]. With this growing list of requirements, designers of voting protocols face two problems: if they do not know the

---

[***] Basic Research in Computer Science (www.brics.dk),
 funded by the Danish National Research Foundation.
[†] www.cryptomathic.com

M. Jakobsson, M. Yung, J. Zhou (Eds.): ACNS 2004, LNCS 3089, pp. 46–60, 2004.

literature well they may miss a security requirement, and even if they do cover all known requirements this does not guarantee that new yet to be discovered requirements are satisfied by their voting scheme.

To partially solve these problems we suggest evaluating voting schemes in the universal composability (UC) framework of Canetti [3]. In the UC framework, an execution of a multi-party computation protocol is compared to an execution where a trusted ideal functionality handles the data and produces the output. A protocol is said to be secure if an adversary operating in a real-life model can be simulated in the ideal process model with the ideal functionality. In the case of voting, the ideal functionality takes as input the votes and outputs the result of the election. This ideal functionality corresponds to the old method of voters marking their choice on paper and putting the ballot in a box, which is opened once the election is over.

Let us see how this solution addresses some of the properties that we mentioned. Privacy and accuracy are automatically satisfied since it is a part of the model that input to the ideal functionality is not revealed in any way to the adversary and the ideal functionality does compute the result correctly. Robustness follows too; in the UC framework, we can corrupt parties and still have a good simulation in the ideal process. Fairness follows from the fact that the ideal functionality does not reveal any partial tallies during the process.

Our approach has the advantage that it covers many security requirements in a single security model. This simplifies security proofs since we only need to prove universal composability to prove all these specific security requirements. Our approach is also pro-active in the sense that using a general security model may mean that security requirements yet to be discovered are covered.

We do not claim to solve all security issues with this approach. In particular, universal composability of a voting scheme does not guarantee universal verifiability, incoercibility, receipt-freeness or protection against hackers. However, considering that many security issues are dealt with, and considering that the properties dealt with are often defined vaguely in papers dealing with voting schemes, we do find that this application of the UC framework is worthwhile to investigate.

The UC framework allows for modular composition. In short, this means that if we take a hybrid protocol, where part of the protocol is specified by an ideal functionality, then we can freely plug in any protocol that securely realizes this ideal functionality. Most voting schemes presented in the literature make shortcuts. They assume we have a broadcast channel with memory or an anonymous broadcast channel. Often they also assume some public keys are set up and assume that voters are registered without specifying how this is done. We take this approach too and assume these things are provided through an ideal functionality. The modular composition theorem of the UC framework tells us that this is a sound approach and that we may later insert any protocol that realizes this functionality to get a full-blown election protocol.

The specific class of voting protocols we look at in this paper is based on homomorphic threshold encryption. Many such schemes have been proposed in the literature [4,5,6,7], only the first one of these offers a security proof. We prove that indeed these schemes realize an ideal voting functionality when the adversary is non-adaptive. The schemes are not secure against adaptive adversaries, however, we propose a simple modification to make them secure against adaptive adversaries in the erasure model. Furthermore, in the full paper [8] we suggest another modification based on Paillier encryption that gives security against adaptive adversaries in the erasure-free model.

2   Preliminaries

In this section, we present the various tools used in the class of voting schemes we intend to investigate. Before doing so, we offer a brief introduction to the idea behind this class of voting protocols.

The idea behind voting based on homomorphic encryption. We assume that the parties have access to a message board where everybody may post messages, everybody can read the messages posted on the message board, messages cannot be deleted, and all messages are authenticated, for instance with digital signatures. All communication will take place through this message board. Public data pertaining to the election is also posted on the message board. In particular, a public key pk for a cryptosystem is posted.

In this example, we assume for simplicity that the voters only have two choices. We encode "yes" as 1, while "no" is encoded as 0. A voter casts his vote by encrypting the vote and posting it on the message board, i.e., posting $E_{pk}(0)$ or $E_{pk}(1)$. Since the messages are authenticated, everybody can check whether an eligible voter cast the vote.

The cryptosystem should have a homomorphic property:

$$E_{pk}(m_1; r_1) \cdot E_{pk}(m_2; r_2) = E_{pk}(m_1 + m_2; r_1 + r_2).$$

When everybody has cast his vote we may therefore compute the product of all the ciphertexts and get an encryption of the number of "yes" votes.

Now the authorities must decrypt this ciphertext containing the result of the election. For this purpose, we assume that the cryptosystem has threshold decryption. The authorities each hold a secret share of the private key and if sufficiently many of them cooperate, they may decrypt the ciphertext. However, no coalition below the threshold value is able to decrypt any of the encrypted votes; this preserves privacy.

To prevent cheating we require that voters attach a non-interactive zero-knowledge proof that their ciphertext contains either 0 or 1. Otherwise, it would for instance be easy to cast 100 "yes"-votes by posting $E_{pk}(100)$. Standard non-interactive zero-knowledge proofs are too cumbersome to be used in practice, therefore this is typically done through a 3-move honest verifier zero-knowledge proof of correctness of a vote made non-interactive through the Fiat-Shamir heuristic.

In this section, we define Σ-protocols [9], the type of 3-move honest verifier zero-knowledge proofs that we use. We then note that these proofs in the random oracle model [10] can be transformed into non-interactive zero-knowledge proofs. We prove that in the random oracle model, we are dealing with a proof of knowledge, and for any prover there exists an emulator that also produces corresponding witnesses. This can be seen as a random oracle parallel of witness extended emulation as defined by Lindell [11]. Finally, we define the kind of homomorphic threshold encryption that we need.

Σ-protocols. A Σ-protocol is a special type of 3-move proof system. Say we have an element x and a language L. The prover P knows a witness w for $x \in L$ and wants to convince the verifier V that $x \in L$. We assume that both parties have access to a common reference string σ chosen with a suitable distribution. Some Σ-protocols do not require this, and in that case, we can of course just let σ be the empty string. The protocol goes like this: The prover sends an initial message a, receives a random challenge e and produces an answer z. V can now evaluate (σ, x, a, e, z) and decide whether to accept or reject the proof.

A Σ-protocol satisfies the following properties.

Completeness: Given (x, w) where w is a witness for $x \in L$ the prover will with overwhelming probability convince the verifier, if they both follow the protocol.

Special Soundness: There exists an efficient extractor that for any x given two acceptable proofs (a, e, z) and (a, e', z') with the same initial message but different challenges can compute a witness w for $x \in L$.

Special Honest Verifier Zero-Knowledge: There exists an efficient simulator that given x, e can create a "proof" (a, e, z) for $x \in L$, which is indistinguishable from a real proof with challenge e.

Non-interactive zero-knowledge proofs. Given access to a random oracle $\mathcal{O}$ we can transform a Σ-protocol into a non-interactive proof system. To get the challenge e we form the initial message a, query $\mathcal{O}$ with (x, a, aux) to get the challenge e and then compute the answer z.[1] The proof is then (a, z, aux). To verify such a proof query $\mathcal{O}$ with (x, a, aux) to get e and then run the verifier from the Σ-protocol.

Using standard techniques, we can prove that we get a non-interactive proof system with the following properties:

Completeness: Given (x, w) where w is a witness for $x \in L$ the verifier will accept if both the prover and the verifier follow the protocol.

Soundness: A dishonest prover cannot convince the verifier if $x \notin L$.

Zero-Knowledge: There exist a simulator $S^{\mathcal{O}}$ that given $x \in L$ can create a convincing proof (a, z, aux) indistinguishable from a real proof provided it has the following ability to modify the oracle. It may give (x, a, aux, e) to $\mathcal{O}$

---

[1] Typically, *aux* will contain the identity of the prover in order to prevent somebody else to duplicate the proof and claim to have made it.

and provided (x, a, aux) has not been queried before $\mathcal{O}$ assigns the value e to be the answer to query (x, a, aux).

The random oracle model is an idealization of the Fiat-Shamir heuristic, see [10]. In the Fiat-Shamir heuristic the prover uses a cryptographic hash-function to produce the challenge as $e = \text{hash}(x, a, aux)$.

Witness extended emulation in the random oracle model. A Σ-protocol is a proof of knowledge in the random oracle model. We formulate this in the form of witness extended emulation in the following way. Given some adversary that produces a vector of elements $x \in L$ and valid proofs of memberships of L, there is an emulator E_A that produces identically distributed elements together with the corresponding witnesses for memberships of L.

Theorem 1. *For all adversaries A there exists an expected polynomial time emulator E_A such that for all distinguishers D (even unbounded ones) we have*

$$P[(\boldsymbol{x}, \boldsymbol{p}, s) \leftarrow A^{\mathcal{O}}(z) : (\boldsymbol{x}, \boldsymbol{p}) \in V \wedge D^{\mathcal{O}}(\boldsymbol{x}, \boldsymbol{p}, s, z) = 1]$$
$$\approx P[(\boldsymbol{x}, \boldsymbol{p}, \boldsymbol{w}, s) \leftarrow E_A^{\mathcal{O}}(z) : (\boldsymbol{x}, \boldsymbol{p}) \in V \wedge (\boldsymbol{x}, \boldsymbol{w}) \in W \wedge D^{\mathcal{O}}(\boldsymbol{x}, \boldsymbol{p}, s, z) = 1],$$

where z is some advice with length bounded by a polynomial in k, $\mathcal{O}$ is a random oracle, V is the set of vector pairs $(\boldsymbol{x}, \boldsymbol{p})$ such that $\boldsymbol{p}$ contains valid proofs for the elements in $\boldsymbol{x}$ belonging to L, and W is the set of pairs $(\boldsymbol{x}, \boldsymbol{w})$ where $\boldsymbol{w}$ contains witnesses for the elements of $\boldsymbol{x}$ belonging to L.[2]

The theorem follows from standard rewinding techniques. A proof can be found in the full paper [8].

Homomorphic threshold encryption. A (t, n)-threshold cryptosystem is a public key cryptosystem where the secret key is shared between n authorities $A_1, \ldots, A_n$. If t of them cooperate they may decrypt ciphertexts, but any group of less than t authorities cannot learn anything about the contents of a ciphertext.

We use a key generation algorithm K to generate the keys. In general, all elements of the cryptosystem, messages, randomness and ciphertexts belong to suitable groups. We write the ciphertext space with multiplicative notation and the other groups with additive notation. The key generation algorithm produces

---

[*] It is instructive to consider this theorem in connection with the cryptosystem TDH0 in [12]. TDH0 is a cryptosystem where a Σ-protocol made non-interactive with a random oracle is used to prove knowledge of the plaintext. Intuitively one might argue CCA2 security by saying that the adversary already knows the answer when submitting decryption requests. However, Gennaro and Shoup show that this argument fails since rewinding is used to get the plaintexts, and since decryption requests may depend on oracle queries made before several other oracle queries we risk an exponential blow-up when tracking back through the decryption requests. Our theorem does not solve this problem. What our theorem can be used to prove, however, is that TDH0 is non-malleable.

a public key pk which is used for encryption, secret keys $sk_1, \ldots, sk_n$ used for decryption, and verification keys $vk_1, \ldots, vk_n$ that are public and used for verifying that the authorities act according to the protocol.

Encryption works as usual. To decrypt a ciphertext the authorities use their secret keys to produce decryption shares. Given t decryption shares anybody can combine them to get the plaintext. The verification keys are used by the authorities to make a zero-knowledge proof that they have provided the correct decryption shares.

We require that the cryptosystem have the following properties.

Semantic security: The cryptosystem must be semantically secure.

Errorless decryption: With overwhelming probability, the key generation algorithm selects keys such that there is probability 1 for the decryption to yield the message encrypted.[3]

Homomorphicity: For all messages m_1, m_2 and randomizers r_1, r_2 we have $E_{pk}(m_1 + m_2; r_1 + r_2) = E_{pk}(m_1; r_1) \cdot E_{pk}(m_2; r_2)$.

Simulatability of decryption: There is an algorithm S that takes as input a ciphertext c, a message m and the secret shares of any group of $t - 1$ authorities and produces simulated decryption shares for all the remaining authorities that c decrypts to m. S must be such that even with knowledge of the corresponding $t - 1$ keys the simulated decryption shares are indistinguishable from real decryption shares.

3   Universal Composability

The universal composability framework is described in details in [3]. The main gist is to compare a real-life execution of a protocol with an ideal process. We say a real-life protocol π realizes an ideal functionality $\mathcal{F}$ if an adversary $\mathcal{A}$ in the real-life model cannot gain more than an adversary $\mathcal{S}$ in the ideal process does. More precisely, we have an environment $\mathcal{Z}$ that gives inputs to parties, sees outputs from parties and learns which parties are corrupted, and we say π securely realizes $\mathcal{F}$ if $\mathcal{Z}$ cannot distinguish the real-life protocol with adversary $\mathcal{A}$ from the ideal process with simulator $\mathcal{S}$.

In the ideal process, the ideal functionality handles everything taking place in the protocol. The parties in the protocol hand their inputs from $\mathcal{Z}$ directly and securely to $\mathcal{F}$. $\mathcal{F}$ computes the parties outputs and sends it to them. When a party receives a message from $\mathcal{F}$, it outputs this message. $\mathcal{S}$ is restricted to corrupting some of the parties and blocking messages from $\mathcal{F}$ to the honest parties. On the other hand, in the real-life execution the parties carry out the protocol π to produce their outputs.

One main feature in this framework is security under modular composition. Let us say we have a protocol ρ that realizes the ideal functionality $\mathcal{F}$. Say that

---

[.] Most known cryptosystems have this property. However, in the notion of deniable encryption [13] the goal is to make it possible to deny that a particular thing was encrypted by producing honest looking randomness for an entirely different plaintext.

ρ is used as a sub protocol in π and write this as π^ρ. We may then form the hybrid $\pi^{\mathcal{F}}$ where calls to ρ are replaced with calls to $\mathcal{F}$. It is a theorem that π^ρ securely realizes $\pi^{\mathcal{F}}$.

Key generation and message board hybrid model. We will take advantage of the modular composition theorem and work in a hybrid model where we assume we have protocols that realize the key generation and message board functionality described in Figure 1. For distributed key generation protocols refer to [14,15, 16,17]. This enables us to concentrate on the voting protocol itself.

Functionality $\mathcal{F}$. .

$\mathcal{F}$. . proceeds as follows, running with parties $V., \ldots, V_m, A., \ldots, A_n$ and an adversary $\mathcal{A}$.

- Generate keys for the homomorphic threshold cryptosystem $(pk, vk., \ldots, vk_n, sk., \ldots, sk_n)$. Send (**public key**, sid, pk) to all parties and $\mathcal{A}$. Send (**verification keys**, $sid, vk., \ldots, vk_n$) to all the authorities and $\mathcal{A}$. For $i = 1, \ldots, n$ send (**secret share**, sid, sk_i) to A_i.
- Upon receiving (**message**, sid, m) from party V_i store (**message**, sid, V_i, m) and send it to $\mathcal{A}$.
- Upon receiving (**no-block**, sid, V_i, m) from $\mathcal{A}$ check whether (**message**, sid, V_i, m) has been stored. In that case, store (**post**, sid, V_i, m) and ignore subsequent (**no-block**, $sid, V_i, \ldots$) messages from $\mathcal{A}$.
- Upon receiving (**tally**, sid) from $\mathcal{A}$, send all stored (**post**, sid, V_i, m) messages to $A., \ldots, A_n$. Ignore subsequent (**tally**, sid) and (**no-block**, $\ldots$) requests.
- Upon receiving (**post**, sid, m) from party A_i send (**post**, sid, A_i, m) to $A., \ldots, A_n$ and $\mathcal{A}$.

Fig. 1. The key generation and message board functionality, $\mathcal{F}$. . .

We note that in $\mathcal{F}_{\mathrm{KM}}$ we allow $\mathcal{A}$ to block voters' messages. This is to cover all the benign and malicious failures that may occur when voters try to cast their vote; everything from the Internet connection being unstable to an adversary deliberately cutting the cables to groups of voters with a particular political opinion. A typical requirement of a voting system is that it should be available, i.e., voters wanting to vote should have access to vote. This covers protecting against denial of service attacks, etc., but is not part of what the cryptographic protocol can accomplish. Therefore, we specifically allow the adversary to block votes. We quantify over all adversaries in the security proof, so in particular the security proof also holds for non-blocking adversaries that do not block messages, i.e., it holds for voting systems with the availability property. In contrast, for simplicity we do not allow the adversary to block inputs from the authorities. This choice is reasonable since any voting system must have appropriate back-up procedures to ensure that all authorities can communicate as needed.

Another remark pertains to resubmission of votes. Depending on the requirements, sometimes dictated by law, it may or may not be allowed for voters to change their votes. For simplicity, we treat the case where voters cannot change their mind, and therefore we only allow a single message not to be blocked. Security can be proved quite similarly in the case where we allow voters to change their mind.

Functionality $\mathcal{F}\cdots\cdots$

$\mathcal{F}\cdots\cdots$ proceeds as follows, running with parties $V\cdot,\dots,V_m, A\cdot,\dots,A_n$ and an adversary $\mathcal{S}$.

- Upon receiving (**vote**, sid, V_i, v) from V_i store it and send (**vote**, sid, V_i) to $\mathcal{S}$. Ignore future (**vote**, $sid,\dots$) messages from V_i.
- Upon receiving (**no-block**, sid, V_i) from $\mathcal{S}$ check whether some (**vote**, sid, V_i, v) has been stored. In that case, add v to the result and ignore subsequent (**no-block**, sid, V_i) messages from $\mathcal{S}$.
- Upon receiving (**result**, sid) from $\mathcal{S}$ compute the result and send (**result**, sid, result) to $\mathcal{S}$ and $A\cdot,\dots,A_n$ and halt.

Fig. 2. The voting functionality, $\mathcal{F}\cdots\cdots$.

Voting protocol. Before describing the protocol that we use to realize the ideal voting functionality in Figure 2, we need to discuss how to encode the voters' choice as a plaintext to be encrypted. In [5,6,7] this is done by assigning each candidate a number $j \in \{0,\dots,L-1\}$ and encoding the candidate as M^j, where M is a strict upper bound on the number of votes any candidate can receive. Adding many such votes gives a result on the form $\sum_{j=0}^{L-1} v_j M^j$ where v_j is the number of votes on candidate number j. Votes and result can be embedded in a message space on the form $\mathbb{Z}_N$ provided $N \geq M^L$. More generally we require that there is an encoding such that:

- Each valid vote v can be encoded as Encode(v).
- The sum of the encodings yields an encoding of the result, Encode(result).
- It is possible to efficiently extract the result from an encoding.
- The encodings can be embedded in the message space of the cryptosystem.

We describe the voting protocol based on homomorphic threshold encryption in Figure 3. Examples of such voting protocols can be found in [4,5,6,7].

Ideal process adversary. To prove security of the voting protocol we need to provide an ideal process adversary $\mathcal{S}$ that fares as well as $\mathcal{A}$ does in the $\mathcal{F}_{\text{KM}}$-hybrid model. $\mathcal{S}$ is described in Figure 4.

Theorem 2. *The voting protocol hybrid $\pi_{\text{VOTING}}^{\mathcal{F}_{\text{KM}}}$ securely realizes $\mathcal{F}_{\text{VOTING}}$ for the class of non-adaptive adversaries that corrupt less than t authorities.*

Voting Protol $\pi_{\cdot,\cdot,\cdot}^{\mathcal{F}_{KM}}$

The voting protocol for voters $V_{\cdot}, \ldots, V_m$ and authorities $A_{\cdot}, \ldots, A_n$ with access to ideal functionality $\mathcal{F}_{\cdot\cdot}$ and random oracle $\mathcal{O}$ is as follows.

1. Invoke $\mathcal{F}_{\cdot}$ to give each voter $V_{\cdot}, \ldots, V_m$ the public key and give each authority $A_{\cdot}, \ldots, A_n$ all the verification keys and its own secret key.
2. Each voter V_i with a public key pk on the incoming message tape and a valid vote v_i on the input tape computes $c_i \leftarrow E_{pk}(\text{Encode}(v_i))$. He creates a proof p_i for the vote being correct using a Σ-protocol with $\mathcal{O}$'s answer on (c_i, a_i, pk, sid, V_i) as the challenge e_i.
   He sends (**message**, sid, c_i, p_i) to $\mathcal{F}_{\cdot\cdot}$.
3. Authority A_j with the public key and the verification keys on its tape and a secret share of the private key on its tape does the following. When receiving a bunch of broadcast votes it computes C as the product of all the votes with valid proofs. Then it computes the decryption share ds_j. It also forms a proof p_j for the decryption share being correct using the verification key vk_j. The challenge in this proof is computed with $\mathcal{O}$.
   It sends (**post**, sid, ds_j, p_j) to $\mathcal{F}_{\cdot\cdot}$.
4. Each authority picks the first t decryption shares with valid proofs that it receives and computes the plaintext of C.
   It interprets the plaintext as Encode(result) and outputs (**result**, sid, result).

Fig. 3. The voting protocol $\pi_{\cdot,\cdot,\cdot}^{\mathcal{F}_{KM}}$

Proof. We will take a walk one step at a time from the $\mathcal{F}_{KM}$-hybrid model to the ideal process. In doing so we will use expected polynomial-time algorithms and rewind the environment. This is all right as long as we do not do this in the $\mathcal{F}_{KM}$-hybrid model or the ideal process itself.

Exp₁. Define Exp_1 to be the following modification of the $\mathcal{F}_{KM}$-hybrid model. After $\mathcal{A}$ has submitted the command (**tally**, sid) to $\mathcal{F}_{KM}$ we use the honest authorities' secret shares to decrypt the encrypted votes with valid proofs sent by $\mathcal{A}$ on behalf of corrupt voters. We look at the tapes of the honest voters and if they are not blocked by $\mathcal{A}$, we add their votes to the corrupt voters' votes. This gives us the result of the election.

By the simulation property of the threshold cryptosystem, we may now simulate the honest authorities' decryption shares such that they fit with the result. To do this simulation we do not need knowledge of the honest authorities' secret shares. Using our ability to control the random oracle, we may also simulate proofs of these decryption shares being correct.

$\text{HYB}_{\pi,\mathcal{Z},\mathcal{A}}^{\mathcal{F}_{KM}} \approx P_1$. We define P_1 to be the probability of $\mathcal{Z}$ outputting 1 in Exp_1. It is not possible for $\mathcal{Z}$ to distinguish whether it is running in the $\mathcal{F}_{KM}$-hybrid model or experiment Exp_1. The result is the same in both cases and indistinguishability follows from the zero-knowledge property of the proofs and the simulation property of the threshold cryptosystem.

Ideal process adversary $\mathcal{S}$

$\mathcal{S}$ operates in the ideal process with dummy voters $\tilde{V}., \ldots, \tilde{V}_m$ and dummy authorities $\tilde{A}., \ldots, \tilde{A}_n$. It has input z. It controls the random oracle $\mathcal{O}$ in the sense that it may assign a response e to a query q. This means that it can simulate proofs.
$\mathcal{S}$ runs a simulated $\mathcal{F}.$. -hybrid execution with simulated adversary $\mathcal{A}$. We write $V., \ldots, V_m$ and $A., \ldots, A_n$ to denote simulated parties.

- $\mathcal{S}$ forwards all messages between $\mathcal{A}$ and $\mathcal{Z}$.
- $\mathcal{S}$ simulates the invocation of $\mathcal{F}.$ . . Having done this it knows the secret shares of the private key of all the authorities, in other words $\mathcal{S}$ may decrypt messages encrypted under the public key.
- Suppose $\mathcal{A}$ on behalf of a corrupt V_i sends (**message**, sid, c_i, p_i) and sends (**no-block**, sid, V_i, c_i, p_i) to $\mathcal{F}.$ . . $\mathcal{S}$ checks whether the proof is valid and in that case it decrypts c_i to get a vote v_i. It submits (**vote**, sid, V_i, v_i) to $\mathcal{F}. . . ..$ on behalf of $\tilde{V}_i$ and sends (**no-block**, sid, V_i) to $\mathcal{F}. . . ..$.
- Upon receiving (**vote**, sid, V_i) from $\mathcal{F}. . . ..$ it knows that $\tilde{V}_i$ got (**vote**, sid, V_i, v_i) as input from $\mathcal{Z}$. It does not know the actual vote v_i. As long as V_i has not received the public key for the election $\mathcal{S}$ ignores the problem, but if V_i has or gets the public key for the election $\mathcal{S}$ must simulate V_i trying to cast a vote. It forms $c_i = E_{pk}(0)$ and simulates a proof p_i for c_i containing a valid vote. It simulates V_i sending (**message**, sid, V_i, c_i, p_i) to $\mathcal{F}.$. and sends the resulting (**message**, sid, V_i, c_i, p_i) to the copy of $\mathcal{A}$. If it later receives (**no-block**, sid, V_i, m) from $\mathcal{A}$, $\mathcal{S}$ simulates $\mathcal{F}.$. receiving this message, and it sends (**no-block**, sid, V_i) to $\mathcal{F}. . . ..$.
- Upon $\mathcal{A}$ sending (**tally**, sid) to $\mathcal{F}.$. , $\mathcal{S}$ lets the simulated $\mathcal{F}.$. send the list of stored messages (**post**, sid, V_i, c_i, p_i) to $A., \ldots, A_n$.
  It sends (**tally**, sid) to $\mathcal{F}. . . ..$ and learns the result.
  Let C be the product of all the c_i's. $\mathcal{S}$ uses the simulation property of the threshold cryptosystem to simulate shares ds_j for the honest A_j's such that C decrypts to the actual result. Furthermore, it also simulates proofs p_j of the shares being correct.
- After $\mathcal{A}$ has delivered both the keys and the messages to honest A_j, $\mathcal{S}$ simulates that A_j sends the decryption share (**post**, sid, A_j, ds_j, p_j) to $\mathcal{F}.$ . .
- When A_j has received both the public keys and t decryption shares, then $\mathcal{S}$ delivers the (**result**, sid, result) message from $\mathcal{F}. . . ..$ to $\tilde{A}_j$.

Fig. 4. The ideal process adversary $\mathcal{S}$.

Exp_2. Define Exp_2 as the following modification of Exp_1. We look at the execution in the interval between key generation having been done and $\mathcal{A}$ not yet having submitted (**tally**, sid) to $\mathcal{F}_{KM}$. After the key generation, we may for each honest voter and each possible vote it can get as input pre-generate the (**message**, sid, c_i, p_i) message.

Let A be an algorithm that takes as input the tapes of $\mathcal{A}$, $\mathcal{Z}$ and the pre-generated encrypted votes. It runs the entire execution in this interval, and in the end, it outputs the views of $\mathcal{A}$ and $\mathcal{Z}$. From the views, we may read off the states of $\mathcal{A}$ and $\mathcal{Z}$, restart them, and continue the experiment.

According to Theorem 1 we may replace A with an expected polynomial time algorithm E_A that indistinguishably outputs the same as A, but in addition provides the witnesses for the proofs made by corrupt voters. These witnesses include the votes of these corrupt parties and therefore we do not need to decrypt anything with the honest authorities' secret shares of the private key.

$P_1 \approx P_2$. We define P_2 as the probability that $\mathcal{Z}$ outputs 1 at the end of experiment Exp_2. It follows from Theorem 1 that $P_1 \approx P_2$.

Exp₃. Define Exp_3 the following way. Instead of letting the honest voters encrypt their votes and proving in zero-knowledge that the ciphertexts contain correct votes, we let them encrypt 0 and simulate the proofs of correctness. For each possible vote that $\mathcal{Z}$ could give to an honest voter V_i, we construct such a 0-vote and feed A with these ciphertexts and simulated proofs.

$P_2 \approx P_3$. Let P_3 be the probability that $\mathcal{Z}$ outputs 1 after experiment Exp_3. In Exp_3, we still use the real votes to fit the result in the end, and we do not at any point use the honest authorities' shares of the private key. Therefore, by the semantic security of the cryptosystem, the result is the same and $\mathcal{Z}$ cannot distinguish the two experiments. Neither does it allow us to distinguish the views of $\mathcal{A}$ and $\mathcal{Z}$ that A produces, so these transcripts must still look like correct views of $\mathcal{A}$ and $\mathcal{Z}$ acting according to their programs.

Exp₄. We define Exp_4 as a modification of Exp_3 where we go back to using decryption to get $\mathcal{A}$'s votes. Instead of using the votes supplied by E_A, we decrypt the corrupt voters' ciphertexts with valid proofs and use these votes. We may now replace E_A with A since we do not need the votes directly. By definition, A produces valid transcripts of how $\mathcal{A}$ and $\mathcal{Z}$ behave with these inputs and we may therefore replace A with the execution of $\mathcal{A}$ and $\mathcal{Z}$.

$P_3 \approx P_4$. By Theorem 1 we may shift back from E_A to A without being able to tell the difference. Since A produces two good transcripts for how $\mathcal{A}$ and $\mathcal{Z}$ work we may now go back to using $\mathcal{A}$ and $\mathcal{Z}$ also in the interval between key generation and $\mathcal{A}$ submitting (**tally**, *sid*) to $\mathcal{F}_{\text{KM}}$.

$P_4 \approx \text{IDEAL}_{\mathcal{F}_{\text{VOTING}}, \mathcal{Z}, \mathcal{S}}$. The ideal process and Exp_4 are actually the same experiment. In Exp_4 we submit 0-votes on behalf of honest parties and simulate the proofs, just as $\mathcal{S}$ does. When $\mathcal{A}$ submits (**vote**, *sid*, V_i, c_i, p_i) on behalf of an honest voter we check the proof and decrypt just as $\mathcal{S}$ does. To create something that looks as decryption shares that produce the result we simulate this just as $\mathcal{S}$ does. □

Recycling keys. One could ask whether the keys can be reused for several elections. The security proof fails in this case for the same reasons as described in [12] and Footnote 2. The problem is that we can prove non-malleability of the cryptosystem used to encrypt votes but not prove security with respect to general adaptive chosen ciphertext attacks. If we use the same keys in several elections, we give the adversary access to a decryption of the ciphertexts containing the results and therefore an adaptive chosen ciphertext attack. While we see no way to use this attack in practice, we cannot guarantee security.

If we really want to use the keys for several elections that is possible though. We can simply demand that the voter makes a proof of knowledge where votes can be straight-line extracted. For instance, the voter can encrypt votes under a second public key and prove that this has been done correctly. Then votes may be extracted directly from this ciphertext and no rewinding is needed. The authorities tally the votes by stripping away the extra proof and ciphertext and carrying out the usual tallying procedure with the remaining ciphertext.

4   Adaptive Adversaries

An adaptive adversary is one that decides during the execution of the protocol which parties to corrupt. After corruption of a party, the adversary may learn some data from earlier computations. To guard against such problems we may specifically specify in protocols that parties should erase certain data. We call this the erasure model. Sometimes the more strict erasure-free security model is preferred. In this model, the party's entire computational history is revealed upon corruption.

The voting schemes are not adaptively secure. The schemes [4,5,6,7] are in fact not secure in the adaptive setting, even when we allow erasures. Let us sketch a counter-argument for the case of a yes/no election using the scheme in [4] with 2 voters, 3 authorities and a threshold $t = 2$. We refer the reader to [4] for a description of the scheme.

Consider an environment $\mathcal{Z}$ and adversary $\mathcal{A}$, where $\mathcal{A}$ forwards everything it sees to $\mathcal{Z}$ and follows instructions from $\mathcal{Z}$ on how to behave. $\mathcal{Z}$ first asks $\mathcal{A}$ to activate the key-generation step of $\mathcal{F}_{KM}$ and to deliver all the keys to the relevant parties. Then $\mathcal{Z}$ selects at random that all voters should vote yes or all voters should vote no. It lets the first voter post its vote and then it flips a coin to decide whether to block the second voter or not. If both voters were allowed to post their votes, $\mathcal{Z}$ carries out the entire election according to the protocol. If only the first voter was allowed to post his vote, $\mathcal{Z}$ lets $\mathcal{A}$ activate A_1 to obtain its decryption share. Then it flips a coin and corrupts either A_2 or A_3. From the secret share it obtains it may now compute the result of the election. If everything works out OK, $\mathcal{Z}$ outputs 1. If we are operating in the real-life model everything will work out OK and $\mathcal{Z}$ will output 1 with 100% probability.

To finish the argument we will show that any $\mathcal{S}$ cannot make $\mathcal{Z}$ accept with more than 50% probability. First, $\mathcal{S}$ must provide public keys $g, h = g^s$ for an

ElGamal cryptosystem. Second it must provide verification keys $h_1 = g^{s_1}, h_2 = g^{s_2}, h_3 = g^{s_3}$ to the authorities. Here s, s_1, s_2, s_3 may or may not be known to $\mathcal{S}$ and may or may not be chosen according to the protocol. Having given these keys to $\mathcal{Z}$ $\mathcal{S}$ must now produce the vote (x, y) for the first voter. At this point it cannot know the result since if it queries $\mathcal{F}_{\text{VOTING}}$ for the result, then $\mathcal{Z}$ has 50% probability of letting the second voter vote, and then the result will be wrong and $\mathcal{Z}$ will be able to distinguish. From now on, we look at the case where (x, y) has been produced without knowledge of the result, and where this is the only vote to be cast. $\mathcal{S}$ must try to make it look like (x, y) decrypts to the result. First, it must produce a decryption share w_1 for the first authority. Then depending on $\mathcal{Z}$'s coin-flip, it must give either s_2 or s_3 to $\mathcal{Z}$ according to which authority $\mathcal{Z}$ decides to corrupt. To make $\mathcal{Z}$ accept with more than 50% probability, $\mathcal{S}$ must be able to make it look like (x, y) decrypts to the result in both cases. In other words, we have

$$G^{\text{result}} = y/w_1^{\lambda_{1,\{1,2\}}} x^{s_2 \lambda_{2,\{1,2\}}} = y/w_1^{\lambda_{1,\{1,3\}}} x^{s_3 \lambda_{3,\{1,3\}}},$$

where the Lagrange coefficients are $\lambda_{1,\{1,2\}} = 2, \lambda_{2,\{1,2\}} = -1, \lambda_{1,\{1,3\}} = 3/2, \lambda_{3,\{1,3\}} = -1/2$. This implies that we can compute $w_1 = x^{2s_2-s_3}$ and $y = G^{\text{result}} x^{3s_2-2s_3}$. However, since (x, y) was chosen before the result was known to $\mathcal{S}$ there is at least 50% probability that $\mathcal{S}$ could not have done this. $\mathcal{Z}$ only has 50% probability of outputting 1 in the ideal process and it can therefore distinguish.

Adaptive security in the erasure model. We can deal with an adversary that may adaptively corrupt voters quite easily. The voters simply erase the plaintext vote and the randomness after they have computed the encrypted vote. This way an adaptive adversary does not learn anything by corrupting a voter. We find the erasure model to be somewhat reasonable since a good voting system should specify that voters delete the randomness and the vote used in order to give some rudimentary receipt-freeness.

To guard against adversaries that adaptively corrupt authorities we can use techniques from [18,19,20]. Let us briefly sketch how to do this. All the homomorphic cryptosystems in [4,6,5,7] require that in the decryption process we raise the ciphertext C or part of the ciphertext to a secret value s. In the abovementioned schemes we share s using a polynomial f of degree $t - 1$, and give each authority a share $s_i = f(i)$. Lagrange interpolation can then be used to perform the decryption. As we saw before, this technique causes trouble in the adaptive setting. However, if we instead use a linear secret sharing of s, i.e., select $s_1, \ldots, s_{n-1}$ at random and $s_n = s - \sum_{i=1}^{n-1} s_i$, then we can cope with an adaptive adversary. To recover If an authority fails to provide its decryption share, we also use polynomials $f_1, \ldots, f_n$ of degree $t - 1$ to secret share $s_1, \ldots, s_n$. I.e., $f_i(0) = s_i$ and $s_{i,j} = f_i(j)$. Authority j knows all the shares $\{s_{i,j}\}_{i=1,\ldots,n}$. The verification keys now also include trapdoor commitments, for instance Pedersen commitments, to the $s_{i,j}$'s. In the simulation, we pick all the shares $s_1, \ldots, s_n$ at random. When the first honest authority is about to compute its share, it computes the share such that it fits with the result and all the other authorities' shares, and it simulates a proof of correctness. The authorities have to go through a more complicated protocol to compute the result and anybody wishing to verify the result also has to do more work, but it is still well within what is practical. The voters do not pay any performance penalty when having to use this type of voting scheme instead of the original type of voting scheme, for them the protocol looks the same.

Adaptive security in the erasure-free model. To obtain a protocol security against adaptive adversaries in the erasure-free model we can use the UC threshold cryptosystem of Damgård and Nielsen [21]. One problem in this scheme is that they use the UC commitments of [22], which require that each voter receive an individual commitment key. [23] suggested to solve this problem using non-malleable commitments, and better efficiency can be obtained if we use simulation sound commitments [24]. We can combine the protocols with zero-knowledge proofs of the type in [7] to prove correctness of the votes. Making it all non-interactive using the Fiat-Shamir heuristic, we obtain a fairly efficient voting scheme, which is secure against adaptive adversaries in the erasure-free setting. More details on this scheme are offered in [8].

Acknowledgment. Thanks to Ivan Damgård for asking whether the schemes based on homomorphic threshold encryption are secure in the universal composability framework.

References

1. Burmester, M., Magkos, E.: Towards secure and practical e-elections in the new era. In Gritzalis, D., ed.: Secure Electronic Voting. Kluwer Academic Publishers (2003) 63–72
2. Lambrinoudakis, C., Gritzalis, D., Tsoumas, V., Karyda, M., Ikonomopoulos, S.: Secure electronic voting: The current landscape. In Gritzalis, D., ed.: Secure Electronic Voting. Kluwer Academic Publishers (2003) 101–122
3. Canetti, R.: Universally composable security: A new paradigm for cryptographic protocols. In: FOCS 2001. (2001) 136–145 Full paper available at http://eprint.iacr.org/2000/67.
4. Cramer, R., Gennaro, R., Schoenmakers, B.: A secure and optimally eficient multi-authority election scheme. In: proceedings of EUROCRYPT '97, LNCS series, volume 1233. (1997) 103–118
5. Damgård, I., Jurik, M.J.: A generalisation, a simplification and some applications of paillier's probabilistic public-key system. In: 4th International Workshop on Practice and Theory in Public Key Cryptosystems, PKC 2001, LNCS series, volume 1992. (2001)
6. Baudron, O., Fouque, P.A., Pointcheval, D., Poupard, G., Stern, J.: Practical multi-candidate election scheme. In: PODC '01. (2001) 274–283
7. Damgård, I., Groth, J., Salomonsen, G.: The theory and implementation of an electronic voting system. In Gritzalis, D., ed.: Secure Electronic Voting. Kluwer Academic Publishers (2003) 77–100

8. Groth, J.: Evaluating security of voting schemes in the universal composability framework. Cryptology ePrint Archive, Report 2002/002 (2002)

9. Cramer, R., Damgård, I., Schoenmakers, B.: Proofs of partial knowledge and simplified design of witness hiding protocols. In: proceedings of CRYPTO '94, LNCS series, volume 893. (1994) 174–187

10. Bellare, M., Rogaway, P.: Random oracles are practical: A paradigm for designing efficient protocols. In: ACM Conference on Computer and Communications Security 1993. (1993) 62–73

11. Lindell, Y.: Parallel coin-tossing and constant round secure two-party computation. In: proceedings of CRYPTO '01, LNCS series, volume 2139. (2001) 408–432

12. Shoup, V., Gennaro, R.: Securing threshold cryptosystems against chosen ciphertext attack. Journal of Cryptology 15 (2002) 75–96

13. Canetti, R., Dwork, C., Naor, M., Ostrovsky, R.: Deniable encryption. In: proceedings of CRYPTO '97, LNCS series, volume 1294. (1997) 90–104

14. Boneh, D., Franklin, M.K.: Efficient generation of shared rsa keys. In: proceedings of CRYPTO '97, LNCS series, volume 1294. (1997) 425–439

15. Gennaro, R., Jarecki, S., Krawczyk, H., Rabin, T.: Secure distributed key generation for discrete-log based cryptosystems. In: proceedings of EUROCRYPT '99, LNCS series, volume 1592. (1999) 293–310

16. Fouque, P.A., Stern, J.: Fully distributed threshold rsa under standard assumptions. In: proceedings of ASIACRYPT '01, LNCS series, volume 2248. (2001) 310–330

17. Algesheimer, J., Camenisch, J., Shoup, V.: Efficient computation modulo a shared secret with application to the generation of shared safe-prime products. In: proceedings of CRYPTO '02, LNCS series, volume 2442. (2002) 417–432

18. Canetti, R., Gennaro, R., Jarecki, S., Krawczyk, H., Rabin, T.: Adaptive security for threshold cryptosystems. In: proceedings of CRYPTO '99, LNCS series, volume 1666. (1999) 98–115

19. Jarecki, S., Lysyanskaya, A.: Adaptively secure threshold cryptography: Introducing concurrency, removing erasures. In: proceedings of EUROCRYPT '00, LNCS series, volume 1807. (2000) 221–242

20. Lysyanskaya, A., Peikert, C.: Adaptive security in the threshold setting: From cryptosystems to signature schemes. In: proceedings of ASIACRYPT '01, LNCS series, volume 2248. (2001) 331–350

21. Damgård, I., Nielsen, J.B.: Universally composable efficient multiparty computation from threshold homomorphic encryption. In: proceedings of CRYPTO '03, LNCS series, volume 2729. (2003) 247–264

22. Damgård, I., Nielsen, J.B.: Perfect hiding and perfect binding universally composable commitment schemes with constant expansion factor. In: proceedings of CRYPTO '02, LNCS series, volume 2442. (2002) 581–596

23. Damgård, I., Groth, J.: Non-interactive and reusable non-malleable commitment schemes. In: STOC '03. (2003) 426–437

24. Garay, J.A., MacKenzie, P.D., Yang, K.: Strengthening zero-knowledge protocols using signatures. In: proceedings of EUROCRYPT '03, LNCS series, volume 2656. (2003) 177–194 Full paper available at htpp://eprint.iacr.org/2003/037.

Verifiable Shuffles: A Formal Model and a Paillier-Based Efficient Construction with Provable Security

Lan Nguyen[1], Rei Safavi-Naini[1], and Kaoru Kurosawa[2]

. School of Information Technology and Computer Science
University of Wollongong, Wollongong 2522, Australia
{ldn01,rei}@uow.edu.au
. Department of Computer and Information Sciences
Ibaraki University 4-12-1 Nakanarusawa, Hitachi, Ibaraki, 316-8511, Japan
kurosawa@cis.ibaraki.ac.jp

Abstract. We propose a formal model for security of verifiable shuffles and prove security of a number of recently proposed shuffle schemes in this model. The model is general and can be extended to mix-nets and verifiable shuffle decryption. We propose a new efficient verifiable shuffle system based on Paillier encryption scheme and prove its security in the proposed model.

Keywords: Privacy, verifiable shuffles, formal security model, mix-nets, Paillier public-key system.

1 Introduction

A *shuffle* takes an input list of ciphertexts and outputs a permuted and re-encrypted version of the input list. Re-encryption of a ciphertext can be defined for encryption systems such as El Gamal and Paillier encryption systems, and allows generation of ciphertexts c' from a given ciphertext c such that both ciphertexts correspond to the same plaintext m under the same *public key*.

The main application (motivation for the study) of shuffles is to construct *mix-nets*, a cryptographic system introduced by Chaum [3] for providing communication unlinkability and anonymity. Mix-nets are among the most widely used systems for providing communication privacy, and have found applications in anonymous email system [3], Web browsing [9], electronic voting [18], anonymous payment systems [4], location privacy for mobile networks [16] and mobile IP [4], secure multiparty computation [14] and privacy in advertisements [15].

A mix-net consists of a number of mix-centres that collectively permute and decrypt the mix-net input list. Shuffles are used to implement mix-centres. A basic shuffle permutes its input list of ciphertexts through re-encryption. Mix-centres may also partially decrypt the list, hence called *shuffle decryption*. Mix-nets that use shuffle decryption could be more efficient but in case of failure of one of the mix-centres, they need more computation to recover [8].

M. Jakobsson, M. Yung, J. Zhou (Eds.): ACNS 2004, LNCS 3089, pp. 61–75, 2004.

The main security property of shuffle systems is providing *unlinkability* of elements of its input to the elements of the output list for outsiders, and so effectively keeping the permutation secret. We refer to this property as *shuffle privacy*. A second important property of shuffles is *verifiability*: that is providing a proof that the output is correctly constructed. Verifiability of shuffles is used to provide *robustness* for the mix-net: that is ensuring that the mix-net works correctly even if a number of mix-servers are malicious. This is an important property of mix-nets and so verifiability of shuffles has received much attention. Shuffles must be efficient and the cost is measured in terms of the amount of computation and communication that is required for providing privacy for n users.

In this paper we focus on *verifiable shuffles*. Privacy of shuffles has traditionally been equated to the zero-knowledge property of the proof system used for verifying correctness. Recently a number of efficient constructions for verifiable shuffles have been proposed. In Crypto'01, Furukawa and Sako [6] gave a characterisation of permutation matrices in terms of two equations that can be efficiently proved, hence proposing an efficient (3 round proof system) verifiable shuffle. However in a subsequent paper [7], they noted that the proof system was not zero-knowledge. They however gave a definition of privacy for shuffles and showed that the protocol satisfied that definition. The definition requires that the verifier cannot learn anything about the 'relation' between the output of the shuffle and its input, using the transcript of the protocol. Neff [18,19] and later Groth [13] proposed shuffles that provide zero-knowledge property for their proofs.

As noted above the notion of privacy varies among shuffles and no formal model for verifiable shuffles has been suggested so far. Such a formalisation will be also important for formalising security of mix-nets. Recently proposed attacks [1,20,25] against mix-nets clearly demonstrate the need for such a model.

The *first contribution* of this paper is to give a formal model for shuffles that allows us to have a unified approach for assessment of shuffle systems. Our definition of shuffle privacy is motivated by observing the similarity between a shuffle hiding the permutation, and an encryption system hiding the input message. We consider adaptive attacks by an active adversary that uses a *chosen permutation attack (CPA$_S$)* (similar to chosen plaintext) and *chosen transcript attack (CTA$_S$)* (similar to chosen ciphertext). A subtle difference between this model and the model of a traditional encryption system is that in this case the adversary does not only specify the distribution of challenge permutation (i.e. plaintext) but also another input, the list of input ciphertexts. We allow the adversary to choose this input ciphertext list adaptively and also know the corresponding plaintext list. Using this approach, notions of privacy can be defined in line with semantic security and indistinguishability. We prove that these two notions of privacy are equivalent and can be interchangeably used. The definition of verifiability is based on the notion of completeness and soundness of the proof system. We note that the prover, the shuffle, does not have access to the private key of encryption. This is the first complete model for shuffle security with active adversary and under CPA$_S$ and CTA$_S$. The model can be extended to verifiable shuffle decryption and mix-nets, and so providing a unified framework for security evaluation of these systems. We prove security of Furukawa-Sako, Neff and Groth schemes in this model.

A *second contribution* of this paper is proposing a new efficient verifiable shuffle based on Paillier encryption system [22]. Paillier encryption system provides semantic security against adaptive chosen plaintext attack (CPA) in standard model and similar to El Gamal cryptosystem, it is possible to define a re-encryption operation for it. The shuffle uses Furukawa-Sako approach for characterisation of permutation matrices but has computations over a composite modulus which complicates security proofs (We have to prove Theorem 6 and Theorem 7). We prove privacy and verifiability of the shuffle in our proposed model. The proof technique can also be used to prove privacy of Furukawa-Sako, Neff and Groth schemes in our model. Compared to Furukawa-Sako and Groth, our proof system has a more efficient initialisation phase and similar to Groth's shuffle, does not require the message space to be prime (a product of two primes instead). By using the NM-CCA robust threshold version of Paillier encryption scheme [5], a robust mix-net can be constructed from our verifiable shuffle, as will be shown in the full version of our paper [21].

The organization of the paper is as follows. In section 2, we recall some background on public-key encryption schemes and shuffles. Section 3 provides our formal definitions of verifiable shuffles and its security requirements. Section 4 gives a verifiable shuffle based on Paillier public-key system, its security proofs and efficiency analysis.

2   Background

2.1   Public-Key Encryption Schemes

A public-key encryption scheme consists of three probabilistic polynomial time (PPT) algorithms (G, E, D). The key generation algorithm G on input 1^l outputs (pk, sk) where pk is a public key, sk is the secret key and l is a security parameter. The encryption algorithm E takes as input the public key pk and a plaintext and outputs a ciphertext. The decryption algorithm D takes as input the secret key sk and a ciphertext and outputs a plaintext. A public-key encryption scheme may have a *re-encryption* function. Following the definition in [24], this means there is a PPT algorithm R that takes as input the public key pk and a ciphertext and outputs another ciphertext such that for every plaintext m and its ciphertexts c and c': $Pr[c' = R_{pk}(c)] = Pr[c' = E_{pk}(m)]$ (2.1). A public-key scheme with a re-encryption function is denoted by (G, E, D, R). Note that we write $E_{pk}(m)$, $D_{sk}(c)$ and $R_{pk}(c)$ instead of $E(pk, m)$, $D(sk, c)$ and $R(pk, c)$ respectively.

Due to space limitation, for a discussion about encryption security requirements, including semantic security (SS), indistinguishability (IND) and non-malleability (NM) against chosen plaintext attacks (CPA) and chosen ciphertext attacks (CCA), we refer to the full version of this paper [21].

2.2   Paillier Public-Key System

Key generation: Let $N = pq$, where p and q be large primes. Denote λ as Carmichael value of N, so $\lambda = lcm(p - 1, q - 1)$. The public key is $pk = N$ and the secret key is $sk = \lambda$. Hereafter, unless stated otherwise we assume all modular computations are in modulo N^2.

Encryption: Plaintext $m \in Z_N$ can be encrypted by choosing an $r \in_R Z_N^*$ (i.e. chosen randomly and with uniform distribution from Z_N^*) and computing the ciphertext $g = r^N(1 + mN)$. [1]

Re-encryption: A Paillier ciphertext g for a plaintext m can be re-encrypted as $g' = r'^N \times g$ for the same plaintext m, where $r' \in_R Z_N^*$. The re-encryption satisfies the condition (2.1) above.

Decryption: Ciphertext $g \in Z_{N^2}^*$ can be decrypted as $m = L(g^\lambda \bmod N^2)/\lambda \bmod N$, where the function L takes its input from the set $\{u < N^2 | u = 1 \bmod N\}$ and is defined as $L(u) = (u - 1)/N$.

Decisional Composite Residuosity Assumption (DCRA): A number $z \in Z_{N^2}^*$ is said to be an *e-th residue mod N^2* if there exists a number $y \in Z_{N^2}^*$ such that $z = y^e$. DCRA states that there is no polynomial time distinguisher for the N-th residues modulo N^2.

Security: Paillier encryption scheme has SS-CPA if and only if DCRA holds.

NM-CCA robust threshold encryption scheme: Using the twin-encryption paradigm of [17], Shamir sharing scheme [23], the proof of equality of discrete logs and a simulation-sound proof of equality of plaintexts, Fouque and Pointcheval [5] proposed a NM-CCA robust threshold encryption scheme based on Paillier public-key system that is proved secure in the random oracle model. This encryption system can be used to construct a robust mix-net.

2.3   Furukawa-Sako Shuffle

Furukawa and Sako [6] proposed an efficient verifiable shuffle based on El Gamal public-key system. In their scheme, a permutation is represented as a matrix (Definition 1) and their proof system is based on proving two equations based on the matrix (Theorem 1). However, Furukawa-Sako's proof of zero-knowledgeness is not correct [7].

Definition 1. *A matrix $(A_{ij})_{n \times n}$ is a permutation matrix modulo k if it satisfies the following for some permutation π*

$$A_{ij} = \begin{cases} 1 \bmod k \text{ if } \pi(i) = j \\ 0 \bmod k \text{ otherwise} \end{cases}$$

---

[*] Paillier encryption is originally defined as $g = r^N e^m$, where $e \in Z_{N^2}^*$ and its order in modulo N^* is a non-zero multiple of N. For efficiency we use $e = 1 + N$. Our results do not depend on this choice and are true for all values of e.

Theorem 1. *A matrix* $(A_{ij})_{n \times n}$ *is a permutation matrix modulo* q, *where* q *is a prime, if and only if for all* i, j *and* k, *both*

$$\sum_{l=1}^{n} A_{li} A_{lj} = \begin{cases} 1 \ mod \ q \ if \ i = j \\ 0 \ mod \ q \ otherwise \end{cases}$$

$$\sum_{l=1}^{n} A_{li} A_{lj} A_{lk} = \begin{cases} 1 \ mod \ q \ if \ i = j = k \\ 0 \ mod \ q \ otherwise \end{cases}$$

hold.

3   Security of Verifiable Shuffles

3.1   Notation and Terminology

For a list L of elements, $|L|$ denotes the size of the list, $L[i]$ denotes the ith element of the list and $\pi(L)$ the list of elements in L permuted by a permutation π. Let T_n denote the set of all permutations on $\{1, ..., n\}$. A *positive polynomial* is a polynomial for which the leading coefficient is positive. Let $poly(n)$ refer to some fixed but unspecified polynomial and U_n denote a random variable uniformly distributed over $\{0, 1\}^n$. When a PPT algorithm M takes an input x and produces an output y, we write $y \xleftarrow{R} M(x)$ and denote $C_M^{x,y}$ the probabilistic input (sequence of internal random coin tosses) of M. For example, if Paillier ciphertext $g = r^N(1 + mN)$, then $C_E^{(N,m),g} = r$. We can abuse this notation by writing $C_{E_{pk}}^{m,c}$ instead of $C_E^{(pk,m),c}$ and similar for D_{sk} and R_{pk}. We use $C_M^{L_x, L_y}$ to denote the list of probabilistic inputs of M where the ith element of the list is the probabilistic input that takes the ith element of the list L_x to the ith element of the list L_y. The set of possible outputs of M on input x is denoted by $[M(x)]$.

The adversary is modelled by an *oracle machine* which is a Turing machine with additional tapes and states allowing access to some *oracles* that provide answers to queries of the defined types. An interactive proof system $(\mathcal{P}, \mathcal{V})$ consists of two party: a prover $\mathcal{P}$ and a verifier $\mathcal{V}$. Each party can be modelled by an *interactive machine*, which is a Turing machine with additional tapes and states allowing joint communication and computation with another interactive machine. Formal descriptions of oracle machines and interactive machines can be found in [10]. For a proof system $(\mathcal{P}, \mathcal{V})$, $View_{\mathcal{V}}^{\mathcal{P}}(x)$ denotes all that $\mathcal{V}$ can see from the execution of the proof system on input x (in other words, the transcript of the proof system on input x).

3.2   Syntax of Shuffles

First, we define a language to describe that a list of ciphertexts is a permuted and re-encrypted version of another ciphertext list.

Definition 2. *Suppose* $\mathcal{RP} = (G, E, D, R)$ *is a public-key scheme with a re-encryption function. Define a language* $\mathcal{L}_{\mathcal{RP}}$ *of tuples* (pk, L_1, L_2) *such that pk is a public key generated by* G *and* L_2 *is a permutation of re-encryptions of ciphertexts in* L_1 *produced by* R_{pk}. *The witness* $w(pk, L_1, L_2)$ *includes the permutation and the list of probabilistic inputs of* R_{pk}.

$$\mathcal{L}_{\mathcal{RP}} = \{(pk, L_1, L_2) | (|L_1| = |L_2|) \wedge$$
$$(\exists \pi \in T_{|L_1|}, \forall i \in \{1, ..., |L_1|\} : L_2[\pi(i)] \in [R_{pk}(L_1[i])])\}$$
$$w(pk, L_1, L_2) = (\pi, C_{R_{pk}}^{\pi(L_1), L_2})$$

A shuffle takes a list of ciphertexts and outputs a permuted list of their re-encryptions. If verifiable, it then runs a proof system to prove that the output is really a permutation of the re-encryptions of input ciphertexts. This can be formally defined as follows.

Definition 3. *A shuffle is a pair,* $(\mathcal{RP}, S)$, *such that:*

- $\mathcal{RP}$ *is a public-key scheme with a re-encryption function* (G, E, D, R). *Suppose the algorithm* G *generates a pair* (pk, sk).
- *The PPT algorithm* S *takes as input a public key pk, a list of n input ciphertexts* L_{in} *and a random permutation* $\pi \in T_n$, *and outputs a list of n output ciphertexts* L_{out}. *S performs correctly if* L_{out} *is a list of re-encryptions of ciphertexts in* L_{in} *permuted by* π.

Definition 4. *A verifiable shuffle is a tuple,* $(\mathcal{RP}, S, (\mathcal{P}, \mathcal{V}))$, *such that:*

- $\mathcal{RP}$ *and* S *are defined as in Definition 3.*
- *The proof system* $(\mathcal{P}, \mathcal{V})$ *takes input pk,* L_{in} *and* L_{out} *from* S *and proves that* $(pk, L_{in}, L_{out}) \in \mathcal{L}_{\mathcal{RP}}$. *The private input to* $\mathcal{P}$ *includes only the witness* $w(pk, L_{in}, L_{out})$ *and does not include the private key sk.*

3.3   Security Definitions

There are 2 security requirements. Privacy requires an honest shuffle to protect its secret permutation whereas verifiability requires that any attempt by a malicious shuffle to produce an incorrect output must be detectable.

We assume an honest verifier for the proof system $(\mathcal{P}, \mathcal{V})$.

Verifiability. The proof system proves that the output of the shuffle is a permutation of the re-encryptions of the input ciphertexts. In other words, it is a proof system for the language $\mathcal{L}_{\mathcal{RP}}$. The proof system should satisfy two conditions, completeness and soundness. The completeness condition states that for all $x \in \mathcal{L}_{\mathcal{RP}}$, the proof system accepts with overwhelming probability. The soundness condition means that for all $x \notin \mathcal{L}_{\mathcal{RP}}$ the proof system accepts with negligible probability. In both definitions of completeness and soundness, we capture the non-uniform capability of the adversary by using a (non-uniform) auxiliary input t.

The private input y of the prover does not include the private key sk but may include information about the lists of plaintexts $L_{in}^{(p)}, L_{out}^{(p)}$ and the corresponding probabilistic inputs $C_{E_{pk}}^{L_{in}^{(p)}, L_{in}}, C_{E_{pk}}^{L_{out}^{(p)}, L_{out}}$. The following definition is for interactive proof systems but can be trivially modified for non-interactive proof systems.

Definition 5. *A shuffle $(\mathcal{RP}, S, (\mathcal{P}, \mathcal{V}))$ is verifiable if its proof system $(\mathcal{P}, \mathcal{V})$ has a polynomial-time $\mathcal{V}$ and satisfies two conditions:*

- *Completeness: For every PPT algorithm A and every positive polynomial $p()$, there exists an l_0 such that for all $l > l_0$ and $t \in \{0,1\}^{poly(l)}$, it holds that*

$$
Pr\left[
\begin{array}{l}
\langle \mathcal{P}(y), \mathcal{V} \rangle (pk, L_{in}, L_{out}) = 1 \text{ given } (pk, L_{in}, L_{out}) \in \mathcal{L_{RP}} \\
\text{where } (pk, sk) \xleftarrow{R} G(1^l), \\
(L_{in}, L_{out}) \xleftarrow{R} A(pk, t), \\
y \leftarrow w(pk, L_{in}, L_{out})
\end{array}
\right] > 1 - \frac{1}{p(l)}
$$

- *Soundness: For every interactive machine B, every PPT algorithm A and every positive polynomial $p()$, there exists an l_0 such that for all $l > l_0$ and $t \in \{0,1\}^{poly(l)}$, it holds that*

$$
Pr\left[
\begin{array}{l}
\langle \mathcal{B}(y), \mathcal{V} \rangle (pk, L_{in}, L_{out}) = 1 \text{ given } (pk, L_{in}, L_{out}) \notin \mathcal{L_{RP}} \\
\text{where } (pk, sk) \xleftarrow{R} G(1^l), \\
(\pi, L_{in}, L_{out}) \xleftarrow{R} A(pk, t), \\
y \leftarrow (\pi, L_{in}^{(p)}, C_{E_{pk}}^{L_{in}^{(p)}, L_{in}}, L_{out}^{(p)}, C_{E_{pk}}^{L_{out}^{(p)}, L_{out}})
\end{array}
\right] < \frac{1}{p(l)}
$$

Privacy. First assume the algorithm S performs correctly and the aim is to model concealment of the permutation. The shuffle is a public key transformation that hides the permutation through re-encryption. This can be viewed as 'encryption' of permutation through the process of re-encryption hence using notions of 'concealment' of plaintexts in encryption systems to model privacy. We consider 2 types of *adaptive attacks* by active adversaries. *Chosen permutation attack (CPA_S)* is similar to chosen plaintext attacks and the adversary can obtain transcripts of the shuffle executions corresponding to permutations that the adversary adaptively chooses. *Chosen transcript attack (CTA_S)* is similar to chosen ciphertext attacks and the adversary obtains permutations that correspond to valid shuffle transcripts that it adaptively chooses. The transcript of a verifiable shuffle's execution consists of the lists of input ciphertexts and output ciphertexts and the transcript of the proof system. An *adaptive attack* has 4 steps.

- *Key generation:* A trusted party generates the keys $(pk, sk) \xleftarrow{R} G(1^l)$. The adversary is given $(1^l, pk)$. (sk is used for decryption and is also not given to the shuffle.)

- *Oracle queries:* The adversary (adaptively) uses the information obtained so far to make queries to some oracles. The types of oracles determine the type of the attack (CPA$_S$ and CTA$_S$). After making a number of such queries, the adversary moves to the next stage.

- *Challenge generation:* Using the information obtained so far, the adversary specifies a *challenge template*, according to which an actual challenge will be generated.

- *Additional oracle queries:* Based on the information obtained so far, the adversary makes additional queries as in Step 2 and then, produces an output and halts.

The adversary's strategy consists of two stages, each represented by a PPT oracle machine, and corresponding to its action before and after generation of the actual challenge. The first part, denoted by A_1, captures the adversary's behavior during Step 2 and 3. A_1 is given the public key pk, and its output is a pair (τ, δ), where τ is the challenge template generated at the beginning of Step 3 and δ is the state information passed to the second part of the adversary. The second part of the adversary, denoted by A_2, captures the adversary's behavior during Step 4. A_2 is given the state information δ and the actual challenge o generated in Step 3, and produces the adversary's output. We let each oracle machine to have a (nonuniform) auxiliary input t. This is to capture the nonuniform power of the adversary. It suffices to give t to only the first machine as A_1 can pass this input to the second machine as part of the state information δ. A similar argument shows that it suffices to provide the public key only to A_1. We write $(\tau, \delta) \overset{R}{\leftarrow} A_1^{Oracles}(pk, t)$, and $v \overset{R}{\leftarrow} A_2^{Oracles}(\delta, o)$. where $Oracles$ specifies oracles that are available to the adversary.

Notions of Privacy: We consider two notions of privacy. *Semantic privacy* formalizes the intuition that whatever is computable about the permutation from a shuffle execution transcript must be also computable without the transcript. In formalising this notion under CPA$_S$ and CTA$_S$ we consider the following challenge templates. The challenge template includes a triplet of polynomial-size circuits Π_n, h_n, f_n and a list of n ciphertexts L_{in}. Π_n specifies a distribution on the set T_n (of all permutations on $\{1, ..., n\}$): it takes $poly(l)$-bit (l is the security parameter) input and outputs a permutation $\pi \in T_n$. The information regarding the permutation that the adversary tries to obtain is captured by f_n, whereas the a-priori partial information about the permutation is captured by h_n. The actual challenge includes the list of output ciphertexts L_{out}, the transcript of the proof system, $View_{\mathcal{V}}^{\mathcal{P}}(pk, L_{in}, L_{out})$, the partial information $h_n(\pi)$, the list of n input ciphertexts L_{in}, the list of n corresponding plaintexts $L_{in}^{(p)}$ and the list of probabilistic inputs $C_{E_{pk}}^{L_{in}^{(p)}, L_{in}}$. The inclusion of $L_{in}^{(p)}$ and $C_{E_{pk}}^{L_{in}^{(p)}, L_{in}}$ models the fact that the adversary can somehow know all the plaintexts of the input ciphertexts to the shuffle. The adversary's goal is to guess $f_n(\pi)$.

The second notion of privacy is *indistinguishability* and means that it is infeasible to distinguish transcripts of two shuffle executions that correspond to two permutations of the same size. In the definitions of IND-CPA$_S$ and IND-

CTA_S, the challenge template consists of a pair of permutations $\pi_{(1)}, \pi_{(2)} \in T_n$ and a list of n ciphertexts L_{in}. The actual challenge is the transcript of the shuffle execution corresponding to one of the permutations and consists of the list of output ciphertexts L_{out}, the transcript of the proof system $View_{\mathcal{V}}^{\mathcal{P}}(pk, L_{in}, L_{out})$, the lists of input ciphertexts L_{in} and the corresponding plaintexts $L_{in}^{(p)}$, and the probabilistic inputs $C_{E_{pk}}^{L_{in}^{(p)}, L_{in}}$ of the input ciphertexts. The adversary's goal is to distinguish the two possible cases.

Attacks: We consider two attacks.

(Chosen permutation attack) The adversary has access to two oracles. The first oracle takes a permutation and a list of input ciphertexts and produces a ciphertext list output by the algorithm S and corresponding to the input list, and the transcript of the proof system $(\mathcal{P}, \mathcal{V})$ when the shuffle interacts with an honest verifier. The second oracle takes a plaintext and returns the ciphertext encrypted by algorithm E_{pk} corresponding to plaintext. The adversary is adaptive and queries are chosen by taking the results of all previous queries into account. We note that in CPA_S the adversary can compute all answers to the queries using public information however using oracles provides consistency in our presentation.

Definition 6. *A verifiable shuffle $(\mathcal{RP}, S, (\mathcal{P}, \mathcal{V}))$ is said to have **semantic privacy under chosen permutation attack (SP-CPA$_S$)** if for every pair of PPT oracle machines, A_1 and A_2, there exists a pair of PPT algorithms, A_1' and A_2', such that the following two conditions hold:*

1. *For every positive polynomial $p()$, there exists an l_0 such that for all $l > l_0$ and $t \in \{0, 1\}^{poly(l)}$, it holds that*

$$Pr\left[\begin{array}{l} v = f_n(\pi) \text{ where} \\ \quad (pk, sk) \xleftarrow{R} G(1^l), \\ \quad ((\Pi_n, h_n, f_n, L_{in}), \delta) \xleftarrow{R} A_1^{(S,(\mathcal{P},\mathcal{V})),E_{pk}}(pk, t), \\ \quad L_{out} \xleftarrow{R} S(pk, L_{in}, \pi) \text{ where } \pi \leftarrow \Pi_n(U_{poly(l)}), \\ \quad o \leftarrow (L_{out}, View_{\mathcal{V}}^{\mathcal{P}}(pk, L_{in}, L_{out}), h_n(\pi), L_{in}, L_{in}^{(p)}, C_{E_{pk}}^{L_{in}^{(p)}, L_{in}}), \\ \quad v \xleftarrow{R} A_2^{(S,(\mathcal{P},\mathcal{V})),E_{pk}}(\delta, o) \end{array}\right]$$

$$< Pr\left[\begin{array}{l} v = f_n(\pi) \text{ where} \\ \quad ((\Pi_n, h_n, f_n), \delta) \xleftarrow{R} A_1'(1^l, t), \\ \quad \pi \leftarrow \Pi_n(U_{poly(l)}), \\ \quad v \xleftarrow{R} A_2'(\delta, 1^n, h_n(\pi)) \end{array}\right] + \frac{1}{p(l)}$$

2. *For every l and t above, the parts (Π_n, h_n, f_n) in the random variables $A_1^{(S,(\mathcal{P},\mathcal{V})),E_{pk}}(pk, t)$ and $A_1'(1^l, t)$ are identically distributed.*

Definition 7. *A verifiable shuffle $(\mathcal{RP}, S, (\mathcal{P}, \mathcal{V}))$ is said to provide **indistinguishability under chosen permutation attack (IND-CPA$_S$)** if for every pair of PPT* *oracle machines, A_1 and A_2, for every positive polynomial $p()$, there exists an l_0 such that for all $l > l_0$ and $t \in \{0,1\}^{poly(l)}$, it holds that*

$$|p_{l,t}^{(1)} - p_{l,t}^{(2)}| < \frac{1}{p(l)}$$

where

$$p_{l,t}^{(i)} \triangleq Pr \begin{bmatrix} v = 1 \text{ where} \\ (pk, sk) \overset{R}{\leftarrow} G(1^l), \\ ((\pi_{(1)}, \pi_{(2)}, L_{in}), \delta) \overset{R}{\leftarrow} A_1^{(S,(\mathcal{P},\mathcal{V})),E_{pk}}(pk, t), \\ L_{out} \overset{R}{\leftarrow} S(pk, L_{in}, \pi_{(i)}), \\ o \leftarrow (L_{out}, View_{\mathcal{V}}^{\mathcal{P}}(pk, L_{in}, L_{out}), L_{in}, L_{in}^{(p)}, C_{E_{pk}}^{L_{in}^{(p)}, L_{in}}), \\ v \overset{R}{\leftarrow} A_2^{(S,(\mathcal{P},\mathcal{V})),E_{pk}}(\delta, o) \end{bmatrix}$$

where $\pi_{(1)}, \pi_{(2)} \in T_n$.

The following theorem shows the equivalence of SP-CPA$_S$ and IND-CPA$_S$. The proof is similar to the proof of the equivalence of SS-CPA and IND-CPA [11].

Theorem 2. *A verifiable shuffle $(\mathcal{RP}, S, (\mathcal{P}, \mathcal{V}))$ provides SP-CPA$_S$ if and only if it provides IND-CPA$_S$.*

(Chosen transcript attack) In this attack, in addition to two oracles described before, the adversary has access to another oracle T, that takes a transcript of a shuffle execution and returns the corresponding permutation if the transcript is valid, and an error symbol, otherwise. We assume that in step 4, the adversary can not use the transcript in the actual challenge as the query to T.

We note that if the shuffle does not provide verifiability, then the adversary can always learn the permutation. This is because the shuffle transcript consists of an input and an output ciphertext list and the adversary can use re-encryption to generate another input and output ciphertext list that he can present to T and obtain the permutation. For verifiable shuffles, the attack can be prevented by using proof systems. For example, informally, by adding proofs of knowledge in the verifiability proof, construction of new valid transcripts from old ones can be prevented.

Definitions of SP-CTA$_S$ and IND-CTA$_S$ and the theorem stating their equivalence are quite similar to Definition 6, 7 and Theorem 2 and can be found in the full version of this paper [21].

3.4   Applications to Some Verifiable Shuffles

The following theorems shows security of the Furukawa-Sako [6], Neff [19] and Groth [13] verifiable shuffles. The proof of Verifiability (Theorem 3) can be constructed from proofs of Completeness and Soundness in the corresponding papers. The proof of SP-CPA$_S$ (Theorem 4) is similar to the verifiable shuffle in the next section.

Theorem 3. *Furukawa-Sako shuffle provides Verifiability if Discrete Log Assumption holds. Neff shuffle achieves Verifiability with overwhelming probability. Groth shuffle provides Verifiability if the encryption scheme provides SS-CPA and the commitment scheme is secure.*

Theorem 4. *Furukawa-Sako and Neff shuffles provide SP-CPA$_S$ if Decisional Diffie-Hellman Assumption holds. Groth shuffle provides SP-CPA$_S$ under conditions specified in Theorem 3.*

4   A Verifiable Shuffle Based on Paillier Public-Key System

4.1   Description

In our verifiable shuffle, the public-key re-encryption scheme $\mathcal{RP}$ is the Paillier scheme. The public key is $pk = N$ and the secret key is $sk = \lambda$. The algorithm S takes pk, a list of Paillier ciphertexts $g_1, ..., g_n \in Z_{N^2}^*$ and a permutation π and outputs another list of Paillier ciphertexts $g_1', ..., g_n' \in Z_{N^2}^*$. The proof system $(\mathcal{P}, \mathcal{V})$ is described in the next subsection.

4.2   Proof System

The proof system $(\mathcal{P}, \mathcal{V})$ proves that the prover $\mathcal{P}$ knows permutation π and $r_1, ..., r_n \in Z_N^*$ so that $g_i' = r_i^N g_{\pi^{-1}(i)}$. The input to the proof system is N, $\{g_i\}$, $\{g_i'\}$, $i = 1, ..., n$. Suppose there is a publicly known set $\{\tilde{g}_i\}_{i=1}^n$ of elements in $Z_{N^2}^*$, which is generated randomly and independently from the ciphertexts. Therefore if $DCRA$ holds, then it is easy to show that without knowing the secret key sk, it is infeasible to obtain non-trivial $\{a_i\}$ so that there exists $z \in Z_N^*$ satisfying $\prod_{i=1}^n \tilde{g}_i{}^{a_i} = z^N$ in polynomial time. Represent the permutation π by a permutation matrix $(A_{ij})_{n \times n}$, the protocol is as follows:

1. $\mathcal{P}$ generates: $\alpha_i \in_R Z_N, \alpha, \tilde{r}_i, \tilde{\alpha}, \delta_i, \rho, \rho_i, \tau, \tau_i \in_R Z_N^*, \ i = 1, ..., n$
2. $\mathcal{P}$ computes:

$$\tilde{g}_i' = \tilde{r}_i{}^N \prod_{j=1}^n \tilde{g}_j{}^{A_{ji}}; \ \dot{w}_i = \tau_i^N (1 + N \sum_{j=1}^n 2\alpha_j A_{ji}), \ i = 1, ..., n; \ g' = \alpha^N \prod_{j=1}^n g_j{}^{\alpha_j}$$

$$\tilde{g}' = \tilde{\alpha}^N \prod_{j=1}^n \tilde{g}_j{}^{\alpha_j}; \ \dot{v} = \rho^N (1 + N \sum_{j=1}^n \alpha_j^3); \ \dot{w} = \tau^N (1 + N \sum_{j=1}^n \alpha_j^2)$$

$$\dot{t}_i = \delta_i^N (1 + N \sum_{j=1}^n 3\alpha_j A_{ji}); \ \dot{v}_i = \rho_i^N (1 + N \sum_{j=1}^n 3\alpha_j^2 A_{ji}), \ i = 1, ..., n$$

3. $\mathcal{P} \longrightarrow \mathcal{V}: \{\tilde{g}_i'\}, \tilde{g}', g', \{\dot{t}_i\}, \{\dot{v}_i\}, \dot{v}, \{\dot{w}_i\}, \dot{w}, \ i = 1, ..., n$
4. $\mathcal{P} \longleftarrow \mathcal{V}:$ challenge $\{c_i\}, \ c_i \in_R Z_N, \ i = 1, ..., n$

5. $\mathcal{P} \longrightarrow \mathcal{V}$: the following responses

$$s_i = \sum_{j=1}^{n} A_{ij}c_j + \alpha_i \bmod N, i = 1, ..., n; \; \tilde{s} = \tilde{\alpha} \prod_{i=1}^{n} \tilde{r}_i^{c_i} \tilde{g}_i^{d_i} \bmod N$$

$$s = \alpha \prod_{i=1}^{n} r_i^{c_i} g_i^{d_i} \bmod N; \; u = \rho \prod_{i=1}^{n} \rho_i^{c_i} \delta_i^{c_i^2} \bmod N; \; v = \tau \prod_{i=1}^{n} \tau_i^{c_i} \bmod N$$

where $d_i = (\sum_{j=1}^{n} A_{ij}c_j + \alpha_i - s_i)/N$, $i = 1, ..., n$ (so d_i can only be 0 or 1)

6. $\mathcal{V}$ verifies:

$$\tilde{s}^N \prod_{j=1}^{n} \tilde{g}_j^{s_j} = \tilde{g}' \prod_{j=1}^{n} \tilde{g}_j'^{c_j}; \; u^N (1 + N \sum_{j=1}^{n} (s_j^3 - c_j^3)) = \dot{v} \prod_{j=1}^{n} \dot{v}_j^{c_j} \dot{t}_j^{c_j^2}$$

$$s^N \prod_{j=1}^{n} g_j^{s_j} = g' \prod_{j=1}^{n} g_j'^{c_j}; \; v^N (1 + N \sum_{j=1}^{n} (s_j^2 - c_j^2)) = \dot{w} \prod_{j=1}^{n} \dot{w}_j^{c_j}$$

4.3 Security

The proposed shuffle provides Verifiability and SP-CPA$_S$ under DCRA, as stated in Theorem 5 and Theorem 8.

Theorem 5. *The shuffle achieves Verifiability if DCRA holds.*

To prove Theorem 5, we need Theorem 6 and Theorem 7. The rest of the proof of Theorem 5 is quite similar to the Completeness and Soundness proofs of Furukawa-Sako scheme [6] and can be found in the full version of this paper [21].

Theorem 6. *A matrix* $(A_{ij})_{n \times n}$ *is a permutation matrix modulo* N *or there exists* i', j' *such that* $\gcd(A_{i'j'}, N) = p$, *if for all* i, j, k, *both*

$$\sum_{l=1}^{n} A_{li} A_{lj} = \begin{cases} 1 \bmod N \text{ if } i = j \\ 0 \bmod N \text{ otherwise} \end{cases} \tag{1}$$

$$\sum_{l=1}^{n} A_{li} A_{lj} A_{lk} = \begin{cases} 1 \bmod N \text{ if } i = j = k \\ 0 \bmod N \text{ otherwise} \end{cases} \tag{2}$$

hold.

Proof. Suppose a matrix (A_{ij}) satisfying (1) and (2), then (A_{ij}) is a permutation matrix mod p and also a permutation matrix mod q, based on Theorem 1. Therefore, if (A_{ij}) is not a permutation matrix mod N, then there exists i', j' such that $A_{i'j'} = 0 \bmod p$ and $A_{i'j'} = 1 \bmod q$. It leads to $\gcd(A_{i'j'}, N) = p$.

Theorem 7. *Denote* $\langle S \rangle_k$ *the vector space spanned by a set of vectors* S *in modular* k *and* $|S|$ *the number of elements in* S. *Suppose a set of vectors* $S_n = \{(1, c_1, ..., c_n)|(c_1, ..., c_n \in Z_N) \wedge (\nexists Q_n \subseteq S_n : |Q_n| = n + 1 \wedge \langle Q_n \rangle_p = Z_p^{n+1} \wedge \langle Q_n \rangle_q = Z_q^{n+1})\}$. *Then* $|S_n| \leq (p + q)N^{n-1}$.

Proof. It is proved by induction as follows

- $n = 1$: Suppose a set of vectors $S_1 \subseteq \{(1,c)|c \in Z_N\}$ satisfying $|S_1| > (p+q)$; and a vector $(1, c_1) \in S_1$. Consider a set $R_1 = \{(1, c_1 + kp \bmod N)|k \in Z_q\} \cup \{(1, c_1 + kq \bmod N)|k \in Z_p\}$. As $|R_1| = p+q-1$, there exists $c_1' \in Z_N$ so that $(1, c_1') \in S_1$ but $(1, c_1') \notin R_1$. Then $Q_1 = \{(1, c_1), (1, c_1')\}$ satisfying $|Q_1| = 2 \wedge \langle Q_1 \rangle_p = Z_p^2 \wedge \langle Q_1 \rangle_q = Z_q^2)\}$.
- Assume it is right for n. We prove it is also right for $n+1$. Let a set $S_{n+1} = \{(1, c_1, ..., c_{n+1})|(c_1, ..., c_{n+1} \in Z_N) \wedge (\nexists Q_{n+1} \subseteq S_{n+1} : |Q_{n+1}| = n+2 \wedge \langle Q_{n+1} \rangle_p = Z_p^{n+2} \wedge \langle Q_{n+1} \rangle_q = Z_q^{n+2})\}$. Consider $S_n' = \{(1, c_1, ..., c_n)|\exists c_{n+1} \in Z_N : (1, c_1, ..., c_n, c_{n+1}) \in S_{n+1}\}$, there are two possibilities:
  1. If $\nexists Q_n' \subseteq S_n' : |Q_n'| = n+1 \wedge \langle Q_n' \rangle_p = Z_p^{n+1} \wedge \langle Q_n' \rangle_q = Z_q^{n+1}$, then $|S_n'| \leq (p+q)N^{n-1}$, as the theorem is right for n. So $|S_{n+1}| \leq |S_n'|N \leq (p+q)N^n$.
  2. If $\exists Q_n' \subseteq S_n' : |Q_n'| = n+1 \wedge \langle Q_n' \rangle_p = Z_p^{n+1} \wedge \langle Q_n' \rangle_q = Z_q^{n+1}$, select a set T of $n+1$ vectors $(1, c_{i1}, ..., c_{i(n+1)}) \in S_{n+1}$, $i = 1, ..., n+1$ so that $Q_n' = \{(1, c_{i1}, ..., c_{in})\}$

  Let $d = det \begin{pmatrix} 1 & c_{11} & \cdots & c_{1n} \\ .. & .. & .. & .. \\ 1 & c_{(n+1)1} & \cdots & c_{(n+1)n} \end{pmatrix} \bmod N$, then $gcd(d, N) = 1$, so d^{-1}

  mod N exists.

  For each vector $x = (1, x_1, ..., x_{n+1}) \in S_{n+1}$ (including those in T), let

  $$d_x = det \begin{pmatrix} 1 & c_{11} & \cdots & c_{1(n+1)} \\ .. & .. & .. & .. \\ 1 & c_{(n+1)1} & \cdots & c_{(n+1)(n+1)} \\ 1 & x_1 & \cdots & x_{n+1} \end{pmatrix} = dx_{n+1} - F(x_1, ..., x_n) \bmod N$$

  for some function F. The conditions of S_{n+1} leads to either $d_x = 0 \bmod p$ or $d_x = 0 \bmod q$.

  Suppose $d_x = 0 \bmod p$, then $x_{n+1} = d^{-1}F(x_1, ..., x_n) \bmod p$, so the number of possible vectors $x = (1, x_1, ..., x_{n+1})$ is no more than qN^n. Similar for the case $d_x = 0 \bmod q$, the number of possible vectors $x = (1, x_1, ..., x_{n+1})$ is no more than pN^n. So $|S_{n+1}| \leq (p+q)N^n$.

Theorem 8. *The shuffle achieves SP-CPA$_S$ if and only if DCRA holds.*

Based on Theorem 2, proving Theorem 8 is equivalent to proving Theorem 9 below. We need Definition 8 and Lemma 1 to prove Theorem 9. Proof of Lemma 1 can be found in the full version of this paper [21].

Definition 8. *Define R_m to be the set of tuples of m elements in $Z_{N^2}^*$ and subset D_m of R_m to be the set of tuples of m N-th residues modulo N^2. We then define the problem of distinguishing instances uniformly chosen from R_m and those from D_m by DCRA$_m$.*

Lemma 1. *For any $m \geq 1$, DCRA$_m$ is easy if and only if DCRA is easy.*

Theorem 9. *The shuffle achieves IND-CPA$_S$ if and only if DCRA holds.*

Proof. Suppose the challenge template includes two permutations $\pi_{(1)}, \pi_{(2)} \in T_n$ and a list of ciphertexts $L_{in} = (g_1, ..., g_n)$. The actual challenge o to the adversary includes L_{in}, the list of corresponding plaintexts $L_{in}^{(p)}$, $C_{E_{pk}}^{L_{in}^{(p)}, L_{in}}$, a list of re-encryption ciphertexts $L_{out} = (g'_1, ..., g'_n)$ and

$$View_\mathcal{V}^\mathcal{P}(pk, L_{in}, L_{out}) = (\{\tilde{g}_i\}, \{\tilde{g}_i'\}, \tilde{g}', g', \{\dot{t}_i\}, \{\dot{v}_i\}, \{\dot{w}_i\}, \dot{v}, \dot{w}, \{c_i\}, \{s_i\}, \tilde{s}, s, u, v)$$

satisfying: $g' = s^N \prod_{j=1}^n g_j^{s_j} g_j'^{-c_j}$, $\dot{v} = u^N (1 + N \sum_{j=1}^n (s_j^3 - c_j^3)) \prod_{j=1}^n \dot{v}_j^{-c_j} \dot{t}_j^{-c_j^2}$, $\tilde{g}' = \tilde{s}^N \prod_{j=1}^n \tilde{g}_j^{s_j} \tilde{g}_j'^{-c_j}$, $\dot{w} = v^N (1 + N \sum_{j=1}^n (s_j^2 - c_j^2)) \prod_{j=1}^n \dot{w}_j^{-c_j}$.

Compute $I_{\pi_{(1)}} = (h_1, .., h_n, \tilde{h}_1, .., \tilde{h}_n, \overline{t}_1, .., \overline{t}_n, \overline{v}_1, .., \overline{v}_n, \overline{w}_1, .., \overline{w}_n)$, where

$$\alpha_i = s_i - c_{\pi_{(1)}(i)} \bmod N; \; h_i = g'_i / g_{\pi_{(1)}^{-1}(i)}, \; i = 1, ..., n$$

$$\tilde{h}_i = \tilde{g}_i' / \tilde{g}_{\pi_{(1)}^{-1}(i)}; \; \overline{t}_i = \dot{t}_i / (1 + N3\alpha_{\pi_{(1)}^{-1}(i)}), \; i = 1, ..., n$$

$$\overline{v}_i = \dot{v}_i / (1 + N3\alpha_{\pi_{(1)}^{-1}(i)}^2); \; \overline{w}_i = \dot{w}_i / (1 + N2\alpha_{\pi_{(1)}^{-1}(i)}), \; i = 1, ..., n$$

Then $\pi_{(1)}$ is the permutation used for the actual challenge o if and only if $I_{\pi_{(1)}} \in D_{5n}$. Therefore, based on Lemma 1, if the actual challenge o is computationally distinguishable under chosen shuffle attacks, then DCRA is easy, and vice-versa.

4.4 Efficiency

The proposed shuffle has the round efficiency (3 rounds) and the number of exponentiations (about $18n$) of Furukawa-Sako protocol, compared to Groth's protocol with a 7 round proof. The shuffle has less rounds and requires smaller number of exponentiations compared to Neff's protocol with 7 rounds and $23n$ exponentiations. (Note that exponentiations in our case is modulo N^2 which is more expensive than modulo p and so the number of bit operations in Furukawa-Sako's shuffle is smaller.) Compared with Furukawa-Sako and Groth's proof system, our proposed proof system has a more efficient initialization phase. In both those systems for El Gamal ciphertexts, a set of subgroup elements is used. Construction of these elements in general is computationally expensive [19]. Our proof system also relies on a set ($\{\tilde{g}_1, ..., \tilde{g}_n\}$) of elements of $Z_{N^2}^*$ that are just randomly generated.

References

1. M. Abe and H. Imai. Flaws in Some Robust Optimistic Mix-nets. ACISP 2003, LNCS 2727, pp. 39-50.
2. S. Brands. An efficient off-line electronic cash system based on the representation problem. CWI Technical Report CS-R9323, 1993.
3. D. Chaum. Untraceable electronic mail, return addresses, and digital pseudonyms. Communications of the ACM, 24(2):84-88, 1981.

4. S. Choi and K. Kim. Authentication and Payment Protocol Preserving Location Privacy in Mobile IP. GLOBECOM 2003.
5. P. Fouque and D. Pointcheval. Threshold Cryptosystems Secure against Chosen-Ciphertext Attacks. Asiacrypt 2001, LNCS 2248, pp. 351-369.
6. J. Furukawa and K. Sako. An Efficient Scheme for Proving a Shuffle. Crypto 2001, LNCS 2139, pp. 368-387.
7. J. Furukawa, H. Miyauchi, K. Mori, S. Obana and K. Sako. An Implementation of a Universally Verifiable Electronic Voting Scheme based on Shuffling. Financial Cryptography 2002, LNCS 2357.
8. J. Furukawa. Efficient, Verifiable Shuffle Decryption and Its Requirement of Unlinkability. PKC 2004, LNCS 2947, pp. 319-332.
9. E. Gabber, P. Gibbons, Y. Matias, and A. Mayer. How to make personalized Web browsing simple, secure, and anonymous. Financial Cryptography 1997, LNCS 1318, pp. 17-31.
10. O. Goldreich. Foundations of Cryptography, Basic Tools. Cambridge University Press 2001.
11. O. Goldreich. Foundations of Cryptography, Basic Applications. Cambridge University Press 2004.
12. P. Golle, S. Zhong, D. Boneh, M. Jakobsson and A. Juels. Optimistic Mixing for Exit-Polls. Asiacrypt 2002, LNCS 2501, pp. 451-465.
13. J. Groth. A Verifiable Secret Shuffle of Homomorphic Encryptions. PKC 2003, LNCS 2567, pp. 145-160.
14. M. Jakobsson and A. Juels. Mix and match: Secure function evaluation via ciphertexts. Asiacrypt 2000, LNCS 1976, pp. 162-177.
15. A. Juels. Targeted advertising and privacy too. RSA Conference Cryptographers' Track 2001, LNCS 2020, pp. 408-425.
16. J. Kong and X. Hong. ANODR: ANonymous On Demand Routing with Untraceable Routes for Mobile Ad-hoc Networks. Fourth ACM International Symposium on Mobile Ad Hoc Networking and Computing (MobiHoc) 2003, pp. 291-302.
17. M. Naor and M. Yung. Public-Key Cryptosystems Provably Secure against Chosen Ciphertexts Attacks. ACM STOC 1990, pp. 427-437.
18. A. Neff. A verifiable secret shuffle and its application to e-voting. ACM CCS 2001, pp. 116-125.
19. A. Neff. Verifiable Mixing (Shuffling) of ElGamal Pairs. http://www.votehere.org/vhti/documentation/egshuf.pdf.
20. L. Nguyen and R. Safavi-Naini. Breaking and Mending Resilient Mix-nets. Privacy Enhancing Technologies workshop (PET) 2003, LNCS 2760, pp. 66-80.
21. L. Nguyen, R. Safavi-Naini and K. Kurosawa. Verifiable Shuffles: A Formal Model and a Paillier-based Efficient Construction with Provable Security. Full version. Email: ldn01@uow.edu.au.
22. P. Paillier. Public-Key Cryptosystems Based on Composite Degree Residuosity Classes. Eurocrypt 1999, LNCS 1592, pp. 223-239.
23. A. Shamir. How to Share a Secret. Communications of the ACM, 22:612-613, 1979.
24. D. Wikstrom. The security of a mix-center based on a semantically secure cryptosystem. Indocrypt 2002, LNCS 2551, pp. 368-381.
25. D. Wikstrom. Five Practical Attacks for "Optimistic Mixing for Exit-Polls". SAC 2003, LNCS 3006.

On the Security of Cryptosystems with All-or-Nothing Transform

Rui Zhang, Goichiro Hanaoka, and Hideki Imai

Institute of Industrial Science, University of Tokyo
{zhang,hanaoka}@imailab.iis.u-tokyo.ac.jp, imai@iis.u-tokyo.ac.jp

Abstract. An AONT is an efficiently computable transform with two properties. Given all the bits of its output, it is easy to retrieve the message. On the other hand, if sufficiently many bits of the output are missing, it is computationally infeasible for an polynomial-time adversary to learn any information about the message. The natural intuition then may be deduced that if an secure AONT is used in a cryptosystem, the whole system will be secure as long as sufficiently many bits are "protected". However, we show this is not enough. Our results are three-fold: First we answer an open problem raised in [6], showing that previous definitions are not sufficient to guarantee a provably secure cryptosystem with strong data privacy, namely, indistinguishability against chosen ciphertext attack (IND-CCA). Second, we give a new definition to AONT, showing this definition suffices to guarantee an AONT integrated with any encryption functions to acquire IND-CCA secure cryptosystems. Third, we give concrete constructions that satisfy the new definition.

1   Introduction

THE CONCEPT. All-or-Nothing transform (AONT) was introduced by Rivest in [17] to increase the cost of brute force attacks on block ciphers without changing the key length. As originally defined in [17], an AONT is a randomized transform T that can be computed efficiently mapping sequences of blocks $(x_1, ..., x_n)$ to sequences of blocks $(y_1, ..y_{n'})$, with the following properties:

- If all the $T(x_1, ..., x_n) = (y_1, ..., y_{n'})$ blocks are given, it is easy to compute $(x_1, ..., x_n)$.
- Even if one of the blocks of output $(y_1, ..., y_{n'})$ is missing, it is infeasible to find out any information of any of the original blocks $(x_1, ..., x_n)$.

If such a transform is applied to a message producing a sequence of output blocks, and each of these blocks is encrypted by a block cipher, interestingly, an adversary will have no information unless it can decrypt all the cipher blocks. Thus the attack will be slowed down by a factor of n' without even changing the length of the secret key. However, since the security of AONT and the data privacy of a cryptosystem were independently developed in literature, one may naturally ask the following questions: Is a cryptosystem secure if it is composed by a "secure" AONT with an encryption component? In other words, how can we safely utilize an AONT in a cryptosystem? In this paper, we try to give an answer to such questions.

M. Jakobsson, M. Yung, J. Zhou (Eds.): ACNS 2004, LNCS 3089, pp. 76–90, 2004.

APPLICATIONS OF AONT. First possible category of applications, as has been addressed already, can be used as a mode of operation for block cipher to enhance the security against exhaustive search attack security without increasing key length, as proposed in [17,8]. AONT can also be combined with cryptosystems to reduce the computation cost of a bandwidth limited device. This was also known as remotely keyed encryption. If an AONT is performed on a long message to be sent, because of the nice property of AONT, only a small proportion, say a few blocks of output of AONT needs to be encrypted, as shown by Jakobsson, Stern and Yung [13]. In [14] for inclusion in the IEEE P1363a standard, an ANOT was proposed to make fixed-block size encryption schemes more efficient. The authors further claim that this method is encryption algorithm independent, that is, any asymmetric or symmetric key encryption. However, this needs *more careful discussions*, as we shall show later.

With AONT, one can design a cryptosystem with separate component, say, a smart card, which holds the secret key independent from the main system. By updating the secret keys from time to time, one can acquire strong key-insulated cryptosystem [9]. It was further generalized in [21] in constructing a parallel construction of multiple encryption to enhance the security of a single component cipher. Besides, as pointed out in [6], one might use AONT for gradual exchange of information. Suppose two users Alice and Bob want to exchange the secrets they hold. One possible problem is that the secret might be of different lengths. Then we can apply AONT to "pad" both secrets to equal length. Additional zero-knowledge proof should be attached to prevent cheating.

AONT ENHANCES DATA PRIVACY? From above discussion, one may naturally think that if a secure AONT is used in the system, the data privacy can be protected, as long as the underlying AONT is secure and efficiently many bits of the transformed message are protected by the encryption component. However, we argue that this intuition may be *not* true. At least, it may be fallacious according to chosen ciphertext security (CCA), which is considered as a standard security notion for practical cryptosystems. For why chosen ciphertext security is important, one may refer to [18]. We have noticed that in the context of authenticated encryption, it has been pointed out in [3] that for several construction methods by combining a secure message authentication code (MAC) with a secure encryption scheme, the resulting authenticated encryption may be insecure at all.

PREVIOUS DEFINITIONAL EFFORTS AND RELATED PRIMITIVES. The first definition was given in Rivest's original work [17], however, the definition simply mentions the case where the adversary "loses" a particular message block. It did not, however, mention the exact information that an adversary learn about the input with several bits invisible and how the adversary learns the information of the input related to bits that the adversary holds regarding the output was not addressed yet.

Desai studied AONT in the context of the security of symmetric key encryption against key search attack [8], and gave a definition of AONT. Again, in his model the security is defined in a block-wise manner: if there are some missing blocks cannot be learned by the adversary, it is considered secure. He claims that this suffices in building an operation mode of block ciphers secure in the terms of non-separability of keys. Stinson has considered AONT from the point of view of unconditional security [20]. However, his treatment is also considered the amount of information leaked by a particular block and the definition is just straightforward formalization of Rivest's definition in the information-theoretic security.

Aware of this shortage, Boyko [6] gave a new definition, namely, indistinguishability [12] against adaptive attack in the random oracle model [11,4]. In this model, an adversary can adaptively choose the positions of bits of the output of AONT to learn, however, below a certain threshold. It is also proved in [6] that OAEP, which was proposed by Bellare and Rogaway [5] with a different goal to obtain IND-CCA secure encryption schemes [12,16,15,10,2], is a secure implementation satisfying this definition, moreover, no AONT can do significantly better that OAEP. Later, Canetti et al. [7] gave a similar definition in the standard model (cf. random oracle model), furthermore, they constructed secure AONT under their definition based on exposure-resilient functions (ERF). They also proved the existence of ERF is equivalent to that of oneway functions. Though the existence of special class of exposure-resilient functions that are used in their OAEP-like construction is still left open.

A similar notion, *concealment*, was proposed in the context of remotely keyed authenticated encryption by An and Dodis [1]. Both of these two notions provide secrecy of the message, when even most of the blocks are given to the adversary. The difference is that concealment also provides authentication (knowledge of the plaintext), while an AONT does not necessarily need.

1.1   Our Contribution

ADJUSTED SECURITY NOTION ON AONT. We show that previous definitions of AONT are insufficient to guarantee cryptosystems with strong security, e.g., IND-CCA. We demonstrate that there exist cryptosystems, with an AONT secure in the sense of above definitions, however, are not secure against CCA attack. This also answers an open problem raised in [6] negatively, where Boyko wondered if OAEP can be replaced by an arbitrary AONT in the construction of a CCA secure encryption scheme. We pointed out previous definitions of AONT were either defined in a scenario where only chosen plaintext attack (CPA) is considered, or operates with some "ideal" encryption component, e.g., block cipher (often modeled as random permutation), or IND-CCA secure encryption component (strongest security for public key encryption). The security of AONT joined with arbitrary encryption component against adaptive attacks has not been thoroughly considered yet.

NEW DEFINITION REGARDING AONT. Actually, since AONT is only a randomized transform, which contains no secret key information, it may lead to fallacious conclusion if the security of the whole system is considered merely based on the security of AONT. In the real world an active attacker, who may be a legal user of this system, is capable of launching adaptive attacks. Thus we suggest that the security of the system should be considered as a joint contribution of AONT and the encryption component. We give a new definition of AONT based on indistinguishability, called *extended-indistinguishability*, which is defined together with encryption component. A straightforward consequence turns out that if an AONT with extended-indistinguishability is used in a cryptosystem together with arbitrary encryption scheme, the resulting cryptosystem is IND-CCA secure.

CONSTRUCTION OF EXTENDED-INDISTINGUISHABLE AONTS. We also give two constructions of AONT satisfying the new definition. The first one, provably secure in the random permutation model, is capable for deterministic encryption primitives. The second one, provably secure in the random oracle model, is capable for probabilistic encryption primitives.

2 Preliminary

2.1 Notations and Model

Throughout this paper, we limit our scope within "efficiently computable" algorithms, which means that algorithms have expected polynomial execution time. A function $f : \mathsf{D} \to \mathbf{R}$ is called *negligible* if for every constant $l \geq 0$ there exists an integer k such that $f(k) \leq k_c^{-l}$ for all $k \geq k_c$, denoted by $\mathsf{neg}(k)$.

$X \approx Y$ denotes that probability distribution X are computationally indistinguishable from Y. We shall use $x \xleftarrow{R} X$ to denote x is uniformly selected from distribution X. Suppose X is an algorithm, $x \leftarrow X$ denotes x is set to the output of X. We also use $x \oplus y$ to denote bit-wise XOR of two binary strings x and y. Let Ω be all the mappings from set of infinite strings $\{0,1\}^\infty$ to set of finite strings $\{0,1\}^*$, then $G, H \leftarrow \Omega$ denotes two random function G and H are selected uniformly from Ω, whose input and output sizes should be restricted accordingly in proper context. For an integer n and $L \in [1, n]$, we define $h_{n,L} : \{0,1\}^n \to \{0,1\}^{n-|L|}$ as for an input binary string of length n, $h_{n,L}$ returns a punctured string with the bit positions that is indicated by label L.

2.2 Public Key Encryption

A public key encryption scheme $\mathcal{E}$ is a 3-tuple algorithm: $\mathcal{E} = (\mathsf{Enc\text{-}Gen}, \mathsf{Enc}, \mathsf{Dec})$. $\mathsf{Enc\text{-}Gen}(1^k)$ is a probabilistic algorithm, where k is the security parameter, with internal random coin flipping outputs a pair of keys (pk, sk). pk is the encryption key which is made public, and sk is the decryption which is kept secret. Enc may be a probabilistic algorithm that takes as input a key pk and a message m from associated message space $\mathcal{M}$, and internally flips some coins and outputs a ciphertext c, denoted by $c \leftarrow \mathsf{Enc}_{pk}(m)$, in short $c \leftarrow \mathsf{Enc}(m)$. Dec is a deterministic algorithm takes as input the ciphertext c and the secret key sk, and outputs some message $m \in \mathcal{M}$, or "$\perp$" in case c is "invalid". We denote it by $m \leftarrow \mathsf{Dec}_{sk}(c)$, in short $m \leftarrow \mathsf{Dec}(c)$.

Indistinguishability under chosen-ciphertext attack (IND-CCA), is defined as: if no PPT adversary $\mathcal{A}$ can distinguish encryptions of any two messages (M_0, M_1)

of equal length chosen by it with negligible advantage than random guess in the following game. We require that $\mathcal{A}$ runs in two stages $\mathcal{A}_{\text{find}}$ and $\mathcal{A}_{\text{guess}}$, in which $\mathcal{A}_{\text{find}}$ gets side information α from the queries and output a pair of challenge messages, and $\mathcal{A}_{\text{guess}}$ outputs a guess $\tilde{b}$ on b according to the ciphertext C_b encrypted by the Encryption Oracle with randomly chosen $b \in \{0, 1\}$. According to the ability of the adversary, $\mathcal{A}_{\text{find}}$ and $\mathcal{A}_{\text{guess}}$ can be assisted by an Decryption Oracle $\mathcal{DO}$ that returns the plaintext for a decryption query other than the target ciphertext. Note that according to the adversary's ability, sometimes $\mathcal{DO}$ is unavailable, (this can be equivalently denoted by $\mathcal{DO}$ outputting an empty string ϵ). In our analysis, it is sufficient to consider the case where $\mathcal{DO}$ is available. We denote this as:

$$\Pr\left[b = \tilde{b} \,\middle|\, \begin{array}{l} (pk, sk) \leftarrow \text{Enc-Gen}(1^k), (M_0, M_1, \alpha) \leftarrow \mathcal{A}_{\text{find}}^{\mathcal{DO}}(pk), \\ b \xleftarrow{R} \{0, 1\}, C_b \leftarrow \text{Enc}(M_b), \tilde{b} \leftarrow \mathcal{A}_{\text{guess}}^{\mathcal{KE}, \mathcal{DO}}(C_b, \alpha) \end{array} \right] \le \frac{1}{2} + \text{neg}(k)$$

If no such PPT adversary exists against $\mathcal{E}$, then we call $\mathcal{E}$ IND-CCA secure.

2.3 Previous Definitions on AONT

Definition from [6] In fact, in [6], several definitions are presented based on semantic security and indistinguishability [12], against adaptive and non-adaptive attacks. From the quantitive results given in [6], we notice that the upper bounds of semantic security and indistinguishability against adaptive attacks are essentially the same. It is sufficient to only consider the indistinguishability-based security definition.

Definition 1. *AONT is a randomized transform* $T(x) : \{0, 1\}^n \to \{0, 1\}^{n'}$, *which is efficiently computable. with all bits of the output, there is an inverse function I, which can uniquely recover x:* $I(T(x)) = x$. *Suppose an adversary runs the experiment in the following stages:*

1. Select: *The adversary is given l and access to Γ. It selects l bit positions and outputs labels of positions $L \in \{^{n'}_l\}$ and side-information $c_s \in \{0, 1\}^*$.*
2. Find: *The adversary is given c_s and access to Γ. It outputs $x_0 \in \{0, 1\}^n$, $x_1 \in \{0, 1\}^n$ and side-information $c_f \in \{0, 1\}^*$.*
3. Guess: *The adversary is given c_f and for random bit b, $\text{AONT}^{\Gamma}(x_b)$ with bit positions L missing. The adversary has access to Γ and tries to guess b.*

Let AONT be a randomized transform mapping n-bit messages to n'-bit outputs and using random oracle Γ. Let l between 1 and n'. An adversary $\mathcal{A}$ is said to succeed in (T, q_Γ, ϵ)-adaptively-distinguishing AONT with l missing bits if

$$\Pr\left[\tilde{b} = b \,\middle|\, \begin{array}{l} \Gamma \leftarrow \Omega, (L, c_s) \leftarrow \mathcal{A}_{\text{select}}^{\Gamma}(l), (x_0, x_1, c_f) \leftarrow \mathcal{A}_{\text{find}}^{\Gamma}(c_s), \\ b \xleftarrow{R} \{0, 1\}, y \leftarrow \text{AONT}^{\Gamma}(x_b), \tilde{b} \leftarrow \mathcal{A}_{\text{guess}}^{\Gamma}(h_{n', L}(y), c_f)] \end{array} \right] \ge \frac{1}{2} + \epsilon$$

and moreover, in the experiment above, A runs at most T steps and makes at most q_Γ queries to Γ. Then the AONT is secure if no probabilistic polynomial time adversary exists.

Furthermore, it is proved that OAEP [5] is a secure implementation of AONT in the above sense in the random oracle model.

Definition from [7] We can see this definition is significantly the same as the Definition 1, except that the latter can only be defined in the random oracle model. Definition 2 indicates more general case. In addition, [7] also divides the output y of an AONT into two sections: one is called the *public part* y_2, which does not need protection, that is, it can be revealed to the adversary. The other section is called *secret part* y_1, which needs some protection. The security guarantee is: as long as l bits of the secret output y_1 remain hidden, while all the bit of y_2 can be revealed, the adversary should have no information about the message.

Definition 2. *A randomized polynomial time computable function $T(x) : \{0,1\}^k \rightarrow \{0,1\}^{n'}$ is l-AONT if*

1. *T is efficiently invertible, i.e., there is a polynomial time machine I such that for any $x \in \{0,1\}^k$ and any $y \in T(x)$, we have $I(y) = x$.*
2. *For any label $L \in \{^{n'}_l\}$ and any $x_0, x_1 \in \{0,1\}^k$ chosen by the adversary adaptively, we have*

$$\langle x_0, x_1, [T(x_0)]_L \rangle \approx \langle x_0, x_1, [T(x_1)]_L \rangle$$

The construction of [7] makes use of *exposure-resilient functions* (ERF). Informally, an l-ERF is a special type of pseudorandom generator whose output remains computationally indistinguishable from a random sequence as long as l bits of its seed remain hidden. Refer [7] for formal definition and construction of ERF. A construction satisfying above Definition 2 was proposed and has been proved secure (theorem 5.1 of [7]).

3   AONT Enhances Data Privacy?

As we know, since an AONT contains no secret information itself, and it does no encryption, when integrated in a cryptosystem, the security of the whole system rather than AONT itself should be considered. Above two definitions [6,7] have considered AONT against adaptive attacks, however, the security of other component of the cryptosystem, especially the security of the encryption component is never confronted with.

Actually, definitions given in [6,7] are sufficient for a chosen plaintext attack (CPA). A simple reasoning is listed here: if the attacker can break the security of the cryptosystem then it can be used as a subroutine, to break either the indistinguishability of the AONT or the encryption component. A similar argument in proving the CPA security of a generic construction for key-insulated cryptosystem can be found in [9], yet in a different context.

However, the same argument is not applicable in discussing the CCA security of the cryptosystem. Problems may occur when an AONT meeting security definitions of [6,7] works with a malleable encryption scheme. Here we demonstrate two examples.

3.1   Example 1

The first example is an attack on OAEP, which was first exhibited by Shoup [19] in disproving the original secure result of OAEP. OAEP can be described as follows: two hash functions G, H are considered as random functions, a message m is masked by: $s = m \oplus G(r)$, $t = r \oplus H(s)$. Then the ciphertext is $c = \varphi_{pk}(s, t)$, where φ is oneway trapdoor function defined by pk and sk. For decryption, one computes

$$(s, t) = \varphi_{sk}(s, t), \quad r = t \oplus H(s), \quad m = s \oplus G(r).$$

Suppose there exists XOR-malleable f (refer [19] for precise definition), which is oneway trapdoor function with following properties: Given $\varphi_{pk}(x) = (s, f(t))$, one can efficiently compute $f(x \oplus \Delta x)$, where Δx is any binary string with the same length as x.

For any challenge ciphertext $c_b = (s, f(t))$ given by the encryption oracle in the IND-CCA game, the adversary can choose any random string Δx and compute $s' = s \oplus \Delta x$ and $f(t') = f(t \oplus H(s) \oplus H(s'))$, which yields a new ciphertext c'. If the adversary queries c' at the Decryption Oracle, which will returns $m_b \oplus \Delta x$, and the adversary can easily recover m_b and guess b correctly. The reason why this attack works is that the adversary can make the ciphertext malleable.

From above description, one can see that if OAEP is used as AONT in a cryptosystem, and the encryption component (encrypting t or part of t) happens to be XOR-malleable, the whole system is not IND-CCA secure.

3.2   Example 2

The second example is more straightforward. The following construction is given in [7]: Let $f : \{0, 1\}^n \to \{0, 1\}^{n'}$ be computational l-ERF. Define $T : \{0, 1\}^k \to \{0, 1\}^n \times \{0, 1\}^k$ (with n random bits r) as follows: $T(x; r) = \langle r, f(r) \oplus x \rangle$. Then T is l-AONT with secret part r and public part $f(r) \oplus x$.

For this one-time pad like construction, with the same seed r as the secret part and $f(r) \oplus x$ as the public part (without any encryption), one can compute $f(r) \oplus x \oplus \Delta x$, where Δx is any binary string. The resulting ciphertext becomes $E(r)$ (secret part under encryption) and $f(r) \oplus x \oplus \Delta x$ (public part to transmit in plaintext). Again, it is easily seen that the whole cryptosystem is not IND-CCA secure, either.

4   New Definition Regarding AONT

We have manifested that under present definition of AONT, it is not sufficient to guarantee CCA security of the whole cryptosystem. However, the fact that there are no obvious attacks to the security of previous constructions of AONT seems to contradict above counterexamples. We figure that AONT was originally proposed for block cipher, and in the theoretical analysis block cipher is usually modeled as random permutation. One may think that a random permutation is somehow a transform with authentication, at least in a weak sense. For block cipher, informally speaking chosen ciphertext attack is almost the same as chosen plaintext attack, for the random permutation will leave the ciphertext non-malleable. On the other hand, for a public key cryptosystem, chosen ciphertext attack is more powerful attack. In a cryptosystem with AONT, whenever the encryption component is malleable, the security of the whole system, regardless of that of AONT, may be insecure.

Then two natural questions arise that how should one consider the security of AONT and how should it be implemented in designing a secure cryptosystem? We proceed to solve these problems.

4.1   Public Key Encryption Schemes with AONT

Before we can formalize our solutions, we would like to give a new syntax on public key encryption scheme with AONT, which leads to better model practice.

Definition 3. *A public key encryption scheme with AONT as a component is an encryption scheme with following algorithms: (K, S, E, Com, D), where:*

- *K is the key generation algorithm, necessarily to be randomized. It calls the key generation algorithm of a public key encryption scheme $\mathsf{Gen\text{-}Enc}(1^k)$, where k is the security parameter, and outputs a pair (pk, sk) of keys defining a oneway trapdoor permutation. It also pick an $AONT = (T, I)$, where T is a randomized transform algorithm, taking a message m, with internal randomness r, outputs $y = T(m)$ as the output; I is the deterministic inverse algorithm, takes a binary string $\bar{y}$, and return $\bar{m} = I(\bar{y})$.*
- *S is the deterministic plaintext split algorithm, taking $y = T(m)$ as input, returning two section y_1 and y_2, called secret part and public part respectively.*
- *E may be a probabilistic algorithm, calls the encryption algorithm Enc of a normal public key encryption with (y_1, pk) as input, outputs the ciphertext c_1 that returns by Enc.*
- *Com is a deterministic combine algorithm, output $C = (c_1, y_2)$ as the final ciphertext.*
- *D is the deterministic decryption algorithm. It first takes $\bar{C}$ as input, splits it into two parts: $(\bar{c}_1$ and $\bar{y}_2)$, then calls Dec of the public key encryption with $(\bar{c}_1, sk)$ as input, and gets $\bar{y}_1$, otherwise $\perp$ if "invalid" and terminates right away. It then returns $\bar{m} = I(\bar{y}_1, \bar{y}_2)$ as plaintext and terminates.*

4.2   Extended-Indistinguishability

We solve the first question by giving a new definition, called extended-indistin guishability, on AONT, where besides what the adversary can get in previous model, some additional side-information is given to it. The justification lies in that, the adversary not only has the resources he could in the previous game, e.g., Definition 1, additionally, it also has access to c_1, the output of the encryption component. The adversary then plays the a modified game with oracle queries. The adversary wins if it can distinguish the input of the AONT, which also turns out to be the plaintext of the whole system. Note that the side-information may be useless for the adversary, for instance, in the case that the cryptosystem is IND-CCA secure.

We are now ready to give the new definition. Suppose an probabilistic polynomial time adversary $\mathcal{A}$ attacking a cryptosystem with AONT is engaged in the following game:

Definition 4. *At the beginning the key generation K algorithm is run, (pk, sk) are generated. The adversary schedules the attack in two phase* find *and* guess, *where it has decryption oracle access for polynomial times. At the end of* find *phase, the adversary outputs a pair of messages and writes some internal information s to its tape. An encryption oracle randomly chooses a bit b and generates the challenge ciphertext C_b. At the end of* guess *phase, the adversary outputs its guess on b. The adversary cannot query C_b on decryption oracle and an AONT has* extended-indistinguishability *if the adversary's advantage of correctly guessing b is negligible than random guess.*

$$\Pr\left[\tilde{b} = b \middle| \begin{array}{l} (pk, sk) \leftarrow K, (m_0, m_1, s) \leftarrow \mathcal{A}^{\mathcal{DO}}_{\mathsf{find}}(pk), \\ b \xleftarrow{R} \{0, 1\}, y_b \leftarrow T(m_b), \\ (y_{1b}, y_{2b}) \leftarrow S(y_b), c_{1b} \leftarrow E(y_{1b}), \\ C_b \leftarrow Com(c_{1b}, y_{2b}), \tilde{b} \leftarrow \mathcal{A}^{\mathcal{DO}}_{\mathsf{guess}}(C_b, s) \end{array}\right] \leq 1/2 + neg(k)$$

Theorem 1. *Suppose a cryptosystem is integrated by an extended-indistinguishable AONT with an encryption component that is at least oneway, then the resulting cryptosystem is* IND-CCA *secure.*

Proof. From definition, obvious.   □

4.3   Relations among Definitions for AONT

We briefly discuss how the new definition relates to previous definitions. Since Definition 2 completely catches the essence of Definition 1, we focus on the relation between Definition 2 and Definition 4. As we have mentioned, when AONT is combined with an IND-CCA component, there is no gap between these two definitions for an static adversary. We give a more detailed discussion here.

Suppose (T, I) is a secure AONT in the sense of Definition 2, we want to show for secret part y_1 protected by an IND-CCA secure encryption component, T is also secure in the sense of extended-indistinguishability. Actually, if this AONT is not extended-indistinguishable, an adversary $\mathcal{B}$ attacking this AONT in the sense of Definition 2 can simply be constructed as follows:

Suppose $\mathcal{A}$ is an adversary breaks extended-indistinguishability of the AONT. When $\mathcal{A}$ as for decryption queries, $\mathcal{B}$ can simply choose random c_1, together with public part y_2 complete the input message m. Since the encryption component is IND-CCA secure, which implies that for any c_1, y_1 is independent with c_1, which implies $\mathcal{B}$ simulation is perfect. Then in the end of the game, $\mathcal{B}$ outputs whatever bit b $\mathcal{A}$ outputs, thus gets the same advantage as $\mathcal{A}$. On the other hand, AONT with extended-indistinguishability is also secure under Definition 2 with similar discussion.

Remark 1. Similar analysis applies to the case of block cipher. Above analysis explains the correctness of practical schemes built on AONTs secure in the sense of previous definitions.

5   Secure Constructions

Present public key encryption primitives can be divided into two categories: the deterministic ones and the probabilistic ones. However, different treatments should be performed on these primitives respectively, because probabilistic encryption primitive requires additional randomness. If this randomness is not carefully controlled, or more exactly, if the encryption component is malleable regarding the underlying AONT, then an adversary can still create a malleable ciphertext, thus the cryptosystem is not IND-CCA secure. We give two constructions according to the types of primitives: the first is based on random permutation and suitable for deterministic encryption component. The second is based on random oracle and suitable for probabilistic encryption component. We remark that for the latter, generic construction based on non-interactive zero-knowledge proof is also capable, however, to make the ciphertext compact and computationally efficient, we adopt the random oracle.

5.1   Construction 1

The first is a Full-Domain Permutation based construction. We note the permutation is public random permutation and not oneway.

DESCRIPTION. Intuitively, one can think the random permutation as a bijective random oracle. A random permutation family is a family of permutations, $\pi : Keys(\pi) \times Dom(\pi) \to Rang(\pi)$, where $Dom(\pi)$ and $Rang(\pi)$ denotes the input domain space and output range space of π. Fixing each key k, $P_k : \{0,1\}^n \to \{0,1\}^n$ is a bijective mapping over the same space. By random permutation, in fact, we mean there doesn't not exist two keys k_1 and k_2, such that P_{k_1} is the same as P_{k_2}. Thus a random permutation family of domain $\{0,1\}^n$ has the key size 2^n. Since the permutation is public, given $P_k(m)$ and k, one can easily and uniquely recover

$$m = P_k^{-1}(P_k(m)).$$

The construction is very simple: for a random permutation over space $\{0,1\}^n$, where n is the size of message space, pick key k_r, and compute $P_{k_r}(m)$, then $(k_r, P_{k_r}(m))$ is an AONT with secret part k_r and public part $P_{k_r}(m)$.[1] The following theorem guarantees the security of this construction:

Theorem 2. *An AONT from Construction 1 is extended-indistinguishable.*

---

[*] In fact choice of places of bits to encrypt can be flexible, if sufficiently many bits are protected.

PROOF IDEA. The goal of the proof is to simulate the oracles P and P^{-1}, such that the adversary cannot distinguish this from the real oracles. In the simulation. If a new query is encountered, for P is a random permutation, we have to reply with a new random value in order to keep the simulation consistent. On simulation of decryption oracle queries, if the pre-image of the encryption component is asked, there will be a small error probability. However, we prove this is negligible, and the simulation is almost perfect. On the other hand, the challenge of m_b from the pair (m_0, m_1) is independent of the simulation, thus the adversary has no advantage. If there exist such an adversary breaks the extended-indistinguishability, then we can construct an adversary breaks the onewayness of the encryption component.

Proof. Assume there exists an adversary $\mathcal{A}$ that breaks the extended-indistin guishability of above construction. We can then construct an adversary $\mathcal{B}$ that breaks the onewayness of the encryption component denoted as φ. Namely, on input $c^* = \varphi_{pk}(r^*)$, $\mathcal{B}$ outputs r^*.

CONSTRUCTION OF $\mathcal{B}$. The key generation algorithm is run, generating (pk, sk). $\mathcal{B}$ maintains an ordered P-list of 4 data-entry (m, r, p, c) as follows:

On P query on $m \in \{0,1\}^n$ from $\mathcal{A}$ for P, $\mathcal{B}$ chooses $r \overset{R}{\leftarrow} \{0,1\}^n$, replies $p = P_r(m)$, computes the corresponding ciphertext $\varphi_{pk}(r)$ and stores $(m, r, p, \varphi_{pk}(r))$ in P-list. On P^{-1} query on $p \in \{0,1\}^n$, $\mathcal{B}$ chooses $r \overset{R}{\leftarrow} \{0,1\}^n$, replies $m = P^{-1}(p)$, and stores $m, r, p, \varphi_{pk}(r)$ in the P-list.

On decryption query on $C = (p, c)$, $\mathcal{B}$ searches in P-list whether there exists entry with (p, c). If there exists such entry, answers with m and quits. If there is no such entry, replies $m \overset{R}{\leftarrow} \{0,1\}^n$, computes $r = P^{-1}(p)$ and writes (m, r, p, c) to P-list.

On encryption oracle query with chosen messages (m_0, m_1) by $\mathcal{A}$, $\mathcal{B}$ chooses random p^*. Instead of giving correct challenge to $\mathcal{A}$, $\mathcal{B}$ takes his challenge $c^* = \varphi_{pk}(m^*)$, replies the challenge $C_b = (p^*, c^*)$.

When $\mathcal{A}$ terminates and outputs a guess b, $\mathcal{B}$ then searches in the P-list and if there is an entry (m,r,p,c) with $c = c^*$, then it outputs $m^* = m$ as the pre-image of $c^* = \varphi_{pk}(m^*)$. If $\mathcal{A}$ does not terminate in polynomial time or it encounters an error, $\mathcal{B}$ aborts the simulation and chooses random m from the list as output. Define some probability events as:

- PBad: $\mathcal{B}$ answers one P or P^{-1} query incorrectly.
- DBad: $\mathcal{B}$ answers one decryption query incorrectly.

Suppose the $\mathcal{A}$ issues Q_P direct P-oracle and P^{-1}-oracle queries and Q_D decryption queries respectively. Since P is a random permeation, then when a new entry is added to the list, it fails when there is already one entry with the same r, c in the list. Then this time, the simulation aborts. This implies the probability of failing to simulate of P or P^{-1} queries are:

$$\Pr[\text{PBad}] \leq Q_P \cdot 2^{-n}$$

For $|r| = n$, the only exception on decryption query is when the corresponding ciphertext is $C = (p, \varphi_{pk}(r^*))$, that is, $\mathcal{A}$ is asking on $\varphi_{pk}(r^*)$ and gets a wrong reply from $\mathcal{B}$, for r^* is unknown to the simulator because of onewayness of encryption component $\varphi(r^*)$. This time we have:

$$\Pr[\text{DBad}] \leq (Q_P + Q_D)^2 \cdot 2^{-n}$$

Since there is $Q_P + Q_D$ elements on the P-list, the fail probability of simulation of adversary $\mathcal{B}$ denoted as $\Pr[\text{BadB}]$ is given as:

$$\Pr[\text{BadB}] = \Pr[\text{DBad} \vee \text{PBad}] \leq \Pr[\text{DBad}] + \Pr[\text{PBad}] \qquad (1)$$

Define advantage of $\mathcal{A}$ as ε_1 and $\mathcal{B}$ as ε, which is non-negligible, since the challenge is completely independent of (m_0, m_1), since C is independent from m_0 and m_1, the success probability of $\mathcal{A}$ should be exactly $1/2$.

$$\Pr[\text{SucA} \wedge \neg\text{BadB}] = 1/2 \qquad (2)$$

On the other hand, we have

$$\Pr[\text{BadB}] \geq \Pr[\text{SucA} \wedge \text{BadB}] \geq \Pr[\text{SucA}] - 1/2 = \varepsilon_1 \qquad (3)$$

For failed simulation, if there is an entry (m, r, p, c^*) in the list there will appear a collision. In this case, the simulation fails but $\mathcal{B}$ can know it has already inverted $\varphi_{pk}(r)$. Now from (1,2,3), we have:

$$\varepsilon \geq \Pr[\text{SucA} \wedge \text{BadB}] - \Pr[\text{PBad}] - \Pr[\text{PBad}]$$
$$\geq \varepsilon_1 - Q_P \cdot 2^{-n} - (Q_P + Q_D)^2 \cdot 2^{-n}$$

This implies $\mathcal{B}$ successfully inverts φ_{pk} with non-negligible probability and the execution time of $\mathcal{B}$ is within polynomial time. Proof completes. $\square$

5.2   Construction 2

DESCRIPTION. For probabilistic public key encryption primitive, we would like to propose another construction based on random oracles. The second construction works as follows: G, H, H' are three hash functions treated as random oracles. For a message m, and randomness r, let the transform be

$$s = G(r) \oplus x, \quad t = H(s) \oplus r$$

which takes $y = s\|t$ as output. Additionally, compute $H'(r, m)$ as the randomness used in for the probabilistic encryption component ψ. We note that only a part of y needs to be encrypted. Suppose the split algorithm works as: $y = y_1\|y_2$, we require $y_1 << s$ and 2^{-y_1} is negligible. Then the probabilistic encryption component ψ takes y_1 as input, using randomness $H'(r, m)$, producing partial ciphertext $c_1 = \psi_{pk}(y_1)$.

In decryption phase, after recovering y_1, one can divide y as (s, t). Set $\bar{r} = H(s) \oplus t$ and compute $\bar{m} = s \oplus G(r)$. Check whether the ciphertext is formed correctly by computing $H'(r, \bar{m})$ and encrypt y_1 again. If this test is passed, output $\bar{m}$ as plaintext, otherwise "$\perp$".

Theorem 3. *An AONT from Construction 2 is extended-indistinguishable.*

PROOF IDEA. The idea lies in that, because of the checksum $H'(r, m)$ can be reconstructed, with re-encryption, most of the invalid decryption queries will be rejected. Thus an adversary can simulate the decryption oracle almost perfect. All correct decryption queries are "plaintext aware", in other words, the adversary gains no help from the decryption oracle. On the other hand, the adversary should simulate the random oracle queries. This is achieved by letting the adversary maintain three lists. We try to prove that the simulated oracles are in fact indistinguishable from real oracles.

Proof. From assumptions, if there exists an adversary $\mathcal{A}$ breaks the extended-indistinguishability of the AONT, another adversary $\mathcal{B}$ can be built as follows:

The key generation algorithm is run, generating (pk, sk). $\mathcal{B}$ maintains three lists, named G-list, H-list and H'-list respectively. On each random oracle query on a, $\mathcal{B}$ flips coins and selects random number as output $b \in \{0, 1\}^*$. Here $\{0, 1\}$ should be understood as proper length according to different contexts. $\mathcal{B}$ then write the pair (a, b) to corresponding list. We also denote the data entries in each list as: $g, G(g)$, $h, H(h)$ and $h', H'(h')$ respectively.

On answering decryption queries c_1, $\mathcal{B}$ first searches for the pair G-list and H-list, and finds pairs $g, G(g)$ and $h, H(h)$, such that $s \| t = h \| g \oplus H(h)$. It then sets $r = g$ and $m = h \oplus G(r)$. If there is an entry in H'-list such that $h' = r \| m$, it splits $s \| t$ as $y_1 \| y_2$, and encrypts y_1 with the public key pk to get $c_1 = \psi_{pk}(y_1)$ with $H'(h')$ as randomness for ψ_{pk}. Otherwise, it outputs "$\perp$". Denote the bit length of y_1 as k_1, length of h as k_2 and length of g as k_3.

When $\mathcal{A}$ queries the encryption oracle with two chosen messages (m_0, m_1), $\mathcal{B}$ converts the message into two sub-ciphertexts (y_{10}, y_{11}) with the same random r as its chosen message and outputs to its encryption oracle. When the challenge c_{1b} is returned by its encryption oracle, $\mathcal{B}$ selects random y_2 and completes the challenge to $\mathcal{A}$ as (c_{1b}, y_2). We can see that since y_2 is selected independent of (m_0, m_1), in fact $\mathcal{A}$ has no advantage in the game.

Obviously, the simulation random oracle query is perfect except that $\mathcal{A}$ issues a decryption query containing the real challenge c_{1b} or a random oracle query contains the real m_b. For this time, $\mathcal{B}$ cannot distinguish which one is the case.

Denote some events as:

- AskG: g is asked to G before h is asked to H.
- AskH: h is asked to H before g is asked to G.
- AskH': h' is asked to H' before AskG and AskH happen.
- SucA: $\mathcal{A}$ succeeds in guessing b.
- DBad: $\mathcal{B}$ fails to answer decryption query.

Suppose $\mathcal{A}$ issues Q_G and Q_H for G-oracle and H-oracle queries respectively. Also $\mathcal{A}$ issues Q_D decryption oracle queries. We can count the probability of simulation failure as follows.

$$\Pr[\mathsf{SucA}] \leq \Pr[\mathsf{AskG} \vee \mathsf{AskH} \vee \mathsf{DBad}] + 1/2 \tag{4}$$

$$\Pr[\mathsf{AskG} \vee \mathsf{AskH} \vee \mathsf{AskH'} \vee \mathsf{DBad}] \geq \Pr[\mathsf{SucA}] - 1/2 = \varepsilon_1 \tag{5}$$

For random oracle queries, by definition, $\Pr[\mathsf{AskG} \wedge \mathsf{AskH}] = 0$

$$\Pr[\mathsf{AskG} \vee \mathsf{AskH}] = \Pr[\mathsf{AskG}] + \Pr[\mathsf{AskH}]$$

For G queries, the probability of one G query "happens" to be the real challenge is 2^{-k_3} and for H to be 2^{-k_2}, accordingly. Then for total Q_G queries and Q_H queries. We have:

$$\Pr[\mathsf{AskG}] \geq 1 - (1 - 2^{-k_3})^{Q_G} = Q_G \cdot 2^{-k_3}$$
$$\Pr[\mathsf{AskH}] \geq 1 - (1 - 2^{-k_2})^{Q_H} = Q_H \cdot 2^{-k_2}$$

It is time to count the decryption oracle query. In above construction, we can see easily that similar analysis applies to failure of decryption query. Since most of the invalid queries will be rejected. We omit the details here. The probability of rejected a correctly formed ciphertext is:

$$\Pr[\neg\mathsf{DBad}] \geq 1 - (1 - 2^{-k_1})^{Q_D} = Q_D \cdot 2^{-k_1}$$

Then from Equation 5,

$$
\begin{aligned}
\Pr[\mathsf{AskG} \vee \mathsf{AskH} \vee \mathsf{AskH}' \vee \mathsf{DBad}] &= \Pr[\mathsf{AskG} \vee \mathsf{AskH} \vee \mathsf{AskH}'] \\
&\quad - \Pr[\mathsf{AskG} \vee \mathsf{AskH} \vee \mathsf{AskH}' \wedge \neg\mathsf{DBad}] \\
&= \Pr[\mathsf{AskH}] - (\Pr[\mathsf{AskG}] + \Pr[\mathsf{AskH}] - \Pr[\neg\mathsf{DBad}]) \\
&\leq \Pr[\mathsf{AskH}] - (Q_G \cdot 2^{-k_3} + Q_H \cdot 2^{-k_2}) \quad (6)
\end{aligned}
$$

When AskH happens, $\mathcal{B}$ must have known c_{1b}, thus breaks the indistinguishability of ψ_{pk}. So we have

$$\varepsilon \geq \Pr[\mathsf{AskH}] \geq \varepsilon_1 + Q_H \cdot 2^{-k_2} + Q_G \cdot 2^{-k_3}$$

It is obvious that $\mathcal{B}$ works within polynomial time and wins the game with non-negligible advantage. This completes the proof. □

6 Conclusion

A "secure" AONT of previous definitions may not yield CCA secure cryptosystem. Our new definition on AONT abstracts the essential nature of AONT when used in a practical cryptosystem. Moreover, we give concrete constructions of extended-indistinguishable AONT according to different types of encryption primitive. We remark that this justifying is important in designing real life system.

References

1. J. H. An and Y. Dodis. Concealment and Its Applications to Authenticated Encryption. In *Eurocrypt'03*, volume 2656 of *LNCS*, pages 312–329. Springer-Verlag, 2003.

2. M. Bellare, A. Desai, D. Pointcheval, and P. Rogway. Relations among Notions of Security for Public-Key Encryption Schemes. In *Crypto'98*, volume 1462 of *LNCS*. Springer-Verlag, 1998.
3. M. Bellare and C. Namprempre. Authenticated Encryption: Relations among Notions and Analysis of the Generic Composition Paradigm. In *Asiacrypt'00*, volume 1976 of *LNCS*. Springer-Verlag, 2000.
4. M. Bellare and P. Rogaway. Random Oracles are Practical: a Paradigm for Designing Efficient Protocols. In *1st ACM Conference on Computer and Communications*, pages 62–73. ACM Press, 1993.
5. M. Bellare and P. Rogaway. Optimal Asymmetric Encryption. In *Eurocrypt'94*, volume 590 of *LNCS*, pages 92–111. Springer-Verlag, 1994.
6. V. Boyko. On the Security Properties of the OAEP as an All-or-Nothing Transform. In *Crypto'99*, volume 1666 of *LNCS*, pages 503–518. Springer-Verlag, 1999.
7. R. Canetti, Y. Dodis, S. Halevi, E. Kushilevitz, and A. Sahai. Exposure-Resilient Functions and All-or-Nothing Transforms. In *Eurocrypt'00*, volume 1807 of *LNCS*, pages 453–469. Springer-Verlag, 2000.
8. A. Desai. The Security of All-or-Nothing Encryption: Protecting against Exhaustive Key Search. In *Crypto'00*, volume 1880 of *LNCS*, pages 359–375. Springer-Verlag, 2000.
9. Y. Dodis, J. Katz, S. Xu, and M. Yung. Key-insulated Public Key Cryptosystems. In *Eurocrypt'02*, volume 2332 of *LNCS*, pages 65–82. Springer-Verlag, 2002.
10. D. Dolev, C. Dwork, and M. Naor. Non-Malleable Cryptography. In *STOC'91*. ACM, 1991.
11. A. Fiat and A. Shamir. How to Prove Yourself: Practical Solutions to Identification and Signature Problems. In *Crypto'86*, volume 263 of *LNCS*, pages 186–194. Springer-Verlag, 1987.
12. S. Goldwasser and S. Micali. Probabilistic Encryption. *Journal of Computer and System Science*, 28(2):270–299, 1984.
13. M. Jakobsson, J. Stern, and M. Yung. Scramble All, Encrypt Small. In *FSE'99*, volume 1636 of *LNCS*, pages 95–111. Springer-Verlag, 1999.
14. D. Johnson, S. Matyas, and M. Peyravian. Encryption of Long Blocks Using a Short-Block Encryption Procedure. Available at:
    http://grouper.ieee.org/groups/1363/contributinos/peyrav.ps, 1997.
15. M. Naor and M. Yung. Public-key Cryptosystems Provably Secure against Chosen Ciphertext Attacks. In *STOC'90*, pages 427–437. ACM, 1990.
16. C. Rackoff and D. Simon. Noninteractive Zero-Knowledge Proof of Knowledge and Chosen Ciphertext Attack. In *Advances in Cryptology-Crypto'91*, volume 576 of *LNCS*, pages 433–444. Springer-Verlag, 1991.
17. R.L. Rivest. All-Or-Nothing Encryption and The Package Transform. In *FSE'97*, volume 1267 of *LNCS*, pages 210–218. Springer-Verlag, 1997.
18. V. Shoup. Why Chosen Ciphertext Security Matters. Technical Report RZ 3076, IBM Research, 1998.
19. V. Shoup. OAEP Reconsidered. In *Crypto'01*, volume 2139 of *LNCS*, pages 239–259, 2001.
20. D.R. Stinson. Some Considerations on All-Or-Nothing Transforms. Available at:
    http://cacr.math.uwaterloo.ca/~dstinson/papers/AON.ps, 1998.
21. R. Zhang, G. Hanaoka, J. Shikata, and H. Imai. On the Security of Multiple Encryption or CCA-security+CCA-security=CCA-security? In *PKC'04*, volume 2947 of *LNCS*, pages 360–374. Springer-Verlag, 2004.

Centralized Management of Virtual Security Zones in IP Networks

Antti Peltonen, Teemupekka Virtanen, and Esa Turtiainen

. Ericsson Finland
antti.peltonen@ericsson.fi
. Helsinki University of Technology
teemupekka.virtanen@hut.fi
. Ericsson Finland
esa.turtiainen@ericsson.fi

Abstract. The growing security awareness among business users of networks based on Internet Protocol has emerged a need to control the security policies of the network nodes. The nodes can be distributed all over the Internet. The node configuration that is used to enforce the security policy is typically set by hand which is time consuming and error prone. Thus there is a need for centralized management system of the security policies of the nodes.

In this paper we suggest that the roles of network and security administrators should be separated. We have designed a system for centralized security policy management and made a prototype implementation of it. With our system we can control security policies of the nodes securely and remotely from a centralized management node.

Keywords: Virtual Security Zones, Security Policy Management

1 Introduction

According to Computer Emergency Response Team (CERT) Coordination Center the most common cause for firewall security breaches is misconfigurations [7] and the configuration for the firewall is put in place by the firewall's administrator. Separating the roles of network and security administration would make the situation much simpler as the network administrators no more needed to be aware of security requirements and vice versa.

One of the biggest threats for an enterprise becomes from within the company. Insider attacks are far more common than believed, because companies try to avoid the bad publicity that could follow if the incidents were reported. According to year 2003 CSI/FBI Computer Crime and Security Survey [9] eighty percent of survey respondents had detected insiders abusing the company's network access. By enforcing strong security policies for the hosts in the company's network lowers the possibility for this kind of abuse, along with preventing the flow of highly sensitive data out of the network.

M. Jakobsson, M. Yung, J. Zhou (Eds.): ACNS 2004, LNCS 3089, pp. 91–102, 2004.
© Springer-Verlag Berlin Heidelberg 2004

In order to reach this higher level of protection some additional mechanisms are needed to existing networks. In this study we will identify the enabling technologies and the components that are needed to control security policies of nodes in a public Internet. We will also present a method to separate security management from general system management and divide network into several virtual zones. We have implemented these methods and present the implementation.

2   Security Policy Enforcement

Security policy enforcement is the deployment strategy to put the security policy defined by the security administrator in action. The point where the policy decisions are made is called a Policy Decision Point (PDP) [19]. The actual enforcement point is called a Policy Enforcement Point (PEP) [19].

Security policy enforcement can be done either in the end-point or in the network. In the end-point based approach the node itself acts as a PEP or there is a dedicated PEP device in place. A good example of the end-point based approach is the distributed firewall concept. Another possibility for policy enforcement is to use the network based approach. In this approach there exists a certain node in the network that the end-point needs to contact before being able to contact the desired host. In other words the PEP resides at the end-point, while the PDP is somewhere in the network.

We noticed that policy enforcement approaches can be divided by using two parameters – is the approach dependent on the network topology and does the approach use strong authentication. With strong authentication we mean that the hosts trust each other explicitly. Trust relationship can be established for example by using PKI or web of trust. In weak authentication hosts base their trust directly to other host's identifier that may be for example an IP address or a host name. Based on this categorization we have identified one approach that fits into every class. Our results are presented in Table 1.

Table 1. Approaches to policy enforcement

	Weak authentication	Strong authentication
Topology dependent	Conventional firewall	Security clearance server with firewall
Topology independent	Host identity protocol	Distributed firewall

3   Existing Administration Tools and Current Technology

The SNMPv3 provides authorization, authentication and confidentiality protection [17], thus being the recommended version for all network management applications. The data items for different devices are specified in the Management

Information Base (MIB) specifications. MacFaden et al. discuss the configuration of networks using the SNMP protocol in [14]. This document represents the best practices for designing MIB modules, implementation of SNMP configuration agents, and discusses deployment and security issues as well.

Extensible Markup Language (XML) [18] is a language for describing flexible common information formats and the related data. XML may be used to present almost anything, including also security policies. The DAXFi project [1] has devised a dynamic XML firewall that uses XML to specify the firewall security policy. By using XML, the security policies can be defined in a vendor independent manner, and then later translated to vendor specific commands. We see this approach as one of the best solutions for describing security policies in multivendor environments.

An interesting approach to firewall policy definition is presented by Bartal et al. in their paper about Firmato a novel firewall management toolkit [3]. The Firmato constitutes of a Model Definition Language (MDL), Entity-Relationship (E/R) model, a model compiler and a visualization component. The basic concept in Firmato is a role. Roles define the capabilities of initiating and accepting services. We think that the abstraction layer that the Firmato brings into firewall rule definition is a huge step forward in firewall management. The security administrator is no more obliged to do the tedious configuration work using low level configuration files, but instead use a modelling language.

Conventional firewalls depend on the topology of the network. If a host is moved beyond the firewall perimeter the policy enforcement does not apply anymore. The PEP and PDP both reside in the firewall and the policy decisions are based on preconfigured filter lists.

In order to have a topology independent approach that uses strong authentication an approach like distributed firewall may be applied. In distributed firewall the PEP is located at the host, while the PDP may be located at the same place or somewhere else in the network. The concept of distributed firewall was first introduced by Steven M. Bellovin in his paper Distributed Firewalls [4].

Host Identity Protocol (HIP)[15] is an attempt to break the binding between the host's identity and its location. This is achieved by introducing a new cryptographic name space and protocol layer between the transport and network layers. In HIP each end-point has a distinguishing Host Identifier (HI). In order to communicate between a pair of end-points the initiating end-point must learn one of the IP addresses the other end-point is associated to. This is achieved using an address resolution service.

KeyNote [6][5] is a trust management system that provides a language with the same name for defining policy rules conveniently. The purpose of trust-management system is to provide a standard mechanism for specifying application security policies and credentials. [6]

In our opinion the concept of a trust-management system is quite easily applicable to networking, too. An important point is that the trust management should be done on stream not on packet basis. On packet basis this would consume too much processing time. However, every stream passing a compliance checker once would be no problem. Hedbom et al. noticed that the security of a firewall or Intrusion Detection System (IDS) itself is very important [12].

Virtual Private Network (VPN) is a very widely and wildly used concept. It is used in several different contexts to mean different things. In this paper we will understand the VPN as a way to transfer private data traffic using a public network without exposing it to public. VPNs provide a more cost effective way to provide private networking for multi-site communication than traditional approaches such as leased lines. Tunneling is one of the principles used in VPN networks to carry traffic over the IP backbone network. [10] Tunneling is especially useful when the payload traffic have no relation to underlying IP addressing. This is the case when the payload traffic is multiprotocol or private IP addressing [16] is in use.

4   Virtual Security Zones

4.1   Design

The general level architecture for the system is depicted in the Figure 1. The central component of the system is the security policy server, which is the server hosting the software component for managing the virtual security zones. In close connection to the security policy server work the directory servers, which are used as distribution points for security policy definition files. In addition to these, a certificate authority is used for assigning certificates for the security policy server and managed nodes. These certificates act as digital identities of their owners. PKI was chosen for the trust establishment system as it provides the best scalability and availability.

We have also a natural hierarchy in our system as every node needs to trust the central point – the security policy server. Mutual authentication between the security policy server and the managed nodes is achieved using CA assigned certificates. In the managed node, a small program is needed to fetch the security policy definition files from one of the directory servers, and interpret the acquired file into executable commands.

Local administrator is the person responsible for local administrative tasks on the node. These tasks include hardware and software installation and configuration of the node. The local administrator also initiates the certificate enrollment for acquiring the certificate for the node. Network administrator is the person responsible for configuring the general network infrastructure. He will assign the IP addresses that the nodes will use either manually or automatically using the DHCP protocol. If the node is supposed to be part of a virtual security zone, the network administrator will pass the information about the node to the security policy server.

Security administrator is the person responsible for setting up the security zones. He is also responsible for administration of the network administrators' access rights to the central management node. Security administrator trusts that the certificates assigned by the certificate authority are valid.

Certificate Authority is the entity who assigns the digital certificates for security policy server and managed nodes. It will act as a trusted third party between the security policy server and the nodes. In the case that security policy server and the managed nodes are below different PKIs a cross certification process [2] is needed to establish the trust between the two PKIs.

Security Policy Manager (SPM) is the software component for the centralized management of the security policies in the security zones. The component is located in the security policy server. It will assemble the security policy configuration files for managed nodes and delegate the distribution of these files to the directory servers.

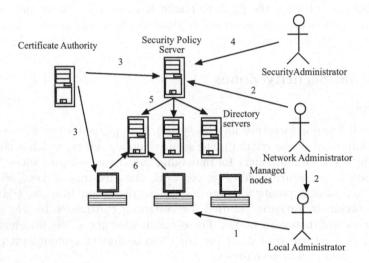

Fig. 1. General architecture for the system

Security Policy Agent (SPA) is the software component installed in the managed nodes for retrieving and processing the configuration information written by the SPM. The SPA together with firewall and VPN software acts as a software based policy enforcement point (PEP).

Directory Servers act as distribution points for security policy configuration files. Managed nodes will contact one of the directory servers to acquire their own configuration.

Managed nodes form security zones according to security policies defined by the security policy administrator. Managed nodes listen for policy updates from security policy server and fetch their configuration files from directory servers.

4.2   Policy Transfer

The policy decision can be made either in the central management node or at the managed PEP. However, the former approach is unreasonable in our case. Because the policy decisions are made per packet basis, the traffic towards the central management node would become outrageously high. We therefore chose to combine the PDP with the PEP. This way the security policy information needs to be transferred to the managed node only during system startup and when the security policy is changed.

Based on the literature study we examined the different possibilities for transferring the policy from central management node to the PEP. The most promising methods we identified were using SNMP for policy transfer, or using XML or configuration commands to describe the policy, and other means to transfer it. We wanted to make the presentation of the policy independent from the transfer process, which then left us with the last two choices. If the policy is mapped to low level commands already at the SPM, the SPM needs to exactly know the target environment. However, often this information is not easily available or it would require extra work from one of the administrators to figure it out. Therefore we chose to use the XML language as the high level policy description language, which is used in the policy transfer. The XML based message is then mapped to environment specific low level configuration commands at the PEP in the managed node.

The Document Type Definition (DTD) for the XML file used for policy transfer is depicted in Figure 2. The root element, the policy, can have any number of ipsec groups (ipsec group) in it. The ipsec groups consists of a pre-shared key (psk) and any number of end-points (end point). End-points always have an IP address (remote ip) and they may have a tunneling configuration (tunnel). If a tunneling configuration is present the tunnel element will include the virtual IP address of the remote node (remote vip) and a corresponding virtual IP address for the local node (own vip). The tunneling can be used to create an extra logical layer on top of the public IP network.

We used a similar process to that used in PGP [62] to sign and encrypt the configuration information. Data is first compressed to enhance the resistance against cryptanalysis [21].

To be able to notify the managed node about a change in the security policy two mechanisms can be used - server push or client pull. In our system the configuration changes do not occur often, therefore the server push is the preferred method, as it creates less network traffic compared to client pull. However, the server push generates a heavy load on the security policy server if the number of clients in the security zone is high. Therefore we chose to use a slightly modified server push approach.

```
<?xml version="1.0" encoding="utf-8"?>
<!-- DTD forsecurity policy presentation -->
<!ELEMENT policy(ipsec_group*)>
<!ELEMENT ipsec_group(psk, end_point*)>
<!ELEMENT psk(#PCDATA)>
<!ELEMENT end_point(remote_ip, tunnel?)>
<!ELEMENT remote_ip(#PCDATA)>
<!ELEMENT tunnel(remote_vip, own_vip)>
<!ELEMENT remote_vip(#PCDATA)>
<!ELEMENT own_vip(#PCDATA)>
```

Fig. 2. The DTD for policy presentation

When the security policy is changed the server sends a short notification message to the client. This will initiate the client side update process. The listening daemon process in the managed node - the SPA - wakes up and starts the configuration process for the node.

4.3   Security Policy Manager

Security Policy Manager (SPM) is the software component that is used for managing the security policies of the distributed managed nodes. The SPM process is hosted by the security policy server. We will next formulate the requirements for the SPM in the form of use cases.

The primary actors using services of the system are administrators and nodes. The administrator actor is extended with two special types of administrator – network administrator and security administrator. Every administrator needs to login into the system before being able to do any other type of action.

The network administrator has a use case for inserting node into system and for removing node from the system. Using these two functions the Network administrator can join and remove nodes from the group of managed nodes.

The security administrator has use cases for creating, modifying and deleting security zones. The create zone allows security administrator to define new security zone and its parameters. The parameters include the name of the zone, the shared secret the nodes in the zone will use for mutual authentication, and optionally the private address space to be used in the zone. The modify zone is used for adding or removing nodes from an existing security zone, and the delete zone removes the whole security zone. All these three use cases use the notify node use case for notifying managed nodes about configuration changes.

Only one use case was defined for managed node actor. This is called get configuration. It allows the managed node to retrieve its configuration information from the SPM. The storage of configuration files need not be at the same server the SPM is located, but the task can be delegated for directory servers as we depicted earlier in the system architecture.

When considering a node inside a security zone, certain information about these entities need to be maintained. We begin by modeling the node. The managed node has a name that is used by the network and security administrators to identify it. It has also an unique IP-address that can be used for distinguishing the nodes from each other. The node can also be a member of any number of security zones. A security zone has a distinguished name that is used for identifying it. In addition, a shared secret that the nodes use for identifying members of the zone is required. Optionally the nodes may communicate using private address space instead of the public IP addresses. Therefore also the private address space, or virtual address space as we call it, is stored in the database. The security zone can have any number of nodes in it.

4.4   Security Policy Agent

Security Policy Agent is the software component located in the managed nodes. It is responsible for retrieving configuration files from SPM and putting the received security policy in action.

The configuration update of the client consists of the following phases: (1) Node downloads the compressed and encrypted configuration file, content encryption key and signature of the configuration file from one of the directory servers. (2) Node decrypts the content encryption key with its private key. (3) Node decrypts the configuration file with the content encryption key. (4) Node verifies the signature of the decrypted configuration file. (5) Node decompresses the configuration file. (6) Node maps the XML based policy contained in the configuration file to environment specific commands. (7) Node executes the commands.

After executing all the aforementioned steps the node will be running with the new configuration. If there is a problem in any step, the configuration update will fail and the program will return to its initial state. One reason for a failed configuration update could be a network failure.

4.5   Security Policy Enforcement

Instead of presenting another high level policy definition language (see [8] [5]) we took a hands- on approach to solving the problem of security policy management in distributed network. We will include in our prototype implementation the support for configuring firewall and VPN policies.

Although any protocol capable of traffic encryption could be used, we chose the IPSec for encrypting the traffic in the virtual security zones. The IPSec being a part of the forthcoming IPv6 standard, will most probably have a strong position in encrypting future network traffic, not forgetting its already wide use in the IPv4 networks. We also wanted to combine the VPNs with the distributed firewall concept to provide a totally isolated VPN or virtual security zone.

A comprehensive security solution can not depend solely on a packet filtering firewall although the firewall can be a crucial part of it. To secure a node we need to control several different things. We have listed some of the most important ones in the following list: user or program access rights, filtering incoming and leaving traffic, encrypting the leaving traffic, user authentication and authorization, and intrusion detection

Firewall's purpose is to enforce the security policy defined by the security administrator. It accomplishes this by filtering the traffic at packet, stream or application level. According to Ziegler in Linux Firewalls [20], a packet filtering firewall can protect you against the following threats: some source address spoofing, useful information revealed in response to port scan, malformed broadcast packets used to identify UNIX systems, some forms of network mapping, some denial-of-service attacks, source-routed packets, some forms of fragmentation bombs, local mistakes that affect remote sites, access to private Local Area Network (LAN) services, and additional protection against local server misconfigurations

However, as we pointed out already in the introductory chapter, a firewall can only be as good as its administrator is. In a centralized remote configuration, the hopefully highly competent security administrator can verify that the configuration is really error free before distributing the configuration to managed nodes. Centralized administration also makes it easy to change the configuration very rapidly throughout the network if a flaw is found.

4.6   Communication Model between the Managed Nodes

We wanted to let the managed nodes communicate using a private address space, while on the other hand we wanted to provide a secure communication channel over the public network. Analysis of the different VPN technologies lead us to the combination of two of these – namely GRE with IPSec. GRE provides the tunneling of the private addresses, while IPSec handles the data encryption and integrity protection.

Using this approach we can form logically separate networks from the underlying public IP address space. Only the virtual IP-address is provided for applications, thus making those independent from the underlying public IP-address. In other words, we will use the public IP-addresses of the nodes just for packet transmission and decapsulate the virtual IP-address at the receiving node. Combining the end point firewalls to this structure will lead us to the construction of a virtual security zone.

5   Implementation

J2EE was chosen as the server implementation environment because it supports the Java servlet and Java Server Pages (JSP) technologies, and thus enables easy development of web frontends.

Java servlets are server side components that handle the client requests in an efficient and highly versatile way. JSPs are used to create the presentation front-end for the data that the servlets provide. JSP files are interpreted by the Apache Tomcat to Hypertext Markup Language (HTML) pages that can be shown by the client in a web browser. The actual data is stored inside a relational database system. Apache Ant [11] is a build tool for Java, developed in the Apache Jakarta Project. It uses feature rich XML based configuration language to describe the build and deployment process. All build scripts for our project were written using the scripting language of the Ant.

5.1   Software Components

In Figure 3 we have depicted the classes for the SPM server and how they are divided into packages. The web package consists of the two servlet classes which handle the requests made by the security and network administrators from their web browsers. These classes work in close connection with the classes in the util package.

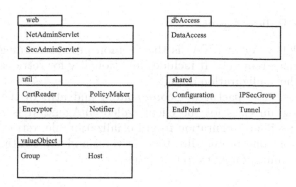

Fig. 3. Classes and packages for Security Policy Manager

The util package includes most of the advanced functionality embedded into the system. In advance to having the actual logic for forming the XML based configuration files for managed nodes (PolicyMaker), it includes worker classes for reading certificates from keystore (CertReader), encrypting data (Encryptor) and notifying the client hosts about configuration changes (Notifier). The data acquired from database is handled using the classes in the valueObject package.

Configuration data is saved into object structure which corresponds to the XML presentation we have introduced. The corresponding classes are located in the shared package, which as the name indicates, is shared between the SPM and SPA applications. A configuration may have any number of IPSec groups and each IPSec group may have any number of end-points. End-points can have a tunnel dependency if the private IP addressing is in use. Data persistence is handled by the DataAccess class in the dbAccess package. It provides methods for storing, querying and deleting data. The actual database access is naturally done using SQL language.

5.2   User Interface for Administrators

The Security Policy Manager provides a convenient web-based user interface for network and security administrators. Being web-based, the interface is available everywhere there is a web-browser. The connection between the web-browser and the server is protected with TLS/SSL and the administrators are authenticated using username and password.

The security administrator can conveniently select the nodes he wants in the zone by clicking the radio box next to the hostname and IP address. He also needs to define a name for the zone and a shared secret that the zone members will use to authenticate each other. This secret should probably be generated automatically by the system because the administrator is likely to choose easy and too short shared secrets. The last field allows the administrator to give a virtual network address space for the chosen managed nodes.

5.3   Security Policy Agent

The Security Policy Agent (SPA) is the daemon process running in the nodes we want to manage remotely. It includes functionality for retrieving, processing and installing the configuration data.

The SPA has three packages – core, shared and util. In the core package is the main program class for the client called SPAgent. It is responsible for reading client specific configuration from initialization file, retrieving the initial configuration from one of the directory servers, and for starting the process listening for incoming configuration updates.

6   Conclusions

In this study we constructed a system for centralized management of virtual security zones. The choice for policy transfer from centralized management node to the managed nodes was an XML based policy file. The integrity and confidentiality of the file was protected using strong cryptography. The actual policy enforcement was done by the policy enforcement point in the managed node. To prevent users and local administrator from changing the security policy the security administrator has set, the policy enforcement point should be tamper resistant.

We also presented a new concept called a virtual security zone. The members of the virtual security zone are isolated from the underlying public IP network using tunneling and encryption. In our implementation the traffic inside the virtual security zone was encrypted using the IPSec protocol. Applications running on the nodes can be separated into different zones using virtual IP addresses provided by the GRE tunneling.

The management of security policies in a distributed environment has traditionally been a task including lot of handwork. By handwork we mean that the configurations of the hosts are either locally or remotely set up using a command line interface. Our system provides an easy way to define virtual security zones that can span hosts in multiple mutually untrusted networks in a centralized manner. The configuration is done securely by using strong cryptography to provide confidentiality as well as integrity protection for the configuration data. We also provided a web based management front-end for the administrators, that made the security administration independent from time and place.

One interesting area for further research would be the support for the mobility of the managed hosts. While our system could provide limited mobility with slight modifications, further research in the area would be needed to enable the managed hosts move freely while still maintaining the security policy the security administrator had set in the first place.

References

1. DAXFi - Dynamic XML Firewall http://daxfi.sourceforge.net
2. C. Adams and S. Farrel: Internet X.509 Public Key Infrastructure Certificate Management Protocols. IETF RFC 2510. March 1999.
3. Yair Bartal, Alain Mayer, Kobbi Nissim, and Avishal Wool: A Novel Firewall Management Toolkit, in Proceedings of the 20th IEEE Symposium on Security and Privacy, 1999.
4. Steven Bellovin: Distributed firewalls, ;login: 24(Security), November 1999.
5. M. Blaze, J. Feigenbaum, J. Ioannidis, and A. Keromytis The KeyNote Trust-Management System Version 2. IETF RFC 2704. September 1999.
6. Matt Blaze, Joan Feigenbaum, A. Angelos, and D. Keromytis KeyNote: Trust management for public-key infrastructures, in Proceedings of the Cambridge 1998 Security Protocols International Workshop, 1998.
7. CERT. Install firewall hardware and software. http://www.cert.org/security-improvement/ practices/p056.html
8. Nicodemos Damianou, Naranker Dulay, Emil Lupu, Morris Sloman. The Ponder Policy Specification Language, in Proceedings of Workshop on Policies for Distributed Systems and Networks (Policy2001), 2001.
9. Robert Richardson (Editorial Director). Eighth Annual CSI/FBI Computer Crime and Security Survey. 2003. Available at: http://www.gocsi.com
10. Paul Ferguson, Geoff Huston. What is a VPN, The Internet Protocol Journal 1(2), 1998.
11. Apache Software Foundation. Apache Ant. Available at: http://ant.apache.org
12. Hans Hedbom, H Kan Kvarnstr M, Erland Jonsson, A Protection Scheme for Security Policies Using One-Way Functions, tech.rep. 01-3, Chalmers University of Technology, 2001.
13. S. Kent, R. Atkinson. Security Architecture for the Internet Protocol. IETF RFC 2401. November 1998.
14. M. Macfaden, D. Partain, J. Saperia, W. Tackabury. Configuring Networks and Devices with Simple Network Management Protocol (SNMP). IETF RFC 3512. April 2003.
15. Pekka Nikander, Jukka Ylitalo, Jorma Wall. Integrating Security, Mobility, and Multi-Homing in a HIP Way, in Proceedings of Network and Distributed Systems Security Symposium (NDSS'03), page 87–99, Internet Society, San Diego, CA, Feb 2003.
16. Y. Rekhter, B. Moskowitz, D. Karenberg, G. J. De Groot, E. Lear. Address Allocation for Private Internets. IETF RFC 1918. February 1996.
17. William Stallings. SNMPv3: A Security Enhancement for SNMP, IEEE Communications Surveys & Tutorials 1 (Fourth Quarter), 1998. Available at: http://www.comsoc.org/livepubs/surveys/public/4q98issue/stallings.html
18. World Wide Web Consortium (W3C). Extensible Markup Language (XML). Available at: http://www.w3c.org/XML
19. R. Yavatkar, D. Pendarakis, R. Guerin. A Framework for Policy-based Admission Control. IETF RFC 2753. January 2000.
20. Robert L. Ziegler. Linux Firewalls, second edition, New Riders Publishing, 2002.
21. P. R. Zimmermann. The Official PGP User's Guide, MIT Press, 1995.

S-RIP: A Secure Distance Vector Routing Protocol*

Tao Wan, Evangelos Kranakis, and Paul C. van Oorschot

School of Computer Science, Carleton University, Ottawa, Canada
{twan, kranakis, paulv}@scs.carleton.ca

Abstract. Distance vector routing protocols (e.g., RIP) have been widely used on the Internet, and are being adapted to emerging wireless ad hoc networks. However, it is well-known that existing distance vector routing protocols are insecure due to: 1) the lack of strong authentication and authorization mechanisms; 2) the difficulty, if not impossibility, of validating routing updates which are aggregated results of other routers. In this paper, we introduce a secure routing protocol, namely *S-RIP*, based on a distance vector approach. In *S-RIP*, a router confirms the consistency of an advertised route with those nodes that have propagated that route. A reputation-based framework is proposed for determining how many nodes should be consulted, flexibly balancing security and efficiency. Our threat analysis and simulation results show that in *S-RIP*, a well-behaved node can uncover inconsistent routing information in a network with many misbehaving nodes assuming (in the present work) no two of them are in collusion, with relatively low extra routing overhead.

Keywords: Routing Security, Distance Vector, Distance Fraud, Security Analysis

1 Overview

It is well-known that today's Internet is not secure. Both Internet applications and the underlying routing infrastructures are vulnerable to a variety of attacks. Although a majority of incidents reported so far are realized by the exploitation of software vulnerabilities in client and server machines, it has been noted long ago that abusing routing protocols may be the easiest way for launching attacks [2], and a single misbehaving router can completely disrupt routing protocols and cause disaster [23]. This viewpoint has been more recently expressed by a group of network and security experts [4].

There are many factors that make today's routing infrastructures insecure. Three of them are as follows. 1) There are no strong security services built into routing protocols. Many routing protocols only provide weak authentication mechanisms, e.g., plain-text password or system-wide shared keys, for authenticating peers or routing updates. As a result, it is easy for an adversary to gain access to the routing infrastructure and manipulate routing information. 2) Software vulnerabilities and misconfigurations expose routing infrastructures to severe risks. 3) Most routing protocols assume a trustworthy environment. In the case where no authentication mechanisms are implemented, routing updates are accepted with only rudimentary validation. When authentication mechanisms are present, routing updates are verified for the correctness of data origin and integrity

---

* Version: April 12, 2004.

M. Jakobsson, M. Yung, J. Zhou (Eds.): ACNS 2004, LNCS 3089, pp. 103–119, 2004.
© Springer-Verlag Berlin Heidelberg 2004

only. However, after a route update is verified to be "authentic", the routing information conveyed in the update is trusted and used to update the recipient's routing table. This is risky since data origin authentication, which includes data integrity [17], cannot guarantee the factual correctness of a message. A malicious entity or a compromised legitimate entity can send false information in a correctly signed message. A recipient can detect unauthorized alteration of the message, but cannot tell if the information conveyed in the message is factually correct unless the recipient has the perfect knowledge of what it expects to receive.

The difficulty of validating DV routing updates arises due to the fact that they are the distributed computational results of other nodes [22,31]. Mittal and Vigna [18] propose to use intrusion detection sensors for validating routing advertisements by comparing a routing update with a master routing database that is pre-computed off-line. One disadvantage is that their approach cannot prevent fraudulent misinformation from poisoning others' routing tables, although it may be able to detect it. Hu, Perrig, and Johnson [9] propose to use hash chains and authentication trees to authenticate the distance of a route. However, their approach does not address longer distance fraud.

We present a secure DV routing protocol, namely *S-RIP*, based on RIP [15], which can prevent router and prefix impersonation, as well as shorter and longer distance fraud. In *S-RIP*, an advertised route is validated for its factual correctness before being used to update a routing table. Given the difficulty of validating the factual correctness of routing information in a DV routing protocol, we propose to use *consistency* as an approximation of *correctness*. An advertised route is treated as correct if it is consistent among those nodes that have propagated that route. Unless those nodes involved in a consistency check are in collusion, with high confidence a consistent route is correct. By this approach, we hope that nodes surrounding a misbehaving node will uncover inconsistency and prevent misinformation from further spreading.

A reputation-based framework is proposed for determining how many nodes to involve in a consistency check, providing the flexibility for balancing security and efficiency. Firstly, the notion of either trusting or distrusting a node is replaced by *node reputation* measured by a numeric value. Although in an intra-domain routing protocol (e.g., RIP), routers are under a single administrative domain and tend not to be mutually suspicious, they could be compromised due to software flaws. Malicious nodes can also manage to join a routing domain by exploiting routing vulnerabilities. Therefore, fully trusting any individual node even in an intra-domain routing protocol may introduce the vulnerability that a malicious node can call into question the legitimacy of other nodes. Node reputation provides the flexibility to relax this notion, and can be interpreted as an estimation that a node will provide correct information in the near future. Secondly, we propose an efficient method for computing the accumulated confidence in the correctness of a consistent routing update from the reputations of those nodes involved in the consistency check. Combined with confidence thresholds, this method effectively creates a *sized window* for determining how many nodes to involve in a consistency check.

The sequel is organized as follows. Section 2 analyzes RIP vulnerabilities. Section 3 presents security objectives and mechanisms of *S-RIP*. The reputation-based framework is presented in Section 4. *S-RIP* is presented and analyzed in Section 5. Section 6 presents simulation results. Section 7 reviews related work for securing routing protocols, with emphasis on securing DV routing protocols. Further comments and future work are discussed in the last section.

2   Background: RIP Vulnerabilities

RIP (we mean RIPv2) is an Internet Standard intra-domain DV routing protocol (see [15] for details). Despite certain limitations, e.g., the maximum distance between two nodes is 15 hops, it is still used by many small and medium size organizations (including some universities). RIP has several known security vulnerabilities. Five of them are discussed below.

1) An unauthorized node can easily join a routing domain and participate in routing operations. This is referred to as *router impersonation*. RIPv1 [8] does not have any authentication mechanism. RIPv2 only uses a clear-text password for authenticating peers. Since a clear-text password can be easily captured, it provides only marginal additional security in practice. Keyed MD5 has been proposed [1] to replace the password-based authentication mechanism. However, it is still vulnerable in that one compromised router discloses keying materials of every other router in the network.

In addition, RIP does not have any mechanism for preventing a *questionable node* (an unauthorized node or a compromised/malicious legitimate node) from advertising fraudulent routing information about distance or next hop.

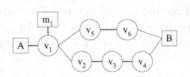

2) A questionable node can claim a zero distance to a non-directly connected network or a nonexistent network. This is often referred as *prefix impersonation*. The proposed MD5 authentication [1] requires a system-wide shared secret key(s). This makes router impersonation harder, but cannot prevent prefix impersonation. Although prefix impersonation is a bigger issue in inter-domain routing protocol (e.g., BGP), it can also cause serious problems in intra-domain routing protocol (e.g., RIP). Figure 1 shows that

Fig. 1. $m.$ advertises a zero distance route for B. As a result, $v.$'s routing table is poisoned by an incorrect route for B. Traffic from A to B will be forwarded by $v.$ to $m.$, which causes service disruption against A since $m.$ does not have a route to B other than the one via $v.$.

a malicious node can easily launch service disruption (a type of denial of service) attacks by prefix impersonation. A similar incident (referred to as a blackhole) has occurred in the ARPANET [16].

3) A questionable node may claim a distance shorter than the actual distance to a destination. This is called *shorter distance fraud*. This fraud can be used to attract traffic to launch a variety of attacks (e.g., eavesdropping, session hijacking).

4) A questionable node can claim a distance longer than the actual distance for a destination. This is called *longer distance fraud*. This fraud can be used to avoid traffic, which may lead to unfair utilization of network links and cause network congestion. Thus, it can be used to launch a denial of service attack. This fraud is different from malicious packet dropping attacks. While they both result in packet dropping, the latter

can be detected by known techniques (e.g., secure traceroute [20]) while the former is more stealthy.

5) A questionable node may advertise arbitrary routing information or carefully crafted routes to poison others' routing tables, e.g., to cause routing loops or have invalid routes installed, and can also provide false information on a next hop.

3   Security Objectives and Mechanisms of S-RIP

To counter security vulnerabilities of RIP, we propose a new secure DV routing protocol, namely *S-RIP*. The security objectives of *S-RIP* include: 1) preventing router impersonation; 2) preventing prefix impersonation; and 3) preventing distance fraud (both shorter and longer). Fraud can be committed by individual nodes or colluding nodes. In this paper, we only consider uncoordinated individual fraud and leave the discussion of collusion to the future work. Our proposed mechanisms for achieving the above objectives are discussed below.

3.1   Preventing Router Impersonation

To prevent *router impersonation*, we require Assumption A1: every router shares a different key with every other router in a RIP domain. With A1 and an authentication algorithm (e.g., keyed MD5), a router can effectively detect router impersonation by validating a message authentication code (MAC) of a routing update message. Pair-wise shared keys make it more difficult for an unauthorized node to impersonate a legitimate node, and ensure that the keying materials of one router will not be disclosed when another router is compromised. Of course, use of shared keys results in additional complexity; due to space limitations, we omit further discussion here.

3.2   Preventing Prefix Impersonation

To prevent *prefix impersonation*, we require Assumption A2: there is a central authority (e.g., a network administrator) with perfect knowledge of which router is physically connected to which subnets in that autonomous system (AS). Such perfect knowledge, or router-prefix mapping, is realistic for an AS since network configurations are administratively controlled by a single authority. The router-prefix mapping is then securely distributed to each router, e.g., it can be pre-configured on each router. Ongoing update (e.g., additions of subnets or routers) can then be done through a secure channel (e.g., SSH) between the central authority and each router. Although network topology may be dynamic (e.g., caused by link failures), we expect router-prefix mapping is relatively static since addition/deletion of subnets usually occurs far less frequently than link failures. Other alternatives can also be used to prevent prefix impersonation, e.g., *address attestation* in S-BGP [14], *authorization certificates* in soBGP [32], etc. However, they may require a public key infrastructure, which has its own drawbacks.

3.3 Preventing Distance Fraud

Shorter and longer distance frauds are difficult to prevent. In a distance vector routing protocol, routing updates received by a node are computational results or aggregated routes of other nodes. Unless a node has perfect knowledge of network topology and dynamics, it appears impossible to validate the factual correctness of aggregated routing updates [22,31].

We propose to use *consistency* as an approximation of correctness. An advertised route is validated by cross checking its consistency with the routing information of those nodes from which this route is derived. If the route is consistent among those nodes, it is treated as correct. Otherwise, incorrect. For example, in Figure 2, when node v_2 advertises to v_1 a 2-hop route for v_5 with v_3 as the next hop, v_1 queries v_3's route for v_5, which is 2 hops. Since v_2's route for v_5 is supposed to be one hop longer than v_3's route for v_5 (this is specifically based on RIP, but can be easily generalized), an inconsistency is detected. Although v_1 does not know which node (v_2 or v_3) provides invalid information, v_1 knows that something is abnormal with this route. Therefore, this route is dropped. If v_2 advertises a 3-hop route for v_5, it is consistent with v_3's 2-hop route. Thus, it may be accepted. §5 presents the algorithm details for consistency checks and analyzes various threats.

To support consistency checks, we require Assumption A3: a node indicates (either voluntarily for direct neighbors or upon request otherwise) the next hop of each route in its routing table. For example, in Figure 2, v_2 should tell v_1 that v_3 is the next hop on the route for v_5. v_3 should also tell v_1 that v_4 is its next hop to v_5 upon request. Requests can be made by RIP

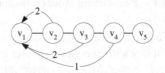

Fig. 2. Consistency Checks

route request or other mechanisms (e.g., SNMP MIB query [3]). If a node fails to provide information on next hops, its behavior is called into question.

One property of a DV routing protocol is that a node only communicates with its direct neighbors and does not need to maintain the network topology beyond its direct neighbors. In a link state (LS) routing protocol, a node advertises its link states to every other node in the network by flooding, and each node maintains a whole view of the network topology. A3 allows a node to query non-direct neighbors, which expands node-to-node communication boundary in a DV routing protocol to a dynamic area (by our reputation-based approach §4).

We thus note that our approach falls in between the DV and LS approaches. Pictorially, the communication range of an LS node covers the whole network (flooding), while the communication range of a traditional DV node only covers its direct neighbors (neighbor-to-neighbor). In *S-RIP*, the communication range of a node is dynamic. Although it is certainly beyond direct neighborhood and could reach the whole network, most likely, it will only cover a nearby neighborhood (e.g., within 2 or 3 hops) dependent on window size (§4.3). Therefore, additional routing overhead generated by non-neighbor querying is limited, as confirmed by our simulation results in §6. Requirement of storage space is also increased in *S-RIP*, but very slightly since an *S-RIP* node only needs to maintain the information of remote nodes when they are being or will be consulted for a consistency check.

Another question which arises is: how does a node query a remote node if it does not have a known route for that node? For example, in Figure 2, for v_1 to validate a route for v_3, v_1 may need to query v_3. However, v_1 cannot talk to v_3 if it does not have a route for v_3. This is a known problem that a secure routing protocol relies upon a routing protocol for node reachability. In *S-RIP*, a temporary routing table is maintained, which contains all routes to be validated. The temporary routing table is only used for route validation (not for routing data traffic). When a route passes a validation, it is moved to the regular routing table and can be used for routing data traffic. In the above example, v_1 first installs the route for v_3 into the temporary routing table, and sends to v_2 a routing request destined for v_3. v_2 should have a route for v_3 since it advertises such a route to v_1 (otherwise, it is misbehaving). When v_3 receives a route request from v_1, it sends back to v_1 a route response via a route either in its temporary routing table or the regular one. This route request and response process incurs additional routing overhead, but also adds another level of assurance that intermediate nodes are actually forwarding packets. If we can make a route request or response message indistinguishable from a normal data packet (e.g., by IPSec ESP [13]), this process may detect forwarding level misbehavior, (i.e., a router advertising correct routes but does not forward data packets).

To implement A3 in RIP, the next hop field in a RIP routing update message can be utilized. In RIP, the next hop field is only used for route optimization (avoiding an extra hop). For example, v_2 will not include v_3 in the next hop field (by setting it to 0) unless it believes that v_1 should forward traffic destined for v_5 directly to v_3. With A3, v_2 voluntarily includes v_3 in the next hop. This changes the meaning of a next hop from *this is your next hop* to *this is my next hop*. Thus, A3 allows a receiving node, instead of an advertising node, to decide which node should be the next hop. Despite the change of the meaning, A3 is still compatible with RIP since a receiving node will ignore the next hop field (treats it as null) if it is not directly reachable. To interoperate with an existing implementation of RIP, an *S-RIP* node may get next hop information from a RIP node by external mechanisms, e.g., SNMP MIB query.

4   Reputation-Based Framework

In this section we present a reputation-based framework, consisting of a reputation update function, an efficient method of computing accumulated confidence, localized rules for processing routing updates, and a sized window method for balancing security and efficiency.

4.1   Reputation Definition

We propose to use node reputation as an estimation of the confidence in that a node will provide correct routing information in the near future. Every node assigns an initial value as the reputation of every other node in a network. A node's reputation is then dynamically updated by Equation 1. The detail of how this equation is derived is given in [30]. Many possibilities exist for $c_i(j, t+1)$. We propose Equation 2 for its simplicity.

$$r_i(j, t+1) = \frac{r_i(j, t)}{2} + c_i(j, t+1) \tag{1}$$

$$c_i(j,t) = \begin{cases} 0.5 & \text{if } j \text{ provides consistent information at time } t \\ 0 & \text{otherwise (e.g., if } j \text{ provides conflicting information at time } t) \end{cases} \quad (2)$$

One property of Equation 1 is that if $r_i(j,t) \neq 1$, $r_i(j,t+1)$ will be always less than 1. Thus, if node i does not assign an initial value of 1 or higher as j's reputation, $r_i(j)$ will always be in the range $[0,1)$. We propose Equation 3 for computing an accumulated confidence from node reputation in the correctness of a routing update consistent among a group of nodes.

Definition 1 (Accumulated Confidence) *Let $r_x(v_1), r_x(v_2), \ldots, r_x(v_n)$ be x's rating of the reputation of nodes $v_1, v_2, \ldots, v_n$, respectively. In the case that routing information from nodes $v_1, v_2, \ldots, v_n$, is consistent, node x's confidence in that information, denoted by $r_x(v[1..n])$, is defined as follows, where $v[1..n]$ denotes $v_1, v_2, \ldots, v_n$:*

$$r_x(v[1..n]) = \begin{cases} r_x(v_1) & \text{if } n = 1 \\ r_x(v_1) + \big(1 - r_x(v_1)\big) \cdot r_x(v_2) & \text{if } n = 2 \\ r_x(v[1..n-1]) + \Big(1 - r_x(v[1..n-1])\Big) \cdot r_x(v_n) & \text{if } n > 2 \end{cases} \quad (3)$$

Although developed independently based on our intuition, it turns out that Equation 3 is consistent with Dempster-Shafer theory (DST) of evidence reasoning [5,27] if we assume that in our case, for all i $(1 \leq i \leq n)$, v_i acquires its information from an independent source. The proof is given in [30]. The advantage of Equation 3 is that it is intuitive and computationally efficient. Although DST is more general, e.g., it can handle conflicting information, it is computationally less inefficient since it involves set operations.

4.2 Validation Rules

We propose a set of rules for determining how to treat routing advertisements based on node reputation. Two thresholds (θ_1, θ_2) are used to divide the reputation domain into three levels, namely low, medium, and high.

Rule 1 *(Low Reputation). If node j's reputation rated by i is in the low range $(0 \leq r_i(j) < \theta_1)$, node i will ignore a routing advertisement from j without cross-checking its consistency with any other node(s).*

Rule 2 *(Medium Reputation). If node j's reputation rated by i is in the medium range $(\theta_1 \leq r_i(j) < \theta_2)$, node i will cross check the consistency of a routing advertisements from j with other node(s).*

Rule 3 *(High Reputation). If node j's reputation rated by node i is in the high range $(\theta_2 \leq r_i(j) \leq 1)$, node i will cross check the consistency of a routing advertisement from j with only one other node.*

4.3 Sized Windows

Since there may be multiple nodes having propagated an advertised route, a mechanism is required to decide how many nodes to involve in a consistency check. The more nodes consulted (which agree with the the advertised route), the higher the confidence acquired in the correctness of that route; but the network overhead will also be higher. We use a *sized window* as a mechanism for balancing the trade-off between security and efficiency. The size of the window is the number of the nodes consulted in a consistency check. The window size starts from 1. In other words, there is only one node in the window before the consistency check of an advertised route, which is the advertiser of that route. The window size grows by one, or an additional node is consulted, if the computed confidence using Equation 3 in the correctness of that route is less than θ_2. The window size keeps growing for the advertised route until 1) an inconsistency occurs, i.e., a node reports conflicting information; or 2) all the nodes in the window agree upon the route, and 2.1) the computed confidence is greater than θ_2; or 2.2) all informed nodes have been involved. In case 1), the route fails the consistency check and is dropped. In case 2), the route succeeds the consistency check and is accepted.

5 Secure Routing Information Protocol (*S-RIP*)

We present the detail and analysis of *S-RIP*. For an advertised route $[dest, dist, nh]$, we use v_0, v_1, and v_n to represent the recipient, the advertiser, and the ultimate destination respectively. To be more specific, we use $dist(v_1, v_n)$ and $nh(v_1, v_n)$ to represent the distance and the next hop respectively from v_1 to v_n for this particular route.

5.1 *S-RIP*

When router v_0 receives from v_1 an advertised route $[v_n, dist(v_1, v_n), nh(v_1, v_n)]$, v_0 validates the route as required by RIP [1]. If the route passes the validation, and will be used to update v_0's routing table, *S-RIP* is triggered to perform additional validations. *S-RIP* will NOT be triggered if the advertised route does not indicate a route change or a topology change. Although the timer associated with this route will be re-initialized, there is no need to re-validate the route since such a validation should have been done when the route was first installed in v_0's routing table. Highlights of *S-RIP* on validating $[v_n, dist(v_1, v_n), nh(v_1, v_n)]$ are given immediately below. More details are presented in the remainder of this section.

1. Is the advertised route self-consistent? If not, drop the route.
2. If $dist(v_1, v_n) = 0$, v_0 performs router or prefix authentication. If the authentication succeeds, v_0 accepts the route. Otherwise, drops it.
3. If $1 \leq dist(v_1, v_n) < 15$, v_0 checks the consistency of $[v_n, dist(v_1, v_n), nh(v_1, v_n)]$. If the consistency check succeeds, v_0 accepts the route. Otherwise, drops it.
4. If $dist(v_1, v_n) \geq 15$, v_0 accepts the route without validating it.

Self-consistency Check. v_0 checks if $[v_n, dist(v_1, v_n), nh(v_1, v_n)]$ is self-consistent. 1) If v_1, v_2, or v_n is not a legitimate entity, the route is dropped. A router is legitimate to v_0 only if v_0 shares a secret key with it. 2) If $dist(v_1, v_n) = 0$, $nh(v_1, v_n)$ should be v_1 itself since the advertised route is for v_1 or a subnet directly attached to v_1. 3) If $1 \leq dist(v_1, v_n) < 15$, the next hop must not be v_0 or v_1. v_1 should not advertise a valid route back to v_0 from which it learns that route. Otherwise, the problem of counting to infinity occurs. Although RIP recognizes this problem and proposes split horizon (or with poisoned reverse) for solving it, a misbehaving node may not follow the rule and intentionally create the problem.

Router/Prefix Authentication. If $dist(v_1, v_n) = 0$, v_1 advertises to v_0 a route for itself or for a subnet directly attached to v_1. If the route is for v_1 itself, message authentication already provides data origin authentication [17]. If the route is for a subnet, the router-prefix mapping (§3.2) is used to validate if v_1 is physically connected to that subnet. If the validation succeeds, the router is accepted. Otherwise, dropped.

Consistency Check. If $1 \leq dist(v_1, v_n) < 15$, v_1 advertises to v_0 a reachable route for v_n. v_0 will check the consistency of that route with $nh(v_1, v_n)$, let's say v_2. v_0 will request from v_2 the routing information from v_2 to v_n and v_1. The message flows are given in Table 1, where * denotes a information field to be provided. The advertised route from v_1 for v_n is treated as consistent with v_2's routing information if $dist(v_2, v_1) = 1$ and $dist(v_1, v_n) = dist(v_2, v_n) + 1$ (based on RIP). Otherwise inconsistent.

If v_1 is consistent with v_2, v_0 will use Equation 3 to compute an accumulated confidence, $r_{v_0}(v_1, v_2)$. If $r_{v_0}(v_1, v_2) \geq \theta_2$, v_0 accepts the advertised route as correct. Otherwise, v_0 will consult with additional nodes based on the next hop information. Before v_0 sends a route request to node v_i,

Table 1. Routing Request and Response

$v_0 \rightarrow v_2$	$[v_n, *, *]$
	$[v_1, *, *]$
$v_0 \leftarrow v_2$	$[v_n, dist(v_2, v_n), nh(v_2, v_n)]$
	$[v_1, dist(v_2, v_1), nh(v_2, v_1)]$

it checks if a network loop has been formed. A network loop is formed if the node (v_i) to be consulted has been consulted before. In the case that a loop is detected, v_0 drops the advertised route. Otherwise, the consistency check continues until one of the following three conditions holds: 1) $r_{v_0}(v[1..k]) \geq \theta_2$. In this case, the advertised route from v_1 is treated as correct by v_0. 2) $r_{v_0}(v[1..k-1]) < \theta_2$, and v_k disagrees with v_{k-1}, i.e., $dist(v_{k-1}, v_n) \neq dist(v_k, v_n) + dist(v_k, v_{k-1})$. In this case, v_0 treats the advertised route as inconsistent. 3) v_n has been consulted. If v_n disagrees with v_{n-1}, the advertised route from v_1 is treated as inconsistent. Otherwise, v_0 will performs router/prefix authentication with v_n. If v_n succeeds the authentication, the advertised route is treated as correct no matter what the value of $r_{v_0}(v[1..n])$ is. Otherwise, the advertised route is dropped as v_n provides incorrect information.

Infinity Route. If $dist(v_1, v_n) \geq 15$, v_1 advertises to v_0 an route for v_n which is infinite from v_0. v_0 does not validate an infinite or unreachable route since it is trivial for v_1 to make a valid route unreachable if it misbehaves, e.g., by disabling a network interface or dropping packets. The consequence of such possible misbehavior is that v_0 will drop the route and will not forward packets to v_n through v_1. If there is only one route in the network from v_0 to v_n and it goes through v_1, v_0 will not be able to communicate with v_n. It seems to be hard to force a misbehaving node forward packets for others if it is determined not to do so. Therefore, we hope a network is designed with redundancy to accommodate a single point of failure. In that case, hopefully v_0 could find an alternative route to v_n, bypassing the misbehaving node v_1.

5.2 Threat Analysis

A node may misbehave in several ways: 1) advertising false routing information; 2) providing false routing information specifically during a consistency check; 3) dropping a validation request/reply message or not responding to a validation request; 4) manipulating a validation request/reply message originated from other nodes; 5) providing correct routing information but not forwarding data traffic.

1) *Advertising false routing information.* Given a route $[v_n, dist(v_1, v_n), nh(v_1, v_n)]$ advertised by node v_1 to v_0, v_1 may provide false information about v_n, $dist$, nh, or any combination.

1.1) *Destination Fraud.* v_1 may advertise a route for a nonexistent destination v_n. Under our proposal, such misbehavior can be detected since v_0 does not share a secret key with v_n if it is not a legitimate entity in the network.

1.2) *Distance Fraud.* v_1 may advertise a fraudulent distance to a destination v_n, e.g., longer or shorter than the actual distance. If $dist(v_1, v_n) = 0$, but v_1 is actually one or more hops away from v_n, in our proposal, v_0 can detect this fraud by router/prefix authentication. Other shorter or longer distance fraud can be detected by cross checking consistency with those nodes which propagated the route in question. There are three scenarios in which a consistency in the corroborating group may not represent correctness: a) the nodes in the corroborating group are simultaneously misled by one or more misbehaving nodes; b) the nodes in the corroborating group are colluding; c) a subset of the corroborating group are colluding and mislead the rest of the nodes. Our idea is that by increasing the size of the corroborating group, it is increasingly unlikely that these scenarios will not be detected.

1.3) *Next Hop Fraud.* Node v_1 may provide a fraudulent next hop to support its claim of a longer or shorter distance. First, v_1 may use fictional nodes as next hops. v_1 then intercepts from v_0 the subsequent validation requests to these nodes and send back false responses on behalf of them. In our scheme, a fictional node can be detected since v_0 does not share a prior secret with it. Second, v_1 may use a remote node (i.e., a node not directly connected to v_1) as the next hop. For example, suppose v_1 is 5 hops away from v_n. If v_1 learns that v_m is one hop away from v_n, it may claim to be two hops away from v_n and use v_m as the next hop. Unless v_m is willing to provide false information (e.g., $dist(v_m, v_1) = 1$) to cover v_1's misbehavior, v_0 will be able to detect this fraud. In the case that v_m is willing to collude with v_1, we treat it as the case that v_1 establishes a virtual link (e.g., TCP connection) with v_m, and they forward packets over the virtual link to each other. This misbehavior is equivalent to the *wormhole* attack studied by Hu, Perrig, and Johnson [10]. *S-RIP* may detect such attack if a prior knowledge of node physical connections is assumed. Otherwise, the proposed *Packet Leashes* defense mechanism [10] should be used.

2) *Providing false routing information* in a consistency check. The fraud could be on distance or next hop. When the false information cause inconsistency, the consequences are: 2.1) correct routing advertisements may be disregarded by well-behaved nodes. We think it is not to the advantage of a misbehaving node to mislead another node by this type of misbehavior since it may be best to avoid a "valid" route through a misbehaving node in any case. By dropping a route involving a misbehaving node, the validation node may take an alternative good route, albeit possibly suboptimal. 2.2) the reputation of a well-behaved node may be decreased as a result of false information arising from a misbehaving node. In the worst case, if node v_0's rating of node v_1's reputation is decreased to the low range, v_0 will disregard v_1's routing advertisements for a certain period of time. Since consistency checks occur only on route changes, a misbehaving node, v_m, may only damage the reputation of v_1's reputation when there is a route change which involves both v_m and v_1 in a consistency check. v_m's own reputation may also be decreased if it provides false information. Therefore, v_m is unable to damage another node's reputation at its will. On the other hand, v_1 has other chances to increase its reputation when it advertises good routes (without going through v_m) to v_0. So the effect of the type of misbehavior depends on the network topology and the location of the misbehaving nodes. If one or more misbehaving nodes are located on the links which can form a network-cut, they may be able to completely separate the network through collusion. It would appear no approach is resilient to such misbehavior.

3) *Dropping a validation request/reply message or not responding to a validation request*. This misbehavior can disrupt a validation process. As a result, the route being validated will be dropped. We do not consider this as a major drawback since dropping a route with misbehaving nodes en route allows an alternative route to be discovered. An adversary may launch this type of attack when it is not willing to forward packets for other nodes. As discussed before, a misbehaving node can avoid traffic by many other ways, e.g., dropping packets based on source or destination addresses, or simply disabling a network interface. We rely upon network redundancy and other mechanisms [20,12] to counter this type of misbehavior.

4) *Manipulating a validation request/response message* originated from other nodes. If all routers are deployed with *S-RIP* and use MD5 for message authentication, validation request/response messages cannot be manipulated en route. However, communication between a secured router and a remote non-secured router is not authenticated. The consequences are: 4.1) A routing response sent back by a remote non-secured router can be modified by an adversary en route. The adversary may modify the routing response in such a way that it would confirm the consistency of a false advertised route. 4.2) An adversary may intercept routing requests sent to a non-secured router, and produce false responses on behave of that router. This vulnerability can be addressed by IP layer security. For example, if IPSec is available, an adversary would not be able to manipulate or intercept routing requests or responses between two remote nodes. It can also be mitigated if we assume that an adversary does not have the capability to launch attacks in packet level. It is easy for an adversary to manipulate a routing table to make a router to broadcast fraudulent routing information. It may not be that easy to manipulate packets transmitted through a router if the adversary does not have sufficient control over that router, e.g., modify and compile source codes, install malicious software, etc.

5) *Providing correct routing information but not forwarding data traffic.* We can make routing request and response messages indistinguishable from normal data traffic to validate forwarding level behavior of intermediate routers. Other detection techniques (e.g., probing [12]) for identifying such misbehaving routers can also be integrated into *S-RIP*, we do not address the issue in this paper.

One characteristic of *S-RIP* is that it does not guarantee that a validated route is optimal. In fact, *S-RIP* only validates route consistency, without considering the cost. *S-RIP* always accepts a consistent route and disregards an inconsistent one regardless of its cost. Therefore, optimal route involving a misbehaving node may not be used. We consider this as a good tradeoff between routing security and efficiency.

5.3   Efficiency Analysis

We consider the worst case here. The efficiency of average cases is analyzed by simulation (§6).

Suppose there are n routers and m subnets in a network. The average length of a route is $l + 1$ hops. For maximum security, every router would validate every route with all other routers on that route. For a single route with a length of $l + 1$ hops, the number of messages required for a consistency check, including requests and responses, is $2 \cdot l$. Each message will travel a number of hops. The first request message is sent to the node in two hops, and will travel 2 hops. The last request message is sent to the node in $l + 1$ hops, and will travel $l + 1$ hops. A response message will travel the same number of hops as the corresponding request message assuming they travel at the opposite direction of a same route. Therefore, the total number of hops (message transmissions) traveled by both request and response messages is $2 \cdot [2 + 3 + \cdots + (l + 1)] = (1 + l) \cdot l$. Assume every router keeps a route for every subnet in the network. Each router would need $(1 + l) \cdot l \cdot m$ message transmissions for validating every route. Over the whole network, the total number of message transmissions in the most secure case is $(1 + l) \cdot l \cdot m \cdot n$.

We use RIP messages for route request and response. Each route request would need two route entries, one for the routing information from the recipient to the ultimate destination, and one from the recipient to its predecessor node on that route. The RIP message header is 24 bytes including authentication data, and each route entry is 20 bytes. Thus, one route request or response is 64 bytes. Plus the UDP header (8 bytes) and IP header (20 bytes), a packet carrying a route request or response is 92 bytes. The total overhead of routing validation, in addition to the overhead of regular routing updates, in the most secure case, is $92 \cdot (1 + l) \cdot l \cdot m \cdot n$ bytes.

As confirmed by our simulation (§6), the validation overhead by *S-RIP* is prohibitively expensive in the maximally secured case. However, *S-RIP* provides the flexibility for balancing security and efficiency via two configurable thresholds θ_1 and θ_2 (§4.2). In practice, we expect that the maximally secured case may only be applied to a small size network (i.e., the number of nodes and network diameter are small). In other scenarios, θ_1, θ_2 can be adjusted to obtain a comfortable level of security and efficiency.

S-RIP validation overhead can also be reduced by optimized implementation (e.g., transmitting several route requests or responses in a single message). For example, if v_1 advertises to v_0 three routes with a same next hop v_2. v_0 can send a single message with 4 route entries to v_2, one for each of three advertised destinations and one for v_1. The size of the packet carrying this message is 132 bytes, considerably less than 276 bytes which are the total size of three standard packets (each has a length of 92 bytes).

5.4   Incremental Deployment

A practical challenge of securing routing protocols is how to make the secured version interoperative with the existing infrastructure. Despite their technical merits, many proposed mechanisms for securing routing protocols are not widely deployed due to the fact that they require significant modifications to existing implementations and/or do not provide backward interoperability. Since it is unrealistic to expect that an existing routing infrastructure can be replaced by a secured version in a very short period of time, ideally a secured version should be compatible with the insecure protocols. It is also desirable that security can be increased progressively as more routers are deployed with the secured protocol.

To this end, *S-RIP* supports incremental deployment. We propose that messages exchanged in *S-RIP* conform to the message format defined in RIP. *S-RIP* can be implemented as a compatible upgrade to the existing RIP, and a *S-RIP* router performs routing functions the same way as a RIP router. Therefore, deploying *S-RIP* on a router only requires a down time for the period of installation and rebooting of RIP processes. Since RIP router responds to a routing request from a non-direct neighbor (a remote node), a *S-RIP* router can successfully get information (albeit not authenticated) from a non-secured router for a consistency check. In other words, a RIP router can participate in a consistency check, but not initiate a consistency check. Thus, even before *S-RIP* is deployed on all routers, the routing table of a *S-RIP* router is partially protected as it is built from validated routing updates. The more routers deployed with *S-RIP*, the more reliable routing tables in the network become. Therefore, we can say that security can be increased incrementally.

6   Simulation

We implemented *S-RIP* in the network simulator NS2 as an as an extension to the distance vector routing protocol provided by NS2. *S-RIP* is triggered if an advertised route is used to update a recipient's routing table. In this section, we present our preliminary simulation results on how routing overhead is affected by different threshold settings and number of misbehaving nodes in *S-RIP*.

Table 2. Simulation Scenarios

Maximally Secured	$\theta_1 = 0$	$\theta_2 = 1$
Partially Secured-1	$\theta_1 = 0.1$	$\theta_2 = 0.9$
Partially Secured-2	$\theta_1 = 0.2$	$\theta_2 = 0.8$
Partially Secured-3	$\theta_1 = 0.3$	$\theta_2 = 0.7$
Not Secured	$\theta_1 = 0$	$\theta_2 = 0$

6.1   Simulation Environment

Network Topology: we simulated *S-RIP* with a number of different network topologies. In this paper, we only present the simulation results for one topology which has 50 routers and 82 network links. *Fraud*: we simulated misbehaving nodes which commit either or both shorter and longer distance fraud (§3.3). We randomly selected 5, 10, 15, 20, and 25 nodes to commit fraud in each run of the simulation. Note that 25 misbehaving nodes represent 50% of the total nodes. Each misbehaving node periodically (every 2.5 seconds) randomly selects a route from its routing table and makes its distance shorter or longer. *Simulation Scenarios*: we simulated 5 scenarios (Table 2) by adjusting the thresholds θ_1 and θ_2. Each simulation runs 180 seconds.

6.2 Routing Overhead

To determine how much network overhead is generated by *S-RIP*, we compared the *S-RIP* overhead to the total routing overhead, which is calculated as the sum of *S-RIP* overhead and regular routing update overhead in RIP. Since the distance vector routing protocol provided by NS2 is not a strict implementation of RIP RFCs, we could not obtain network overhead directly from the NS2 trace file. We use $\frac{92x}{92x+632y}$ to calculate the ratio of *S-RIP* overhead and the total routing overhead, where x is the total number of *S-RIP* message transmissions, y is the total number of rounds of regular routing updates, 92 bytes is the size of the packet carrying a *S-RIP* message (see §5.3), and 632 bytes is the overhead generated by one router in one round of regular routing updates. x and y are derived from simulation outputs, which are used to generate Figure 3.

6.3 Simulation Results

By looking at the output data from the simulation, we observed that an advertised malicious route can be successfully detected by a consistency check. This is precisely what we expected.

Figure 3 compares the *S-RIP* overhead in different scenarios. 1) In a maximally secured network, *S-RIP* overhead is very high (about 40% of the total routing overhead). The *S-RIP* overhead stays relatively flat when the number of misbehaving nodes increases. This is because every node needs to validate every route with every other node on that route. In our implementation, a new route is not considered if the current route is being checked for consistency. Since it takes long time for a consistency check to complete, most new route changes (malicious or non-malicious) are not checked for their consistency. Therefore, overhead increased by new malicious updates is insignificant. This indicates that the speed of network convergence is significantly slowed down. We expect that it would make no difference in terms of overhead if we allow a new route to interrupt an ongoing consistency check as several uncompleted consistency checks would generate similar amount of *S-RIP*

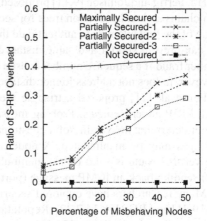

Fig. 3. *S-RIP* Routing Overhead.

overhead as a completed one does. 2) In the three partially secured scenarios, *S-RIP* overhead is relatively low (less than 8.6%) when there are only 10% of misbehaving nodes. *S-RIP* overhead increases significantly when the number of misbehaving nodes increases. Since the number of nodes involved in a consistency check is relatively low in these scenarios, it takes less time to complete. Thus more malicious updates will trigger more consistency checks and result in more *S-RIP* overhead. *S-RIP* overhead decreases when θ_1 and θ_2 are moved toward each other because: a) the number of nodes involved in a consistency check decreases; b) the number of routes dropped without being checked for consistency increases when more than 20% of the nodes misbehave. 3) There is no *S-RIP* overhead in a non-secured network since *S-RIP* is never triggered.

7 Related Work

Significant work has been done in securing routing protocols. Perlman [22] is the first to study the problem of securing routing protocols. Perlman classified router failures into *simple failures* and *byzantine failures*, and proposed use of public key signatures, source routing, and other mechanisms, for achieving robust flooding and robust routing.

Smith et al. [29] proposed use of digital signatures, sequence numbers, and a loop-free path finding algorithm for securing DV routing protocols. One disadvantage is that it cannot prevent longer or shorter distance fraud.

Mittal and Vigna [18] proposed to use sensor-based intrusion detection for securing DV routing protocols. One notable advantage of their approach is that it does not require modifications to the routing protocol being secured. Thus, it allows incremental deployment. One disadvantage is that it cannot prevent fraudulent routing advertisements from poisoning others' routing tables, although it may be able to detect them.

Hu, Perrig and Johnson [9,11] proposed several efficient mechanisms using one-way hash chains and authentication trees for securing DV routing protocols. Their approach is one of the first attempts to authenticate the factual correctness of DV routing updates, and can prevent shorter and same distance fraud. It can also prevent newer sequence number fraud if a sequence number is used to indicate the freshness of a routing update. However, it does not address longer distance fraud.

Pei et al. [21] proposed a triangle theorem for detecting potentially or probably invalid RIP advertisements. Probing messages based on UDP and ICMP are used to further determine the validity of a questionable route. One disadvantage is that probing messages may be manipulated. A node advertising an invalid route can convince a receiver that route is valid by: 1) manipulating the TTL value in a probing message; or 2) sending back an ICMP message (port unreachable) on behalf of the destination.

Many researchers have explored securing link state routing protocols (e.g., OSPF) [22,19,31] and BGP [28,14,7,32]. Reputation-based systems have been used to facilitate trust in electronic commerce [25,33].

8 Concluding Remarks

We expect our framework can be applied to other non-trustworthy environments, e.g., inter-domain routing protocols and wireless ad hoc networks. Future research includes:

1) performing detailed analysis of *S-RIP* and comparing it with other secure DV protocols (e.g., SEAD [11]); 2) applying the framework to securing BGP [24].

Acknowledgments. We thank anonymous reviewers for comments which significantly improved this paper. The first author is supported in part by Alcatel Canada, NCIT (National Capital Institute of Telecommunications), and MITACS (Mathematics of Information Technology and Complex Systems). The second author is supported in part by NSERC (Natural Sciences and Engineering Research Council of Canada) and MITACS. The third author is Canada Research Chair in Network and Software Security, and is supported in part by an NSERC Discovery Grant and the Canada Research Chairs Program.

References

[1] F. Baker and R. Atkinson. RIP-II MD5 Authentication. RFC 2082, January 1997.

[2] S.M. Bellovin. Security Problems in the TCP/IP Protocol Suite. *ACM Computer Communications Review*, 19(2): 32-48, April 1989.

[3] J. Case, M. Fedor, M. Schoffstall, and J. Davin. A Simple Network Management Protocol (SNMP). RFC 1157. May 1990.

[4] S. Deering, S. Hares, C. Perkins, and R. Perlman. Overview of the 1998 IAB Routing Workshop (RFC 2902). August, 2000.

[5] A.P. Dempster. Upper and Lower Probabilities Induced by a Multivalued Mapping. *The Annals of Statistics*, 28: pages 325-339, 1967.

[6] J.J. Garcia-Luna-Aceves and S. Murthy. A Loop-Free Algorithm Based on Predecessor Information. In *Proceedings of IEEE INFOCOM* , Boston, MA, USA. April 1995.

[7] G. Goodell, W. Aiello, T. Griffin, J. Ioannidis, P. McDaniel, and A. Rubin. Working around BGP: An Incremental Approach to Improving Security and Accuracy in Interdomain Routing. In *Proc. of NDSS'03*, San Diego, USA. Feb 2003.

[8] C. Hedrick. Routing Information Protocol. RFC 1058. June 1988.

[9] Y.C. Hu, A. Perrig, and D.B. Johnson. Efficient Security Mechanisms for Routing Protocols. In *Proc. NDSS'03*, San Diego, USA. Feb 2003.

[10] Y.C. Hu, A. Perrig, and D.B. Johnson. Packet Leashes: A Defense against Wormhole Attacks in Wireless Networks. In *Proc. of IEEE INFOCOM 2003*, San Francisco, USA. April 2003.

[11] Y.C. Hu, D.B. Johnson, and A. Perrig. SEAD: Secure Efficient Distance Vector Routing for Mobile Wireless Ad Hoc Networks. In *Ad Hoc Networks Journal*, 1 (2003):175-192.

[12] M. Just, E. Kranakis, and T. Wan. Resisting Malicious Packet Dropping in Wireless Ad Hoc Networks. In *Proc. of ADHOCNOW'03*, Montreal, Canada, Oct 2003.

[13] S. Kent and R. Atkinson. IP Encapsulating Security Payload. RFC 2406, Nov 1998.

[14] S. Kent and C. Lynn and K. Seo. Secure Border Gateway Protocol (Secure-BGP). *IEEE Journal on Selected Areas in Communications*, 18(4): 582-592, April 2000.

[15] G. Malkin. RIP Version 2. RFC 2453 (Standard), November 1998.

[16] J.M. McQuillan, G. Falk, and I. Richer. A Review of the Development and Performance of the ARPANET Routing Algorithm. *IEEE Trans. on Comm.*, 26(12): 1802-1811, Dec 1978.

[17] A.J. Menezes, P.C. van Oorschot, and S. Vanstone. *Handbook of Applied Cryptography*. CRC Press, 1996.

[18] V. Mittal and G. Vigna. Sensor-Based Intrusion Detection for Intra-Domain Distance-Vector Routing. In *Proc. of CCS'02*, Washington, D.C., USA. Nov 2002.

[19] S.L. Murphy and M.R. Badger. Digital Signature Protection of the OSPF Routing Protocol. In *Proc. of NDSS'96*, San Diego, USA. April 1996.

[20] V.N. Padmanabhan and D.R. Simon. Secure Traceroute to Detect Faulty or Malicious Routing. *ACM SIGCOMM Workshop on Hot Topic in Networks*, Princeton, NJ, USA. Oct 2002.

[21] D. Pei, D. Massey, and L. Zhang. Detection of Invalid Announcements in RIP protocols. *IEEE Globecom 2003*, San Francisco, California, USA. December 2003.

[22] R. Perlman. *Network Layer Protocols with Byzantine Robustness*. PhD thesis, MIT, 1988.

[23] R. Perlman. Interconnections: Bridges and Routers. Addison-Wesley, 1992.

[24] Y. Rekhter and T. Li. A Border Gateway Protocol 4 (BGP-4), RFC 1771, March 1995.

[25] P Resnick, R. Zeckhauser, E. Friedman, and K. Kuwabara. Reputation systems: Facilitating trust in Internet interactions. *Communications of the ACM*, 43(12): 45-48, 2000.

[26] R. Rivest. The MD5 Message-Digest Algorithm, RFC 1321, April 1992.

[27] G. Shafer. *A Mathematical Theory of Evidence*. Princeton University Press, 1976.

[28] B.R. Smith and J.J. Garcia-Luna-Aceves. Securing the Border Gateway Routing Protocol. In *Proceedings of Global Internet 1996*. London, UK. November 1996.

[29] B.R. Smith, S. Murphy, and J.J. Garcia-Luna-Aceves. Securing Distance-Vector Routing Protocols. In *Proc. of NDSS'97*, San Diego, USA. Feb 1997.

[30] T. Wan, E. Kranakis, and P.C. van Oorschot. Secure Routing Protocols Using Consistency Checks and S-RIP. Technical Report TR-03-09, School of Computer Science, Carleton University, Ottawa, Canada. Oct 2003.

[31] F.Y. Wang and F.S. Wu. On the Vulnerablity and Protection of OSPF Routing Protocol. In *Proceedings of IEEE Seventh International Conference on Computer Communications and Networks*, Lafayette, LA, USA. Oct 12-15, 1998.

[32] R. White. Securing BGP Through Secure Origin BGP. *The Internet Protocol Journal*, 6(3): 15-22, September 2003.

[33] B. Yu and M.P. Singh. Distributed Reputation Management for Electronic Commerce. In *Computational Intelligence*, 18(4): 535-549, 2002.

A Pay-per-Use DoS Protection Mechanism for the Web⋆

Angelos Stavrou, John Ioannidis, Angelos D. Keromytis, Vishal Misra, and
Dan Rubenstein

Columbia University
{angel,ji,angelos,misra,danr}@cs.columbia.edu

Abstract. Internet service providers have resisted deploying Denial-of-Service (DoS) protection mechanisms despite numerous research results in the area. This is so primarily because ISPs cannot directly charge users for the use of such mechanisms, discouraging investment in the necessary infrastructure and operational support.
We describe a pay-per-use system that provides DoS protection for web servers and clients. Our approach is based on WebSOS, an overlay-based architecture that uses reverse Turing tests to discriminate between humans and automated processes that are part of an attack. We extend WebSOS with a credential-based micropayment scheme that combines access control and payment authorization in one operation. Contrary to WebSOS, we use Graphic Turing Tests (GTTs) to prevent malicious code, such as a worm, from using a user's micropayment wallet. Our architecture allows ISPs to accurately charge web clients and servers. Clients can dynamically decide whether to use WebSOS, based on the prevailing network conditions.

1 Introduction

One of the main threats against the reliability of the Web services are (DoS) attacks: attacks that produce an excessive surge of bogus service requests against the target forcing it to processing and (or) to link capacity starvation. These attacks have dire consequences for the target's service viability, since availability and quality of service are of critical importance for the majority of the modern on-line services.

Despite considerable research on devising methods for protection against such attacks [15,29,28,26,22,32], so far none of these mechanisms has been widely adopted. Moreover, it has been argued recently [11] that the network DoS problem is inherently impossible to solve without infrastructure support.

However, ISPs seem to be reluctant to deploy such mechanisms. Investment in the necessary infrastructure and operational support are discouraged because such mechanisms represent a poor value proposition: fundamentally, ISPs cannot charge users for the use of such mechanisms. One possible solution would be a system with the ability to both protect against DoS attacks and provide a service payment scheme that would

---

⋆ This work is supported in part by DARPA contract No. F30602-02-2-0125 (FTN program) and by the National Science Foundation under grant No. ANI-0117738 and CAREER Award No. ANI-0133829, with additional support from Cisco and the Intel IT Research Council. Any opinions, findings, and conclusions or recommendations expressed in this material are those of the authors and do not necessarily reflect the views of the National Science Foundation.

M. Jakobsson, M. Yung, J. Zhou (Eds.): ACNS 2004, LNCS 3089, pp. 120–134, 2004.
ⓒ Springer-Verlag Berlin Heidelberg 2004

allow ISPs to recoup their costs and support the continued operation and maintenance of this infrastructure. Such incentives would motivate router manufacturers to provide appropriate support in their products.

In this paper, we describe a pay-per-use system that provides DoS protection for web servers and clients. Our approach is based on WebSOS, an overlay-based architecture that uses reverse Turing tests to discriminate between humans and automated processes that are part of an attack. We extend WebSOS with a credential-based micropayment scheme that combines access control and payment authorization. Our architecture allows ISPs to accurately charge web clients and servers. Clients can dynamically decide whether to use WebSOS, based on the prevailing network conditions.

WebSOS [23], an enriched implementation of the *Secure Overlay Services (SOS)*, is a DoS-protection architecture [22] for web services. WebSOS enhances the resilience of Web services against congestion-based DDoS attacks, acting as a distributed firewall and filtering attack traffic before it reaches the target. The network immediately surrounding attack targets is protected by high- performance routers that aggressively filter and block all incoming connections from hosts that are not approved. Only a small number of secretly selected secure access points within WebSOS are allowed to contact the target directly. The rest of the nodes use the overlay network as a routing mechanism to forward the requests to these secret nodes (the identity of which varies in time). WebSOS uses Graphic Turing Tests [33] as a means to differentiate anonymous users from automated zombies. Upon connection to the access point, the user was prompted with a GTT test. By preventing large-scale automated attacks, these tests allowed enough time for the overlay system to heal in case of an attack. Contrary to WebSOS, we use Graphic Turing Tests (GTTs) after to prevent malicious code, such as a worm, from using a user's micropayment wallet. This change in order can be done because our service is not anonymous: we have a means of authenticating the user credentials.

We extend WebSOS to include a lightweight offline electronic payment scheme. Although practically any micropayment system can be used in our model, we chose a payment system that can inter-operate with WebSOS' distributed architecture and provide the necessary user credentials. OTPchecks [16] encompasses all these properties: it is a simple distributed scheme, intended for general Internet-based micropayments that produces bank-issued users' credentials which can in turn used to acquire small-valued payment tokens. It has very low transaction overhead and can be tuned to use different risk strategies for different environments making it a suitable payment solution for a wide range of on-line services.

The remainder of this paper is organized as follows: Section 2 gives an overview of Secure Overlay Services (SOS) and discusses the specifics of the WebSOS architecture giving an overview of the Graphics Turing Tests. At the end of this section we provide details on OTPchecks, our micropayment scheme, and its risk strategies. Section 3 presents a detailed description of the extended WebSOS system. The related work is presented in section 4. Section 5 concludes the paper.

2   Background

Since our approach is based on the Secure Overlay Services (SOS) [22] architecture, we will start by giving a brief overview of its important aspects.

2.1   Overview of SOS

Fundamentally, the goal of the SOS infrastructure is to distinguish between authorized and unauthorized traffic. The former is allowed to reach the destination, while the latter is dropped or is rate-limited. Thus, at a very basic level, SOS requires the functionality of a firewall "deep" enough in the network that the access link to the target is not congested. This imaginary firewall performs access control by using protocols such as IPsec [21]. This generally pre-supposes the presence of authentication credentials (*e.g.,* X.509 [6] certificates) that a user can use to gain access to the overlay.

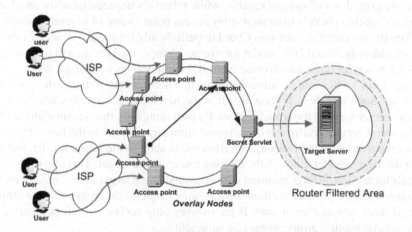

Fig. 1. Basic SOS architecture. Access Points represent an entry point to the SOS overlay. SOS nodes can serve any of the roles of secure access point, beacon or Secret Servlet.

Since traditional firewalls themselves are susceptible to DoS attacks, what is really needed is a distributed firewall [2,17]. To avoid the effects of a DoS attack against the firewall connectivity, instances of the firewall are distributed across the network. Expensive processing, such as cryptographic protocol handling, is farmed out to a large number of nodes. However, firewalls depend on topological restrictions in the network to enforce access-control policies. In what we have described so far, an attacker can launch a DoS attack with spoofed traffic purporting to originate from one of these firewalls, whose identity cannot be assumed to remain forever secret. The insight of SOS is that, given a sufficiently large group of such firewalls, one can select a very small number of these as the designated authorized forwarding stations: only traffic forwarded from these will be allowed through the filtering router. In SOS, these nodes are called *secret servlets*. All other firewalls must forward traffic for the protected site to these servlets. Figure 1 gives a high-level overview of a SOS infrastructure that protects a target node or site so that it only receives legitimate transmissions. Note that the secret servlets can change over time, and that multiple sites can use the same SOS infrastructure.

To route traffic inside the overlay, SOS uses Chord [30], which can be viewed as a routing service that can be implemented atop the existing IP network fabric, *i.e.*, as a network overlay. Consistent hashing [19] is used to map an arbitrary identifier to a unique destination node that is an active member of the overlay.

SOS uses the IP address of the target (*i.e.*, web server) as the identifier to which the hash function is applied. Thus, Chord can direct traffic from any node in the overlay to the node that the identifier is mapped to, by applying the hash function to the target's IP address. This node, where Chord delivers the packet, is not the target, nor is it necessarily the secret servlet. It is simply a unique node that will be eventually be reached, after up to $m = \log N$ overlay hops, regardless of the entry point. This node is called the *beacon*, since it is to this node that packets destined for the target are first guided. Chord therefore provides a robust and reliable, while relatively unpredictable for an adversary, means of routing packets from an overlay access point to one of several beacons.

Finally, the secret servlet uses Chord to periodically inform the beacon of the secret servlet's identity. Should the servlet for a target change, the beacon will find out as soon as the new servlet sends an advertisement. If the old beacon for a target drops out of the overlay, Chord will route the advertisements to a node closest to the hash of the target's identifier. Such a node will know that it is the new beacon because Chord will not be able to further forward the advertisement. By providing only the beacon with the identity of the secret servlet, traffic can be delivered from any firewall to the target by traveling across the overlay to the beacon, then from the beacon to the secret servlet, and finally from the secret servlet, through the filtering router, to the target. This allows the overlay to scale for arbitrarily large numbers of overlay nodes and target sites. *Unfortunately, this also increases the communication latency, since traffic to the target must be redirected several times across the Internet.* If the overlay only serves a small number of target sites, regular routing protocols may be sufficient.

2.2 Graphic Turing Tests

Graphic Turing Tests(GTTs) are tests designed to provide a way of differentiating a human from a machine by presenting the user with a set of images and asking a questions about the content of the images. CAPTCHA (Completely Automated Public Turing test to Tell Computers and Humans Apart) is a program that generates and grade GTTs [33].

The particular CAPTCHA realization we use is PIX. It consists of a large database of labeled images. All of these images are pictures of concrete objects (a horse, a table, a house, a flower, etc). The program picks an object at random, finds 6 random images of that object from its database, distorts them at random, presents them to the user and then asks the question "what are these pictures of?" as shown in Figure 2. PIX relies on the fact that humans can relate the objects within the distorted image and current automated tools cannot. The human authenticates himself/herself by entering as the description of the object in ASCII text. Graphic Turing Tests are an independent component of our architecture and thus we can update it without changing any other component.

124   A. Stavrou et al.

CAPTCHA Implementation

What are these pictures of?

[Enter]

The Captcha library was obdained from CMU CAPTCHA Project

Fig. 2. Web Challenge using CAPTCHA PIX. The challenge in this case is "baby or babies".

Although recent advances in visual pattern recognition [24] can defeat some of the CAPTCHAs, there is no solution to date that can recognize complicated images or relation between images like PIX or Animal-PIX. Although for demonstration purposes in our prototype we use PIX, we can easily substitute it with any other instance of graphic turing test in case a solution to the problem presented by this specific CAPTCHA is discovered.

2.3 WebSOS

WebSOS is the first instantiation of the SOS architecture. The access points participating in the overlay are implemented using Web proxies with SSL to provide two layers of encryption. A source that wants to communicate with the target contacts a random overlay node, the Secure Access Point. After authenticating and authorizing the request via the CAPTCHA test, the overlay node securely proxies all traffic from the source to the target via one of the beacons. The Secure overlay access point(*SOAP*) (and all subsequent hops on the overlay) can proxy the HTTP request to an appropriate beacon in a distributed fashion using Chord, by applying the appropriate hash function(s) to the target's IP address to identify the next hop on the overlay. To minimize delays in future requests, the client is issued a short-duration X.509 certificate, bound to the SOAP and the client's IP address, that can be used to directly contact the proxy-server component of the SOAP without requiring another CAPTCHA test.

In WebSOS, routing decisions are made on a per-connection basis. Any subsequent requests over the same connection (when using HTTP 1.1) and any responses from the web server can take the reverse path through the overlay. While this makes the implementation simpler, it also introduces increased latency, as the bulk of the traffic will also traverse the overlay. To deal with this issue, an adaptation of the initial implementation was created: rather than transporting the request and response through the full overlay network, only routing information travels through the overlay. As before, the requester makes a proxy request to the SOAP. At that point, the SOAP sends a UDP message into the overlay, specifying the target. The message is routed to the beacon, which responds directly to the SOAP with information on the secret servlet for that target. The SOAP then connects to the servlet, which proxies the request as before, in effect creating a *shortcut* through the overlay.

The SOAP caches the servlet information for use in future requests. That information is timed out after a period of time to allow for changes to propagate correctly. The same basic UDP protocol is used by servlets to announce their presence to (and periodically update) the beacons for the various targets.

2.4 OTPchecks Micropayment System

The general architecture of this microbilling system is shown in figure 3. In 3, the Check Guarantor plays the role of *Provisioning*, the Network User plays the role of *Payer*, and the Network Storage Provider (or another NU acting as an NSP) plays the role of the *Merchant*. *Clearing* is done either by a financial institution (if real money is used) or by a selected user of the system (when loyalty points or "play money" are used).

In this system, The *Provisioning* agent issues KeyNote[4] credentials to *Payers* and *Merchants*. These credentials describe the conditions under which a Payer is allowed to perform a transaction, and the fact that a Merchant is authorized to participate in a particular transaction. When a Payer wants to buy something from a Merchant, the Merchant first encodes the details of the proposed transaction into an *offer* which is transmitted to the Payer.

If the Payer wishes to proceed, she must issue to the Merchant a microcheck for this offer. The microchecks are also encoded as KeyNote credentials that authorize payment for a specific transaction. The Payer creates a KeyNote credential signed with her public key and sends it, along with her Payer credential, to the Merchant. This credential is effectively a check signed by the Payer (the Authorizer) and payable to the Merchant (the Licensee). The conditions under which this check is valid match the offer sent to the Payer by the Merchant. Part of the offer is a nonce, which maps payments to specific transactions, and prevents double-depositing of microchecks by the Merchant.

To determine whether he can expect to be paid (and therefore whether to accept the payment), the Merchant passes the action description (the attributes and values in the offer) and the Payer's key along with the Merchant's policy (that identifies the Provisioning key), the Payer credential (signed by Provisioning) and the microchecks credential (signed by the Payer) to his local KeyNote compliance checker. If the compliance checker authorizes the transaction, the Merchant is guaranteed that Provisioning will allow payment. The correct linkage among the Merchant's policy, the Provisioning key, the Payer key, and the transaction details follow from KeyNote's semantics[4].

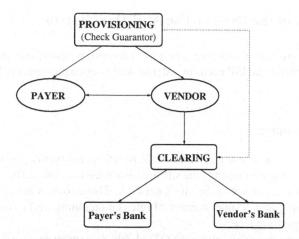

Fig. 3. Microbilling architecture diagram. We have the generic terms for each component, and in parentheses the corresponding players in 3. The arrows represent communication between the two parties: Provisioning issues credentials to Payers and Merchants; these communicate to complete transactions; Merchants send transaction information to Clearing which verifies the transaction and posts the necessary credits/charges or arranges money transfers. Provisioning and Clearing exchange information on the status of Payer and Merchant accounts.

If the transaction is approved, the Merchant should give the item to the Payer and store a copy of the microcheck along with the payer credential and associated offer details for later settlement and payment. If the transaction is not approved because the limits in the payer credentials have been exceeded then, depending on their network connectivity, either the Payer or the Merchant can request a transaction-specific credential that can be used to authorize the transaction. Observe that this approach, if implemented transparently and automatically, provides a continuum between online and offline transactions tuned to the risk and operational conditions.

Periodically, the Merchant will 'deposit' the microchecks (and associated transaction details) it has collected to the *Clearing and Settlement Center (CSC)*. The CSC may or may not be run by the same company as the Provisioning, but it must have the proper authorization to transmit billing and payment records to the Provisioning for the customers. The CSC receives payment records from the various Merchants; these records consist of the Offer, and the KeyNote microcheck and credential from the payer sent in response to the offer. In order to verify that a microcheck is good, the CSC goes through the same procedure as the Merchant did when accepting the microcheck. If the KeyNote compliance checker approves, the check is accepted. Using her public key as an index, the payer's account is debited for the amount of the transaction. Similarly, the Merchant's account is credited for the same amount.

The central advantage of this architecture is the ability to encode risk management rules for micropayments in user credentials. Other electronic systems have focused on preventing fraud and failure, rather than on managing it. In many cases with such systems, the prevention mechanisms can be too expensive for micropayments, making the risk management approach particularly attractive.

3 Overview of the Pay-per-Use Anti-DoS System

To illustrate the overall system, we now give a thorough description of the necessary software and hardware an ISP needs in order to deploy our a pay-per-use DoS protection mechanism.

3.1 ISP Provisioning

The ISP first creates an overlay network of WebSOS access points ('servlets'). In addition, the routers at the perimeter of the site are instructed to allow traffic only from these servlets to reach the interior of the site's network. These routers are powerful enough to do filtering using only a small number of rules on incoming traffic without adversely impacting their performance.

For a payment scheme, we chose the OTPchecks system because of its inherent flexibility to accommodate different services and its ability to interoperate with a distributed system like WebSOS. Refer to the roles presented in the OTPchecks functional description, in Figure 3; the Payer is the client connecting to the access points, the Vendor is the ISP providing the DoS protection service, and the web service provider (Target) is the clearing entity. The web service provider controls the usage of the service provided via the ISP's network by having the access points delegate payment credentials to each of the clients. In this manner, the service payment can be charged either to the client or to the web service provider. The ISP, using the same transaction information, charges the site providing the web service. The web service itself may charge the user at the same or even a higher rate for the DoS protection and possibly for other Internet commodities (bandwidth, time *etc.*) using the data presented by the access points. The overall system is presented in Figure 4.

3.2 System Operation

We now describe the steps involved in a client using the micropayment scheme in the context of WebSOS. For more details on WebSOS system operation, the reader is referred to [23].

Initialization – System setup. When a WebSOS node is informed that it will act as a secret servlet for a site (and after verifying the authenticity of the request, by verifying the certificate received during the SSL exchange), it computes the key k for a number of well-known consistent hash functions, based on the target site's network address. Each of these keys will identify a number of overlay nodes that will act as beacons for that web server.

Having identified the beacons, the servlets or the target will contact them, notifying them of the servlets' association with a particular target. Beacons will store this information and use it to answer the routing queries of the access points who want to connect to the target. By providing only the beacon with the identity of the secret servlet, traffic can be delivered from any firewall to the target by traveling across the overlay to the

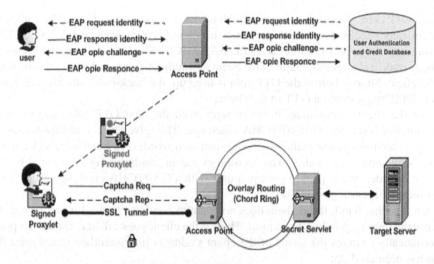

Fig. 4. Pay-per-use DoS protection system operation overview. The user is connected to an access point that in turn authenticates the user credentials and issues an X.509 certificate and a signed proxylet that allows the user to connect securely to the web service for a limited amount time.

beacon, then from the beacon to the secret servlet, and finally from the secret servlet, through the filtering router, to the target.

Since the standard EAP protocol is used, it is possible to use any or all the EAP sub-protocols. However, since neither EAP or EAPoL provide any cryptographic protection themselves, the security of the system depends on the security of the underlying network and on the properties of the EAP sub-protocol. Thus, the risks and the protections must be matched to provide the desired level of security.

Buying OTP coins. Whenever a new client host wants to access a service that the ISP protects from DoS attacks, the access point attempts to run the EAPoL protocol with the client. The status of the client is kept unauthenticated as long as the client fails to authenticate through EAPoL. In our case, we provide unauthenticated clients limited access so that they can buy OTP coins, used for the actual EAPoL level authentication (see below).

Using OTP coins. Once the Client has acquired a set of OTP coins, it runs the standard EAPoL protocol towards the local access point. The protocol run is illustrated in Figure 4.

Upon connection, the access point requests a user identifier from the client. The client answers with a string that identifies the microcheck used for buying the OTP coins, and the web service the coins where bought for. This allows the access point to contact the correct back-end authenticator, the web service provider (Target). The microcheck fingerprint identifies the relevant unused OTP coin pile.

Once the back-end authenticator receives the identity response, it checks the OTP coin pile and sends an OPIE request, requesting for the next unused OPIE password, *i.e.,* an OTP coin. The Client responds with the next unused coin, H_{i+1}. The back-end authenticator checks the coin, records it as used, and replies with an EAP SUCCESS message. As the access point receives the EAP SUCCESS message from the back-end authenticator, it changes the status of the client into authenticated, and passes the message to the client. Shortly before the OTP coin is used up, the back-end authenticator sends a new OPIE request and a GTT to the client.

For the client to continue, it has to reply with the next OTP coin, and the user must answer correctly the CAPTCHA challenge. This gives us the ability to have a strong protection against malicious code, such as a worm or a zombie process, using a user's micropayment wallet. The lifetime of a coin can be easily configured by the service provider. We expect to prompt a user with a CAPTCHA challenge every 30 to 45 minutes, depending on the service.

On the other hand, if the client does not want to continue access for any reason, he simply does not respond to the request. Thus, if the client goes off-line, the access point automatically changes the status of the client's address into unauthenticated once the coin has been used up.

The access point then issues a short-lived X.509 [6] certificate. This certificate is signed by the ISP operating the overlay, and authorizes the holder to access the web service that was paid for by the coin. The overlay securely proxies all traffic from the source to the target via one of the beacons. The access point (and all subsequent hops on the overlay) can proxy the HTTP request to an appropriate beacon in a distributed fashion using Chord, by applying the appropriate hash function(s) to the target's IP address to identify the next hop on the overlay.

This scheme is robust against DoS attacks because if an access point is attacked, the confirmed source point can simply choose an alternate access point to enter the overlay. Any overlay node can provide all different required functionalities (access point, Chord routing, beacon, secret servlet). If a node within the overlay is attacked, the node simply exits the overlay and the Chord service self-heals, providing new paths over the re-formed overlay to (potentially new sets of) beacons. Furthermore, no node is more important or sensitive than others — even beacons can be attacked and are allowed to fail. Finally, if a secret servlet's identity is discovered and the servlet is targeted as an attack point, or attacks arrive at the target with the source IP address of some secret servlet, the target can choose an alternate set of secret servlets.

3.3   Experimental Evaluation – Latency Results

One of the main concerns of people using DoS systems is the impact of the latency overhead to the end users. Here we include some of the experimental results of WebSOS [23] that show that the end to end latency increases by a factor of two, as shown in Figure 5.

To complete the overhead analysis we measured the number of public key verifications an access point can perform, which indicates how many microchecks it can validate in unit time. We used a 3 GHz Pentium4 processor machine running Linux with the OpenSSL V 0.9.7c library for the measurements. The contribution of the micropayment system to the overall system latency overhead is minimal, even when we issue 1024-bit RSA certificates for the client credentials, as shown in Table 1. These

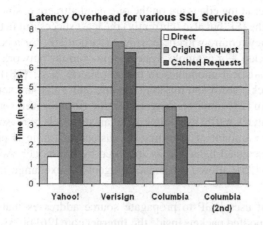

Fig. 5. WebSOS Latency overhead for different SSL-enabled services when using the shortcut routing mechanism

measurements show that the impact of the user verification process on the access points is minimal.

Table 1. Signing and verification times for 1024-bit RSA keys.

Sign	Verify	Sig/sec	Ver/sec
0.0037 sec	0.0002 sec	270.0	5055.9

4 Related Work

Considerable research has been devoted to the problem of network denial of service, with most of the effort focusing on tracing the sources of malicious attacks, filtering out attack traffic at the edges, and filtering inside the network itself.

Methods for tracking down the sources of malicious attacks (*e.g.,* [9,29,12] generally require that routers mark packets or that they "remember" whether particular packets (or flows) have been seen in the recent past. Their primary use is in identifying the real sources of attacks involving spoofed traffic (*i.e.,* traffic purporting to originate from an IP address different from that of the real source). As a value proposition, these mechanisms represent the worst approach for ISPs, since there is no way of quantifying their usefulness.

A variant of the packet marking approaches creates probabilistically unique path-marks on packets without requiring router coordination; end-hosts or firewalls can then easily filter out packets belonging to a path that exhibits anomalous behavior [34]. Although this approach avoids many of the limitations of the pure marking schemes, it requires that core routers "touch" packets (rather than simply switch them). Again, however, it is unclear how ISPs can charge for such a service.

Methods that filter at the edges are on the one hand attractive, since they require no action on the part of the ISP, but also (currently) the least successful in defending against DoS attacks, since they require wide deployment (particularly for mechanisms filtering at the sources of attacks). For example, systems that examine network traffic for known attack patterns or statistical anomalies in traffic patterns (*e.g.*, [28]) can be defeated by changing the attack pattern and masking the anomalies that are sought by the filter. The D-WARD system [28] monitors outgoing traffic from a given source network and attempts to identify attack traffic by comparing against models of reasonable congestion control behavior. The amount of throttling on suspicious traffic is proportional to its deviation from the expected behavior, as specified by the model. An extension of D-WARD, COSSACK [25], allows participating agents to exchange information about observed traffic.

An approach that uses BGP to propagate source addresses that can be used for filtering out source-spoofed packets inside the Internet core [26] places undue burden on the core and is useful only in weeding out spoofed packets; unfortunately, the majority of DDoS attacks do not use spoofed packets. [20] proposes using Class-Based Queuing on a web load-balancer to identify misbehaving IP addresses and place them in lower priority queues. However, many of the DDoS attacks simply cause congestion to the web server's access link. To combat that, the load-balancer would have to be placed closer to the network core. Such detailed filtering and especially state-management on a per-source-IP address basis can have performance implications at such high speeds. In [14], the authors use a combination of techniques that examine packet contents, transient ramp-up behavior and spectral analysis to determine whether an attack is single- or multi-sourced, which would help focus the efforts of a hypothetical anti-DoS mechanism. Another interesting approach is that of [18], which proposes an IP hop-count-based filter to weed out spoofed packets. The rationale is that most such packets will not have a hop-count (TTL) field consistent with the IP addresses being spoofed. In practice, most DoS attacks are launched from subverted hosts.

Mechanisms involving filtering inside the network itself (*i.e.*, inside an ISP's infrastructure), such as Pushback [15] require ISP investment (in infrastructure, man power, and operational support). In Pushback, routers push filter towards the sources of an attack, based on the ingress traffic they observe on their various interfaces. Unfortunately, it is unclear how an ISP can charge for such a service; one possibility is as a subscription service, or measuring the number of times a client site invokes the service.

Another approach to mitigating DoS attacks against information carriers is to massively replicate the content being secured around the entire network. To prevent access to the replicated information, an attacker must attack all replication points throughout the entire network — a task that is considerably more difficult than attacking a small number of, often co-located, servers. Replication is a promising means to preserve information that is relatively static, such as news articles. However, there are several reasons why replication is not always an ideal solution. For instance, the information may require frequent updates complicating large-scale coherency (especially during DoS attacks), or may be dynamic by its very nature (*e.g.*, a live web-cast). Another concern is the security of the stored information: engineering a highly-replicated solution without leaks of information is a challenging endeavor.

An extension of the ideas of SOS [22,23] appears in [1]. There, the two main facets of the SOS architecture: filtering and overlay routing, are explored separately, and several alternative mechanisms are considered. It is observed that in some cases, the various security properties offered by SOS can still be maintained using mechanisms that are simpler and more predictable. However, some second-order properties, such as the ability to rapidly reconfigure the architecture in anticipation of or in reaction to a breach of the filtering identity are compromised. In most other respects, the two approaches are very similar.

The NetBouncer project [32] considers the use of client-legitimacy tests for filtering attack traffic. Such tests include packet-validity tests (*e.g.,* source address validation), flow-behavior analysis, and application-specific tests, including Graphic Turing Tests. However, since their solution is end-point based, it is susceptible to large link-congestion attacks.

[3] examines several different DDoS mitigation technologies and their interactions. Among their conclusions, they mention that requiring the clients to do some work, *e.g.,* [10], can be an effective countermeasure, provided the attacker does not have too many resources compared to the defender. Gligor [11] disagrees with this conclusion, noting that computational client puzzles cannot provide hard bounds (guarantees) on client wait time.

Although we use a particular micropayment system [5], other schemes can also be used, including digital cash systems (*e.g.,* [7]), scrip-based micropayments (*e.g.,* [27]), and offline micropayment protocols (*e.g.,* [31]). MiniPay [13] is particularly attractive, since it was developed primarily for use with a web browser, with considerable effort gone into the user interface aspect. Risk management is implemented as a decision to perform an online check with the billing server based on the total spending by the customer that day, and some parameter set by the merchant. We believe that general transactional payment schemes (*e.g.,* [8]) may prove too heavy-weight for our purposes.

5   Conclusion

We present the first pay-friendly DoS protection system that furnishes ISPs with a better value proposition for deploying anti-DoS systems: a way to turn DoS protection into a commodity. Our pay-per-use system is based on the WebSOS DoS protection architecture, extended to include OTPchecks, a light-weight and flexible pay-per-use micropayment scheme. Its hardware and software deployment can be done without changing any of the current ISP infrastructure. The initial investment and maintenance cost can regulated and scaled depending on the actual services protected.

From the end user perspective, the system acts almost transparently: no modifications are required in the browsers since we are taking advantage of browser extensibility. Moreover, the target site offering the web service can have a more fine-grained control of the users that it serves without altering any of its current servers' protocols. Finally, we allow a web service to charge its clients for the DoS protection service or provide the service as an added value feature.

References

1. D. G. Andersen. Mayday: Distributed Filtering for Internet Services. In *4th USENIX Symposium on Internet Technologies and Systems USITS*, March 2003.
2. S. M. Bellovin. Distributed Firewalls. *;login: magazine, special issue on security*, pages 37–39, November 1999.
3. W. J. Blackert, D. M. Gregg, A. K. Castner, E. M. Kyle, R. L. Hom, and R. M. Jokerst. Analyzing Interaction Between Distributed Denial of Service Attacks and Mitigation Technologies. In *Proceedings of DISCEX III*, pages 26–36, April 2003.
4. M. Blaze, J. Feigenbaum, J. Ioannidis, and A. D. Keromytis. The KeyNote Trust Management System Version 2. RFC 2704, September 1999.
5. M. Blaze, J. Ioannidis, and A. D. Keromytis. Offline Micropayments without Trusted Hardware. In *Proceedings of the Fifth International Conference on Financial Cryptography*, pages 21–40, 2001.
6. CCITT. *X.509: The Directory Authentication Framework*. International Telecommunications Union, Geneva, 1989.
7. D. Chaum. Achieving Electronic Privacy. *Scientific American*, pages 96–101, August 1992.
8. B. Cox, D. Tygar, and M. Sirbu. NetBill security and transaction protocol. In *Proceedings of the First USENIX Workshop on Electronic commerce*. USENIX, July 1995.
9. D. Dean, M. Franklin, and A. Stubblefield. An Algebraic Approach to IP Traceback. In *Proceedings of the Network and Dsitributed System Security Symposium (NDSS)*, pages 3–12, February 2001.
10. D. Dean and A. Stubblefield. Using client puzzles to protect TLS. In *Proceedings of the 10th USENIX Security Symposium*, August 2001.
11. V. D. Gligor. Guaranteeing Access in Spite of Distributed Service-Flooding Attacks. In *Proceedings of the Security Protocols Workshop*, April 2003.
12. M. T. Goodrich. Efficient Packet Marking for Large-Scale IP Traceback. In *Proceedings of the 9th ACM Conference on Computer and Communications Security (CCS)*, pages 117–126, November 2002.
13. A. Herzberg. Safeguarding Digital Library Contents. *D-Lib Magazine*, January 1998.
14. A. Hussain, J. Heidemann, and C. Papadopoulos. A Framework for Classifying Denial of Service Attacks. In *Proceedings of ACM SIGCOMM*, August 2003.
15. J. Ioannidis and S. M. Bellovin. Implementing Pushback: Router-Based Defense Against DDoS Attacks. In *Proceedings of the Network and Distributed System Security Symposium (NDSS)*, February 2002.
16. J. Ioannidis, S. Ioannidis, A. D. Keromytis, and V. Prevelakis. Fileteller: Paying and Getting Paid for File Storage. In *Proceeding of Financial Cryptography (FC) Conference*, pages 282–299, March 2002.
17. S. Ioannidis, A. Keromytis, S. Bellovin, and J. Smith. Implementing a Distributed Firewall. In *Proceedings of Computer and Communications Security (CCS)*, pages 190–199, November 2000.
18. C. Jin, H. Wang, and K. G. Shin. Hop-Count Filtering: An Effective Defense Against Spoofed DoS Traffic. In *Proceedings of the 10th ACM International Conference on Computer and Communications Security (CCS)*, pages 30–41, October 2003.
19. D. Karger, E. Lehman, F. Leighton, R. Panigrahy, M. Levine, and D. Lewin. Consistent Hashing and Random Trees: Distributed Caching Protocols for Relievig Hot Spots on the World Wide Web. In *Proceedings of ACM Symposium on Theory of Computing (STOC)*, pages 654–663, May 1997.
20. F. Kargl, J. Maier, and M. Weber. Protecting web servers from distributed denial of service attacks. In *World Wide Web*, pages 514–524, 2001.

21. S. Kent and R. Atkinson. Security Architecture for the Internet Protocol. RFC 2401, Nov. 1998.
22. A. D. Keromytis, V. Misra, and D. Rubenstein. SOS: Secure Overlay Services. In *Proceedings of ACM SIGCOMM*, pages 61–72, August 2002.
23. W. G. Morein, A. Stavrou, D. L. Cook, A. D. Keromytis, V. Misra, and D. Rubenstein. Using Graphic Turing Tests to Counter Automated DDoS Attacks Against Web Servers. In *Proceedings of the 10th ACM International Conference on Computer and Communications Security (CCS)*, pages 8–19, October 2003.
24. G. Mori and J. Malik. Recognizing Objects in Adversarial Clutter: Breaking a Visual CAPTCHA. In *Computer Vision and Pattern Recognition CVPR'03*, June 2003.
25. C. Papadopoulos, R. Lindell, J. Mehringer, A. Hussain, and R. Govindan. COSSACK: Co-ordinated Suppression of Simultaneous Attacks. In *Proceedings of DISCEX III*, pages 2–13, April 2003.
26. K. Park and H. Lee. On the Effectiveness of Route-based PAcket Filtering for Distributed DoS Attack Prevention in Power-law Internets. In *Proceedings of ACM SIGCOMM*, pages 15–26, August 2001.
27. T. Poutanen, H. Hinton, and M. Stumm. NetCents: A Lightweight Protocol for Secure Micro-payments. In *Proceedings of the Third USENIX Workshop on Electronic Commerce*. USENIX, September 1998.
28. P. Reiher, J. Mirkovic, and G. Prier. Attacking DDoS at the source. In *Proceedings of the 10th IEEE International Conference on Network Protocols*, November 2002.
29. S. Savage, D. Wetherall, A. Karlin, and T. Anderson. Network Support for IP Traceback. *ACM/IEEE Transactions on Networking*, 9(3):226–237, June 2001.
30. I. Stoica, R. Morris, D. Karger, F. Kaashoek, and H. Balakrishnan. Chord: A Scalable Peer-To-Peer Lookup Service for Internet Application. In *Proceedings of ACM SIGCOMM*, August 2001.
31. L. Tang. A Set of Protocols for MicroPayments in Distributed Systems. In *Proceedings of the First USENIX Workshop on Electronic Commerce*. USENIX, July 1995.
32. R. Thomas, B. Mark, T. Johnson, and J. Croall. NetBouncer: Client-legitimacy-based High-performance DDoS Filtering. In *Proceedings of DISCEX III*, pages 14–25, April 2003.
33. L. von Ahn, M. Blum, N. J. Hopper, and J. Langford. CAPTCHA: Using Hard AI Problems For Security. In *Proceedings of EUROCRYPT'03*, 2003.
34. A. Yaar, A. Perrig, and D. Song. Pi: A Path Identification Mechanism to Defend against DDoS Attacks. In *Proceedings of the IEEE Symposium on Security and Privacy*, May 2003.

Limited Verifier Signature from Bilinear Pairings

Xiaofeng Chen[1], Fangguo Zhang[2], and Kwangjo Kim[1]

[1] International Research center for Information Security (IRIS)
Information and Communications University(ICU),
103-6 Munji-dong, Yusong-ku, Taejon, 305-714 KOREA
{crazymount,kkj}@icu.ac.kr
[2] Department of Electronics and Communication Engineering,
Institute of Information Security Technology,
Sun Yat-Sen University,
Guangzhou 510275, P.R.China
isdzhfg@zsu.edu.cn

Abstract. Motivated by the conflict between authenticity and privacy in the digital signature, the notion of limited verifier signature was introduced [1]. The signature can be verified by a limited verifier, who will try to preserve the privacy of the signer if the signer follows some specified rules. Also, the limited verifier can provide a proof to convince a judge that the signer has indeed generated the signature if he violated the predetermined rule. However, the judge cannot transfer this proof to convince any other party. Also, the limited verifier signature should be converted into an ordinary one for public verification if required.
In this paper, we first present the precise definition and clear security notions for (convertible) limited verifier signature, and then propose two efficient (convertible) limited verifier signature schemes from bilinear pairings. Our schemes were proved to achieve the desired security notions under the random oracle model.

Keywords: Undeniable signature, Designated verifier signature, Limited verifier signature, Bilinear pairings.

1 Introduction

Undeniable signature, introduced by Chaum and van Antwerpen [10], is a kind of digital signature which cannot be verified without interacting with the signer. It is useful in a case where the validity of a signature must not be verified universally. For example, a software vendor might embed his signature into his products and only allow the paying customers to verify the authentication of the products. If the vendor signed a message (product), he must provide some proofs to convince the customer of the fact. Also, these proofs must be non-transferable, *i.e.*, once a verifier (customer) is convinced that the vendor signed (or did not sign) the message, he cannot transfer these proofs to convince any third party. After the initial work of Chaum and van Antwerpen, several undeniable signature schemes were proposed [9,17,15,22]. Also, Boyar *et al.* [5] introduced the notion of convertible undeniable signature.

M. Jakobsson, M. Yung, J. Zhou (Eds.): ACNS 2004, LNCS 3089, pp. 135–148, 2004.
© Springer-Verlag Berlin Heidelberg 2004

In some cases, it will be a disadvantage that the signature can be verified only with the cooperation of the signer. If the signer should be unavailable, or should refuse to cooperate, then the recipient cannot make use of the signature. This facilitates the concept of "designated confirmer signature" [8]. The designated confirmer can confirm the signature even without the cooperation of the signer when a dispute occurs.

In some applications, it is important for the signer to decide not only *when* but also *by whom* his signatures can be verified due to the blackmailing [13, 20] and mafia [12] attacks. For example, the voting center presents a proof to convince a certain voter that his vote was counted while without letting him to convince others (*e.g.*, a coercer) of his vote, which is important to design a receipt-free electronic voting scheme preventing vote buying and coercion. This is the motivation of the concept of "designated verifier signature" [21]. The designated verifier will trust the signer indeed signed a message with a proof of the signer. However, he cannot present the proof to convince any third party because he is fully capable of generating the same proof by himself.

Recently, motivated by privacy issues associated with dissemination of signed digital certificate, Steinfeld *et al.* [26] introduced the conception of "universal designated verifier signature", which can be viewed as an extended notion of designated verifier signature. Universal designated verifier signature allows any holder of the signature (not necessarily the signer) to designate the signature to any desired designated verifier. The verifier can be convinced that the signer indeed generated the signature, but cannot transfer the proof to convince any third party. For example, a user Alice is issued a signed certificate by the CA. When Alice wishes to send her certificate to a verifier Bob, she uses Bob's public key to transfer the CA's signature into a universal designated verifier signature to Bob. Bob can verifier the signature with CA's public key but is unable to use this designated signature to convince any third party that the certificate is issued by the CA, even if Bob is willing to reveal his secret key to the third party.

In some applications, it is also important for the recipient to decide *when* and *whom* the signer's signature should be verified. For example, a credit company will try his best to preserve the client's privacy in order to get his trust, provided that the client obeys the rules of the company. So, it is sufficient for the company only to be convinced the validity of the client's signature for his dishonorable message such as a bill. Furthermore, the company will preserve the client's privacy if he pays the bill in a certain time. However, if the client violated the rules, the company can provide a proof to convince a Judge of the client's treachery while the Judge cannot transfer the proof to convince any other third party.

It is obvious that undeniable signature and designated verifier signature are unsuitable for these situations. In the undeniable signatures, the signature can be verified only the cooperation of the signer. In the designated verifier signature, the designated verifier can never transfer the signature or the proof to convince any third party even he would like to reveal his secret key. This is because the designated verifier is fully capable to generate a "signature" himself which is indistinguishable from the real signature of the signer.

Araki *et al.* [1] introduced the concept of "limited verifier signature" to solve these problems. The limited verifier signature can only be verified by a limited verifier, who will try to preserve the signer's privacy (especially some dishonorable message) unless the signer violated some rules. When a later dispute occurs, the limited verifier can convince a third party, usually a Judge, that the signer indeed generated a signature. We argue that the goal of the limited verifier is not to make the signature to be verified publicly, but force the signer to obey the rules. In some cases, the signer may not intentionally violate the rules and the limited verifier should give the signer some chances to correct his fault. Therefore, the Judge should not transfer this proof to convince any other party.

In some situations, the signer's privacy is closely related to the recipient's privacy. For example, a spy, Carol, has a certificate with a signature of the President, which can be verified by Carol herself. Also, Carol can provide a proof to prove her real identity to a third party in case of an emergency. However, the signature and the proof cannot be transferred by the third party to convince any other party in order to ensure Carol's safety. Therefore, limited verifier signature can be used in any cases that the signer's signature *should* be protected by the recipient.

Some official documents, which is treated as limited verifier signature, should be verified by everyone after a period of time if necessary. This is the motivation of "convertible limited verifier signatures", also introduced by Araki *et al.* [1]. Convertible limited verifier signatures enable the limited verifier to convert the signature into an ordinary one for public verification.[1]

In the convertible limited verifier signature [1], the conversion of the signature requires the cooperation of the original signer, who must release some information. This might not be workable if the original signer is unwilling or inconvenient to cooperate. Furthermore, Zhang and Kim [28] proposed a universal forgery attack on this scheme. Wu *et al.* [24] proposed a convertible authenticated encryption scheme, which overcomes some disadvantages of Araki *et al.*'s scheme. However, if the recipient publishes the message and signature together, anyone can be convinced that the signer generated the signature. It does not satisfy the non-transferability. There seems no secure convertible limited verifier signature scheme to the best of our knowledge.

In this paper, we first present the precise definition and clear security notions for (convertible) limited verifier signature. Based on the power of different adversaries, we then propose two efficient (convertible) limited verifier signature schemes from bilinear pairings. Moreover, the conversion of the proposed limited verifier signature schemes does not need the cooperation of the original signer.

The rest of the paper is organized as follows: Some preliminary works are given in Section 2. In Section 3, the precise definition and notions of security for

---

[*] Convertible limited verifier signature is different from the notion of converted undeniable signature, where only the signer can release some information to convert his originally undeniable signature into an ordinary one.

limited verifier signature are presented. Our efficient limited verifier signature schemes from bilinear pairings are given in Section 4. In Section 5, the security and efficiency analysis of our schemes are given. Finally, conclusions will be made in Section 6.

2   Preliminary Works

In this section, we will briefly describe the basic definition and properties of bilinear pairings and gap Diffie-Hellman group.

2.1   Bilinear Pairings

Let G_1 be a cyclic additive group generated by P, whose order is a prime q, and G_2 be a cyclic multiplicative group of the same order q. Let a and b be elements of Z_q^*. We assume that the discrete logarithm problems (DLP) in both G_1 and G_2 are hard. A bilinear pairing is a map $e : G_1 \times G_1 \to G_2$ with the following properties:

1. Bilinear: $e(aP, bQ) = e(P, Q)^{ab}$.
2. Non-degenerate: There exists P and $Q \in G_1$ such that $e(P, Q) \neq 1$.
3. Computable: There is an efficient algorithm to compute $e(P, Q)$ for all $P, Q \in G_1$.

2.2   Gap Diffie-Hellman Group

Let G_1 be a cyclic additive group generated by P, whose order is a prime q. Assume that the inversion and multiplication in G_1 can be computed efficiently. We introduce the following problems in G_1.

1. Discrete Logarithm Problem (DLP): Given two elements P and Q, to find an integer $n \in Z_q^*$, such that $Q = nP$ whenever such an integer exists.
2. Computation Diffie-Hellman Problem (CDHP): Given P, aP, bP for $a, b \in Z_q^*$, to compute abP.
3. Decision Diffie-Hellman Problem (DDHP): Given P, aP, bP, cP for $a, b, c \in Z_q^*$, to decide whether $c \equiv ab \bmod q$.
4. Bilinear Diffie-Hellman Problem (BDHP): Given P, aP, bP, cP for $a, b, c \in Z_q^*$, to compute $W = e(P, P)^{abc} \in G_2$.

We call G_1 a gap Diffie-Hellman group if DDHP can be solved in polynomial time but there is no polynomial time algorithm to solve CDHP with non-negligible probability. Such group can be found in supersingular elliptic curve or hyperelliptic curve over finite field, and the bilinear pairings can be derived from the Weil or Tate pairings. For more details, see [3,7,14,19].

3   Limited Verifier Signature (LVS) Scheme

3.1   Precise Definition

The limited verifier signature scheme involves a signer, a limited verifier (the designated recipient of the signature) and a certain third party (the Judge). It consists of six algorithms and a specific protocol.

- **System Parameters Generation:** on input a security parameter k, outputs the common system parameters SP.
- **Key Generation:** on input the common system parameters SP, outputs a secret/public key pair (sk, pk) for each user.
- **Limited Verifier Signing:** on input the key pair (sk_s, pk_s) of the signer, message m and the public key pk_v of the limited verifier, outputs a limited verifier signature σ.
- **Limited Verifier Verification:** on input the key pair (sk_v, pk_v) of the limited verifier, the public key pk_s of the signer, and a limited verifier signature σ, outputs a verification decision $b \in \{0, 1\}$. If $b = 1$, the verifier accepts the signature.
- **Confirmation Protocol:** a protocol between the limited verifier and a third party such as a Judge. The limited verifier provides a proof to convince the third party that a signature is indeed generated by a certain signer while the third party cannot transfer this proof to convince any other party even he can always eavesdrop the information between the signer and the limited verifier.
- **Convertible Limited Verifier Signing:** on input the secret key sk_v of the limited verifier, the public key pk_s of the signer, the message m and a limited verifier signature σ, outputs a convertible limited verifier signature σ'.
- **Public Verification:** on input the public key pk_v of the limited verifier, the public key pk_s of the signer, the message m and a convertible limited verifier signature σ', outputs a verification decision $b \in \{0, 1\}$. If $b = 1$, anyone can be convinced that the signer indeed generated the signature σ' for the message m.

3.2   Adversarial Model

The only assumption in the LVS scheme is that the limited verifier will try his best to preserve the signer's privacy unless the signer violates some rules or an emergency occurs. But the limited verifier should never be able to forge a signature of the signer to frame him. Therefore, "unforgeability" is the basic cryptographic requirement of LVS scheme. There are three kind of forgers in LVS scheme: "limited verifier", "outsiders" and "colluders". In the proposed schemes, we only consider the strongest adversarial model for unforgeability: an adversary can collude with the limited verifier.

On the other hand, an adversary should not be able to forge a proof to convince any other party that the signer indeed generated a signature. "Non-transferability" is another basic cryptographic requirement in LVS scheme. Similarly, we think the adversary can collude with the Judge. Also, we suppose the adversary can also eavesdrop all the information between the limited verifier and signer. This is the strongest adversarial model for non-transferability. In this case, the adversary should not collude with the limited verifier anymore because the limited verifier wants to convince only the Judge of the fact.

3.3   Security Requirements

3.3.1 Unforgeability

Similar to universal designated verifier signature scheme, there are two type of unforgeability in LVS scheme. The first is identical to the usual existential unforgeability notion under the chosen message attack. This prevents an adversary to frame the signer by "generating" a signature of the signer. The second requires that it is difficult for an adversary (usually the limited verifier) to forge a proof, which can be used to convince a third party (usually a Judge) that the signer generated a signature for a message. Because LVS scheme should be converted into an ordinary one for public verification when necessary, the limited verifier only forges a proof to frame a signer is meaningless even he can.[2] In this sense, we only consider the first unforgeability in LVS scheme.

Definition 1. *A LVS scheme is said to secure against an existential forgery for adaptive chosen message attack if no polynomial bounded adversary $\mathcal{A}$ win the following game with a non-negligible advantage.*

1. The challenger $\mathcal{C}$ runs the System Parameter Generation algorithm with a security parameter k and sends the system parameters SP to the adversary $\mathcal{A}$.
2. The limited verifier $\mathcal{V}$ runs the Key Generation algorithm to generate his key pair $(pk_{\mathcal{V}}, sk_{\mathcal{V}})$ and publishes $pk_{\mathcal{V}}$. Also, the adversary $\mathcal{A}$ is allowed to access the secret key $sk_{\mathcal{V}}$.
3. The adversary $\mathcal{A}$ performs a polynomial bounded number of queries to challenger $\mathcal{C}$.
4. Finally, the adversary $\mathcal{A}$ outputs a valid message-signature pair (m, s). We said that $\mathcal{A}$ wins the game if m is never queried by $\mathcal{A}$ in step 3.

3.3.2 Non-transferability

The property of non-transferability in LVS scheme can be automatically reduced from universal designated verifier signature scheme.

---

[*] This is different from universal designated verifier signature scheme, where it is enough for the third party to be convinced by such a proof.

Definition 2. *Let $P(\mathcal{V}, \mathcal{J})$ be a protocol between the limited verifier $\mathcal{V}$ and a Judge $\mathcal{J}$. The outputs of $P(\mathcal{V}, \mathcal{J})$ is a proof $\mathcal{P}$ presented by $\mathcal{V}$ which can convince $\mathcal{J}$ the truth of a statement Θ. We said the proof is non-transferable if $\mathcal{J}$ is fully able to generate an indistinguishable proof $\mathcal{P}'$. In this case, no one can be convinced of the truth of a statement Θ even if $\mathcal{J}$ would like to reveal his secret key $sk_{\mathcal{J}}$.*

4 Our Proposed LVS Schemes from Bilinear Pairings

In this section, we propose two efficient LVS schemes from bilinear pairings based on the power of different adversaries. Furthermore, we present a general construction of LVS scheme.

4.1 Our Scheme (I)

– **System Parameters Generation:** Let G_1 be a gap Diffie-Hellman group generated by P, whose order is a prime q, and G_2 be a cyclic multiplicative group of the same order q. A bilinear pairing is a map $e : G_1 \times G_1 \to G_2$. Define two cryptographic hash functions $H_1 : \{0,1\}^l \to G_1$, $H_2 : G_2 \to Z_q$ and $h : \{0,1\}^l \times G_2 \to Z_q$, where l denotes a bound on the message bit-length. The system parameters are $SP = \{G_1, G_2, e, q, P, H_1, H_2, h, l\}$.
– **Key Generation:** The user U randomly chooses $r_U \in_R Z_q^*$ as the secret key and computes the public key $r_U P$.
– **Limited Verifier Signing:** Suppose Alice wants to sign the message m for Bob. She does as follows:
  • Randomly choose a point $Q \in_R G_1$ and compute $c = e(Q, r_A P)$.
  • Compute $s = Q - r_A k H_1(m)$, where $k = h(m, e(Q, P))$.
  • Compute $t = H_2(e(r_A Q, r_B P))^{-1} s$.
  The signature for message m is the pair $S = (c, k, t)$.
– **Limited Verifier Verification:** On receiving the limited verifier signature S, Bob computes:
  • $s = H_2(c^{r_B})t$.
  • $d = e(s, P)e(H_1(m), r_A P)^k$.
  • Output "accept" if and only if $k = h(m, d)$.
– **Confirmation Protocol:** When Alice does not obey some rules, **only** Bob can provide a proof to convince a Judge that Alice indeed signed a message with a confirmation protocol.[3] However, the Judge cannot transfer this proof to convince any other party.
  • Bob computes $a = e(s, r_J P)$.
  • Bob sends (a, d) and the message m to Judge.
  • Let $k = h(m, d)$. Judge computes $l = (d^{r_J}/a)^{k^{-1}}$ and accepts the proof if and only if $l = e(H_1(m), r_A P)^{r_J}$.

. Note that any adversary cannot compute s without the information of r_B even he can eavesdrop all the information between Bob and Alice and Judge unless he can solve CDHP in G. .

Actually, $l = e(r_A H_1(m), r_J P)$, which is a universal designated verifier signature for the message m [26]. Therefore, the Judge will be convinced that Alice signed the message while he cannot transfer this proof to convince any other party.

We explain this in more details. The Judge can simulate Bob to generate an indistinguishable pair (a, d) for any message m as follows:

- He randomly chooses an element $d \in G_2$, and computes $k = h(m, d)$.
- He computes $l = (e(H_1(m), r_A P))^{r_J}$.
- He computes $a = d^{r_J} / l^k$, and outputs (a, d).

- **Convertible Limited Verifier Signing:** In some situations, the limited verifier signature should be converted into an ordinary signature for public verification. In Araiki *et al.*'s scheme, the conversion of the signature requires the cooperation of the original signer. However, it might be unworkable if the signer is unwilling or inconvenient to cooperate. In our scheme, both the signer and limited verifier can convert a limited verifier signature into an ordinary one:

  - Alice (or Bob) publishes the message m and the pair (k, s).

- **Public Verification:** Anyone can be convinced that the signer indeed generated the the signature for the message m:

  - The verifier computes $d = e(s, P)e(H_1(m), r_A P)^k$.
  - Output "accept" if and only if $k = h(m, d)$.

4.2   Our Scheme (II)

In some situations, the message m, *e.g.*, an official document, also should be confidential. Signcryption, firstly introduced by Zheng [29], provides simultaneously both message confidentiality and unforgeablity at a lower computational and communication overhead compare to *Encrypt-and-Sign* method. Signcryption protocol usually should satisfy the property of public verifiability, *i.e.*, if a recipient Bob can recover the signer Alice's signature, anyone can verify the signature based on a given signature scheme.[4] However, in the limited verifier signcryption algorithm, the signature can only be verified by himself even after the recipient recovered the message-signature pair. Also, it should satisfy the property of non-transferability, *i.e.*, the recipient can provide a proof to convince a third party that the signer generated a signature while the third party cannot transfer the proof to convince any other party. Therefore, the signature on the message must be invisible in the ciphertext because the adversary can eavesdrop all the information between the recipient and others. If the adversary knows the signature, the message and the proof, he can convince any party that the signer indeed generated the signature. We will explain this later in more details.

We construct limited verifier signature protocol based on "*Sign-then-Encrypt*" methodology [6]. Without loss of generality, let Alice is the signer and Bob is the recipient (limited verifier).

---

[*] Shin *et al.* [25] defined this "**SIG-verifiability**".

- **System Parameters Generation:** Let G_1 be a gap Diffie-Hellman group generated by P, whose order is a prime q, and G_2 be a cyclic multiplicative group of the same order q. A bilinear pairing is a map $e : G_1 \times G_1 \to G_2$. Define five cryptographic hash functions $H_1 : \{0,1\}^l \to G_1$, $H_2 : G_2 \to Z_q$, $H_3 : Z_q \to G_1$, $H_4 : G_1 \to \{0,1\}^l$, and $h : \{0,1\}^l \times Z_q \to Z_q$, where l denotes a bound on the message bit-length. The system parameters are $SP = \{G_1, G_2, e, q, P, H_1, H_2, H_3, H_4, h, l\}$.

- **Key Generation:** The user U randomly chooses $r_U \in_R Z_q^*$ as his secret key and computes the public key $r_U P$.

- **Limited Verifier Signing (Signcryption):** Suppose Alice wants to sign the message m for Bob. She does as follows:
  - Randomly choose an integer $c \in_R Z_q$ and compute $S = c r_A H_1(m)$.
  - Compute $k = h(m, c)$.
  - Compute $U = H_2(e(r_A P, r_B P)^k) \oplus c$.
  - Compute $V = H_3(c) \oplus S$.
  - Compute $W = H_4(S) \oplus m$.

  The signature for message m is the ciphertext $C = (kP, U, V, W)$.

- **Limited Verifier Verification (Unsigncryption):** On receiving the limited verifier signature C, Bob computes:
  - $c = U \oplus H_2(e(r_A P, kP)^{r_B})$.
  - $S = V \oplus H_3(c)$.
  - $m = W \oplus H_4(S)$.
  - Verify that $kP = h(m, c)P$. If not, output "reject".
  - Output "accept" if and only if $e(S, P)^{c^{-1}} = e(H_1(m), r_A P)$.

- **Confirmation Protocol:** Bob can convince a Judge that Alice indeed signed a message with the following confirmation protocol.[5] From the property of universal designated verifier signature, the Judge cannot transfer this proof to convince any other party.
  - Bob computes $a = e(S, r_J P)^{c^{-1}}$.
  - Bob sends a and the message m to Judge.
  - Judge outputs "accept" if and only if $a = e(H_1(m), r_A P)^{r_J}$.

  Note that the Judge is fully able to generate the indistinguishable proof $e(H_1(m), r_A P)^{r_J}$. Therefore, he cannot use this proof to convince any other party.

- **Convertible Limited Verifier Signing:** Both the signer and limited verifier can convert a limited verifier signature into an ordinary one:
  - Alice (or Bob) publishes the message m and the signature $T = c^{-1} S$.

- **Public Verification:** Anyone can be convinced that the signer indeed generated the the signature for the message m:
  - Outputs "accept" if and only if $e(T, P) = e(H_1(m), r_A P)$.

---

[*] Any adversary cannot compute c to recover $r_A H. (m)$ without the information of r_B even he can eavesdrop all the information between Bob and Alice and Judge unless he can solve BDHP in $G.$.

4.3   Generalization

Our Scheme (II) can be extended to design a general construction of (convertible) limited verifier signature.[6] The signer generates a universal designated verifier signature s on the message m and then encrypts the concatenation of m and s with the limited verifier's public key PK_v by using a semantically secure probabilistic encryption algorithm ENC. The ciphertext $C = \text{ENC}_{PK_v}(m||s)$ is the limited verifier signature for the message m.

The limited verifier decrypts the ciphertext with his secret key and can then designate it to any Judge as in the universal designated verifier signature scheme. For public verification, the limited verifier (or the signer) publishes m and s, and anyone can be convinced that the signer generated the the signature s for the message m.

Recently, Steinfeld et al. [27] extended standard Schnorr/RSA signatures into universal designated verifier signatures. Therefore, we can use the general construction to design (convertible) limited verifier signature scheme without pairings.

5   Analysis of the Proposed Schemes

5.1   Security

Lemma 1. *Under the strongest adversarial model, if an adversary $\mathcal{A}$ in scheme (I) can forge a valid signature (m, c, k, t) with the advantage ε within time T, then he can forge the valid signature (m, c, k, s) with the same advantage ε within time T, and vice versa.*

Proof. Suppose the adversary $\mathcal{A}$ can forge a valid signature (m, c, k, t) with the advantage ε within time T, then he can compute $s = H_2(c^{r_B})t$ since he can access the secret key r_B of the limited verifier Bob, i.e., he can forge the valid signature (m, c, k, s) with the same advantage ε within time T, and vice versa. □

Theorem 1. *In the random oracle, if there exists an adversary $\mathcal{A}$ that can succeed in an existential forgery against the proposed LVS scheme (I) with an advantage ϵ within a time T and when performing n queries on signature oracle and hash oracles h and H_1, then there exists an algorithm $\mathcal{C}$ can solve the CDHP in G_1 with an advantage $\epsilon' \geq \epsilon/n$ within a time $T' \leq 84480nT/\varepsilon$.*

Proof. Let P is a generator of G_1, the following algorithm $\mathcal{C}$ can be used to compute abP for a randomly given triple (P, aP, bP). Define the public key of the signer is aP.

Randomly choose $x_i \in Z_q, y_i \in Z_q$ and $k_i \in Z_q$ for $i = 1, 2, \cdots, n$. Denote by m_i the (partial) input of the i-th query to h and H_1. We show how the queries of $\mathcal{A}$ can be simulated.

---

* An anonymous reviewer suggested the general approach.

Choose an index $r \in \{1, 2, \cdots, n\}$ randomly. Define

$$c_i = e(x_i P, aP)$$

$$h(m_i, e(x_i P, P)) = k_i$$

$$H_1(m_i) = \begin{cases} bP, & \text{if } i = r \\ y_i P, & \text{if } i \neq r \end{cases}$$

$$s_i = \begin{cases} \text{"Fail"}, & \text{if } i = r \\ x_i P - y_i k_i(aP), & \text{if } i \neq r \end{cases}$$

Suppose the output of $\mathcal{A}$ be (m, c, k, s). If $m = m_r$ and (m, c, k, s) is valid, output (m, c, k, s). Otherwise, output "Fail" and halt.

By replays of with the same random tape but different choices of oracle h, as done in the Forking Lemma [23], we can obtain two valid signatures (m, c, k, s) and (m, c, k', s') with respect to different hash oracles h and h'. Note that $s = Q - akH_1(m)$ and $s' = Q - ak'H_1(m)$, we have $abP = (s - s')/(k' - k)$.

Because h and H_1 are the random oracles, the adversary $\mathcal{A}$ cannot distinguish the simulation of algorithm $\mathcal{C}$ from the real signer. Also, since r is independently and randomly chosen, the success of probability of $\mathcal{C}$ is ε/n. The total running time T' of algorithm $\mathcal{C}$ is equal to the running time of the Forking Lemma [23] which is bound by $84480nT/\varepsilon$. □

In our scheme (II), the proposed signcryption algorithm is based on "Sign-then-Encrypt" methodology, which can be viewed as the standard version of Boyen's ID-based signcryption algorithm [6]. Therefore, we have

Theorem 2. *In the random oracle, the proposed signcryption algorithm in our scheme (II) is semantically secure against adaptively chosen ciphertext attacks and unforgeable secure against adaptively chosen message attacks based on the assumption BDHP is intractable.*

Theorem 3. *Our proposed LVS schemes are both satisfy the property of non-transferability based on the assumption of BDHP is intractable.*

Proof. Firstly, the third party can be convinced by the proof that the signer indeed generate a signature. From the result of [26], we know that it is impossible for the limited verifier to forge a universal designated verifier signature to cheat the Judge.

Secondly, the Judge cannot transfer the proof to convince any other party. In scheme (I), the proof is the pair (a, d). We have proved that the Judge is fully able to generate an indistinguishable pair. In scheme (II), the proof is just a universal designated verifier signature. Therefore, the non-transferability of both schemes is obvious. □

5.2   Efficiency

We compare the efficiency of our schemes with that of Araki *et al.*'s scheme. In Table 1, we denote $\mathcal{P}$ the pairings operation, $\mathcal{M}$ the point scalar multiplication in G_1, $\mathcal{E}$ exponentiation in G_2 and $\mathcal{R}$ reversion in Z_q. We ignore other operations such as hash in all schemes.

Table 1. Comparison of computation cost

	Araki's scheme	Our scheme (I)	Our scheme (II)
Signing	$1\mathcal{E} + 2\mathcal{R}$	$2\mathcal{P} + 3\mathcal{M} + 1\mathcal{R}$	$1\mathcal{P} + 2\mathcal{M}$
Verification	$2\mathcal{E} + 1\mathcal{R}$	$2\mathcal{P} + 1\mathcal{M} + 1\mathcal{E}$	$2\mathcal{P} + 1\mathcal{E} + 1\mathcal{R}$
Confirmation	$11\mathcal{E} + 1\mathcal{R}$	$2\mathcal{P} + 2\mathcal{E} + 2\mathcal{R}$	$2\mathcal{P} + 2\mathcal{E}$
Denial	$24\mathcal{E}$	/	/
Convertion	$3\mathcal{E} + 1\mathcal{R}$	$2\mathcal{P} + 1\mathcal{E}$	$2\mathcal{P}$

   In Araki *et al.*'s scheme, both of the confirmation and denial protocol need rounds of interactive communication. However, the confirmation protocol in our schemes is performed in a non-interactive manner. Moreover, our scheme does not require the denial protocol. The Judge can be convinced by a proof that the signer indeed generated a signature. Because the proposed scheme can be converted into an ordinary one for public verification when necessary, the signer cannot repudiate his signature.

   Suppose the length of a point in G_1 is $|q|$, and the length of an element of G_2 and the message m is $|p|$. Table 2 presents the comparison of communication cost between Araki *et al.*'s scheme and ours.

Table 2. Comparison of communication cost

	Araki's scheme	Our scheme (I)	Our scheme (II)
Signing	$1|p| + 1|q|$	$2|p| + 2|q|$	$1|p| + 3|q|$
Confirmation	$3|p| + 3|q|$	$3|p|$	$2|p|$
Denial	$6|p| + 6|q|$	/	/
Convertion	$2|p| + 1|q|$	$1|p| + 2|q|$	$1|p| + 1|q|$

6   Conclusions

The ordinary digital signature provides the functions of integration, authentication, and non-repudiation for the signed message. Anyone can verify the signature with the signer's public key. However, it is unnecessary for anyone to be convinced the validity of the signature in some situations. It is sufficient for a designated recipient, who will try to preserve the signer's privacy if the signer follow some specified rules, to verify the signature. Limited verifier signature was introduced to solve this problem. If the signer violated the rules, the designated recipient (namely, limited verifier) can provide a proof to convince a judge that the signer indeed generated the signature for the message. Also, the limited verifier can also convert the signature into an ordinary one for public verification when necessary. In this paper, we firstly present the precise definition and clear security notions for (convertible) limited verifier signature, and then propose two new (convertible) limited verifier signature schemes from bilinear pairings. Moreover, we proved that our schemes achieved the desired security notions in the random oracle.

In our schemes, the confirmation protocol does not need the interactive communication and the conversion does not need the cooperation of the original signer. Therefore, they are much efficient than previous scheme.

Acknowledgement. The authors are grateful to the anonymous reviewers for their valuable suggestions and comments to this paper. This work was supported by a grant No.R12-2003-004-01004-0 from the Ministry of Science and Technology, Korea.

References

1. S. Araki, S. Uehara, and K. Imamura, *The limited verifier signature and its application*, IEICE Trans. Fundamentals, vol.E82-A, No.1, pp. 63-68, 1999.
2. P.S.L.M. Barreto, H.Y. Kim, B.Lynn, and M.Scott, *Efficient algorithms for pairings-based cryptosystems*, Advances in Cryptology-Crypto 2002, LNCS 2442, pp.354-368, Springer-Verlag, 2002.
3. D. Boneh and M. Franklin, *Identity-based encryption from the Weil pairings*, Advances in Cryptology-Crypto 2001, LNCS 2139, pp.213-229, Springer-Verlag, 2001.
4. D. Boneh, B. Lynn, and H. Shacham, *Short signatures from the Weil pairings*, Advances in Cryptology-Asiacrypt 2001, LNCS 2248, pp.514-532, Springer-Verlag, 2001.
5. D. Boyar, D. Chaum, and D. Damgård, *Convertible undeniable signatures*, Advances in Cryptology-Crypto 1990, LNCS 537, pp.183-195, Springer-Verlag, 1991.
6. X. Boyen, *Multipurpose identity-based signcryption: a Swiss army knife for identity-based cryptography*, Advances in Cryptology-Crypto 2003, LNCS 2729, pp.382-398, Springer-Verlag, 2003.
7. J.C. Cha and J.H. Cheon, *An identity-based signature from gap Diffie-Hellman groups*, Public Key Cryptography-PKC 2003, LNCS 2567, pp.18-30, Springer-Verlag, 2003.
8. D. Chaum, *Designated confirmer signatures*, Advances in Cryptology-Eurocrypt 1994, LNCS 950, pp.86-91, Springer-Verlag, 1994.
9. D. Chaum, *Zero-knowledge undeniable signatures*, Advances in Cryptology-Eurocrypt 1990, LNCS 473, pp.458-464, Springer-Verlag, 1991.
10. D. Chaum and H. van Antwerpen, *Undeniable signatures*, Advances in Cryptology-Crypto 1989, LNCS 435, pp.212-216, Springer-Verlag, 1989.
11. D. Chaum and T.P. Pedersen, *Wallet databases with observers*, Advances in Cryptology-Crypto 1992, LNCS 740, pp.89-105, Springer-Verlag, 1993.
12. Y. Desmedt, C. Goutier, and S. Bengio, *Special uses and abuses of the Fiat-Shamir passport protocol*, Advances in Cryptology-Crypto 1987, LNCS 293, pp.21-39, Springer-Verlag, 1988.

13. Y. Desmedt and M. Yung, *Weaknesses of undenaiable signature schemes*, Advances in Cryptology-Eurpcrypt 1991, LNCS 547, pp.205-220, Springer-Verlag, 1992.
14. S. D. Galbraith, K. Harrison, and D. Soldera, *Implementing the Tate pairings*, ANTS 2002, LNCS 2369, pp.324-337, Springer-Verlag, 2002.
15. S. Galbraith, W. Mao, and K. G. Paterson, *RSA-based undeniable signatures for general moduli*, Advances in CT-RSA 2002, LNCS 2271, pp.200-217, Springer-Verlag, 2002.
16. S. Galbraith and W. Mao, *Invisibility and anonymity of undeniable and confirmer signatures*, Advances in CT-RSA 2003, LNCS 2612, pp.80-97, Springer-Verlag, 2003.
17. S. Gennaro, H. Krawczyk, and T. Rabin, *RSA-based undeniable signatures*, Advances in Cryptology-Crypto 1997, LNCS 1294, pp.132-149, Springer-Verlag, 1997.
18. C. Gentry and A. Silverberg, *Hierarchical ID-Based Cryptography*, Advances in Cryptology-Asiacrypt 2002, LNCS 2501, pp.548–566, Springer-Verlag, 2002.
19. F. Hess, *Efficient identity based signature schemes based on pairingss*, Proc. 9th Workshop on Selected Areas in Cryptography-SAC 2002, LNCS 2595, Springer-Verlag, pp.310-324, 2002.
20. M. Jakobsson, *Blackmailing using undeniable signatures*, Advances in Cryptology-Eurocrypt 1994, LNCS 950, pp.425-427, Springer-Verlag, 1994.
21. M. Jakobsson, K. Sako, and R. Impagliazzo, *Designated verifier proofs and their applications*, Advances in Cryptology-Eurocrypt 1996, LNCS 1070, pp.143-154, Springer-Verlag, 1996.
22. B. Libert and J. Quisquater, *ID-based undeniable signatures*, Advances in CT-RSA 2004, LNCS 2694, pp.112-125, Springer-Verlag, 2004.
23. D. Pointcheval and J. Stern, *Security arguments for digital signatures and blind signatures*, Journal of Cryptography, Vol.13, No.3, pp.361-396, Springer-Verlag, 2000.
24. T. Wu and C. Hsu, *Convertible authenticated encryption scheme*, The Journal of Systems and Software, Vol.62, No.3, pp.205-209, 2002.
25. J. Shin, K. Lee, and K. Shim, *New DSA-verifiable signcryption schemes*, ICISC 2002, LNCS 2587, pp.35-47, Springer-Verlag, 2003.
26. R. Steinfeld, L. Bull, H. Wang, and J. Pieprzyk, *Universal designated-verifier signatures*, Advances in Cryptology-Asiacrypt 2003, LNCS 2894, pp.523-542, Springer-Verlag, 2003.
27. R. Steinfeld, H. Wang, and J. Pieprzyk, *Efficient extension of standard Schnorr/RSA signatures into universal designated-verifier signatures*, Public Key Cryptography-PKC 2004, LNCS 2947, pp.86-100, Springer-Verlag, 2004.
28. F. Zhang and K. Kim, *A universal forgery on Araki et al.'s convertible limited verifier signature scheme*, IEICE Trans. Fundamentals, vol.E86-A, No.2, pp. 515-516, 2003.
29. Y. Zheng, *Digital signcryption or how to achieve cost (signature & encryption) << cost (signature)+ cost (encryption)*, Advances in Cryptology-Crypto 1997, LNCS 1294, pp.165-179, Springer-Verlag, 1997.

Deniable Ring Authentication Revisited

Willy Susilo and Yi Mu

Centre for Information Security Research
School of Information Technology and Computer Science
University of Wollongong
Wollongong 2522, AUSTRALIA
{wsusilo,ymu}@uow.edu.au

Abstract. Ring signatures allow a signer in an ad-hoc group to authenticate a message on behalf of the group without revealing which member actually produced the signature [8]. Recently, this notion has been extended by Naor by introducing *Deniable Ring Authentication*: it is possible to convince a verifier that a member of an ad-hoc subset of participants is authenticating a message without revealing which member has issued the signature, and the verifier V cannot convince any third party that message m was indeed authenticated. Unfortunately, the scheme proposed in [7] requires an *interactive* protocol, which requires an assumption that an anonymous routing channel (eg. MIX-net) exists. Having this restriction, the primitive cannot be used in practice without the existence of the anonymous routing channel. In this paper, we introduce a non-interactive version of deniable ring authentication. This work proposes a deniable ring authentication without any interactive protocol required (cf. [7]). We present a generic construction that can convert *any* existing ring signature schemes to deniable ring authentication schemes. Our generic construction combines *any* ring signature scheme with an ID-based chameleon hash function. We also present three ID-based chameleon hash functions and show that our schemes outperform the construction proposed in [2].

1 Introduction

A ring signature scheme [8] can be used to convince a verifier that a document is legally signed by one of the n possible independent signers without revealing the identity of the signer. This signature scheme can be seen as a simple group signature scheme that has no group manager who can revoke the identity of the signer in the case of forgery. To produce a ring signature, the signer constructs an ad-hoc collection of signers that includes himself, and computes the signature entirely by himself using only secret key and the others' public keys. This primitive is formalized by Rivest, Shamir and Tauman in [8], and the construction presented in [8] is based on RSA.

In [1], Abe, Ohkubo and Suzuki presented a scheme to use public-keys of several different signature schemes (that are based on discrete logarithm problem

M. Jakobsson, M. Yung, J. Zhou (Eds.): ACNS 2004, LNCS 3089, pp. 149–163, 2004.

and/or factorization) to generate a ring signature scheme (that they call 1-out-of-n signature scheme). Unlike the previous construction, their contribution allows a mixture of DL-type keys and RSA-type keys in the ring signature construction.

Recently, Naor extended this work to introduce a new primitive called *Deniable Ring Authentication* [7]. Deniable Ring Authentication allows a signer, who forms an ad-hoc collection of participants, to convince a single verifier, V, that a member of an ad-hoc group is authenticating a message m, without revealing which one. Moreover, the verifier V cannot convince any third party that message m was indeed authenticated. This is done by showing that the verifier V could have produced such signature by himself, without any interaction with the signers.

The primitive introduced in [7] is particularly useful in the case where the signer would like to *designate* his authenticated message to a particular verifier. The construction provided in [7] is based on the assumption that users have public-keys of some good encryption schemes. However, the drawbacks of the presented scheme are as follows. Firstly, the scheme requires an interactive zero knowledge protocol. It is assumed that an anonymous channel routing (eg. MIX-net) exists and can be used. Secondly, the message size is longer compared to a normal ring signature. This is due to the interactivity required in the protocol.

In this paper, we provide a generic construction for Deniable Ring Authentication that does not require any interaction. We provide a generic construction for Deniable Ring Authentication that is non-interactive. By removing the interactivity of the protocol, the primitive can be used more widely in practice (cf. [7]).

1.1 Related Work

In [8], the definition of *ring signatures* was formalized and an efficient scheme based on RSA was proposed. A ring signature scheme is based on trapdoor one-way permutations and an ideal block cipher that is regarded as a perfectly random permutation. A ring signature scheme allows a signer who knows at least one secret information (or trapdoor information) to produce a sequence of n random permutations and form them into a ring. This signature can be used to convince any third party that one of the participants in the group (who knows the trapdoor information) has authenticated the message on behalf of the group. The authentication provides *signer ambiguity*, in the sense that no one can identify who has actually signed the message.

In [1], a method to construct a ring signature from different types of public keys, such as these for integer factoring based schemes and discrete log based schemes, was proposed. The proposed scheme is more efficient than [8]. The formal security definition of a ring signature is also defined in [1].

Dwork, Naor and Sahai proposed *deniable authentication* in [5]. Deniable authentication provides a system that addresses the deniability aspects, i.e. the protocol does not leave any paper trail for the authentication of the message. This work allows a single signer to achieve this property.

In [7], the notion of ring signatures was combined with deniable authentica-ton [5]. The result is called *Deniable Ring Authentication* that allows a signer to authenticate a message m on behalf of an ad hoc collection of users and to con-vince a verifier that this authentication is done correctly. Moreover, the verifier cannot convince any third party that the message m was indeed authenticated. There is no 'paper trail' of the conversation, other than what could be produced by the verifier alone, as in zero-knowledge [7]. However, the verification is done interactively, and hence, the requirement of having an anonymous routing, such as MIX-nets, is essential. Moreover, as a result of the requirement of this new notion, the message size is longer compared to a normal ring signature.

In [11], we constructed a non-interactive version of deniable ring authenti-cation scheme. The scheme uses a combination of a ring signature scheme and a chameleon hash function. However, we assume that the verifier has setup a chameleon hash function before a message can be sent to him/her, and this is certainly not practical.

Our Contributions

Essentially, we provide a generic construction for non-interactive deniable au-thentication schemes. Our schemes follow all the requirements defined in [7], but there is no interactivity involved. The recipient of the deniable ring au-thentication can verify the correctness of an authenticated message without any interaction with the ad-hoc signers. This will certainly improve the usage of de-niable ring authentication in practice. The size of the our signature scheme is the same as the original ring signature scheme together with a random number. This is significantly shorter compared to the previous construction in [7]. Our scheme is an ID-based scheme, which means that the only requirement for the verifier (or signature recipient) is to have his ID (such as email address, a per-son's address, etc) published. We assume that there is a trusted authority TA, that is only required when the verifier wants to generate his secret key based on his ID. We note that this assumption always exists in ID-based cryptography, as pointed out in its seminal paper in [10]. As pointed out in [7], the verifier V does not necessary have to setup his public-private key before a signer (on behalf of an ad-hoc group) decides to send him a message. Based on our generic construction, we can convert *any* ring signature schemes to deniable ring authen-tication schemes. We note that as in any other ID based system, our scheme is very applicable in a closed network [10] where a TA trusted by all participants exists.

The rest of this paper is organized as follows. In the next section, we will review some cryptographic tools that are required in this paper. In section 3, we present three constructions of ID-based Chameleon Hashing that are based on the difficulty of factorization problem. We evaluate the efficiency of our schemes and show that they are more efficient than the scheme proposed in [2]. In section 4, we present our generic construction for deniable ring authentication schemes that do not require any interaction with the signers to verify the authenticity of the message. We also present an example of such construction in the same section. Section 5 concludes the paper.

2   Cryptographic Tools

2.1   Chameleon Hashing and ID-Based Chameleon Hashing

Chameleon hashing (or *trapdoor commitment*) is basically non-interactive commitment schemes as proposed by Brassard, Chaum and Crepeau [3]. The idea of chameleon hash functions was introduced and formalized in [6] in the construction of their chameleon signature schemes. The name "chameleon" refers to the ability of the owner of the trapdoor information to change the input to the function to any value of his choice without changing the resulting output.

A chameleon hash function is associated with a pair of public and private keys and has the following properties [6]: (1) Anyone who knows the public key can compute the associated hash function. (2) For people who do not have the knowledge of the trapdoor (i.e. the secret key), the hash function is collision resistant: it is infeasible to find two inputs which are mapped to the same output. (3) The trapdoor information's holder can easily find collisions for every given input.

Several constructions of chameleon hashing have been proposed in [6], which are based on discrete log and [4], which is based on the hardness of deciding whether an element is a "small" e-th residue modulo N^2.

The idea of chameleon hashing has been extended in [2] to construct an Identity-based chameleon hash. An ID-based chameleon hash scheme is defined by a family of efficiently computable algorithms (Setup, Extract, Hash, Forge) as follows.

- Setup: A probabilistic algorithm that is run by a trusted authority TA to generate a pair of keys $\mathcal{SK}$ and $\mathcal{PK}$ defining the scheme. TA publishes $\mathcal{PK}$ and keeps $\mathcal{SK}$ secret.
- Extract: A deterministic algorithm that accepts $\mathcal{SK}$ and an identity string ID and outputs the trapdoor information $\mathcal{T}$ associated with the identity ID.
- Hash: A probabilistic algorithm that accepts $\mathcal{PK}$, an identity string ID and a message m to produce a hash value h.
- Forge: An algorithm that, on input $\mathcal{PK}$, an identity string ID, the trapdoor information $\mathcal{T}$ associated with ID, a message m', and a hash value $h = $ Hash$(\mathcal{PK}, \mathsf{ID}, m')$, outputs a sequence of random bits that correspond to a valid computation of Hash$(\mathcal{PK}, \mathsf{ID}, m')$ yielding a collision on the same target value h.

Related to this definition is the notion of *collision forgery* defined [2] as follows.

Definition 1. *A collision forgery strategy is a probabilistic algorithm that given identity string* ID, *a message* m *and random bits* r, *outputs another message* m' *and random bits* r', *where* $m \neq m'$ *and* $r \neq r'$, *such that* Hash$(\mathsf{ID}, m, r) = $ Hash(ID, m', r') *with non-negligible probability.*

A hashing scheme is said to be *secure against existential collision forgery by passive attacks* if no collision-forgery strategy against it exists.

The semantic security for chameleon hashing scheme is defined as follows [2].

Definition 2. *The chameleon hashing scheme is said to be semantically secure if for all identity strings* ID *and all pairs of messages* (m, m'), *the probability distributions of the random variables* $\mathsf{Hash}(\mathsf{ID}, m, r)$ *and* $\mathsf{Hash}(\mathsf{ID}, m', r')$ *are computationally indistinguishable.*

In [2], an ID-based chameleon hash function based on factorization is proposed. It is also shown an application of ID-based chameleon hash function for a sealed-bid auction system.

2.2 Ring Signature Schemes

For convenience of presentation, we review ring signature schemes in this section. We use the notation proposed in [1] to define ring signature schemes. We note that the ring signature schemes are referred to 1-out-of-n in [1].

Definition 3. *[1] A ring signature scheme consists of three polynomial time algorithms*

- $(s_k, p_k) \leftarrow \mathcal{G}(1^\kappa)$: *A probabilistic algorithm that takes security parameter κ and outputs private key s_k and public key p_k.*
- $\sigma \leftarrow \mathcal{S}(m, s_k, L)$: *A probabilistic algorithm that takes a message m, a list L that contains public keys including the one that corresponds to s_k and outputs a signature σ.*
- {**True** *or* $\perp$} $\leftarrow \mathcal{V}(m, \sigma, L)$: *A deterministic algorithm that takes a message m and a signature σ, and outputs either* **True** *or* $\perp$ *meaning accept or reject, respectively. It is required to have* **True** $\leftarrow \mathcal{V}(m, \mathcal{S}(m, s_k, L), L)$ *with an overwhelming probability.*

A ring signature scheme that allows a mixture of factorization and discrete log based public keys has been constructed in [1].

2.3 Deniable Ring Authentication

The notion of *deniable ring authentication* is formalized in [7]. The setup and requirements of a deniable ring authentication scheme is summarized as follows.
Setup. We assume that the participants have published their public keys. The public keys are generated via a standard public key generation algorithm. We define the *ring* as follows.

A ring $\mathbb{S}$ contains any subset of participants. An authenticator $\mathsf{S}_i \in \mathbb{S}$ can sign on behalf of $\mathbb{S}$. The verifier of a message, V, is an arbitrary party. We require that $\mathsf{V} \not\subset \mathbb{S}$. We assume that both verifier and the authenticator have access to the public keys of all members $\mathsf{S}_i \subset \mathbb{S}$. The verifier V can verify an authenticated message. In Naor's construction in [7], the verification must be done interactively with the help of the ad-hoc group $\mathbb{S}$. However, as we will show in this paper, we can remove this requirement by allowing the verifier V to test the authenticity of the signature by himself.

In the following definition, we denote $< s_{k_i}, p_{k_i} >$ as a pair of secret and public key according to a specific algorithm, that is owned by S_i. A deniable authentication scheme consists of the following algorithms:

- DeniableSign(m, s_k, L, V): is a probabilistic polynomial time algorithm that takes a message $m \in \{0, 1\}^*$ and a list L that contains a set of public keys, including the one that corresponds to the secret key, s_k, and outputs a signature σ, that can only be verified by V.
- DeniableVerify(m, σ, L): is a deterministic non-interactive polynomial-time algorithm that takes a message m, a signature σ and a list of public keys L, and outputs either True or $\perp$ meaning accept or reject, respectively. We require that

$$\Pr \left(\begin{matrix} \{m, \sigma, L\} : \sigma \leftarrow \text{DeniableSign}(m, s_k, L, \mathsf{V}); \\ \text{True} \leftarrow \text{DeniableVerify}(m, \sigma, L) \end{matrix} \right) = 1.$$

L includes public keys based on different security parameters, and the security of DeniableSign (m, s_k, L, V) is set to the smallest one among them. L can include several types of public-keys at the same time, such as for RSA and Schnorr in a particular construction.

We note that the verifier V cannot convince any other third party about the authenticity of the message because he can always forge the signature by creating the required proof in the verification by himself [7].

As presented in [7], the verification requires V to interact with the ad-hoc group of participants to test the authenticity of the message. This restriction requires an existence of an anonymous routing channel [7]. The purpose of this work is to remove this requirement and to allow V to verify the authenticity of the signature without any communication with S.

Intuitively, our idea is to *combine* any ring signature scheme with an ID-based chameleon hash function to obtain a deniable ring authentication scheme. In the following section, we will present three novel constructions of ID-based chameleon hash functions, that are based on the hardness of factorization problem, and we will proceed with our generic construction for deniable authentication schemes in section 4.

3   Three Constructions of ID-Based Chameleon Hash Schemes Based on Factorization

In this section, we will present three ID-based chameleon hash functions. We will also show that our schemes are more efficient than the one proposed in [2]. The settings for the three ID-based chameleon hash functions are as follows.

Model
We assume there is a trusted authority TA which exists to assist the receiver to "extract" his secret key whenever needed. As noted in [10], the existence of TA can be completely removed after this process. Let ID denote an identity

string associated to some party. We note that this ID can be an email address, a person's address, etc. that can uniquely determine the party [10]. Let $\mathcal{H}_{ID}$ be a secure public one way hash function (for instance, the hash function as defined and used in the ID-based signature scheme in [10]) or a public secure hash-and-encode scheme (eg. EMSA-PSS encoding defined in [9]).

3.1   Scheme 1: An ID-Based Chameleon Hash Based on Factorization

Setup: Following the above setting, the TA generates two safe prime numbers p and q (where $p = 2p' + 1, q = 2q' + 1$, and p', q' are also prime) and computes $n = pq$. Then, he selects a random element $\alpha \in \mathbb{Z}_n^*$, where $ord_n(\alpha) = p'q'$. The public key $\mathcal{PK}$ is (n, α). TA's secret key $\mathcal{SK}$ is (p, q).

Extract: To extract his secret key, a party obtains his identity ID and applies the public hash function $\mathcal{H}_{ID}$ to obtain $Q_{ID} = \mathcal{H}_{ID}(ID)$. The secret key is extracted as $\mathcal{T} = \alpha^{Q_{ID}^{-1}}$ (mod n). Note that this value can only be computed by TA who knows the factorization of n, because Q_{ID}^{-1} is computed modulo $\phi(n)$.

Hash: The Hash($\cdot$) algorithm is defined as

$$\mathcal{H}(ID, m, r) = \alpha^{h(m)} r^{Q_{ID}} \pmod{n}$$

where $h(\cdot)$ is a secure hash function and $Q_{ID} = \mathcal{H}_{ID}(ID)$.

Forge: The Forge algorithm is defined as follows.

$$\text{Forge}(ID, Q_{ID}, m, r, h, m') = r' = \mathcal{T}^{h(m) - h(m')} r \pmod{n}.$$

Completeness. The completeness of the Forge algorithm is justified as follows.

$$\begin{aligned}
\text{Hash}(ID, m', r') &= \alpha^{h(m')} (r')^{Q_{ID}} \pmod{n} \\
&= \alpha^{h(m')} \left\{ \mathcal{T}^{h(m) - h(m')} r \right\}^{Q_{ID}} \pmod{n} \\
&= \alpha^{h(m')} \left\{ \alpha^{Q_{ID}^{-1}(h(m) - h(m'))} r \right\}^{Q_{ID}} \pmod{n} \\
&= \alpha^{h(m')} \left\{ \alpha^{(h(m) - h(m'))} r^{Q_{ID}} \right\} \pmod{n} \\
&= \alpha^{h(m)} r^{Q_{ID}} \pmod{n} \\
&= \text{Hash}(ID, m, r).
\end{aligned}$$

We note that the owner of the secret key can always produce a collision in the hash function with an overwhelming probability. $\diamond$

Security Analysis
As noted in [2], we need to show the following security requirement.

Theorem 1. *Our first ID-based chameleon hash function is resistant to forgery, assuming that RSA signature scheme is resistant.*

Proof. We will prove our argument with a contradiction. Firstly, we assume there is an algorithm $\mathcal{F}$ that can produce a collision for our first ID-based chameleon hash function without the knowledge of the trapdoor information $\mathcal{T}$, and we will build an algorithm $\mathcal{A}$ that uses $\mathcal{F}$ to generate an RSA signature without the trapdoor information. The algorithm $\mathcal{F}$ can produce a collision such that

$$\mathsf{Hash}(\mathsf{ID}, m, r) = \mathsf{Hash}(\mathsf{ID}, m', r')$$

for a given $c = \mathsf{Hash}(\mathsf{ID}, m, r)$, a pair of messages (m, m') and a random number r. We build the algorithm $\mathcal{A}$ as follows.

- Run algorithm $\mathcal{F}$ given (c, m, m', r) to produce $r' \neq r$.
- From this collision, $\alpha^{h(m)}(r)^{\mathsf{Q}_{\mathsf{ID}}} = \alpha^{h(m')}(r')^{\mathsf{Q}_{\mathsf{ID}}}$ (mod n) holds. That means, $(r/r')^{\mathsf{Q}_{\mathsf{ID}}} = \alpha^{h(m')-h(m)}$ (mod n).
- From the above knowledge, we can compute $(r/r') = \left(\alpha^{(h(m')-h(m))\mathsf{Q}_{\mathsf{ID}}^{-1}}\right)$ (mod n), which was assumed to be infeasible without the knowledge of the factorization of n.

We note that by running our algorithm $\mathcal{A}$, we have successfully "extract" an RSA signature on $\alpha^{h(m')-h(m)}$ (with a "public key" Q_{ID} associated with n) without the knowledge of the factorization of n. This result contradicts with the assumption that it is infeasible to compute an RSA signature on a message without the knowledge of the factorization of n (the difficulty of finding the e-th root modulo n). $\diamond$

3.2   Scheme 2: An ID-Based Chameleon Hash Based on RSA

In this section, we design an ID-based chameleon hash function based on RSA. Essentially, this construction simplifies the construction proposed in [2]. We note that our construction is inspired by Shamir's ID based signature scheme proposed in [10]. The Setup and Extract algorithms follow the same setting as the construction in [10].

Setup: The TA generates two safe prime numbers p and q (where $p = 2p' + 1, q = 2q' + 1$, and p', q' are also prime). Then, he generates an RSA-key pair (e, d), where $d = e^{-1}$ (mod $4p'q'$), together with computing $n = pq$. The published values, $\mathcal{PK}$, are (e, n), and d is kept secret by TA (as TA's $\mathcal{SK}$). We note that in several occasions, we also would like to keep p and q as part of the secret information (eg. to make the computation faster with Chinese Remainder Theorem).

Extract: To extract his secret key, a party obtains his identity ID and applies the public hash function $\mathcal{H}_{\mathsf{ID}}$ to obtain $\mathsf{Q}_{\mathsf{ID}} = \mathcal{H}_{\mathsf{ID}}(\mathsf{ID})$. The secret key is extracted as $\mathcal{T} = \mathsf{Q}_{\mathsf{ID}}^d$ (mod n). Note that this process can only be performed by TA

who knows the secret key d, under the published public key (e, n). The values p and q are discarded afterwards.

Hash: The Hash($\cdot$) algorithm is defined as follows.

$$\mathsf{Hash}(\mathsf{ID}, m, r) = \mathsf{Q_{ID}}^{h(m)} r^e \pmod{n}$$

where $h(\cdot)$ is a secure hash function, and $\mathsf{Q_{ID}} = \mathcal{H}_{\mathsf{ID}}(\mathsf{ID})$.

Forge: The Forge algorithm is defined as follows.

$$\mathsf{Forge}(\mathsf{ID}, \mathsf{Q_{ID}}, m, r, h, m') = r' = \mathcal{T}^{h(m)-h(m')} r \pmod{n}.$$

Completeness. The completeness of the Forge algorithm for Scheme 2 is justified as follows.

$$
\begin{aligned}
\mathsf{Hash}(\mathsf{ID}, m', r') &= \mathsf{Q_{ID}}^{h(m')} (r')^e \pmod{n} \\
&= \mathsf{Q_{ID}}^{h(m')} \left\{ \mathcal{T}^{h(m)-h(m')} r \right\}^e \pmod{n} \\
&= \mathsf{Q_{ID}}^{h(m')} \left\{ \mathsf{Q_{ID}}^{(h(m)-h(m'))d} r \right\}^e \pmod{n} \\
&= \mathsf{Q_{ID}}^{h(m')} \left\{ \mathsf{Q_{ID}}^{(h(m)-h(m'))} r^e \right\} \pmod{n} \\
&= \mathsf{Q_{ID}}^{h(m)} r^e \pmod{n} \\
&= \mathsf{Hash}(\mathsf{ID}, m, r).
\end{aligned}
$$

$\diamond$

Security Analysis

Theorem 2. *Our ID-based chameleon hash function based on RSA is resistant to forgery, assuming that RSA signature scheme is resistant.*

Proof. We assume there is an algorithm $\mathcal{F}$ that can produce a collision for our ID-based chameleon hash function, without the knowledge of the trapdoor information $\mathcal{T}$. We will construct an algorithm $\mathcal{A}$ that will use the algorithm $\mathcal{F}$ to generate an RSA signature as follows.

We assume that there exists an algorithm $\mathcal{F}$ can produce a collision

$$\mathsf{Hash}(\mathsf{ID}, m, r) = \mathsf{Hash}(\mathsf{ID}, m', r')$$

for a given $c = \mathsf{Hash}(\mathsf{ID}, m, r)$, a pair of messages (m, m') and a random number r. We construct our algorithm $\mathcal{A}$ as follows.

- Run algorithm $\mathcal{F}$ given (c, m, m', r), to produce $r' \neq r$, so that the collision occurs.
- From this collision, we will obtain $\mathsf{Hash}(\mathsf{ID}, m, r) = \mathsf{Hash}(\mathsf{ID}, m', r')$, or $\mathsf{Q_{ID}}^{h(m)} r^e = \mathsf{Q_{ID}}^{h(m')} (r')^e \pmod{n}$.

- From the above equation, we obtain

$$(r/r')^e = \mathsf{Q_{ID}}^{h(m')-h(m)} \pmod{n}.$$

- The above equation will be equivalent to

$$(r/r') = \left\{\mathsf{Q_{ID}}^{h(m')-h(m)}\right\}^d \pmod{n}.$$

- Note that $\left\{\mathsf{Q_{ID}}^{h(m')-h(m)}\right\}^d$ is an RSA signature on $\mathsf{Q_{ID}}^{h(m')-h(m)}$, which is assumed to be infeasible to compute without the knowledge of the trapdoor d.
- Hence, we have successfully "extract" an RSA signature on $\mathsf{Q_{ID}}^{h(m')-h(m)}$ without the knowledge of d.

We note that the success probability of the algorithm $\mathcal{A}$ is the same as the algorithm $\mathcal{F}$. Assuming that RSA is secure, then our ID-based scheme is also secure.   ◇

3.3   Scheme 3: An ID-Based Chameleon Hash Based on Factorization

In this section, we design an ID-based chameleon hash function based on factorization. Unlike the previous two constructions, the TA does not require to keep any information other than the factorization of n as his secret keys, $\mathcal{SK}$.

Setup: The TA generates two safe prime numbers p and q, and compute $n = pq$. The public key $\mathcal{PK}$ is n, and the secret key $\mathcal{SK}$ is (p, q).

Extract: To extract his secret key, a party obtains his identity ID and applies the public hash function $\mathcal{H}_{ID}$ to obtain $\mathsf{Q_{ID}} = \mathcal{H}_{ID}(ID)$. The secret key is extracted as $\mathcal{T} = \mathsf{Q_{ID}}^{\mathsf{Q_{ID}}^{-1}} \pmod{n}$. Note that the computation $\mathsf{Q_{ID}}^{-1}$ is performed under modulo $\phi(n)$ which is infeasible to be performed without the knowledge of the factorization of n.

Hash: The Hash$(\cdot)$ algorithm is defined as follows.

$$\mathcal{H}(ID, m, r) = \mathsf{Q_{ID}}^{h(m)} r^{\mathsf{Q_{ID}}} \pmod{n}$$

where $h(\cdot)$ is a secure hash function, and $\mathsf{Q_{ID}} = \mathcal{H}_{ID}(ID)$.

Forge: The Forge algorithm is defined as follows.

$$\mathsf{Forge}(ID, \mathsf{Q_{ID}}, m, r, h, m') = r' = \mathcal{T}^{h(m)-h(m')} r \pmod{n}.$$

Completeness. The completeness of the Forge algorithm for Scheme 3 is justified as follows.

$$\mathsf{Hash}(ID, m', r') = \mathsf{Q_{ID}}^{h(m')}(r')^{\mathsf{Q_{ID}}} \pmod{n}$$

$$= \mathsf{Q_{ID}}^{h(m')} \left\{ \mathcal{T}^{h(m)-h(m')} r \right\}^{\mathsf{Q_{ID}}} \pmod{n}$$

$$= \mathsf{Q_{ID}}^{h(m')} \left\{ \mathsf{Q_{ID}}^{\mathsf{Q_{ID}}^{-1}(h(m)-h(m'))} r \right\}^{\mathsf{Q_{ID}}} \pmod{n}$$

$$= \mathsf{Q_{ID}}^{h(m')} \left\{ \mathsf{Q_{ID}}^{h(m)-h(m')} r^{\mathsf{Q_{ID}}} \right\} \pmod{n}$$

$$= \mathsf{Q_{ID}}^{h(m)} r^{\mathsf{Q_{ID}}} \pmod{n}$$

$$= \mathsf{Hash}(\mathsf{ID}, m, r).$$

Theorem 3. *Our third scheme is resistant to forgery, assuming that RSA signature scheme is resistant.*

Proof. The proof is very similar to Theorem 1 and Theorem 2. Therefore, we omitted the proof.   ◇

3.4 Efficiency Comparison

In this section we compare efficiency of our proposed schemes with the scheme proposed in [2]. Efficiency of ID-based chameleon hash functions can be measured in terms of the parameters lengths: the length of TA's public key, the length of TA's secret key and the length of recipient's secret key (after Extract). To compare two ID-based chameleon hash functions, we fix the level of security provided by the two schemes and find the size of the three length parameters. Table 1 gives the results of comparison of four ID-based chameleon hash functions. We fix the size of the prime numbers p and q, and without losing generality, assume that their size are equal. Let $\tau = |p|_2 \approx |q|_2$. Therefore, we have $|n|_2 \approx 2\tau$. We assume that the length of the elements to construct the secret/public key parameters are represented by κ. The first scheme refers to the scheme proposed in [2]. We refer this scheme as AM scheme (that stands for "Ateniese-Medeiros" scheme). The next three columns refer to the three schemes presented earlier.

In the scheme proposed in [2], TA's public key $\mathcal{PK}$ is (n, v), where $n = pq$, and v is a random integer. The secret key $\mathcal{SK}$ is (p, q, w), where $vw + z(p-1)(q-1) = 1$. The Hash function is defined as $\mathsf{Hash}(\mathsf{ID}, m, r) = \mathsf{Q_{ID}}^{h(m)} r^v \pmod{n}$. The recipient's secret key is extracted from $\mathsf{Q_{ID}}^w \pmod{n}$.

As shown in Table 1, our schemes outperform the scheme proposed in [2]. In particular, scheme 2 requires the shortest $\mathcal{SK}$ length for the TA and scheme 3 requires TA's $\mathcal{PK} = TA$'s $\mathcal{SK} = $ Recipient's $\mathcal{SK} = 2\tau$.

4   Generic Construction for Deniable Ring Authentication Schemes

In this section, we describe our generic construction for deniable ring authentication schemes. Our construction is based on the ID-based chameleon hash functions $\mathcal{H}_{\mathsf{ID}}(\cdot)$ described in the previous section. Let V_{ID} be the recipient of the deniable ring authentication, who has his identity ID published. The construction is defined as follows.

Table 1. Comparison of Efficiency Parameters

	AM scheme [2]	Scheme 1	Scheme 2	Scheme 3
TA's $\mathcal{PK}$ length	$2\tau + \kappa$	$2\tau + \kappa$	$2\tau + \kappa$	2τ
TA's $\mathcal{SK}$ length	$2\tau + \kappa$	2τ	κ	2τ
Recipient's $\mathcal{SK}$ length	2τ	2τ	2τ	2τ
Hash(ID, m, r) (mod n)	$Q_{\text{ID}}^{h \cdot m \cdot} r^v$	$\alpha^{h \cdot m \cdot} r^{Q_{\text{ID}}}$	$Q_{\text{ID}}^{h \cdot m \cdot} r^e$	$Q_{\text{ID}}^{h \cdot m \cdot} r^{Q_{\text{ID}}}$
Extract($\cdot$) (mod n)	Q_{ID}^w	$\alpha^{Q_{\text{ID}}^{-1}}$	Q_{ID}^d	$Q_{\text{ID}}^{Q_{\text{ID}}^{-1}}$
Underlying hard problem	Factorization	RSA	RSA	Factorization

1. Define:
$$\text{DeniableSign}(m, s_k, L, \mathsf{V_{ID}}) \triangleq \begin{cases} \tilde{h} \leftarrow \mathcal{H}_{\mathsf{V_{ID}}}(\mathsf{ID}, m, r), \text{for a random } r; \\ \sigma_1 \leftarrow \mathcal{S}(\tilde{h}, s_k, L); \\ \sigma \leftarrow (\sigma_1 || r). \end{cases}$$

The signed message is $\sigma \triangleq (m, \sigma)$.
2. Define:
$$\text{DeniableVerify}(m, \sigma, L) \triangleq \begin{cases} (\sigma_1 || r) \leftarrow \sigma; \\ \tilde{h} \leftarrow \mathcal{H}_{\mathsf{V_{ID}}}(\mathsf{ID}, m, r); \\ \text{Result} \leftarrow \mathcal{V}(\tilde{h}, \sigma_1, L). \end{cases}$$

The result of the verification is defined as

$$\text{Result} \leftarrow \text{DeniableVerify}(m, \sigma, L)$$

which is either **True** or $\perp$, meaning **accept** or **reject**, respectively.

Theorem 4. *The resulting signature is non-transferable.*

Proof. We note that the resulting deniable ring authentication does not allow the verifier V to convince any third party about this fact. This is due to the use of ID-based chameleon hash function $\mathcal{H}(\cdot)$. The verifier V can always contact the TA to extract his secret key and execute the **Forge** algorithm to create a valid pair of (m', r'), for $m' \neq m$, that will pass under the ring signature verification algorithm. $\diamond$

Theorem 5. *A signer S can always create an ad-hoc group $\mathbb{S}$ and generate a deniable ring authentication without contacting the verifier V.*

Proof. Due to the use of ID-based chameleon hash function, the verifier does not need to have her public key setup before receiving a message that is signed with a deniable ring authentication scheme. The signer is only required to contact TA if he wants to 'forge' a signature. $\diamond$

We note that an interesting property of the above deniable ring authentication scheme is to allow a signer to form an ad-hoc group and sign on behalf of the group without contacting the verifier. The verifier is only obliged to contact TA if he wants to 'forge' a signature. However, since there is no way to know whether the verifier has contacted TA or not, then the resulting signature cannot be used to convince any other third party (*non-transferability* property).

4.1   Comparison with Other Schemes

In this section, we provide a complete comparison between our scheme and the other deniable authentication schemes, namely RST scheme proposed in [8] (achieved by adding the verifier to the ring) and Naor's scheme proposed in [7]. The result of this comparison is illustrated in Table 2. In the comparison below, we assume that the length of any ring signature scheme is denoted by $|l|_2$. The length of the random number r required in our scheme is denoted by $|r|_2$.

Table 2. Comparison of Deniable Authentication Schemes

	RST Scheme [8]	Naor's Scheme [7]	Our Scheme
Additional Assumption	The verifier V is required to have his public key setup	An anonymous routing channel exists (for interactive protocol)	n/a
Implication of the Assumption	The verifier V can be added to the ring $\mathbb{S}$	An Interactive Protocol	n/a
Requirements	$V \subset \mathbb{S}$	$V \not\subset \mathbb{S}$	$V \not\subset \mathbb{S}$
Protocol	Non interactive	Interactive	Non interactive
Signature Length	$|l|.$	at least $2|l|.$	$|l|. + |r|.$
Size of the ring $\mathbb{S}$	2 (can be extended to n)	n	n

From the comparison table above, we can conclude that our scheme is *the only* scheme that satisfies all the requirements of deniable authentication schemes [7] but without any interactive protocol required. In the scheme proposed in [8], although a non interactive protocol is used, it is assumed that $V \subset \mathbb{S}$, which violates the original assumption proposed in [7]. Our scheme also produces a shorter signature compared to [7].

4.2   An Example

We present a sample conversion of the ring signature scheme proposed in [1] to construct a deniable ring authentication scheme as described in previous section. We will use a ring signature scheme based on RSA proposed in [1], together with our ID-based chameleon hash function based on RSA presented in section 3.2. The ID-based chameleon hash function is defined as

$$\mathsf{Hash}(\mathsf{ID}, m, r) = \mathsf{Q_{ID}}^{h(m)} r^e \pmod{n}.$$

For $i = 0, \cdots, N-1$, let (e_i, n_i) be RSA public keys and $H_i : \{0,1\}^* \to \mathbb{Z}_{n_i}$ be hash functions. Let L be a list of these public-keys. TA has published his public key (e, n) as described in section 3.2. We assume that the verifier V has his ID, ID, published. For simplicity, we also assume a signer S_k would like to send a deniable ring authenticated message to V. Let the size of the ring be N.

A signer S_k who owns the private key d_k generates a signature for a message m as follows.

- Obtain the identity of the recipient, ID, and compute $\mathsf{Q_{ID}} = \mathcal{H}_{\mathsf{ID}}(\mathsf{ID})$.
- Select a random number $r \in \mathbb{Z}_n$ and compute

$$\tilde{h} = \mathsf{Q_{ID}}^{h(m)} r^e \pmod{n}.$$

- Select N random numbers $r_1 \in \mathbb{Z}_{n_1}, \cdots, r_n \in \mathbb{Z}_{n_N}$.
- From r_k, $k \in \{1, \cdots, N\}$, compute $c_{k+1} = H_{k+1}(L, \tilde{h}, r_k)$.
- For $i = k+1, \cdots, N-1, 0, 1, \cdots, k-1$, select $s_i \in \mathbb{Z}_{n_i}$ and compute $c_{i+1} = H_{i+1}(L, \tilde{h}, c_i + s_i^{e_i} \pmod{n_i}))$.
- Compute $s_k = (r_k - c_k)^{d_k} \pmod{n_k}$.

The resulting signature is $(r, c_0, s_1, s_1, \cdots, s_{N-1})$.
To verify a signature, the verifier V performs the following.

- Generate $\mathsf{Q_{ID}} = \mathcal{H}_{\mathsf{ID}}(\mathsf{ID})$ for his ID.
- Compute $\tilde{h} = \mathsf{Q_{ID}}^{h(m)} r^e \pmod{n}$.
- For $i = 0, \cdots, N-1$, compute
  - $r_i = c_i + s_i^{e_i} \pmod{n_i}$;
  - $c_{i+1} = H_{i+1}(L, \tilde{h}, r_i)$ if $i \neq N-1$.
- Accept if $c_0 \stackrel{?}{=} H_0(L, \tilde{h}, r_{n-1})$ holds. Otherwise, reject.

Theorem 6. *The above signature scheme is a non-interactive deniable ring authentication scheme.*

Proof (sketch). The proof can be derived from the use of ID-based chameleon hash function described in section 3.2. The verifier V can contact TA to retrieve his secret key $\mathcal{T}$. Obtaining his secret key, he can select any message $m' \neq m$ and execute the Forge algorithm to retrieve the associated $r' \neq r$ that will pass the verification test. The underlying ring signature used remains the same, and hence, we have obtained a deniable ring authentication scheme.   ◇

5   Conclusions

In this paper, we presented a novel construction of deniable ring authentication scheme that does not require any interaction to verify the authenticity of the message. Our scheme combines *any* ring signature schemes with an ID-based chameleon hash function that allows the resulting signature to be *non-transferable*. In our construction, the verifier V (or the signature recipient) does not necessarily need to retrieve the associated secret key that is related to his published identification, ID, unless he wants to 'forge' a signature. Based on this idea, the resulting signature becomes non-transferable, since any third party cannot determine whether the verifier has retrieved his secret key and produce a collision on the hash function or not. We presented a generic construction of deniable ring authentication schemes. Unlike the construction proposed in [7], our scheme produces a shorter signature size (cf. [7]). We presented three ID-based chameleon hash functions that outperform the construction proposed in [2].

References

1. M. Abe, M. Ohkubo, and K. Suzuki. 1-out-of-n Signatures from a Variety of Keys. *Advances in Cryptology - Asiacrypt 2002, Lecture Notes in Computer Science 2501,* pages 415 – 432, 2002.
2. G. Ateniese and B. de Medeiros. Identity-based Chameleon Hash and Applications. *Financial Cryptography 2004,* 2004 (to appear).
3. G. Brassard, D. Chaum, and C. Crépeau. Minimum Disclosure Proofs of Knowledge. *JCSS, 37(2),* pages 156–189, 1988.
4. D. Catalano, R. Gennaro, N. Howgrave-Graham, and P. Q. Nguyen. Paillier's Cryptosystem Revisited. *ACM CCS 2001,* 2001.
5. C. Dwork, M. Naor, and A. Sahai. Concurrent Zero-Knowledge. *Proc. 30th ACM Symposium on the Theory of Computing,* pages 409–418, 1998.
6. H. Krawczyk and T. Rabin. Chameleon hashing and signatures. *Network and Distributed System Security Symposium, The Internet Society,* pages 143–154, 2000.
7. M. Naor. Deniable Ring Authentication. *Advances in Cryptology - Crypto 2002, Lecture Notes in Computer Science 2442,* pages 481–498, 2002.
8. R. L. Rivest, A. Shamir, and Y. Tauman. How to Leak a Secret. *Advances in Cryptology - Asiacrypt 2001, Lecture Notes in Computer Science 2248,* pages 552–565, 2001.
9. RSA Labs. RSA Cryptography Standard: EMSAPPS - PKCS # 1 v2.1. June 2002.
10. A. Shamir. Identity-based cryptosystems and signature schemes. *Advances in Cryptology - Crypto '84, Lecture Notes in Computer Science 196,* pages 47–53, 1985.
11. W. Susilo and Y. Mu. Non-Interactive Deniable Ring Authentication. *The 6th International Conference on Information Security and Cryptology (ICISC 2003),* pages 397–412, 2003.

A Fully-Functional Group Signature Scheme over Only Known-Order Group

Atsuko Miyaji and Kozue Umeda

1-1, Asahidai, Tatsunokuchi, Nomi, Ishikawa, 923-1292, Japan
{kozueu, miyaji}@jaist.ac.jp

Abstract. The concept of group signature allows a group member to sign message anonymously on behalf of the group. In the event of a dispute, a designated entity can reveal the identity of a signer. Previous group signature schemes use an RSA signature based membership certificate and a signature based on a proof of knowledge(SPK) in order to prove the possession of a valid membership certificate. In these schemes, SPK is generated over an unknown-order group, which requires more works and memory compared with a publicly-known-order group. Recently, a group signature based on a known-order group is proposed. However, it requires an unknown-order group as well as a known-order group. Furthermore, unfortunately, it does not provide the function of revocation. In this paper, we propose the group signature scheme based on only publicly-known-order groups. Our scheme improves the Nyberg-Rueppel signature to fit for generating membership certificates and uses SPKs over a cyclic group whose order is publicly known. As a result, our scheme reduces the size of group signature and the computational amount of signature generation and verification.

1 Introduction

A group signature proposed by Chaum and van Heyst[10], allows a group member to sign messages anonymously on behalf of the group. A group signature has a feature of tracing, that is, the identity of a signer can be revealed by a designated entity in case of dispute. A group signature consists of three entities: group members, a group manager, and an escrow manager. The group manager is responsible for the system setup, registration and revocation of group members. The escrow manager has an ability of revealing the anonymity of signatures with the help of a group manager.

A group signature consists of six functions, setup, registration of a user, revocation of a group member, signature generation, verification, and tracing, which satisfy the following features:

Unforgeability : Only group members are able to generate a signature on a message;

Exculpability : Even if the group manager, the escrow manager, and some of group members collude, they can not generate a signature on behalf of other group members;

M. Jakobsson, M. Yung, J. Zhou (Eds.): ACNS 2004, LNCS 3089, pp. 164–179, 2004.

Anonymity : Nobody can identify a group member who generated a signature
on a message;

Traceability : In the case of a dispute, the identity of a group member is revealed
by the cooperation of both the group manager and the escrow manager;

Unlinkability : Nobody can decide whether or not two signatures have been
issued by the same group member;

Revocability : In the case of withdrawal, the group manager can revoke a member, and a signature generated by the revoked member can not pass the
verification;

Anonymity after revocation : Nobody can identify a group member who generated a signature on a message even after a group member was revoked;

Unlinkability after revocation : Nobody can decide whether or not two signatures have been issued by the same group member even after a group member
was revoked.

The efficiency of a group signature scheme is considered by the size of public key
and signature, the work complexity of signature generation and verification, and
administration complexity of revocation and registration of a group member.

Various group signature schemes have been proposed[5,6,9,8,1,4,16,3,7,2].
These group signature schemes are classified into two types, a *public-key-registration* type, and a *certificate-based* type. In the former type, [5,6] are constructed by using only known-order groups. However, in their schemes, both a
group public key and the signature size depend on the number of group members. It yields a serious problem for large groups. In the latter type, [9,8,1,4,
16,7,3,2] give a membership certificate to group members, and the group signature is based on the zero-knowledge proof of knowledge(SPK) of membership
certificate. Therefore, neither a group public key nor signature size depends on
the number of group members. In these previous certificate-based type group
signature schemes, the membership certificate has used an RSA signature over
an unknown-order group, and, thus, the size of group signature becomes huge.

In this paper, we present an efficient group signature scheme based on a
Nyberg-Rueppel signature. This is the first scheme that is constructed on only
known-order groups and that realizes the full features of unforgeability, exculpability, anonymity, traceability, unlinkability, and revocability. As a result, the
signature size and computation amount of signature generation and verification are reduced. We also give the security proof of membership certificate and
group signature. Furthermore, our scheme also applies the *Certificate Revocation
List(CRL)-based* revocation which proposed by Ateniese and Tsudik[3] with a
slightly few additional work.

This paper is organized as follows. In the next section, we provide an overview
of related work. In Section 2, we summarize some notations and definitions used
in this paper. In Section 3, we propose our new group signature scheme. Section 4
discusses the security of our scheme. Features and efficiency of our scheme are
analyzed in Section 5. Finally, Section 6 concludes our paper.

1.1 Related Work

Various certificate-based type group signature schemes have been proposed in [1,3,4,7,8,9,16]. These schemes are based on the following mechanisms. A user, denoted by M_i, who wants to join the group, chooses a random secret key x_i, and computes $y_i = f(x_i)$, where f is a suitable one-way function. M_i commits to y_i (for instance, M_i signed on y_i) and sends both y_i and the commitment to the group manager denoted by GM, who returns M_i with a membership certificate $cer_i = \mathrm{Sig}_{\mathrm{GM}}(y_i)$. To sign a message m on behalf of the group, M_i encrypts y_i to c_i using the public key of the escrow manager denoted by EM, and generates a signature based on the proof of knowledge which shows the knowledge of both x_i and cer_i such that $cer_i = \mathrm{Sig}_{\mathrm{GM}}(f(x_i))$. The verification is done by checking the signature of knowledge. The escrow manager can easily reveal the anonymity of a group signature by decrypting c_i.

These group signature schemes are classified into two types, a *public-key-registration* type and a *certificate-based* type. Public-key-registration type group signature schemes[5,6] use only known-order groups and can easily realize the revocation by removing the group member's public key. However, both a group public key and the signature size depend on the number of group members. It becomes serious if we apply them on large group. On the other hand, the group signature schemes of certificate-based type must make the member's certificate invalid when they revoke member. However, since the previous schemes [9,8,1, 2] do not provide any function of revocation, they can not realize the feature of revocability. The schemes [4,16,3,7] provide the function of revocation. In Song's scheme[16], a membership certificate is valid for a limited period. Therefore, each group member has to update his/her membership certificate in each time period. Camenisch and Lysyanskaya's scheme[7] needs to update a membership certificate in both cases of registration and revocation. Thus, their scheme requires additional cost to manage the valid member although their verification does not depend on the number of registered or revoked member. Bresson and Stern's scheme[4] uses a CRL to realize revocation. CRL is a public list of information related with revoked-member certificates. This scheme does not have to update a membership certificate, but the size of group signature and the cost of signature generation and verification depends on the number of revoked members. Ateniese and Tsudik proposed quasi-efficient solution for CRL-based revocation[3]. CRL-based revocation scheme is based on the following mechanisms. The group manager computes $V_j = f'(cer_j)$ for each revoked member M_j by using a suitable one-way function f' and publishes V_j together with the current CRL. In the signing phase, a signer M_i also sends $T = f''(f'(cer_i))$ with a signature by using a suitable one-way function f''. In the verification phase, a verifier checks that $T \neq f''(V_j)$ for $^\forall V_j \in \mathcal{CRL}$. The signature size and the cost of signature generation does not depend on the number of revoked members, but the cost of verification depends on the number of revoked members. To sum up, there are certificate-update-based revocation and CRL-based revocation. In the former, the cost of verification does not depend on the number of revoked members, but each group member needs to update a membership certificate. In the latter, each group member does not need to update a membership certificate, but the cost of verification depends on the number of revoked members.

In the certificate-based type group signature schemes, the membership certificate has used an RSA signature over an unknown-order group, and thus the size of group signature becomes huge. Recently, Nyberg-Rueppel signature was applied to a group signature[2]. However, their scheme requires an unknown-order group and must hide the membership certificate by a random value in order to satisfying the feature of anonymity and unlinkability. Thus, although a known-order group is introduced, it suffers from much work complexity and complicated interaction. Furthermore, since it does not provide the function of revocation, much administrative complexity might be required in order to revoke a member.

1.2 Our Contribution

Our proposed scheme is constructed on only known-order groups and that realizes full feature of unforgeability, exculpability, traceability, unlinkability, and revocability. In our scheme, a membership certificate is generated by Nyberg-Rueppel signature, and the features of anonymity and unlinkability are realized by zero-knowledge proof of knowledge which does not have to be hidden by a random value in contrast to [2]. Thus, our group signature is rather simple than [2]. As a result, the signature size and computation amount of signature generation and verification are reduced from [2]. Furthermore, our scheme also provides the CRL-based revocation with a slightly few additional work to group members. We also give the security proof of membership certificate and group signature.

2 Preliminaries

2.1 Notation

In this section, we summarize facts used in this paper. Let the empty string be $\tilde{0}$. For a set A, $a \in_R A$ means that a is chosen randomly and uniformly from A, and $A \setminus \{a\}$ means that $A - \{a\} = \{x \in A | x \neq a\}$. For a group $G \ni g$, $\text{ord}(g)$ means order of g in G. The bit length of a is denoted by $|a|$. Let $c[j]$ be the j-th bit of a string c. We use a collision resistant hash function $\mathcal{H} : \{0,1\}^* \rightarrow \{0,1\}^k$.

2.2 Proof of Knowledge

A signature based on a zero-knowledge proof of knowledge(SPK), denoted by $SPK\{(\alpha_1, \cdots, \alpha_w) : Predicates\}$, is used for proving that a signer knows $\alpha_1, \cdots, \alpha_w$ satisfying $Predicates$. We borrow three SPKs over known-order groups from [11,15,6], SPK of representations and a double discrete logarithm.

Let q, p and $\tilde{p}$ be primes with $q|(p-1)$ and $p|(\tilde{p}-1)$. We use two cyclic groups $\mathbb{G}_p$ of order q with $\mathbb{G}_p \subset \mathbb{Z}_p^*$ and $\mathbb{G}_{\tilde{p}}$ of order p with $\mathbb{G}_{\tilde{p}} \subset \mathbb{Z}_{\tilde{p}}^*$.

Definition 1. *Let* $g_1, \cdots, g_u, y_1, \cdots, y_v \in \mathbb{G}_p$. *An SPK proving the knowledge of representations of* $y_1, \cdots, y_v$ *to the base* $g_1, \cdots, g_u$ *on a message* $m \in \{0,1\}^*$ *is denoted as*

$$SPK\{(\alpha_1, \cdots, \alpha_w) : y_1 = \prod_{j=1}^{J_1} g_{b_{1j}}^{\alpha_{a_{1j}}} \bmod p \wedge \cdots \wedge y_v = \prod_{j=1}^{J_v} g_{b_{vj}}^{\alpha_{a_{vj}}} \bmod p\}(m),$$

where $J_i \in [1, \cdots, u]$ *are the number of bases of* y_i, $a_{ij} \in [1, \cdots, w]$ *are indexes of the elements* $\alpha_{a_{ij}}$, *and* $b_{ij} \in [1, \cdots, u]$ *are indexes of the bases* $g_{b_{ij}}$, *which consists of a set of* $(c, s_1, \cdots, s_w) \in \{0,1\}^k \times \mathbb{Z}_q^w$ *satisfying* $c = \mathcal{H}(g_1 || \cdots || g_u || y_1 || \cdots || y_v ||$ $y^c \prod_{j=1}^{J_1} g_{b_{1j}}^{s_{a_{1j}}} \bmod p || \cdots || y_v^c \prod_{j=1}^{J_v} g_{b_{vj}}^{s_{a_{vj}}} \bmod p || m)$.

If a signer knows $x_1, \cdots, x_w \in \mathbb{Z}_q$ *such that* $y = \prod_{j=1}^{J_1} g_{b_{1j}}^{x_{a_{1j}}} \bmod p, \cdots, y_v = \prod_{j=1}^{J_v} g_{b_{vj}}^{x_{a_{vj}}} \bmod p$, *then a signature on a message* m *can be computed as follows:*

1. choose random exponents $r_d \in \mathbb{Z}_q^*$ for $1 \leq d \leq w$,
2. compute $c = \mathcal{H}(g_1 || \cdots || g_u || y_1 || \cdots || y_v || \prod_{j=1}^{J_1} g_{b_{1j}}^{r_{a_{1j}}} \bmod p || \cdots || \prod_{j=1}^{J_v} g_{b_{vj}}^{r_{a_{vj}}}$ $\bmod p || m)$ and
3. compute $s_d = r_d - c x_d \bmod q$ for $1 \leq d \leq w$.

Definition 2. *Let* $\tilde{g}, \tilde{y} \in \mathbb{G}_{\tilde{p}}$ *and* $g \in \mathbb{G}_p$. *An SPK proving the knowledge of double discrete logarithm of* $\tilde{y}$ *to the base* $\tilde{g}$ *and* g *on a message* $m \in \{0,1\}^*$ *is denoted as*

$$SPK\{(\alpha) : \tilde{y} = \tilde{g}^{g^\alpha} \bmod \tilde{p} \}(m),$$

which consists of a set of $(c, s_1, \cdots, s_k) \in \{0,1\}^k \times \mathbb{Z}_q^k$ *satisfying* $c = \mathcal{H}(g || \tilde{g} || \tilde{y} ||$ $(\tilde{y}^{c[1]} \tilde{g}^{1-c[1]})^{g^{s_1}} \bmod \tilde{p} || \cdots || (\tilde{y}^{c[k]} \tilde{g}^{1-c[k]})^{g^{s_k}} \bmod \tilde{p} || m)$.

A signer who knows the secret key $x \in \mathbb{Z}_q$ with $\tilde{y} = \tilde{g}^{g^x} \bmod \tilde{p}$ can compute a signature $(c, s_1, \cdots, s_k) = SPK\{(\alpha) : \tilde{y} = \tilde{g}^{g^\alpha} \bmod \tilde{p} \}(m)$ on a message m as follows:

1. choose random exponents $r_j \in \mathbb{Z}_q^*$ for $1 \leq j \leq k$,
2. compute $c = \mathcal{H}(g || \tilde{g} || \tilde{y} || \tilde{g}^{g^{r_1}} \bmod \tilde{p} || \cdots || \tilde{g}^{g^{r_k}} \bmod \tilde{p} || m)$, and
3. compute $s_j = r_j - c[j] x \bmod q$ for $1 \leq j \leq k$.

3   Proposed Scheme

We present the group signature scheme based on a Nyberg-Rueppel signature after we define a new SPK and a new problem based on DLP, and modify the Nyberg-Rueppel signature.

3.1   New SPK of a Common Discrete Logarithm over Different Groups

Let us define a new SPK which proves the knowledge of a common discrete logarithm over different groups. Let P be a product pq of prime p and $q|(p-1)$, $\tilde{P}$ be a prime with $P|(\tilde{P}-1)$. We also use two cyclic groups $\mathbb{G}_P$ of order q with $\mathbb{G}_P \subset \mathbb{Z}_P^*$ and $\mathbb{G}_{\tilde{P}}$ of order P with $\mathbb{G}_{\tilde{P}} \subset \mathbb{Z}_{\tilde{P}}^*$.

Definition 3 (SPK of a common discrete logarithm over different groups). *Let* $g, y \in \mathbb{G}_P$ *with* $ord(g) = ord(y)$ *and* $\tilde{g}, \tilde{y} \in \mathbb{G}_{\tilde{P}}$ *with* $ord(\tilde{g}) = ord(\tilde{y})$. *An SPK proving the knowledge of common discrete logarithm of* y *to the base* g *and* $\tilde{y}$ *to the base* $\tilde{g}$ *on a message* $m \in \{0,1\}^*$ *is denoted as*

$$SPK\{(\alpha) : y = g^\alpha \bmod P \ \wedge \ \tilde{y} = \tilde{g}^\alpha \bmod \tilde{P} \ \wedge \ \alpha \in \mathbb{Z}_P \}(m),$$

which consists of a set of $(c, s) \in \{0,1\}^k \times \mathbb{Z}_P$ *satisfying* $c = \mathcal{H}(g\|y\|\tilde{g}\|\tilde{y}\| y^c g^s \bmod P \| \tilde{y}^c \tilde{g}^s \bmod \tilde{P} \| m)$.

If a signer knows such an integer $x \in \mathbb{Z}_P$ that both $y = g^x \bmod P$ and $\tilde{y} = \tilde{g}^x \bmod \tilde{P}$ hold, a signature on a message m corresponding to public keys y and $\tilde{y}$ can be computed as follows:

1. choose a random exponent $r \in \mathbb{Z}_P^*$,
2. compute $c = \mathcal{H}(g\|y\|\tilde{g}\|\tilde{y}\|g^r \bmod P\|\tilde{g}^r \bmod \tilde{P}\|m)$, and
3. compute $s = r - cx \bmod P$.

Lemma 1. *The interactive protocol corresponding to* $SPK\{(\alpha) : y = g^\alpha \bmod P \ \wedge \ \tilde{y} = \tilde{g}^\alpha \bmod \tilde{P} \ \wedge \ \alpha \in \mathbb{Z}_P \}(m)$ *is a honest-verifier perfect zero-knowledge proof of knowledge of common discrete logarithm of* y *to the base* g *and* $\tilde{y}$ *to the base* $\tilde{g}$.

Proof : The proof on the perfect zero-knowledge part is quite standard. We restrict our attention to the proof of knowledge part. By using the fact that the equivalent protocol[15] is a proof of knowledge, it is sufficient to show that the knowledge extractor can compute the witness once he has found two accepting sets (t_1, t_2, c, s) and (t_1, t_2, c', s'). Since both $t_1 = y^c g^s = y^{c'} g^{s'} \pmod{P}$ and $t_2 = \tilde{y}^c \tilde{g}^s = \tilde{y}^{c'} \tilde{g}^{s'} \pmod{\tilde{P}}$ hold, we have $y = g^{\frac{s'-s}{c-c'}} \pmod{P}$ and $\tilde{y} = \tilde{g}^{\frac{s'-s}{c-c'}} \pmod{\tilde{P}}$. From these equations, we have

$$\begin{cases} x_q = \frac{s'-s}{c-c'} \bmod q, \\ x_p = \frac{s'-s}{c-c'} \bmod p \end{cases}.$$

On the other hand, we can compute such an integer $x \in \mathbb{Z}_P$ that

$$\begin{cases} x \equiv x_q \bmod q \\ x \equiv x_p \bmod p \end{cases}$$

by using Chinese Remainder Theorem. Then both $y = g^x \bmod P$ and $\tilde{y} = \tilde{g}^x \bmod \tilde{P}$ hold. Therefore, $SPK\{(\alpha) : y = g^\alpha \bmod P \ \wedge \ \tilde{y} = \tilde{g}^\alpha \bmod \tilde{P} \ \wedge \ \alpha \in \mathbb{Z}_P \}(m)$ is a honest-verifier perfect zero-knowledge proof of knowledge of common discrete logarithm of y to the base g and $\tilde{y}$ to the base $\tilde{g}$. $\qquad\square$

3.2   The Multiple Discrete Logarithm Problem

Before presenting our scheme, we define the Multiple Discrete Logarithm Problem(MDLP), which is used for the security proof of our scheme. Let k be a security parameter, q and p be primes with $|q| = k$ and $q|(p-1)$, P be a product of q and p, g_1, g_2 and g_3 be elements in $\mathbb{Z}_P^*$ with order q.

Problem 1 (MDLP) *Given $\mathbb{Z}_P$ and g_1, g_2 and $g_3 \in \mathbb{Z}_P^*$ with order q such that the discrete logarithms based on each other element are unknown, find a pair $(x_1, x_2, x_3) \in \mathbb{Z}_P \times \mathbb{Z}_q \times \mathbb{Z}_q$ such that $x_1 g_1^{x_1} g_2^{x_2} = g_3^{x_3} \pmod{P}$.*

Assumption 1 (MDL Assumption) *There is no probabilistic polynomial-time algorithm P that can solve the Problem 1.*

3.3   The Modified Nyberg-Rueppel Signature Scheme

Let us summarize the original Nyberg-Rueppel signature scheme[14]. For a q-order element $g \in \mathbb{Z}_p^*$, a signer chooses his secret key $x \in_R \mathbb{Z}_q$ and computes his public key $y = g^x \bmod p$. A signature $(r, s) \in \mathbb{Z}_p \times \mathbb{Z}_q$ on a message $m \in \mathbb{Z}_p^*$ is computed as $r = mg^{-w} \bmod p$ and $s = w - rx \bmod q$ for a random integer $w \in_R \mathbb{Z}_q$, which is verified by recovering the message m as $m = ry^r g^s \bmod p$.

Message recovery signature schemes are subject to an existential forgery, in which an attacker cannot control a message. In a sense, it is not a serious problem because we can avoid such a forgery by restricting a message to a particular format. However, suppose that we want to use it for a membership certificate of DLP-based key like $m = g^t \bmod p$. Then, by using a valid signature for a message $m = g^t \bmod p$ with a known discrete logarithm t, it is easy to obtain a forged signature for some known message $m' = g^{t'} \bmod p$, in which an attacker can control a message of m'. Therefore, we must remove such a defect from the original Nyberg-Rueppel signature to generate a membership certification of a DLP-based key.

In order to generate a membership certificate of a DLP-based key securely, we introduce another base $h \in \mathbb{Z}_p^*$ with order q such that the discrete logarithm of h to the base g is unknown. We restrict the message space for Nyberg-Rueppel signature to $\{h^t \bmod p \mid t \in \mathbb{Z}_q\}$. In our scheme, GM or M_i computes each public key as $y = g^{x_{GM}} \bmod p$ or $z_i = h^{x_i} \bmod p$, respectively. Then, a membership certificate $(r_i, s_i) \in \mathbb{Z}_p \times \mathbb{Z}_q$ of M_i's public key $z_i = h^{x_i} \bmod p$ is given as $z_i = r_i y^{r_i} g^{s_i} \pmod{p}$.

3.4   Functional Description

A group signature scheme with CRL-based revocation consists of the following procedures:

Setup: A probabilistic polynomial-time algorithm that on input a security parameter k outputs the group public key $\mathcal{Y}$ (including all system parameters), the secret key $\mathcal{S}$ of the group manager, and the initial certificate revocation list $\mathcal{CRL}$.

Registration: A protocol between the group manager and a user that registers a user as a new group member. The group manager outputs the renewed member list $\mathcal{ML}$. The user outputs a membership key with a membership certificate.

Revocation: A probabilistic polynomial-time algorithm that on input the renewed revoked member list $\mathcal{RML}$ outputs a renewed certificate revocation list $\mathcal{CRL}$ corresponding to $\mathcal{RML}$.

Sign: A probabilistic polynomial-time algorithm that on input a group public key $\mathcal{Y}$, a membership key, a membership certificate, and a message m outputs a group signature σ.

Verification: A boolean-valued algorithm that on input a message m, a group signature σ, a group public key $\mathcal{Y}$, and a current certificate revocation list $\mathcal{CRL}$ returns 1 if and only if σ was generated by some valid group member.

Tracing: An algorithm that on input a valid group signature σ, a group public key $\mathcal{Y}$, the group manager's secret key, and the member list $\mathcal{ML}$ outputs the identity of a signer.

3.5   Scheme Intuition

Our scheme must permit M_i to prove knowledge of his membership certificate (r_i, s_i) corresponding his membership key x_i without revealing any information of x_i, r_i or s_i. However, there has not been any SPK which proves the knowledge of the membership certificate directly. So, we modify Nyberg-Rueppel signature as follows. Let $\tilde{P}$ be a prime with $P|(\tilde{P} - 1)$, $P = pq$ and $q|(p - 1)$ and q-order elements g_1 and $g_2 \in \mathbb{Z}_P^*$. GM issues a membership certificate (A_i, b_i) of M_i's public key $z_i = g_2^{x_i} \bmod P$ as $g_2^{x_i} = A_i y^{A_i} g_1^{b_i} \pmod{P}$. This exactly means that our membership certificate is based on MDLP. To forge a valid membership certificate is equivalent to solve MDLP. Under the Assumption 1, it is difficult to find a set of $\{x_i, (A_i, b_i)\}$ such that $g_2^{x_i} = A_i y^{A_i} g_1^{b_i} \bmod P$ without knowing the discrete logarithm of g_1, g_2 and y based on each other elements. Therefore, the membership certificate (A_i, b_i) corresponding to a membership key x_i can be obtained by only the interactive protocol between GM and M_i. In the signing phase, we employ a base $\tilde{g} \in \mathbb{Z}_{\tilde{P}}^*$ with order P to protect any information of the membership certificate (A_i, b_i) and corresponding membership key x_i, M_i computes a random base $T = \tilde{g}^W \bmod \tilde{P}$ for a random integer $W \in_R \mathbb{Z}_P$ and generates a signature based on the proof of knowledge of $\{x_i, (A_i, b_i)\}$ such that $T^{g_2^{x_i}} = T^{A_i y^{A_i} g_1^{b_i}} \bmod \tilde{P}$ holds. This can be constructed by using SPK which defined in Section 2.2.

3.6   Our Group Signature Scheme

We present a new group signature scheme with CRL-based revocation, which uses only known-order groups. Let k be the security parameter and the initial member list $\mathcal{ML}$, the initial revoked member list $\mathcal{RML}$ and the initial membership certificate revocation list $\mathcal{CRL}$ be null.

Setup(k)
1. Choose a random k-bit prime q, a random prime p of such that $q|(p-1)$ and set $P = pq$.
2. Choose a random prime $\tilde{P}$ of such that $P|(\tilde{P}-1)$.
3. Set each cyclic subgroup $\mathbb{G}_P \subset \mathbb{Z}_P^*$ with order q and $\mathbb{G}_{\tilde{P}} \subset \mathbb{Z}_{\tilde{P}}^*$ with order P.
4. Choose random elements g_1, g_2, g_3 and $g_4 \in_R \mathbb{G}_P \setminus \{1\}$ such that the discrete logarithms based on each other elements are unknown.
5. Choose a random element $\tilde{g} \in_R \mathbb{G}_{\tilde{P}} \setminus \{1\}$.
6. Compute $y_1 = g_1^{x_{GM}} \bmod P$ and $y_2 = g_3^{x_{GM}} \bmod P$ for a secret key $x_{GM} \in_R \mathbb{Z}_q$.
7. Output the group public key $\mathcal{Y} = \{q, P, \tilde{P}, g_1, g_2, g_3, g_4, \tilde{g}, y_1, y_2\}$ and the secret key $\mathcal{S} = \{x_{GM}\}$.

Registration($\mathcal{Y}, \mathcal{S}, \mathcal{ML}$)
1. M_i chooses a membership key $x_i \in_R \mathbb{Z}_q$, sets $z_i = g_2^{x_i} \bmod P$, and sends z_i with $\sigma_i = SPK\{(\alpha) : z_i = g_2^\alpha \bmod P \}(\tilde{0})$ to GM[1].
2. GM checks the validity of σ_i, chooses a random integer $w_i \in_R \mathbb{Z}_q$, computes $A_i = z_i g_1^{-w_i} \bmod P$ and $b_i = w_i - A_i x_{GM} \bmod q$, and sends $(A_i, b_i) \in \mathbb{Z}_P \times \mathbb{Z}_q$ to M_i through a secure cannel.
3. GM adds (A_i, b_i) with M_i's identity ID_i to the member list $\mathcal{ML}$.
4. M_i verifies that $A_i y_1^{A_i} g_1^{b_i} = z_i \pmod{P}$.
5. GM outputs the renewed member list $\mathcal{ML} = \{(ID_i, A_i, b_i)\}$.
6. M_i possesses a membership key x_i and a membership certificate $(A_i, b_i) \in \mathbb{Z}_P \times \mathbb{Z}_q$.

In order to revoke a new subset of members whose revoked member list is $\mathcal{RML} = \{(ID, b)\}$ with $|\mathcal{RML}| = u$, GM renews the certificate revocation list $\mathcal{CRL}$ by running the following Revocation protocol.

Revocation($\mathcal{RML}$)
1. Choose a new revocation base $g_4 \in_R \mathbb{G}_P \setminus \{1\}$ and update $\mathcal{Y}$.
2. Compute $V_j = g_4^{b_j} \bmod P$ for $b_j \in \mathcal{RML}$ $(1 \le j \le u)$.
3. Output the renewed certificate revocation list $\mathcal{CRL} = \{V_j \mid 1 \le j \le u\}$.

Sign($\mathcal{Y}, g_4\ x_i, A_i, b_i, m$)
1. Choose a random integer $w \in_R \mathbb{Z}_q$.
2. Compute $T_1 = \tilde{g}^{g_3^w} \bmod \tilde{P}$, $T_2 = T_1^{g_4^{b_i}} \bmod \tilde{P}$, $T_3 = g_3^{b_i} g_4^w \bmod P$, $T_4 = A_i g_3^w \bmod P$, and $T_5 = y_2^w \bmod P$.
3. Generate

$$\sigma_1 = SPK\{(\alpha_1, \alpha_2) : T_1 = \tilde{g}^{g_3^{\alpha_2}} \bmod \tilde{P} \wedge T_2 = T_1^{g_4^{\alpha_1}} \bmod \tilde{P} \wedge$$
$$T_3 = g_3^{\alpha_1} g_4^{\alpha_2} \bmod P \}(m)$$
$$= (c_1, s_{11}, \cdots, s_{1k}, s_{21}, \cdots, s_{2k}) \in \{0,1\}^k \times \mathbb{Z}_q^{2k}$$

as follows:

---

* We can also add an interactive protocol to make a member's secret key jointly by a member and GM.

- choose random integers ω_{1j}, $\omega_{2j} \in_R \mathbb{Z}_q$ for $1 \leq j \leq k$,
- compute
  - $t_{1j} = \tilde{g}^{g_3^{\omega_{2j}}} \bmod \tilde{P}$, $t_{2j} = T_1^{g_4^{\omega_{1j}}} \bmod \tilde{P}$, and $t_{3j} = g_3^{\omega_{1j}} g_4^{\omega_{2j}} \bmod P$ for $1 \leq j \leq k$,
  - $c_1 = \mathcal{H}(g_3||g_4||\tilde{g}||T_1||T_2||T_3||t_{11}||\cdots||t_{1k}||t_{21}||\cdots||t_{2k}||t_{31}||\cdots||t_{3k} ||m)$,
  - $s_{1j} = \omega_{1j} - c_1[j]b_i \bmod q$ and $s_{2j} = \omega_{1j} - c_1[j]w \bmod q$ for $1 \leq j \leq k$.

4. Generate

$$\sigma_\cdot = SPK\{(\alpha_\cdot, \alpha_\cdot, \alpha_\cdot, \alpha_\cdot) : \ \alpha_\cdot \in \mathbb{Z}_P \wedge T_\cdot = g_\cdot^{\alpha_4} g_\cdot^{\alpha_6} \bmod P \wedge$$

$$T_\cdot = y_\cdot^{-\alpha_3} g_\cdot^{-\alpha_4} g_\cdot^{\alpha_5} g_\cdot^{\alpha_6} \bmod P \wedge T_\cdot = y_\cdot^{\alpha_6} \bmod P \wedge \tilde{g}^{T_4} = T_\cdot^{\alpha_3} \bmod \tilde{P}\}(m)$$

$$= (c_\cdot, s_\cdot, s_\cdot, s_\cdot, s_\cdot) \in \{0,1\}^k \times \mathbb{Z}_q^* \times \mathbb{Z}_P$$

as follows:
- choose $\omega_3 \in_R \mathbb{Z}_P$, $\omega_4, \omega_5, \omega_6 \in_R \mathbb{Z}_q$,
- compute
  - $t_4 = g_3^{\omega_4} g_4^{\omega_6} \bmod P$, $t_5 = y_1^{-\omega_3} g_1^{-\omega_4} g_2^{\omega_5} g_3^{\omega_6} \bmod P$, $t_6 = y_2^{\omega_6} \bmod P$, and $t_7 = T_1^{\omega_3} \bmod \tilde{P}$,
  - $c_2 = \mathcal{H}(g_1||g_2||g_3||g_4||\tilde{g}||y_1||y_2||T_1||T_3||T_4||T_5||t_4||t_5||t_6||t_7||m)$,
  - $s_3 = \omega_3 - c_2 A_i \bmod P$, $s_4 = \omega_4 - c_2 b_i \bmod q$, $s_5 = \omega_5 - c_2 x_i \bmod q$ and $s_6 = \omega_6 - c_2 w \bmod p$.

5. Output a group signature $\sigma = \{T_1, T_2, T_3, T_4, T_5, \sigma_1, \sigma_2\}$.

Verification($\mathcal{Y}$, $\mathcal{CRL}$, m, σ)
1. Check the validity of σ_1 and σ_2.
2. If $T_1^{V_j} \neq T_2 \bmod \tilde{P}$ for $^\forall V_j \in \mathcal{CRL}$, then accept the signature otherwise reject the signature.

Tracing(x_{GM}, $\mathcal{ML}$, σ)
1. Recover A_i by $A_i = T_4/T_5^{1/x_{\mathrm{GM}}} \bmod P$.
2. Identify a signer M_i from A_i by using the member list $\mathcal{ML}$.
3. Output the signer's identity ID_i.

In our scheme, in order to realize the features of anonymity and unlinkability, GM has to keep $\mathcal{ML}$ secretly and send a membership certificate to a group member through a secure cannel. This assumption is required in the CRL-based revocation as in [3]. To reduce the features of anonymity and unlinkability to GM, GM may be separated to two managers, the group manager and the escrow manager by applying techniques of multi-party computation to generate a membership certificate.

4 Security Consideration

We use two different signature schemes in our group signature scheme. One is the modified Nyberg-Rueppel signature scheme that generates the membership certificate, and the other is SPK that generates the group signature. In this section, we consider the security of a membership certificate and the group signature.

4.1   Security Proof on the Membership Certificate

The security of the membership certificate in our scheme is based on the difficulty of the MDLP. We show the membership certificate is secure against any
probabilistic polynomial-time adversaries.

Let us define one more security assumption. For the security parameter k,
primes p and q with $|q| = k$ and $q|(p-1)$, $P = pq$ and g_1, g_2, $g_3 \in \mathbb{Z}_P^*$ with order
q, a set of solutions of Problem 1 is denoted as

$$\mathcal{X}(\mathbb{Z}_P, g_1, g_2, g_3) = \{(x_1, x_2, x_3) \in \mathbb{Z}_P \times \mathbb{Z}_q \times \mathbb{Z}_q \mid x_1 g_1^{x_1} g_2^{x_2} = g_3^{x_3} \pmod{P}\}$$

where the discrete logarithms of g_1, g_2, and g_3 based on each other element is
not known.

Problem 2 (Strong-MDLP) *Given $\mathbb{Z}_P$, g_1, g_2, and $g_3 \in \mathbb{Z}_P^*$ such that the
discrete logarithm based on each other element is not known and any subset
$X \subset \mathcal{X}(\mathbb{Z}_P, g_1, g_2, g_3)$ with the polynomial order $|X|$, find a pair $(x_1, x_2, x_3) \in
\mathbb{Z}_P \times \mathbb{Z}_q \times \mathbb{Z}_q$ such that $x_1 g_1^{x_1} g_2^{x_2} = g_3^{x_3} \pmod{P}$ and $(x_1, x_2, x_3) \notin X$.*

Assumption 2 (Strong-MDLP Assumption) *There is no probabilistic
polynomial-time algorithm P that can solve the Problem 2.*

More formally, the following experiment is executed with algorithm A.

```
Break-strong-MDLP(A, k, q, P, g_1, g_2, g_3)
```
1. Choose a polynomial-order subset $X \subset \mathcal{X}(\mathbb{Z}_P, g_1, g_2, g_3)$.
2. $(x_1, x_2, x_3) \leftarrow A^X(k, g_1, g_2, g_3, q, P)$.
3. If $(x_1, x_2, x_3) \in \mathbb{Z}_P \times \mathbb{Z}_q \times \mathbb{Z}_q$, $g_3^{x_3} = x_1 g_1^{x_1} g_2^{x_2} \pmod{P}$, and
   $(x_1, x_2, x_3) \notin X$
   then return 1,
   else return 0.

The strong MDLP assumption is that the maximum success probability of Break-
strong-MDLP$(A, k, q, P, g_1, g_2, g_3)$ over all the probabilistic polynomial-time adversary is negligible in k.

By using Assumption 2, we can formalize the security of the membership
certificate as follows. Let us define A be a probabilistic polynomial-time oracle
Turing machine, which gets input $\mathcal{Y}$ and runs with a *membership certificate oracle*
$O_C(t, \mathcal{Y}, \mathcal{S}, \cdot)$, which on input $z \in \mathbb{Z}_P^*$ outputs a membership certificate (A, b).
The adversary A may query the oracle adaptively. Eventually, adversary outputs
a new membership certificate (A', b') for a public key z' and the corresponding
membership key x'. The adversary wins if z' was not queried and $A' y^{A'} g_1^{b'} = z'$
$(\mod P)$. More formally, the following experiment is executed with the algorithm
A.

```
Adversary (A, k)
```
1. Set $(\mathcal{S}, \mathcal{Y}) \leftarrow$ Setup(k)

2. Set $(A', b', z', x') \leftarrow \mathsf{A}^{O_C}(k, \mathcal{Y})$
3. If $A'y^{A'}g_1{}^{b'} \neq z' \pmod{P}$ or z' was queried to O_C,
   then return "adversary failed",
   else return "adversary succeeded".

From the above discussion, the security of our certificate is proved as follows.

Theorem 1. *Let* A *be a probabilistic polynomial-time adversary of time complexity* τ *with at most* Q *queries to an oracle* O_C. *If the adversary successfully forges a new certificate, then there exists an adversary* B *performing an attack against the strong MDLP with at least the same advantage. Furthermore the time complexity of* B *is at most* τ.

4.2 Security Proof on the Group Signature

We show the security of the group signature.

Theorem 2. *The interactive protocol underlying the group signature scheme is a honest-verifier perfect zero-knowledge proof of knowledge of a membership certificate and corresponding membership key. Furthermore, it proves that the a pair* (T_4, T_5) *encrypts the membership certificate under the group manager's public key* y_2.

Proof : The proof that the perfect zero-knowledge part is quite standard. We restrict our attention to the proof of knowledge part. By the properties of the SPK protocol, the signer can produce values of $\alpha_1, \alpha_2, \alpha_3, \alpha_4,\ \alpha_5$ and α_6 such that

$$T_1 = \tilde{g}^{g_3^{\alpha_2}} \bmod \tilde{P} \tag{1}$$

$$T_2 = T_1^{g_4^{\alpha_1}} \bmod \tilde{P} \tag{2}$$

$$T_3 = g_3^{\alpha_1} g_4^{\alpha_2} = g_3^{\alpha_4} g_4^{\alpha_6} \bmod P \tag{3}$$

$$T_4 = y_1^{-\alpha_3} g_1^{-\alpha_4} g_2^{\alpha_5} g_3^{\alpha_6} \bmod P \tag{4}$$

$$T_5 = y_2^{\alpha_6} \bmod P \tag{5}$$

$$\tilde{g}^{T_4} = T_1^{\alpha_3} \bmod \tilde{P} \tag{6}$$

$$\alpha_3 \in \mathbb{Z}_P \tag{7}$$

hold, in which $\alpha_1 = \alpha_4$ and $\alpha_2 = \alpha_6$ hold from Equation (3). Thus, Equations (1) and (2) represent

$$T_1 = \tilde{g}^{g_3^{\alpha_6}} \bmod \tilde{P} \tag{8}$$

and

$$T_2 = T_1^{g_4^{\alpha_4}} \bmod \tilde{P}. \tag{9}$$

From Equations (4) and (8), we can rewrite Equation (6) as

$$\tilde{g}^{y_1^{-\alpha_3}} g_1^{-\alpha_4} g_2^{\alpha_5} g_3^{\alpha_6} = (\tilde{g}^{g_3^{\alpha_6}})^{\alpha_3} \pmod{\tilde{P}}$$
$$\Leftrightarrow \qquad y_1^{-\alpha_3} g_1^{-\alpha_4} g_2^{\alpha_5} g_3^{\alpha_6} \equiv g_3^{\alpha_6} \alpha_3 \pmod{P}$$
$$\Leftrightarrow \qquad g_2^{\alpha_5} \equiv \alpha_3 y_1^{\alpha_3} g_1^{\alpha_4} \pmod{P}. \qquad (10)$$

Thus, a set of $\{\alpha_5, (\alpha_3, \alpha_4)\}$ is coincident with the valid membership certificate and corresponding membership key. From using Equation (10), Equation (4) represents

$$T_4 = \alpha_3 g_3^{\alpha_6} \pmod{P}.$$

Thus, a pair of (T_4, T_5) is an encryption of α_3 by the group manager's public key y_2. Therefore, the group signature is a honest-verifier perfect zero-knowledge proof of knowledge of a membership certificate and corresponding membership key, and it proves that the a pair (T_4, T_5) is an encryption of the membership certificate by the group manager's public key y_2.   □

5   Analysis of Our Scheme

5.1   Features

Here we show that our scheme satisfies all features necessary for group signatures.

Unforgeability : From the proof of Theorem 2, a set of $(T_1, T_2, T_3, T_4, T_5)$ is an unconditional binding commitment to a valid membership certificate (A_i, b_i) and corresponding membership key x_i. Under the Assumption 2, it is infeasible to find a certificate (A_i, b_i) corresponding a membership key x_i without knowledge of the group manager's secret key. Therefore, only group members who have a valid membership certificate are able to generate a signature on a message;

Exculpability : GM knows a member's membership certificate, but he can not get any information about the corresponding membership key x_i. Hence, even if GM colludes with some group members, they cannot sign on behalf of M_i.

Anonymity : Assuming that the function $\mathcal{H}$ is a random function, the SPKs of σ_1 and σ_2 do not leak any information since their interactive counterparts are based on the honest-verifier perfect zero-knowledge. To decide whether some group member with certificate (A_i, b_i) generated, it is required to decide whether $\log_{\tilde{g}} T_1 = T_4/A_i$, $\log_{T_1} T_2 = g_4^{b_i}$ or $\log_{g_4} T_3/g_3^{b_i} = \log_{g_3} T_4/A_i = \log_{y_2} T_5$. However, these are impossible under the decision Diffie-Hellman assumption[12], and hence anonymity is guaranteed.

Traceability : When the signature is valid, (T_4, T_5) is coincident with the encryption of the membership certificate A_i, which can be uniquely recovered by GM. Therefore, a member can be traced in case of dispute. On the other hand, in order to impersonate another signer with (A_i', b_i'), they must forge the membership certificate (A_i', b_i'). Under the Assumption 2, it is infeasible.

Unlinkability : In order to decide whether or not two signatures $\{T_1, T_2, T_3, T_4,$ $T_5, \sigma_1, \sigma_2\}$ and $\{T_1', T_2', T_3', T_4', T_5', \sigma_1', \sigma_2'\}$ were generated by the same group member, we need to decide whether or not $\log_{\tilde{g}} T_1/T_1' = T_4/T_4'$, $(\log_{T_1} T_2)/$ $(\log_{T_1'} T_2') = 1$ or $\log_{g_4} T_3/T_3' = \log_{g_3} T_4/T_4' = \log_{y_2} T_5/T_5'$ holds. However, these are impossible under the decision Diffie-Hellman assumption[12], and hence group signatures are unlinkable each other.

Revocability : Each group signature must prove the knowledge of b_i with $T_2 = T_1^{g_4^{b_i}} \mod \tilde{P}$, where GM publishes revoked member's membership certificate as $V = g_4^b \mod \tilde{P}$. Therefore, if a signer is a revoked member (i.e., $b_i = b$), then $T_1^V = T_2 \mod \tilde{P}$ for some V holds. The verifier can check the equation and judge whether the signer has been revoked or not. In order to forge the group signature that passes verification, a revoked member must substitute another b' for a part of membership certificate b, but it is impossible under Assumption 2. We can say that a revoked member can not generate a valid group signature.

Anonymity after revocation : A CRL certificate, however do not leak any information of group member. Therefore nobody can identify a group member who generated a signature on a message even after a group member was revoked.

Unlinkability after revocation : In order to decide whether or not two signatures σ and σ' based on different-time CRL CRL and CRL' were generated by the same member M_j whose certificate is in CRL', we need to decide whether or not $\log_{g_4} log_{T_1} T_2 = \log g_4' V_j'$ holds. However, this is impossible under the decision Diffie-Hellman assumption[12], and thus group signatures are unlinkable even after a group member was revoked.

5.2 Efficiency

We compare our scheme with previous schemes [3] from the viewpoints of both computational work and signature size in Table 1. Let P or q be 1200 or 160 bits, respectively. Here M denotes the computational work of a multiplication over an 1200-bit modulus. We assume the binary method or the extended binary method to compute the exponentiation or multiple exponentiations[13], respectively.

Table 1 shows that our scheme reduces both of signature size and verification work by about 1/3 than [3], maintaining the same security level. Furthermore, our scheme is slightly more efficient than even the group signature scheme based on known-order cyclic groups proposed by G. Ateniese and B. de Medeiros[2], which does not satisfy the feature of revocability as mentioned in Section 1. Although revocability can be easily added in a simple way[3], it just increases both the signature size and computational work. Our scheme is optimized under such a condition that realizes all features, including the revocability. Therefore, our scheme is much better than a scheme combined [2] with the revocation function of [3].

Since our scheme uses the SPK of double discrete logarithms, it seems to require much computational work in contrast to group signature schemes with revocation[5,6] which do not use SPK of double discrete logarithms. However, their group public key and signature size depend on the number of group members, and thus these schemes are less efficient than our scheme for large groups like of 1000 members.

Table 1. Comparison of the efficiency

	Work		Signature Size
	Sign	Verification	Signature
[2] with [3]	$2020.3 \times 10^{*}$ M	$(2031.3 + 1.8u) \times 10^{*}$ M	101.6 KByte
[5]***	$200n + 760$M	$200(n + 1)$ M	$380 + 20n$ KByte
Our scheme	$705.1 \times 10^{*}$ M	$(700.4 + 1.8u) \times 10^{*}$ M	31.3 KByte

(1) The number of group member denoted by n.

6   Conclusion

We have proposed the group signature with CRL-based revocation. In our scheme, the membership certificate is constructed by using improved Nyberg-Rueppel signature with appendix. As a result, the signature size and computational work of signature generation and verification can be reduced because all secret data can be computed by using the knowledge of order of group.

Our scheme uses the proof of knowledge involving double discrete logarithm in the same way as previous group signatures, which requires many computational work. Furthermore our scheme uses a membership certificate based on a special assumption of Multiple DLP. Developing a membership certificate based on standard assumptions is a challenging open problem. Another interesting open question is to find the relation ship among the Multiple DLP, DLP.

References

1. G. Ateniese and J. Camenisch and M. Joye and G. Tsudik, "A practical and provably secure Coalition-Resistant group signature scheme", Advances in Cryptology-Proceedings of CRYPTO2000, LNCS 1880(2000), pp. 255-270.
2. G. Ateniese and B. de Medeiros, "Efficient group signatures without trapdoors", Cryptology ePrint Archive, available from
   http://citeseer.nj.nec.com/ateniese02efficient.html.
3. G. Ateniese and G. Tsudik, "Quasi-efficient revocation of group signatures", In the proceeding of FC2002, 2002.
4. E. Bresson and J. Stern, "Group signatures with efficient revocation", In proceeding of PKC2001, LNCS 1992(2001), pp. 190-206.
5. J. Camenisch, "Efficient and generalized group signature", Advances in Cryptology – Proceedings of EUROCRYPT'97, LNCS 1233(1997), pp. 465-479.

6. J. Camenisch, "Group signature schemes and payment systems based on the discrete logarithm problem", PhD thesis, vol. 2 of ETH-Series in Information Security an Cryptography, Hartung-Gorre Verlag, Konstanz, 1998, ISBN 3-89649-286-1.
7. J. Camenisch and A. Lysyanskaya, "Dynamic accumulators and application to efficient revocation of anonymous credentials", Advances in Cryptology-Proceedings of CRYPTO2002, LNCS 2442(2002), pp. 61-76.
8. J. Camenisch and M. Michels, "A group signature scheme based on an RSA-variant", preliminary version in Advances in Cryptology - ASIACRYPT'98, Tech. Rep., RS-98-27, BRICS, 1998.
9. J. Camenisch and M. Stadler, "Efficient group signature schemes for large group", Advances in Cryptology-Proceedings of CRYPTO'97, LNCS 1296(1997), pp. 410-424.
10. D. Chaum and E. van Heyst, "Group signatures", Advances in Cryptology-Proceedings of EUROCRYPT'91, LNCS 547(1991), pp. 257-265.
11. D. Chaum, J. H. Evertse and J. van de Graaf, "An improved protocol for demonstration possession of discrete logarithms and some generalizations", Advances in Cryptology-Proceedings of EUROCRYPT'87, LNCS 304(1987), pp. 127-141.
12. W. Diffie and M. E. Hellman, "New directions in cryptography", IEEE Transaction on Information Theory IT-22, 1976, pp. 664-654.
13. D. E. Knuth, "The Art of Computer Programming", Addison-Wesley Publishing Co.,, 1981.
14. K. Nyberg and R. A. Rueppel, "Message recovery for signature scheme based on the discrete logarithm problem", Advances in Cryptology-Proceedings of EUROCRYPT'94, 1994, pp. 182-193.
15. C. P. Schnorr, "Efficient signature generation for smart cards", Journal of Cryptology, Vol. 4(3), 1991, 239-252.
16. D. Song, "Practical Forward-Secure group signature schemes", In proceeding of 2001 ACM Symposium on Computer and Communication Security, 2001.

Some Observations on Zap and Its Applications*

Yunlei Zhao[1,2], C.H. Lee[1], Yiming Zhao[2], and Hong Zhu[2]

* Department of Computer Science
City University of Hong Kong
HONG KONG
{csylzhao, chlee}@cityu.edu.hk
* Department of Computer Science
Fudan University, Shanghai
P. R. China
{zhym, hzhu}@fudan.edu.cn

Abstract. In this paper we make some observations on the zaps and their applications developed by Dwork and Naor [13]. We clarify the relations among public-coin witness indistinguishability (WI), public-coin honest verifier zero-knowledge (HVZK) and public-coin special honest verifier zero-knowledge (SHVZK). Specifically, we observe that the existence of zaps under the existence of one-way permutations actually strictly separates public-coin WI and public-coin SHVZK assuming $\mathcal{NP} \nsubseteq \mathcal{BPP}$. We also show that public-coin HVZK does not implies WI assuming the existence of one-way permutations. For zap-based applications, we present an improved Dwork-Naor 2-round timed deniable authentication scheme that improves the communication and computation complexity of the original protocol presented by Dwork and Naor [13]. Specifically, in the improved protocol the first message (from the verifier to the authenticator) is independent on the message to be authenticated by the authenticator.

Keywords: Zap, public-coin honest verifier zero-knowledge, deniable authentication, timed commitment, witness indistinguishability

1 Introduction

Zap, first introduced by Dwork and Naor [13], is itself a 2-round public-coin witness indistinguishable (WI) proof system for $\mathcal{NP}$. Zaps are a very powerful cryptographic tool to significantly simplify many cryptographic tasks. As a notable example, it is used to achieve the first 2-round timed deniable authentication scheme [13].

Deniable authentication first appears in [10,12], and is then formalized in [14]. Roughly speaking, a deniable authentication scheme is a *public-key interactive* authentication scheme in which an authenticator AP convinces a second party V,

---

* This research is supported by a research grant of City University of Hong Kong (No. 7001358).

M. Jakobsson, M. Yung, J. Zhou (Eds.): ACNS 2004, LNCS 3089, pp. 180–193, 2004.

only accessing to AP's public-key, that AP is willing to authenticate a message m. However, different from the case of digital signatures, deniable authentication does not permit V to convince a third party that AP has authenticated m. That is, there is no "paper trail" of the conversation other than what could be produced by V alone. Several 4-round timed deniable authentication protocols appear in [14,15] and the first 2-round timed deniable authentication is presented by Dwork and Naor in [13].

We remark that before the emergence of zaps, when we use public-coin WI proofs in fulfilling cryptographic tasks we actually use public-coin special honest verifier zero-knowledge (SHVZK) proofs. Public-coin honest verifier zero-knowledge (HVZK) and public-coin SHVZK are introduced by Cramer, Damgard and Schoenmakers [5] and it is shown there that any public-coin SHVZK protocol is also WI[1]. Roughly, a public-coin protocol is called honest verifier zero-knowledge if there is a simulator S such that the output of S on input x is computationally indistinguishable from the real transcript between honest prover and honest verifier on common input x. A public-coin protocol is called SHVZK if for any *given* random challenges of honest verifier the simulator S can take the given random challenges as inputs and output a transcript that is consistent with the given random challenges and is computationally indistinguishable from the real transcript between the honest prover and the honest verifier. We remark that public-coin SHVZK protocols are a very powerful cryptographic tool and are widely used in numerous important cryptographic applications. As a notable example, Σ-protocols, which are 3-round public-coin SHVZK protocols with some special (knowledge-extraction) soundness property, play a critical role in achieving secure digital signatures in the random oracle model (by using the famous Fiat-Shamir methodology [18]) and efficient electronic payment systems [4]. For a good survey of Σ-protocols and their applications, readers are referred to [7,4].

1.1   Our Contributions

In this paper, we clarify the relations among public-coin WI, public-coin SHVZK and public-coin HVZK. Specifically, we have the following observations:

Observation 1. The existence of zaps (under the existence of one-way permutations) actually strictly separates public-coin WI and public-coin SHVZK. Specifically, we show that although any public-coin SHVZK is also public-coin WI [5], but the zap, which is itself a 2-round public-coin WI proof system for $\mathcal{NP}$ and can be constructed under the existence of one-way permutations, cannot be public-coin SHVZK assuming $\mathcal{NP} \nsubseteq \mathcal{BPP}$. This observation is proven by showing that only languages in $\mathcal{BPP}$ have a 2-round public-coin SHVZK protocol.

---

[*] The fact that any public-coin SHVZK protocol is also WI is proved in the Proposition 1 of [5]. We note that the Proposition states that any public-coin honest verifier zero-knowledge (rather than any public-coin SHVZK) is WI. But the proof of the Proposition in [5] is actually for the public-coin SHVZK case. In this paper we show that public-coin HVZK does not necessarily imply WI.

Observation 2. Public-coin HVZK does not necessarily imply WI. Specifically, we show that under the existence of one-way permutations there exists a 2-round public-coin proof system for $\mathcal{NP}$ that is public-coin HVZK but not WI.

For the first zap-based 2-round Dwork-Naor timed deniable authentication protocol [13], we have the following observation:

Observation 3. In the first message (from the verifier to the authenticator) of the 2-round timed deniable authentication scheme [13], the verifier needs to send a public-key encryption (using the authenticator's public-key) of the message, m, to be authenticated by the authenticator. This implicitly means that the first (verifier's) message depends on the message to be authenticated by the authenticator. Since in practice the message to be authenticated is normally large and public-key encryption may also be time-consuming so the inclusion of the public-key encryption of m may increase both the communication complexity and the computation complexity. In this paper we observe that the above dependence in the first verifier message can be avoided by using collision-resistant hash functions.

2   Preliminaries

In this section we recall the definitions and the cryptographic tools used in this paper.

We use standard notations and conventions below for writing probabilistic algorithms and experiments. If A is a probabilistic algorithm, then $A(x_1, x_2, \cdots ; r)$ is the result of running A on inputs $x_1, x_2, \cdots$ and coins r. We let $y \leftarrow A(x_1, x_2, \cdots)$ denote the experiment of picking r at random and letting y be $A(x_1, x_2, \cdots ; r)$. If S is a finite set then $x \leftarrow S$ is the operation of picking an element uniformly from S. If α is neither an algorithm nor a set then $x \leftarrow \alpha$ is a simple assignment statement.

Definition 1 (interactive proof system). *A pair of probabilistic machines,* $\langle P, V \rangle$, *is called an interactive proof system for a language L if V is polynomial-time and the following conditions hold:*

- *Completeness. For every $x \in L$, $\Pr[\langle P, V \rangle(x) = 1] = 1$.*
- *Soundness. For all sufficiently large n and every $x \notin L$ of length n and every interactive machine B (even with unbounded computational power), $\Pr[\langle B, V \rangle(x) = 1]$ is negligible in n.*

An interactive protocol is called a *public-coin* system if at each round the prescribed (honest) verifier can only toss coins (random string) and send their outcomes to the prover. An interactive protocol is called an argument if the soundness is only guaranteed for probabilistic polynomial-time (PPT) malicious provers.

Definition 2 (public-coin HVZK and SHVZK). *Let $\langle P, V \rangle$ be a public-coin interactive protocol (argument or proof) for a language $L \in \mathcal{NP}$ in which the prescribed honest verifier V is supposed to send m, $m \geq 1$, random challenges,* and let R_L be the corresponding $\mathcal{NP}$ witness relation for L. Denote by c_i, $1 \leq i \leq m$, the i-th random challenge of the honest verifier and α_i, $1 \leq i \leq m+1$ the i-th message of honest prover. We denote by $view_V^{P(w)}(x)$ a random variable describing the transcript of all messages exchanged between the honest verifier V and the honest prover P in an execution of the protocol on common input x while P has the auxiliary input w.

Such a public-coin protocol is called honest verifier zero-knowledge (HVZK) if there exists a probabilistic polynomial time simulator S such that for any sufficiently large x and its witness w (satisfying $(x, w) \in R_L$) the following ensembles are computationally indistinguishable: $\{S(x)\}_{x \in L}$ and $\{view_V^{P(w)}(x)\}_{x \in L}$. This public-coin protocol is called special honest verifier zero-knowledge (SHVZK) if for any sufficiently large x and for any given random challenges of the honest verifier, $c_1, c_2, \cdots, c_m$, the following ensembles are computationally indistinguishable: $\{S(x, c_1, c_2, \cdots, c_m)\}_{x \in L}$ and $\{view_V^{P(w)}(x)\}_{x \in L}$, where $\{S(x, c_1, c_2, \cdots, c_m)\}_{x \in L}$ is of the following forms: $(x, \alpha_1, c_1, \alpha_2, c_2, \cdots, \alpha_m, c_m, \alpha_{m+1})$ for the case that the prover sends the first message, or $(x, c_1, \alpha_1, c_2, \alpha_2, \cdots, c_m, \alpha_m)$ for the case that the verifier sends the first message.

Definition 3 (witness indistinguishability WI). Let $\langle P, V \rangle$ be an interactive proof system for a language $L \in \mathcal{NP}$, and let R_L be the fixed $\mathcal{NP}$ witness relation for L. That is $x \in L$ if there exists a w such that $(x, w) \in R_L$. We denote by $view_{V^*(z)}^{P(w)}(x)$ a random variable describing the transcript of all messages exchanged between a (possibly malicious) verifier V^* and the honest prover P in an execution of the protocol on common input x, when P has auxiliary input w and V^* has auxiliary input z. We say that $\langle P, V \rangle$ is witness indistinguishability for R_L if for every PPT interactive machine V^*, and every two sequences $W^1 = \{w_x^1\}_{x \in L}$ and $W^2 = \{w_x^2\}_{x \in L}$, so that $(x, w_x^1) \in R_L$ and $(x, w_x^2) \in R_L$, the following two probability distributions are computationally indistinguishable by any non-uniform PPT algorithm: $\{x, view_{V^*(z)}^{P(w_x^1)}\}_{x \in L, z \in \{0,1\}^*}$ and $\{x, view_{V^*(z)}^{P(w_x^2)}\}_{x \in L, z \in \{0,1\}^*}$.

Definition 4 (zap [13]). Under a security parameter n, a zap is a 2-round public-coin witness-indistinguishable interactive proof system for proving membership of $t \in L$ of length n, where L is a language in $\mathcal{NP}$. Furthermore the first round (verifier to prover) message, denoted ρ which is assumed to be a random string, can be fixed once and for all common inputs of length n . Denote by π the second-round (prover to verifier) response. Formally, a zap satisfies the following conditions:

- Completeness. Given t and a witness $w \in W_L(x)$, and a first-round ρ, the prover, running in time polynomial in $|t|$, can generate a proof π that will be accepted by the verifier with overwhelming probability.

- *Soundness. With overwhelming probability over choice of ρ, there exists no $t' \notin L$ and round-2 message π such that verifier accepts (t', ρ, π).*
- *Witness-Indistinguishability. Let $w, w' \in W_L(t)$ for $t \in L$. Then $\forall \rho$, the distribution on π when the prover has input (t, w) and the distribution on π when the prover has input (t, w') are non-uniform polynomial-time indistinguishable.*

We remark that zaps are a very powerful cryptographic tool to greatly simplify many cryptographic tasks, such as deniable authentication schemes, oblivious transfer, verifiable pseudorandom generator, concurrent-zero-knowledge, resettable zero-knowledge, quasi-polynomial time simulatable zero-knowledge and so on [13,16,24,26].

Definition 5 (non-interactive zero-knowledge NIZK). *Let NIP and NIV be two interactive machines and NIV is also probabilistic polynomial-time, and let $NI\sigma Len$ be a positive polynomial. We say that $\langle NIP, NIV \rangle$ is an NIZK proof system for an $\mathcal{NP}$ language L, if the following conditions hold:*

- *Completeness. For any $x \in L$ of length n, any σ of length $NI\sigma Len(n)$, and $\mathcal{NP}$-witness w for x, it holds that*

$$\Pr[\Pi \xleftarrow{R} NIP(\sigma, x, w) : NIV(\sigma, x, \Pi) = YES] = 1.$$

- *Soundness. $\forall x \notin L$ of length n,*

$$\Pr[\sigma \xleftarrow{R} \{0,1\}^{NI\sigma Len(n)} : \exists \Pi \text{ s.t. } NIV(\sigma, x, \Pi) = YES] \text{ is negligible in } n.$$

- *Zero-Knowledgeness. $\exists$ a PPT simulator NIS such that, $\forall$ sufficiently large n, $\forall x \in L$ of length n and $\mathcal{NP}$-witness w for x, the following two distributions are computationally indistinguishable: $[(\sigma', \Pi') \xleftarrow{R} NIS(x) : (\sigma', \Pi')]$ and $[\sigma \xleftarrow{R} \{0, 1\}^{NI\sigma Len(n)}; \Pi \xleftarrow{R} NIP(\sigma, x, w) : (\sigma, \Pi)].$*

Non-interactive zero-knowledge proof systems for $\mathcal{NP}$ can be constructed based on any one-way permutation [17]. An efficient implementation based on any one-way permutation is presented in [21] and readers are referred to [8] for recent advances of NIZK.

Definition 6 (NIZK proof of knowledge [9]). *An NIZK proof system $\langle NIP, NIV \rangle$ for a language $L \in \mathcal{NP}$ with witness relation R_L (as defined above) is NIZK proof of knowledge (NIZKPOK) if there exists a pair of PPT machines (E_1, E_2) and a negligible function ε such that for all sufficiently large n:*

- *Reference String Uniformity. The distribution on reference strings produced by $E_1(1^n)$ has statistical distance at most $\varepsilon(n)$ from the uniform distribution on $\{0,1\}^{NI\sigma Len(n)}$.*
- *Witness Extractability. For all adversaries A, we have that $\Pr[\textbf{Expt}_A^E(n) = 1] \geqslant \Pr[\textbf{Expt}_A(n) = 1] - \varepsilon(n)$, where the experiments $\textbf{Expt}_A(n)$ and $\textbf{Expt}_A^E(n)$ are defined as follows:*

$\textbf{Expt}_A(n)$:	$\textbf{Expt}_A^E(n)$:
$\sigma \xleftarrow{R} \{0,1\}^{NI\sigma Len(n)}$	$(\sigma, \tau) \longleftarrow E_1(1^n)$
$(x, \Pi) \longleftarrow A(\sigma)$	$(x, \Pi) \longleftarrow A(\sigma)$
$return\ NIV(x, \sigma, \Pi)$	$w \longleftarrow E_2(\sigma, \tau, x, \Pi)$
	$return\ 1\ if\ (x, w) \in R_L$

NIZK proofs of knowledge for $\mathcal{NP}$ can be constructed assuming the existence of one-way permutations and dense secure public-key cryptosystems [9].

Definition 7 (deniable authentication). *A deniable authentication scheme is a public-key interactive protocol in which an authenticator AP convinces a verifier V who only has access to AP's public-key that AP is willing to authenticate a message m. However, deniable authentication does not permit V to convince a third party that AP has authenticated m. Specifically, a deniable authentication protocol should satisfy:*

- *Completeness. For any message m, if the prover (authenticator) and the verifier follow the protocol for authenticating m, then the verifier accepts.*
- *Soundness (Existential Unforgeability Against Chosen Message Attack). Suppose that the copies of AP are willing to authenticate any polynomial number of messages $m_1, m_2, \cdots$, which may be chosen adaptively by an adversary A. We say that A successfully attacks the scheme if a forger C, under control of A and pretending to be AP, succeeds in authenticating to a third party D (running the protocol of the original verifier V) a message $m \neq m_i, i = 1, 2, \cdots$. The soundness requirement is that all probabilistic polynomial time A can succeed with at most negligible probability.*
- *Deniability (zero-knowledge). Consider an adversary A as above and suppose that the copies of AP are willing to authenticate any polynomial number of messages. Then for each A and each message m to be authenticated there exists a polynomial time simulator that outputs an indistinguishable transcript.*

Definition 8 (CCA2-secure non-malleable public-key cryptosystem). *Let $\Pi = (\mathcal{K}, \mathcal{E}, \mathcal{D})$ be a public-key encryption scheme and let $A = (A_1, A_2)$ be an adversary. For $k \in \mathbb{N}$ define*

$$\text{ADV}_{A,\Pi}(k) \stackrel{\text{def}}{=} \Pr[\textbf{Expt}_{A,\Pi}(k) = 1] - \Pr[\widetilde{\textbf{Expt}}_{A,\Pi}(k) = 1]$$

where

$\textbf{Expt}_{A,\Pi}(k):$	$\widetilde{\textbf{Expt}}_{A,\Pi}(k):$
$(pk, sk) \leftarrow \mathcal{K}(1^k)$	$(pk, sk) \leftarrow \mathcal{K}(1^k)$
$(M, s) \leftarrow A_1^{\mathcal{D}_{sk}(\cdot)}(pk)$	$(M, s) \leftarrow A_1^{\mathcal{D}_{sk}(\cdot)}(pk)$
$x \leftarrow M$	$x, \widetilde{x} \leftarrow M$
$y \leftarrow \mathcal{E}_{pk}(x)$	$\widetilde{y} \leftarrow \mathcal{E}_{pk}(\widetilde{x})$
$(R, \mathbf{y}) \leftarrow A_2^{\mathcal{D}_{sk}(\cdot)}(s, y),$	$(R, \widetilde{\mathbf{y}}) \leftarrow A_2^{\mathcal{D}_{sk}(\cdot)}(s, \widetilde{y}),$
where $\mathbf{y}$ *is a vector*	*where* $\widetilde{\mathbf{y}}$ *is a vector*
$\mathbf{x} \leftarrow \mathcal{D}_{sk}(\mathbf{y})$	$\widetilde{\mathbf{x}} \leftarrow \mathcal{D}_{sk}(\widetilde{\mathbf{y}})$
$return\ 1\ iff\ (y \notin \mathbf{y}) \wedge R(x, \mathbf{x})$	$return\ 1\ iff\ (\widetilde{y} \notin \widetilde{\mathbf{y}}) \wedge R(x, \widetilde{\mathbf{x}})$

We say that Π is secure against chosen-ciphertext attacks in the post-processing model if for every polynomial $p(k)$: if A runs in time $p(k)$, outputs a valid message space M sampleable in time $p(k)$, and outputs a relation R computable in time $p(k)$, then $\mathsf{ADV}_{A,\Pi}(k)$ is negligible. It is understood that A_2 is not allowed to ask its oracle for the decryption of the challenge ciphertext y.

The above definition is almost verbatim from [1,2]. There are another equivalent definition of non-malleable public-key cryptosystem secure against chosen-ciphertext attack in the post-processing model (CCA2) [1,2,22].

Definition 9 (indistinguishability of CCA2-secure encryptions). *A public-key encryption scheme $(\mathcal{G}, \mathcal{E}, \mathcal{D})$ is indistinguishable under CCA2 attacks if for every pair of probabilistic polynomial-time oracle machines $A = (A_1, A_2)$,*

$$|\Pr[\mathbf{Expt}_A(0) = 1] - \Pr[\mathbf{Expt}_A(1) = 1]| < \mu(n)$$

where μ is a negligible function and $\mathbf{Expt}_A(b)$ is defined as follows for $b \in \{0, 1\}$:

1. *$(pk, sk) \leftarrow \mathcal{G}(1^n)$: generate a pair of public key and a secret key.*
2. *$(m_0, m_1, a) \leftarrow A_1^{D_{sk}}(pk)$, where $|m_0| = |m_1|$: A_1 receives a decryption oracle and outputs a pair of plaintexts for the challenge, and state information a for A_2.*
3. *$c \leftarrow \mathcal{E}_{pk}(m_b)$: compute the challenge ciphertext.*
4. *$b' \leftarrow A_2^{D_{sk}^{\neg c}}(c, a)$: A_2 receives the challenge ciphertext, access to a (restricted) decryption oracle (A_2 can not ask c to the decryption oracle as a query) and the state information a from A_1, and outputs a guess b' for b.*
5. *Output b'.*

The general construction of CCA2-secure public-key cryptosystem is first achieved by Dolev, Dwork and Naor [10] and was refined by Sahai and Lindell [25,22] by following the technique introduced by Naor and Yung in [23] and using simulation sound non-interactive zero-knowledge [25,8,22]. The first practical CCA2-secure public-key cryptosystem is achieved by Cramer and Shoup [6]. A good survey for this field can be found in [22].

2.1   Using Time in the Design of Protocols

In the following, we introduce the (α, β) time assumption for cryptographic protocol designs and the timed commitment scheme.

(α, β) (where $\alpha \leq \beta$) time assumption is introduced in [14] which essentially assumes that all good parties have clocks satisfying the following constraint: for any two (possibly the same) non-faulty parties P_1 and P_2, if P_1 measures α elapsed time on its local clock and P_2 measures β elapsed time on its local clock, and P_2 begins its measurement in real time after P_1 begins, then P_2 will finish after P_1 does.

Recent works have shown the power of time in the design of cryptographic protocols through the use of an (α, β) assumptions [11,12,14,15,3,13,19]. In this work, we implicitly use time via the *timed commitment* introduced in [3].

The following description of timed commitment is almost verbatim from [3]. Let ε be a negligible function, a (T, t, ε) *timed commitment* scheme for a string $y \in \{0,1\}^n$ enables Alice (the committer) to give Bob (the verifier) a commitment to the string y. At a later time Alice can prove to Bob that the committed string is y. However, if Alice refuses to reveal y, Bob can spend time T to forcibly retrieve y. Alice is assured that within time t on a parallel machine with polynomially many processors, where $t < T$, Bob will succeed in obtaining y with probability at most ε. Formally, a (T, t, ε) timed commitment scheme consists of three phases:

Commit phase: To commit to a string $y \in \{0,1\}^n$ Alice and Bob execute a protocol whose outcome is a commitment string ζ which is given to Bob.

Open phase: At a later time Alice may reveal the string y to Bob. They execute a protocol so that at the end of the protocol Bob has a proof that y is the committed value.

Forced open phase: Suppose Alice refuses to execute the *open* phase and does not reveal y. Then there exists an algorithm, called *forced-open*, that takes the commitment string ζ as input and outputs y and a proof that y is the committed value by computing a moderately hard function. Specifically, for every valid commitment ζ, it is possible, through moderately hard computation, to recover a pair (y, π) such that π is an easily checked witness to the fact that ζ is a commitment to y. The set of valid commitments is in $\mathcal{NP}$: for every valid commitment ζ there is a witness π to the statement "ζ is a valid commitment to a string that can be recovered through the *forced open phase*". The running time of the algorithm is T. We remark that the forced open time is relatively large compared to the time of all other operations in the protocol (such as, constructing ζ, verifying a correctly decommitted value, verifying future recoverability, etc.). Thus, we think of all other operations as "easy" while recovery is "moderately hard".

And, the commitment scheme must satisfy a number of security constraints:

Binding: During the *open* phase, Alice can not convince Bob that ζ is commitment to $y' \neq y$.

Soundness: At the end of the *commit* phase Bob is convinced that, given ζ, the *forced-open* algorithm will produce the committed value y in time T.

Privacy: Every *PRAM* algorithm A whose running time is at most t for $t < T$ on polynomially many processors, will succeed in distinguishing y from a random string r, given the transcript of the commit protocol as input, with advantage at most ε. In other words,

$$|\Pr[A(transcript, y) = \text{``yes''}] - \Pr[A(transcript, r) = \text{``yes''}]| < \varepsilon(n)$$

where the probability is over the random choice of y and r and the random bits used to create ζ from y during the *commit* phase.

3   Public-Coin WI vs. Public-Coin HVZK and Public-Coin SHVZK

In this section, we clarify the relations among public-coin WI, public-coin HVZK and public-coin SHVZK. It is well-known that any public-coin SHVZK protocol is also public-coin WI [5]. In this section, we show that the existence of zaps for $\mathcal{NP}$ (under the existence of one-way permutations) actually strictly separates public-coin WI and public-coin SHVZK. We also show that public-coin HVZK does not imply public-coin WI assuming the existence of one-way permutations.

Theorem 1. *Assuming one-way permutations exists and $\mathcal{NP} \nsubseteq \mathcal{BPP}$, there exists a public-coin proof system for $\mathcal{NP}$ that is WI but not public-coin special honest verifier zero-knowledge.*

Proof. We first note that the zap [13] is itself a 2-round public-coin WI proof for $\mathcal{NP}$ and can be constructed under the assumption that one-way permutations exist. Then all the left is to show that zaps cannot be public-coin SHVZK assuming $\mathcal{NP} \nsubseteq \mathcal{BPP}$. Actually, using the idea of [20] we can show the following lemma.

Lemma 1. *Let L be a language for which there exists a 2-round public-coin SHVZK proof system, then $L \in \mathcal{BPP}$.*

Proof. For any language L that has a 2-round public-coin SHVZK proof system, suppose S be the special honest verifier zero-knowledge simulator. We construct a $\mathcal{BPP}$ machine M that decides L as follows.

On common input x, machine M randomly chooses a random string r and runs $S(x, r)$. If $S(x, r)$ outputs an accepting conversation in polynomial time then M decides $x \in L$, otherwise, $x \notin L$.

Completeness of M: If $x \in L$, then according to the completeness of the underlying 2-round public-coin SHVZK proof system, the conversation between honest prover and honest verifier on x will be an accepting one with overwhelming probability. Then according to the definition of public-coin SHVZK, $S(x, r)$ will also generate an accepting conversation in polynomial time with overwhelming probability, and so M decides correctly $x \in L$ with overwhelming probability.

Soundness of M: If $x \notin L$, then $S(x, r)$ cannot generate an accepting conversation in polynomial time with non-negligible probability since otherwise it will violate the soundness of the underlying 2-round public-coin SHVZK proof system. This means that if $x \notin L$ then M will correctly decide $x \notin L$ with overwhelming probability.   □

The theorem follows from the above lemma.   □

Although 2-round public-coin SHVZK proofs cannot exist for non-trivial languages (out of $\mathcal{BPP}$), there do exist 2-round public-coin HVZK proofs for $\mathcal{NP}$ assuming the existence of one-way permutaions. Furthermore, such 2-round public-coin HVZK proofs cannot be public-coin WI.

Theorem 2. *Assuming the existence of one-way permutations, there exists a 2-round public-coin proof system for $\mathcal{NP}$ that is public-coin HVZK but not public-coin WI.*

Proof. We first note that there exists a transformation that from any 2-round public-coin HVZK protocol for a language L produces another 2-round public-coin protocol for same language L that is still HVZK but not WI. Given a 2-round public-coin HVZK protocol, the idea is just to modify the given HVZK protocol so that the prover outputs the witness if the verifier's first message are all zeros. This modification does not hurt the ZK property with respect to honest verifier but it's certainly not WI.

Then all the left is to present a 2-round public-coin HVZK protocol for $\mathcal{NP}$ under the assumption that one-way permutations exist. Let $\langle NIP, NIV \rangle$ be a non-interactive zero-knowledge proof system for $\mathcal{NP}$ that can be constructed assuming the existence of one-way permutations. Consider the following 2-round public-coin proof system $\langle P, V \rangle$ for $\mathcal{NP}$:

Round 1. On common input x of length n, V randomly selects a string r from $\{0,1\}^{NI\sigma Len(n)}$ and sends r to P.

Round 2. Using r as the common random string, P gives back a non-interactive zero-knowledge proof that there exists a w such that $(x, w) \in R_L$. Specifically, P sends back $NIP(x, r)$ to V.

The completeness and soundness of $\langle P, V \rangle$ is followed from the completeness and soundness of the underlying NIZK system.

$\langle P, V \rangle$ is public-coin HVZK by observing that the non-interactive zero-knowledge simulator of $\langle NIP, NIV \rangle$ is also an honest verifier zero-knowledge simulator for $\langle P, V \rangle$. $\qquad\square$

4   Improved Two-Round Timed Deniable Authentication

We now describe our improved 2-round deniable authentication scheme. We remark that the following three cryptographic tools play a critical role in the original Dwork-Naor 2-round timed deniable authentication [13]: non-malleable public-key cryptosystem secure against chosen-ciphertext attacks in the post-processing model, zap and timed commitment. Besides the above three cryptographic tools, in this paper we also use collision-resistant hash functions which map strings of different lengths to short, fixed-sized output. Informally, a function $H : \{0,1\}^* \rightarrow \{0,1\}^l$ is collision-resistant if it is infeasible for any (non-uniform polynomial-time) adversary to find two strings x and x' such that $H(x) = H(x')$. Collision-resistance is a basic property of cryptographic hash functions, such as MD5 or SHA-1. We remark that hashing is a much faster operation in comparison with public-key encryption and even with block ciphers.

Let AP be the authenticator and V be the verifier. The AP has a public-key E_1, E_2, ρ, H, where E_1 and E_2 are public encryption keys chosen according to a public-key cryptosystem generator that is non-malleable against chosen-ciphertext attacks in the post-processing mode, ρ is a first-round message of a zap and H is a collision-resistant hash function: $\{0,1\}^* \to \{0,1\}^n$. AP's private-keys are (D_1, D_2) corresponding to (E_1, E_2). The verifier V uses a timed commitment scheme denoted TC.

Round 1. The verifier chooses random strings y_0, y_1, r from $\{0,1\}^n$ and sends to the authenticator $c \in_R E_1(r)$ and timed commitments $\zeta_0 \in_R TC(y_0)$ and $\zeta_1 \in_R TC(y_1)$. In addition, using ρ, the verifier gives a zap π that at least one of the ζ_i is valid. Finally, the verifier also sends to the authenticator a first-round message ρ' for a zap.

Round 2. The authenticator checks the zap (ρ, π) and aborts if verification fails. Otherwise, let m be the message to be authenticated, the authenticator computes $H(m)$ and sends to the verifier $m, \eta \in_R E_1(r \oplus H(m)), \delta \in_R E_2(s)$ for a randomly chosen s in $\{0,1\}^n$. Using ρ', the prover sends a zap π' that at least one of the following holds: $\eta \in E_1(r \oplus H(m))$ or $s \in \{y_0, y_1\}$. The witness used in creating π' is the set of random bits in creating η.

The verifier V accepts if and only if both (1) the zap (ρ', π') is accepted and (2) AP's response is received in a *timely* fashion, satisfying in the following (α, β) timing constraint.

(α, β)-**Timing constraint:** AP's Round 2 message must arrive within time α on V's local clock from the time at which V sent its Round 1 message. α and β are chosen to satisfy $\alpha \leq \beta$ and $\beta + \gamma < T$, where the value T is the time below which it is safe to assume that the timed commitment cannot be broken, even by a PRAM, and γ is an upper bound on the time it takes to create a zap by a program that is given a witness. For completeness, α must be sufficiently large to permit the necessary computation by AP, and the round-trip message delay.

Theorem 1. *The above protocol is a 2-round timed deniable authentication scheme.*

Proof.

The completeness can be easily checked. Here we only focus on soundness and deniability of the scheme.

Soundness. After having asked the authenticator to authenticate any polynomial number of messages $m_1, m_2, \cdots$, suppose the adversary is trying to forge a message m, $m \neq m_i, i = 1, 2, \cdots$. Then, for a Round 1 message $(E_1(r), TC(y_0), TC(y_1), \pi, \rho')$ received from the verifier, there are three cases for the adversary to successfully respond it:

Case 1. $H(m) = H(m_i)$, for some $i = 1, 2, \cdots$.

Case 2. $H(m) \neq H(m_i), i = 1, 2, \cdots$, and the zap (ρ', π') is created by using $H(m) \oplus r$ as the witness.

Case 3. $H(m) \neq H(m_i), i = 1, 2, \cdots$, and the zap (ρ', π') is created by using $y_i, i \in \{0, 1\}$, as the witness.

It is clear that the probability for the adversary succeeds in Case 1 is negligible due to the collision-resistance property of the hash function used. By the non-malleability of E_1 the adversary also cannot compute out $H(m) \oplus r$, otherwise, the adversary can completely break E_1. So the probability of Case 2 is also negligible. In the following, we focus on the analysis of Case 3.

According to above arguments, we know that given that the adversary successfully provides the zap (ρ', π'), with overwhelming probability it is the case that $s = y_i$ for some $i \in \{0, 1\}$. Furthermore, the adversary responds in a timely way satisfying the timing constraints specified above. Then, together the adversary and the real authenticator (who knows the corresponding decryption-key of E_2, D_2) we can construct a non-uniform PPT algorithm that breaks the timed commitment scheme TC with probability negligibly close to $1/2$ as follows: given $TC(y)$, choose y' at random and give $TC(y')$; then, using the witness based on y', give a zap that at least one of $TC(y)$ or $TC(y')$ is recoverable. By definition, such a zap can be constructed within time γ. If the adversary successfully gives back the Round 2 message $(m, \eta, \delta, \rho', \pi')$ within time α, then with probability negligibly close to $1/2$ we will get y by decrypting δ. This means that TC has been broken in time at most $\beta + \gamma < T$, which contradicts the privacy property of the timed commitment used. Thus, the probability of Case 3 is also negligible.

Deniability. For each message m to be authenticated, after receiving $(E_1(r), TC(y_0), TC(y_1), \pi, \rho')$ from the verifier the simulator first check the zap (ρ, π) and aborts if verification fails. Otherwise, the simulator *freezes* the clocks and extracts from $TC(y_0)$ and $TC(y_1)$ either y_0 or y_1 by using the forced-open algorithm of the timed commitment. It then creates $E_1(r')$ for a random r' and creates $E_2(y_i)$ and uses it as a witness to a zap π' that $\eta \in E_1(H(m) \oplus r)$ or $s = y_i$.

Now consider four classes of transcripts: they differ according to the values encrypted by E_1 and E_2 and which witness is used in creating the zap π': $H(m) \oplus r$ or y_i.

1. $(E_1(H(m) \oplus r), E_2(s), \pi'(H(m) \oplus r))$, where s is a random string and $\pi'(H(m) \oplus r)$ denotes that the zap π' is created using $H(m) \oplus r$ as the witness.
2. $(E_1(H(m) \oplus r), E_2(y_i), \pi'(H(m) \oplus r))$.
3. $(E_1(H(m) \oplus r), E_2(y_i), \pi'(y_i))$.
4. $(E_1(r'), E_2(y_i), \pi'(y_i))$.

The real transcripts are the first class. The simulator outputs the fourth class. Class 1 is indistinguishable from Class 2 according to the indistinguishability of public-key cryptosystem secure against chosen-ciphertext attacks in the post-processing model. For the same reason, Class 3 is also indistinguishable from Class 4. Class 2 and Class 3 are indistinguishable by the witness-indistinguishability of zaps. Hence Class 1 and Class 4 are computationally indistinguishable. $\square$

We comment that the main difference between our protocol and the original Dwork-Naor scheme is that in the original protocol of Dwork and Naor [13] the verifier sends $E_1(m \circ r)$ rather than only $E_1(r)$ as in our protocol. This means the dependence of the first verifier message in the original scheme (on the message to be authenticated) is avoided.

Acknowledgement. We are full of gratitude to Xiaotie Deng and Frances Yao for their valuable suggestions and discussions. The first author is grateful to Damgard and Dwork for their kindly clarifications on Σ-protocols and zaps.

References

1. M. Bellare, A. Desai, D. Pointcheval and P. Rogaway. Relations Among Notions of Security for Public-Key Encryption Schemes In *H. Krawczyk (Ed.): Advances in Cryptology-Proceedings of CRYPTO 1998, LNCS 1462*, pages 26-45. Springer-Verlag, 1998.
2. M. Bellare and A. Sahai. Non-Malleable Encryption: Equivalence between Two Notions and an Indistinguishability-Based Characterization. In *M. J. Wiener (Ed.): Advances in Cryptology-Proceedings of CRYPTO 1999, LNCS 1666*, pages 519-536. Springer-Verlag, 1999.
3. D. Boneh and M. Naor. Timed Commitments and Applications. In *M. Bellare (Ed.): Advances in Cryptology-Proceedings of CRYPTO 2000, LNCS 1880*, pages 236-254. Springer-Verlag, 2000.
4. R. Cramer and I. Damgard. On Electronic Payment Systems. A lecture note for the course of Cryptographic Protocol Theory at Aarhus University, 2003. Available from: http://www.daimi.au.dk/~ivan/CPT.html
5. R. Cramer, I. Damgard and B. Schoenmakers. Proofs of Partial Knowledge and Simplified Design of Witness Hiding Protocols. In *Y. Desmedt (Ed.): Advances in Cryptology-Proceedings of CRYPTO 1994, LNCS 839*, pages 174-187. Springer-Verlag, 1994.
6. R. Cramer and V. Shoup. A Practical Public-Key Cryptosystem Provably Secure Against Adaptive Chosen Ciphertext Attack. In *H. Krawczyk (Ed.): Advances in Cryptology-Proceedings of CRYPTO 1998, LNCS 1462*, pages 13-25. Springer-Verlag, 1998.
7. I. Damgard. On Σ-protocols. A lecture note for the course of Cryptographic Protocol Theory at Aarhus University, 2003. Available from: http://www.daimi.au.dk/~ivan/CPT.html
8. A. D. Santis, G. D. Crescenzo, R. Ostrovsky, G. Persiano and A. Sahai. Robust Non-Interactive Zero-Knowledge. In *J. Kilian (Ed.): Advances in Cryptology-Proceedings of CRYPTO 2001, LNCS 2139*, pages 566-598. Springer-Verlag, 2001.
9. A. D. Santis and G. Persiano. Zero-Knowledge Proofs of Knowledge Without Interaction. In *IEEE Symposium on Foundations of Computer Science*, pages 427-436, 1992.
10. D. Dolev, C. Dwork and M. Naor. Non-Malleable Cryptography. In *ACM Symposium on Theory of Computing*, pages 542-552, 1991.
11. C. Dwork and M. Naor. Pricing via Processing-or-Combatting Junk Mail. In *E. F. Brickell (Ed.): Advances in Cryptology-Proceedings of CRYPTO 1992, LNCS 740*, pages 139-147. Springer-Verlag, 1992.
12. C. Dwork and M. Naor. Method for Message Authentication from Non-Malleable Crypto Systems. US Patent No. 05539826, issued Aug. 29th 1996.
13. C. Dwork and M. Naor. Zaps and Their Applications. In *IEEE Symposium on Foundations of Computer Science*, pages 283-293, 2000. Available on-line from: http://www.wisdom.weizmann.ac.il/~naor/
14. C. Dwork, M. Naor and A. Sahai. Concurrent Zero-Knowledge. In *ACM Symposium on Theory of Computing*, pages 409-418, 1998.

15. C. Dwork and A. Sahai. Concurrent Zero-Knowledge: Reducing the Need for Timing Constraints. In *H. Krawczyk (Ed.): Advances in Cryptology-Proceedings of CRYPTO 1998, LNCS 1462*, pages 442-457. Springer-Verlag, 1998.

16. C. Dwork and L. Stockmeyer. 2-Round Zero-Knowledge and Proof Auditors. In *ACM Symposium on Theory of Computing*, pages 322-331, 2002.

17. U.Feige, D. Lapidot and A. Shamir. Multiple Non-Interactive Zero-Knowledge Proofs Under General Assumptions. *SIAM Journal on Computing*, 29(1): 1-28, 1999.

18. A. Fiat and A. Shamir. How to Prove Yourself: Practical Solutions to Identification and Signature Problems. In *A. Odlyzko (Ed.): Advances in Cryptology-Proceedings of CRYPTO'86, LNCS 263*, pages 186-194. Springer-Verlag, 1986.

19. O. Goldreich. Concurrent Zero-Knowledge with Timing, Revisited. In *ACM Symposium on Theory of Computing*, pages 332-340, 2002.

20. O. Goldreich and Y. Oren. Definitions and Properties of Zero-Knowledge Proof Systems. *Journal of Cryptology*, 7(1):1-32, 1994.

21. J. Kilian, E. Petrank. An Efficient Non-Interactive Zero-Knowledge Proof System for $\mathcal{NP}$ with General Assumptions. *Journal of Cryptology*, 11(2): 24, 1998.

22. Y. Lindell. A Simple Construction of CCA2-Secure Public-Key Enryption Under General Assumptions. In *E. Biham (Ed.): Advances in Cryptology-Proceedings of EUROCRYPT 2003, LNCS 2656* , pages 241-255. Springer-Verlag, 2003.

23. M. Naor and M. Yung. Public-Key Cryptosystems Provably Secure Against Chosen Ciphertext Attacks. In *ACM Symposium on Theory of Computing*, pages 427-437, 1990.

24. R. Pass. Simulation in Quasi-Polynomial Time, and Its Application to Protocol Composition. In *E. Biham (Ed.): Advances in Cryptology-Proceedings of EUROCRYPT 2003, LNCS 2656* , pages 160-177. Springer-Verlag, 2003.

25. A. Sahai. Non-Malleable Non-Interactive Zero Knowledge and Adaptive Chosen Ciphertext Security. In *IEEE Symposium on Foundations of Computer Science*, pages 543-553, 1999.

26. Y. Zhao, X. Deng, C. H. Lee and H. Zhu. Resettable Zero-Knowledge in the Weak Public-Key Model. In *E. Biham (Ed.): Advances in Cryptology-Proceedings of EUROCRYPT 2003, LNCS 2656,* pages 123-140. Springer-Verlag, 2003.

Security Measurements of Steganographic Systems

Weiming Zhang and Shiqu Li

Department of Applied Mathematics, University of Information Engineering,
P.O.Box 1001-747, Zhengzhou 450002, P.R. China
{nlxd_990, ShiquLi}@yahoo.com.cn

Abstract. Different security measurements for a steganographic system, i.e. security (detectability), robustness and secrecy (difficulty of extraction), are discussed in this paper. We propose a new measurement for the security of stegosystems using variational distance which can upper bound the advantage for passive attackers. It is proved that the hiding capacity, which is also the measurement for robustness, is limited by security. We think the extracting attack essentially is a kind of cryptanalysis and define the secrecy of stegosystems as an analogue of secrecy of cryptosystems. The relations of secrecy with capacity and security are analyzed in the terms of unicity distance. And it is shown that there is a tradeoff between secrecy and capacity while there is some kind of consistency between secrecy and security.

1 Introduction

This paper is about steganography which is the oldest branch of information hiding. The scientific study of steganography began with Simmons' "Prisoners' Problem" [1]. The survey about the history and current development of it can be found in [2] and [3]. A general model of a steganographic system (i.e. stegosystem) can be described as follows. The embedded data M is the message that Alice wants to send secretly to Bob. It is hidden in an innocuous message $\tilde{X}$, usually named cover-object, in the control of a stego-key K, producing the stego-object X. And the receiver can extract M from X with the stego-key K.

The attacks to a stegosystem mainly include passive attack, active attack, and extracting attack. A passive attacker only wants to detect the existence of the embedded message, while an active attacker wants to destroy the embedded message. The purpose of an extracting attacker is to obtain the message hidden in the stego-object. So there are three kinds of security measurements for the different attackers respectively, i.e. detectability, robustness and difficulty of extraction. Usually the problem of steganography only concerns the detectability so in many literatures detectability is referred to as the security of a stegosystem. In this paper, we also call the detectability as security of a stegosystem and the difficulty of extraction as secrecy of it. But so far the definitions of the three security measurements are still tangly and relations of them are still unclear. The

M. Jakobsson, M. Yung, J. Zhou (Eds.): ACNS 2004, LNCS 3089, pp. 194–204, 2004.

main purpose of this paper is just to distinguish their definitions and analyze relations between them.

So far there have been several literatures that define the security (detectability) of stegosystems, such as [4,5,6,7], and the one of C.Cachin [5] is most influential. Cachin formulates the steganography problem as a hypothesis testing problem and defines the security using the statistic distance between the cover-object and stego-object which indeed catches the key of detectability. But, he uses the relative entropy as the security measurement which, to some extent, seems not appropriate. According to Cachin's definition the stegosystem is ε-secure when the relative entropy $D(\widetilde{X}\|X) \leq \varepsilon$, and perfectly secure when $\varepsilon = 0$. Supposing the false alarm probability (the probability of a cover-object being mistaken as a stego-object) equals zero, Cachin uses the relative entropy to estimate the lower bound of missing probability (the probability of a stego-object being mistaken as a cover-object). However, it is evident that the adversary will not use a rule such that he makes the false alarm probability very small, because this means he will leak the illegal messages in a large probability. For instance, in Cachin's model, when the stegosystem is perfect security, the probability of the adversary finding the stego-object equals zero. But the fact is that even guessing randomly, he could success with probability $\frac{1}{2}$.

S.Katzenbeisser and F.A.Petitcolas [8] defines security in computational settings, and their definition still need a security measurement which is referred as to the advantage for a adversary, i.e. the probability of the adversary's successful detection minus $\frac{1}{2}$. This description for stegosystem's security is reasonable, but it is a description in words. And the definition of R.Chandramouli and N.D.Memon [9] can be though of as a mathematic version of description in [8], and their definition is related with the strategy of attackers. In fact we hope there is a metric that can reflect the adversaries' advantage, and in this paper we will propose such a metric with variational distance.

Information hiding with active attackers were analyzed by P.Moulin and J.A.O'Sullivan [10] and M.Ettinger [11]. They defines the robustness using "hiding capacity". Robustness is mainly concerned in watermarking problem, but as the measure of efficiency, capacity is also important for steganography. I.S.Moskoxitz et al. [7] proposed a two dimension security measure for steganography, i.e. $capability = (P, D)$ where P is the payload size and D is detectability threshold. In this paper, we prove that the capacity is limited by detectability, and for stegosystems with active attackers this shows a tradeoff between the security and robustness.

The security and robustness have been greatly concerned. However there is scarcely any literature about extracting attacks. We only know that R.Chandramouli ever studied how to extract the hidden message for some kind of scenario in [12], and J.Fridrich et al. recently presented a methodology for identifying the stego-key in [13]. In fact, for most of stegosystems the message is asked to be encrypted before it is embedded into the cover-object, so the secrecy is guaranteed by the cryptographic algorithm. So stegoanalysts only concern detection and think extraction is the task of cryptanalysts, while the latter only process encrypted data. But how to extract the hidden message is a very difficult problem itself. We think the extracting attack essentially is a kind of cryptanalysis. When facing the model of "encrytion+hiding", a cryptanalyst has to analyze a "multiple cipher": he should extract the hidden messag (the ciphertexts) from stego-objects, and then extract the plaintexts from the hidden message. In this paper, we distinguish the secrecy of steganography from that of cryptography. If the message has been encrypted, the extraction attacker is successful as long as he can extract the cipertexts. So the secrecy of steganography is just the difficulty of extraction. Because extracting attack is a kind of cryptanalysis, we define the secrecy of steganography imitating Shannon's definition for unconditional security of cryptosystems [14], i.e. measuring the secrecy with mutual information $I(M; X)$ or $I(M; X, \widetilde{X})$. And we will analyze the relations between security, capacity and secrecy.

The rest of this paper is organized as follows: Section 2 defines the security of stegosystems with variational distance and estimates the upper bound of the advantage for passive adversaries. Section 3 proves the tradeoff between the security and capacity. Section 4 defines the perfect secrecy for only stego-object extracting attack and known cover-object extracting attack respectively, and analyzes the relations between capacity, security and secrecy in terms of unicity distance. The paper concludes with a discussion in Sect. 5.

2   Security of Stegosystems

2.1   Notations and Statement of Problem

We use the following notations. Random variables are denoted by capital letters (e.g. X), and their realizations by respective lower case letters (e.g. x). The domains over which random variables are defined are denoted by script letters (e.g. $\mathcal{X}$). Sequences of n random variables are denoted with a superscript n (e.g. $X^n = (X_1, X_2, \cdots, X_n)$ which takes its values on the product set $\mathcal{X}^n$). The probability mass function (p.m.f.) of random variable X is denoted by $P_X(x)$, and when no confusion is possible, we drop the subscript.

Definition 1. [15] *Let $\widetilde{X}$ and X are two random variables on a discrete universe $\mathcal{X}$, then the variational distance between $\widetilde{X}$ and X is defined to be*

$$VD(\widetilde{X}, X) = \max_{S \subseteq \mathcal{X}} |P_{\widetilde{X}}(S) - P_X(S)| \ .$$

Lemma 1. [16] *Let $\widetilde{X}$ and X are two random variables on a discrete universe $\mathcal{X}$, and $\mathcal{T}$ is another discrete universe, then for any function $f : \mathcal{X} \to \mathcal{T}$, $VD(f(\widetilde{X}), f(X)) \leq VD(\widetilde{X}, X)$.*

In this paper, $\widetilde{X}$ stands for cover-object, taking values in $\mathcal{X}$. M denotes the hidden message, K is the stego-key (embedding key). X, which is also defined in $\mathcal{X}$, denotes the stego-object. Here hidden message is what will ultimately be embedded into the cover-object which usually is encrypted data. And the stego-key only refers to the embedding key excluding the encrytion key. E is the embedding algorithm, with which the sender Alice embeds m into $\widetilde{x}$ to get x using k, i.e. $x = E(\widetilde{x}, m, k)$. And D is the extracting algorithm used by receiver Bob, which satisfies $m = D(x, k) = D(E(\widetilde{x}, m, k), k)$. We denote a stegosystem by a set with 6 elements: $stegosystem(\widetilde{X}, X, M, K, E, D)$.

The present paper mainly follows the view of Cachin [5] who formulated the steganography problem with passive attackers as a hypothesis testing problem. Alice, who maybe uses a stegosystem, sends data to Bob. The passive adversary Wendy observes the data and makes a hypothesis testing. Here the original hypothesis H_0 is that the data is generated according to $\widetilde{X}$, i.e. Alice sent a cover-object. And the opposite hypothesis H_1 is that the data is generated according to X, i.e. Alice sent a stego-object. The probability that Wendy fails to detect a stego-object is called missing probability and denoted by β. And the probability that she thinks of a cover-texts as a stego-object is called false alarm probability and denoted by α.

2.2   Security of Stegosystem

Variational distance can reflect the statistic difference of two probability distributions as relative entropy does. What's more, Variational distance is a distance in the sense of mathematics and take values between zero and one. So with variational distance as the measurement, we can compare the security of different stegosystems. We define the security of a stegosystem as follows.

Definition 2. *A* $stegosystem(\widetilde{X}, X, M, K, E, D)$ *is called ε-secure, if*

$$VD(\widetilde{X}, X) \leq \varepsilon .$$

And when $\varepsilon = 0$, the system is called perfectly secure.

With relative entropy as the security measure, Cachin [5] yields a lower bound on the missing probability β, i.e. if $D(\widetilde{X}\|X) \leq \varepsilon$ and the false alarm probability $\alpha = 0$, then $\beta \geq 2^{-\varepsilon}$. But, as the analysis in the Sect. 1, what we need is the estimation about the advantage for adversaries. To do this, we define the event of successful attack as

$$SUCC = \{H_0 \text{ is true and Wendy accepts } H_0\}$$
$$\cup \{H_1 \text{ is true and Wendy accepts } H_1\} .$$

And its complementary event is defined to be

$$\overline{SUCC} = \{H_0 \text{ is true and Wendy accepts } H_1\}$$
$$\cup \{H_1 \text{ is true and Wendy accepts } H_0\} .$$

It is reasonable for Wendy to suppose the prior probability of both H_0 and H_1 is that $P(H_0) = P(H_1) = \frac{1}{2}$, because the event that which kind of object

Alice will send is random for Wendy who wants to get some advantage through the observed data. So the advantage for the adversary (Adv) is defined by

$$Adv = |P(SUCC) - \frac{1}{2}| . \tag{1}$$

As for Adv, using the security measurement in definition 2 we can yield the following result.

Theorem 1. *If a stegosystem$(\widetilde{X}, X, M, K, E, D)$ is ε-secure, then the advantage for the adversary satisfies $Adv \leq \frac{\varepsilon}{2}$. And when the system is perfectly secure, i.e. $\varepsilon = 0$, then $Adv = 0$.*

Proof. Note that the probabilities of two type errors made by Wendy are just that $\alpha = P\{Wendy\ accepts\ H_1|H_0\ is\ true\}$, and $\beta = P\{Wendy\ accepts\ H_0|H_1\ is\ true\}$.
Combing these two equalities with the fact $P(H_0) = P(H_1) = \frac{1}{2}$, we have $P(\overline{SUCC}) = \frac{1}{2}(\alpha + \beta)$ and then

$$P(SUCC) = 1 - \frac{1}{2}(\alpha + \beta) . \tag{2}$$

The probabilities of the two type errors, α and β can induce two $0 - 1$ random variables as follows:

	0	1
$\widetilde{X}'$	α	$1 - \alpha$
X'	$1 - \beta$	β

$\widetilde{X}'$ and X' can be get through a same function from $\widetilde{X}$ and X, so using Lemma 1 we can obtain that $VD(\widetilde{X}', X') \leq VD(\widetilde{X}, X)$, i.e. $1 - \varepsilon \leq \alpha + \beta \leq 1 + \varepsilon$, which with (2) implies that $\frac{1}{2} - \frac{\varepsilon}{2} \leq P(SUCC) \leq \frac{1}{2} + \frac{\varepsilon}{2}$, i.e. $Adv \leq \frac{\varepsilon}{2}$. □

Theorem 1 shows that if a stegosystem is ε-security the advantage for a passive adversary using any decision rule over the adversary guessing randomly will not larger than $\frac{\varepsilon}{2}$. And if the stegosystem is perfectly secure, then any decision rule used by the adversary will not more effective than guessing randomly. That means that the knowledge the adversary get through observing data about whether Alice has sent stego-object or not is zero. So the metric given in Definition 2 accurately depicts the security of stegosystems.

3   Tradeoff between Security and Capacity

Moulin and O'Sullivan. [10] and Ettinger [11] view the information hiding problem as a capacity game between the users of a stegosystem and the active attacker. According to formulations in [10], a strategy of the sender is just a "covert channel", i.e. a conditional p.m.f $\widetilde{Q}(x, u|\widetilde{x}, k)$, subject to distortion D_1. Here U is an auxiliary random variable. $\widetilde{Q}$ is the set of all such cover channels. The attacker's output is denoted by Y, and a strategy of the attacker is described as a "attack channel", i.e. a conditional p.m.f $Q(y|x)$, subject to distortion D_2. And The set of all such attack channels is denoted by $\mathcal{Q}$. The hiding capacity is defined as the upper-bound of rates of reliable transmission of the hidden message. Moulin and O'Sullivan obtained a expression for the hiding capacity as follows:

$$C = \max_{\widetilde{Q} \in \widetilde{\mathcal{Q}}} \min_{Q \in \mathcal{Q}} [I(U; Y|K) - I(U; \widetilde{X}|K)] \ . \tag{3}$$

where $(U, \widetilde{X}, K) \to X \to Y$ is a Markov chain.

In this section, we discuss the relation between the detectability (security) and the capacity (robustness) of general information hiding problems. We think the detectability of a information hiding code should include two parts: one is the sensual detectability (transparency) which is needed by any information hiding problem such as watermarking, steganography and fingerprint, the other is statistic detectability which is just the security of steganography. The former means the stego-object is a good estimation of the cover-object, so it can be measured by the probability $p_e = P(X \neq \widetilde{X})$ which is relative with the conditional entropy $H(\widetilde{X}|X)$, and the latter can be measured by the advantage for adversaries which, as we have proved in Sect. 2, is relative with the varational distance $VD(\widetilde{X}, X)$. Theorem below shows that there is a tradeoff between the detectability and the capacity.

Lemma 2. [16] *Let X and $\widetilde{X}$ are random variables on a discrete universe $\mathcal{X}$, and $VD(\widetilde{X}, X) = \varepsilon$. Then $|H(X) - H(\widetilde{X})| \leq H(\varepsilon) + \varepsilon \log_2(|\mathcal{X}| - 1)$.*

Theorem 2. *For a stegosystem$(\widetilde{X}, X, M, K, E, D)$, if $P(X \neq \widetilde{X}) = p_e$, $VD(\widetilde{X}, X) = \varepsilon$ and the hiding capacity is C, then we have*

$$C \leq H(p_e) + H(\varepsilon) + (p_e + \varepsilon) \log_2(|\mathcal{X}| - 1) \ . \tag{4}$$

Proof.

$$I(U; Y|K) - I(U; \widetilde{X}|K)$$

$$\overset{(a)}{\leq} I(U; X|K) - I(U; \widetilde{X}|K)$$

$$= [I(U; \widetilde{X}, X|K) - I(U; \widetilde{X}|X, K)] - [I(U; \widetilde{X}, X|K) - I(U; X|\widetilde{X}, K)]$$

$$= I(U; X|\widetilde{X}, K) - I(U; \widetilde{X}|X, K)$$

$$\leq I(U; X|\widetilde{X}, K)$$

$$\leq H(X|\widetilde{X}, K)$$

$$\leq H(X|\widetilde{X})$$

$$= H(X) - I(X; \widetilde{X})$$

$$= [H(X) - H(\widetilde{X})] + H(\widetilde{X}|X)$$

$$\overset{(b)}{\leq} H(\varepsilon) + \varepsilon \log_2(|\mathcal{X}| - 1) + H(p_e) + p_e \log_2(|\mathcal{X}| - 1)$$

$$= H(p_e) + H(\varepsilon) + (p_e + \varepsilon) \log_2(|\mathcal{X}| - 1) \ .$$

Where (a) follows from the data processing inequality applied to the Markov chain $(U, \widetilde{X}, K) \to X \to Y$. *(b) is obtained from the Lemma 2 and Fano's inequality. And combining the inequality above with (3) just proves the theorem.*   □

On account of the meaning of p_e and Theorem 1, it is reasonable for us to suppose that $p_e \leq \frac{1}{2}$ and $\varepsilon \leq \frac{1}{2}$. Under this condition, the right of (4) increases with p_e and ε. So Theorem 2 shows a tradeoff between the capacity and detectability. And the upper-bound of hiding capacity includes two symmetrical parts: the first part is a function of sensual detectability, i.e. $H(p_e) + p_e \log_2(|\mathcal{X}| - 1)$, and the second part is a function of statistic detectability (security), i.e. $H(\varepsilon) + \varepsilon \log_2(|\mathcal{X}| - 1)$. Given p_e, Theorem 2 means a tradeoff between the security and capacity, and for information hiding problems with active attackers this is just the tradeoff between the security and robustness.

4   The Relations between Capacity, Security, and Secrecy

Since the extracting attack to a stegosystem in principle is a kind of cryptanalysis, we define the secrecy of stegosystems simulating the one of Shannon's [14] for cryptosystems.

Definition 3. *a stegosystem*$(\widetilde{X}, X, M, K, E, D)$ *is perfectly secret for only stego-object extracting attack if* $I(M; X) = 0$, *and is perfectly secret for known cover-object extracting attack if* $I(M; X, \widetilde{X}) = 0$.

J.Zölner et al. [4] ever defined the security of stegosystem using $I(M; X, \widetilde{X})$, but what they wanted to describe was the detectability, which seemed not appropriate because of the difference between the security and secrecy.

In this section, we only discuss the steganographic problem without active attackers. And suppose that stego-key K is independent with M and X. In this scenario, the result of [10] combined with the discussion in [17] implies that the hiding capacity

$$C = \max_{P(X|\widetilde{X})} H(X|\widetilde{X}) . \tag{5}$$

We also suppose that both the source of cover-objects and the channel $P(X|\widetilde{X})$ are memoryless. This seems not realistic, but we can think that X and $\widetilde{X}$ are both stand for block data, and usually supposing blockwise memoryless is reasonable.

What the extracting attacker ultimately wants to obtain is just the stego-key. Therefore we analyze the relations between capacity, security and secrecy in the terms of unicity distance for the stego-key. And we begin with the known cover-object extracting attack.

Lemma 3. *For a stegosystem*$(\widetilde{X}, X, M, K, E, D)$, *if* K *is independent with* $\widetilde{X}$, *then* $H(K|\widetilde{X}, X) = H(K) + H(M|\widetilde{X}, K) - H(X|\widetilde{X})$.

Proof. Because X can be determined by $(\widetilde{X}, M, K)$, and M can be determined by (X, K), we have $H(X|\widetilde{X}, M, K) = 0$, and $H(M|X, K) = 0$. *So*

$$H(\widetilde{X}, M, K) = H(\widetilde{X}, M, K) + H(X|\widetilde{X}, M, K)$$
$$= H(\widetilde{X}, X, M, K)$$
$$= H(\widetilde{X}, X, K) + H(M|\widetilde{X}, X, K)$$
$$= H(\widetilde{X}, X, K) \ .$$

Since K is independent with $\widetilde{X}$, using the chain rules we have

$$H(\widetilde{X}, M, K) = H(K) + H(\widetilde{X}|K) + H(M|\widetilde{X}, K)$$
$$= H(K) + H(\widetilde{X}) + H(M|\widetilde{X}, K) \ ,$$

and

$$H(\widetilde{X}, X, K) = H(\widetilde{X}) + H(X|\widetilde{X}) + H(K|\widetilde{X}, X) \ .$$

Combining the three equalities above, we can get

$$H(K|\widetilde{X}, X) = H(K) + H(M|\widetilde{X}, K) - H(X|\widetilde{X}) \ .$$

$\square$

Theorem 3. *For a stegosystem$(\widetilde{X}, X, M, K, E, D)$, if K is independent with $\widetilde{X}$ and M, and both source of cover-objects and cover channel are memoryless, then for given long enough sequence (the length is n) of pairs of cover-objects and stego-objects, the expectation of spurious stego-keys $\overline{S}_n$ for known cover-object extracting attack has the lower bound such that*

$$\overline{S}_n \geq \frac{2^{H(K)}}{2^{nC}} - 1 \ , \tag{6}$$

where $C = \max_{P(X|\widetilde{X})} H(X|\widetilde{X})$ is the hiding capacity.

Proof. For a given sequence of pairs of cover-objects and stegotexts $(\widetilde{x}^n, x^n) \in (\mathcal{X}^n \times \mathcal{X}^n)$, defining the set of possible stego-keys as

$$K(\widetilde{x}^n, x^n) = \{k \in \mathcal{K} | \text{there is } m^n \in \mathcal{M}^n \text{ such that } P(m^n) > 0, E(\widetilde{x}^n, m^n, k) = x^n\} \ .$$

So the number of spurious stego-keys for observed $(\widetilde{x}^n, x^n)$ is $|K(\widetilde{x}^n, x^n) - 1|$, and the expectation of spurious stego-keys is given by

$$\overline{S}_n = \sum_{(\widetilde{x}^n, x^n)} P(\widetilde{x}^n, x^n)(|K(\widetilde{x}^n, x^n) - 1|) = \sum_{(\widetilde{x}^n, x^n)} P(\widetilde{x}^n, x^n)|K(\widetilde{x}^n, x^n)| - 1 \ .$$

Using Jesen's inequality, we can get

$$H(K|\widetilde{X}^n, X^n) = \sum_{(\widetilde{x}^n, x^n)} P(\widetilde{x}^n, x^n) H(K|\widetilde{x}^n, x^n)$$

$$\leq \sum_{(\widetilde{x}^n, x^n)} P(\widetilde{x}^n, x^n) \log_2 |K(\widetilde{x}^n, x^n)|$$

$$\leq \log_2 \sum_{(\widetilde{x}^n, x^n)} P(\widetilde{x}^n, x^n) |K(\widetilde{x}^n, x^n)|$$

$$= \log_2(\overline{S}_n + 1) \ .$$

On the other hand, Lemma 3 and the fact that source of cover-objects and cover channel are memoryless implies that

$$H(K|\widetilde{X}^n, X^n) = H(K) + \quad H(M^n|\widetilde{X}^n, K) - H(X^n|\widetilde{X}^n)$$
$$\geq H(K) - H(X^n|\widetilde{X}^n)$$
$$= H(K) - nH(X|\widetilde{X}) \ .$$

Combing the two inequalities above, we have $\log_2(\overline{S}_n + 1) \geq H(K) - nH(X|\widetilde{X})$, i.e.

$$\overline{S}_n \geq \frac{2^{H(K)}}{2^{nH(X|\widetilde{X})}} - 1 \ .$$

Since $C = \max_{P(X|\widetilde{X})} H(X|\widetilde{X})$, we have

$$\overline{S}_n \geq \frac{2^{H(K)}}{2^{nC}} - 1 \ .$$

□

Definition 4. *The unicity distance n_0 for a stegosystem with known cover-object extracting attackers is the length of pairs of cover-objects and stego-objects at which one expects that the expectation of spurious stego-keys equals zero. And the unicity distance n_1 for a stegosystem with only stego-object extracting attackers is the length of stego-objects at which one expects that the expectation of spurious stego-keys equals zero.*

It is easy to know that $n_1 \geq n_0$, because $H(K|X) \geq H(K|\widetilde{X}, X)$. What's more, in (6), let $\overline{S}_n = 0$ and we have

$$n_1 \geq n_0 \geq \frac{H(K)}{C} \ . \tag{7}$$

Inequality (7) with Theorem 2 implies that

$$n_1 \geq n_0 \geq \frac{H(K)}{H(p_e) + H(\varepsilon) + (p_e + \varepsilon) \log_2(|\mathcal{X}| - 1)} \ . \tag{8}$$

For a stegosystem, (7) shows a tradeoff between the secrecy and capacity, while (8) shows some king of consistency of secrecy with security.

5   Conclusion

In this paper, three kind of security measuremeasures of stegosystems are discussed together. The relations and differences between them are analyzed with information theoretic method. We substitute variational distance for relative entropy to measure the security (detectability) of a stegosystem. This new measurement can upper bound the advantage for passive attackers. And it is proved out that the capacity (i.e. the robustness for stegosystems with active attackers) is limited by security. So an interesting problem is what the expression of hiding capacity subject to some security level ε is. Recently, P.Moulin and Y.Wang derived the capacity expression for perfectly secure (i.e. $\varepsilon = 0$) steganographic systems [20].

Our definition for secrecy is an analogue of Shannon's for cryptosystems. And it is shown that there is a tradeoff between secrecy and capacity but some kind of consistency of secrecy with security. However, the lower bound for unicity distance in Sect. 4 is rough. And a more useful lower bound will be discussed with the redundancy of cover channel in our upcoming paper.

Extracting attack is a problem that cryptanalysts have to face. So far there have been many literatures about passive attacks (i.e. steganalysis) such as [18, 19], while there is few about extracting attack which should rely on the techniques of both steganalysis and cryptanalysis. Our further work will also include the study of different kinds of extracting attacks to stegosystems.

References

1. Simmons, G. J.: The prisoners' problem and the subliminal channel. in Advances in Cryptology: Proceedings of Crypto' 83. Plenum Press (1984) 51–67
2. Petitcolas, F. A., Anderson, R. J., Kuhn, M. G.: Information hiding-a survey. Proceedings of the IEEE, Special Issue on Idenntification and Protection of Multimedia Information, vol. 87. (1999) 1062–1078
3. Anderson, R. J., Petitcolas, F. A.,: On the limits of steganography. IEEE Journal of Selected Areas in communications, vol. 16. (1998) 474–481
4. Zölner, J., Federrath, H., Klimant, H., Pfitzmann, A., Piotraschke, R., Westfeld, A., Wicke, G., Wolf, G.: Modeling the security of steganographic systems. in Information Hiding, Second International Workshop, Lecture Notes in Computer Science, vol. 1525. Springer-Verlag, Berlin Heidelberg New York (1998) 344–354
5. Cachin, C.: An information-theoretic model for steganography. in Information Hiding: Second International Workshop, Lecture Notes in Computer Science, vol. 1525. Springer-Verlag, Berlin Heidelberg New York (1998) 306–318
6. Mittelholzer, T.: An information-theoretic approach to steganography and watermarking. In: Pfitzmann A. (eds.): 3rd International Workshop. Lecture Notes in Computer Science, vol. 1768. Springer-Verlag, Berlin Heidelberg New York (2000) 1–16
7. Moskowitz, I. S., Chang, L., Newman, R. E.: Capacity is the wrong paradigm. Available: http://chacs.nrl.navy.mil/publications/CHACS/2002/2002moskowitz-capacity.pdf (2002)
8. Katzenbeisser, S., Petitcolas, F. A.: Defining security in steganographic systems. Proc. Electronic Imaging, Photonics West, SPIE, San Jose, California (2002)

9. Chandramouli, R., Memon, N. D.: Steganography capacity: A steganalysis perspective. Proc. SPIE Security and Watermarking of Multimedia Contents. Available: http://www.ece.stevens-tech.edu/~mouli/res.html (2003)

10. Moulin, P., O'Sullivan, J. A.: Information theoretic analysis of information hiding. IEEE Trans. on Information Theory, vol. 49. (2003) 563–593

11. Ettinger, M.: Steganalysis and game euilibria. in Information Hiding: Second International Workshop, Lecture Notes in Computer Science, vol. 1525. Springer-Verlag, Berlin Heidelberg New York (1998) 319–328

12. Chandramouli, R.: A mathematical framework for active steganalysis. In ACM Multimedia Systems Journal, Special Issue on Multimedia Watermarking. Available: http://www.ece.stevens-tech.edu/ mouli/res.html (2003)

13. Fridrich, J., Goljan, M., Soukal, D.: Searching for the stego key. Proc. EI SPIE San Jose, CA, Vol. 5306. (2004)

14. Shannon, C. E.: Communication theory of secrecy system. Bell Syst. Tech. J., vol. 28. (1949) 656–715

15. Cover, T. M., Thomas, J. A.: Elements of Information Theory. Wiley Series in Telecommunications, John Wiley & Sons Inc., 2nd edition. (1991)

16. Vadhan, S. P.: A study of statistical zero-knowledge proofs. Ph.D. dissertation. Department of Mathematics, Cambridge University (1999)

17. Somekh-Baruch, A., Merhav, N.: On the Capacity Game of Public Watermarking Systems. Available: http://tiger.technion.ac.il/~merhav/papers/p71.ps (2002)

18. Westfeld, A., Pfitzmann, A.: Attacks on Steganographic Systems. In: Pfitzmann A. (eds.): 3rd International Workshop. Lecture Notes in Computer Science, vol. 1768. Springer-Verlag, Berlin Heidelberg New York (2000) 61–75

19. Fridrich, J. Goljan, M., Hogea, D.: Steganalysis of JPEG Images: Breaking the F5 Algorithm. 5th Information Hiding Workshop, Lecture Notes in Computer Science, vol. 2578. Springer-Verlag, Berlin Heidelberg New York (2003) 310–323

20. Moulin, P., Wang, Y.: New results on steganographic capacity. Proceeding of CISS 2004. University of Princeton, Princeton, New Jersey (2004)

X²Rep: Enhanced Trust Semantics for the XRep Protocol

Nathan Curtis, Rei Safavi-Naini, and Willy Susilo

Centre for Information Security Research
School of Information Technology and Computer Science
University of Wollongong
Wollongong 2522, Australia
{nathanc,rei,wsusilo}@uow.edu.au

Abstract. Peer-to-peer file sharing networks are a popular means of sharing a diverse range of resources and information. Many of today's most widely used file sharing networks are built on the Gnutella file sharing protocol. The open, insecure nature of such networks means that they are susceptible to the distribution of malicious, unauthentic or low quality resources. XRep is a reputation-based trust management system designed to reduce the number of malicious or low quality resources distributed in a Gnutella file sharing network. XRep is significant in that it can be integrated into a Gnutella environment with minimal disruption. This is achieved primarily through the use of the same message passing mechanism as in the standard Gnutella protocol. We demonstrate that the trust semantics algorithm employed by XRep has a number of weaknesses and does not produce correct trust values when used against a range of strategies that can be employed by malicious agents. We describe an enhanced trust semantics algorithm called X* Rep that can be seamlessly incorporated into the XRep protocol. We demonstrate that this algorithm is robust against such strategies, offers a high degree of expressiveness in voting and vote evaluation and significantly reduces the network communications required by the XRep protocol.

1 Introduction

Peer-to-peer (P2P) file sharing networks have become a popular way of distributing a diverse range of resources and information. P2P systems are truly decentralized systems that are believed to reflect society better than other types of computer architectures. In a P2P network each node is a client and server both, and by participating in the network allows others to access its computing resources. P2P networks have a number of attractive properties including scalability, anonymity and fault-tolerance, that are much harder to achieve in traditional networks. Nodes can join and leave the network without leaving any trace and while active can initiate downloads and respond to queries. However due to the lack of accountability, such networks have tremendous potential to be misused. For example a malicious peer can use the network to distribute malicious code [7].

M. Jakobsson, M. Yung, J. Zhou (Eds.): ACNS 2004, LNCS 3089, pp. 205–219, 2004.

Another important problem is *authenticity* and *quality* of downloaded resources. Unauthentic or poor quality resources could be deliberately shared by the casual user. A peer that has requested a resource may receive one or more response(s) and needs to decide which one, if any, to download. In the absence of any mechanism to differentiate between good and poor quality resources a peer may have to download a resource many times and this will result not only to the high network cost but also contribute to network load and slower downloads.

Traditional methods of providing security in networks cannot be implemented effectively as the heavy use of cryptography will not only slow down the network but also may be unacceptable to users with less powerful computers. An approach to increase reliability of P2P networks without loosing their essential properties including anonymity is to use *reputation* systems to identify the quality of peers and resources. A reputation system collects, processes and distributes information about entities based on their history in the system [7]. For example in a P2P system, a peer's reputation may be determined by its behaviour in previous transactions, and a resource reputation may be determined by the evaluation of peers who have downloaded the resource.

In [5], a reputation based trust management system for the Gnutella protocol was proposed that has a number of attractive properties. The system uses reputation of peers and resources both, to assist a requesting peer in selecting which resource to download. The reputations generated by the system allow a user to have an indication of the level of risk associated with the download, hence enabling him to make the required provisions. This is the first system that includes reputations of resources and is shown that because of this inclusion a number of known attacks can be prevented. An important feature of the system is that the reputation system can be incorporated into the Gnutella protocol and the additional information be piggybacked onto the existing Gnutella protocol.

1.1 Our Contribution

We present a trust semantics algorithm called X^2Rep that extends the XRep protocol. The purpose of X^2Rep is to address the weaknesses of XRep. We demonstrate that our algorithm provides substantial improvements against these weaknesses using extensive simulations. We give more expressive power to peers to express their opinion about resources that they have downloaded and the peers that they have downloaded from. We allow collusions of malicious peers to use a range of strategies and use the reputation to protect against these attacks.

A major challenge to the development of a reputation system is to ensure the reliability of gathered reputation information. In particular, it is vital that any "vote spoofing" activity is as difficult or expensive as possible for malicious agents. The XRep protocol uses a complex process of challenge and response messages to ensure that a vote is supplied by a 'real' peer. We eliminate this complexity by employing extensive vote generation and evaluation system that makes use of voter *credibility* information. Voter credibility is an additional piece of information that helps an evaluating peer to determine the trustworthiness of a voter's vote through the evaluation of the voter's previous voting activity.

1.2 Related Work

Reputation-based trust management systems must address issues at two levels
[2]: 1) Data Management, and 2) Trust semantics. Data management is concerned with the storage and dissemination of reputation information in a distributed environment with no centralised control. Trust semantics specify the
model for the evaluation of 'trust' through the computation of gathered reputation information.

Data management techniques used in distributed reputation-based trust
management systems fall into two broad categories:

1. Peers maintain repositories of their experiences and make it available to
   others through a voting mechanism;
2. Reputation information is held in the network and is accessed through an
   additional network overlay, such as a distributed hash table (DHT).

Work in the former category includes XRep [5] and its predecessor, P2PRep [4].
In both protocols the reputation information is piggybacked onto the Gnutella
P2P file sharing protocol. In the P2PRep protocol reputation information is
associated only with peers.

Work in the latter category includes EigenRep [6] that uses a distributed
hash table as its network overlay. Another system in this category is proposed
by Aberer and Despotovic [2] and uses a P-Grid [1] as its network overlay. A novel
aspect of this system is the use of a complaint system for assigning reputations.

The rest of this paper is organised as follows. In Section 2.1 we give a
brief overview of the Gnutella protocol and XRep protocol. Section 3 gives our
analysis of the system and its shortcomings. Section 4 defines the properties
that must be found in a reputation system. Section 5 describes X^2Rep, our
trust semantics algorithm. Finally, Section 6 concludes the paper.

2   Peer-to-Peer File Sharing

Recent years have seen a tremendous growth in the popularity of peer-to-peer
(P2P) file-sharing networks [9]. Traditionally, the term P2P has been used to
describe a decentralised network architecture in which all peers have equal roles
and responsibilities, and follow the same behavioural patterns. In a P2P network,
a peer acts as both client and server and exchanges information and services
directly with other peers. Often, a peer also acts as a router, forwarding messages
it receives to directly connected neighbours.

Each peer in a P2P file-sharing network participates by offering files for
downloading by other peers. A file exchange interaction follows two phases; a
search phase in which the enquirer attempts to locate a peer offering the desired
file, and a *download phase* in which the peer connects directly with the offerer to
initiate the download, commonly using traditional protocols such as HTTP or
FTP. Many of todays most widely used P2P file sharing applications are based
on the Gnutella protocol [8].

2.1   XRep Protocol

XRep [5] is a notable reputation based trust management system that can be straightforwardly piggybacked onto the Gnutella P2P file sharing protocol. XRep defines a secure protocol for the exchange of reputation information using the same message passing mechanisms as used in standard Gnutella Query andQueryHit exchanges. Thus, to provide XRep functionality, current Gnutella implementations require only modest modifications.

In XRep reputation information is associated with both peers and resources. XRep requires resources and peers to be uniquely identifiable. This is achieved by using the digest of a resource's content as the $resource_{id}$, and the digest of the public key of a peer as the $peer_{id}$. Using a cryptographic hash function ensures that the resources and the peers are uniquely identifiable.

When considering a file download in Gnutella, the user selects the resource that best satisfies the request (using information such as the standard resource meta data string and offerers connection speed). To assist the user in making the download decision, the network is 'polled' for any available reputation information on that resource and the peers that offer it. Poll messages are broadcast in the same way as Gnutella Query messages. All peers maintain repositories of their experiences (both good and bad) of resources they have downloaded and the peers with whom they have interacted. When a peer receives a Poll message, it checks its repositories for matching resource and peer identifiers. If it has some information to offer, it generates a set of binary votes based on its experiences, and returns them to the enquirer as a PollReply message.

The resource and peer votes are then processed and combined to produce a single value to the user as a reputation value for the download under consideration. Based on this reputation value, the user can make a decision whether or not to initiate a download.

Prior to the download, the offering peer for whom the highest peer reputation value was calculated is contacted directly to verify that it has really offered the target resource. This exchange is known as the Best Peer Check.

We note the following about the protocol.

Phase 1. A minor change to the Gnutella Query exchange is required; the resource identifier is added to the resource information contained in the ResultSet of the QueryHit message. This allows the polling peer to uniquely identify each offered resource.

Phase 2. The poll message consists of the identifier of the resource under consideration and the set of peers that offer it. Also included is a public key Pk_{poll} for which only the polling peer knows the private key. This may be a persistent key pair or a pair generated on the fly for each poll. Voting peers return their votes for some or all of the entities listed in the Poll message together with their IP address. The message is encrypted with Pk_{poll} to ensure confidentiality.

Phase 3. Once a set of votes are received, the polling peer must try to ensure the reliability of the votes and the honesty of the voters. The polling peer attempts this by carrying out the following steps.

- Decrypt each PollReply message and detect any tampering that may have taken place.
- Group votes from voters that are from the same IP network.
- Select a portion of peers from each group send a *TrueVote* challenge, from which the poller expects to receive a *TrueVoteReply*. This ensures that at least some of the votes are from genuine peers and not merely spoofed votes from non-existent IP addresses.

Phase 4. At this stage the polling peer has evaluated trust for all the entities under consideration. The poller now carries out one further phase to ensure that the peer with the best trust evaluation exists and actually offers the resource. It is important for two reasons:

- A malicious peer is prevented from 'hijacking' the identity ($peer_{id}$) of a reputable peer.
- If it can be established that the resource has a good reputation and is offered by a peer with a good reputation, then it is possible to download that resource from any offerer and be assured that the resource is reliable. This can be considered as a load balancing technique.

3 Evaluating XRep

XRep uses the same constrained broadcast and back propagation mechanisms as used in the standard Gnutella Query and QueryHit exchange and therefore effectively doubles the amount of traffic required to complete a single transaction. A number of additional messages must also be exchanged to ensure vote reliability and the existence of voting peers.

The main shortcoming of XRep is the inadequacy of trust semantic and calculation of reputation values. In XRep a peer's experience repository consists of a table that contains a binary value for each resource describing the peer's opinion, good (+) or bad (-), about the resource, and a peer repository, which includes triplets of ($peer_{id}$, num_{plus}, num_{minus}) that records the number of good and bad download counts for each peer.

When polled, a peer converts these experiences into a binary vote for each entity matched in the poll message. Although these values are adequate to provide rudimentary information on whether a peer or resource is good or bad, finer evaluations such as the voter's judgement on the quality of a resource cannot be expressed. This results in the reputation calculation becoming ineffective against a range of malicious strategies. Important successful malicious strategies are the following.

- The generation of "spoofed" positive votes from fake peer identities.
- The systematic generation of positive votes for other members of a voting clique.
- The generation of negative votes for genuine peers in order to reduce their evaluated trust value.

The XRep protocol attempts to ensure the reliability of votes and protect against votes originating from colluding peers. This is by identifying voting cliques through clustering the votes that are provided by voters with the same network portion of their IP address. Such a correlation between colluding peers and IP addresses is tenuous because,

- Users connecting via a proxy server will share the same network part of their IP address and will therefore be considered as part of a voting collusion. It is therefore likely that a substantial number of legitimate votes will be treated as malicious.
- It is highly likely that, in the real world, malicious agents will have completely different IP addresses, for example, if they subscribe to different providers. These agents will therefore be able to continue generating spurious votes unchallenged.
- The protocol requires that a portion of the clustered peers be directly contacted to ensure that the they have actually voted. It is impractical to directly contact any more than a very small proportion of peers from each cluster and therefore a large amount of spurious voting activity could potentially continue unchallenged.

XRep provides some safeguards against ID Stealth attacks. These attacks take place when a malicious peer 'hijacks' the identity ($peer_{id}$) of a reputable peer in order to deceive another peer into a malicious download. In such cases, the downloading peer believes it is interacting a peer with a good reputation. XRep provides safeguards against this attack in the **Best Peer Check** message exchange. Prior to downloading a resource, the downloading peer challenges the offering peer as to whether it really does offer the resource under consideration. The offering peer sends a response that is signed using its private key, and also supplies its public key. The downloading peer can be certain of the identity of the offering peer, firstly by verifying the signature of the message, and secondly by taking a cryptographic hash of the provided public key and comparing it against the $peer_{id}$ of the offering peer. If all verification is successful the downloading peer can initiate the download.

3.1   Malicious Strategies

We focus on three basic strategies that can be employed by a single malicious peer or a group (collusion) of malicious peers with the intention of circumventing or degrading the reputation system in order to continue to share malicious resources unchallenged. We outline these strategies in the following sections.

Strategy A. This strategy is the simplest way for a malicious peer to share malicious resources. The peer actively participates in the network by offering good resources. However occasionally the malicious peer will offer malicious resources. The malicious peer must carefully monitor the amount of good and bad resources it supplies in order to maintain a network-wide reputation that is sufficiently high for other peers to deem it trustable.

Strategy B. In this strategy a malicious agent attempts to degrade the quality of the reputation system by generating spurious votes when polled. The principal objective of this strategy may either be to simply degrade the correctness of reputation values to the point where these information are no longer trustable, or to attempt to increase the peer's relative standing by voting positively for itself and negatively for all others.

Strategy C. This strategy shares a similar objective with Strategy B. The principal differentiator is that more effort and resources are required on the part of the malicious peer(s) and such activity is harder to counteract by the reputation system. A group of peers systematically vote positively for each other whilst sharing malicious resources. Each peer in the group may also share some good resources in order to enhance its own reputation. The difficultly in detection of this strategy results from the evaluating peer receiving what appears to be a set of valid votes sent by real peers.

Other strategies hybrids of the basic strategies identified above to further increase their effectiveness.

4   Reputation-Based Trust Management for Peer to Peer Networks

The aim of a reputation system is to provide some kind of 'rating' that can be used by users to select a resource and a peer from which the resource will be downloaded. The reputation system, at each time t, will result in a number $\sigma^x(t)$, the reputation score for x, such that a high score represents the genuineness of x (peer or resource) and low score, shows the opposite, and t is the time. A reputation system must satisfy the following properties.

1. Correctness and Soundness: the system must ensure that genuine entities x will eventually receive high σ_0^x and fake entities (malicious peer or resource) will eventually receive low σ_0^x, where σ_0^x denotes a *True Score*.

2. Dynamic behaviour: Reputation scores vary over time. We require that the reputation of an entity x to *stabilize* to a *True Score*, σ_0^x. That is although the instant value of reputations will change but after a transient phase their values will be within an ϵ error from the True Score. We are also interested in the transient behaviour of the function $\sigma^x(t)$ with time: that is the rate of convergence of $\sigma^x(t)$ to σ_0^x. This is a measure of effectiveness of the system.

There are a number of conflicting requirements on the dynamic behaviour of the system.

1. *Start up*: A reputation system must provide a strategy for a genuine entity (resource or peer) to join the system (resource to be chosen for download, and peer be selected to download from). However the start-up strategy must prevent malicious agents from entering the system.

2. *Runtime protection*: A reputation system must ensure that an existing malicious entity will loose its reputation, even if it starts with high reputation value, after a defined length of time.

The strategies that are used to speed up Runtime behaviour in general will make the start up phase of genuine entities slower. Balancing the two requirements must be done for each particular system.

$\sigma^x(t)$ converges to σ_0^x in minimum time. We accept that since reputation is a function of time over a period of time, its value could be different from its true value. We require that the system can be stabilized to its true value.

4.1   Requirements of a Reputation System

Reputation values are evaluated through the past experience of a peer and its response to a current query. Applying the above principles to an XRep type reputation system for P2P file sharing we will have the following groups of requirements.

Security Requirements

S1 Honest peers should be able to join the network and introduce resources in the network as they wish. The reputation of both resource and peer should raise to a level τ, determined by the network designer, that gives them a reasonable chance of being chosen by other peers.

S2 Reputations must be calculated and and propagated through the network securely, and at a sufficient rate to allow timely identification of malicious resources and/or peers.

We note that requirement S2 implies that a secure communication environment exists. However following XRep approach we will not assume a secure communication layer and will incorporate the required security as part of the reputation system. This includes protection against the deletion of and tampering with recommendations whilst in transit. We note that we need not consider source authentication because of the anonymous nature of the system.

One may assume such a layer to be able to focus on the design and behaviour of reputation functions and their dynamics.

Operational Requirements

1. A reputation system should maintain the essential properties of the underlying P2P system. In the case of Gnutella, this includes a decentralised architecture, network transitivity, and anonymity of participants.

2. Reputation system can assist with balancing the load in the system. That is, use reputation values as a mechanisms to ensure avoidance of unnecessary bottlenecks by using harsh assessments of entities (for example by using only zero and one for reputation values).

A reputation system will add some communication and computation cost to the original system.

Efficiency

1. The reputation system must not produce excessive network traffic to the extent that the service provided by the underlying network is degraded.

2. A reputation system must not require excessive storage space and computation power from peers in the network.

In the following section we propose modifications to XRep protocol to provide protection against the malicious strategies outlined in Section 3. We describe how this can be achieved at little cost to each peer, requiring only a modest amount of additional storage space and computational power. We also describe how the introduction of voter credibility allows XRep network communications to be simplified, reducing network traffic.

5   X' Rep

X^2Rep is designed to address the weaknesses of the XRep protocol. The X^2Rep reputation system provides safeguards against threats posed by collusions of malicious peers, attempting to circumvent the system and causing malicious downloads. The algorithm achieves its security goal whilst reducing communications overhead. This is achieved by determining the trustworthiness of voters by using voter credibility, rather than by clustering voters and requiring that a portion of them confirm their vote.

5.1 X^2Rep Trust Semantics Algorithm

We describe the system by breaking it down into four logical parts: 1) Local Reputation Repository; 2) Voting; 3) Evaluating Ratings for Downloads; and 4) Updating State on a Peer. Each of these is described in detail in the following sections.

Local Reputation Repository. Each peer will store data expressing its experiences with peers and resources that it has interacted with. For each downloaded resource with identification string $Resource_{id}$, it stores a pair $(Resource_{id}, \lambda_{Resource_{id}})$, where $\lambda_{Resource_{id}}$ is a real value between 0 (poor or malicious) and 1 (good), that is a measure of satisfaction of the peer with the resource.

For each peer P_j that P_i has interacted with, P_i maintains a vector of length n storing its past n experiences with that peer . The peer Experience Vector v_{ij} is denoted by $v_{ij} = (P_j, (q_{ij,1}, q_{ij,2}, q_{ij,3}...q_{ij,n}))$ where $q_{ij,k}, k = 1, \cdots n$ are real values between 0 (poor or malicious) and 1 (good).

On completion of each transaction with the peer P_j, P_i evaluates the transaction and generates a number that reflects his satisfaction and appends it to the end of the Experience Vector associated with peer P_j. The vector stores the results of the most recent n experiences and so as new experiences are appended the oldest ones are removed. During the initialization phase all data items will be set to zero.

Voting

Resource Vote. The vote of peer P_i for a resource with ID (*resource*$_{id}$ is simply $\lambda_{resource_{id}}$). This allows the polling peer to learn precisely how the voting peer rated the resource.

Peer Vote. Voting for a peer uses the content of the Experience Vector associated with that peer. This information will be used to generate a vote that is a number in the interval $[0, 1]$. The function that is used to calculate the vote must cater for conflicting requirements. On one hand it must harshly treat peers who have resulted in a bad experience so that opportunities for malicious agents to share malicious resources while still enjoying a good reputation are reduced. On the other hand the system must provide tolerance for situations in which an otherwise good peer inadvertently shares a bad resource, perhaps by downloading it from a malicious peer and leaving it in its shared directory. In such a circumstance, the innocent peer should not be penalized to such an extent to exclude it from all subsequent transactions.

To reconcile the above conflicting requirements we will use a vote evaluation function that uses all elements of the $E(i, j)$ and reduces the effect of low ratings by using the square function. To generate the vote $\nu_{i,j}$ of peer P_i for peer P_j, we use the following:

$$\nu_{ij} = \sum_k \tilde{v}_{ij,k}/n$$

One may use other criteria, for example giving more importance to more recent experiences or emphasizing bad experiences. To implement the function in the former case higher weights (multipliers) may be used for more recent experiences, and for the latter case a higher power function (x^n), can be used.

Using the Experience Vector and the above method of calculating votes, provides a conservative method of admitting newcomers to the system with reputation built over time. Experience vectors are initialised to zero, resulting in votes for newcomers to be low until the experience vector for that peer is filled with real experience values. Using this method, a newcomer must make some effort in order to gain a good reputation. One way this can be achieved is for a newcomer to share popular resources that already have a good reputation. Similarly, new resources can build a good reputation by being offered by reputable peers. Malicious agents must also undertake this effort to gain a positive reputation and it is a primary consideration of the X^2Rep protocol that the speed with which malicious activity is identified, that this effort is not worthwhile.

Evaluating Ratings for Downloads. After a specified time period (set in a configuration file) the polling peer will have received zero or more PollReply messages (votes). The peer must now convert these votes into an evaluation for a possible transaction. Each transaction is specified by a *resource*$_{id}$ and a *peer*$_{id}$.

If rating evaluation is only based on the votes received from other peers, the polling peer implicitly assumes the voting peers are honest. However a received vote may have been spoofed, or may be generated as part of a malicious strategy used by a group of colluding peers. To reduce this implicit trust in voting peers we introduce an additional factor called *credibility*. Credibility focuses on the reliability of peers with respect to the voting process and is an indication of the confidence that a polling peer places in the votes provided by other peers. The experience vector reflects the satisfaction of P_i with respect to transactions with a specific peer and combines quality of the downloaded resource and the peer. The credibility c_{ij} is given by the peer P_i for the peer P_j that has provided votes in previous transactions and will be stored in the Local Credibility Repository of the peer P_i. Credibility c_{ij} is a real number in the interval $[0, 1]$ and is initialised to zero for an unknown peer.

On completion of a transaction, credibility of all the peers who had participated in the voting phase of the transaction are updated. The updating policy may vary. The aim of this policy is to reward the peers who have voted correctly, that is in accordance with the assessment of the transaction after the download, and punish those whose votes were contrary to this assessment. Voter credibility is updated for all peers who participated in the voting process, whether the peer voted for the resource, offering peer(s) or both.

Credibility values will be used to adjust a peers' votes for the current download. A peer P_i that sent a resource vote μ to polling peer P_j, will have the Adjusted Resource Vote $\tilde{\mu}_i$ as $\tilde{\mu} = \mu c_{ij}$. A peer P_i, that sent a peer vote ν_{ij} about offering peer P_j to peer P_l, will have the Adjusted Peer Vote $\tilde{\nu}_{ij}$ as: $\tilde{\nu}_{ij} = \nu_{ij} c_{li}$.

To collate these voting information to produce a single value for the rating of each entity (resource, or peer) one may use an average value. However this could result in attacks by large collusions to succeed. We noted that a collusion of malicious peers may degrade the reputation of an entity (resource or peer) by all providing bad votes during the polling phase. The X^2Rep protocol mechanism to detect and counter such activities is to identify agents that vote inaccurately and punish them by reducing their credibility to zero. As such, a vote cast by an agent with no credibility will have little effect on the summation the of adjusted votes. However, if we are not careful in this approach, a large number of votes of this nature will significantly reduce the calculated trust value. To negate this attack we choose not to include votes from peers for which there is no credibility rating or peers whose credibility rating is zero. Thus:

- Resource Trust Value $R\tau_i = \sum \tilde{\mu}_i$ where c_i is not 0
- Peer Trust Value $P\tau_j = \sum \tilde{\nu}_{ij}$ where c_i is not 0

$R\tau_i$ and the set of $P\tau_j$ will be used to find the most trustworthy offering peer and to determine whether the transaction can be considered trustworthy overall. A simple approach will be to use *threshold* values to define trust categories and determine the category of an entity with a given calculated trust by comparing it against this threshold. For example running averages of all previous $R\tau$ and $P\tau_{ij}$ can be maintained and the difference of the calculated trust and these values be used as to determine the category of the current entity.

The final trust value presented to the user will be a combination of the resource and peer trust values. The simplest approach would be to find the average of the two values. Users can use trust categories combined with other criteria, for example accepted level of risk, to make the final decision.

Updating State on a Peer. After the completion of a transaction, the state information of the downloading peer must be updated. This includes the following.

- Updating the downloading peer's Local Reputation Repository with peer and resource evaluation values.
- For each peer that provided a vote:
  - If the voting peer P_i provided an accurate vote $c_i = c_i + 0.05$.
  - If the voting peer P_i provided an inaccurate vote $c_i = 0$.

Although reducing c_i to zero for a single inaccurate vote may seem harsh but this will protect against a malicious agent who plans to build credibility and then subsequently use that credibility to provide inaccurate votes over an extended period. Reducing credibility to zero after a single inaccurate vote will minimise the success chance of such peers. This is an important feature as it is relatively easy to build credibility. Clearly, an unfortunate consequence is that a well-intentioned peer that mistakenly provides an inaccurate vote will have its credibility reduced to zero on the downloading peer.

5.2   XRep Protocol Modifications

X^2Rep requires that the PollReply message in *phase 2* of the XRep protocol be modified to include the identity of the sending peer. Thus we define the message as: PollReply $(\{[\text{peer}_{id}, \text{votes}]\text{Sk}_{voter}, \text{Pk}_{voter}\}\text{Pk}_{poll})$.

The voting peer sends it *peer$_{id}$* and the set of votes signed using its private key Sk$_{voter}$, and its public key Pk$_{voter}$. The entire message is encrypted with the public key of the polling peer Pk$_{poll}$ which had been sent in the Poll message.

This modification to the PollReply message is significant because it allows the polling peer to be certain that the *peer$_{id}$* provided belongs to the voting peer and thus it can find the correct credibility rating. This assurance is made in what will now be *phase 3* of the XRep protocol as follows:

1. The polling peer decrypts the message using its private key Sk$_{poll}$. This provides confidentiality to the message and votes cast.
2. The polling peer verifies the signature of the *peer$_{id}$* and votes token using the public key provided by the voting peer Pk$_{voter}$. This ensures that integrity of the token.
3. The polling peer finds the digest of the public key provided by the voting peer Pk$_{voter}$ using a secure hash function and compares the result to the *peer$_{id}$* provided by the voting peer. If these values are equal then the polling peer can be assured that *peer$_{id}$* provided in the message really belongs to the voting peer.

The polling peer can then search its Local Credibility Repository for a rating for that voting peer. Obviously, there is nothing to stop a malicious agent creating a new *peer$_{id}$* and key pair with which to vote, but the polling peer will have no credibility rating for that $peer_{id}$ and the vote will not carry any weight in the trust evaluation. We note that $peer_{id}$ is an opaque identifier and does not affect the anonymity provided by the underlying system.

As a result of this modification, a number of alterations can be made to the XRep protocol.

- Vote clustering techniques in *phase 3* of the XRep protocol are no longer required. Such techniques offer little protection against the activities of collusions of malicious agents. X^2Rep provides a more robust approach, combining the verification of the $peer_{id}$ provided in the PollReply message and the use of voter credibility ratings.
- The *TrueVote* and *TrueVoteReply* message exchange in *Phase 3* is no longer required as the verification of votes and authentication of the $peer_{id}$ are now provided in the PollReply message.
- For the same reason *phase 4*, the Best Peer Check message exchange is also not required.

These modifications significantly reduce the amount of message exchanges required by the protocol, whilst providing more a robust approach to combat malicious strategies. It should be noted that the X^2Rep algorithm requires an additional signature in the PollReply message. The extra computation required for this signature is not negligible but we argue that it still remains more efficient than the network communication that it replaces.

The XRep protocol with X^2Rep extensions is summarised in table 1.

5.3   Consideration of X^2Rep Properties

In this section we consider how the X^2Rep extensions measure against the properties of a reputation system, as defined in section 4.

Firstly we analyse the effects of the X^2Rep extensions on efficiency. A major design goal of X^2Rep is to reduce the amount of network communications required to determine trust. This is to ensure that the system is as scalable as possible within the constraints of the underlying architecture [9,3]. This is achieved by making redundant several unnecessary XRep network communication phases. This considerable benefit is reached as a result of a small amount of additional storage and computation resource use on each host machine. Given the processing power and amount of disk space available on modern PCs, we believe this trade off is reasonable.

Both XRep and X^2Rep fullfil the operational requirements of a reputation system. Neither system requires any modifications to the underlying network architecture or its dynamics. Furthermore, the inherent anonymity provided by the network is retained. This is achieved through the use of opaque identifiers, which cannot be traced to individual participants.

X^2Rep provides significant improvements over XRep in its security properties. X^2Rep utilises the cryptographic security features provided by XRep that prevent vote tampering. This is obtained through the use of digital signatures.

Table 1. XRep Protocol with X˙Rep extensions

Phase	Description
1 Resource Searching	*Poller to Network: Query (search_string, min_speed)* *Offerer to Poller: QueryHit (no_hits, IP, speed, ResultSet, trailer, peer_{id})*
2 Resource Selection and Vote Polling	Poller to Network: Poll $((resource\_id, \{peer.\, ,....peer_n\}, Pk_{poll})$ *Voter to Poller: PollReply $(\{[peer_{id}, votes]Sk_{voter}, Pk_{voter}\}Pk_{polr})$*

3 Vote Evaluation	Actions:
	
	    – Find credibility ratings for voting peers and adjust votes accordingly.
	    – Create Adjusted Resource and Peer votes and compare them with each other and with the Trust Threshold values.

4 Resource Download	Actions:
	
	    – Select peer from which to download
	    – After download, check the resource's digest
	    – Update repositories and credibility ratings

Legend (Pk_i, Sk_i) pair of public and private keys where i can be a peer or poll request $\{M\}_k$ encryption of message M under key k $[M]_k$ signature of message M under key k	

Furthermore, the smarter vote evaluation algorithm protects against generation of false reputations through the execution of malicious strategies. We have explored this improvement in our simulation. However, due to the page limitation, we omit the detail in this paper and we refer the reader to the full version of this paper.

X^2Rep continues to deliver the same safeguards as XRep against ID Stealth attacks. The primary modification is that X^2Rep requires that the offering peer provides both its public key and *peer_{id}* within the PollReply message, and that the message is signed by its private key. Prior to initiating a download from a selected offering peer the downloading peer can carry out the same verification as previously described in the Best Peer Check phase of the XRep protocol.

6   Conclusion

We have presented X^2Rep, a trust semantics algorithm that extends the XRep reputation-based trust management protocol. X^2Rep provides reliable evaluation of trust even against a number of hostile environments. We started by describing the XRep protocol and identified some weaknesses. We then outlined our algorithm by describing the semantics for the storage of experience information, the generation of votes and the evaluation of trust. We gave detailed descriptions of how X^2Rep improves on the XRep protocol, including how two of the XRep message exchanges can be dropped. We then demonstrated through simulation that although the performance of a simplistic trust semantics algorithm is comparable to X^2Rep in an environment where no malicious strategies are imposed, X^2Rep displays far more accuracy and robustness when such strategies are introduced. Our conclusion is that when X^2Rep is integrated into the XRep protocol, a significant improvement in trust evaluation reliability can be obtained. Furthermore, this improvement is achieved whilst reducing network traffic and the complexity of the protocol.

References

1. Aberer, Cudré-Mauroux, Datta, Despotovic, Hauswirth, Punceva, Schmidt, and Wu. Advanced Peer-to-Peer networking: The P-grid system and its applications. *EPFL Technical Report IC/2002/73*, 2002.
2. Aberer and Despotovic. Managing trust in a Peer-2-Peer information system. *Proc of the Ninth International Conf on Information and Knowledge Management*, 2001.
3. Anderson. Analysis of the traffic on the gnutella network. March 2001.
4. Cornelli, D. C. di Vimercati, Paraboschi, and Samarati. Choosing reputable servents in a P2P network. May 2002.
5. Damiani, C. di Vimercati, Paraboschi, Samarati, and Violante. A reputation-based approach for choosing reliable resources in peer-to-peer networks. November 2002.
6. Kamvar, Schlosser, and Garcia-Molina. Eigenrep: Reputation management in p2p networks. 2002.
7. Resnick, Zeckhauser, Friedman, and Kuwabara. Reputation systems: Faciliating trust in internet interactions. 2000.
8. C. D. S. Services. The gnutella protocol specification v0.4 document revision 1.2.
9. K. Sripanidkulchai. The popularity of gnutella queries and its implications on scalability. 2001.

One-Round Protocols for Two-Party Authenticated Key Exchange

Ik Rae Jeong[1]*, Jonathan Katz[2]**, and Dong Hoon Lee[1]

* Center for Information Security Technologies (CIST),
Korea University, Seoul, Korea. jir@cist.korea.ac.kr, donghlee@korea.ac.kr
* Dept. of Computer Science, University of Maryland, College Park, MD, USA.
jkatz@cs.umd.edu

Abstract. Cryptographic protocol design in a two-party setting has often ignored the possibility of *simultaneous* message transmission by each of the two parties (i.e., using a duplex channel). In particular, most protocols for two-party key exchange have been designed assuming that parties alternate sending their messages (i.e., assuming a bidirectional half-duplex channel). However, by taking advantage of the communication characteristics of the network it may be possible to design protocols with improved latency. This is the focus of the present work.

We present a number of provably-secure protocols for two-party authenticated key exchange (AKE) which require only a single round. Our first protocol provides *key independence* only, and is analyzed in the random oracle model. This scheme matches the most efficient AKE protocols among those found in the literature. Our second scheme additionally provides *forward secrecy*, and is also analyzed in the random oracle model. Our final protocol provides the same strong security guarantees, but is proven secure in the standard model. This scheme is only slightly less efficient (from a computational perspective) than the previous ones. These last two schemes are the first provably-secure *one-round* protocols for authenticated 2-party key exchange which provide forward secrecy.

Keywords: Authenticated key exchange, Forward secrecy, Round complexity, Diffie-Hellman key exchange.

1 Introduction

Key-exchange protocols are among the most basic and widely used cryptographic protocols. Such protocols are used to derive a common *session key* between two (or more) parties; this session key may then be used to communicate securely over an insecure public network. Thus, secure key-exchange protocols serve as basic building blocks for constructing secure, complex, higher-level protocols. For this reason, the computational efficiency, communication requirements, and

* Work supported by the Ministry of Information & Communications, Korea, under the Information Technology Research Center (ITRC) Support Program.
** Work supported by NSF Trusted Computing Grant #ANI-0310751.

M. Jakobsson, M. Yung, J. Zhou (Eds.): ACNS 2004, LNCS 3089, pp. 220–232, 2004.

round complexity of key-exchange protocols are very important and have received much attention, both in the two-party [16,22,5,17,4,3,6,7,14] and multi-party (i.e., group) [18,13,26,20,2,12,10,9,21] settings.

This paper concerns protocols for *authenticated* key exchange (AKE); achieving such authentication is only possible if some out-of-band initialization phase is assumed prior to execution of the protocol. One common assumption is that each communicating party has an associated public-/private-key pair, with the public key known to all other parties in the network (of course, this includes the adversary). We assume this model here.

Most protocols for two-party key exchange have been designed and analyzed assuming that parties alternate sending messages (equivalently, that the parties communicate over a bidirectional *half-duplex* channel). However, in many common applications parties can actually transmit messages simultaneously (i.e., they have access to a bidirectional *duplex* channel). Of course, any protocol designed and proven secure in the former model may be used in the latter; however, it may be possible to design protocols with improved round complexity by fully exploiting the communication characteristics of the underlying network, and in particular the possibility of simultaneous message transmission.

As a simple example, consider the traditional Diffie-Hellman key-exchange protocol [16] (which does *not* provide any authentication). Traditionally, this is presented as a two-round protocol in which Alice first sends g^a and Bob then replies with g^b. However, in this particular case Alice and Bob can send their messages simultaneously, thereby "collapsing" this protocol to a single round. However, the situation is more complex when authentication is required. For instance, *authenticated* Diffie-Hellman typically involves one party signing messages sent by the other party; this may be viewed as a type of "challenge-response" mechanism. (For example, the work of Bellare, et al. [3] suggests implementing "authenticated channels" in exactly this way.) When this is done, it is no longer possible to collapse the protocol to a single round.

Motivated by the above discussion, we explore the possibility of designing protocols for authenticated key exchange which can be implemented in only a single round (assuming simultaneous message transmission). Of course, we will also ensure that our protocols are efficient with respect to other measures, including communication complexity and computational efficiency.

1.1 Our Work in Relation to Prior Work

Before relating our work to prior works, we briefly recall various notions of security for key exchange protocols (formal definitions are given below). At the most basic level, an authenticated key-exchange scheme must provide secrecy of a generated session key. Yet to completely define a notion of security, we must define the class of adversarial behaviors tolerated by the protocol. A protocol achieving *implicit authentication* simply ensures secrecy of session keys for an adversary who passively eavesdrops on protocol executions and may also send messages of its choice to the various parties. A stronger notion of security (and the one that is perhaps most often considered in the cryptographic literature) is

key independence, which means that session keys are computationally independent from each other. A bit more formally, key independence protects against
"Denning-Sacco" attacks [15] involving compromise of multiple session keys (for
sessions other than the one whose secrecy must be guaranteed). Lastly, protocols
achieving *forward secrecy* maintain secrecy of session keys even when an adversary is able to obtain long-term secret keys of principals who have previously
generated a common session key (in an honest execution of the protocol, without
any interference by the adversary).

The original two-party key-exchange scheme of Diffie and Hellman [16] is
secure against passive eavesdroppers, but not against active attacks; indeed,
that protocol provides no authentication at all. Several variations of the scheme
have been suggested to provide security against active attacks [22,23,24,7], but
these schemes have either been found to be flawed or have not yet been proven
secure. There are only a few provably secure schemes in the literature which
provide both key independence and forward secrecy. Most such schemes seem to
be "overloaded" so as to provide explicit authentication along with key independence and forward secrecy. (For example, the schemes of [1,6,3] use signatures
and/or message authentication codes to authenticate messages in a way that
achieves explicit authentication.) However, in some cases explicit authentication
may be unnecessary, or may be provided anyway by subsequent communication.
Thus, one may wonder whether more efficient protocols (say, with reduced round
complexity) are possible if explicit authentication is not a requirement.

We first propose and analyze a very simple one-round scheme, $\mathcal{TS}1$, which
provides key independence but not forward secrecy (security is based on the computational Diffie-Hellman assumption in the random oracle model). In Table 1
we compare our scheme to a scheme of Boyd and Nieto [9] which achieves the
same level of security in the same number of rounds. (Boyd and Nieto actually
propose a protocol for group AKE, but their protocol can of course be instan-
tiated for the case of two parties.) Our scheme is (slightly) more efficient than
the scheme of Boyd and Nieto and has other advantages as well: our protocol is
simpler and is also symmetric with respect to the two parties.

Table 1. Comparison of the Boyd-Nieto scheme [9] to $\mathcal{TS}1$. Efficiency of the Boyd-
Nieto scheme depends on the instantiation of its generic components; the above are
rough estimates assuming the random oracle model and "discrete-log-based" components using an order-q subgroup of $\mathbb{Z}_p^*$.

	Boyd-Nieto*	$\mathcal{TS}1$
Modular exponentiations (per party)	2	1
Communication (total)	$2|p| + |q|$	$2|q|$
Security	KI	KI
Assumptions	(varies)	CDH in random oracle model

Table 2. Comparison of key-exchange protocols achieving key independence and forward secrecy. Efficiency of some schemes depends on instantiation details; the above represent rough estimates assuming "discrete-log-based" instantiations using an order-q subgroup of $\mathbb{Z}_p^*$.

	[1,6]	Auth. DH		$\mathcal{TS}2$	$\mathcal{TS}3$
		(cf. [3])	(cf. [21])		
Modular exponentiations (par party)	3	4	4	3	3
Rounds	3	3	2	1	1
Communication (total)	$2\|p\| + 2\|q\|$	$4\|p\|$	$4\|p\| + 2\|q\|$	$2\|p\|$	$2\|p\| + 2\|q\|$
Model	R.O.	standard	standard	R.O.	standard

We next propose a modification of this scheme, $\mathcal{TS}2$, which provides both key independence and forward secrecy, yet still requires only a single round of communication (security is again proved based on the CDH assumption in the random oracle model). We are not aware of any previous one-round protocol achieving this level of security. $\mathcal{TS}2$ requires only 3 modular exponentiations per party and uses neither key confirmation nor digital signatures, and hence the protocol is more efficient than previous schemes in terms of computation and communication as well. A drawback of $\mathcal{TS}2$ is that its security is analyzed only in the random oracle model. For this reason, we propose a third protocol, $\mathcal{TS}3$, which provides the same level of security in the same number of rounds but whose security can be analyzed in the standard model based on the stronger, but still standard, *decisional* Diffie-Hellman assumption. This protocol is only slightly less efficient than $\mathcal{TS}2$ (it uses message authentication codes, whose efficiency is negligible compared to modular exponentiations). We compare both of these protocols to previous work in Table 2.

1.2 Outline

In Section 2 we define our security model for authenticated key exchange. We present our two-party authenticated key-exchange protocols in Section 3. Proofs of security for each of our protocols are deferred to the full version of this paper.

2 Security Model for Authenticated Key Exchange

We use the standard notion of security as defined in [4] and used extensively since then. We assume that there are N parties, and each party's identity is denoted as P_i. Each party P_i holds a pair of private and public keys. We consider a key-exchange protocol in which two parties want to exchange a session key using their public keys. Π_i^k represents the k-th instance of player P_i. If a key-exchange protocol terminates, then Π_i^k generates a session key $sk_{\Pi_i^k}$. A session identifier of an instance, denoted $sid_{\Pi_i^k}$, is a string different from those of all other sessions in the system (with high probability). We assume that $sid_{\Pi_i^k}$ is a concatenation of all transmitted messages of a session in Π_i^k, where the sequence of messages is determined *by the (lexicographic, say) ordering of the owners*. Note that ordering messages by their appearance cannot be used in our setting, because two parties may send their messages simultaneously.

We denote the identity set of the communicating parties in a session $sid_{\Pi_i^k}$ by $C_{\Pi_i^k}$, where $|C_{\Pi_i^k}| = 2$ in our case, and the index set of identities of the communicating parties in a session $sid_{\Pi_i^k}$ is denoted by $I_{\Pi_i^k} = \{i|P_i \in C_{\Pi_i^k}\}$. We say that Π_i^k and Π_j^l are *matching* if i and $j(\neq i)$ are in $I_{\Pi_i^k}$, and $sid_{\Pi_i^k}$ and $sid_{\Pi_j^l}$ are equal. Any protocol should satisfy the following correctness condition: if two instances are matching, then the session keys computed by those instances are equal.

To define a notion of security, we define the capabilities of an adversary. We allow the adversary to potentially control all communication in the network via access to a set of oracles as defined below. We consider an *experiment* in which the adversary asks queries to oracles, and the oracles answer back to the adversary. Oracle queries model attacks which an adversary may use in the real system. We consider the following types of queries in this paper.

- A query Initiate(C) models an invocation of a key-exchange protocol in the real system in which each $P_i \in C$ initiates a key exchange protocol with other entities in C and sends the first message of the protocol.

- A query Send(Π_i^k, M) is used to send a message M to instance Π_i^k. When Π_i^k receives M, it responds according to the key-exchange protocol. An adversary may use this query to perform *active* attacks by modifying and inserting the messages of the key-exchange protocol. Impersonation attacks and man-in-the-middle attacks are also possible using this query.

- A query Execute(C) represents passive eavesdropping of the adversary on an execution of the protocol by the parties in C. Namely, the parties specified in C execute the protocol without any interference from the adversary, and the adversary is given the resulting transcript of the execution. (Although the output of an Execute query can be simulated via repeated Initiate and Send oracle queries, this particular query is needed to define forward secrecy.)

- A query Reveal(Π_i^k) models *known key* attacks (or Denning-Sacco attacks) in the real system. The adversary is given the session key for the specified instance.

- A query Corrupt(P_i) models exposure of the long-term key held by player P_i. The adversary is assumed to be able to obtain long-term keys of players, but cannot control the behavior of these players directly (of course, once the adversary has asked a query Corrupt(P_i), the adversary may impersonate P_i in subsequent Send queries.)

- A query Test(Π_i^k) is used to define the advantage of an adversary. When an adversary $\mathcal{A}$ asks a *test* query to an instance Π_i^k, a coin b is flipped. If b is 1, then the session key $sk_{\Pi_i^k}$ is returned. Otherwise, a random string is returned. The adversary is allowed to make a single Test query, at any time during the experiment.

At the end of the experiment, the adversary $\mathcal{A}$ outputs a bit b'. The advantage of $\mathcal{A}$, denoted $\mathsf{Adv}_{\mathcal{A}}(\cdot)$, is defined as $|2 \cdot \Pr[b' = b] - 1|$.

To define a meaningful notion of security, we must first define *freshness*.

Definition 1. An instance Π_i^k is *fresh* if both the following conditions are true at the conclusion of the experiment described above:

(a) For all $P_j \in C_{\Pi_i^k}$, the adversary has not queried $\mathsf{Corrupt}(P_j)$.
(b) The adversary has not queried $\mathsf{Reveal}(\Pi_i^k)$, nor has it queried $\mathsf{Reveal}(\Pi_j^\ell)$ where Π_j^ℓ and Π_i^k are matching.

In all cases described below, the adversary is only allowed to ask its Test query to a fresh instance. Generically speaking, a protocol is called "secure" if the advantage of any PPT adversary is negligible. The following notions of security may then be considered, depending on the types of queries the adversary is allowed to ask:

(1) IA (Implicit Authentication): An adversary $\mathcal{A}$ can ask neither Reveal nor Corrupt queries.
(2) KI (Key Independence): An adversary $\mathcal{A}$ can ask Reveal queries, but can not ask Corrupt queries.
(3) FS (Forward Secrecy): An adversary $\mathcal{A}$ can ask *corrupt* queries, but can not ask *reveal* queries. The freshness condition (a) in this case is changed as follows: either the adversary did not query $\mathsf{Corrupt}(P_j)$ for any $P_j \in C_{\Pi_i^k}$, or the adversary did not query $\mathsf{Send}(P_j, \star)$ for any $P_j \in C_{\Pi_i^k}$ (and thus must have instead queried $\mathsf{Execute}(C_{\Pi_i^k})$).

Of course, the strongest notion of security requires both key independence and forward secrecy.

If a key exchange scheme satisfies (1), it is called a IA-secure key exchange scheme. If a key exchange scheme satisfies (2), it is called a KI-secure key exchange scheme. If a key exchange scheme satisfies (3), it is called a FS-secure key exchange scheme. If a key exchange scheme satisfies both (2) and (3), it is called a KI&FS-secure key exchange scheme.

For an adversary $\mathcal{A}$ attacking a scheme in the sense of XX (where XX is one of IA, KI, FS, or KI&FS), we denote the advantage of this adversary (as a function of k) by $\mathsf{Adv}_{\mathcal{A}}^{XX}(k)$. For a particular protocol P, we may define its security via:

$$\mathsf{Adv}_P^{XX}(k, t) = \max_{\mathcal{A}}\{\mathsf{Adv}_{\mathcal{A}}^{XX}(k)\},$$

where the maximum is taken over all adversaries running in time t. A scheme P is said to be XX-secure if $\mathsf{Adv}_P^{XX}(k, t)$ is negligible (in k) for any $t = \mathrm{poly}(k)$.

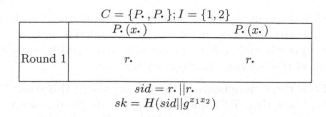

$$C = \{P_\bullet, P_\bullet\}; I = \{1, 2\}$$

	$P_\bullet(x_\bullet)$	$P_\bullet(x_\bullet)$
Round 1	$r_\bullet$	$r_\bullet$

$$sid = r_\bullet \| r_\bullet$$
$$sk = H(sid \| g^{x_1 x_2})$$

Fig. 1. An example of an execution of $\mathcal{TS}1$

3   One-Round Protocols for Authenticated Key Exchange

We assume that parties can be ordered by their names (e.g., lexicographically) and write $P_i < P_j$ to denote this ordering. Let k be a security parameter, and let G be a group of prime order q (where $|q| = k$) with generator g. Let H be a hash function such that $H : \{0,1\}^* \to \mathbb{Z}_q$. We assume that each party P_i has a public-/private-key pair $(y_i = g^{x_i}, x_i)$ which is known to all other parties in the network (alternately, these keys may be certified by a central CA). Recall that the standard definition of security (discussed above) does not include the possibility of "malicious insiders"; thus, in particular, we assume that all public-/secret-keys are honestly generated.

We now present our first protocol $\mathcal{TS}1$:

$\mathcal{TS}1$

Setup: Assume P_i wants to establish a session key with $P_j \neq P_i$, and $P_i < P_j$. Let (y_i, x_i) (respectively, (y_j, x_j)) denote the public-/private-keys of player P_i (respectively, P_j).

Round 1: P_i selects a random number $r_i \in_R \{0,1\}^k$ and transmits it (and P_j acts analogously).

Computation of session key: P_i forms a session identifier by concatenating the messages according to the ordering of P_i, P_j. That is, $sid_{\Pi_i} = sid_{\Pi_j} = r_i \| r_j$. Party P_i computes the session key $sk_{\Pi_i} = H(sid_{\Pi_i} \| y_j^{x_i})$ (and P_j acts analogously).

An example of an execution of $\mathcal{TS}1$ is shown in Fig. 1. In the example we assume that $P_1 < P_2$. The following theorem states the security achieved by this protocol.

Theorem 1. Under the CDH assumption, $\mathcal{TS}1$ is a KI-secure key-exchange protocol when H is modeled as a random oracle. Concretely,

$$\mathsf{Adv}_{\mathcal{TS}1}^{KI}(k, t, q_{re}, q_H) \leqslant 2 \cdot q_H \cdot N^2 \cdot \mathsf{Adv}^{CDH}(k, t) + \frac{4q_s^2}{2^k},$$

where t is the maximum total experiment time including the adversary's execution time, and the adversary makes q_{re} Reveal queries and q_H hash queries. Here, N is an upper bound on the number of parties, and q_s is an upper bound on the number of the sessions an adversary initiates.

The proof of this theorem appears in the full version of this paper [19].

It is easy to see that $\mathcal{T}\mathcal{S}1$ does not provide forward secrecy. To provide forward secrecy, we add an ephemeral Diffie-Hellman exchange to $\mathcal{T}\mathcal{S}1$. The resulting protocol, $\mathcal{T}\mathcal{S}2$, is given below:

$\mathcal{T}\mathcal{S}2$

Setup : Same as in $\mathcal{T}\mathcal{S}1$.

Round 1 : P_i selects a random number $\alpha_i \in_R \mathbb{Z}_q$ and sends $B_i = g^{\alpha_i}$ to the other party. (Party P_j acts analogously.)

Computation of session key : P_i forms a session identifier by concatenating the messages according to the ordering of P_i, P_j. That is, $sid_{\Pi_i} = sid_{\Pi_j} = B_i \| B_j$. P_i computes the session key $sk_{\Pi_i} = H(sid_{\Pi_i} \| B_j^{\alpha_i} \| y_j^{x_i})$. (Party P_j acts analogously.)

An example of an execution of $\mathcal{T}\mathcal{S}2$ is shown in Fig. 2. In the example we assume that $P_1 < P_2$.

$$C = \{P_., P_.\}; I = \{1, 2\}$$

	$P_.(x_.)$	$P_.(x_.)$
Round 1	g^{α_1}	g^{α_2}

$$sid = g^{\alpha_1} \| g^{\alpha_2}$$
$$sk = H(sid \| g^{\alpha_1 \alpha_2} \| g^{x_1 x_2})$$

Fig. 2. An example of an execution of $\mathcal{T}\mathcal{S}2$

The following characterizes the security of $\mathcal{T}\mathcal{S}2$.

Theorem 2. Under the CDH assumption, $\mathcal{T}\mathcal{S}2$ is a KI&FS-secure key-exchange protocol when H is modeled as a random oracle. Concretely,

$$\mathsf{Adv}_{\mathcal{T}\mathcal{S}2}^{KI\&FS}(k, t, q_{re}, q_{co}, q_H) \leqslant 2 \cdot q_H \cdot (N^2 + q_s) \cdot \mathsf{Adv}^{CDH}(k, t) + \frac{4q_s^2}{q},$$

where t is the maximum total experiment time including an adversary's execution time, and an adversary makes q_{re} Reveal queries, q_{co} Corrupt queries, and q_H hash queries. N is an upper bound of the number of parties, and q_s is the upper bound on the number of the sessions an adversary initiates.

The proof of this theorem appears in the full version of this paper [19].

The security of $\mathcal{TS}2$ (and $\mathcal{TS}1$, for that matter) is proven in the random oracle model. Next, we present protocol $\mathcal{TS}3$ which may be proven secure in the standard model (under the stronger DDH assumption):

$\mathcal{TS}3$

Setup: Same as in $\mathcal{TS}1$.

Round 1: P_i computes $k_{i,j} = k_{j,i} = y_j^{x_i}$ which it will use as a key for a secure message authentication code. (Of course, $k_{i,j}$ may need to be hashed before being used; we ignore this technicality here.) Next, P_i chooses a random number $\alpha_i \in_R \mathbb{Z}_q$, computes $\tau_i \leftarrow \mathsf{MAC}_{k_{i,j}}(P_i\|P_j\|g^{\alpha_i})$, and sends $B_i = g^{\alpha_i}\|\tau_i$ to the other party. (Party P_j acts analogously.)

Computation of session key: P_i verifies the MAC of the received message. If verification fails, no session key is computed. Otherwise, P_i computes a session key $sk_{\Pi_i} = (g^{\alpha_j})^{\alpha_i}$. The session identifier, computed by concatenating the messages, is $sid_{\Pi_i} = B_i\|B_j$. (Party P_j acts analogously.)

An example of an execution of $\mathcal{TS}3$ is shown in Fig. 3. In the example we assume that $P_1 < P_2$.

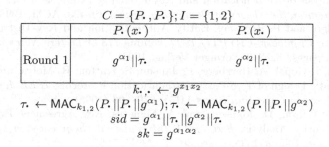

Fig. 3. An example of an execution of $\mathcal{TS}3$

The following characterizes the security of $\mathcal{TS}3$.

Theorem 3. Let M be an unforgeable MAC scheme. Then $\mathcal{TS}3$ is a KI&FS-secure key exchange scheme under the DDH assumption. Concretely,

$$\mathsf{Adv}^{KI\&FS}_{\mathcal{TS}3}(k, t, q_{re}, q_{co}) \leqslant (q_s + 2 \cdot N^2 + 2 \cdot q_s^2) \cdot \mathsf{Adv}^{DDH}(k, t)$$
$$+ N^2 \cdot \mathsf{Adv}^{SUF}_M(k, t, 2 \cdot q_s) + \frac{4q_s^2}{q},$$

where t is the maximum total experiment time including an adversary's execution time, and an adversary makes q_{re} Reveal queries and q_{co} Corrupt queries. N is an upper bound on the number of parties, and q_s is an upper bound of the number of the sessions an adversary initiates.

The proof of this theorem appears in the full version of this paper [19]. We note that the concrete security bound given here can be improved using random self-reducibility of the DDH problem.

A variant. In the above description of $\mathcal{TS}3$, each party computes a key $k_{i,j}$ which it then uses to authenticate its message using a message authentication code. It is also possible to have each party P_i *sign* its messages using, for example, its public key y_i as part of a Schnorr signature scheme. In this case, the party should sign (P_i, P_j, g^{α_i}) (in particular, it should sign the recipient's identity as well) to ensure that the signed message will be accepted only by the intended partner. The proof of security for this modified version is completely analogous to (and, in fact, slightly easier than) the proof of $\mathcal{TS}3$.

References

1. R. Ankney, D. Johnson, and M. Matyas. The Unified Model. Contribution to ANSI X9F1, October 1995.
2. G. Ateniese, M. Steiner, and G. Tsudik. New Multi-Party Authentication Services and Key Agreement Protocols. *IEEE Journal of Selected Areas in Communications*, volume 18, No. 4, pages 628–639, 2000.
3. M. Bellare, R. Canetti, and H. Krawczyk. A Modular Approach to the Design and Analysis of Authentication and Key Exchange Protocols. *Proc. 30th Annual Symposium on the Theory of Computing*, pages 419–428, ACM, 1998.
4. M. Bellare and P. Rogaway. Entity Authentication and Key Distribution. *Advances in Cryptology-CRYPTO 1993*, volume 773 of *Lecture Notes in Computer Science*, pages 232–249, Springer Verlag, 1993.
5. R. Bird, I. Gopal, A. Herzberg, P. Janson, S. Kutten, R. Molva, and M. Yung. Systematic Design of Two-Party Authentication Protocols. *IEEE Journal on Selected Areas in Communications* 11(5): 679–693 (1993).
6. S. Blake-Wilson, D. Johnson, and A. Menezes. Key Agreement Protocols and their Security Analysis. *Sixth IMA International Conference on Cryptography and Coding*, volume 1335, pages 30–45, ACM, 1997.
7. S. Blake-Wilson and A. Menezes. Authenticated Diffie-Hellman Key Agreement Protocols. *Selected Areas in Cryptography*, volume 1556 of *Lecture Notes in Computer Science*, pages 339–361, Springer Verlag, 1998.
8. C. Boyd. On Key Agreement and Conference Key Agreement. *ACISP 1997*, volume 1270 of *Lecture Notes in Computer Science*, page 294–302, Springer Verlag, 1997.
9. C. Boyd and J.M.G. Nieto. Round-Optimal Contributory Conference Key Agreement. *Public Key Cryptography*, volume 2567 of *Lecture Notes in Computer Science*, pages 161–174, Springer Verlag, 2003.
10. E. Bresson, O. Chevassut, and D. Pointcheval. Provably Authenticated Group Diffie-Hellman Key Exchange — The Dynamic Case. *Advances in Cryptology-ASIACRYPT 2001*, volume 2248 of *Lecture Notes in Computer Science*, pages 290–309, Springer Verlag, 2001.

11. E. Bresson, O. Chevassut, and D. Pointcheval. Dynamic Group Diffie-Hellman Key Exchange under Standard Assumptions. *Advances in Cryptology-EUROCRYPT 2002*, volume 2332 of *Lecture Notes in Computer Science*, pages 321–336, Springer Verlag, 2002.

12. E. Bresson, O. Chevassut, D. Pointcheval, and J.-J. Quisquater. Provably Authenticated Group Diffie-Hellman Key Exchange. *ACM Conference on Computer and Communications Security*, pages 255–264, 2001.

13. M. Burmester and Y. Desmedt. A Secure and Efficient Conference Key Distribution System. *Advances in Cryptology-EUROCRYPT 1994*, volume 950 of *Lecture Notes in Computer Science*, pages 275–286, Springer Verlag, 1994.

14. R. Canetti and H. Krawczyk. Universally Composable Notions of Key Exchange and Secure Channels. *Advances in Cryptology-Eurocrypt 2002*, volume 2332 of *Lecture Notes in Computer Science*, pages 337–351, Springer Verlag, 2002.

15. D. Denning and G. M. Sacco. Timestamps in Key Distribution Protocols. *Comm. ACM* 24(8): 533–536, 1981.

16. W. Diffie and M. Hellman. New Directions in Cryptography. *IEEE Transactions on Information Theory*, volume 22, Issue 6, pages 644–654, 1976.

17. W. Diffie, P. van Oorschot, and M. Wiener. Authentication and Authenticated Key Exchanges. *Designs, Codes, and Cryptography* 2(2): 107–125 (1992).

18. I. Ingemarasson, D.T. Tang, and C.K. Wong. A Conference Key Distribution System. *IEEE Transactions on Information Theory*, volume 28, Issue. 5, pages 714–720 , 1982.

19. I.R. Jeong, J. Katz, and D.H. Lee. Full version of this paper. Available at http://cist.korea.ac.kr/e_cist/e_index.htm.

20. M. Just and S. Vaudenay. Authenticated Multi-Party Key Agreement. *ASIACRYPT 1996*, volume 1163 of *Lecture Notes in Computer Science*, page 36–49, Springer Verlag, 1996.

21. J. Katz and M. Yung. Scalable Protocols for Authenticated Group Key Exchange. *Advances in Cryptology — CRYPTO 2003*.

22. L. Law, A. Menezes, M. Qu, J. Solinas, and S. Vanstone. An Efficient Protocol for Authenticated Key Agreement. Technical report CORR 98-05, University of Waterloo, 1988.

23. T. Matsumoto, Y. Takashima, and H. Imai. On Seeking Smart Public-Key Distribution Systems. *The Transactions of the IECE of Japan*, E69, pages 99–106, 1986.

24. National Security Agency. SKIPJACK and KEA algorithm specification. Version 2.0, May 29, 1998.

25. V. Shoup. On Formal Models for Secure Key Exchange. Available at http://eprint.iacr.org.

26. M. Steiner, G. Tsudik, and M. Waidner. Diffie-Hellman Key Distribution Extended to Group Communication. *ACM Conference on Computer and Communications Security*, page 31–37, 1996.

27. W.-G. Tzeng. A Practical and Secure-Fault-Tolerant Conference-Key Agreement Protocol. *Public Key Cryptography 2000*, volume 1751 of *Lecture Notes in Computer Science*, page 1–13, Springer Verlag, 2000.

A   Primitives

A.1   Computational Diffie-Hellman Problem

Let $\mathcal{GG}$ be a group generator which generates a group G whose prime order is q and a generator g. Let $k \in N$ be a security parameter. Consider the following experiment:

$$
\begin{array}{|l|}
\hline
\textbf{Exp}_{\mathcal{A}_{\text{CDH}}}^{\text{CDH}}(k) \\
\quad (G, q, g) \leftarrow \mathcal{GG}(k) \\
\quad u_1, u_2 \in_R [1, q-1] \\
\quad U_1 \leftarrow g^{u_1}; U_2 \leftarrow g^{u_2} \\
\quad W \leftarrow \mathcal{A}_{\text{CDH}}(U_1, U_2) \\
\quad \text{if } W = g^{u_1 u_2} \text{ return } 1 \\
\quad \text{else return } 0 \\
\hline
\end{array}
$$

The advantage of an adversary $\mathcal{A}_{\text{CDH}}(k)$ is defined as follows:

$$Adv_{\mathcal{A}_{\text{CDH}}}^{\text{CDH}}(k) = Pr[\textbf{Exp}_{\mathcal{A}_{\text{CDH}}}^{\text{CDH}}(k) = 1]$$

The advantage function is defined as follows:

$$Adv^{\text{CDH}}(k, t) = \max_{\mathcal{A}} \{Adv_{\mathcal{A}_{\text{CDH}}}^{\text{CDH}}(k)\},$$

where $\mathcal{A}_{\text{CDH}}$ is any adversary with time complexity t. The CDH assumption is that the advantage of any adversary $\mathcal{A}_{\text{CDH}}$ with time complexity polynomial in k is negligible.

For simplicity we consider a subgroup G, whose prime order is q and a generator is g, of a cyclic group Z_p^* where p is a prime.

A.2   Decisional Diffie-Hellman Problem

Let $\mathcal{GG}$ be a group generator which generates a group G whose prime order is q and a generator g. Let $k \in N$ be a security parameter. Consider the following experiment:

$$
\begin{array}{|l|}
\hline
\textbf{Exp}_{\mathcal{A}_{\text{DDH}}}^{\text{DDH}}(k) \\
\quad (G, q, g) \leftarrow \mathcal{GG}(k) \\
\quad u_1, u_2, w \in_R [1, q] \\
\quad U_1 \leftarrow g^{u_1}; U_2 \leftarrow g^{u_2} \\
\quad d \xleftarrow{R} \{0, 1\} \\
\quad \text{if } d = 1 \text{ then } W \leftarrow g^{u_1 u_2} \\
\quad \text{else } W \leftarrow g^w \\
\quad d' \leftarrow \mathcal{A}_{\text{DDH}}(U_1, U_2, W) \\
\hline
\end{array}
$$

The advantage of an adversary $\mathcal{A}_{\text{DDH}}(k)$ is defined as follows:

$$Adv_{\mathcal{A}_{\text{DDH}}}^{\text{DDH}}(k) = 2 \cdot Pr[d = d'] - 1.$$

The advantage function is defined as follows:

$$Adv^{\mathrm{DDH}}(k,t) = \max_{A}\{Adv^{\mathrm{DDH}}_{\mathcal{A}_{\mathrm{DDH}}}(k)\},$$

where $\mathcal{A}_{\mathrm{DDH}}$ is any adversary with time complexity t. We assume that the advantage of any adversary $\mathcal{A}_{\mathrm{DDH}}$ with time complexity polynomial in k is negligible.

For simplicity we consider a subgroup G, whose prime order is q and a generator is g, of a cyclic group Z_p^* where p is a prime.

A.3   Strong Unforgeability (SUF) of MAC

A MAC scheme consists of $M = (M.key, \mathsf{MAC}, \mathsf{Vrfy})$. $M.key$ generates a MAC key for the users. MAC computes a MAC for the message using the MAC key. Vrfy verifies the message-MAC pair with the MAC key and returns 1 if valid or 0 otherwise.

Let $k \in N$ be a security parameter. Let M be a MAC scheme. Consider the following experiment:

> $\mathbf{Exp}^{\mathrm{SUF}}_{M,\mathcal{A}}(k)$
> $\quad sk \leftarrow M.key(1^k)$
> $\quad (M,\tau) \leftarrow \mathcal{A}^{\mathsf{MAC}_{sk}(\cdot)}(1^k)$
> $\quad$ if $\mathsf{Vrfy}_{sk}(M,\tau) = 1$ and oracle $\mathsf{MAC}_{sk}(\cdot)$
> $\quad\quad$ never returned τ on input M then return 1
> $\quad$ else return 0

The advantage of an adversary $\mathcal{A}_{\mathrm{SUF}}(k)$ is defined as follows:

$$\mathsf{Adv}^{\mathrm{SUF}}_{M,\mathcal{A}}(k) = \Pr[\mathbf{Exp}^{\mathrm{SUF}}_{M,\mathcal{A}_{\mathrm{SUF}}}(k) = 1]$$

The advantage function of the scheme is defined as follows:

$$\mathsf{Adv}^{\mathrm{SUF}}_{M}(k,t,q_g) = \max_{A}\{\mathsf{Adv}^{\mathrm{SUF}}_{M,\mathcal{A}}(k)\},$$

where $\mathcal{A}_{\mathrm{SUF}}$ is any adversary with time complexity t and making at most q_g MAC queries. The scheme M is SUF secure if the advantage of any adversary $\mathcal{A}_{\mathrm{SUF}}$ with time complexity polynomial in k is negligible.

Password Authenticated Key Exchange Using Quadratic Residues

Muxiang Zhang

Verizon Communications Inc.
40 Sylvan Road, Waltham, MA 02451, USA
muxiang.zhang@verizon.com

Abstract. This paper investigates the feasibility of designing password-authenticated key exchange protocols using quadratic residues. To date, most of the published protocols for password-authenticated key exchange were based on the Diffie-Hellman key exchange. It appears inappropriate to design password-authenticated key exchange protocols using other public-key cryptographic techniques. In this paper, we show that protocols for password-authenticated key exchange can be constructed using quadratic residues and we present the first protocol of this type. Under the factoring assumption and the random oracle model, we show that our protocol is provably secure against off-line dictionary attacks. We also discuss the use of cache technique to improve the efficiency of our protocol.

1 Introduction

Password-authenticated key exchange protocols allow two entities who only share a human-memorable password to authenticate each other and agree on a large session key between them. Such protocols are attractive for their simplicity and convenience and have received much interest in the research community. A major challenge in designing password-authenticated key exchange protocols is to deal with the so-called exhaustive guessing or off-line dictionary attacks [22], as passwords are generally drawn from a small space enumerable, off-line, by an adversary. In 1992, Bellovin and Merritt [2] presented a family of protocols, known as *Encrypted Key exchange* (EKE), which was shown to be secure against off-line dictionary attacks. Using a combination of symmetric and asymmetric (i.e. public-key) cryptographic techniques, EKE provides insufficient information for an adversary to verify a guessed password and thus defeats off-line dictionary attacks. Following EKE, a number of protocols for password-based authentication and key exchange have been proposed, e.g., [3-5,8-9,12,14-18,21]. A comprehensive list of such protocols can be found in Jablon's research link [13].

Unlike other public-key based key exchange protocols such as SSL, the EKE-like protocols do not rely on the existence of a public key infrastructure (PKI). This is appealing in many environments where the deployment of a public key infrastructure is either not possible or would be overly complex. Over the last decade, many researchers have investigated the feasibility of implementing EKE

M. Jakobsson, M. Yung, J. Zhou (Eds.): ACNS 2004, LNCS 3089, pp. 233–247, 2004.

using different types of public-key cryptosystems, e.g., RSA, ElGamel, and Diffie-Hellman key exchange. Nonetheless, most of the well-known and secure variants of EKE are based on Diffie-Hellman key exchange. It seems that EKE works well with Diffie-Hellman key exchange, but presents subtleties one way or the other when implemented with RSA and other public-key cryptographic systems. In their original paper [2], Bellovin and Merritt pointed out that the RSA-based EKE variant is subject to a special type of dictionary attack, called *e-residue attack*. In 1997, Lucks [17] proposed an RSA-based password-authenticated key exchange protocol (called OKE) which was claimed to be secure against the e-residue attack. Later, Mackenzie et al [18] found that the OKE protocol is still subject to the e-residue attack. In [18], Mackenzie et al proposed an RSA-based EKE variant (called $SNAPI$) and provided a formal security proof in the random oracle model. Although the SNAPI protocol only allows using a public exponent e which is larger than the RSA modulus n, it is interesting to see that secure password-authenticated key exchange protocols can be constructed based on a diverse of public-key cryptosystems.

In this paper, we investigate the feasibility of designing password authenticated key exchange protocols using quadratic residues. A nice feature of this type of protocols is that the overhead for the protocol setup is minimal, since entities only need to share a password in *advance*; they do not need to establish other common parameters such as a prime number p and a generator g of the cyclic group modulo p. Based on number-theoretic techniques, we show that password-authenticated key exchange protocols can be constructed using quadratic residues and we present the first protocol of this type. Our protocol, called $QR\text{-}EKE$, involves two entities (say, Alice and Bob) who share a short password and one of the entity (say, Alice) also possess a Blum integer $n = pq$, where p and q are distinct prime numbers each congruent to 3 modulo 4. Using quadratic residues of n, both entities perform authentication and key establishment without leaking useful information about the password. We show that our protocol $QR\text{-}EKE$ is secure against the residue attacks as described in [2]. We also provide a formal security analysis of $QR\text{-}EKE$ under the factoring assumption and the random oracle model.

To reduce the computational load on communication entities (i.e., Alice and Bob), we present a variant of $QR\text{-}EKE$, called $QR^c\text{-}EKE$. In the protocol $QR^c\text{-}EKE$, one of the entity, say Bob, caches a hashed value of the public parameter n used by Alice in previous sessions. In a new session, Bob checks if the same parameter n is used by Alice. If yes, Bob only needs to compute two quadratic residues in the current run of the protocol $QR^c\text{-}EKE$. If else, Bob executes exactly as in the protocol $QR\text{-}EKE$ and at the end of a successful protocol run, Bob updates the cache using the new public parameter. When Alice uses the same parameter n in multiple sessions, the computational load on Bob will be greatly reduced.

The rest of the paper is organized as follows. In Section 2, we review basic concepts of number theory used throughout this paper. We provide an overview of the security model for password-authenticated key exchange in Section 3. We present the protocol QR-EKE In Section 4 and investigate its security against residue attacks. In Section 5, we improve the efficiency of QR-EKE using cache technique. In Section 6, we prove the security of QR-EKE under the factoring assumption and the random oracle model.

2 Preliminaries

Let $\{0,1\}^n$ denote the set of binary strings of length n and $\{0,1\}^*$ denote the set of binary strings of finite length. Without confusion, we sometimes use s_1, s_2 to denote the concatenation of two strings s_1 and s_2. A real-valued function $\epsilon(k)$ of non-negative integers is called *negligible* (in k) if for every $c > 0$, there exists $k_0 > 0$ such that $\epsilon(k) \leq 1/k^c$ for all $k > k_0$.

For every positive integer n, $n > 1$, it is well know that n can be expressed as a product of nontrivial powers of distinct primes, i.e., $n = p_1^{a_1} p_2^{a_2} \ldots p_r^{a_r}$, where $p_1, p_2, \ldots, p_r$ are primes and $a_1, a_2, \ldots, a_r$ are positive integers. Up to a rearrangement of the prime powers, this *prime-power factorization* is unique. Let $\mathbb{Z}_n$ denote the set of non-negative integers less than n and let $\mathbb{Z}_n^*$ denote the set consisting of integers in $\mathbb{Z}_n$ that are relatively prime to n. The number of integers in $\mathbb{Z}_n^*$ is equal to the *Euler phi-function* $\phi(n)$.

Let a, b, and n be integers such that $n > 0$ and $\gcd(a,n) = c$. If $c \nmid b$, the congruence $ax \equiv b \pmod{n}$ has no solutions. If $c \mid b$, then $ax \equiv b \pmod{n}$ has exactly c incongruent solutions modulo n. Let x_0 denote one of the solutions, then the c incongruent solutions are given by

$$x = x_0 + j(n/c), \quad j = 0, 1, \ldots, c-1. \tag{1}$$

Let g and n be positive integers relatively prime to each other. The least positive integer i such that $g^i \equiv 1 \pmod{n}$ is called the *order of g modulo n*. If the order of g is equal to $\phi(n)$, then g is called a *primitive root of n*. It is known (see [1,20]) that a positive integer n, $n > 1$, possesses a primitive root if and only if $n = 2, 4, p^t$ or $2p^t$, where p is an odd prime and t is a positive integer. When the positive integer n has a primitive root g, then the integers $g^0, g^1, g^2, \ldots, g^{\phi(n)-1}$ form a cyclic group under the modulo n multiplication. Due to this fact, we see that if a is a positive integer relatively prime to n, then there exists a unique integer i, $0 \leq i \leq \phi(n) - 1$, such that $a = g^i \bmod n$. The integer i is called the *index of a to the base g modulo n*, and is denoted by $\text{ind}_g a$. With this notation, we have $a = g^{\text{ind}_g a} \bmod n$.

If n and e are positive integers and a is an integer relatively prime to n, then we say that a is a *e-th power residue of n* if the congruence $x^e \equiv a \pmod{n}$ has a solution. If a is a second power residue of n, it is also called a *quadratic residue* of n. If a is not a quadratic residue of n, it is called a *quadratic non-residue* of n. We use Q_n to denote the set of all quadratic residues of n. The set of all quadratic non-residue of n is denoted by $\bar{Q}_n$. Let p be an odd prime and a be an integer not divisible by p. The *Legendre symbol* $\left(\frac{a}{p}\right)$ is defined to be 1 if $a \in Q_p$; and -1 if $a \in \bar{Q}_p$.

3 Security Model

We consider two-party protocols for authenticated key-exchange using human-memorable passwords. In its simplest form, such a protocol involves two entities, say *Alice* and *Bob* (denoted by A and B), both possessing a secret password drawn from a small password space $\mathcal{D}$. Based on the password, Alice and Bob can authenticate each other and upon a successful authentication, establish a session key which is known to nobody but the two of them. There is present an active adversary, denoted by $\mathcal{A}$, who intends to defeat the goal for the protocol. The adversary has full control of the communications between Alice and Bob. She can deliver messages out of order and to unintended recipients, concoct messages of her own choosing, and create multiple instances of entities and communicate with these instances in parallel sessions. She can also enumerate, off-line, all the passwords in the password space $\mathcal{D}$. She can even acquire session keys of accepted entity instances. Our formal model of security for password-authenticated key exchange protocols is based on that of [5]. In the following, we review the operations of the adversary and formulate the definition of security. For details as well as motivations behind the model, please refer to [5].

INITIALIZATION. Let I denote the identities of the protocol participants. Elements of I will often be denoted A or B (Alice and Bob). We emphasis that A and B are variables ranging over I and not fixed members of I. Each pair of entities, $A, B \in I$, are assigned a password w which is randomly selected from the password space $\mathcal{D}$. The initialization process may also specify a set of cryptographic function (e.g., hash functions) and sets a number of cryptographic parameters.

RUNNING THE PROTOCOL. Mathematically, a protocol Π is a probabilistic polynomial-time algorithms which determines how entities behave in response to received input. For each entity, there may be multiple instances running the protocol in parallel. We denote the i-th instance of entity A as Π_A^i. The adversary $\mathcal{A}$ can make queries to any instance; she has an endless supply of Π_A^i oracles ($A \in I$ and $i \in \mathbb{N}$). In response to each query, an instance updates its internal state and gives its output to the adversary. At any point in time, the instance may accept and possesses a session key sk, a session id sid, and a partner id pid. The query types, as defined in [5], include:

- Send(A, i, M): This sends message M to instance Π_A^i. The instance executes as specified by the protocol and sends back its response to the adversary. Should the instance accept, this fact, as well as the session id and partner id will be made visible to the adversary.
  Execute(A, i, B, j): This call carries out an honest execution between two instances Π_A^i and Π_B^j, where $A, B \in I, A \neq B$ and instances Π_A^i and Π_B^j were not used before. At the end of the execution, a transcript is given to the adversary, which logs everything an adversary could see during the execution (for details, see [5]).
- Reveal(A, i): The session key sk_A^i of Π_A^i is given to the adversary.

- Test(A, i): The instance Π_A^i generates a random bit b and outputs its session key sk_A^i to the adversary if $b = 1$, or else a random session key if $b = 0$. This query is allowed only once, at any time during the adversary's execution.
- Oracle(M): This gives the adversary oracle access to a function h, which is selected at random from some probability space Ω. The choice of Ω determines whether we are working in the standard model, or in the random-oracle model (see [5] for further explanations).

In additional to the above query types, we introduce another query type:

- Impersonate$(A, i, \pi, paras)$: This replaces the password and the parameters of the instance Π_A^i by π and $paras$, respectively, where Π_A^i was not used before. After this query, the internal state of Π_A^i is visible to the adversary. Each query of this type is also called an *impersonation attempt*.

We use the Impersonate type to model an impersonation attack, which allows the adversary to test a guessed password on-line. In an impersonation attack, the adversary picks a password π as her guess and then impersonates as an instance Π_A^i to start the protocol towards another instance Π_B^j. By observing the decision of Π_B^j (i.e., accepts or rejects), the adversary can test the correctness of the guessed password π. Furthermore, by analyzing, off-line, the transcript of the execution, the adversary may be able to test passwords other than π. For a secure protocol, we expect that the adversary can only test a single password in each impersonation attempt. Certainly, the impersonation attack can be implemented by solely using the Send query type. The number of Send queries called by the adversary, however, may vary with different protocols. Using the Impersonate type, we can *explicitly* defines the number of impersonation attempts performed by the adversary. We assume that the adversary always use an impersonated instance to launch an impersonation attack.

DEFINITION. Let Π_A^i and Π_B^i, $A \neq B$, be a pair of instances. We say that Π_A^i and Π_B^i are *partnered* if both instances have accepted and hold the same session id sid and the same session key sk. Here, we define the sid of Π_A^i (or Π_B^i) as the concatenation of all the messages sent and received by Π_A^i (or Π_B^i). We say that Π_A^i is *fresh* if: i) it has accepted; ii) it is not impersonated; and iii) a Reveal query has not been called either on Π_A^i or on its partner. With these definitions, we now define the advantage of the adversary $\mathcal{A}$ in attacking the protocol. Let Succ denote the event that $\mathcal{A}$ asks a single Test query on a fresh instance, outputs a bit b', and $b' = b$, where b is the bit selected during the Test query. The advantage of the adversary $\mathcal{A}$ is defined as $\mathsf{Adv}_{\mathcal{A}}^{ake} = 2Pr(\mathsf{Succ}) - 1$.

Definition 1. *A protocol Π is called a secure password-authenticated key exchange protocol if for every polynomial-time Adversary $\mathcal{A}$ that makes at most v impersonation attempts, the following two conditions are satisfied:*

1) *Except with negligible probability, each oracle call Execute(A, i, B, j) produces a pair of partnered instances Π_A^i and Π_B^j.*
2) *$\mathsf{Adv}_{\mathcal{A}}^{ake} \leq v/|\mathcal{D}| + \varepsilon$, where $|\mathcal{D}|$ denotes the size of the password space and ε is a negligible function.*

4   The Protocol

In this section, we present a new password-authenticated key exchange protocol called $QR\text{-}EKE$. In the protocol $QR\text{-}EKE$, there are two entities, Alice and Bob, who share a password w drawn at random from the password space $\mathcal{D}$ and Alice also possess a Blum integer $n = pq$, where p and q are primes of (about) the same size and $p \equiv q \equiv 3 \pmod 4$. Let A and B denote the identities of Alice and Bob, respectively. Before describing the protocol, let's review some of the facts about quadratic residues of Blum integers.

Let n be the product of two distinct primes p and q, $p \equiv q \equiv 3 \pmod 4$. Then for every quadratic residue a of n, i.e., $a \in Q_n$, the congruence $x^2 \equiv a \pmod n$ has four solutions x_1, x_2, x_3, x_4 in $\mathbb{Z}_n^*$. For any integer $\gamma \in \mathbb{Z}_n^*$, there is a unique square root $x_i, 1 \le i \le 4$, such that $x_i \gamma$ is also a quadratic residue of n, that is, $(\frac{x_i}{p}) = (\frac{\gamma}{p})$ and $(\frac{x_i}{q}) = (\frac{\gamma}{q})$. Moreover, the function $f : Q_n \to Q_n$ defined by $f(x) = x^2 \bmod n$ is a permutation. The inverse function of f is:

$$f^{-1}(y) = y^{((p-1)(q-1)+4)/8} \bmod n. \tag{2}$$

It is clear that for every positive integer t, the function $f_t : Q_n \to Q_n$ defined by

$$f_t(x) = x^{2^t} \bmod n \tag{3}$$

is also a permutation. For $z \in Q_n$, we can certainly compute the inverse $f_t^{-1}(z)$ by applying f^{-1} to z for t times. In fact, there is a more efficient algorithm (see [19]) for $f_t^{-1}(z)$.

Define hash functions $H_1, H_2, H_3 : \{0,1\}^* \to \{0,1\}^k$ and $H : \{0,1\}^* \to \mathbb{Z}_n$, where k is a security parameter, e.g., $k = 160$. Note that H can be implemented using a standard hash function $h : \{0,1\}^* \to \{0,1\}^l$, where l is the length of n, i.e., $l = \lceil \log_2 n \rceil$. On input x, $H(x) = h(x)$, if $h(x) < n$, and $H(x) = h(x) - \lceil n/2 \rceil$ if else. Assume that h is a random function, then for any integer $z \in \mathbb{Z}_n$, it can be proved that $|Pr(H(x) = z) - \frac{1}{n}| < 2^{-l}$; the bias is negligible. We will assume that H_1, H_2, H_3 and H are independent random functions.

The protocol $QR\text{-}EKE$ is described in Fig. 1. Alice starts the protocol by sending her public parameter n and a random number $r_A \in_R \{0,1\}^k$ to Bob. Bob then verifies if n is an odd integer. If n is not odd, Bob rejects; otherwise, Bob computers an integer $t = \lfloor \log_2 n \rfloor$ and selects a random number $r_B \in_R \{0,1\}^k$. Bob also selects a quadratic residue α at random from Q_n. To do this, Bob may select a random number from $\mathbb{Z}_n^*$ and raise it to the power of 2. Bob then computes $\gamma = H(w, r_A, r_B, A, B, n)$ and checks if $\gcd(\gamma, n) = 1$. If yes, Bob assigns γ to the variable λ; otherwise, Bob assigns a random number of $\mathbb{Z}_n^*$ to λ. Next, Bob computes $z = (\lambda \alpha^2)^{2^t} \bmod n$ and sends z and r_B to Alice. Subsequently, Alice computes γ using her password w and checks if γ and n are relatively prime. If $\gcd(\gamma, n) \ne 1$, Alice assigns a random number of $\mathbb{Z}_n$ to the variable β. If $\gcd(\gamma, n) = 1$ and z is a quadratic residue, Alice sets $\beta = (\sigma \gamma^{-1})^{((p-1)(q-1)+4)/8} \bmod n$, where σ is a square root of $f_{t-1}^{-1}(z)$ such that $\sigma \gamma$ is a quadratic residue of n. Next, Alice and Bob authenticate each other using

α and β and generate the session key sk upon a successful authentication. In the protocol $QR\text{-}EKE$, both Alice and Bob intend to reject when they detect that $\gcd(\gamma, n) \neq 1$. To avoid leaking any information about this event, Alice and Bob use random numbers to compute their responses μ, z, and η. When p and q are large primes of about the same size, the probability of such an event is negligible.

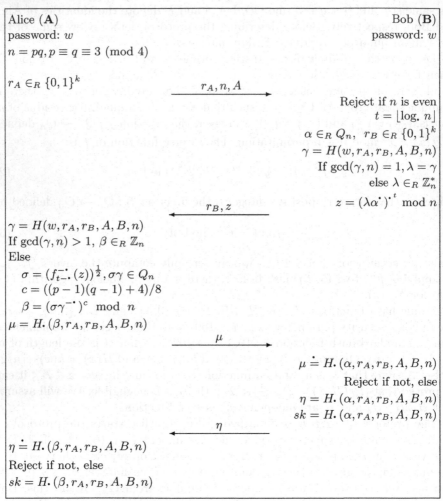

Fig. 1. The Protocol $QR\text{-}EKE$

Theorem 1. *Let n be the product of two distinct primes p and q, $p \equiv q \equiv 3$ (mod 4). Then for any integers $z \in Q_n, \gamma \in \mathbb{Z}_n^*$, and $t > 1$, the congruence $(\gamma x^2)^{2^t} \equiv z$ (mod n) has a unique solution in Q_n, which is given by*

$$\beta = (\sigma\gamma^{-1})^{((p-1)(q-1)+4)/8} \mod n,$$

where σ is a square root of $f_{t-1}^{-1}(z)$ such that $\sigma\gamma \in Q_n$.

Proof. Let z be a quadratic residue of n and t be a positive integer greater than 1. Since the function $f_{t-1} : Q_n \to Q_n$ as defined by $f_{t-1}(x) = (x)^{2^{t-1}} \bmod n$ is a permutation, there is a unique integer $v \in Q_n$ such that $z = (v)^{2^{t-1}} \bmod n$, i.e., $v = f_{t-1}^{-1}(z)$. For any integer $\gamma \in \mathbb{Z}_n^*$, there is a unique square root of v, denoted σ, such that $\sigma\gamma$ is a quadratic residues of n, or equivalently $\sigma\gamma^{-1} = \sigma\gamma \cdot \gamma^{-2}$ is a quadratic residue of n. By (2), $\sigma\gamma^{-1}$ has a unique square root in Q_n. Thus, the congruence $(\gamma x^2)^{2^t} \equiv z \pmod{n}$ has a unique solution in Q_n, which is given by β. □

Theorem 1 implies that when $\gamma = H(w, r_A, r_B, A, B, n)$ is relatively prime to n, Alice and Bob agree on a secret number $\beta = \alpha$ and can thus use the secret number to authenticate each other and establish a shared session key. Note that in the protocol $QR\text{-}EKE$, Bob only verifies that the integer n received from Alice is an odd number; he does not verify that n is the product of two distinct primes p and q and $p \equiv q \equiv 3 \pmod{4}$. This may foster the so-called residue attack as described in [2]. In such an attack, an adversary, say, *Eva*, selects a password π_0 at random from $\mathcal{D}$ and an odd integer n which may not necessarily be a Blum integer. Then Eva impersonates as Alice and starts the protocol by sending r_E, n, A to Bob. After receiving r_B and z from Bob, Eva Computes μ and sends it back to Bob. If Bob accepts, then Eva has a successful guess of Alice's password. If Bob rejects, on the other hand, Eva excludes her guess (i.e., π_0) from the password space $\mathcal{D}$. Furthermore, Eva may exclude more passwords by repeating, *off-line*, the following three steps:

1) Eva selects a password π from $\mathcal{D}$.
2) Eva computes $\gamma = H(\pi, r_E, r_B, A, B, n)$.
3) Eva tests if $\gcd(\gamma, n) = 1$. If not, Eva returns to step 1; otherwise, Bob verifies if the congruence $(\gamma x^2)^{2^t} \equiv z \pmod{n}$ has a solution in Q_n. If the congruence has a solution, Eva returns to step 1. If the congruence has no solution in Q_n, then Eva is ensured that π is not the password of Alice. Next Eva excludes π from $\mathcal{D}$ and returns to step 1.

We say that Eva succeeds if she can exclude more than one password in each residue attack as described above. In the following, we show that our protocol $QR\text{-}EKE$ is secure against residue attacks.

Theorem 2. *Let n, $n > 1$, be an odd integer with prime-power factorization $n = p_1^{a_1} p_2^{a_2} \ldots p_r^{a_r}$ and let $t = \lfloor \log_2 n \rfloor$. If z is a 2^t-th power residue modulo n, then for any $\gamma \in \mathbb{Z}_n^*$, the congruence $(\gamma x^2)^{2^t} \equiv z \pmod{n}$ has a solution in Q_n.*

Proof. To prove that $(\gamma x^2)^{2^t} \equiv z \pmod{n}$ has a solution in Q_n, we only need to prove that, for each prime power $p_i^{a_i}$ of the factorization of n, the following congruence

$$(\gamma x^2)^{2^t} \equiv z \pmod{p_i^{a_i}} \tag{4}$$

has a solution in $Q_{p_i^{a_i}}$.

Let $n_i = p_i^{a_i}, 1 \le i \le r$. Then $\phi(n_i) = p_i^{a_i - 1}(p_i - 1)$. Since n is odd, p_i is an odd prime. Hence, the integer n_i possesses a primitive root. Let g be a primitive root of n_i, then $g^{\phi(n_i)} \equiv 1 \pmod{n_i}$. Let $\gcd(2^t, \phi(n_i)) = 2^m, 1 \le m \le t$. We consider the following two cases:

(1) If $m = 1$, then $d = \phi(n_i)/2$ must be an odd integer. For any integer $a \in \mathbb{Z}^*_{n_j}$, $a^{2d} \equiv 1 \pmod{n_i}$, which implies that $a^d \equiv 1$ or $-1 \pmod{n_i}$. We claim that $a^d \equiv -1 \pmod{n_i}$ if and only if a is a quadratic non-residue of n_i. If $a^d \equiv -1 \pmod{n_i}$, it is obvious that $a \in \bar{Q}_{n_i}$. On the other hand, if $a \in \bar{Q}_{n_i}$, then there exists an odd integer s such that $a = g^s \bmod n_i$ since g is the primitive root of n_i. As the order of g is $2d$, not d, we have $a^d = (g^d)^s = -1 \bmod n_i$. Similarly, we can also prove that, if $a \in Q_{n_i}$, then the congruence $x^2 \equiv a \pmod{n_i}$ has two solutions, with one solution in Q_{n_i} and another in $\bar{Q}_{n_i}$. Hence, for any $\gamma \in \mathbb{Z}^*_n$, there exists a solution x_j, $0 \le j \le 1$, such that $x_j\gamma \in Q_{n_i}$, that is, $(x_j\gamma)^q = -1 \pmod{n_i}$. Following the proof of Theorem 1, it is clear that the congruence (4) has a solution in Q_{n_i}.

(2) Next, we consider the case that $2 \le m \le t$. Since z is a 2^t-th power residue modulo n, the congruence $x^{2^t} \equiv z \pmod{n}$ has solutions in $\mathbb{Z}^*_n$. By the Chinese Remainder Theorem, the following congruence

$$y^{2^t} \equiv z \pmod{n_i} \tag{5}$$

has solutions in $\mathbb{Z}^*_{n_i}$. Let $\mathrm{ind}_g z$ denote the index of z to the base g modulo n_i and let $y \in \mathbb{Z}^*_{n_i}$ be a solution of (5). Then, $g^{2^t \mathrm{ind}_g y - \mathrm{ind}_g z} \equiv 1 \pmod{n_i}$. Since the order of g modulo n_i is $\phi(n_i)$, it follows that

$$2^t \mathrm{ind}_g y \equiv \mathrm{ind}_g z \pmod{\phi(n_i)} \tag{6}$$

Also since $\gcd(2^t, \phi(n_i)) = 2^m$, equation (6) has exactly 2^m incongruent solutions modulo $\phi(n_i)$ when taking $\mathrm{ind}_g y$ as variable. This indicates that equation (5) has exactly 2^m incongruent solutions modulo n_i. Let y_0 be one of the solutions of equation (5), by (1), the 2^m incongruent solutions of (6) are given by

$$\mathrm{ind}_g y = \mathrm{ind}_g y_0 + j\phi(n_i)/2^m \bmod \phi(n_i), \quad 0 \le j \le 2^m - 1.$$

For any $\gamma \in \mathbb{Z}^*_n$, we have

$$\mathrm{ind}_g y - \mathrm{ind}_g \gamma = \mathrm{ind}_g y_0 - \mathrm{ind}_g \gamma + j\phi(n_i)/2^m \bmod \phi(n_i), \quad 0 \le j \le 2^m - 1.$$

Without loss of generality, let's assume that $\mathrm{ind}_g y_0 - \mathrm{ind}_g \gamma \ge 0$; otherwise we consider $\mathrm{ind}_g \gamma - \mathrm{ind}_g y$. Since $t = \lfloor \log_2 n \rfloor$ and $\phi(n_i) < n$, it is clear that $\phi(n_i)/2^m$ is an odd integer. Hence, there exist an integer $j, 0 \le j \le 3 \le 2^m - 1$, such that

$$\mathrm{ind}_g y_0 - \mathrm{ind}_g \gamma + j\phi(n_i)/2^m \equiv 0 \pmod{4},$$

which implies that there exists an integer $y \in \mathbb{Z}^*_{n_i}$ such that $y^{2^t} \equiv z \pmod{n_i}$ and $y\gamma^{-1}$ is a 4-th power residue of n_i. Therefore, the congruence (4) has a solution in Q_{n_i}, which proves the theorem. □

Theorem 2 demonstrates that, by repeating the three steps, Eva could not exclude any password from the space $\mathcal{D}$. Hence, in each residue attack , Eva could not exclude more than one password when Bob rejects. So, our protocol QR-EKE is secure against the residue attack as described in [2]. In Section 6, we will provide a formal analysis of QR-EKE within the security model described in Section 3. In each run of QR-EKE, Bob performs one gcd operation and $t+1$ squaring operations. As $t = \lfloor \log_2 n \rfloor$, the computation time for the $t+1$ squaring operations is $\mathcal{O}((\log_2 n)^3)$. It is easy to show that the computation time for Alice is about the same. When n is large, e.g., $n \approx 2^{1024}$, the computational load is high both on Alice and on Bob. In the next section, we describe an effective way to reduce the computational load on Alice and Bob.

5   Efficiency Improvement Using Cache

In practice, Alice (who may act as a server) would most likely use the same public parameter n in many sessions, although for perfect forward secrecy, Alice would need to select a new parameter in each session. Based on this observation, we let Bob cache a hashed value of Alice's public parameter n used in previous runs of QR-EKE, that is, $V = h(n, A)$. The initial value of V is set to be empty. Based on the cache, we describe a computationally-efficient variant of QR-EKE, which is called QR^c-EKE and is described in Fig. 2.

   In QR^c-EKE, Bob computes the hashed value $h(n, A)$ of the public parameter n received from Alice and compares it with the number in the cache. If they are equal, Bob is ensured that Alice's public parameter n has not changed. In this case, Bob sets $t = 1$ and computes the number z using only two squaring operations. If the hashed value $h(n, A)$ is not equal to the number in the cached, then Bob sets $t = \lfloor \log_2 n \rfloor$ and the protocol run is identical to that of QR-EKE. At the end of a successful run, Bob updates the cache using the hashed value $h(n, A)$. In QR^c-EKE, Bob also sends the number t explicitly to Alice. Alice performs the right computation for $f_{t-1}^{-1}(z)$ based on the received number t. To show that the protocol QR^c-EKE works correctly, we have the following proposition. Its proof follows directly from that of Theorem 1 and is omitted.

Proposition 1. *Let n be the product of two distinct primes p and q, $p \equiv q \equiv 3$ (mod 4). If z is a quadratic residue of n, then for any integer $\gamma \in \mathbb{Z}_n^*$, the congruence $(\gamma x^2)^2 \equiv z$ (mod n) has a unique solution in Q_n, which is given by*

$$\beta = (\sigma \gamma^{-1})^{((p-1)(q-1)+4)/8} \mod n,$$

where σ is a square root of z such that $\sigma \gamma \in Q_n$.

   We need to point out that the use of cache in QR^c-EKE is different than the use of *public password* (also called *hand-held certificate*) in the Halevi-Krawczyk protocol [10]. A public password, which is the hashed value of an public key, must be computed beforehand and will not be changed during its life time. The owner of the public password needs to either remember its value or carry it using a memory device. In the protocol QR^c-EKE, however, the cache does not need to be set beforehand; its initial value is empty. Moreover, Bob does not need to remember the number in the cache, either; Bob can provision the cache using the protocol itself. When Alice does not change the public parameter n, Bob only needs to compute two squaring operations in each protocol run. In this case, the computation time for Bob is $\mathcal{O}((\log_2 n)^2)$, which is greatly reduced in comparison with that in $QR\text{-}EKE$.

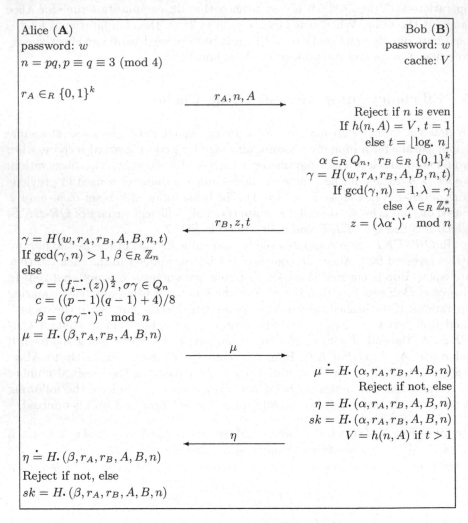

Fig. 2. The Protocol $QR^c\text{-}EKE$ with a Cache

6   Formal Security Analysis

In this section, we analyze the security of $QR\text{-}EKE$ within the formal model of security given in Section 3. Our analysis is based on the random-oracle model [6,7]. In this model, a hash function is modeled as an oracle which outputs a random number for each new query. If the same query is asked twice, identical answers are returned by the oracle. In our analysis, we also assume the intractability of integer factorization.

Factoring Assumption: Let MG be a probabilistic polynomial-time algorithm that on input 1^ℓ returns a product of two distinct primes of length $\ell/2$. For any probabilistic polynomial-time algorithm C, the following probability

$$Pr(C(n) = (p, q), pq = n | n \leftarrow \mathsf{MG}(1^\ell))$$

is negligible (in ℓ).

Theorem 3. *Let $\mathcal{A}$ be a polynomial-time adversary who makes v impersonation attempts in attacking the protocol $QR\text{-}EKE$. Let $\pi_1, \pi_2, \ldots, \pi_v$ denote her guesses of the password (shared between A and B) in the v impersonation attempts and let E_v denote the event that one of her guesses, say π_i, is a correct guess. Under the condition that E_v is false, the adversary's success probability in attacking the protocol is equal to $Pr(\mathsf{Succ}|_{\neg E_v}) = 1/2 + \zeta$, where ζ is negligible.*

Proof. Assume that the adversary $\mathcal{A}$ makes a Test query on a *fresh* instance, which is either Π_A^i or Π_B^j, and succeeds with probability $Pr(\mathsf{Succ})$. Without loss of generality, we assume that random numbers generated by instances Π_A^i and Π_B^j and by random oracles H, H_1, H_2, H_3 never repeat. To prove that $Pr(\mathsf{Succ}|_{\neg E_v}) - 1/2$ is negligible, we consider the following two cases:

Case 1: Test query is called on Π_A^i. First, we show that, except with negligible probability, r_B, z and η could not be sent by an instance which is impersonated by $\mathcal{A}$. If r_B, z and η were sent by an instance Π_B^j which was impersonated by A, then the instance Π_B^j queried the oracle H_2 on the input $\alpha, r_A, r_B, A, B, n$ and obtained the answer η, where α is a random number selected by Π_B^j. Let λ' denote the answer of the oracle H on the input π, r_A, r_B, A, B, n, where π is the adversary's guess of the password of A. Under the condition that E_v is false, we have $\lambda' \neq \lambda$. Hence, the probability that $(\lambda'/\lambda)^{2^t} \equiv 1 \pmod{n}$ is negligible. Due to the uniqueness of the solution of $(\lambda x^2)^{2^t} \equiv z \pmod{n}$ in Q_n, it is clear that the probability $Pr(\beta = \alpha)$ is negligible also. Therefore, the probability that r_B, z and η were sent by Π_B^j is negligible.

Next, let us assume that r_B, z and η were sent by an instance Π_B^j which is not impersonated by $\mathcal{A}$. Then Π_B^j is partnered with Π_A^i. Under the assumption that random numbers generated by entity instances and by random oracles never repeat, it is clear that Π_B^j is the only instance partnered with Π_A^i. Thus, the session key sk_A^i could not be held by any instance other than Π_A^i and Π_B^j. Due to the randomness assumption of H_3, the session key sk_A^i is just a random session key for anyone without knowing β. To recover β, the only thing that the adversary could do is to perform off-line dictionary attacks, that is, the adversary selects a random password π, obtains a solution α of the congruence $(\lambda' x^2)^{2^t} \equiv z \pmod{n}$, and then tests the correctness of α using μ or η, where $\lambda' = H(\pi, r_A, r_B, A, B, n)$. Let E_β denote the event that the adversary $\mathcal{A}$ correctly recovers β in the off-line dictionary attacks. Assume that the probability $Pr(E_\beta)$ is non-negligible.

Then for any $\lambda \in \mathbb{Z}_n^*$ and $z \in Q_n$, the adversary $\mathcal{A}$ can obtain the solution of $(\lambda x^2)^{2^t} \equiv z \pmod{n}$ in Q_n with non-negligible probability. In this case, we can construct a factoring algorithm C for n as follows: the algorithm C selects $\rho \in \bar{Q}_n$ and $\lambda \in \mathbb{Z}_n^*$ and gives λ and $z = (\lambda \rho^2)^{2^t} \mod n$ to $\mathcal{A}$. The adversary $\mathcal{A}$ solves the congruence $(\lambda x^2)^{2^t} \equiv z \pmod{n}$ and returns $\beta \in Q_n$. Under our assumption, it can be concluded that $Pr((\lambda \beta^2)^{2^t} \equiv (\lambda \rho^2)^{2^t} \pmod{n}) = Pr(E_\beta)$. Thus, $Pr(\beta^{2^{t+1}} \equiv \rho^{2^{t+1}} \pmod{n}) = Pr(E_\beta)$. Note that $f(x) = 2^{2^t} \mod n$ is a permutation on Q_n. Hence, $Pr(\beta^2 \equiv \rho^2 \pmod{n}) = Pr(E_\beta)$. Since $\rho \in \bar{Q}_n$ and $\beta \in Q_n$, the algorithm C can find the factorization of n by computing $\gcd(n, \rho + \beta)$ and $\gcd(n, \rho - \beta)$, which contradicts the factoring assumption. Hence, $Pr(E_\beta)$ must be negligible.

Finally, let Auth denote the event that r_B, z and η were sent by an instance Π_B^j which is not impersonated by $\mathcal{A}$. Then $Pr(\neg\mathsf{Auth}|_{\neg E_v})$ is negligible. Moreover,

$$
\begin{aligned}
Pr(\mathsf{Succ}|_{\neg E_v}) &= Pr(\mathsf{Succ}|_{\neg\mathsf{Auth}})Pr(\neg\mathsf{Auth}|_{\neg E_v}) + Pr(\mathsf{Succ}|_{\mathsf{Auth}})Pr(\mathsf{Auth}|_{\neg E_v}) \\
&\le Pr(\neg\mathsf{Auth}|_{\neg E_v}) + Pr(\mathsf{Succ}|_{\mathsf{Auth}}) \\
&= Pr(\neg\mathsf{Auth}|_{\neg E_v}) + Pr(\mathsf{Succ}|_{E_\beta})Pr(E_\beta) + Pr(\mathsf{Succ}|_{\neg E_\beta})Pr(\neg E_\beta) \\
&= Pr(\neg\mathsf{Auth}|_{\neg E_v}) + Pr(E_\beta) + 0.5(1 - Pr(E_\beta)) \\
&= 0.5 + Pr(E_\beta)/2 + Pr(\neg\mathsf{Auth}|_{\neg E_v})
\end{aligned}
$$

which demonstrates that $Pr(\mathsf{Succ}|_{\neg E_v}) - 1/2$ is negligible.

Case 2: Test query is called on Π_B^j. Assume that the instance Π_B^j sent out r_B and z after receiving r_A, n, A in the first flow, where $z = (\lambda \alpha^2)^{2^t} \mod n$, $\alpha \in Q_n$, and $\lambda = H(w, r_A, r_B, A, B, n)$. The instance Π_B^j accepted after receiving μ, which is equal to the value of $H_1(\alpha, r_A, r_B, A, B, n)$. As in Case 1, wee first show that, except with negligible probability, r_A, n, A and μ were not sent by an instance Π_A^i which is impersonated by $\mathcal{A}$.

If r_B, z and η were sent by an instance Π_A^i which is impersonated by A, then the integer n may not necessarily be a Blum integer. In addition, the adversary has knowledge of the factorization of n. Let π denote the adversary's guess of the password of B and let λ' denote the answer of the oracle H on the input π, r_A, r_B, A, B, n. Under the condition that E_v is false, we have $\lambda' \ne \lambda$. By Theorem 1, the congruence $(\lambda' x^2)^{2^t} \equiv z \pmod{n}$ has solutions in Q_n for every integer $\lambda' \in \mathbb{Z}_n^*$. Thus, the probability that the adversary could obtain α by solving the congruence is $1/|Q_n|$. Let $n = P_1^{a_1} P_2^{a_2} \ldots P_r^{a_r}$ denote the prime-power factorization of n. By [11], $r \sim \ln\ln n$, which demonstrates that $1/|Q_n| \sim (\ln n)/\phi(n)$. On the other hand, it is known that (see [19]), for all integers $n \ge 5, \phi(n) > n/(6\ln\ln n)$. Hence, the probability that the adversary could recover α is negligible. Therefore, the probability that r_B, z and η were sent by Π_B^j is negligible. Next, following the analysis in Case 1, we can also show that $Pr(\mathsf{Succ}|_{\neg E_v}) - 1/2$ is negligible in Case 2. $\qquad\square$

Theorem 4. *The protocol QR-EKE is a secure password-authenticated key exchange protocol under the factoring assumption and the random oracle model.*

Proof. It is easy to verify that the protocol QR-EKE satisfies the first condition of Definition 1. To prove that protocol QR-EKE also satisfies the second condition of Definition 1, let us fix a polynomial-time adversary $\mathcal{A}$ who makes v impersonation attempts in attacking the protocol QR-EKE. Let $\pi_1, \pi_2, \ldots, \pi_v$ denote her guesses of the password in the v impersonation attempts. Let E_v denote the event that one of the guesses, say π_i, is a correct guess. Under the condition that E_v is true, it is clear that the adversary's success probability $Pr(\mathsf{Succ})$ in attacking the protocol QR-EKE is equal to 1, i.e., $Pr(\mathsf{Succ}|_{E_v}) = 1$. Let $\neg E_v$ denote that event that E_v is false, i.e., $\pi_1, \pi_2, \ldots, \pi_v$ are incorrect password-guesses. By Theorem 3, $\zeta = Pr(\mathsf{Succ}|_{\neg E_v}) - 1/2$ is negligible. Hence,

$$\begin{aligned}
\mathsf{Adv}_{\mathcal{A}}^{ake} &= 2Pr(\mathsf{Succ}) - 1, \\
&= 2Pr(\mathsf{Succ}|_{E_v})Pr(E_v) + 2Pr(\mathsf{Succ}|_{\neg E_v})Pr(\neg E_v) - 1, \\
&= 2v/|\mathcal{D}| + 2(0.5 + \zeta)(1 - v/|\mathcal{D}|) - 1, \\
&= v/|\mathcal{D}| + 2\zeta(1 - v/|\mathcal{D}|).
\end{aligned}$$

which indicates that QR-EKE satisfies the second condition of Definition 1 and thus is a secure password-authenticated key exchange protocol.   □

Similarly, we can also prove that QR^c-EKE is a secure password-authenticated key exchange protocol under the factoring assumption and random oracle model.

References

1. E. Bach and J. Shallit, *Algorithmic Number Theory*, vol. 1: *Efficient Algorithms*, MIT Press, 1997.
2. S. M. Bellovin and M. Merritt, Encrypted key exchange: Password-based protocols secure against dictionary attacks, *Proc. of the IEEE Symposium on Research in Security and Privacy*, Oakland, May 1992, pp. 72-84.
3. S. M. Bellovin and M. Merritt, Augmented encrypted key exchange: A password-based protocol secure against dictionary attacks and password file compromise, *Proc. of the 1st ACM Conference on Computer and Communications Security*, ACM, November 1993, pp. 244-250.
4. V. Boyko, P. MacKenzie, and S. Patel, Provably secure password authenticated key exchange using Diffie-Hellman, *Advances in Cryptology - EUROCRYPT 2000 Proceedings*, Lecture Notes in Computer Science, vol. 1807, Springer-Verlag, 2000, pp. 156-171.
5. M. Bellare, D. Pointcheval, and P. Rogaway, Authenticated key exchange secure against dictionary attack, *Advances in Cryptology - EUROCRYPT 2000 Proceedings*, Lecture Notes in Computer Science, vol. 1807, Springer-Verlag, 2000, pp. 139-155.
6. M. Bellare and P. Rogaway. Random oracles are practical: A paradigm for designing efficient protocols, *Proc. First Annual Conference on Computer and Communications Security*, ACM, 1993, pp. 62-73.
7. M. Bellare and P. Rogaway, Entity Authentication and key distribution, *Advances in Cryptology - Crypto 93 Proceedings*, Lecture Notes in Computer Science Vol. 773, Springer-Verlag, 1994, pp. 22-26.

8. R. Gennaro and Y. Lindell, A framework for password-based authenticated key exchange, *Advances in Cryptology - Eurocrypt 2003 Proceedings*, Lecture Notes in Computer Science Vol. 2656, Springer-Verlag, 2003, pp.524-542.

9. O. Goldreich and Y. Lindell, Session-key generation using human passwords only, *Advances in Cryptology - Crypto 2001 Proceedings*, Lecture Notes in Computer Science Vol. 2139, Springer-Verlag, 2001, pp.408-432.

10. S. Halevi and H. Krawczyk, Public-key cryptography and password protocols, *Proc. of the Fifth ACM Conference on Computer and Communications Security*, 1998, pp. 122-131,

11. G. H. Hardy, *Ramanujan: Twelve Lectures on Subjects Suggested by His Life and Work*, 3rd ed., New York: Chelsea, 1999.

12. D. Jablon, Strong password-only authenticated key exchange, *Computer Communication Review, ACM SIGCOMM*, vol. 26, no. 5, 1996, pp. 5-26.

13. D. Jablon, http://www.integritysciences.com.

14. J. Katz, R. Ostrovsky, and M. Yung, Efficient password-authenticated key exchange using human-memorable passwords, *Advances in Cryptology – Eurocrypt'2001 Proceedings*, Lecture Notes in Computer Science, Vol. 2045, Springer-Verlag, 2001.

15. K. Kobara and H. Imai, Pretty-simple password-authenticated key-exchange under standard assumptions, *IEICE Trans.*, vol. E85-A, no. 10, 2002, pp. 2229-2237.

16. T. Kwon, Authentication and key agreement via memorable passwords, *Proc. Network and Distributed System Security Symposium*, February 7-9, 2001.

17. S. Lucks, Open key exchange: How to defeat dictionary attacks without encrypting public keys, *Proc. Security Protocol Workshop*, Lecture Notes in Computer Science, Vol. 1361, Springer-Verlag, 1997, pp. 79-90.

18. P. MacKenzie, S. Patel, and R. Swaminathan, Password-authenticated key exchange based on RSA, *Advances in Cryptology—ASIACRYPT 2000 Proceedings*, Lecture Notes in Computer Science, vol. 1976, Springer-Verlag, 2000, pp. 599–613.

19. A. Menezes, P. C. van Oorschot, S. A. Vanstone, *Handbook of Applied Cryptography*, CRC Press, 1997.

20. K. H. Rosen, *Elementary Number Theory and Its Applications*, 4th ed., Addison Wesley Longman, 2000.

21. T. Wu, The secure remote password protocol , *Proc. Network and Distributed System Security Symposium*, San Diego, March 1998, pp. 97-111.

22. T. Wu, A real-world analysis of Kerberos password security, *Proc. Network and Distributed System Security Symposium*, February 3-5, 1999.

Key Agreement Using Statically Keyed Authenticators

Colin Boyd[1*], Wenbo Mao[2**], and Kenneth G. Paterson[3***]

[*] Information Security Research Centre, Queensland University of Technology,
Brisbane, Australia
[*] Hewlett-Packard Laboratories, Filton Road, Stoke Gifford, Bristol BS34 8QZ, UK
[*] Information Security Group, Royal Holloway, University of London, Egham, Surrey
TW20 0EX, UK

Abstract. A family of authenticators based on static shared keys is
identified and proven secure. The authenticators can be used in a variety of settings, including identity-based ones. Application of the authenticators to Diffie-Hellman variants in appropriate groups leads to
authenticated key agreement protocols which have attractive properties
in comparison with other proven-secure protocols. We explore two key
agreement protocols that result.

1 Introduction

There is a vast range of protocols for key establishment. Historically such protocols have been regarded as difficult to design correctly and the literature is
replete with broken examples. This has led to the realisation that a proof of
security is an almost essential property of any new protocol. In recent years
the number of key establishment protocols that carry a security proof has increased enormously. Most popular has been the model introduced by Bellare and
Rogaway [3,4] and later refined by themselves and others.

In the modular approach to protocol design and proof [2], Bellare, Canetti
and Krawczyk introduced the notion of an *authenticator* as a protocol translator.
Protocols may be proven secure in an ideal model (the so-called authenticated
links model, or simply the AM) in which the adversary is prevented from fab-
ricating messages coming from uncorrupted principals. The role of the authenticator is to transform a protocol secure in the AM, into one that is secure in
the more realistic unauthenticated links model (the UM). A major advantage of
using this modular approach is that authenticators may be re-used with different AM protocols. This facilitates an engineering approach to protocol design,
where components may be selected as appropriate to the application at hand. A

---

[*] Work supported by the Australian Research Council through Discovery Project
DP0345775.
[**] Research partially funded by the EU Fifth Framework Project IST-2001-324467
"CASENET".
[***] Supported by the Nuffield Foundation, NUF-NAL 02.

M. Jakobsson, M. Yung, J. Zhou (Eds.): ACNS 2004, LNCS 3089, pp. 248–262, 2004.

potential disadvantage of the approach is that for some protocols there may not exist any efficient decomposition into an AM protocol and an authenticator. We remark that, despite the extensive theoretical framework that has been built up, there have been few new protocols proven secure as a result of this technique.

Bellare *et al.* [2] designed two general-purpose authenticators, one based on signatures and the other based on public key encryption. They showed how these authenticators can be used to generate efficient protocols with similar properties to some existing ones, but with the benefit of a formal security proof. In a later refinement of the technique, Canetti and Krawczyk [9] designed a MAC-based authenticator which uses a pre-existing shared secret as the MAC key.

In our earlier work [7], we focussed on deniability properties of protocols resulting from taking an identity-based approach to obtaining keys for the MAC-based authenticator of Canetti and Krawczyk [9]. In this paper, we provide a more detailed study of provable security aspects of MAC-based authenticators. We focus on two methods for obtaining the MAC key. The first uses static Diffie-Hellman keys (supported by certificates). The second uses an identity-based non-interactive key distribution protocol due to Sakai *et al.* [16]. We show that both authenticators have the security properties required to make them usable in the Canetti-Krawczyk methodology. By applying these authenticators to a basic Diffie-Hellman protocol that is secure in the AM, and using various optimisations, we obtain two concrete protocols that are provably secure in the UM. We compare our first protocol with the Unified Model protocol [5] and with the SIGMA protocol of Krawczyk [13]. We compare our second protocol to recent protocols of Chen and Kudla [10]. Analysis shows that our protocols are competitive with these existing protocols in terms of efficiency and security properties. Our protocols show that taking a systematic approach to the use of protocol components can bring new ideas to this heavily researched area.

The rest of this paper is structured as follows. In the next section we provide an overview of the modular approach to protocol proofs. Section 3 provides security proofs for our two MAC-based authenticators. In Sections 4 and 5 we develop and analyse the two key exchange protocols that result from using these two authenticators on the basic Diffie-Hellman protocol.

2   Authenticators and the Canetti–Krawczyk Model

In this section we describe the modular approach to protocol proofs [2] and the Canetti–Krawczyk (CK) model [9]. We aim to give an informal understanding of how the approach works, sufficient to follow the rest of the paper. However, we necessarily omit the formal details and refer the interested reader to the original papers [2,9].

The CK model is based on the idea of *message driven* protocols. In such protocols a set of principals $P_1, P_2, \ldots, P_n$ are activated either by:

- messages from the network;
- external requests to initiate a protocol run.

The output of a protocol consists of the cumulative output of all protocol principals as well as the output of the adversary.

In the AM, the adversary $\mathcal{A}$, a probabilistic polynomial time algorithm, controls the principals $P_1, \ldots, P_n$. The possible actions of $\mathcal{A}$ are:

activate a principal with incoming message m. This includes the ability to start a protocol session.
corrupt a principal and obtain its internal information.
session-key query to obtain the session key agreed in a completed session.
session-state reveal to obtain the internal state of a principal corresponding to an incomplete session. For example, this can include ephemeral parameters deleted after the session is complete.

In the AM, the adversary $\mathcal{A}$ may only activate principals with incoming messages that have already been sent by another principal to that principal. A set M of undelivered messages is defined. When a principal P_i sends a message m to another principal P_j then m is stored in M. Later m can be used by $\mathcal{A}$ to activate P_j (and no other party) and then m is deleted from M. All messages in the protocol are different; this is enforced by appending a session identifier that is unique for each session.

In the UM an adversary $\mathcal{U}$ has the same capabilities as $\mathcal{A}$ except that any message calculated by $\mathcal{U}$ may be used to activate principals. An important part of every protocol is an *initialisation function*, I, that sets up the public keys and associated parameters. An adversary is allowed to perform a special *test session* query by identifying an uncorrupted session whose principals are uncorrupted. The adversary is then given either the correct session key for this session or a random string of the same length, each with probability $1/2$. The definition of protocol security is essentially the same in both the AM and the UM and is based on indistinguishability of these two strings.

Definition 1. *A protocol is called* SK-secure *if:*

- *two uncorrupted parties that complete sessions with matching identifiers both accept the same session key;*
- *the probability that the adversary can distinguish between the correct key in a test session and a random string of the same length is no more than $1/2$ plus a negligible function in the security parameter.*

Canetti and Krawczyk [9] show that a protocol that is SK-secure in the AM is transformed into an SK-secure protocol in the UM if an authenticator is used. In order to explain what an authenticator is, we must first define the concept of emulation.

Definition 2. *A protocol π' in the UM, emulates a protocol π in the AM if given any adversary $\mathcal{U}$ against protocol π', there exists an adversary $\mathcal{A}$ against π such that the output of π' with adversary $\mathcal{U}$ is indistinguishable from π with $\mathcal{A}$.*

Definition 3. *An* authenticator *is a mapping of protocols that transforms a protocol* π *in the AM to a protocol* π' *in the UM such that* π' *emulates* π.

In common with Bellare *et al.* [2], we require the indistinguishability in Defn. 2 to be computational. That is, there should be no efficient algorithm that can distinguish the output of the two protocols.

All the authenticators we talk about in this paper take the special form, known as *message transmission authenticators*, or simply MT-authenticators. The message transmission protocol, MT, is the protocol in the AM that simply transmits a message between two principals. Formally, any party P_i may be activated with (P_j, m) in order to send (P_i, P_j, m) to P_j and then has output 'P_i sent m to P_j'. If party P_j is activated with (P_i, P_j, m) from P_i then P_j has output 'P_j received m from P_i'. Note that sending and receiving of a message m entails it being first stored in, and then removed from, the message store M.

A UM protocol is an MT-authenticator if it emulates the AM protocol MT. Bellare *et al.* [2] showed that the mapping of protocols obtained by replacing each message M in an AM protocol by an MT-authenticator corresponding to M is an authenticator. Therefore, given an SK-secure protocol in the AM, we can convert it to an SK-secure protocol in the UM simply by replacing each separate message of the AM protocol by the MT-authenticator for that message. It is often desirable to optimise the protocol that results from the naive use of this approach when there is more than one message in the basic AM protocol. This optimisation typically consists of piggy-backing flows from one authenticated message onto flows from another and reordering independent protocol messages. Further optimisation is often possible, and can be argued heuristically not to disturb the protocol security.

3   Two Authenticators

Our MT-authenticators can be viewed as variants of the MT-authenticator based on MACs that was proposed by Canetti and Krawczyk [9]. The format of our authenticators is shown in Fig. 1. On successful completion of the protocol, B will output 'B received m from A'. In Fig. 1 k is a security parameter, m is the message to be transmitted and H is a hash function with a k bit output which we replace by a random oracle in our security proofs. In the MAC-based MT-authenticator of Canetti and Krawczyk it is assumed that the key F_{AB} is already shared between A and B during the initialisation phase. In our authenticators F_{AB} is generated by A and B from the long-term keying material which is established in the initialisation phase. We consider two different methods for achieving this: static Diffie-Hellman and an identity-based approach. The main purpose of this section is to prove that our two methods of generating F_{AB} still produce authenticators (in the sense of Defn. 3). A second difference between our approach and that of Canetti and Krawczyk [9] is that we replace the MAC by a hash function where the static shared key is included as an input to the hash. The reason for this is that it makes both the authenticator and the proof a little simpler. We can only do this by modelling the hash function as a random oracle, but in any case we would need to use the random oracle assumption in our proofs even if a MAC were used.

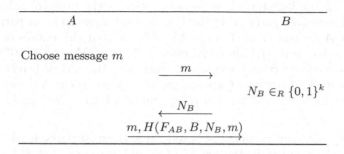

Fig. 1. Statically keyed MT-authenticator

3.1   Authenticator Using Static Diffie-Hellman

Here, the initialisation function I, on input security parameter k, generates for each party P_i a long-term key pair consisting of private key x_i and public key $y_i = g^{x_i}$, where g generates a group $\mathbb{G}$ of prime order q. The shared secret between principals P_i and P_j is $F_{P_iP_j} = g^{x_ix_j}$. When this key is used in the protocol of Figure 1, we name the resulting protocol λ_{SDH}. The fact that λ_{SDH} is an MT-authenticator relies on the difficulty of the following well known problem.

Computational Diffie-Hellman Problem (CDHP): Let $\mathbb{G}$, g and q be as above. The CDHP in $\mathbb{G}$ is as follows: Given g, g^x, g^y with $x, y \in \mathbb{Z}_q$, compute $g^{xy} \in \mathbb{G}$. An algorithm $\mathcal{A}$ has advantage ϵ in solving the CDHP if

$$\Pr\left[\mathcal{A}(g, g^x, g^y) = g^{xy}\right] = \epsilon.$$

Here the probability is measured over random choices of x, y in $\mathbb{Z}_q$ and the random operations of $\mathcal{A}$. We will use the Computational Diffie-Hellman (CDH) Assumption, which states that ϵ is negligible in the security parameter k for all efficient algorithms $\mathcal{A}$.

Theorem 1. *Suppose that H is a random oracle. Then protocol λ_{SDH} emulates MT if the CDH Assumption holds.*

Proof. We follow [2] in our proof structure. Our aim is to take any adversary $\mathcal{U}$ against the protocol λ_{SDH} and construct $\mathcal{A}$ in the AM against MT such that the outputs of the two are indistinguishable. The first step in the proof is to show that most of the actions of $\mathcal{U}$ can be emulated by $\mathcal{A}$ in the 'obvious' way, then leaving the bulk of the proof to show that the exceptional case (which prevents completion of the obvious emulation) happens with only negligible probability in the security parameter.

The scenario is that $\mathcal{A}$ runs $\mathcal{U}$ and attempts to emulate the protocol output. For any party P in the AM we denote the corresponding party in the UM as P'. Note that $\mathcal{A}$ simulates the actions of all parties in the UM. Firstly $\mathcal{A}$ chooses and distributes all the long-term keys for all parties in the protocol using function I. When $\mathcal{U}$ activates party A' in the UM to send message m to party B' then $\mathcal{A}$ activates A to send m to B in the AM. (Recall that this entails m being put into the message store M.) Similarly, when B' in the UM outputs 'B' received m from A'', $\mathcal{A}$ activates B with message m from A in the AM. When $\mathcal{U}$ corrupts a party in the UM, $\mathcal{A}$ corrupts the corresponding party in the AM and hands the information (including the long-term key which $\mathcal{A}$ has) to $\mathcal{U}$. Finally $\mathcal{A}$ outputs whatever $\mathcal{U}$ outputs.

The only obstacle occurs if $\mathcal{A}$ wants to activate a party in the AM with a message which is not in the set M of stored messages. Let $\mathcal{B}$ be the event that, for uncorrupted parties A' and B', B' outputs 'B' received m from A'' and either A was not activated by $\mathcal{A}$ to send m to B, or B previously output 'B received m from A'. Suppose that $\mathcal{B}$ occurs with non-negligible probability $\epsilon(k)$. We will show that if this is the case then it is possible to solve the CDHP with non-negligible probability. This will contradict our CDH Assumption.

From now we assume the existence of an efficient algorithm $\mathcal{U}$ that runs the protocol in the UM such that event $\mathcal{B}$ occurs with non-negligible probability $\epsilon(k)$. We also assume that $\mathcal{U}$ will complete in finite time $\mathcal{T}(k)$. We construct an algorithm $\mathcal{V}$ that interacts with $\mathcal{U}$ in order to solve the CDHP. $\mathcal{V}$ simulates the actions of all parties $P_1, P_2, \ldots, P_n$ and must be able to respond properly to all actions of $\mathcal{U}$. $\mathcal{V}$ also mediates calls to the random oracle H.

$\mathcal{V}$ is given as input a tuple $(\mathbb{G}, g, q, g^x, g^y)$ and is tasked with the problem of finding g^{xy}. Let $n(k)$ be a polynomial bound (in the security parameter k) on the number of principals that might be activated by $\mathcal{U}$. Firstly $\mathcal{V}$ chooses two parties P_f, P_g with $f \neq g$ randomly from the set of all parties $P_1, \ldots, P_n$. $\mathcal{V}$ then generates long-term secret keys x_i chosen randomly from $\mathbb{Z}_q$ for all parties P_i except P_f and P_g. The protocol parameters given to $\mathcal{U}$ are the group parameters $(\mathbb{G}, g, q)$, the public keys $y_i = g^{x_i}$ for parties P_i different from P_f and P_g, and g^x, g^y for parties P_f and P_g respectively.

When $\mathcal{U}$ activates any party, $\mathcal{V}$ follows the protocol specification on behalf of that party, choosing a random value for the output of all queries made to H in that process. $\mathcal{V}$ stores all the hash values output, together with the inputs to H, in a list L and uses L to consistently reply to H queries. Note that for H queries resulting from protocol runs between P_f and P_g, $\mathcal{V}$ does not know the value g^{xy} and so cannot calculate the correct entry to place on the list L. Instead, $\mathcal{V}$ places the symbolic string "$F_{P_f P_g}$" on L along with a record of the other values that should have been input to H in that query. $\mathcal{V}$ can then use these entries to recognize subsequent queries of the same type. $\mathcal{U}$ may also make H queries not associated with any particular protocol run; $\mathcal{V}$ responds to these as above, using the list L to ensure that queries are answered consistently. If $\mathcal{U}$ corrupts any party P_i apart from P_f and P_g then $\mathcal{V}$ can answer with x_i. If $\mathcal{U}$ corrupts P_f or P_g, then $\mathcal{V}$ terminates with failure.

The simulation continues until $\mathcal{U}$ halts, or time $\mathcal{T}(k)$ has passed. In the latter cases $\mathcal{V}$ simply aborts $\mathcal{U}$. Finally, $\mathcal{V}$ chooses α randomly from the prefixes of all oracle queries in L, and returns α as its guess for g^{xy}.

Let $\mathcal{J}$ denote the event that $\mathcal{V}$ is successful. We must now evaluate $\Pr(\mathcal{J})$.

It is easy to see that because H is a random oracle, the simulation provided by $\mathcal{V}$ is indistinguishable from what $\mathcal{U}$ would see in a real attack, unless $\mathcal{U}$ makes an oracle query prefixed by the value g^{xy} at some point in the simulation, or unless $\mathcal{U}$ corrupts P_f or P_g. In the former case, $\mathcal{V}$ may not consistently reply to oracle queries since $\mathcal{V}$ cannot "recognise" the input g^{xy}. Then $\mathcal{U}$'s behaviour is strictly speaking undefined, but this is catered for in our simulation because $\mathcal{V}$ will eventually halt $\mathcal{U}$.

Let $\mathcal{E}$ denote the event that $\mathcal{U}$ makes an oracle query prefixed by the value g^{xy}. Let $\mathcal{F}$ denote the event that $\mathcal{B}$ occurs with $\{A', B'\} = \{P_f, P_g\}$. In other words, $\mathcal{F}$ is the event that a message was passed between P_f and P_g that was not previously sent or already received by one of these parties. Since f and g were chosen at random from $\{1, \ldots, n(k)\}$, we have $\Pr(\mathcal{F}) = \epsilon(k)/\binom{n(k)}{2}$. Let $\mathcal{G}$ denote the event that $\mathcal{U}$ corrupts P_f or P_g. Notice that if event $\mathcal{F}$ occurs, then P_f and P_g must be uncorrupted. Hence if $\mathcal{F}$ occurs, then so must the event $\neg\mathcal{G}$.

After event $\mathcal{E}$, $\mathcal{V}$'s simulation may no longer be correct, but up until the point that $\mathcal{E}$ occurs, it is, so long as $\mathcal{G}$ does not occur. Therefore the probability that $\mathcal{E}$ occurs in the simulation is the same as the probability that it does in $\mathcal{U}$'s real attack, provided $\mathcal{G}$ does not occur. Note too that $\mathcal{V}$'s probability of success $\Pr(\mathcal{J})$ is equal to $\Pr(\mathcal{E} \wedge \neg\mathcal{G})/q_H(k)$ where $q_H(k)$ is a polynomial bound on the number of hash queries made during the simulation. This is because of the way that $\mathcal{V}$ selects an entry at random from the list L and because $\mathcal{V}$ aborts if event $\mathcal{G}$ occurs.

Now suppose that event $\mathcal{F}$ occurs. This means that either P_f or P_g has accepted a value which equals the output of a query to H prefixed with g^{xy}. Then either $\mathcal{U}$ has successfully guessed an output of H without making the relevant query to H, an event of probability 2^{-k}, or event $\mathcal{E}$ occurs. Notice too that if $\mathcal{F}$ occurs, then so does $\neg\mathcal{G}$. Hence we have $\Pr(\mathcal{F}) \le 2^{-k} + \Pr(\mathcal{E} \wedge \neg\mathcal{G})$, from which we deduce $\Pr(\mathcal{E} \wedge \neg\mathcal{G}) \ge \Pr(\mathcal{F}) - 2^{-k} := \epsilon_1(k)$, a non-negligible quantity. Hence we have

$$\Pr(\mathcal{J}) = \Pr(\mathcal{E} \wedge \neg\mathcal{G})/q_H(k) \ge \epsilon_1(k)/q_H(k).$$

We see that $\Pr(\mathcal{J})$, the probability that $\mathcal{V}$ is successful, is non-negligible in the security parameter k. This completes the proof. $\qquad\square$

Remark. The reduction in the proof may be tightened if we assume, instead of the CDH Assumption, that the gap-DH problem is hard. With this assumption we may allow $\mathcal{V}$ access to an oracle that will distinguish between Diffie-Hellman triples and random triples in $\mathbb{G}$. The gap-DH assumption [15] is that CDHP is still hard even given access to this oracle. In this case $\mathcal{V}$ can test if $\mathcal{U}$ has asked a critical query (one involving g^{xy}) of the random oracle and can abort the protocol run with certainty of the correct answer at that point. Therefore we can improve the success probability to the following:

$$\Pr(\mathcal{J}) \geq \epsilon_1(k).$$

3.2 Authenticator Using Identity-Based Static Keys

Using the notation of Boneh and Franklin [6], we let $\mathbb{G}_1$ be an additive group of prime order q and $\mathbb{G}_2$ be a multiplicative group of the same order q. We assume the existence of an efficiently computable, non-degenerate, bilinear map $\hat{e}$ from $\mathbb{G}_1 \times \mathbb{G}_1$ to $\mathbb{G}_2$. Typically, $\mathbb{G}_1$ will be a subgroup of the group of points on an elliptic curve over a finite field, $\mathbb{G}_2$ will be a subgroup of the multiplicative group of a related finite field and the map $\hat{e}$ will be derived from either the Weil or Tate pairing on the elliptic curve. By $\hat{e}$ being bilinear, we mean that for $Q, W, Z \in \mathbb{G}_1$, both

$$\hat{e}(Q, W + Z) = \hat{e}(Q, W) \cdot \hat{e}(Q, Z) \quad \text{and} \quad \hat{e}(Q + W, Z) = \hat{e}(Q, Z) \cdot \hat{e}(W, Z).$$

By $\hat{e}$ being non-degenerate, we mean that for some element $P \in \mathbb{G}_1$, we have $\hat{e}(P, P) \neq 1_{\mathbb{G}_2}$.

When $a \in \mathbb{Z}_q$ and $Q \in \mathbb{G}_1$, we write aQ for Q added to itself a times, also called scalar multiplication of Q by a. As a consequence of bilinearity, we have that, for any $Q, W \in \mathbb{G}_1$ and $a, b \in \mathbb{Z}_q$:

$$\hat{e}(aQ, bW) = \hat{e}(Q, W)^{ab} = \hat{e}(abQ, W).$$

We refer to [1,6,11] for a more comprehensive description of how these groups, pairings and other parameters should be selected in practice for efficiency and security.

In this setting, the initialisation function I on input a security parameter k selects suitable groups $\mathbb{G}_1$, $\mathbb{G}_2$ and map $\hat{e}$. Then I generates a random key $s \in \mathbb{Z}_q$. This key will play the role of the master secret of the Trusted Authority in the ID-based system. Then I distributes to each party P_i with identity ID_i a long-term key pair consisting of public key $Q_i = H_1(ID_i)$ and private key $S_i = sQ_i$. Here H_1 is a hash function mapping identities $ID_i \in \{0,1\}^*$ onto $\mathbb{G}_1$.

With this initialisation, any two principals P_i, P_j with identities ID_i, ID_j can efficiently calculate the shared key $F_{ij} = \hat{e}(Q_i, Q_j)^s = \hat{e}(S_i, Q_j) = \hat{e}(S_j, Q_i)$. This method of *identity-based, non-interactive key distribution* is due to Sakai *et al.* [16]. When this key is used in the protocol of Figure 1, we call the resulting protocol λ_{SBDH}. The fact that λ_{SBDH} is an MT-authenticator relies on the difficulty of the following problem.

Bilinear Diffie-Hellman Problem (BDHP): Let $\mathbb{G}_1$, $\mathbb{G}_2$ and $\hat{e}$ be as above. The BDHP in $\langle \mathbb{G}_1, \mathbb{G}_2, \hat{e} \rangle$ is as follows: Given $\langle P, xP, yP, zP \rangle$ with $P \in \mathbb{G}_1$ and $x, y, z \in \mathbb{Z}_q$, compute $\hat{e}(P, P)^{xyz} \in \mathbb{G}_2$. An algorithm $\mathcal{A}$ has advantage ϵ in solving the BDHP in $\langle \mathbb{G}_1, \mathbb{G}_2, e \rangle$ if

$$\Pr\left[\mathcal{A}(\langle P, xP, yP, zP \rangle) = \hat{e}(P, P)^{xyz}\right] = \epsilon.$$

Here the probability is measured over random choices of $P \in \mathbb{G}_1$, $x, y, z \in \mathbb{Z}_q$ and the random operations of $\mathcal{A}$. We will use the Bilinear Diffie-Hellman Assumption, which states that, for all efficient algorithms $\mathcal{A}$, the advantage ϵ is negligible as a function of the security parameter k used in generating $\langle \mathbb{G}_1, \mathbb{G}_2, \hat{e} \rangle$.

Theorem 2. *Suppose that H and H_1 are random oracles. Then protocol λ_{SBDH} emulates* MT *if the Bilinear Diffie-Hellman Assumption holds.*

Proof. The proof is the same as for Theorem 1 until we assume the existence of an efficient algorithm $\mathcal{U}$ which runs the protocol in the UM such that event $\mathcal{B}$ occurs with non-negligible probability ϵ. We construct an algorithm $\mathcal{V}$ that interacts with $\mathcal{U}$ in order to solve the BDHP.

This time $\mathcal{V}$ is given as input $\langle \mathbb{G}_1, \mathbb{G}_2, \hat{e} \rangle$ and a tuple $\langle P, xP, yP, zP \rangle$ with the aim of finding $\hat{e}(P, P)^{xyz}$. The idea is that z will take the role of s and xP and yP will be the public keys of two entities, P_f and P_g, where f and g are selected randomly from $\{0, 1, \ldots, n(k)\}$. Protocol parameters $\langle \mathbb{G}_1, \mathbb{G}_2, \hat{e} \rangle$ are given to $\mathcal{U}$À t any point, $\mathcal{U}$ generates the public key for entity P_i with identity ID_i by making an H_1 query on ID_i. $\mathcal{V}$ handles these H_1 queries as follows. When $i \neq f, g$, $\mathcal{V}$ responds with $H_1(ID_i) = h_i P$ where $h_i \in \mathbb{Z}_q$ is selected at random. $\mathcal{V}$ then sets the private key for entity P_i to $S_i = h_i \cdot zP$. When $i = f$, $\mathcal{V}$ responds with xP and when $i = g$, $\mathcal{V}$ responds with yP.

When $\mathcal{U}$ activates any party, $\mathcal{V}$ follows the protocol specification on behalf of that party, choosing a random value for the output of all queries made to H in that process. $\mathcal{V}$ stores all the hash values output, together with the inputs to the H, in a list L and uses L to consistently reply to H queries. Note that for H queries resulting from protocol runs between P_f and P_g, $\mathcal{V}$ does not know the value $\hat{e}(P, P)^{xyz}$ and so cannot calculate the correct entry to place on the list L. Instead, $\mathcal{V}$ places the symbolic string "$F_{P_f P_g}$" on L along with a record of the other values that should have been input to H in that query. $\mathcal{V}$ can then use these entries to recognize subsequent queries of the same type. $\mathcal{U}$ may also make H queries not associated with any particular protocol run; $\mathcal{V}$ responds to these as above, using the list L to ensure that queries are answered consistently. If $\mathcal{U}$ corrupts any party P_i apart from P_f and P_g then $\mathcal{V}$ can answer with S_i. If $\mathcal{U}$ corrupts P_f or P_g then $\mathcal{V}$ terminates with failure.

The simulation continues until $\mathcal{U}$ halts or time $\mathcal{T}(k)$ has passed. In the latter case $\mathcal{V}$ simply aborts $\mathcal{U}$. Finally, $\mathcal{V}$ chooses α randomly from the prefixes of all oracle queries in L, and returns α as its guess for $\hat{e}(P, P)^{xyz}$.

The rest of the proof is the same as that of Theorem 1, with the value $\hat{e}(P, P)^{xyz}$ replacing the value g^{xy}. $\square$

4   An Authenticated Key Agreement Protocol

In this and the following section we will examine the effect of applying our authenticators to the basic Diffie-Hellman protocol in the AM in order to derive SK-secure protocols in the UM. We present optimised versions of the protocols rather than the protocols that result by naively applying the authenticators to each AM protocol message. The latter protocols automatically carry a security proof but are not very efficient. In contrast, our optimised protocols rely on heuristic arguments that the proofs are preserved in making the various optimisations.

Canetti and Krawczyk [9] proved that Diffie-Hellman with ephemeral keys is an SK-secure protocol in the AM as long as the Decision Diffie-Hellman (DDH)

Assumption holds in the group in which it is executed.[1] Although we could use groups for which the DDH Assumption is believed hard, we can instead use the weaker CDH Assumption and hash the Diffie-Hellman key with a hash function modelled as a random oracle. So for our *basic Diffie-Hellman protocol*, A and B choose random values r_A and r_B respectively, exchange the values g^{r_A} and g^{r_B}, and calculated the shared secret $Z_{AB} = H_2(g^{r_A r_B})$ where H_2 is a random oracle. Since we are already using the random oracle model for the authenticators, it seems logical to use it here too. This also allows us to be more flexible in our choice of groups.

The following theorem may be proven in a standard way. We emphasise that although Canetti and Krawczyk use the stonger DDH Assumption they do not use the random oracle assumption, so their result on the AM security of Diffie-Hellman is not weaker.

Theorem 3. *The basic Diffie-Hellman protocol is SK-secure in the AM given the CDH Assumption and that H_2 is a random oracle.*

Here, we leave the details of the ephemeral Diffie-Hellman group flexible, assuming only that it is a cyclic group of prime order in which the CDH Assumption holds. Natural choices for this group will arise in the context of each of our two authenticators.

4.1   Key Agreement from Static Diffie-Hellman

We have shown in Section 3 how an MT-authenticator can be obtained from static Diffie-Hellman key exchange. The general result of Canetti and Krawczyk [9] and Theorem 3 ensure that using this MT-authenticator to replace each message of the basic Diffie-Hellman protocol results in a protocol that is SK-secure in the UM. We present an optimised version of this protocol as Protocol 1. The group $\mathbb{G}$ already needed for the authenticator is a natural choice for the basic Diffie-Hellman exchange, and we have selected it here. In Protocol 1, parties A and B generate ephemeral secrets r_A and r_B, and exchange values $t_A = g^{r_A}$ and $t_B = g^{r_B}$. In the optimisation process, messages have been piggy-backed upon one another and values t_A and t_B play dual roles as both messages and the random nonces of A and B respectively. In addition the pair (t_A, t_B) form a unique session identifier which is required for all protocols. We have also added the identities of the sender in the first two messages in plaintext. This will be a functional necessity in case either party does not initially know with which partner it is running the protocol. Both A and B can compute the shared secret Z_{AB} which is then used to calculate a session key using a suitable key derivation function.

---

[*] The DDH Assumption says that Diffie-Hellman triples (g^x, g^y, g^{xy}) cannot be efficiently distinguished from triples (g^x, g^y, g^z), where x, y, z are random exponents.

Shared Information: Static Diffie-Hellman key: $F_{AB} = g^{x_A x_B}$.

$$A \qquad\qquad\qquad\qquad\qquad\qquad B$$

$$r_A \in_R \mathbb{Z}_q$$
$$t_A = g^{r_A} \qquad \xrightarrow{\quad A, t_A \quad} \qquad r_B \in_R \mathbb{Z}_q$$
$$t_B = g^{r_B}$$

$$\xleftarrow{\quad B, t_B, H(F_{AB}, B, t_A, t_B) \quad}$$

Verify hash

$$\xrightarrow{\quad H(F_{AB}, A, t_B, t_A) \quad} \qquad \text{Verify hash}$$

$$Z_{AB} = H \cdot (t_B^{r_A}) \qquad\qquad\qquad Z_{AB} = H \cdot (t_A^{r_B})$$

Protocol 1: Key agreement protocol based on static Diffie-Hellman

4.2   Comparison with Related Protocols

The most similar proven secure protocol to Protocol 1 is the Unified Model Protocol (UMP) analysed by Blake-Wilson and Menezes [5] in the Bellare–Rogaway model. In the variant of the UMP that we consider, the shared secret Z_{AB} is equal to $g^{r_A r_B}||F_{AB}$, the concatenation of ephemeral and static Diffie-Hellman keys. A MAC key (for confirmation) and session key are both derived from Z_{AB} using independent hash functions.

Protocol 1 and the UMP have similar properties and efficiency which we will summarise below. Another proven secure protocol that is worth examining is the SIGMA protocol of Krawczyk [13] which was used as the basis of the Internet Key Exchange (IKE) protocol and which has also been proposed as the basis for its replacement. It is interesting to note that when it comes to additional properties SIGMA and Protocol 1 are in some senses complementary. We will give further details below.

Efficiency. In Protocol 1, each principal has to complete three exponentiations in total. The computational requirements of Protocol 1 are almost identical to those of the UMP. However, one difference is that both parties can complete Protocol 1 before computing the ephemeral secret Z_{AB}. This means that Protocol 1 can be completed more quickly than the UMP.

Protocol 1 has better computational and bandwidth efficiency than SIGMA. An exact comparison relies on the details of the signature scheme used in SIGMA and the size of various parameters. The MQV protocol [14] has slightly smaller computational requirements in total but currently has no published security proof. In terms of bandwidth, Protocol 1 and the UMP also seem to be optimal. The only components included are the ephemeral key and the MAC or hash. In contrast, the SIGMA protocol includes both a MAC and a digital signature sent by each party, in addition to the Diffie-Hellman ephemeral key.

Identity Protection and Knowledge of Peer Entity. One of the main distinctive properties of SIGMA, which motivated its design, is strong identity protection. This property allows the protocol principals to hide their identities from adversaries. In contrast to SIGMA, Protocol 1 and the UMP do not seem well suited to provide identity protection, since each party must know the identity of the other in order to calculate F_{AB} and authenticate to the other.

As a consequence of its strong identity protection, a property that is missing from the SIGMA protocol, but which is held by Protocol 1 and the UMP, is what is often called 'knowledge of the peer entity'. This means that party A in SIGMA can complete the protocol without any indication that B is prepared to communicate. By simply deleting the final message, A will accept the session key, apparently shared with B, even though B may never have received any indication of the existence of A. Krawcyzk discusses the possibility of adding an extra acknowledgement message from B to add knowledge of the peer entity to SIGMA, but this has obvious drawbacks.

Key Compromise Impersonation and Deniability. Although SIGMA is more flexible in providing identity protection, Protocol 1 fares much better than SIGMA when it comes to another desirable feature: deniability. This is the property that each party should be able to deny having taken part in the protocol run. Krawczyk pointed out that although SIGMA provides deniability when both parties cooperate with each other, if one party defects by revealing its random input, then the other cannot deny taking part.

Following the definition of *deniable encryption* by Canetti *et al.* [8] we may say that a two-party protocol is *deniable* for party A, if a legitimate party B could have simulated the protocol without the presence of A. Since all protocols using our authenticators can be simulated perfectly by either party the protocols can be seen to provide very strong deniability: there is no situation in which one party can prevent the other from denying having been involved.

Another property that may be useful is resistance to key compromise impersonation (KCI). It is obvious that in the situation when the adversary obtains the long-term key of a party A, the adversary can masquerade as A; KCI is possible if the adversary can masquerade as other parties to A in this event. Such an attack could potentially allow compromise of A's private key to go undetected.

The SIGMA protocols provide protection against KCI since any partner of A needs to demonstrate knowledge of its own private key through generation of a new signature. However, Protocol 1 and the UMP do not protect against KCI. This is because knowledge of either party's private key is enough to complete the protocol. The mechanisms used to prevent KCI and allow undeniability are in conflict. In SIGMA, signatures protect against KCI but prevent deniability, while in Protocol 1 and the UMP, the mechanism used to provide deniability allows KCI.

5   Identity-Based Key Agreement

There has been considerable recent interest in identity-based key agreement based on pairings. In this section we give more detail of how to apply our identity-based authenticator to derive an identity-based key agreement protocol. We compare this protocol with a protocol proven secure in [10].

We assume the same algebraic setting as in Section 3.2. In principle we can use Diffie-Hellman in any group for the AM protocol. However, it is practical to choose a group that is already implemented for the authenticator. The group $\mathbb{G}_1$ is an obvious choice if we make the natural assumption that the CDHP is hard in $\mathbb{G}_1$: we are already making the stronger assumption that the BDHP is hard for $\langle \mathbb{G}_1, \mathbb{G}_2, \hat{e} \rangle$ to obtain a secure authenticator anyway. We can use any non-zero element $P \in \mathbb{G}_1$ as the base for the Diffie-Hellman protocol. The result of applying our identity-based MT-authenticator to the basic Diffie-Hellman protocol and then optimising is the identity-based key agreement protocol shown as Protocol 2. Its properties are explored in detail in [7], in particular its strong deniability feature.

Shared Information:
Fixed key F_{AB} derived from static Diffie-Hellman key: $F_{AB} = H. (\hat{e}(Q_A, Q_B)^s)$;
A generator P of $\mathbb{G}.$.

A		B
$r_A \in_R \mathbb{Z}_q$		
$T_A = r_A P$	$\xrightarrow{\quad A, T_A \quad}$	$r_B \in_R \mathbb{Z}_q$
		$T_B = r_B P$
	$\xleftarrow{B, T_B, H(F_{AB}, B, T_A, T_B)}$	
Verify hash		
	$\xrightarrow{H(F_{AB}, A, T_B, T_A)}$	Verify hash
$Z_{AB} = H. (r_A T_B)$		$Z_{AB} = H. (r_B T_A)$

Protocol 2: Identity-based key agreement protocol

The most efficient identity-based key agreement protocol with confirmation and enjoying a security proof currently seems to be that due to Chen and Kudla [10, Protocol 4]. Their proof is in the Bellare–Rogaway model but makes the strong restriction that the adversary reveals no session keys in the course of its attack. In [10, Protocol 4], the parties exchange ephemeral values $r_A Q_A$ and $r_B Q_B$ and calculate the shared secret $Z_{AB} = \hat{e}(Q_A, Q_B)^{s(r_A+r_B)}$. MACs are used in a standard way to provide key confirmation.

Protocol 4 of [10] requires each party to compute one elliptic curve pairing and two elliptic curve multiplications (equivalent to exponentiations in a multiplicative group). Therefore the computational effort required is the same as that in Protocol 2. However, if many protocol instances take place between the same parties, Protocol 2 can cache and re-use the same F_{AB} value and therefore requires only one pairing for all of these protocols. In contrast Protocol 4 of [10] requires one pairing for every protocol run, even between the same parties.

Although Protocol 4 of [10] does not provide forward secrecy, Chen and Kudla do provide alternatives with this property. With regard to additional properties discussed in Section 4, Protocol 4 of [10] seems to share some similarity with our protocol and some similarity with the SIGMA protocol. Chen and Kudla establish that their protocol protects against KCI attacks, though only in a security model where no reveal queries are made by the adversary. Their protocol also provides deniability: it is easy to see that either party can simulate a protocol run. Identity protection is not discussed by Chen and Kudla, but their protocols require each party to know the identity of the other party in order to derive the session key. Therefore it seems that, like our protocols, identity protection against active adversaries cannot be efficiently achieved. Protocol 4 of [10] does provide confirmation of knowledge of the peer entity.

6 Conclusion

We have shown that the CK model can be profitably used to design novel, provably secure key exchange protocols. We obtain protocols that have not been proven secure before; subsequent optimisation yields protocols with efficiency properties equal to or better than all known similar protocols. We have also examined the additional properties that our protocols possess. Our work illustrates that a systematic approach to design of provable security can have other benefits apart from the proofs themselves. It may be profitable to augment our authenticators with more examples by using different ways of deriving static keys. The self-certified keys of Girault [12] are one promising example. In addition we reiterate that our authenticators can also be used with any other proven secure AM protocol to provide new SK-secure protocols. One AM protocol that could be used is the key transport protocol proven SK-secure by Canetti and Krawcyzk [9]. A particularly interesting key transport protocol results if only identity-based components are used in the construction.

References

1. P. S. L. M. Barreto, H. Y. Kim, B. Lynn, and M. Scott. Efficient algorithms for pairing-based cryptosystems. In *Advances in Cryptology - CRYPTO 2002*, LNCS. Springer-Verlag, 2002.
2. M. Bellare, R. Canetti, and H. Krawczyk. A modular approach to the design and analysis of authentication and key exchange protocols. In *Proceedings of the thirtieth annual ACM symposium on theory of computing*, pages 419–428. ACM Press, 1998.
3. M. Bellare and P. Rogaway. Entity authentication and key distribution. In D.R. Stinson, editor, *Advances in Cryptology – CRYPTO'93*, volume 773 of *LNCS*, pages 232–249. Springer-Verlag, 1994.

4. M. Bellare and P. Rogaway. Provably secure session key distribution – the three party case. In *27th ACM Symposium on Theory of Computing*, pages 57–66. ACM Press, 1995.
5. S. Blake-Wilson, D. Johnson, and A. Menezes. Key agreement protocols and their security analysis. In M. Darnell, editor, *Crypography and Coding - 6th IMA Conference*, pages 30–45. Springer-Verlag, 1997. LNCS Vol. 1355.
6. D. Boneh and M. Franklin. Identity-based encryption from the Weil pairing. *SIAM Journal of Computing*, 32(3):585–615, 2003.
7. C. Boyd, W. Mao, and K.G. Paterson. Deniable authenticated key establishment for Internet protocols. In *Proceedings of 11th International Workshop on Security Protocols*, LNCS. Springer-Verlag, to appear.
8. R. Canetti, C. Dwork, M. Naor, and R. Ostrovsky. Deniable encryption. In B. Kaliski, editor, *Advances in Cryptology – Crypto'97*, volume 1294 of *LNCS*, pages 90–104. Springer-Verlag, 1997.
9. R. Canetti and H. Krawczyk. Analysis of key-exchange protocols and their use for building secure channels. In B. Pfitzmann, editor, *Advances in Cryptology – Eurocrypt 2001*, volume 2045 of *LNCS*, pages 453–474. Springer-Verlag, 2001.
10. L. Chen and C. Kudla. Identity based authenticated key agreement protocols from pairings. In *IEEE Computer Security Foundations Workshop*, pages 219–233. IEEE Computer Society Press, 2003. Updated version at Cryptology ePrint Archive, Report 2002/184.
11. S.D. Galbraith, K. Harrison, and D. Soldera. Implementing the Tate pairing. In C. Fieker and D.R. Kohel, editors, *Algorithmic Number Theory - ANTS-V*, volume 2369 of *LNCS*, pages 324–337. Springer-Verlag, 2002.
12. M. Girault. Self-certified public keys. In D. W. Davies, editor, *Advances in Cryptology – EUROCRYPT 1991*, volume 547 of *LNCS*, pages 490–497. Springer-Verlag, 1992.
13. H. Krawczyk. SIGMA: The SIGn and MAc approach to authenticated Diffie-Hellman and its use in the IKE protocols. In D. Boneh, editor, *Advances in Cryptology – Crypto 2003*, volume 2729 of *LNCS*, pages 400–425. Springer-Verlag, 2003.
14. L. Law, A. Menezes, M. Qu, J. Solinas, and S. Vanstone. An efficient protocol for authenticated key agreement. *Designs, Codes and Cryptography*, 28(2):119–134, March 2003.
15. T. Okamoto and D. Pointcheval. The gap-problems: a new class of problems for the security of cryptographic schemes. In K. Kim, editor, *Public Key Cryptography (PKC'01)*, volume 1992 of *LNCS*, pages 104–118. Springer-Verlag, 2001.
16. R. Sakai, K. Ohgishi, and M. Kasahara. Cryptosystems based on pairing. In *The 2000 Sympoium on Cryptography and Information Security*, Okinawa, Japan, January 2000.

Low-Latency Cryptographic Protection
for SCADA Communications

Andrew K. Wright[1], John A. Kinast[2], and Joe McCarty[2]

* Cisco Systems, 12515 Research Blvd., Austin, TX USA 78759
akwright@acm.org
* Gas Technology Institute, 1700 S. Mount Prospect Rd.,
Des Plaines, IL USA 60018
{john.kinast,joe.mccarty}@gastechnology.org

Abstract. Supervisory Control And Data Acquisition (SCADA) systems are real-time process control systems that are widely deployed throughout critical infrastructure sectors including power, gas, oil, and water. However, SCADA networks generally have little protection from the rising danger of cyber attack. A retrofit solution to protect existing SCADA communications links must assure the integrity of commands and responses that are typically transmitted over serial lines at speeds from 300 to 19200 bits per second, while introducing minimal additional latency into the real-time SCADA traffic.

This paper describes the key aspects of a cryptographic protocol for retrofit SCADA link protection that leverages the Cyclic Redundancy Checks (CRC) transmitted by existing SCADA equipment to achieve strong integrity while introducing minimal latency. The protocol is based on a new *position embedding* encryption mode which, for a b-bit block cipher, ensures that any unauthentic message an adversary can construct (*i*) includes at least b randomly chosen bits, and therefore, by a new result proved for error detection by systematic shortened cyclic codes, (*ii*) contains a correct h-bit CRC with probability 2^{-h}. The low speed of the communications channel limits the rate at which an adversary can make trials, enabling detection of potential attacks before enough trials can be made to achieve any significant likelihood of success. The protocol avoids the need for a decrypting link protection module to buffer decrypted data until an end-of-message integrity check is verified, which would otherwise add significant latency.

1 Introduction

Supervisory Control And Data Acquisition (SCADA) systems are real-time process control systems that monitor and control local or geographically remote devices. They are in wide use throughout a variety of critical infrastructure sectors, including power, gas, oil, and water, and are a critical component of operations. As illustrated in Fig. 1, a typical SCADA system consists of an *operations console*, a SCADA *master*, and one or more *remote units* that share a communications link. The SCADA master runs a program that polls the remote

M. Jakobsson, M. Yung, J. Zhou (Eds.): ACNS 2004, LNCS 3089, pp. 263–277, 2004.

units, receives and interprets responses, reports system status on the operations console, and issues commands automatically or in response to operator actions. The communications link is commonly a dedicated serial line, a dialup serial line, or a radio link, and operates at low speeds such as 300 to 19200 bits per second. Remote units read temperatures, pressures, flows, voltages, currents, frequencies, or other physical quantities, and control valves, circuit breakers, or other devices that influence physical processes. SCADA devices are environmentally hardened to withstand extremes in temperature, humidity, electromagnetic interference, etc. and typically have service lifetimes measured in decades. They are considerably more expensive than comparable commodity devices, and utilities throughout the world have extensive investments in serial-based SCADA hardware.

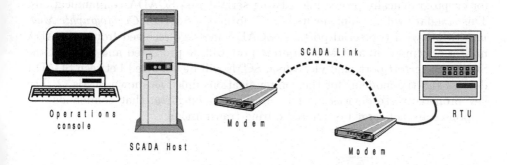

Fig. 1. Typical SCADA System

Due to the nature of the physical processes that SCADA systems control, malicious attacks directed against SCADA systems have the potential to cause significant disruption and damage to critical infrastructures and the markets they supply. SCADA masters and operations consoles are generally well-protected by physical security measures such as perimeter fences and armed guards. Operations consoles generally require at least password authentication. Historically, SCADA masters have not been connected to other computer networks that may have a path to the Internet.[1] SCADA remotes have some physical security, being located at such sites as the tops of telephone poles and transmission towers, and in unmanned stations secured by barbed wire and padlocks. However, SCADA communications links are particularly vulnerable to cyber attack. An adversary with no physical access to any part of a SCADA system can easily compromise dialup links. Compromising radio links requires only proximity and an appropriate transmitter. Leased lines are easily tapped from various points in the telephone network. While most of the over 150 widely deployed SCADA

---

[*] This is beginning to change with the introduction of SCADA systems that communicate using IP (Internet Protocol), and is a very serious but different problem.

protocols use a Cyclic Redundancy Code (CRC) to detect communications errors caused by noise, CRCs provide no protection against a malicious adversary. Some SCADA protocols require device passwords be transmitted along with commands, but these passwords are usually transmitted in the clear where they are easily snooped. We are aware of no SCADA protocols that include strong provisions to assure the integrity of SCADA traffic against a malicious adversary.

Recognizing the vulnerability of SCADA communications, the American Gas Association (AGA) is preparing a series of recommendations for protecting those communications [1]. The extensive investments utilities have made in existing equipment necessitate a retrofit solution to protect these systems. The diversity of deployed equipment, the ages of deployed hardware, and the limited computational power of deployed devices preclude building protection directly into existing systems. Thus one of AGA's key recommendations will be a standard for cryptographically protecting existing serial-based SCADA communications. This standard will be implemented in the form of a *SCADA Cryptographic Module* (SCM) with two serial ports. A SCADA message received from a SCADA master or remote on a SCM's *plaintext* port will be protected and sent out the SCM's *ciphertext* port, and vice versa. SCMs will be deployed between SCADA devices and the modems for the communications links, as shown in Fig. 2. The key property these devices must assure is *data integrity*: that commands and responses are not forged or altered during transmission.

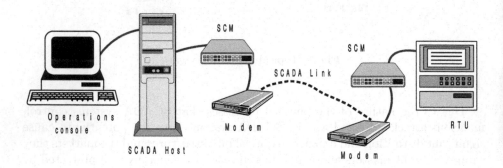

Fig. 2. SCADA System with SCMs Deployed

The constraints imposed by retrofit requirements make designing a protocol to assure integrity more complex than it might first appear. The protocol must introduce minimal additional latency between the SCADA master and remote to avoid impacting the real-time nature of the traffic carried over this low speed channel. The obvious solution of appending to each message some form of integrity check value such as a Message Authentication Code (MAC) would require the receiving SCM to buffer the entire message and check its MAC before forwarding the message out the SCM's plaintext port. Forwarding the buffered message would take as long as receiving it, since both SCM ports will generally operate at the same baud rate, and would thus double the communications latency. Many SCADA environments are unable to tolerate this much additional latency.

The solution we propose leverages the CRC check performed by the receiving SCADA device. Both sending and receiving SCMs buffer only enough data to fill one block of a block cipher, and forward the encrypted or decrypted block as soon as the block is complete. Thus for a 128-bit block cipher such as AES [2], our protocol introduces 16 characters of latency at each of the sender and the receiver, regardless of message length. Our protocol encrypts a SCADA message using a new encryption mode we call *position embedding* (PE) mode. PE-mode encryption ensures that an any attempt to modify ciphertext blocks or to splice together a new message from ciphertext blocks taken from older messages will result in at least one ciphertext block decrypting to random bits. By a new result we prove for error detection by systematic shortened cyclic codes, this in turn ensures that the unauthentic message contains a valid h-bit CRC with probability 2^{-h}. The low speed of the communications channel limits the rate at which the adversary can make trials, and a MAC checked *after* the message has been forwarded permits SCMs to detect potential attacks before enough trials can be made to achieve any significant likelihood of success. Our protocol avoids the need for the decrypting SCM to buffer decrypted data until an end-of-message integrity check is verified.

The remainder of the paper is organized as follows. Section 2 discusses requirements for a satisfactory solution. Section 3 presents our protocol, establishes a security theorem, and discusses its impact on latency. We discuss implementation considerations in Section 4, and review related work in Section 5. We conclude with our expectations for deployment of this protocol in the field.

2   Requirements for SCADA Communications Protection

To be effective, a protocol for retrofit protection of SCADA communications must address the three classical security properties of confidentiality, integrity, and availability. Since SCADA systems measure and control physical processes that are generally of a continuous nature, and since SCADA systems are simple and repetitive, SCADA commands and responses are relatively easy to predict. Thus confidentiality is secondary in importance to data integrity. To assure data integrity, the protocol must prevent an adversary from constructing unauthentic messages, modifying messages that are in transit, reordering messages, replaying old messages, or destroying messages without detection. Given the predictable nature of SCADA commands and responses, the protocol must be designed to address these issues with the recognition that known plaintext attacks are not only possible but likely. Guaranteeing availability of the communications link is more difficult. Unlike the Internet, SCADA communications networks seldom have redundant communications paths. Thus an adversary with access to the communications link can flood the link to deny communications, or even selectively jam specific messages. However, most SCADA masters monitor link quality and will report excessive errors to the operator. The protocol should either ensure that this link monitoring facility continues to function, or should provide an alternative.

Many SCADA systems communicate at rates as low as 19200, 1200, or even 300 bits per second. At these speeds, the time required to transmit a single character is significant. Character overhead in message formatting must be kept to a minimum and full message buffering must be avoided if at all possible to limit impact on message latency. Message buffering at the receiving SCM particularly impacts latency since the plaintext port of the SCM will generally operate at the same speed as its ciphertext port, and thus forwarding the decrypted message will take as long as receiving it. Since many SCADA installations continuously cycle amongst devices, initiating a new status poll as soon as a response is received, any increase in latency directly affects the rate at which system state is updated. On the other hand, most embedded CPUs suitable for use in SCMs have more than adequate computation power for cryptographic operations at these speeds. The low communication rate also works to our advantage in limiting the rate at which an adversary can make online trials.

Finally, the retrofit communications protection system must be easy to deploy and manage, and must not adversely impact safe operation of the SCADA system.

3   Retrofit Protection for SCADA Communications

In this section we present an overview of our protocol designed for retrofit protection of SCADA communications, describe the encryption method, including our new position-embedding encryption mode, establish its security, and analyze the latency the protocol introduces.

3.1   Protocol Overview

We consider a simple point-to-point scenario where two SCMs are deployed to protect the communications between a SCADA master and a single remote device. The two SCMs initially share session establishment keys and use these to negotiate shared session keys. The session negotiation procedure is fairly standard and not our focus, so we will not describe it further. The result of session negotiation is that the two SCMs share an encryption key and an authentication key.

A SCM has two communication ports. A SCM receives and transmits *SCADA messages* on its plaintext port. SCADA messages comprise commands, responses, acknowledgments, negative acknowledgments, keep-alive messages, etc. generated by the SCADA system, and are all treated by the SCM in the same manner. A SCM must be able to recognize the beginning and end of a SCADA message, but for this scenario needs no other knowledge of the format of a SCADA message.[2] We assume the SCADA message contains a CRC that is checked by the receiving SCADA device.

A SCM transmits and receives *ciphertext messages* on its ciphertext port. Once a session has been negotiated, a SCM sends a ciphertext message to its peer SCM only when it receives a SCADA message on its plaintext port. If a ciphertext message is damaged or lost in transit, our protocol does not attempt to retry it. In this way, whatever methods the SCADA system uses to recover from communication errors and to avoid collisions will continue to operate as usual.

When the first characters of a SCADA message are received on a SCM's plaintext port, the SCM immediately begins transmitting a ciphertext message header that includes a sequence number to its peer. Each time enough characters are received on the plaintext port to fill a cipher block, the SCM encrypts and transmits a block of ciphertext. Finally the SCM transmits a trailer that includes a message authentication code (MAC).

At the receiving SCM, an incoming ciphertext message header signals the start of a new message. The receiving SCM checks that the sequence number in the header is greater than the last sequence number it received. If this comparison fails, the SCM ignores the remainder of the ciphertext message. Otherwise, each time enough characters are received on the ciphertext port to fill a cipher block, the SCM decrypts the block and immediately begins forwarding the decrypted characters via its plaintext port to the receiving SCADA unit. When the trailer of the ciphertext message is received, the SCM computes and checks the MAC. By this time, the decrypted SCADA message may have already been forwarded in its entirety to the receiving SCADA unit. If the authentication check fails, it is too late to prevent forwarding the unauthentic message. Thus the authentication code only alerts the SCM to a possible failure of data integrity. The crux of our design is to encrypt in such a way that an adversary attempting to modify or inject an unauthorized ciphertext message can at best hope to construct one in which no fewer than one cipher block will decrypt to random bits, and thus the h-bit SCADA CRC will be correct with probability 2^{-h}.

3.2   Encryption

Our protocol uses a block cipher encryption algorithm that operates on b-bit blocks, such as AES for which b is 128. We require this cipher to have *real-or-random indistinguishability* [3]: modification of any of the bits of a ciphertext block makes the result of decryption appear uniformly random. Typical block ciphers have this property [4, p. 228]. We denote the single-block encryption and decryption functions for key k by $E_k[\cdot]$ and $D_k[\cdot]$ respectively. We also use a message authentication algorithm such as HmacSHA-1 or CBC-MAC. We denote the authentication function for key k' by $MAC_{k'}[\cdot]$. We assume the sender and receiver have previously negotiated the shared session keys k and k'.

---

[*] In a multidrop scenario where several remote devices share the communications link, a sending SCM will need to parse the header of the SCADA message in order to select the appropriate encryption key for the receiver.

A SCM maintains a *send sequence* state variable in order to assign a *sequence number* to each ciphertext message it sends. The send sequence variable is initialized to one at session negotiation, and is incremented with every ciphertext message sent. Let S be a SCADA message containing an h-bit CRC. The SCM prepends a sequence number i to the SCADA message S to form a *plaintext message* $P = i\,S$, where juxtaposition denotes concatenation. Let a *padding sequence* z be a sequence of bits beginning with a '1' bit and followed by from 0 to $b - 1$ '0' bits [5]. The SCM appends to $P = i\,S$ a padding sequence z such that the concatenation $S\,z$ is a multiple of b bits long. The SCM formats $S\,z$ into $n = \lceil(|S| + 1)/b\rceil$ plaintext blocks $p_1, \ldots, p_n$, where $|S|$ denotes the length of S in bits, as follows:

$$P\,z \;=\; i\,S\,z \;=\; i\,p_1\,p_2\,\cdots\,p_n$$

The resulting padded plaintext message is thus $nb + |i_{\max}|$ bits long, where $|i_{\max}|$ is the fixed number of bits used to represent a sequence number.

The sending SCM enciphers $P\,z$ to the ciphertext message C as follows:

$$C \;=\; i\,c_1\,c_2\,\cdots\,c_n\,a$$
$$\text{where}$$
$$c_j \;=\; \mathrm{E}_k\,[p_j \oplus \mathrm{E}_k\,[i\,j\,0\ldots]]$$
$$a \;=\; \mathrm{MAC}_{k'}\,[i\,p_1\,p_2\,\cdots\,p_n]$$

Here $\mathrm{E}_k\,[i\,j\,0\ldots]$ denotes the encryption of i concatenated with j concatenated with enough zeros to fill b bits, and $\oplus$ denotes *exclusive or* (bitwise addition mod 2). The SCM outputs each ciphertext block c_j as soon as it is available. Thus the SCM transmits on its ciphertext port the sequence number i, followed by a sequence of cipher blocks, followed by the MAC a. A simple character escaping mechanism, the details of which are not important here, enables the receiver to parse this message into its header i, body $c_1\,c_2\,\cdots\,c_n$, and trailer a. Including the sequence number in the message's header allows the receiver to decrypt the message regardless of whether any preceding messages were damaged by either line noise or an adversary's actions.

Let $\overline{C}$ be the ciphertext message that the receiving SCM sees. If $\overline{C}$ differs from C, this may be due to line noise or malicious actions of an adversary. A SCM receiving $\overline{C}$ formats the message into a sequence number, a sequence of cipher blocks, and a MAC as follows:

$$\overline{C} \;=\; \overline{i}\,\overline{c}_1\,\overline{c}_2\,\cdots\,\overline{c}_n\,\overline{a}$$

The SCM maintains a *receive sequence* state variable in order to record the sequence number of the last authenticated message that it received. The receive sequence variable is initialized to zero at session negotiation. Before decrypting the following ciphertext blocks, the SCM checks that the sequence number $\overline{i}$ contained in the message is greater than the SCM's receive sequence variable. If it isn't, the SCM discards the remainder of the message. This check ensures that an adversary cannot replay old messages. Provided the sequence number check succeeds, the SCM decrypts the message as follows:

$$\overline{P}\,\overline{z} \;=\; \overline{i}\,\overline{S}\,\overline{z} \;=\; \overline{i}\,\overline{p}_1\,\overline{p}_2\,\ldots\,\overline{p}_n$$

where

$$\overline{p}_j \;=\; \mathrm{D}_k\left[\overline{c}_j\right] \oplus \mathrm{E}_k\left[\overline{i}\,j\,0\ldots\right]$$

The SCM forwards the decrypted plaintext blocks $\overline{p}_j$ to the SCADA system as soon as they are available, stripping the padding from the last block. Finally, the SCM computes the MAC for the message as follows:

$$\widetilde{a} \;=\; \mathrm{MAC}_{k'}\left[\overline{i}\,\overline{p}_1\,\overline{p}_2\,\ldots\,\overline{p}_n\right]$$

and compares it to the MAC $\overline{a}$ received with the message. If the two match, the SCM updates its receive sequence variable to the sequence number $\overline{i}$ of the received message, and otherwise it logs an error.

Our encryption algorithm is essentially a cascade cipher composed of two block ciphers, each using a different NIST-approved encryption mode [5]. The plaintext is first encrypted using *counter* (CTR) mode with a counter that depends on both the message sequence number and the block position within the message. The result is reencrypted using *electronic codebook* (ECB) mode. We call this combination *position embedding* (PE) mode since it embeds the position of a plaintext block into its corresponding cipher block. The properties of PE mode allow us to leverage the underlying SCADA CRC to assure data integrity.

3.3   SCADA Model

We model the operation of a SCADA unit receiving a decrypted SCADA message $\overline{S}$ with the total function PAYLOAD. This function checks the format of $\overline{S}$, calculates and verifies the CRC, and either returns a substring of $\overline{S}$ that represents the actual SCADA data with header and formatting stripped, or the distinguished token **error** indicating that the message was either incorrectly formatted or the CRC check failed. We assume that for all $\overline{S}$ for which PAYLOAD returns a non-**error** message substring, PAYLOAD returns either the same substring or **error** for all prefixes of $\overline{S}$. That is, PAYLOAD finds the shortest prefix of $\overline{S}$ that can be interpreted as a valid SCADA message. Extra bits beyond the end of that substring are either ignored or result in **error**. This assumption is realistic as shortest-prefix decoding corresponds to what most SCADA systems implement. Furthermore, any SCADA system in which a prefix of a valid message was also a valid message would be susceptible to the longer message being transformed into the shorter one by line errors.

3.4   Security

We consider the security of our protocol in the face of known plaintext attacks. We do not consider chosen plaintext attacks because the adversary's principal goal is to disrupt the operation of the SCADA system and the physical processes it controls. If the adversary is able to inject chosen plaintext messages into the plaintext port of a SCM, the adversary has physical access to the SCADA system and can likely perform far greater disruption and damage by other means.

To assure the integrity of SCADA messages, our protocol must guard against an adversary injecting an unauthentic ciphertext message into the communications link, modifying a ciphertext message during its transmission, reordering messages, or replaying an old message. Forging and alteration are prevented by ensuring that an unauthentic ciphertext has a low probability of decrypting to a SCADA message containing a valid CRC. Reordering and replay are prevented by ensuring that an alteration of the sequence number will likewise result in a low probability that the ciphertext decrypts to a SCADA message containing a valid CRC. The following theorem captures this security property more precisely.

Theorem 1. *Let* **CP** *be a collection of corresponding ciphertext, plaintext message pairs defined as in Section 3.2. Let PAYLOAD, as defined in Section 3.3, return non-***error** *for each plaintext message, and utilize an h-bit CRC whose generating polynomial has the form* $g(x) = g_h x^h + g_{h-1} x^{h-1} + \cdots + g_1 x + g_0$ *where* $g_h = 1$ *and* $g_0 = 1$*. Let* $E_k[\cdot]$ *and* $D_k[\cdot]$ *be the encryption and decryption functions of the b-bit block cipher used to form the ciphertexts in* **CP**, *with* $b \geq h$. *Let* $\overline{C} = \overline{i}\,\overline{c}_1 \ldots \overline{c}_{\overline{n}}$ *be a ciphertext message, different from any of the ciphertexts in* **CP**, *constructed by an adversary who knows* **CP** *but not the cipher key* k. *Decrypt* $\overline{C}$ *to* $\overline{P}\,\overline{z} = \overline{i}\,\overline{S}\,\overline{z} = \overline{i}\,\overline{p}_1 \ldots \overline{p}_{\overline{n}}$ *where* $\overline{p}_j = D_k[\overline{c}_j] \oplus E_k[\overline{i}\,j\,0\ldots]$. *If* $\overline{P}$ *is not one of the plaintexts in* **CP**, *then* $PAYLOAD(\overline{S})$ *returns non-***error** *with probability at most* 2^{-h}.

The proof of this theorem relies on a new result on error detection by systematic shortened cyclic codes that differs from any of the results that we have found in the literature.

Lemma 1. *Let* **H** *be a systematic shortened cyclic binary code with generator polynomial* $g(x) = g_h x^h + g_{h-1} x^{h-1} + \cdots + g_1 x + g_0$ *where* $g_h = 1$ *and* $g_0 = 1$. *Let* w *be any bit string of length at least* h. *If any* h *consecutive bits of* w *are selected uniformly and independently at random, then* w *is a codeword of* **H** *with probability* 2^{-h}.

Proof of Lemma 1.   First, consider the long division process that is used to encode or decode a message [6]. The function $\mathcal{M}_1(\cdot,\cdot)$ represents one intermediate step of the division process:

$$\mathcal{M}_1(b_{n-1}\cdots b_0,\, g_h\cdots g_0) = b_{n-1}\cdots b_0 \qquad \text{if } n = h$$

$$\mathcal{M}_1(b_{n-1}\cdots b_0,\, g_h\cdots g_0) = b_{n-2}\cdots b_0 \qquad \text{if } n > h \text{ and } b_{n-1} = 0$$

$$\mathcal{M}_1(b_{n-1}\cdots b_0,\, g_h\cdots g_0) = (b_{n-2} - g_{h-1})\cdots(b_{n-h-1} - g_0)\, b_{n-h-2}\cdots b_0$$
$$\text{if } n > h \text{ and } b_{n-1} = 1$$

To encode a message bit string m, h zero bits are first appended to it, and then $\mathcal{M}_1$ is repeatedly applied until the result is h bits wide. Let $\mathcal{M}$ denote the repeated application of $\mathcal{M}_1$ until the result is h bits wide (transitive closure). The concatenation $m\,\mathcal{M}(m\,0_{h-1}\cdots 0_0)$ is a codeword. A received bit string w is a codeword if and only if $\mathcal{M}(w) = 0_{h-1}\cdots 0_0$.

Fix l and consider the set of all bit strings $\{b_{h-1}\cdots b_0\,0_{l-1}\cdots 0_0\}$. This set has cardinality 2^h. We will show by induction on l that the set of remainders after repeated application of $\mathcal{M}_1$ has cardinality 2^h. The base case where $l = 0$ is straightforward. For the induction step, we need to show that the set $\{\mathcal{M}_1(b_{h-1}\cdots b_0\,0_{l-1}\cdots 0_0\,,\,g_h\cdots g_0)\}$ has cardinality 2^h. To see this, consider the two cases for the values of b_{h-1}. If b_{h-1} is 0, we have

$$\mathcal{X}_0 = \{\mathcal{M}_1(b_{h-1}\cdots b_0\,0_{l-1}\cdots 0_0\,,\,g_h\cdots g_0)\}$$
$$= \{b_{h-2}\cdots b_0\,0\,0_{l-2}\cdots 0_0\}$$

and $\mathcal{X}_0$ has cardinality 2^{h-1}. If b_{h-1} is 1, we have

$$\mathcal{X}_1 = \{\mathcal{M}_1(b_{h-1}\cdots b_0\,0_{l-1}\cdots 0_0\,,\,g_h\cdots g_0)\}$$
$$= \{(b_{h-2}-g_{h-1})\cdots(b_0-g_1)\,(0-g_0)\,0_{l-2}\cdots 0_0\}$$
$$= \{(b_{h-2}-g_{h-1})\cdots(b_0-g_1)\,1\,0_{l-2}\cdots 0_0\} \qquad \text{since } g_0 = 1$$

and $\mathcal{X}_1$ has cardinality 2^{h-1}. Since $\mathcal{X}_0$ and $\mathcal{X}_1$ do not intersect, their union has cardinality 2^h.

Consider a bit string $w = \overline{w} + (b_{h-1}\cdots b_0\,0_{l-1}\cdots 0_0)$ where $|w| = |\overline{w}| \geq h+l$ and bits $b_{h-1},\ldots,b_0$ are selected uniformly and independently at random. Then

$$\mathcal{M}(w) = \mathcal{M}(\overline{w} + (b_{h-1}\cdots b_0\,0_{l-1}\cdots 0_0))$$
$$= \mathcal{M}(\overline{w}) + \mathcal{M}(b_{h-1}\cdots b_0\,0_{l-1}\cdots 0_0).$$

Now, $\mathcal{M}$ takes each element of $\{b_{h-1}\cdots b_0\,0_{l-1}\cdots 0_0\}$ to a different image, by the cardinality argument above. Hence $\mathcal{M}(b_{h-1}\cdots b_0\,0_{l-1}\cdots 0_0)$ is uniformly distributed. Hence $\mathcal{M}(w)$ is uniformly distributed. Since $\mathcal{M}(w)$ has h bits, the probability that w is a valid codeword is 2^{-h}. $\square$

CRCs are systematic shortened cyclic codes. Figure 3 gives the generator polynomials for a number of CRC codes in widespread use, and all of those we have encountered satisfy the prerequisites of Lemma 1. With Lemma 1 in hand, we return to the proof of our security theorem.

Proof of Theorem 1.   Not knowing the encryption key, an adversary is limited to constructing an unauthentic message $\overline{P}$ by choosing ciphertext blocks at random, or by using ciphertext blocks from **CP** and (i) modifying bits in ciphertext blocks, (ii) changing the sequence number, and/or (iii) splicing together ciphertext blocks from messages in **CP**, including reordering ciphertext blocks, deleting ciphertext blocks, and inserting ciphertext blocks. We first show that some of these cases lead directly to PAYLOAD returning **error** for the decrypted message, while the remaining cases lead to at least one plaintext block of the decrypted message being randomized.

Choosing ciphertext blocks at random or modifying bits in a ciphertext block randomizes the corresponding decrypted plaintext block, due to real-or-random

CRC Code	generator polynomial
CRC-4	$g(x) = x^{\cdot} + x^{\cdot} + x^{\cdot} + x + 1$
CRC-7	$g(x) = x^{\cdot} + x^{\cdot} + x^{\cdot} + 1$
CRC-8$_A$	$g(x) = x^{\cdot} + x^{\cdot} + x^{\cdot} + x^{\cdot} + x^{\cdot} + 1$
CRC-8$_B$	$g(x) = x^{\cdot} + x^{\cdot} + x^{\cdot} + 1$
CRC-12	$g(x) = x^{\cdot\cdot} + x^{\cdot\cdot} + x^{\cdot} + x^{\cdot} + x + 1$
CRC-ANSI	$g(x) = x^{\cdot\cdot} + x^{\cdot\cdot} + x^{\cdot} + 1$
CRC-CCITT	$g(x) = x^{\cdot\cdot} + x^{\cdot\cdot} + x^{\cdot} + 1$
CRC-SLDC	$g(x) = x^{\cdot\cdot} + x^{\cdot\cdot} + x^{\cdot\cdot} + x^{\cdot} + x^{\cdot} + x^{\cdot} + x + 1$
CRC-24	$g(x) = x^{\cdot\cdot} + x^{\cdot\cdot} + x^{\cdot\cdot} + x^{\cdot\cdot} + x^{\cdot} + 1$
CRC-32 (IEEE 802.3)	$g(x) = x^{\cdot\cdot} + x^{\cdot\cdot} + x^{\cdot\cdot} + x^{\cdot\cdot} + x^{\cdot\cdot} + x^{\cdot\cdot} + x^{\cdot\cdot}$
	$+ x^{\cdot\cdot} + x^{\cdot} + x^{\cdot} + x^{\cdot} + x^{\cdot} + x^{\cdot} + x + 1$

Fig. 3. Generator Polynomials for Popular CRC codes [6]

indistinguishability of the cipher used in the term $D_k[\overline{c}_j]$ in the decryption formula.

Changing the sequence number $\overline{i}$ randomizes the term $E_k[\overline{i}\ j\ 0\ldots]$ in the decryption formula, due to the security of the cipher used in this term, and thus randomizes every block of decrypted plaintext.

Using blocks from different messages or moving blocks to different positions within a message again randomizes the term $E_k[\overline{i}\ j\ 0\ldots]$ in the decryption formula, and thus randomizes the decrypted plaintext of any ciphertext blocks from messages other than $\overline{i}$ or ciphertext blocks from $\overline{i}$ that do not occupy their original message positions. Deleting ciphertext blocks from the end of a message shortens the decrypted SCADA message, but by the assumptions in the definition of PAYLOAD, PAYLOAD returns **error** on such a shortened message. Adding ciphertext blocks to the end of a message lengthens the decrypted SCADA message, but again by definition PAYLOAD returns either the same result or **error** for such a lengthened message. Modifying the last ciphertext block can shorten or lengthen the message by changing the padding bits, but again PAYLOAD returns either the same result or **error**. Modifying the last ciphertext block which contains the padding bits could also result in fewer than h bits of the message being randomized. If this is the only portion of the message that is randomized, we can consider this as a burst error of width less than h. An h-bit CRC detects all such cases [6], and thus PAYLOAD returns **error**.

Now, if one or more plaintext blocks of $\overline{S}$ are randomized, we consider the randomized blocks as errors introduced into an originally correct plaintext message. Since $b \geq h$, there is at least one span of h consecutive bits that are randomized. Thus, provided PAYLOAD finds $\overline{S}$ to be correctly formatted, the CRC is correct with probability 2^{-h} by Lemma 1. $\qquad\square$

3.5   Latency

We discuss latency in terms of the time required to transmit a character over the long-haul SCADA communications line. For a typical SCADA configuration of 1200 baud, 8 data bits, 1 start bit, and 1 stop bit, transmitting one character takes 8.3 milliseconds. We assume that the plaintext and ciphertext ports of both SCMs all use the same data rate, and that the SCADA system delivers SCADA messages that are free of gaps. We also assume that SCMs have enough computing power that encryption and decryption have no significant impact on latency.

On the sending side, the SCM must wait to receive an entire block of plaintext from the sending SCADA device before it can encrypt and begin transmitting ciphertext. This requirement introduces a delay of $\frac{b}{8}$ character times, e.g. 16 character times for AES with $b = 128$. However, the SCM can begin transmitting the SCM message header, containing the sequence number i, as soon as it receives the first character of the SCADA message. Provided this header is shorter than the cipher block length, the SCM will complete transmitting the header before it receives enough plaintext characters to encrypt the first block. The transmission time for the header is thereby entirely masked by the time required to receive the first block of plaintext. Thus the latency introduced at the sender is exactly $\frac{b}{8}$ character times.

On the receiving side, the SCM must wait to receive an entire block of ciphertext before it can decrypt and begin forwarding the corresponding cleartext. Again, this requirement introduces a delay of $\frac{b}{8}$ character times. Receiving and checking the MAC in the trailer is performed after (or perhaps during) the forwarding of the decrypted SCADA message to the SCADA system, and hence introduce no additional latency. The total delay introduced at the receiver is thus $\frac{b}{8}$ character times.

In sum, our protocol introduces a fixed latency of $2 \cdot \frac{b}{8}$ character times, regardless of the length of the SCADA message. For AES, this is 32 character times.

4   Implementation

As observed earlier, our position embedding encryption mode is essentially a cascade cipher composed of an ECB-mode cipher and a CTR-mode cipher. Since these block ciphers use the same algorithm and key, during encryption they can share the same special-purpose cipher unit in a hardware-based implementation, or the same state variables and key expansion in a software implementation. During decryption, however, the CTR-mode cipher is used in encryption mode while the ECB-mode cipher is used in decryption mode, and this may preclude sharing hardware units or software modules.

It is possible for both the sender and receiver to optimistically perform CTR-mode encryptions for several blocks of several future messages in advance of the receipt of those messages. While we expect even the least capable of the current generation of embedded processors to provide more than adequate performance for cryptographic operations at SCADA communications rates, this optimization could be useful in other applications.

A Java implementation that codifies many of the details we expect to appear in the AGA recommendation is available as open source [7]. This implementation supports several *cipher suites*, of which one uses the position embedding mode described in this paper. The implementation also includes a cipher suite that relies on the MAC rather than the SCADA CRC to assure integrity, at the cost of requiring the receiver to verify the MAC before delivering the deciphered SCADA message. This cipher suite provides stronger security at the expense of latency, and should be used in deployments where the additional latency can be tolerated. In the future, additional cipher suites may be defined to support different key lengths, MAC lengths, and encryption algorithms.

5 Related Work

Stream ciphers are particularly susceptible to known-plaintext active attacks, and are thus unsuitable for protecting SCADA communications without the additional protection of a MAC. This includes block ciphers used with CTR mode alone. An adversary who knows the plaintext corresponding to an encrypted message can recover the key stream, and then replace the message with a different one that decrypts to a plaintext of his choosing. Even with only partially-known plaintext, the linear nature of CRCs allows an adversary to patch up a CRC underneath a stream cipher by performing operations on the encrypted stream. These problems are well known vulnerabilities in the WEP protocol [8].

Stubblebine and Gligor [9] show how blocks from messages encrypted with a block cipher in CBC mode may be spliced together to form unauthentic messages. Their attack applies even when the plaintext includes a CRC. Thus block encryption with CBC mode alone provides inadequate integrity protection.

Our work has a similar goal to that of *non-malleable cryptography*, which seeks to ensure that given a ciphertext, it is impossible to generate a different ciphertext so that the respective plaintexts are related [10]. Our system achieves a weaker property. While the plaintexts may be related, they will be sufficiently unrelated that the CRC is likely to fail.

Beaver *et al.* [11] describe an encryption scheme that uses the internal state of the cipher to obtain authentication. Authenticated encryption solves a different problem than we are concerned with, namely that of computing authentication cheaply in parallel with encryption. However, the internal properties of their cipher appear to provide similar randomization of the plaintext when the ciphertext is modified, and thus their cipher may be viable alternative to our scheme. Ours has some advantage in being built entirely from NIST approved primitives.

Gligor and Donescu [12] propose an encryption and authentication mode called XCBC that requires only a non-cryptographic integrity check such as a CRC to assure message integrity. Their method may also be a viable alternative to our scheme, however the fact that it is patented could deter broad acceptance of a standard that employed it.

A good deal is known about the properties of cyclic and shortened cyclic codes for detecting various kinds of errors, including burst errors [13] and errors over a binary symmetric channel [14]. However, neither of these types of errors precisely matches the types of errors that an adversary's actions can introduce with our encryption scheme. In particular, the classic results on burst errors, which are sometimes stated imprecisely, apply to errors that occur as one single consecutive string of randomized bits. In our situation, an adversary's actions can produce bursts of error bits separated by segments of non-error bits, to which the classic results do not apply. Our Lemma 1 appears to represent a new result on error detection.

6   Conclusion

The American Gas Association (AGA) develops and publishes standards for the gas industry. In February 2004 the AGA 12 task group distributed for ballot a draft of the first AGA 12 recommendation for protecting SCADA communications [15]. This draft describes general requirements for a solution, and a subsequent recommendation will specify a protocol in detail. Several vendors are planning to build and market SCM devices that implement the final standard. These devices will likely be targeted for use not only in the gas industry but in other industries such as power, oil, and water. It is our hope and expectation that these devices will be widely deployed before a significant cyberterrorism incident makes their need all too evident.

Acknowledgments. We would like to acknowledge the leadership of Bill Rush of the Gas Technology Institute in the AGA-12 effort, the many individuals who have contributed to the AGA-12 standards effort, and Mark Torgerson and Erik Anderson at Sandia National Labs who provided valuable advice and critique.

References

1. Gas Technology Institute: http://www.gtiservices.org/security. (2004)
2. National Institute of Standards and Technology: Federal Information Processing Standards Publication 197 (FIPS PUB 197), Advanced Encryption Standard (AES). (2001)
3. Bellare, M., Desai, A., Jokipii, E., Rogaway, P.: A concrete security treatment of symmetric encryption: Analysis of the DES modes of operation. Proc. 38th Annual Symposium on Foundations of Computer Science (1997)
4. Menezes, A.J., Oorschot, P.C.V., Vanstone, S.A.: Handbook of Applied Cryptography. CRC Press (1997)
5. National Institute of Standards and Technology: NIST SP 800-38A 2001 ED, Recommendation for Block Cipher Modes of Operation. (2001)
6. Wicker, S.B.: Error Control Systems for Digital Communication and Storage. Prentice Hall (1995)

7. Wright, A.K.: http://scadasafe.sourceforge.net. (2004)
8. Borisov, N., Goldberg, I., Wagner, D.: Intercepting mobile communications: The insecurity of 802.11. Proc. MOBICOM (2001)
9. Stubblebine, S.G., Gligor, V.D.: On message integrity in cryptographic protocols. Proc. 1992 IEEE Symposium on Research in Security and Privacy (1992) 85–104
10. Dolev, O., Dwork, C., Naor, M.: Non-malleable cryptography. Proc. 23rd ACM Symposium on Theory of Computing (1991)
11. Beaver, C., Draelos, T., Schroeppel, R., Torgerson, M.: ManTiCore: Encryption with joint cipher-state authentication. IACR Preprint, 2003/154, www.iacr.org (2003)
12. Gligor, V.D., Donescu, P.: Fast encryption and authentication: XCBC encryption and XECB authentication modes. Presented at the 2nd NIST Workshop on AES Modes of Operation, Santa Barbara, CA (2001)
13. Peterson, W.W., Weldon, E.J.: Error correcting codes. MIT Press, Cambridge, MA (1972)
14. Witzke, K.A., Leung, C.: A comparison of some error-detecting CRC code Standards. IEEE Trans. Commun. COM-33, No. 9, 996 (1985)
15. AGA 12 Task Group: Cryptographic protection of SCADA communications: General recommendations (2004)

A Best Practice for Root CA Key Update in PKI

InKyoung Jeun[1], Jongwook Park[1], TaeKyu Choi[1], SangWan Park[1],
BaeHyo Park[1], ByungKwon Lee[1], and YongSup Shin[2]

Korea Information Security Agency,
78, Garak-Dong Songpa-Gu, Seoul, 138-803 Korea
{ikjeun,khopri,tkchoi,shpark,parkbh,byungkle}@kisa.or.kr
Ministry of Information and Communication,
100, Sejong-ro, Chongro-Gu, Seoul, 110-777 Korea
ysshin@mic.go.kr

Abstract. User authentication, data integrity and non-repudiation services using public-key infrastructure(PKI) are based on the assumption of the trust toward the root CA key in its domain. This root CA key which is commonly encoded as a self-signed certificate has a validity period and it must be updated before the expiration date of it. To do so, an appropriate root CA key update procedure must be proceeded. This paper explains the requirements and a concrete procedure for a root CA key update and the related security issues. Also we will provide an effective root CA key update mechanism considering a security and efficiency, which can be a best practice for handling the root CA certificate expiration.

1 Introduction

The basic role of PKI is the management of "trust" which is expressed in certificates and preserved by verifying the validity of the certificates along certificate paths. The beginning point of the stream of the "trust" in hierarchical PKI is the trust for a root CA certificate. Root CA Certificates are the parents of the subordinated CA's certificates which are parents of the end-user's certificates, in general. Hence if a root CA's certificate expires, in effect, so do all its children and henceforth all end user's certificates.

Thus, one of the most important things in PKI is to establish and manage the trust point for the root CA Certificates. X.509 based self-signed certificate is commonly used to establish the trust point of root CA[1,2]. Due to the fact that the trust in such self-signed certificates can only be implicit, the mechanisms to establish and manage the trust point of root CA Certificates must be well prepared and informed.

Very recently, there was widespread disruption of normal internet services, such as online banks in Singapore reportedly went offline, or at least refused to do any banking, etc., and it has been told that all such problems came from root CA's certificate business. Especially, inappropriate handling of the root CA

M. Jakobsson, M. Yung, J. Zhou (Eds.): ACNS 2004, LNCS 3089, pp. 278–291, 2004.

Certificate Expiration[3]. As we've seen from such cases, a best practices for handling the root CA Certificate expiration will be ever more emphasized.

Self-signed certificate contains the root CA public key and the corresponding private key must be stored in the root CA in a secure manner. The validation period of the root CA key is specified in the self-signed certificate. It cannot be no longer used after the expiration date. So the root CA key must be updated before the expiration date of it. Based on the updated root CA key, the root CA certificate will be updated and distributed to each subordinated CAs and subscribers, then it can be effective through the transition procedure of the trust point from the old root CA key to the new root CA key.

Up to our knowledge, the mechanisms which deal with the root CA key update was not published. There are some public documents only on the transition procedure of the trust point. RFC2510 of IETF and CTL(Certificate Trust List)method of Microsoft are some of the publications on the transition procedure of the trust point.

In this paper, we will investigate an effective root CA key update mechanism which can be a best practice for handling the root CA certificate expiration. Furthermore, We shall discuss the requirements, the desirable model and the detailed mechanisms for secure and efficient root CA key update on the hierarchical PKI.

The rest of this paper is organized as follows. We shall describe the preliminaries for the key update and the life cycle of the certificates in Section 2. In Section 3, we shall describe the process of root CA key update mechanism and compare the RFC2510 of IETF and the CTL method as transition procedure of the trust point. In Section 4, we shall specify the requirements for effective root CA key update and give the desirable solutions in terms of each requirement. And this paper will make a conclusion in section 5.

2   Preliminary

We have stressed a necessity of effective mechanism for the root CA key update in section 1. Before presenting the details about the mechanism, it is also useful for us to define a terminologies used in this paper as follows.

Validity period of root CA key: A root CA key which is used for the trust point in PKI has a limited validity period. Limiting the validity period reduce the possibility that an attacker can identify a root CA private key. The longer root CA uses a private key for certificate signing, the more information there will be that an attacker can use for cryptanalystic attack. Generally, the validity period of root CA key is the same as the validity period of self-signed certificate, because the root CA public key is encoded as self-signed certificate. Of course, the validity period of root CA private key is set differently with the validity period of the public key using the Private Key Usage Period extension in certificate[4,5]. In this paper, however, we assume that the validity period of root CA key pair is the same as the validity period of self-signed certificate.

Root CA key update: As mentioned above, the root CA key has a validity period. Therefore, the new root CA key need to be generated in order to replace the ones that are discontinued. It refers to this situation as root CA key update. There is another reason for root CA key update. that's a security problem of root CA key pair. The better computer calculation ability and the hacking skills are continuously increased and advanced, the more threats to root CA key pair are increased. Therefore, the root CA key must be updated when its safety is impeded or judged to do so. If the root CA key is updated due to key expiration, we can use a same root CA key for updating. But the root CA key is updated due to key safety, we must change the root CA key for updating.

Certificate Update: When the root CA key is updated, a new self-signed certificate is needed to distribute the updated root CA key. To do this, the self-signed certificate of root CA must be updated. The subject name included in the updated self-signed certificate can be same or different with the subject name of old self-signed certificate. But the validity period of the updated certificate must be extended.

Certificate life cycle: Certificate has a life cycle such as issuing, updating, renewal and revocation which is defined in certificate policy(CP) or certificate policy statements (CPS) of each PKI domain. These terminologies about the certificate life cycle could be differently used in each countries according to their PKI policy. As mentioned the above, a certificate update is the process that a new certificate is issued in order to replace a certificate which will be expired. Certificate Renewal which is one of the certificate life cycle involves the generation of a new key pair and issuing a certificate of a new public key. It may arise in the case of a key compromise. The existing certificate is expired before the renewal. Finally, certificate modification becomes a modification of the contents of a certificate during the validity period of it. There may be a need to modify the contents of a certificate when the legal name is changed, and the certificate profile is changed as well as the other information. In case of the certificate modification, the validity period of certificate and the key pair cannot be changed [6,7].

3 Root CA Key Update Mechanism

Root CA key update brings the issues of how the self-signed certificate can be updated and how the new root CA public key can be distributed in an authenticated manner. For the self-signed certificate update, we must decide when the root CA key must be updated, whether the root CA key included in a self-signed certificate must be changed or not, and whether the subject name of self-signed certificate must be changed or not. The subject name and the public key in self-signed certificate can be same, and also changed. What kind of problems have occur if we change the subject name or the public key in the case of root CA key update? These issues are very important but haven't defined yet in any specification regarding the root CA key update.

Once a root CA key is updated, it is necessary for all entities in PKI to receive the updated root CA public key in a secure manner in order to prevent an attacker substituting the wrong root CA public key instead the real public key. For a distribution of the update root CA key, we must consider a delivery method of the new self-signed certificate and transition procedure of the trust point from the old root CA key to the new root CA key in a secure and reliable way. We can use different techniques to delivery the self-signed certificate such as HTTP web service, LDAP repository and so on. For the transition procedure of the trust point, there are CMP(Certificate Management Protocol) method which is presented in RFC2510 of IETF and CTL(Certificate Trust List) method which is developed by Microsoft Corp[8,14].

3.1   Certificate Management Protocol(CMP)

As explained above, CMP is one of the standards related to the root CA key update and it states clearly the transition procedure of the trust point using the certificates issued by root CA. CMP is a protocol for issuing, revocation, renewal, and updating of certificate and it is used for certificate management in many PKI products. It is a fundamental concept that the old root CA key ensures a reliability of the new root CA key and new one ensures reliability of the old one. For this, a root CA issues a pair of link certificates simultaneously. The first link certificate contains the new root CA public key signed with the old root CA private key. The second link certificate contains the new root CA public key, and it is signed with the old root CA private key. In this way, subscribers who have a certificate signed with the old root CA private key, and subscribers who have a certificate signed with the new root CA private key, can validate each other's certificates[8].

To update the key of the root CA, certificates are issued as follows.

OldWithOld Certificate: This is containing the old root CA public key signed with the old root CA private key.
OldWithNew Certificate: This is containing the old root CA public key signed with the new root CA private key. This certificate allows the subscriber's certificate signed by the new root CA private key to construct a valid certification path to the certificate previously signed with the old root CA private key.
NewWithOld Certificate: This is containing the new root CA public key signed with the new root CA private key. This certificate allows the subscriber's certificates signed by the old root CA private key to construct a valid certification path to the certificates signed with the new root CA private key.
NewWithNew Certificate: This is containing the new root CA public key signed with the new root CA private key.

The point to pay attention here is that these four kinds of certificates have to be published via repository or other means, like a CAKeyUpdAnn(CA Key Update Announcement) message. CAKeyUpdAnn message includes three types of certificates, OldWithNew certificate, NewWithOld certificate and NewWith-New certificate. When the root CA key is updated, CA may transfer this message to all entities to inform that the root CA key is updated. After all, CMP method uses CAKeyUpdAnn message or repository for delivery of the updated self-signed certificate and uses the link certificates like OldWithNew certificate and NewWithOld certificate for the transition of the trust point to the new root CA public key.

3.2   Certificate Trust List(CTL)

We will show the CTL as one of the transition method of the trust point. CTL is usually used as a mechanism in order to trust a CA certificate of other PKI domain for cross certification. It is a PKCS#7 signed data content which is signed with a trust CA key and is composed of a list which includes fingerprints of the trust certificates as below[14,15].

```
CertificateTrustList ::= SEQUENCE
    Version            Version  DEFAULT v1
    subjectUsage       SubjectUsage,
    listIdentifier     ListIdentifier OPTIONAL,
    sequenceNumber     INTEGER,
    thisUpdate         Time,
    nextUpdate         Time,
    subjectAlgorithm   AlgorithmIdentifier,
    trustedSubjects    TrustedSubjects,
    extensions         Extensions OPTIONAL
```

In the structure of CertificateTrustList, trustedSubjects field is a list of fingerprints of all trust CA certificates. After the self-signed certificate is updated, the fingerprint of it is added in the structure. It is the way that a user who trusts the old root CA key can trust the updated new root CA key by acquiring the CTL signed with the old root CA key. If a fingerprint of the updated self-signed certificate were included in the trustedSubjects list, a user can trust the new root CA public key. For the trust of new root CA key, a user only verify the signature of CTL using the old root CA key and there is no necessity for client to come in a root CA key update procedure. CTL dose not include any public key and just include a fingerprint of certificate. Therefore, there is another need for delivery mechanism of a self signed certificate.

4   Consideration for Root CA Key Update

In this section, we represent a root CA key update procedure which is composed of self-signed certificate update and distribution of the updated root CA key. To develop an appropriate root CA key update mechanism, we must consider the following requirements.

4.1 Selection Criteria for Root CA Key Update Mechanism

Self-signed certificate update. When the self-signed certificate is updated, there is no restriction for choosing the subject name of certificate and key pair. The root CA key pair can be updated using the same key or different key by considering its security. The subject name of self-signed certificate can be same or different by the policy. Also, the update point of the self-signed certificate must be calculated by considering a validity period of the subordinate CA certificate for offering a PKI service securely and continuously.

Delivery of self-signed certificate. Self-signed certificate can be delivered to PKI entities with various ways. The root CA key update mechanism must not restrict the delivery method of updated self-signed certificate, but ensure the security of the delivery procedure.

Transition of the trust point. After the root CA key is the updated and the new self-signed certificate is delivered, PKI entities must trust the updated root CA public key for certificate verification. This trust method should be performed in a reliable way. Also, this transition method of the trust point is practicable without regard to change of the key or other information of self-signed certificate.

4.2 Requirements in Terms of Self-Signed Certificate Update

First, we must consider whether the root CA key should be changed or not for self-signed certificate update as we mentioned above. The root CA key pair can be updated by the same key or different key considering the security of it. In the perspective of every root CA key update, we must examine an environmental factors such as a computing power, hacking technology, and then we must decide to change the algorithm or length of root CA key. There are two factors regarding to the root CA key security, one is a signature algorithm and key length, and the other is the validity period of key.

According to the Data protection security survey of RSA Laboratories in 2003, RSA algorithm is recommended to use 1024 bits until 2010 year, minimum 2048 bits until 2030 year, and after then minimum 3172 bits[10]. Besides that, an announcement about the digital signature in German of RegTP, recommends that the RSA algorithm is safe to the end of year 2007 using minimum 1024 bits(recommend 2048 bits) and to end of year 2008 using minimum 1280 bits(recommend 2048 bits)[11]. Lenstra and Vercheul also recommend that we can use a RSA 1024 bits approximately by 2005 year and use a RSA 2048 bits by 2025 year in Selection Cryptographic Key Size[12]. However, as for these factors, it has been consistently changed according to the environmental factors from time to time, so the safety of a root CA key should be considered by these factors. At the end, the decision of root CA key length, signature algorithm, and validity period becomes a political issue. A PKI policy manager must determine above factors within a possible range in order to make those be accepted.

Secondly, we must decide whether the subject name in updated self-signed certificate is changed or not. The subject name is significantly used for certificate path construction. According to the decision of root CA policy, the subject name can be changed or not. Considering the change of a key and the subject name in the certificate, a self-signed certificate update model can be divided into fore different types as shown Table 1. As we can see from this table, self-signed certificate update is free from the change of a key and subject name.

Table 1. Self-signed certificate update model

Type	Root CA Key Change	Subject name Change
All same	X	X
Only different the subject name	X	O
Only different the root CA key	O	X
All different	O	O

Finally, we must consider the update point of the key. It can be calculated by considering the validity period of subordinate CA certificate[1,5,10,12]. We assume that the validity period of root CA key is KP_{RCA} which is the ranged from the start date of root CA key validity(RK_{START}) to the expire date of root key validity(RK_{END}) and presented [RK_{START} - RK_{END}]. We can also assume that the validity term of subordinate CA certificate, which is issued at current time, is KT_{SCA}, that is a value of the expiration date of subordinate CA certificate validity(SK_{END}) minus the start date of subordinate CA certificate(SK_{START}). The expiration date of root CA key must be longer than expiration date of subordinate CA certificate. That is $SK_{END} < RK_{END}$. If $(RK_{END} - RK_{START}) < KT_{SCA}$, then $SK_{END} > RK_{END}$, and then verification of the subordinate CA certificate error has occurred since RK_{END}. Therefore, the root CA key must be updated before $(RK_{END} - KT_{SCA})$ point. Based on the above assumptions, we can propose some terminologies about the validity period.

Definition 1. *Update Point(UP)*
Update point is the time that the root CA key must be updated. As for this, the representation is possible as follows.
$$UP = RK_{END} - KT_{SCA}$$
The root key must be updated before UP for $SK_{END} < RK_{END}$.

Definition 2. *Valid Period(VP)*
Valid period is when the root CA key is effective, and the verification of a root CA key must be certainly possible during this period. VP is the same as the validity of self-signed certificate signed with the root CA key. That is,

$$VP = KP_{RCA} = [RK_{START} - RK_{END}]$$

The root CA key must be always effective unless the root CA key isn't revoked or hold during VP.

Definition 3. *Active Period(AP)*
Active period is the period when a subordinate CA certificate or subordinate CA certificate revocation list issuing is possible with the root CA key. This is presented as follows.

$$AP = [RK_{START} - UP]$$

Namely, AP is a period from RK_{START} to UP. The security of root CA key must be assured during this period.

Assume that the first root CA key is K1, and then sequentially updated key is K2, and so on. The UP, VP, AP of K1 are shown in Fig 1.

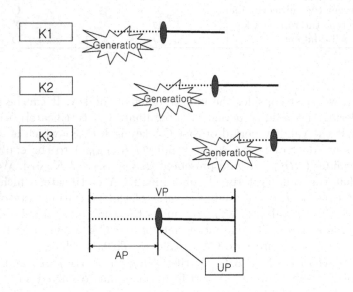

Fig. 1. Valid period of Root Key

4.3   Delivery Methods of Updated Self-Signed Certificate

After the self-signed certificate of root CA is updated, the certificate must be delivered to all subscribers for certificate validation. There are many methods for delivery of updated self-signed certificate and PKI domain can choose the method as they want.

First method for a delivery of self-signed certificate is that root CA may simply post a self-signed certificate on a web site or in repository with or without a secure measures. Subscribers can acquire the self-signed certificate through accessing the web or repository. The other method for delivery a self-signed certificate is to use of subscribers software. Root CA can make arrangements with manufactures of subscribers software to have the root CA public key implemented on the software. When this mechanism is used, the root CA public key have already delivered in a reliable manner to subscribers without the need for special method as repository access. Finally, a root CA or subordinate CA or RA which is trusted by CA may directly provide the updated root CA public key to the relying party during a face-to-face meeting at the time of initial registration[13]. In this case, the self-signed certificate could be contained in a storage device as floppy disk or USB token.

4.4   Transition Procedures of the Trust Point

After all entities like CAs, users, and PKI application servers are received the updated self-signed certificate, there is a necessary for transition procedure of the trust point from the old root CA public key to the new root CA public key contained in the acquired self-signed certificate. As for the transition procedure of the trust point toward the new root CA key, we mentioned CMP and CTL method in the above. In this section, we will compare these two methods in details.

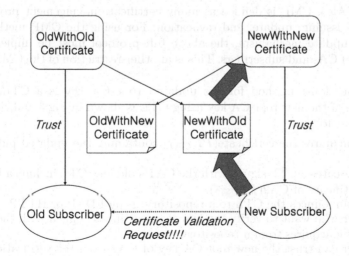

Fig. 2. Transition of the trust point using CMP

Fig.2 is shown that a user who trust the old root CA key can trust a new root CA key using CMP. An old subscriber who have trusted the old root CA key must trust the new root CA key for validation of the new subscriber's certificate which is issued by the new root CA key. To do this, the old subscriber uses the NewWithOld link certificate which is signed with the old root CA key trusted by itself. That is the old root CA key ensures a reliability of the new root CA key using singing. The new subscriber who trust the new root CA key uses the OldWithNew link certificate to trust the old root CA key, vice versa.

If we use the CMP method for trust of updated root CA key, then we will meet some restrictions. The first restriction is the CMP is practicable when the root CA key is updated with the changed key. And in the link certificates which are issued by the root CA, the issuer and subject names are identical. That is, the root CA key must use a different key and a same subject name for updating[2,8]. If the safety of root CA key is ensured enough after updating, and the root CA policy dose not need to change the root CA key, then this method can cause the additional cost along with the root CA key update. It is obvious if we update the root CA key by using a different key, its safety would be relatively improving. However, this is must be set up within a policy range. The root CA key update method using a same key can be needed when the its safety is ensured during the validity period after updating. We already dealt with this issue in section 4.2.

There is another restriction of a CMP mechanism. It is a complexity of procedures for verifying the new root CA key. The users who trust the old root CA key must acquire the NewWithOld link certificate to verify the new root CA key and vice versa. This means the increment of a certificate chain by the link certificates in the existing certificate path chain. This verification method is unsuitable for an application which request very short time for verification of certificate and it causes a implementation complexity of the end entity software. Also, CMP is defined as many certificate management protocols like certificate issuing, update, and revocation. For using the CMP method in the root CA update mechanism, the above full protocol must be implemented in software of CAs and subscribers. This is another restriction of the CMP method.

Another trust method for the updated root CA key is a CTL.The trust procedure of the new root CA key using CTL is shown in Fig.3 and the detailed steps are as follows.

1. CA1 acquires the certificate(PK_{CA2}) containing the updated public key of CA2.
2. CA1 creates a CTL signed with the CA1's old key, CTL include a fingerprint of certificate of CA2(PK_{CA2}).
3. CA1 announces the CTL to a repository using LDAP or HTTP.
4. A user who want to verify the new user certificate signed with the new root CA key acquires from a repository.
5. A user can trust the new root CA key of CA2 from the verification of CTL CA1 public key and confirming that the fingerprint of CA2 self-signed certificate is included in that CTL.

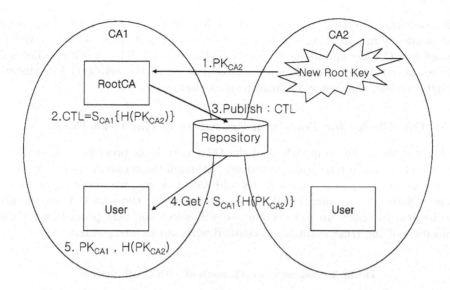

Fig. 3. Transition procedure of the trust point using CTL

The CTL method is similar with the CMP in relation that the old public key ensure the reliability of the new public key. But this mechanism is different with a CMP as the following reasons.

- In the CMP, the NewWithNew certificate or link certificates contain a new root CA public key. But in CTL, only fingerprint of certificate is included. That is, CTL does not contain any public key. So the new public key must be acquired using any other mechanism mentioned in 4.3.
- The number of contained public key in CMP certificate is the only one. Whereas a CTL may contain many fingerprints of the public key certificates. Only one CTL is needed whether the number of root CA public key is one or many.
- In the CMP mechanism, a root CA commonly withdraws the new root CA key by issuing an authority certificate revocation list(ARL). Whereas CTL withdraws the new root CA key by excluding the fingerprint of the new certificate in the trust list.
- The CMP mechanism is standardized by IETF whereas the CTL has not been standardized. But the CTL has been used in many applications like MS explorer.
- The root CA update protocol of CMP is only for the root CA key update, so it needs another method for cross certificate like issuing of cross certificate or certificate trust list[9]. The CTL can be used for the cross certificate too. The hash value of other PKI domain certificate is included in certificate trust list. In this case, the certificate for the cross certificate must be distinguished from the self-signed certificate for the root CA key update.

The most characteristic when we use CTL for trust of a new root CA key is an independency for changing of a root CA key and subject name, so it is available to any root CA key update model mentioned section 4.2. The validity period and the serial number of certificate are changed in all of the self-signed certificate update models, that's why its fingerprint is changed.

4.5   Our Choice for Transition Procedure of the Trust Point

Table 2.is shown the comparison of the CTL transition procedure of the trust point and the CMP transition procedure. Although these two methods are based on the assumption of the trust to the old root CA key, we may find there are some differences. We mentioned our requirements for the root CA key update mechanism in above. In this section, we will select the best procedure for the transition of the trust point to be satisfied with our requirements.

Table 2. Comparison CTL method with CMP method

Issue	CTL method	CMP method
Include the public key	Not included	Included
Basic Assumption	Trust of old root CA key	Trust of old root CA key
Change of root CA key	Independent	Must be changed
Changed of subject name	Independent	Must be identical
Implementation	easy	complex
Scalability to the cross certificate	possible	Impossible
Efficiency	Good	Not good

Our first requirement for the self-signed certificate update is that a root CA key and subject name can be changed or not. A root CA key must be changed in CMP method for root CA key update, but the CTL method satisfies this requirement. That is, the CTL method doesn't require that we must changed the root CA key. Also, a subject name in certificate must not be changed in CMP method, but the CTL method has no restriction for choosing the subject name. That is, the CTL method satisfy our first requirement.

The second requirement is that the updated self-signed certificate could be delivered in many ways. In the CMP method, the self-signed certificate must be posted into repository or transferred by only the CAKeyUpdAnn message. But the CTL method has no restriction for delivering it. The updated certificate can be posted in repository or web, implemented in subscribers software, and directly provided by the root CA as well as the subordinated CA.

The third requirement about the transition of the trust point is satisfied by these two. Besides that, the CTL method is useful for implementation and scalability to the cross certificate. As compared with the CMP, the CTL method holds these merits for efficiency. Because of these reasons, we select CTL method for transition procedure of the trust point in this paper.

5 Conclusion

It is necessary to update the root CA key which is the beginning point of the trust in PKI, due to the validity period expiration of the key and the concern about the safety. If a root CA key is updated by that reason, all of the end entities in relevant PKI domain must receive the updated root CA key in a reliable way and need a transition procedure of the trust point from the old root CA key to the new root CA key. In this paper, we have described the process of root CA key update mechanism which is composed of a self-signed certificate update, distribution of the updated root CA key, and transition procedure of the trust point.

If a root CA key is updated according to the validity period expiration, we must estimate an appropriate update point, considering a validity period of the subordinate CA certificate. Also in the perspective of every root CA key update, the signature algorithm, key length and validity period of the root CA key must be reconsidered in order to ensure its safety. The root CA certificate must be updated after the root CA key is updated and distributed to each subscribers. Then, it can be effective through the transition procedure of the trust point as the CTL method.

For the update of a root CA key, it requires an appropriate change to all entities software of relevant PKI domain, and it causes a consequence for additional cost spending. Through the practical use for this best practice for a root CA key update, each PKI domain is able to establish a root CA key update procedure effectively and safely.

Acknowledgement. We would like to thank Dr. Moti Yung for his valuable suggestion and useful comments.

References

1. Tim Moses, *PKI Trust Models*, available at
   http://www.itu.dk/courses/DSK/E2003/DOCS/PKI-Trust-models.pdf, 2000
2. Russ Housley, Tim Polk, *Planning for PKI*, Wiley Computer Publishing, pp.103-105, 2001
3. Matt Londy, ZDNet(UK), *Last week's mini-Y2K:What went wrong?*, available at
   http://zdnet.com.com/2100-1107-2-5140009.html, January 13, 2004
4. R. Housley et al., *Internet X.509 Public Key Infrastructure Certificate and Certificate Revocation List (CRL) Profile*, RFC3280, IETF, April, 2002
5. ITU-T Recommendation X.509 (1997) | ISO/IEC 9594-8:1998, *Information technology - Open Systems Interconnection - The Directory : Authentication Framework*, 1998
6. Information Security Committee, American Bar Association, *PKI Assessment Guidelines*, June 2001
7. S. Chokhani el al., *Internet X.509 Public Key Infrastructure Certificate Policy and Certification Practices Framework*, RFC2527, IETF
8. C. Adams et al., *Internet X.509 Public Key Infrastructure Certificate Management Protocols*, RFC2510, IETF, 1999

9. Interoperability Working Group, *Asia PKI Interoperability Guideline v1.0*, Asia PKI Forum, March 2003
10. Burt Kaliski, RSA Laboratories *TWIRL and RSA Key Size*, available at http://www.rsasecurity.com/rsalabs/technotes/twirl.html, Revised May 6, 2003
11. RegTP, *Notification in accordance with the Electronic Signature Act and the Electronic Signature Ordinance*, Federal Gazette No 49, pp 4202-4203 of 11 Match 2003
12. Arjen K.Lenstra, Eric R.Verheul, Selecting Cryptographic Key Sizes, 2001
13. Radis Perlman, Sun Microsystems, *An Overview of PKI Trust Models*, IEEE Network, 1999
14. Trevor Freeman, *Certificate Trust List*, Microsoft Corporation
15. A RSA Laboratories, *PKCS7 : Cryptographic Message Syntax Standard*, Revised November 1, 1993

SQLrand: Preventing SQL Injection Attacks

Stephen W. Boyd and Angelos D. Keromytis

Department of Computer Science
Columbia University
{swb48,angelos}@cs.columbia.edu

Abstract. We present a practical protection mechanism against SQL injection attacks. Such attacks target databases that are accessible through a web front-end, and take advantage of flaws in the input validation logic of Web components such as CGI scripts. We apply the concept of instruction-set randomization to SQL, creating instances of the language that are unpredictable to the attacker. Queries injected by the attacker will be caught and terminated by the database parser. We show how to use this technique with the MySQL database using an intermediary proxy that translates the random SQL to its standard language. Our mechanism imposes negligible performance overhead to query processing and can be easily retrofitted to existing systems.

1 Introduction

The prevalence of buffer overflow attacks [3,29] as an intrusion mechanism has resulted in considerable research focused on the problem of preventing [14,11], detecting [35, 23,25], or containing [33,31,21,12] such attacks. Considerably less attention has been paid to a related problem, SQL injection attacks [1]. Such attacks have been used to extract customer and order information from e-commerce databases, or bypass security mechanisms.

The intuition behind such attacks is that pre-defined logical expressions within a pre-defined query can be altered simply by injecting operations that always result in true or false statements. This injection typically occurs through a web form and associated CGI script that does not perform appropriate input validation. These types of injections are not limited strictly to character fields. Similar alterations to the "where" and "having" SQL clauses have been exposed, when the application does not restrict numeric data for numeric fields.

Standard SQL error messages returned by a database can also assist the attacker. In situations where the attacker has no knowledge of the underlying SQL query or the contributing tables, forcing an exception may reveal more details about the table or its field names and types. This technique has been shown to be quite effective in practice [5,27].

One solution to the problem is to improve programming techniques. Common practices include escaping single quotes, limiting the input character length, and filtering the exception messages. Despite these suggestions, vulnerabilities continue to surface in web applications, implying the need for a different approach. Another approach is to use the PREPARE statement feature supported by many databases, which allows a client to pre-issue a template SQL query at the beginning of a session; for the actual queries, the client only needs to specify the variables that change. Although the PREPARE feature was introduced as a performance optimization, it can address SQL injection attacks if the same query is issued many times. When the queries are dynamically constructed (*e.g.*, as a result of a page with several options that user may select), this approach does not work as well.

[22] introduced the concept of instruction-set randomization for safeguarding systems against any type of code-injection attack, by creating process-specific randomized instruction sets (*e.g.*, machine instructions) of the system executing potentially vulnerable software. An attacker that does not know the key to the randomization algorithm will inject code that is invalid for that randomized processor (and process), causing a runtime exception.

We apply the same technique to the problem of SQL injection attacks: we create randomized instances of the SQL query language, by randomizing the template query inside the CGI script and the database parser. To allow for easy retrofitting of our solution to existing systems, we introduce a de-randomizing proxy, which converts randomized queries to proper SQL queries for the database. Code injected by the rogue client evaluates to undefined keywords and expressions. When this is the outcome, then standard keywords (*e.g.*, "or") lose their significance, and attacks are frustrated before they can even commence. The performance overhead of our approach is minimal, adding up to 6.5*ms* to query processing time.

We explain the intuition behind our system, named *SQLrand,* in Section 2, and describe our prototype implementation in Section 3. We give some performance results in Section 4, and an overview of related work in Section 5.

2   SQLrand System Architecture

Injecting SQL code into a web application requires little effort by those who understand both the semantics of the SQL language and CGI scripts. Numerous applications take user input and feed it into a pre-defined query. The query is then handed to the database for execution. Unless developers properly design their application code to protect against unexpected data input by users, alteration to the database structure, corruption of data or revelation of private and confidential information may be granted inadvertently.

For example, consider a login page of a CGI application that expects a user-name and the corresponding password. When the credentials are submitted, they are inserted within a query template such as the following:

```
"select * from mysql.user
    where username=' " . $uid . " ' and
        password=password(' ". $pwd . " ');"
```

Instead of a valid user-name, the malicious user sets the $uid variable to the string: ' or 1=1; - -', causing the CGI script to issue the following SQL query to the database:

```
"select * from mysql.user
    where username='' or 1=1; - -'' and
        password=password('_any_text_');"
```

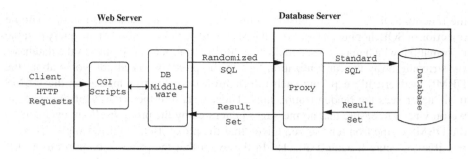

Fig. 1. SQLrand System Architecture

Notice that the single quotes balance the quotes in the pre-defined query, and the double hyphen comments out the remainder of the SQL query. Therefore, the password value is irrelevant and may be set to any character string. The result set of the query contains at least one record, since the "where" clause evaluates to true. If the application identifies a valid user by testing whether the result set is non-empty, the attacker can bypass the security check.

Our solution extends the application of Instruction-Set Randomization [22] to the SQL language: the SQL standard keywords are manipulated by appending a random integer to them, one that an attacker cannot easily guess. Therefore, any malicious user attempting an SQL injection attack would be thwarted, for the user input inserted into the "randomized" query would always be classified as a set of non-keywords, resulting in an invalid expression.

Essentially, the structured query language has taken on new keywords that will not be recognized by the database's SQL interpreter. A difficult approach would be to modify the database's interpreter to accept the new set of keywords. However, attempting to change its behavior would be a daunting task. Furthermore, a modified database would require all applications submitting SQL queries to conform to its new language. Although dedicating the database server for selected applications might be possible, the random key would not be varied among the SQL applications using it. Ideally, having the ability to vary the random SQL key, while maintaining one database system, grants a greater level of security, by making it difficult to subvert multiple applications by successfully attacking the least protected one.

Our design consists of a proxy that sits between the client and database server (see Figure 1). Note that the proxy may be on a separate machine, unlike the figure's depiction.

By moving the de-randomization process outside the DataBase Management System (DBMS) to the proxy, we gain in flexibility, simplicity, and security. Multiple proxies using unique random keys to decode SQL commands can be listening for connections on behalf of the same database, yet allowing disparate SQL applications to communicate in their own "tongue." The interpreter is no longer bound to the internals of the DBMS. The proxy's primary obligation is to decipher the random SQL query and then forward the SQL command with the standard set of keywords to the database for computation. Another benefit of the proxy is the concealment of database errors which may unveil the random SQL keyword extension to the user. A typical attack consists of a simple injection of SQL, hoping that the error message will disclose a subset of the query or table information, which may be used to deduce intuitively hidden properties of the database. By stripping away the randomization tags in the proxy, we need not worry about the DBMS inadvertently exposing such information through error messages; the DBMS itself never sees the randomization tags. Thus, to ensure the security of the scheme, we only need to ensure that no messages generated by the proxy itself are ever sent to the DBMS or the front-end server. Given that the proxy itself is fairly simple, it seems possible to secure it against attacks. In the event that the proxy is compromised, the database remains safe, assuming that other security measures are in place.

To assist the developer in randomizing his SQL statements, we provide a tool that reads an SQL statement(s) and rewrites all keywords with the random key appended. For example, in the C language, an SQL query, which takes user input, may look like the following:

```
select gender, avg(age)
   from cs101.students
      where dept = %d
   group by gender
```

The utility will identify the six keywords in the example query and append the key to each one (*e.g.*, when the key is "123"):

```
select123 gender, avg123 (age)
   from123 cs101.students
      where123 dept = %d
   group123 by123 gender
```

This SQL template query can be inserted into the developer's web application. The proxy, upon receiving the randomized SQL, translates and validates it before forwarding it to the database. Note that the proxy performs simple syntactic validation — it is otherwise unaware of the semantics of the query itself.

3 Implementation

To determine the practicality of the approach we just outlined, we built a proof-of-concept proxy server that sits between the client (web server) and SQL server, de-randomizes requests received from the client, and conveys the query to the server. If an SQL injection attack has occurred, the proxy's parser will fail to recognize the randomized query and will reject it. The two primary components were the de-randomization element and the communication protocol between the client and database system. In order to de-randomize the SQL query, the proxy required a modified SQL parser that expected the suffix of integers applied to all keywords. As a "middle man," it had to conceal its identity by masquerading as the database to the client and vice versa. Although our implementation focused on CGI scripts as the query generators, a similar approach applies when using JDBC.

The randomized SQL parser utilized two popular tools for writing compilers and parsers: flex and yacc. Capturing the encoded tokens required regular expressions that matched each SQL keyword (case-insensitive) followed by zero or more digits. (Technically, it did not require a key; practically, it needs one.) If properly encoded, the lexical analyzer strips the token's extension and returns it to the grammar for reassembly with the rest of the query. Otherwise, the token remains unaltered and is labeled as an identifier. By default, flex reads a source file, but our design required an array of characters as input. To override this behavior, the YY_INPUT macro was re-defined to retrieve tokens from a character string introduced by the proxy. During the parsing phase, any syntax error signals the improper construction of an SQL query using the pre-selected random key. Either the developer's SQL template is incorrect or the user's input includes unexpected data, whether good or bad. On encountering this, the parser returns NULL; otherwise, in the case of a successful parse, the de-randomized SQL string is returned. The parser was designed as a C library.

With the parser completed, the communication protocol had to be established between the proxy and a database. We used MySQL, a popular and widely used open-source database system, to create a fictitious customer database. The record size of the tables ranged from twenty to a little more than eleven thousand records. These sample tables were used in the evaluation of benchmark measurements described in Section 4. The remaining piece involved integrating the database's communication mechanism within the proxy.

Depending upon the client's language of choice, MySQL provides many APIs to access the database, yet the same application protocol. Since the proxy will act as a client to the database, the C API library was suitable. One problem existed: the mysqlclient C library does not have a server-side counterpart for accepting and disassembling the MySQL packets sent using the client API. Therefore, the protocol of MySQL had to be analyzed and incorporated into the proxy. Unfortunately, there was no official documentation; however, a rough sketch of the protocol existed which satisfied the requirements of the three primary packets: the query, the error, and the disconnect packets.

The query packet carries the actual request to the database. The quit message is necessary in cases where the client is abruptly disconnected from the proxy or sends an invalid query to the proxy. In either case the proxy gains the responsibility of discretely disconnecting from the database by issuing the quit command on behalf of the client. Finally, the error packet is only sent to the client when an improper query generates a syntax error, thus indicating a possible injection attack.

The client application needs only to define its server connection to redirect its packets through the proxy rather than directly to the database. In its connection method, this is achieved simply by changing the port number of the database to the port where the proxy is listening. After receiving a connection, the proxy in turn establishes a connection with the database and hands off all messages it receives from the client. If the command byte of the MySQL packet from the client indicates the packet contains a query, the proxy extracts the SQL and passes it to the interpreter for decoding. When unsuccessful, the proxy sends an error packet with a generic "syntax error" message to the client and disconnects from the database. On the other hand, a successful parsing of the SQL query produces a translation to the de-randomized syntax. The proxy overwrites the original, randomized query with the standard query that the database is expecting into the body of the MySQL packet. The packet size is updated in the header and pushed out to the database. The normal flow of packets continues until the client requests another query.

The API libraries define some methods which will not work with the proxy, as they hardcode the SQL query submitted to the database. For example, mysql_list_dbs() sends the query "SHOW databases LIKE <wild-card-input>". Without modification to the client library, the workaround would be to construct the query string with the proper randomized key and issue the mysql_query() method. Presently, binary SQL cannot be passed to the proxy for processing; therefore, mysql_real_query() must be avoided.

4   Evaluation

To address the practicality of using a proxy to de-randomize encoded SQL for a database, two objectives were considered. First, the proxy must prevent known SQL injection vulnerabilities within an application. Second, the extra overhead introduced by the proxy must be evaluated.

4.1   Qualitative Evaluation

First, a sample CGI application was written, which allowed a user to inject SQL into a "where" clause that expected an account ID. With no input validation, a user can easily inject SQL to retrieve account information concerning all accounts. When using the SQLrand proxy, the injected statement is identified and an error message issued, rather than proceeding with the processing of the corrupted SQL query. After testing the reliability of the proxy on a "home grown" example, the next step was to identify an SQL injection vulnerability in a pre-existing application.

An open-source bulletin board, phpBB v2.0.5, presented an opportunity to inject SQL into viewtopic.php, revealing the password of a user one byte at a time. After the attack was replicated in the test environment, the section of vulnerable SQL was randomized and the connection was redirected through the proxy. As expected, the proxy recognized the injection as invalid SQL code and did not send it to the database. The phpBB application did not succumb to the SQL injection attack as verified without the proxy. However, it was observed that the application displays an SQL query to the user by default when zero records are returned. Since an exception does not return any rows, the proxy's encoding key was revealed. Again, the randomization method still requires good coding practices. If a developer chooses to reveal the SQL under certain cases, there is little benefit to the randomization process. Of course, one must remember that the application was not designed with the proxy implementation in mind.

Another content management application prone to SQL injection attacks, Php-Nuke depends on the magic_quotes_gpc option to be turned on to protect against some of them. Without this setting, several modules are open to such attacks. Even with the option set, injections on numeric fields are not protected because the application does not check for numeric input. For example, when attempting to download content from the php-nuke application, the download option d_op is set to 'getit' and accepts an unchecked, numeric parameter name 'lid'. It looks up the URL for the content from the download table based on the lid value and sets it in the HTTP location header statement. If an attacker finds an invalid lid (determined by PHP-Nuke reloading its home page) and appends 'union select pass from users_table' to it, the browser responds with an error message stating that the URL had failed to load, thus revealing the sensitive information. However, when applying the proxy, injection attacks in the affected download module were averted. These vulnerabilities are open in other modules within PHP-Nuke that would also be quickly secured by using the proxy. The same common injection schemes are cited in various applications.

4.2 Performance Evaluation

Next, we quantified the overhead imposed by SQLrand. An experiment was designed to measure the additional processing time required by three sets of concurrent users, respectively 10, 25, and 50. Each class executed, in a round-robin fashion, a set of five queries concurrently over 100 trials. The average length of the five different queries was 639 bytes, and the random key length was thirty-two bytes. The sample customer database created during the implementation was the target of the queries. The database, proxy, and client program were on separate *x86* machines running RedHat Linux, within the same network. The overhead of proxy processing ranged from 183 to 316 microseconds for 10 to 50 concurrent users respectively. Table 1 shows the proxy's performance.

Table 1. Proxy Overhead (in microseconds)

Users	Min	Max	Mean	Std
10	74	1300	183.5	126.9
25	73	2782	223.8	268.1
50	73	6533	316.6	548.8

The worst-case scenario adds approximately 6.5 milliseconds to the processing time of each query. Since acceptable response times for most web applications usually fall between a few seconds to tens of seconds, depending on the purpose of the application, the additional processing time of the proxy contributes insignificant overhead in a majority of cases.

5 Related Work

To date, little attention has been paid to SQL injection attacks. The work conceptually closest to ours is RISE [8], which applies a randomization technique similar to our Instruction-Set Randomization [22] for binary code only, and uses an emulator attached to specific processes. The inherent use of and dependency on emulation makes RISE simultaneously more practical for immediate use and inherently slower in the absence of hardware. [26] uses more general code obfuscation techniques to harden program binaries against static disassembly.

In the general area of randomization, originally proposed as a way of introducing diversity in computer systems [16], notable systems include PointGuard and Address Obfuscation. PointGuard [11] encrypts all pointers while they reside in memory and decrypts them only before they are loaded to a CPU register. This is implemented as an extension to the GCC compiler, which injects the necessary instructions at compilation time, allowing a pure-software implementation of the scheme. Another approach, address obfuscation [10], randomizes the absolute locations of all code and data, as well as the distances between different data items. Several transformations are used, such as randomizing the base addresses of memory regions (stack, heap, dynamically-linked libraries, routines, static data, *etc.*), permuting the order of variables/routines, and introducing random gaps between objects (*e.g.,* randomly pad stack frames or *malloc()*'ed regions). Although very effective against *jump-into-libc* attacks, it is less so against other common attacks, since the amount of possible randomization is relatively small (especially when compared to our key sizes). However, address obfuscation can protect against attacks that aim to corrupt variables or other data. This approach can be effectively combined with instruction randomization to offer comprehensive protection against all memory-corrupting attacks. [13] gives an overview of various protection mechanisms, including randomization techniques, and makes recommendations on choosing obfuscation (of interface or implementation) *vs.* restricting the same.

[6] describes some design principles for safe interpreters, with a focus on JavaScript. The Perl interpreter can be run in a mode that implements some of these principles (access to external interfaces, namespace management, *etc.*). While this approach can somewhat mitigate the effects of an attack, it cannot altogether prevent, or even contain it in certain cases (*e.g.,* in the case of a Perl CGI script that generates an SQL query to the back-end database).

Increasingly, source code analysis techniques are brought to bear on the problem of detecting potential code vulnerabilities. The most simple approach has been that of the compiler warning on the use of certain unsafe functions, *e.g., gets()*. More recent approaches [17,35,23,34,15] have focused on detecting specific types of problems, rather than try to solve the general "bad code" issue, with considerable success. While such tools can greatly help programmers ensure the safety of their code, especially when used in conjunction with other protection techniques, they (as well as dynamic analysis tools such as [25,24]) offer incomplete protection, as they can only protect against and detect *known* classes of attacks and vulnerabilities. Unfortunately, none of these systems have been applied to the case of SQL injection attacks.

Process sandboxing [31] is perhaps the best understood and widely researched area of containing bad code (or its effects), as evidenced by the plethora of available systems like Janus [21], Consh [4], Mapbox [2], OpenBSD's *systrace* [33], and the Mediating Connectors [7]. These operate at user level and confine applications by filtering access to system calls. To accomplish this, they rely on *ptrace(2)*, the */proc* file system, and/or special shared libraries. Another category of systems, such as Tron [9], SubDomain [12] and others [18,20,36,30,37,28,32], go a step further. They intercept system calls inside the kernel, and use policy engines to decide whether to permit the call or not. The main problem with all these is that the attack is not prevented: rather, the system tries to limit the damage such code can do, such as obtain super-user privileges. In the context of a web server, this means that a web server may only be able to issue queries to particular databases or access a limited set of files, *etc.* [19] identifies several common security-related problems with such systems, such as their susceptibility to various types of race conditions.

6   Conclusions

We presented SQLrand, a system for preventing SQL injection attacks against web servers. The main intuition is that by using a randomized SQL query language, specific to a particular CGI application, it is possible to detect and abort queries that include injected code. By using a proxy for the de-randomization process, we achieve portability and security gains: the same proxy can be used with various DBMS back-end, and it can ensure that no information that would expose the randomization process can leak from the database itself. Naturally, care must be taken by the CGI implementor to avoid exposing randomized queries (as is occasionally done in the case of errors). We showed that this approach does not sacrifice performance: the latency overhead imposed on each query was at most 6.5 milliseconds.

We believe that SQLrand is a very practical system that solves a problem heretofore ignored, in preference to the more "high profile" buffer overflow attacks. Our plans for future work include developing tools that will further assist programmers in using SQLrand and extending coverage to other DBMS back-ends.

References

1. CERT Vulnerability Note VU#282403. http://www.kb.cert.org/vuls/id/282403, September 2002.
2. A. Acharya and M. Raje. Mapbox: Using parameterized behavior classes to confine applications. In *Proceedings of the 9th USENIX Security Symposium*, pages 1–17, August 2000.
3. Aleph One. Smashing the stack for fun and profit. *Phrack*, 7(49), 1996.
4. A. Alexandrov, P. Kmiec, and K. Schauser. Consh: A confined execution environment for internet computations, December 1998.
5. C. Anley. Advanced SQL Injection In SQL Server Applications.
   http://www.nextgenss.com/papers/advanced_sql_injection.pdf, 2002.
6. V. Anupam and A. Mayer. Security of Web Browser Scripting Languages: Vulnerabilities, Attacks, and Remedies. In *Proceedings of the 7th USENIX Security Symposium*, pages 187–200, January 1998.
7. R. Balzer and N. Goldman. Mediating connectors: A non-bypassable process wrapping technology. In *Proceeding of the 19th IEEE International Conference on Distributed Computing Systems*, June 1999.
8. E. G. Barrantes, D. H. Ackley, S. Forrest, T. S. Palmer, D. Stefanovic, and D. D. Zovi. Randomized Instruction Set Emulation to Disrupt Binary Code Injection Attacks. In *Proceedings of the 10th ACM Conference on Computer and Communications Security (CCS)*, pages 281–289, October 2003.
9. A. Berman, V. Bourassa, and E. Selberg. TRON: Process-Specific File Protection for the UNIX Operating System. In *Proceedings of the USENIX Technical Conference*, January 1995.

10. S. Bhatkar, D. C. DuVarney, and R. Sekar. Address Obfuscation: an Efficient Approach to Combat a Broad Range of Memory Error Exploits. In *Proceedings of the 12th USENIX Security Symposium*, pages 105–120, August 2003.

11. C. Cowan, S. Beattie, J. Johansen, and P. Wagle. PointGuard: Protecting Pointers From Buffer Overflow Vulnerabilities. In *Proceedings of the 12th USENIX Security Symposium*, pages 91–104, August 2003.

12. C. Cowan, S. Beattie, C. Pu, P. Wagle, and V. Gligor. SubDomain: Parsimonious Security for Server Appliances. In *Proceedings of the 14th USENIX System Administration Conference (LISA 2000)*, March 2000.

13. C. Cowan, H. Hinton, C. Pu, and J. Walpole. The Cracker Patch Choice: An Analysis of Post Hoc Security Techniques. In *Proceedings of the National Information Systems Security Conference (NISSC)*, October 2000.

14. C. Cowan, C. Pu, D. Maier, H. Hinton, J. Walpole, P. Bakke, S. Beattie, A. Grier, P. Wagle, and Q. Zhang. Stackguard: Automatic adaptive detection and prevention of buffer-overflow attacks. In *Proceedings of the 7th USENIX Security Symposium*, Jan. 1998.

15. N. Dor, M. Rodeh, and M. Sagiv. CSSV: Towards a realistic tool for statically detecting all buffer overflows in C. In *Proceedings of the ACM Conference on Programming Language Design and Implementation (PLDI)*, June 2003.

16. S. Forrest, A. Somayaji, and D. Ackley. Building Diverse Computer Systems. In *HotOS-VI*, 1997.

17. J. Foster, M. Fähndrich, and A. Aiken. A theory of type qualifiers. In *Proceedings of the ACM SIGPLAN Conference on Programming Language Design and Implementation (PLDI)*, May 1999.

18. T. Fraser, L. Badger, and M. Feldman. Hardening COTS Software with Generic Software Wrappers. In *Proceedings of the IEEE Symposium on Security and Privacy*, Oakland, CA, May 1999.

19. T. Garfinkel. Traps and Pitfalls: Practical Problems in System Call Interposition Based Security Tools. In *Proceedings of the Symposium on Network and Distributed Systems Security (SNDSS)*, pages 163–176, February 2003.

20. D. P. Ghormley, D. Petrou, S. H. Rodrigues, and T. E. Anderson. SLIC: An Extensibility System for Commodity Operating Systems. In *Proceedings of the 1998 USENIX Annual Technical Conference*, pages 39–52, June 1998.

21. I. Goldberg, D. Wagner, R. Thomas, and E. A. Brewer. A Secure Environment for Untrusted Helper Applications. In *Procedings of the 1996 USENIX Annual Technical Conference*, 1996.

22. G. S. Kc, A. D. Keromytis, and V. Prevelakis. Countering Code-Injection Attacks With Instruction-Set Randomization. In *Proceedings of the ACM Computer and Communications Security (CCS) Conference*, pages 272–280, October 2003.

23. D. Larochelle and D. Evans. Statically Detecting Likely Buffer Overflow Vulnerabilities. In *Proceedings of the 10th USENIX Security Symposium*, pages 177–190, August 2001.

24. E. Larson and T. Austin. High Coverage Detection of Input-Related Security Faults. In *Proceedings of the 12th USENIX Security Symposium*, pages 121–136, August 2003.

25. K. Lhee and S. J. Chapin. Type-assisted dynamic buffer overflow detection. In *Proceedings of the 11th USENIX Security Symposium*, pages 81–90, August 2002.

26. C. Linn and S. Debray. Obfuscation of Executable Code to Improve Resistance to Static Disassembly. In *Proceedings of the 10th ACM Conference on Computer and Communications Security (CCS)*, pages 290–299, October 2003.

27. D. Litchfield. Web Application Disassembly wth ODBC Error Messages. http://www.nextgenss.com/papers/webappdis.doc.

28. P. Loscocco and S. Smalley. Integrating Flexible Support for Security Policies into the Linux Operating System. In *Proceedings of the USENIX Annual Technical Conference, Freenix Track*, pages 29–40, June 2001.

29. M. Conover and w00w00 Security Team. w00w00 on heap overflows. http://www.w00w00.org/files/articles/heaptut.txt, January 1999.
30. T. Mitchem, R. Lu, and R. O'Brien. Using Kernel Hypervisors to Secure Applications. In *Proceedings of the Annual Computer Security Applications Conference*, December 1997.
31. D. S. Peterson, M. Bishop, and R. Pandey. A Flexible Containment Mechanism for Executing Untrusted Code. In *Proceedings of the 11th USENIX Security Symposium*, pages 207–225, August 2002.
32. V. Prevelakis and D. Spinellis. Sandboxing Applications. In *Proceedings of the USENIX Technical Annual Conference, Freenix Track*, pages 119–126, June 2001.
33. N. Provos. Improving Host Security with System Call Policies. In *Proceedings of the 12th USENIX Security Symposium*, pages 257–272, August 2003.
34. U. Shankar, K. Talwar, J. S. Foster, and D. Wagner. Detecting Format String Vulnerabilities with Type Qualifiers. In *Proceedings of the 10th USENIX Security Symposium*, pages 201–216, August 2001.
35. D. Wagner, J. S. Foster, E. A. Brewer, and A. Aiken. A First Step towards Automated Detection of Buffer Overrun Vulnerabilities. In *Proceedings of the ISOC Symposium on Network and Distributed System Security (SNDSS)*, pages 3–17, February 2000.
36. K. M. Walker, D. F. Stern, L. Badger, K. A. Oosendorp, M. J. Petkac, and D. L. Sherman. Confining root programs with domain and type enforcement. In *Proceedings of the USENIX Security Symposium*, pages 21–36, July 1996.
37. R. N. M. Watson. TrustedBSD: Adding Trusted Operating System Features to FreeBSD. In *Proceedings of the USENIX Annual Technical Conference, Freenix Track*, pages 15–28, June 2001.

Cryptanalysis of a Knapsack Based Two-Lock Cryptosystem*

Bin Zhang[1,2], Hongjun Wu[1], Dengguo Feng[2], and Feng Bao[1]

. Institute for Infocomm Research, Singapore 119613
. State Key Laboratory of Information Security,
Graduate School of the Chinese Academy of Sciences,
Beijing, 100039, PRC
{stuzb,hongjun}@i2r.a-star.edu.sg

Abstract. In this paper we break a knapsack based two-lock cryptosystem proposed at ICICS'03 [7]. The two-lock cryptosystem is a commutative encryption algorithm that is very useful for the construction of the general t-out-of-n oblivious transfers and millionaire protocol. However, our analysis shows that the proposed knapsack based two-lock cryptosystem is extremely insecure. The serious flaw is that the sender in the two-lock cryptosystem can retrieve the secret key of the receiver fairly easily. We have implemented the attack on a Pentium 4 2.5 GHz processor. For the parameters given in [7], it takes only several minutes to break that knapsack based two-lock cryptosystem.

Keywords. Cryptanalysis, Two-lock cryptosystem, Knapsack problem.

1 Introduction

Cryptography plays an important role in today's digital world. Many cryptographic techniques have been developed to meet the various requirements arising from applications. Among them oblivious transfer is a very useful cryptographic primitive. The concept of oblivious transfer (OT) was first proposed by Rabin in [6]. In that paper, the sender has one bit secret message and would like the receiver to get it with probability, but the receiver does not want the sender to know whether the secret message being received or not. The 1-out-of-2 OT means that the sender has two secrets and would like the receiver to get one of them at the receiver's choice, meanwhile the receiver does not want the sender to know which secret bit being chosen. The concept of t-out-of-n OT is the generalization of that of 1-out-of-2 OT. The sender can not determine which t messages the receiver obtained, and the receiver can not learn the other $(n - t)$ messages. A millionaire protocol is used to solve the following problem. Two parties, each has a secret integer. Without revealing those two secret integers,

* Supported by National Natural Science Foundation of China (Grant No. 60273027), National Key Foundation Research 973 project (Grant No. G1999035802) and National Science Fund for Distinguished Young Scholars (Grant No. 60025205)

M. Jakobsson, M. Yung, J. Zhou (Eds.): ACNS 2004, LNCS 3089, pp. 303–309, 2004.

they could compare those two integers. In both the t-out-of-n oblivious transfers and millionaire protocol cases, the basic security requirement is that those two parties should not know each other's secret information.

The two-lock cryptosystems proposed in [7] can be used to efficiently construct the t-out-of-n oblivious transfer and/or millionaire protocol. The two-lock cryptosystem consists of two commutative encryption algorithms A and B. Let A and B denote the encryption algorithms belong to Alice and Bob, respectively. A and B satisfy $B_s(A_k(m)) = A_k(B_s(m))$ for any randomly chosen secret keys k and s. This two-lock cryptosystem operates as follows. If the sender Alice wants to send a secret message m to Bob, they communicate with each other as follows:

1. Alice sends to Bob: $Y = A_k(m)$.
2. Bob sends to Alice: $Z = B_s(Y)$.
3. Alice sends to Bob: $C = A_k^{-1}(Z)$.
4. Bob decrypts: $m = B_s^{-1}(C)$.

where $A_k^{-1}(\cdot)$ and $B_s^{-1}(\cdot)$ denote the decryption of $A_k(\cdot)$ and $B_s(\cdot)$ respectively. It is easy to see that at the end Bob can obtain the message m. A two-lock cryptosystem should meet the following security requirements: it should be computationally infeasible for an adversary to recover the keys k or s such that $C = A_k^{-1}(Z)$ or $Z = B_s(Y)$. And it should be computationally impossible for the two parties to recover each other's secret key. The very simple and efficient discrete logarithm based two-lock cryptosystem has been proposed in [1]. In [7], a new knapsack based two-lock cryptosystem was proposed.

In this paper, we show that the knapsack based two-lock cryptosystem proposed in [7] is extremely insecure. The sender in the two-lock cryptosystem can recover the receiver's secret key fairly easily.

This paper is organized as follows. In Section 2, we introduce the proposed knapsack based two-lock cryptosystem with some informal analysis. Our attack against this cryptosystem is given in Section 3. In Section 4, detailed experiment results of our attack are listed with some remarks. Section 5 concludes the paper.

2   The Knapsack Based Two-Lock Cryptosystem

We first recall the definition of knapsack problem. Let $a_1, \cdots, a_l, S, l$ be some integers. The knapsack or subset-sum problem is to determine, given positive integers $a_1, \cdots, a_l, S$, whether there is a subset of the $\{a_j\}$ that sums to S. This is equivalent to determine whether there are variables $x_1, \cdots, x_l \in \{0, 1\}$ satisfying $x_1 a_1 + \cdots + x_l a_l = S$. The density $d(a)$ of the knapsack vector $(a_1, \cdots, a_l)$ is defined as $d(a) = l/\log_2 \max\{a_1, \cdots, a_l\}$. The general knapsack problem is known to be NP-complete [4]. The first knapsack-based cryptosystem was proposed by Merkle and Hellman in 1978 [5], followed by a number of variants. Unfortunately, most of them were broken. The main reason is that although the general knapsack problem is hard, the knapsack algorithm being used in those cryptosystems may not be hard, and the cryptanalyst can deduce the original solvable knapsack from the seemingly random knapsack. A good overview of these systems and their cryptanalysis can be found in [2,3].

The following describes the knapsack based two-lock cryptosystem proposed in [7]. Let t, k, n, l be secure parameters. Alice wish to send Bob a positive integer sequence $m = (m_1, \cdots, m_l) = (u_{1,1}, \cdots, u_{l,1}) + (v_{1,1}, \cdots, v_{l,1})$ where the binary length of m_i is n and $m_i \neq m_j (i \neq j)$. They begin their confidential communication as follows.

1. *Alice:* For $h = 1$ to t, randomly select positive integers e_h, M_h, f_h, N_h such that $M_h > k\max\{u_{1,h}, \cdots, u_{l,h}\}$, $N_h > k\max\{v_{1,h}, \cdots, v_{l,h}\}$, $(e_h, M_h) = 1$, $(f_h, N_h) = 1$ and $(M_h, N_h) = 1$. Compute $u_{j,h+1} = e_h u_{j,h} \bmod M_h$, $v_{j,h+1} = f_h v_{j,h} \bmod N_h$, for $j = 1$ to l. By Chinese remainder theorem, compute $(y_1, \cdots, y_l)$ such that $u_{j,t+1} = y_j \bmod M_t$ and $v_{j,t+1} = y_j \bmod N_t$, for $j = 1, \cdots, l$, i.e. $y_j = u_{j,t+1} N_t^{\phi(M_t)} + v_{j,t+1} M_t^{\phi(N_t)} \bmod M_t N_t$, where $\phi(\cdot)$ is the Euler function. Then select a random integer α and send $Y = (Y_1, \cdots, Y_l) = (y_1 - \alpha, \cdots, y_l - \alpha)$ to Bob.
2. *Bob:* Select a random nonsingular matrix $B = (b_{i,j})_{l \times l}$, where $b_{i,j} \in \{0, 1\}$ and the hamming weight of each column is k. Send $Z = (z_1, \cdots, z_l) = YB$ to Alice.
3. *Alice:* for $h = t$ to 1, compute $d_h = e_h^{-1} \bmod M_h$, $g_h = f_h^{-1} \bmod N_h$. Let $U_{i,t} = d_t(z_i + k\alpha) \bmod M_t$, $V_{i,t} = g_t(z_i + k\alpha) \bmod N_t$ for $i = 1, \cdots, l$. For $h = t-1, \cdots, 1$, calculate $U_{j,h} = d_h U_{j,h+1} \bmod M_h$, $V_{j,h} = g_h V_{j,h+1} \bmod N_h$, for $j = 1, \cdots, l$. Finally, send Bob $C = (c_1, \cdots, c_l) = (U_{1,1} + V_{1,1}, \cdots, U_{l,1} + V_{l,1})$.
4. *Bob:* Compute $(m_1, \cdots, m_l) = (c_1, \cdots, c_l)B^{-1}$.

In [7], the authors argue that if the adversaries intend to find a nonsingular matrix $(b'_{i,j})_{l \times l}$ form $Z = (z_1, \cdots, z_l)$ such that $z_j = b'_{1,j}y_1 + \cdots + b'_{l,j}y_l$, then they will be confronted with a random knapsack problem with density about $l/\log_2(M_t N_t)$. Let $l \geq 1000$, $t \geq 50$, $k = 128$, $n = 100$ and $M_t N_t \leq 2^{900}$, then the density $d(a) > 1$. However, as we will show below, it is the proposed sparse structure of the column vector of $B = (b_{i,j})_{l \times l}$ that leads to the failure of the knapsack based two-lock system.

3 Cryptanalysis of the Knapsack Based Two-Lock Cryptosystem

Our main idea is that if a dishonest Alice deceives Bob with a random-looking vector $(Y_1, \cdots, Y_l)$ of integers, then she can recover the matrix $B = (b_{i,j})_{l \times l}$ by solving easy knapsack problems due to the fact that Alice can choose all the information vectors sent to Bob at her choice. Thus if Alice chooses an easy knapsack and disguise it as a random-looking knapsack, then she can recover the original easy vector she sent to Bob from the vector encrypted by Bob using the knapsack-like encryption scheme. Since the basic security requirement of t-out-of-n oblivious transfers and millionaire protocol is that the two communication parties should not know the counterpart's secret key, the attack above indicates that the proposed knapsack based two-lock cryptosystem is insecure for t-out-of-n oblivious transfers and millionaire protocol applications.

Now we are ready to give the description of our attack in detail. The problem we face is to restore the matrix $B = (b_{i,j})_{l \times l}$ from $Z = (z_1, \cdots, z_l)$ and $Y = (Y_1, \cdots, Y_l)$, where $Z = YB$ and $Y = (Y_1, \cdots, Y_l)$ is chosen at Alice's choice. We wish to recover each column vector $(b_{1,j}, \cdots, b_{l,j})^T$ of hamming weight 128 such that $z_j = b_{1,j}Y_1 + b_{2,j}Y_2 + \cdots + b_{l,j}Y_l$, for $j = 1, 2, \cdots, l$. It is obvious that the better the vector chosen by Alice, the easier it is to recover the matrix B. Since $M_t N_t \leq 2^{900}$, without loss of generality we take the binary representations of the integers Y_i to have 900 bit length. Our attack consists of three stages. At the first stage, Alice chooses a special integer vector $Y' = (Y_1', \cdots, Y_l')$. At the second stage, Alice disguises that special integer vector into a random-looking vector $Y = (Y_1, \cdots, Y_l)$. Finally, Alice recovers the matrix $B = (b_{i,j})_{l \times l}$ from $Z = (z_1, \cdots, z_l)$ and $Y = (Y_1, \cdots, Y_l)$, where Y is encrypted by Bob as $Z = YB$.

3.1 Our Attack

We take the scheme with parameters $l = 2000$, $k = 128$ and $2^{899} < M_t N_t < 2^{900}$ to demonstrate our algorithm. As stated above, the attack consists of three stages, i.e. choosing stage, disguising stage and recovering stage.

Stage 1. Choosing Special Integer Vector Y'. Choose integers $Y_1', \cdots, Y_{2000}'$ such that their binary representations being the row vectors of the following binary matrix (the rightmost bit is the least significant bit):

$$
\begin{pmatrix}
0_{40 \times 18} & 0_{40 \times 18} & \cdots & 0_{40 \times 18} & A_{40 \times 18}^1 \\
0_{40 \times 18} & 0_{40 \times 18} & \cdots & A_{40 \times 18}^2 & 0_{40 \times 18} \\
\vdots & \vdots & \vdots & \vdots & \vdots \\
A_{40 \times 18}^{50} & 0_{40 \times 18} & \cdots & 0_{40 \times 18} & 0_{40 \times 18}
\end{pmatrix}_{2000 \times 900}
\tag{1}
$$

Note that $0_{40 \times 18}$ and $A_{40 \times 18}^i$, $i = 1, \cdots, 50$, are sub-matrices of specified size, i.e. $0_{40 \times 18}$ denotes zero matrix and $A_{40 \times 18}^i$, $i = 1, \cdots, 49$, denote 40×18 matrices such that their row vectors are randomly chosen from the linear vector space $GF(2)^{18}$. $A_{40 \times 18}^{50}$ denotes the matrix such that its leftmost 3 column vectors are the zero vectors and other elements are randomly chose from $GF(2)$ in such a way that the row vectors are all the non-zero vectors. The reason for such a choice of $A_{40 \times 18}^{50}$ is stated in the following stage 2.

Stage 2. Disguising the Special Integer Vector Y'. We use the standard transformation to disguise an easy knapsack into a seemingly more complicated one, i.e. we first select a large integer W such that $(W, M_t N_t) = 1$ and let $Y_i = WY_i' \bmod M_t N_t$. Alice then sends the resultant integer vector to Bob. After receiving the encrypted vector from Bob, Alice reverses the procedure mentioned above using $Y_i' = Y_i W^{-1} \bmod M_t N_t$. Then Alice gets the easy knapsack and recovers the secret key of Bob as stage 3 states. To guarantee recovering the original vector from the encrypted vector successfully, the following condition should be satisfied:

$$\sum_{i=1}^{l} b_{i,j} Y_i' < M_t N_t \tag{2}$$

which results from

$$z_j = \sum_{i=1}^{l} b_{i,j} Y_i = \sum_{i=1}^{l} b_{i,j} (Y_i' W \bmod M_t N_t) \tag{3}$$

Since there are on average at most 2 carriers from $A_{40 \times 18}^i$ to $A_{40 \times 18}^{i+1}$ when the row vectors are summed together, we put the leftmost 3 columns of $A_{40 \times 18}^{50}$ to be zero vectors taking into account that $2^{899} < M_t N_t < 2^{900}$.

Stage 3. Recovering the Matrix B. The problem we now face is, given $z_j' = z_j W^{-1} \bmod M_t N_t$ and $Y_1', \cdots, Y_{2000}'$, to find the column vector $(b_{1,j}, \cdots, b_{2000,j})^T$ of hamming weight 128 such that $z_j' = b_{1,j} Y_1' + b_{2,j} Y_2' + \cdots + b_{2000,j} Y_{2000}'$, for $j = 1, 2, \cdots, 2000$. First rewrite z_j' as binary representation

$$z_j' = (z_{j,900}, \cdots, z_{j,773}, z_{j,772}, \cdots, z_{j,2}, z_{j,1})_2. \tag{4}$$

Then we get

$$
\begin{aligned}
z_j' &= (z_{j,900}, \cdots, z_{j,19}, z_{j,18}, \cdots, z_{j,2}, z_{j,1})_2 \\
&= b_{1,j} Y_1' + b_{2,j} Y_2' + \cdots + b_{2000,j} Y_{2000}' \\
&= b_{1,j}(0_1 \cdots 0_{18} 0_{19} \cdots 0_{864} 0_{865} \cdots 0_{882} *_{883} \cdots *_{900})_2 + \cdots + \\
&\quad\ b_{41,j}(0_1 \cdots 0_{18} 0_{19} \cdots 0_{864} *_{865} \cdots *_{882} 0_{883} \cdots 0_{900})_2 + \cdots + \\
&\quad\ b_{2000,j}(0_1 0_2 0_3 *_4 \cdots *_{18} 0_{19} \cdots 0_{864} 0_{865} \cdots 0_{882} 0_{883} \cdots 0_{900})_2,
\end{aligned}
$$

where the subscripts denote positions and the asterisks denote randomly chosen elements from $GF(2)$. We can see from above equation that the least significant bits $z_{j,18}, \cdots, z_{j,2}, z_{j,1}$ only depend on the sum of $b_{1,j} Y_1' + \cdots + b_{40,j} Y_{40}'$. The bits $z_{j,36}, \cdots, z_{j,20}, z_{j,19}$ depend on $b_{41,j} Y_{41}' + \cdots + b_{80,j} Y_{80}'$ and the carry from $b_{1,j} Y_1' + \cdots + b_{40,j} Y_{40}'$, $\ldots$, and so on. It is obvious from above observations that determining $(b_{1,j}, \cdots, b_{2000,j})^T$ is dependent on the determination of $(b_{1,j}, \cdots, b_{40,j})^T$, for given the knowledge of $(b_{1,j}, \cdots, b_{40,j})^T$, we can follow an iterative way to determine the remaining bits in $(b_{1,j}, \cdots, b_{2000,j})^T$. For the determination of $(b_{1,j}, \cdots b_{40,j})^T$, according to $128 \times 40/2000 = 2.56$, we use an exhaustive search through all the $2 - 3$ combinations of row vectors of $A_{40 \times 18}^1$ to find out the '1' bits in $(b_{1,j}, \cdots, b_{40,j})^T$. The complexity of this procedure is about $\binom{40}{2} \approx 2^{9.60733}$ or $\binom{40}{3} \approx 2^{13.2703}$, which is absolutely negligible on an ordinary PC. We select the true combination of the row vectors, thus determine the '1' bits in $(b_{1,j}, \cdots, b_{40,j})^T$.

Now we give a full description of the attack.

1. *parameters:* $l = 2000$, $k = 128$, $2^{899} < M_t N_t < 2^{900}$, $(z_{900,j}, \cdots , z_{2,j}, z_{1,j}) = z'_j$, $(Y'_1, \cdots , Y'_{2000})$ as defined in the above matrix.
2. $(z^1_{18}, \cdots , z^1_1) = (z_{18,j}, \cdots , z_{1,j})$.
3. For $i = 1$ to 50, make an exhaustive search over the 40 row vectors of $A^i_{40 \times 18}$ to find out about $2 - 3$ rows whose summation's least significant 18 bits are $(z^i_{18}, \cdots , z^i_1)$. Set the elements of $(b_{40(i-1)+1,j}, \cdots , b_{40i,j})$ corresponding to the selected rows as 1, others 0. If $i = 50$ stop else set $(z^{i+1}_{18}, \cdots , z^{i+1}_1)$ be the bits in the position range $[18i + 1, 18(i + 1)]$ of $(z_{900,j}, \cdots , z_{1,j})_2 - \sum^i_{f=1}(b_{40f,j}(Y_{40f,j})_2 + \cdots + b_{40(f-1)+1,j}(Y_{40(f-1)+1,j})_2)$.

Complexity of the attack. From the above algorithm, we can recover the jth column vector $(b_{1,j}, \cdots , b_{2000,j})^T$ of B with $O(2^{20})$ operations on average, i.e. absolutely negligible amount of computations on an ordinary PC, and recover the matrix B with $O(2^{31})$ operations.

3.2   Some Remarks

In the algorithm above, we simply choose $2 - 3$ rows out of the 40 rows in order to clearly illustrate the main structure of our attack. In the experiments, we choose 5 rows out of the 40 rows in order to gain a high success probability. The complexity is also very small as shown in Section 4. In addition, we can also use the method above to attack the case that $l = 1000$, $k = 128$ and $2^{899} < M_t N_t < 2^{900}$, the complexity is $O(2^{27})$ if using partition 18×50 and 20×50. From the discussion above, we know that the insecurity of the proposed knapsack based two-lock cryptosystem is due to the sparseness of the columns of Bob's secret matrix B, which facilitates the attack with the growth of l if the partition of Y'_i's binary representations is properly chosen. Increasing the number of '1' bits in each column could enhance the resistance against our attack, but note that the size of the modulus constrains the number of '1' bits in each column. At Alice's side, modular arithmetic is carried out which means that the summation of Y'_is can not be larger than the modulus; otherwise Bob cannot decrypt correctly. So improving the knapsack based two-lock cryptosystem is nearly impossible.

4   Experiment Results

To check the actual performance as well as the correctness of our cracking algorithm, we have implemented our attack against the proposed knapsack based two-lock cryptosystem in C on the Pentium 4 2.5GHz processor. We use the stream cipher RC4 as the random noise source to supply the integers vector $(Y'_1, Y'_2, \cdots , Y'_{2000})$ and the matrix $B = (b_{i,j})_{l \times l}$ where $l = 2000$. Then we simulate the process in the knapsack based two-lock cryptosystem to get the resulting vector $(z_1, z_2, \cdots , z_l)$. After obtaining $(z_1, z_2, \cdots , z_l)$, we apply our attack algorithm proposed in Subsection 3.1 to restore the matrix $B = (b_{i,j})_{l \times l}$ column-by-column. Instead of making an exhaustive search over the 3 out of 40 row vectors of $A^i_{40 \times 18}$ to find out the correct rows, we made an exhaustive search over the 5 out of 40 row vectors to provide a higher success probability. The probability that there are at most five rows to be summed is

$$\frac{\sum_{i=0}^{5} \binom{40}{i}\binom{1960}{128-i}}{\binom{2000}{128}} \approx 0.961156, \tag{5}$$

where $i = 0$ corresponds to the case that $(b_{1,j}, \cdots, b_{40,j})^T$ happens to be a zero vector. In our experiments, there are on average

$$\binom{40}{5}/2^{18} \approx 2.5101, \tag{6}$$

wrong solutions corresponding to each value of $(z^i_{18}, \cdots, z^i_1)$. Actually, there are some columns where our algorithm only output one solution. We select the very solution with the minimum hamming weight. If some solutions have the same hamming weight, we check every possibility until we find the true key or an equivalent key. In our experiment, one 40-bit segment of one column of the secret key B can be recovered in about 3.6 milliseconds on average. We recovered the whole matrix key in about six minutes on the Pentium 4 2.5GHz processor PC. It is equivalent to about $2^{39.8}$ clock cycles. This experiment result is in expectation since the theoretical complexity given in Section 4 is $O(2^{31})$.

5   Conclusion

We have shown that the recently proposed knapsack based two-lock cryptosystem is insecure for oblivious transfers and millionaire protocol applications. It is an interesting problem to design new secure two-lock cryptosystems based on non-discrete logarithm problems.

References

1. F. Bao, R. Deng, P. Feng. An Efficient and Practical Scheme for Privacy Protection in E-commerce of Digital Goods. *2nd International Conference on Information and Communications Security-ICICS'00*, Springer-verlag, pp. 162-170, 2000.
2. E. F. Brickell, A.M.Odlyzko. Cryptanalysis: A Survey of Recent Results, *Proc. IEEE*, Vol.76, pp. 578-593, 1988.
3. W. Diffie. The First Ten Years of Public-Key Cryptography, *Proc. IEEE*, Vol.76, pp. 560-577, 1988.
4. M. R. Garey, D.S. Johnson. *Computers and Intractability: A Guide to the Theory of NP-Completeness*. W. H. Freeman and Company, San Francisco, 1979.
5. R. C. Merkle, M. Hellman. Hiding Information and Signatures in Trapdoor Knapsack. *IEEE Transactions on Information theory*,Vol.24, No.5, pp. 525-530, 1978.
6. M. Rabin. How to Exchange Secrets by Oblivious Transfer, *Technical Report TR 81*, Aiken computation Laboratory, Harvard University, 1981.
7. Q. Wu, J. Zhang, and Y. Wang. Practical t-out-n Oblivious Transfer and Its Applications. *5th International Conference on Information and Communications Security-ICICS'03*, Springer-verlag, 2003, pp.226-237.

Success Probability in χ^2-Attacks

Takashi Matsunaka*, Atsuko Miyaji**, and Yuuki Takano

Japan Advanced Institute of Science and Technology.
{t-matuna, miyaji, ytakano}@jaist.ac.jp

Abstract. Knudsen and Meier applied the χ^*-attack to RC6. This attack is one of the most effective attacks for RC6. The χ^*-attack can be used for both distinguishing attacks and for key recovery attacks. Up to the present, theoretical analysis of χ^*-attacks, especially the relation between a distinguishing attack and a key recovery attack, has not been discussed. In this paper, we investigate the theoretical relation between the distinguishing attack and the key recovery attack for the first time, and prove the theorem to evaluate the success probability of a key recovery attack by using the results of a distinguishing attack. We also demonstrate the accuracy to χ^*-attack on RC5-64 and RC6 without post-whitening by comparing the implemented results.

Keywords: RC6, RC5-64, χ^* attack, statistical analysis

1 Introduction

The χ^2-attack makes use of correlations between input (plaintext) and output (ciphertext), which is measured by the χ^2-test. The χ^2-attack was originally proposed by Vaudenay as an attack on the Data Encryption Standard (DES) [20], and Handschuh et al. applied that to SEAL [6]. The χ^2-attack can be used for both distinguishing attacks and key recovery attacks. Distinguishing attacks have only to handle plaintexts in such a way that the χ^2-value of a part of ciphertexts becomes significantly a high value. On the other hand, key recovery attacks have to rule out all wrong keys, and single out exactly a correct key by using the χ^2-value. Therefore, key recovery attacks often require more work and memory than distinguishing attacks. In [4,12], the χ^2-attacks were applied to RC6 [18] or a simplified variant of RC6. They focused on the fact that a specific rotation in RC6 causes the correlations between input and output, and estimated their key recovery attack by using only results of a distinguishing attack [4,12,16]. Note that their key recovery attack on RC6 with any round was not implemented because it required too much memory even in the case of small number of rounds. In [5], a key recovery attack on RC5-32 [17] by using the χ^2-attack was proposed. RC5-$w/r/b$ means that two w-bit-word plaintexts are encrypted with r rounds by b-byte keys. The χ^2-attack to RC5-32 was further improved by [15]. Their attack can analyze RC5-32 with 10 rounds by a known

---

* The author is currently with KDDI.
** Supported by Inamori Foundation.

M. Jakobsson, M. Yung, J. Zhou (Eds.): ACNS 2004, LNCS 3089, pp. 310–325, 2004.

plaintext attack with negligible memory. They also pointed out the significant difference between the distinguishing attack and the key recovery attack: The distinguishing attack succeeds if and only if it outputs high χ^2-value, but the key recovery attack does not necessarily succeed even if it outputs high χ^2-value. In fact, a key recovery attack to RC5-32 in [5] outputs higher χ^2-value but recovers a correct key with lower probability than that in [15]. This indicates that the security against the key recovery attack cannot be estimated directly from that against the distinguishing attack. The χ^2-attack to a simplified variant of RC6 are further improved in [16,7], which can work on 4-round simplified variants of RC6.

However, up to the present, any theoretical difference between a distinguishing attack and a key recovery attack in χ^2-attack has not been discussed. Although the theoretical and experimental complexity analysis on the linear cryptanalysis is done by P. Junod in [8], it cannot be applied to the χ^2-attack. His analysis is further generalized by using the normal approximation for order statistics in [19]. However, it is not so sharp or suitable for χ^2-attack.

In this paper, we investigate the theoretical relation between a distinguishing attack and a key recovery attack in χ^2-attack, for the first time, and give the theorem that evaluates the success probability of a key recovery attack by using results of a distinguishing attack. We demonstrate the theorem on a key recovery algorithm against RC5-64, which is given by us, and make sure the accuracy by comparing our approximation to implemented results. We also demonstrate the accuracy to the χ^2-attack against RC6 without post-whitening [7]. As a result, we are able, with our theory, to evaluate the security of key recovery attack in χ^2-attack with less number of plaintexts than expected. We also compare our theory with [19] by applying them on RC5-64 and RC6P, and show our theory is more accurate and more suitable for approximation of χ^2-attack.

This paper is organized as follows. Section 2 summarizes the notation, RC5-64 and RC6 algorithms, the χ^2-test, and statistical facts used in this paper. Section 3 gives the theory of success probability in χ^2-attack and investigates the accuracy by comparing the approximations of success probability to 3-round and 4-round RC5-64 and implemented results. Section 4 applies our theorem to a key recovery algorithm on RC6 without post-whitening. The accuracy of our approximation theorem is compared with that of [19] in Section 5. Conclusion is given in Section 6.

2 Preliminaries

We summarize RC5-64 and RC6 algorithms, the χ^2-test, and statistical facts used in this paper.

2.1 Block Cipher RC5-64

Before showing the encryption algorithm of RC5-64, we give some notation.

$\oplus$: bit-wise exclusive OR;

r: number of rounds ;

$a \lll b$: cyclic rotation of a to the left by b-bit;

$a \ggg b$: cyclic rotation of a to the right by b-bit;

(L_i, R_i): input of the i-th round, (L_0, R_0) and (L_{r+1}, R_{r+1}) are a plaintext and a ciphertext after r-round encryption, respectively;

S_i : i-th subkey (S_{2i} and S_{2i+1} are subkeys of the i-th round);

$\mathrm{lsb}_n(X)$: least significant n-bit of X;

$X[i]$: i-th bit of X.

The encryption algorithm of RC5-64 is reviewed as follows: a plaintext (L_0, R_0) is added with (S_0, S_1) and set to (L_1, R_1); and (L_1, R_1) is encrypted to (L_{r+1}, R_{r+1}) by r iterations of a main loop. The detailed algorithm is given:

Algorithm 1 (RC5-64 Encryption Algorithm)
1. $L_1 = L_0 + S_0$; $R_1 = R_0 + S_1$;
2. for $i = 1$ to r do: $L_{i+1} = ((L_i \oplus R_i) \lll R_i) + S_{2i})$.
   $R_{i+1} = ((R_i \oplus L_{i+1}) \lll L_{i+1}) + S_{2i+1})$.

Two rotations by R_i or L_{i+1} in i-th round are called by first rotation or second rotation, respectively.

2.2 Block Cipher RC6

In addition to notation used in RC5-64, we use the following notation.

(A_i, B_i, C_i, D_i) : input of the i-th round;

(A_0, B_0, C_0, D_0) : plaintext;

$\mathrm{msb}_n(X)$: most significant n-bit of X;

$f(x)$: $x \times (2x + 1)$;

$F(x)$: $f(x) \pmod{2^{32}} \lll 5$;

$x \| y$: concatenated value of x and y.

The detailed algorithm of RC6 is given:

Algorithm 2 (RC6 Encryption Algorithm)
1. $A_{\cdot} = A_{\cdot}$; $B_{\cdot} = B_{\cdot} + S_{\cdot}$; $C_{\cdot} = C_{\cdot}$; $D_{\cdot} = D_{\cdot} + S_{\cdot}$;
2. for $i = 1$ to r do: $t = F(B_i)$; $u = F(D_i)$; $A_{i \cdot \cdot} = B_i$;
   $B_{i \cdot \cdot} = ((C_i \oplus u) \lll t) + S_{\cdot i \cdot \cdot}$; $C_{i \cdot \cdot} = D_i$; $D_{i \cdot \cdot} = ((A_i \oplus t) \lll u) + S_{\cdot i}$;
3. $A_{r \cdot \cdot} = A_{r \cdot \cdot} + S_{\cdot r \cdot \cdot}$; $B_{r \cdot \cdot} = B_{r \cdot \cdot}$; $C_{r \cdot \cdot} = C_{r \cdot \cdot} + S_{\cdot r \cdot \cdot}$; $D_{r \cdot \cdot} = D_{r \cdot \cdot \cdot}$.

Parts 1 and 3 of Algorithm 2 are called pre-whitening and post-whitening, respectively. We call the version of RC6 without post-whitening to, simply, RC6P.

2.3 χ^2-Test

We make use of the χ^2-tests to distinguish a non-uniformly random distribution from uniformly random distribution [10,12,13]. Let $X = X_0, ..., X_{n-1}$ be sets of $\{a_0, ..., a_{m-1}\}$, and $N_{a_j}(X)$ be the number of X which takes on the value a_j.

The χ^2-statistic of X which estimates the difference between X and the uniform distribution is defined as follows:

$$\chi^2(X) = \frac{m}{n} \sum_{i=0}^{m-1} \left(N_{a_i}(X) - \frac{n}{m}\right)^2.$$

Table 1 presents each threshold for 63 degrees of freedom. For example, (level, χ^2) = (0.95, 82.53) in Table 1 means that the value of the χ^2-statistic exceeds 82.53 in the probability of 5%, if the observation X is uniform.

Table 1. χ^*-distribution with 63 degrees of freedom

Level	0.50	0.60	0.70	0.80	0.90	0.95	0.99
χ^*	62.33	65.20	68.37	72.20	77.75	82.53	92.01

2.4 Statistical Facts

Let us describe statistical facts together with the notation.

Theorem 1 (Distribution of the Means [3]). *Let μ and σ^2 be the mean and the variance of a population, respectively. Then the mean and the variance of the distribution of the mean of a random sample with the size n drawn from the population are μ and σ^2/n, respectively.*

Theorem 2 (Central Limit Theorem [3]). *Choose a random sample from a population. If the sample size n is large, then the sampling distribution of the mean is closely approximated by the normal distribution, regardless of the population.*

Theorem 3 (Law of large numbers [3]). *The larger the sample size, the more probable it is that the sample mean comes arbitrarily close to the population mean.*

The probability density function of the normal distribution with the mean μ and the variance σ^2 is given by the following equation,

$$\phi_{(\mu,\sigma^2)}(x) = \frac{1}{\sqrt{2\pi\sigma^2}} exp\left[-\frac{(x-\mu)^2}{2\sigma^2}\right].$$

We also follow commonly used notation: the probability density and the cumulative distribution functions of the standard normal distribution are denoted by $\phi(x)$ and $\Phi(x)$; the probability of distribution X in the range $X \leq I$ is denoted by $\Pr(X \leq I)$; and $\mathcal{N}$ is used for the normal distributions.

3   Theoretical Analysis on χ^2-Attacks

This section presents the theorem of success probability in χ^2-attack, where we use a key recovery algorithm to RC5-64 based on [15].

3.1   Key Recovery Algorithm of RC5-64

The following algorithm recovers the least significant five bits of S_{2r+1}. Let us set $(x, y) = (\mathrm{lsb}_6(L_{r+1}), \mathrm{lsb}_6(R_{r+1}))$, $s = \mathrm{lsb}_5(S_{2r+1})(s = 0, 1, \cdots, 2^5 - 1)$, and $S_{2r+1}[6] = 0$, where x corresponds to the rotation amount in the r-th round.

Algorithm 3
1. Choose a plaintext (L_0, R_0) with $\mathrm{lsb}_6(R_0)$=0, and encrypt it.
2. For each s, decrypt a 6-bit y with a key $S_{2r+1}[6]\|s$ by 1 round to
    a 6-bit z.
3. For each value s, x, and z, update each array by incrementing count$[s][x][z]$.
4. For each s and x, compute $\chi^2[s][x]$.
5. Compute the average $ave[s]$ of $\{\chi^2[s][x]\}_x$ for each s and output s with
    the highest $ave[s]$ as $\mathrm{lsb}_5(S_{r+1})$.

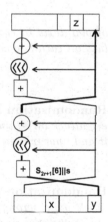

Fig. 1. Algorithm 3

Figure 1 shows the outline of Algorithm 3. Algorithm 3 averages the χ^2-values $\chi^2[s][x]$ by second rotation amount x in the r-th round, in which there are 2^6 rotations.

3.2   Statistical Analysis of χ^2-Attacks

We show the theorem on the success probability of Algorithm 3 by investigating the distribution of χ^2-values for a correct key and wrong keys.

Notation. Let us use the following notation.

- e : recovered-key bit size (There are one correct key and $2^e - 1$ wrong keys.);
- P_S : success probability of a key recovery attack;
- $X_{d[r,n]}$: distributions of χ^2-values on $\text{lsb}_6(R_{r+1})$ of RC5-64 with $\text{lsb}_6(R_0) = 0$ by using 2^n plaintexts;
- $\mu_{d[r,n]}$ $(\sigma^2_{d[r,n]})$: mean (variance) of distribution of χ^2-values on $\text{lsb}_6(R_{r+1})$ of RC5-64 with $\text{lsb}_6(R_0) = 0$ by using 2^n plaintexts;
- $X_{c[r,n]}$ $(X_{w[r,n]})$: distributions of χ^2-values of a key recovery attack to r-round RC5-64 by using a correct key (a wrong key);
- $\mu_{c[r,n]}$ $(\sigma^2_{c[r,n]})$: mean (variance) of distribution of mean of χ^2-values of a key recovery attack in r-round RC5-64 with a correct key by using 2^n plaintexts;
- $f_{c[r,n]}(x)$: probability density function of distribution of χ^2-values with a correct key in r-round RC5-64;
- μ_w (σ^2_w) : mean (variance) of distribution of χ^2-values in a key recovery attack r-round RC5-64 with a wrong key;
- $f_{w[r,n]}(x)$: probability density function of distribution of χ^2-values with a wrong key in r-round RC5-64.

Distributions of χ^2-values. In this section, we put forward three hypotheses on distribution of χ^2-values.

Hypothesis 1 *If the number of plaintexts to compute the χ^2-values is enough large, then the sample of χ^2-values on each key candidate approximately follows a normal distribution.*

Hypothesis 2 (Wrong-Key Randomization Hypothesis 1) *Each distribution of χ^2-values of key-recovery attack on i-th wrong key $X_{w(1)[r,n]}$, $X_{w(2)[r,n]}$, $\cdots$, $X_{w(2^e-1)[r,n]}$ is independent and approximately equal to each other.*

Hypothesis 3 (Wrong-Key Randomization Hypothesis 2) *Distribution of χ^2-values of key-recovery attack on a wrong key $X_{w[r,n]}$ is approximately equal to that of $X_{d[r,n']}$, where n' is the real number of plaintexts that is used for computing χ^2-value of $X_{w[r,n]}$.*

Hypotheses 1 and 2 are simple and natural, which are often used in a statistical analysis of the security, including the differential and linear attack as in [8, 19]. On the other hand, Hypothesis 3 means that the distribution of χ^2-values recovered by using a wrong key is approximately equal to that before recovering. This is considered as a variant of Hypothesis 2, which means that a wrong key randomizes data. We note here that Hypothesis 3 is the ideal case for an attacker, and, thus, the results can be seen as an upper bound for the actual success probability. It also reflects experimental results in [7].

Success probability of χ^2-attacks. We show the theorem on the success probability of Algorithm 3 by investigating the distribution of χ^2-values for a correct key and wrong keys. We may note that χ^2-attacks compute the χ^2-value on a part for every key candidate and output a key with the highest χ^2-value as a correct key.

Lemma 1. *Let $n \geq 6$ and $r \geq 4$. The distribution of χ^2-values on a correct key in Algorithm 3, $X_{c[r,n]}$, follows a normal distribution of $\mathcal{N}(\mu_{d[r-1,n-6]}, \sigma^2_{d[r-1,n-6]}/2^6)$. Therefore, the probability density function of distribution of χ^2-values on a correct key in Algorithm 3, $f_{c[r,n]}(x)$, is given by*

$$f_{c[r,n]}(x) = \phi_{(\mu_{d[r-1,n-6]}, \sigma^2_{d[r-1,n-6]}/2^6)}(x).$$

Proof. The distribution $X_{c[r,n]}$ follows a normal distribution from Hypothesis 1. When a correct key is used in Algorithms 3, six-bit data $\mathrm{lsb}_6(R_{r+1})$ is decrypted correctly by 1 round. χ^2-values are computed for every second rotation in r-th round, where each rotation amount is uniformly distributed on 2^n plaintexts. As a result, the χ^2-values in Algorithm 3 is computed by using roughly 2^{n-6} plaintexts. Putting together the facts and Theorem 1, the distribution $X_{c[r,n]}$ follows a normal distribution $\mathcal{N}(\mu_{d[r-1,n-6]}, \sigma^2_{d[r-1,n-6]}/2^6)$. Thus, we get

$$f_{c[r,n]}(x) = \phi_{(\mu_{d[r-1,n-6]}, \sigma^2_{d[r-1,n-6]}/2^6)}(x).$$

Lemma 2. *Let $n \geq 6$ and $r \geq 4$. The distribution of χ^2-values on a wrong key in Algorithm 3, $X_{w[r,n]}$, follows a normal distribution of $\mathcal{N}(\mu_{d[r,n-6]}, \sigma^2_{d[r,n-6]}/2^6)$. Therefore, the probability density function of distribution of χ^2-values on a wrong key in Algorithm 3, $f_{w[r,n]}(x)$, is given by*

$$f_{w[r,n]}(x) = \phi_{(\mu_{d[r,n-6]}, \sigma^2_{d[r,n-6]}/2^6)}(x).$$

Proof. The distribution $X_{w[r,n]}$ follows a normal distribution $\mathcal{N}(\mu_{d[r,n']}, \sigma^2_{d[r,n']})$ from Hypotheses 1 and 3. Here, n' is the real number of plaintexts that is used for computing χ^2-value of $X_{w[r,n]}$. In the same discussion as Lemma 1, χ^2-values are computed for every second rotation amount in r-th round, which is uniformly distributed on 2^n plaintexts. As a result, the χ^2-values in Algorithm 3 is computed by using roughly 2^{n-6} plaintexts. Putting together the facts and Theorem 1, the distribution $X_{w[r,n]}$ follows a normal distribution $\mathcal{N}(\mu_{d[r,n-6]}, \sigma^2_{d[r,n-6]}/2^6)$. Thus, we get

$$f_{w[r,n]}(x) = \phi_{(\mu_{d[r,n-6]}, \sigma^2_{d[r,n-6]}/2^6)}(x).$$

Using the above preparations, the success probability of the key recovery attack on χ^2-attack is evaluated as follows.

Theorem 4. *The success probability P_S of e-bit key recovery algorithm to r-round RC5-64 with 2^n plaintexts can be evaluated by using $f_{c[r,n]}(x)$ and $f_{w[r,n]}(x)$ as follows,*

$$P_S = \int_{-\infty}^{\infty} f_{c[r,n]}(x) * \left(\int_{-\infty}^{x} f_{w[r,n]}(u)du \right)^{2^e - 1} dx.$$

Proof. The e-bit key can be recovered correctly if and only if the χ^2-value of a correct key is higher than that of all $2^e - 1$ wrong keys. This means that the key recovery algorithm to r-round RC5-64 with 2^n plaintexts succeeds if and only if

$$X_{c[r,n]} > X_{w[r,n]} \ (\forall w).$$

From Hypothesis 2, any distribution on wrong keys is independent and approximately equal to each other, which is denoted by $X_{w[r,n]}$. Thus, the success probability P_S can be evaluated by

$$P_S = \Pr(X_{c[r,n]} > X_{w[r,n]})^{2^e - 1}$$

$$= \int_{-\infty}^{\infty} f_c(x) * \left(\int_{-\infty}^{x} f_w(u) du \right)^{2^e - 1} dx.$$

Theorem 5. *The success probability P_S of e-bit key recovery algorithm to r-round RC5-64 with 2^n plaintexts can be evaluated by using the distributions of χ^2-values in the distinguishing algorithm as follows,*

$$P_S = \int_{-\infty}^{\infty} \phi_{(\mu_{d[r-1,n-6]}, \sigma_{d[r-1,n-6]}^2 / 2^6)}(x) * \left(\int_{-\infty}^{x} \phi_{(\mu_{d[r,n-6]}, \sigma_{d[r,n-6]}^2 / 2^6)}(u) du \right)^{2^e - 1} dx$$

Proof. Theorem 5 follows immediately from Lemmas 1 and 2 and Theorem 4.

Theorem 5 indicates the following two factors for high success probability.

- **(Factor 1)** Maximize the average of χ^2-values computed by a correct key;
- **(Factor 2)** Minimize the variances (the error) of each distribution of χ^2-values computed by each key.

3.3   Accuracy of the Approximations of the Security on RC5-64

We estimate the success probability of Algorithm 3 by using Theorem 5. In the beginning, we conduct the following distinguishing test on 2 - 4 rounds and get the distribution of χ^2-values on $\mathrm{lsb}_6(R_{h+1})$, $X_{d[r,n]}$. Our experiments use 100 kinds of plaintexts and 100 keys and, thus, conduct 10000 trials in total.

Distinguishing Test: The χ^2-test on $\mathrm{lsb}_6(R_{h+1})$ with $\mathrm{lsb}_6(R_0) = 0$.

The experimental results are shown in Table 2.

The success probability of Algorithm 3 to RC5-64, based on Theorem 5, is computed on Table 3. To evaluate the estimation, we also implement Algorithm 3 on 2-round and 3-round RC5-64. Our implementations generate all plaintexts by using M-sequence: Algorithm 3 uses 122-bit random numbers generated by M-sequence, whose primitive polynomial of M-sequence is $x^{122} + x^{108} + x^8 + x + 1$. The platform is IBM RS/6000 SP (PPC 604e/332MHz $\times$ 256) with memory of 32 GB. Table 3 shows the implemented results among 100 keys for RC5-64 with 3 - 4 rounds. Comparing the estimation with the implemented results, we see that our theory can evaluate the success probability of key recovery algorithm of χ^2-attack. Furthermore, the necessary number of plaintexts for this evaluation is reduced by 2^6 from that of Table 3. In summary, our theory can evaluate the success probability in χ^2-attack by using less number of plaintexts.

Table 2. Mean and variance for $X_{d\cdot r,n\cdot}$. ($r = 2, 3, 4$, 10000 trials)

#texts	mean $\mu_{d\cdot r,n\cdot}$ (variance $\sigma_{d\cdot r,n\cdot}$)		
	2 rounds	3 rounds	4 rounds
$2^{\cdot\cdot}$	63.41 (125.83)	63.02 (126.76)	–
$2^{\cdot\cdot}$	63.40 (130.56)	62.91 (125.31)	–
$2^{\cdot\cdot}$	64.03 (132.04)	62.96 (125.09)	–
$2^{\cdot\cdot}$	64.80 (139.10)	62.91 (123.37)	–
$2^{\cdot\cdot}$	66.63 (149.53)	62.97 (125.71)	–
$2^{\cdot\cdot}$	70.02 (178.01)	62.83 (124.80)	–
$2^{\cdot\cdot}$	–	63.09 (124.31)	62.84 (123.69)
$2^{\cdot\cdot}$	–	63.41 (126.33)	62.99 (123.79)
$2^{\cdot\cdot}$	–	63.68 (125.68)	63.01 (122.39)
$2^{\cdot\cdot}$	–	64.39 (130.16)	63.18 (124.95)
$2^{\cdot\cdot}$	–	66.11 (135.60)	63.06 (122.94)
$2^{\cdot\cdot}$	–	69.22 (152.86)	63.05 (124.57)
$2^{\cdot\cdot}$	–	75.43 (174.06)	63.23 (124.58)

Table 3. Comparison of theoretical and implemented results in Algorithm 3

3 rounds				
theoretical results: mean (variance)				implemented results
#texts	correct key	wrong key	P_S	SUC
$2^{\cdot\cdot}$	64.03 (2.06)	62.96 (1.95)	0.128	0.15
$2^{\cdot\cdot}$	64.80 (2.17)	62.91 (1.93)	0.277	0.36
$2^{\cdot\cdot}$	66.63 (2.34)	62.97 (1.96)	0.683	0.62
$2^{\cdot\cdot}$	70.02 (2.78)	62.83 (1.95)	0.991	0.92
4 rounds				
theoretical results: mean (variance)				implemented results
#texts	correct key	wrong key	P_S	SUC
$2^{\cdot\cdot}$	64.68 (1.96)	63.01 (1.91)	0.080	0.09
$2^{\cdot\cdot}$	66.11 (2.12)	63.06 (1.92)	0.552	0.53
$2^{\cdot\cdot}$	69.22 (2.39)	63.05 (1.95)	0.973	0.89
$2^{\cdot\cdot}$	75.43 (2.72)	63.23 (1.95)	1.000	1.000

SUC: the probability of recovered keys in 100 keys

4   Theoretical Analysis on $\chi^{\cdot}$-Attacks to RC6 without Post-whitening

We apply Theorem 5 to a key recovery algorithm on RC6P [7] and investigate the accuracy of approximations by comparing it with implemented results.

4.1   Key Recovery Algorithm of RC6P

Intuitively, a key recovery algorithm [7] fixes some bits out of $\mathrm{lsb}_n(B_0)||\mathrm{lsb}_n(D_0)$, check the χ^2-value of $\mathrm{lsb}_3(A_r)||\mathrm{lsb}_3(C_r)$, and recover $\mathrm{lsb}_2(S_{2r})||\mathrm{lsb}_2(S_{2r+1})$

of r-round RC6P. Here we use the following notation: $(y_b, y_d) = (\mathrm{lsb}_3(B_{r+1}), \mathrm{lsb}_3(D_{r+1}))$, $(x_c, x_a) = (\mathrm{lsb}_5(F(A_{r+1})), \mathrm{lsb}_5(F(C_{r+1})))$, $(s_a, s_c) = (\mathrm{lsb}_2(S_{2r}), \mathrm{lsb}_2(S_{2r+1}))$, $s = s_a || s_c$, and $(S_{2r}[3], S_{2r+1}[3]) = (0, 0)$, where x_a (resp. x_c) is the rotation amounts on A_r (resp. C_r) in the r-th round.

Algorithm 4 ([7])

1. Choose a plaintext (A_0, B_0, C_0, D_0) with $(\mathrm{lsb}_5(B_0), \mathrm{lsb}_5(D_0)) = (0, 0)$ and encrypt it.
2. For each (s_a, s_c), decrypt $y_d || y_b$ with a key $(S_{2r}[3] || s_a, S_{2r+1}[3] || s_c)$ by 1 round
   to $z_a || z_c$, which are denoted by a 6-bit integer $z = z_a || z_c$.
3. For each s, x_a, x_c, and z, update each array by incrementing $\mathrm{count}[s][x_a][x_c][z]$.
4. For each s, x_a, and x_c, compute $\chi^2[s][x_a][x_c]$.
5. Compute the average $ave[s]$ of $\{\chi^2[s][x_a][x_c]\}_{x_a, x_c}$ for each s and output
   s with the highest $ave[s]$ as $\mathrm{lsb}_2(S_{2r}) || \mathrm{lsb}_2(S_{2r+1})$.

Figure 2 shows the outline of Algorithm 4.

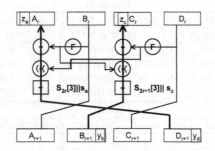

Fig. 2. Algorithm 4

4.2 Success Probability of Algorithm 4

By applying Lemmas 1 and 2 and Theorem 4 to Algorithm 4, we get the theorem of success probability on RC6P. Before showing the theorem, we give some notation, which has the same meaning as that in Section 3.2.

- e : recovered-key bit size (There are one correct key and $2^e - 1$ wrong keys.);
- P_S : success probability of a key recovery attack;
- $X_{d[r,n]}$: distributions of χ^2-values on $\mathrm{lsb}_3(A_{r+1}) || \mathrm{lsb}_3(C_{r+1})$ of RC6P with $\mathrm{lsb}_5(B_0) || \mathrm{lsb}_5(D_0) = 0$ by using 2^n plaintexts;
- $\mu_{d[r,n]}$ $(\sigma^2_{d[r,n]})$: mean (variance) of distribution of χ^2-values on $\mathrm{lsb}_3(A_{r+1}) || \mathrm{lsb}_3(C_{r+1})$ of RC6 with $\mathrm{lsb}_5(B_0) || \mathrm{lsb}_5(D_0) = 0$ by using 2^n plaintexts;

- $X_{c[r,n]}$ $(X_{w[r,n]})$: distributions of χ^2-values of a key recovery attack to r-round RC6P by using a correct key (a wrong key);
- $\mu_{c[r,n]}$ $(\sigma^2_{c[r,n]})$: mean (variance) of distribution of mean of χ^2-values of a key recovery attack to r-round RC6P with a correct key by using 2^n plaintexts;
- $f_{c[r,n]}(x)$: probability density function of distribution of χ^2-values with a correct key in r-round RC6P;
- μ_w (σ^2_w) : mean (variance) of distribution of χ^2-values in a key recovery attack to r-round RC6P with a wrong key;
- $f_{w[r,n]}(x)$: probability density function of distribution of χ^2-values with a wrong key in r-round RC6P.

By assuming three hypotheses on wrong-key distribution in Section 3.2, we get the following lemmas and a theorem in the same way as those of RC5-64. The detailed proof will be given in the final version.

Lemma 3. *Let $n \geq 10$ and $r \geq 4$. The distribution of χ^2-values on a correct key in Algorithm 4, $X_{c[r,n]}$, follows a normal distribution of $\mathcal{N}(\mu_{d[r-1,n-10]}, \sigma^2_{d[r-1,n-10]}/2^{10})$. Therefore, the probability density function of distribution of χ^2-values with a correct key in Algorithm 4, $f_{c[r,n]}(x)$, is given by*

$$f_{c[r,n]}(x) = \phi_{(\mu_{d[r-1,n-10]}, \sigma^2_{d[r-1,n-10]}/2^{10})}(x).$$

Lemma 4. *Let $n \geq 10$ and $r \geq 4$. The distribution of χ^2-values on a wrong key in Algorithm 4, $X_{w[r,n]}$, follows a normal distribution of $\mathcal{N}(\mu_{d[r+1,n-10]}, \sigma^2_{d[r+1,n-10]}/2^{10})$. Therefore, the probability density function of distribution of χ^2-values with a correct key in Algorithm 4, $f_{w[r,n]}(x)$, is given by*

$$f_{w[r,n]}(x) = \phi_{(\mu_{d[r+1,n-10]}, \sigma^2_{d[r+1,n-10]}/2^{10})}(x).$$

Lemma 4 is derived from Hypothesis 3. In the case of Algorithm 4, $X_{d[r,n']}$ defined in Algorithm 3 of Hypothesis 3 corresponds to the distributions of χ^2-values on $\mathrm{lsb}_3(B_{r+1})||\mathrm{lsb}_3(D_{r+1}))$, which are equal to that on $\mathrm{lsb}_3(A_{r+2})||\mathrm{lsb}_3(C_{r+2})$ and thus it corresponds to $X_{d[r+1,n']}$ defined in Algorithm 4.

Theorem 6. *The success probability P_S of e-bit key recovery algorithm to r-round RC6P with 2^n plaintexts can be evaluated by using the distributions of χ^2-values in the distinguishing algorithm as follows,*

$$P_S = \int_{-\infty}^{\infty} \phi_{(\mu_{d[r-1,n-10]}, \sigma^2_{d[r-1,n-10]}/2^{10})}(x) * \left(\int_{-\infty}^{x} \phi_{(\mu_{d[r+1,n-10]}, \sigma^2_{d[r+1,n-10]}/2^{10})}(u)du \right)^{2^e-1} d$$

4.3 Accuracy of the Approximations of the Security on RC6P

We estimate the success probability of Algorithm 4 by using Theorem 6. In the beginning, we conduct the following distinguishing test on 3 and 5 rounds and get the distribution of χ^2-values on $\mathrm{lsb}_3(A_{r+1})\|\mathrm{lsb}_3(C_{r+1})$, $X_{d[r,n]}$. Our experiments use 100 kinds of plaintexts and 100 keys and thus conduct 10000 trials in total.

Distinguishing Test:
The χ^2-test on $\mathrm{lsb}_3(A_{r+1})\|\mathrm{lsb}_3(C_{r+1})$ with $\mathrm{lsb}_3(B_0)\|\mathrm{lsb}_3(D_0) = 0$.

The experimental results are shown in Table 4.

Table 4. Mean and variance for $X_{d \cdot r, n \cdot}$. ($r = 3, 5$, 10000 trials)

	mean $\mu_{d \cdot r, n \cdot}$ (variance $\sigma_{d \cdot r, n \cdot}$)	
#texts	3 rounds	5 rounds
$2^{\cdot}$	63.03(124.25)	63.02(123.82)
$2^{\cdot}$	63.05(125.25)	63.02(125.06)
$2^{\cdot}$	63.12(125.92)	62.99(125.47)
$2^{\cdot}$	63.26(126.89)	63.01(125.82)
$2^{\cdot \cdot}$	63.51(128.07)	63.02(125.97)
$2^{\cdot \cdot}$	64.08(130.62)	62.99(125.97)
$2^{\cdot \cdot}$	65.17(135.41)	63.00(125.98)

The success probability of Algorithm 4 to RC6P, based on Theorem 6, is computed on Table 5. To evaluate the estimation, we implement Algorithm 4 on 4-round RC6P. Our implementations generate all plaintexts by using M-sequence: Algorithm 4 uses 118-bit random numbers generated by M-sequence, whose primitive polynomial of M-sequence is $x^{118}+x^{36}+x^8+x+1$. The platform is the same as that in Section 3.3. Table 5 also shows implemented results among 100 keys for 4-round RC6P. Comparing the estimation with implemented results, we see that our theorem can evaluate the success probability of key recovery algorithm of χ^2-attack. Furthermore, the necessary number of plaintexts for this evaluation is reduced by 2^{10} from that of Table 5. In summary, our theory can also evaluate the success probability in χ^2-attack by using less number of plaintexts.

Table 5. Comparison of theoretical and implemented results in Algorithm 4 to 4-round RC6P

	theoretical results: mean (variance)			implemented results
#texts	correct key	wrong key	P_S	SUC
$2^{\cdot \cdot}$	63.12(0.123)	62.99(0.123)	0.111	0.11
$2^{\cdot \cdot}$	63.26(0.124)	63.01(0.123)	0.185	0.15
$2^{\cdot \cdot}$	63.51(0.125)	63.02(0.123)	0.388	0.40
$2^{\cdot \cdot}$	64.08(0.128)	62.99(0.123)	0.882	0.75
$2^{\cdot \cdot}$	65.17(0.132)	63.00(0.123)	1.000	1.00

SUC: the probability of recovered keys in 100 keys

Table 6. Mean and variance for $X_{d\cdot r,n\cdot}$ ($r = 5, 7$, 10000 trials)

#texts	mean $\mu_{d\cdot r,n\cdot}$ (variance $\sigma_{d\cdot r,n\cdot}$)	
	5 rounds	7 rounds
$2^{\cdot\cdot}$	63.3060(128.796)	63.0142(126.729)
$2^{\cdot\cdot}$	63.3729(126.632)	63.0180(126.843)
$2^{\cdot\cdot}$	63.7322(129.106)	62.8563(126.375)
$2^{\cdot\cdot}$	64.4361(132.361)	62.8587(126.070)
$2^{\cdot\cdot}$	66.0068(141.824)	63.1763(124.279)

Table 7. Approximations of the security on 6-round RC6P

#texts	correct key	wrong key	P_S
$2^{\cdot\cdot}$	63.31(0.126)	63.01(0.124)	0.215
$2^{\cdot\cdot}$	63.37(0.124)	63.02(0.124)	0.263
$2^{\cdot\cdot}$	63.73(0.126)	62.86(0.123)	0.747
$2^{\cdot\cdot}$	64.44(0.129)	62.86(0.123)	0.990
$2^{\cdot\cdot}$	66.01(0.139)	62.86(0.123)	1.000

SUC: the probability of recovered keys in 100 keys

Table 8. Comparison between Theorems 5 and 7 in the accuracy on to RC5-64

#texts	Theorem 5		Theorem 7		SUC
	P_S	error rates	P_{Sel}	error rates	
$2^{\cdot\cdot}$	0.128	15%	0.252	68%	0.15
$2^{\cdot\cdot}$	0.277	23%	0.441	23%	0.36
$2^{\cdot\cdot}$	0.683	10%	0.815	31%	0.62
$2^{\cdot\cdot}$	0.991	8%	0.997	8%	0.92
#texts	Theorem 5		Theorem 7		SUC
	P_S	error rates	P_{Sel}	error rates	
$2^{\cdot\cdot}$	0.080	11%	0.387	330%	0.09
$2^{\cdot\cdot}$	0.552	4%	0.716	35%	0.53
$2^{\cdot\cdot}$	0.973	9%	0.991	11%	0.89
$2^{\cdot\cdot}$	1.000	0%	1.000	0%	1.000

SUC: the probability of recovered keys in 100 keys (implemented results)

4.4   Approximations of the Security on 6-Round RC6P

By using Theorem 6, we can estimate the security on 6-round RC6P theoretically although it is not easy to compute experimentally. The experimental results of distinguishing test on 5- and 7-round RC6P are shown in Table 6. The approximation of the security on 6-round RC6P is shown in Table 7. The results indicate that a correct key on 6-round RC6P can be recovered by using 2^{16} times as many texts as those on 4-round RC6P, which reflects the estimation of security of RC6 or RC6P [11,7].

Table 9. Comparison between Theorems 5 and 7 in the accuracy on to 4-round RC6P

#texts	Theorem 5		Theorem 7		SUC
	P_S	error rates	P_{Sel}	error rates	
$2^{\cdot\cdot}$	0.111	0.9%	0.150	36%	0.11
$2^{\cdot\cdot}$	0.185	23%	0.233	55%	0.15
$2^{\cdot\cdot}$	0.388	3%	0.452	13%	0.40
$2^{\cdot\cdot}$	0.882	18%	0.916	22%	0.75
$2^{\cdot\cdot}$	1.000	0%	1.000	0%	1.00
$2^{\cdot\cdot\cdot\cdot}$	0.889	16%	0.922	20%	0.768
$2^{\cdot\cdot\cdot\cdot}$	0.921	12%	0.947	16%	0.817
$2^{\cdot\cdot\cdot\cdot}$	0.946	12%	0.966	14%	0.846
$2^{\cdot\cdot\cdot\cdot}$	0.966	8%	0.980	9%	0.896
$2^{\cdot\cdot\cdot\cdot}$	0.979	7%	0.989	8%	0.919

SUC: the probability of recovered keys in 100 or 1000 keys (implemented results)

5   Comparison of Approximation Theorems of χ^2-Attack

Another approximation of success probability was proposed in [19]. It is based on order statistics and applied to differential and linear attack. Although it is also applicable to χ^2-attack, the accuracy has not been reported yet. From the point of view of accuracy of success probability in χ^2-attack, we compare our theory to [19].

5.1   Success Probability Based on Order Statistic

The main idea of an analysis based on order statistics is as follows:

1. distributions of a correct key follows a normal distribution;
2. distributions of wrong keys are sorted in increasing order;
3. the highest distribution of wrong keys follows a normal distribution;
4. the success probability is computed as the probability that the distribution of correct key is greater than the highest distribution of wrong keys.

We may note that assumptions on distributions of a correct key and a wrong key is the same as those in Section 3.2. When we apply an analysis of order statistics to e-bit key recovery on RC5-64 or RC6P, the success probability is computed as follows:

1. distributions of a correct key follows a normal distribution $\mathcal{N}(\mu_{c[r,n]}, \sigma^2_{c[r,n]})$;
2. distributions of wrong keys are sorted in increasing order, $X_{w(1)[r,n]}, \cdots, X_{w(2^e-1)[r,n]}$;
3. the highest distribution $X_{w(2^e-1)[r,n]}$ are assumed to follow a normal distribution $\mathcal{N}(\mu_{[r,n]}, \sigma^2_{[r,n]})$, where the average and the variance are given as:

$$\mu_{[r,n]} = \mu_{w[r,n]} + \sigma_{w[r,n]}\Phi^{-1}(1 - 2^{-e}) \text{ and } \sigma_{[r,n]} = \frac{\sigma_{w[r,n]}}{\phi(\Phi^{-1}(1 - 2^{-e}))}2^{-e}.$$

Then, the success probability is computed as the probability that the distribution of correct key is greater than the highest distribution of wrong keys as follows:

Theorem 7 ([19]). *The success probability P_{Sel} of e-bit key recovery algorithm can be evaluated by using the distributions of χ^2-values in the distinguishing algorithm as follows*

$$P_{Sel} = \int_{-\frac{\mu_{c[r,n]} - \mu_{[r,n]}}{\sqrt{\sigma_c^2[r,n] + \sigma_{[r,n]}^2}}}^{\infty} \phi(x)dx,$$

where

$$\mu_{[r,n]} = \mu_{w[r,n]} + \sigma_{w[r,n]}\Phi^{-1}(1 - 2^{-e}) \text{ and } \sigma_{[r,n]} = \frac{\sigma_{w[r,n]}}{\phi(\Phi^{-1}(1 - 2^{-e}))}2^{-e}.$$

5.2 Accuracy of Approximations of Success Probability in χ^2-Attack

We compare approximations of the success probability of 3-round and 4-round RC5-64 and 4-round RC6P based on our theorems to those of Theorem 7, especially. Table 8 or 9 shows results of 3-round and 4-round RC5-64 or 4-round RC6P, respectively. These results indicate that our approximation is more accurate than Theorem 7. Theorem 7 gives rather loose upper bounds. On the other hand, our theorem approximates the success probability more accurately. Especialy when $P_S > 0.8$, our estimation gives a lower upper bound. Our theorem deals with distributions of all wrong keys. On the other hand, Theorem 7 deals with only the highest distribution of wrong keys. This is one reason that our theorem can estimate strictly. Furthermore, Theorem 7 aims at dealing with differential or linear attack rather than χ^2-attack. This is why our theorems are more suitable for computing the success probability in χ^2-attack.

6   Conclusion

In this paper, we have proved the theorems that evaluate the success probability in χ^2-attack by using the distinguishing test. The derived formulae can be computed efficiently and provide a practical analysis for the estimation of the success probability in χ^2-attack. We have also demonstrated that our theorems can estimate success probability in χ^2-attacks against RC5-64 and RC6P.

References

1. A. Biryukov and E. Kushilevitz, "Improved Cryptanalysis of RC5", *Proc. EURO-CRYPT'98*, **1403**(1998), pp. 85–99, Springer-Verlag.
2. J. Borst, B. Preneel, and J. Vandewalle, "Linear Cryptanalysis of RC5 and RC6", *Proc. Fast Software Encryption'99*, **1636**(1999), pp. 16–30, Springer-Verlag.
3. R.J. Freund and W.J. Wilson, *Statistical Method*, Academic Press, San Diego, 1993.

4. H. Gilbert, H. Handschuh, A. Joux, and S. Vaudenay, "A Statistical Attack on RC6", *Proc. Fast Software Encryption'2000*, **1978**(2000), pp. 64–74, Springer-Verlag.
5. J. Hayakawa, and T. Shimoyama, "Correlation Attack to the Block Cipher RC5 and the Simplified Variants of RC6", *Third AES Candidate Conf.*, April 2000.
6. H. Handschuh and H. Gilbert, "χ^* Cryptanalysis of the SEAL Encryption Algorithm", *Proc. Fast Software Encryption*, **1267**(1997), pp.1–12.
7. N. Isogai, T. Matsunaka, and A. Miyaji, "Optimized χ^*-attack against RC6", *Proc. ANCS 2003*, **2846**(2003), to appear in Springer-Verlag.
8. Pascal Junod, "On the Complexity of Matsui's Attack", *Proc. Selected Areas in Cryptography'01*, **2259**(2001), pp. 199–211, Springer-Verlag.
9. B. Kaliski and Y. Lin, "On Differential and Linear Cryptanalysis of the RC5 Encryption Algorithm", *Proc. CRYPTO'95*, **963**(1995), pp. 171–184, Springer-Verlag.
10. J. Kelsey, B. Schneier, and D. Wagner, "Mod n Cryptanalysis, with applications against RC5P and M6", *Proc. Fast Software Encryption'99*, **1636**(1999), pp. 139–155, Springer-Verlag.
11. L. Knudsen and W. Meier, "Improved Differential Attacks on RC5", *Proc. CRYPTO'96*, **1109**(1996), pp. 216–228.
12. L. Knudsen and W. Meier, "Correlations in RC6 with a reduced number of rounds", *Proc. Fast Software Encryption'2000*, **1978**(2000), pp. 94–108, Springer-Verlag.
13. D. Knuth, *The art of computer programming*, vol.2, Seminumerical Algorithms, 2nd ed., Addison-Wesley, Reading, Mass. 1981.
14. A. Menezes, P.C. van Oorschot, and S. Vanstone, *Handbook of applied cryptography*, CRC Press, Inc., Boca Raton, 1996.
15. A. Miyaji, M. Nonaka, and Y. Takii, "Known plaintext correlation attack against RC5", *Proc. RSA'2002 Conf.*, **2271**(2002), pp. 131–148, Springer-Verlag.
16. A. Miyaji and M. Nonaka, "Cryptanalysis of the Reduced-Round RC6", *Proc. ICICS 2002*, **2513**(2002), pp.480-494.
17. R. Rivest, "The RC5 Encryption Algorithm", *Proc. Fast Software Encryption'95*, **1008**(1995), pp. 86–96, Springer-Verlag.
18. R. Rivest, M. Robshaw, R. Sidney, and Y. Yin, "The RC6 Block Cipher. v1.1," August 20, 1998. Available at http://www.rsasecurity.com/rsalabs/rc6/.
19. A. A. Selcuk and A. Bicak, "On probability of success in differential and linear cryptanalysis", *Security in Communication Networks SCN 2002*, Lecture notes in Computer Science, **2576**(2003), 1751-185, Springer-Verlag. Available at http://www.rsasecurity.com/rsalabs/rc6/.
20. S. Vaudenay, "An Experiment on DES Statistical Cryptanalysis", *Proc. 3rd ACM Conference on Computer and Communications Security*, ACM Press, pp.139–147, 1996.

More Generalized Clock-Controlled Alternating Step Generator

Ali A. Kanso

Department of Science
King Fahd University of Petroleum and Minerals (HCC)
P.O. Box 2440, Hail, KSA

Abstract. In this paper a new stream cipher generator, called More Generalized Clock-Controlled Alternating Step Generator is proposed for use in stream cipher applications. The design of the generator is simple, made up of three feedback shift registers which are connected such that one register (FSR A) controls the clocking of the other two registers (FSRs B and C). The generator generates a large family of output sequences using the same key (initial states and/or feedback functions). When the control register (FSR A) generates a de Bruijn sequence of period $K = 2^\kappa$ and the other two registers (FSRs B and C) generate m-sequences of periods $M = (2^m - 1)$ and $N = (2^n - 1)$ respectively, then the output sequences have period $P_Z = 2^\kappa(2^m - 1)(2^n - 1)$, linear complexity L bounded from below by $(m + n)2^{\kappa-\cdot}$ and from above by $(m + n)2^\kappa$. Furthermore, the distribution of short patterns in the output sequences occur equally likely and these sequences are secure against known correlation attacks.

Keywords. Stream Ciphers, Clock-Controlled Registers, Alternating Step Generator, and Clock-Controlled Alernating Step Generator.

1 Introduction

Linear feedback shift registers are known to produce sequences with large period and good statistical properties [1]. But the inherent linearity of these sequences results in susceptibility to algebraic attacks that is the prime reason why LFSRs are not used directly for keystream generation. Pseudorandom sequence generators based on linear feedback shift registers are most common used in practice due to their efficient hardware implementation. Their stucture can be classified into two classes. One class is to apply a boolean fuction in n variables to a set of n LFSRs. The other class is to use one LFSR to control outputs of other LFSRs. There are two different control models. One is the clock-controlled generators such as the stop/go generator [2] [3], Gunther's alternating step generator [4], and Kanso's clock-controlled alternating step generator [5], and the other model is the shrinking generators [6], including self-shrinking generator [7], new self-shrinking generator [8], and clock-controlled shrinking generator [9].

M. Jakobsson, M. Yung, J. Zhou (Eds.): ACNS 2004, LNCS 3089, pp. 326–338, 2004.
© Springer-Verlag Berlin Heidelberg 2004

In this paper, a new clock-controlled generator that is called *More Generalized Clock-Controlled Alternating Step Generator* (and referred to as MGCCASG) is presented. The MGCCASG is a sequence generator composed of three FSRs A, B and C which are interconnected such that at any time t, if the content of the 0th stage of FSR A is 1, then FSR A is clocked once, FSR B is clocked by one plus the integer value represented in selected fixed W_B stages of FSR A, and FSR C is not clocked, otherwise, FSR A is clocked once, FSR B is not clocked, and FSR C is clocked by one plus the integer value represented in selected W_C fixed stages of FSR A. FSR A is called the control register and FSRs B and C are called the generating registers. The output bits of the MGCCASG are produced by adding modulo 2 the output bits of FSRs B and C under the control of FSR A.

Suppose that the control register FSR A has k stages and feedback function R. Similarly, suppose that the generating registers FSRs B and C have m and n stages respectively and feedback functions S and T respectively. Let $\underline{A_0} = A_0(0), A_1(0), ..., A_{k-1}(0)$, $\underline{B_0} = B_0(0), B_1(0), ..., B_{m-1}(0)$, and $\underline{C_0} = C_0(0), C_1(0), ..., C_{n-1}(0)$ be the initial states of A, B and C respectively.

The initial state of the MGCCASG at time $t = 0$ is given by: $\underline{S_0} = (\underline{A_0}, \underline{B_0}, \underline{C_0})$.

Define two functions F_B and F_C that act on the state of FSR A at a given time t to determine the number of times FSR B or FSR C respectively is clocked such that: At any time t,

$$F_B(\underline{A_t}) = [1 + 2^0 A_{i_0}(t) + 2^1 A_{i_1}(t) + ... + 2^{W_B-1} A_{i_{W_B}-1}(t)], \tag{1}$$

and

$$F_C(\underline{A_t}) = [1 + 2^0 A_{j_0}(t) + 2^1 A_{j_1}(t) + ... + 2^{W_C-1} A_{j_{W_C}-1}(t)], \tag{2}$$

for $W_B < k$, $i_0, i_1, ...i_{W_B-1} \in \{1, 2, ..., k-1\}$, and $W_C < k$, $j_0, j_1, ...j_{W_C-1} \in \{1, 2, ..., k-1\}$.

Define two cumulative functions of FSR A, G_A and Q_A: $\{0, 1, 2, ...\} \rightarrow \{0, 1, 2, ...\}$ such that:

$$G_A(t) = \sum_{i=0}^{t-1} A_0(i) F_B(\underline{A_i}), \text{ for } t > 0, \text{ and } G_A(0) = 0, \tag{3}$$

and

$$Q_A(t) = \sum_{i=0}^{t-1} (A_0(i) \oplus 1) F_C(\underline{A_i}), \text{ for } t > 0, \text{ and } Q_A(0) = 0. \tag{4}$$

{Where $\oplus$ denotes addition modulo 2}.

Thus, with initial state $\underline{S}_0 = (\underline{A}_0, \underline{B}_0, \underline{C}_0)$, at time t the state of the MGC-CASG is given by: $\underline{S}_t = (\underline{A}_t, \underline{B}_{G_A(t)}, \underline{C}_{Q_A(t)})$.

At any time t, the output of the MGCCASG is the content of the 0th stage of FSR B added modulo 2 to the content of the 0th stage of FSR C i.e. $B_0(G_A(t)) \oplus C_0(Q_A(t))$.

The MGCCASG may also be described in terms of the three output sequences $(A_t), (B_t)$ and (C_t) of the feedback shift registers A, B and C respectively.

Acting on their own, suppose that FSR A, FSR B and FSR C produce output sequences $(A_t) = A_0, A_1, ...$, $(B_t) = B_0, B_1, ...$, and $(C_t) = C_0, C_1, ...$ respectively. The sequence (A_t) is called the control sequence, and the sequences (B_t) and (C_t) are called the generating sequences of the MGCCASG respectively and referred to these as component sequences.

For an FSR the state sequence is related to the corresponding output sequence of the FSR in the following way: At time t, the state of FSR A, $\underline{A}_t = A_0(t), A_1(t), ..., A_{k-1}(t) = A_t, A_{t+1}, ..., A_{t+k-1}$. Therefore, one can write the functions F_B and F_C in terms of the output bits of A.

The output sequence (Z_t) of the MGCCASG whose control sequence and generating sequences are (A_t), (B_t) and (C_t) respectively is given by: $Z_t = B_{G_A(t)} \oplus C_{Q_A(t)}$.

This paper is constructed as follows. In section 2, the properties of randomness of the output sequences of the generator such as period, linear complexity and statistical properties are established. In section 3, a number of cryptanalytic attacks are considered. In section 4, a comparison between the introduced generator and related works is given. Finally, the last section consists of the conlusion of this paper.

2   Randomness Properties

Suppose that A is an FSR with initial state $\underline{A}_0$ and feedback function R such that the output sequence (A_t) of A is a de Bruijn sequence of span κ and it has period $K = 2^\kappa$ [1]. Suppose that the feedback shift registers B and C are primitive linear feedback shift registers (LFSRs) with non-zero initial states $\underline{B}_0$ and $\underline{C}_0$ respectively, and primitive characteristic feedback polynomials $q(x)$ of degree m and $h(x)$ of degree n respectively (where $g(x)$ and $h(x)$ are associated with the feedback functions S and T respectively) [1]. Let (B_t) and (C_t) denote the output sequences of LFSRs B and C respectively. Then (B_t) and (C_t) are m-sequences of periods $M = (2^m - 1)$ and $N = (2^n - 1)$ respectively [1]. Let (Z_t) be the output sequence of the MGCCASG whose component sequences are (A_t), (B_t) and (C_t).

Note that a de Bruijn sequence of span κ can be easily obtained from an m-sequence generated by a κ-stage primitive LFSR by simply adding a "0" to the end of each subsequence of $(\kappa - 1)$ zeroes occurring in the m-sequence. Since in a full period $K = 2^\kappa$ of (A_t) the number of ones and zeroes is $K_1 = K_0 = 2^{\kappa-1}$ [1]. Thus, after clocking FSR A K times, LFSR B is clocked $G_A(K) = 2^{(\kappa-1)-W_B}(1 + 2 + ... + 2^{W_B}) = 2^{(\kappa-1)-W_B}[2^{W_B-1}(2^{W_B} + 1)] = 2^{\kappa-2}(2^{W_B} + 1)$ times and LFSR C is clocked $Q_A(K) = 2^{\kappa-2}(2^{W_C} + 1)$ times.

In this section, some properties of the output sequences such as period and linear complexity are established. It is shown that, when m and n are positive integers greater than 1 satisfying $gcd(m, n) = 1$, and W_B, W_C satisfy $gcd(2^{W_B} + 1, 2^m - 1) = gcd(2^{W_C} + 1, 2^n - 1) = 1$, then the period of the output sequences is exponential in κ, m and n, and that the linear complexity is exponential in κ. Finally, it is established that the distribution of short patterns in the output sequences of this MGCCASG turns out to be ideal.

2.1   Period and Linear Complexity

The sequence (Z_t) can be seen as two sequences added modulo 2, $(Z_t) = (B_{G_A(t)}) \oplus (C_{Q_A(t)})$, where $(B_{G_A(t)})$ and $(C_{Q_A(t)})$ are generated by the sub-generators whose component sequences are (A_t), (B_t) and (A_t), (C_t) respectively.

In order to establish the period and the linear complexity of (Z_t) one needs to first consider the periods and the linear complexities of the two sequences $(B_{G_A(t)})$ and $(C_{Q_A(t)})$.

In the following two lemmas, the periods of the sequences $(B_{G_A(t)})$ and $(C_{Q_A(t)})$ are considered. Tretter [10] has considered this proof for the output sequences of the stop and go generator [2]. His proof is also valid for the sequences $(B_{G_A(t)})$ and $(C_{Q_A(t)})$.

Lemma 1. *If $gcd(2^{W_B} + 1, 2^m - 1) = 1$, then the period P_G of the sequence $(B_{G_A(t)})$ is $2^\kappa(2^m - 1)$.*

Proof. The sequence $(B_{G_A(t)})$ will repeat whenever the states of the shift registers A and B return to their initial states $\underline{A}_0$ and $\underline{B}_0$ respectively. The register A returns to its initial state once every $K = 2^\kappa$ clock pulses. Thus, for Y cycles of register A, register B is clocked $Y G_A(K)$ times.

Therefore, if for some integers U and Y, $Y G_A(K) = U M$, then the feedback shift registers A and B will simultaneously be in their initial states. The period of the sequence $(B_{G_A(t)})$ corresponds to the smallest integer value that the integer U can take.

Now $U = Y G_A(K)/M$. Therefore, if $gcd(G_A(K), M) = 1$ [i.e. $gcd(2^{\kappa-2}(2^{W_B} + 1), 2^m - 1) = 1$], then the smallest value that U can take is when $Y = M$. Clearly $gcd(2^{\kappa-2}, 2^m - 1) = 1$, hence, if $gcd(2^{W_B} + 1, 2^m - 1) = 1$ then $gcd(G_A(K), M) = 1$.

Thus, in M cycles of register A, register B cycles $G_A(K)$ times and the period of $(B_{G_A(t)})$ is $KM = 2^{\kappa}(2^m - 1)$.

Lemma 2. *If $gcd(2^{W_C} + 1, 2^n - 1) = 1$, then the period P_Q of the sequence $(C_{Q_A(t)})$ is $2^{\kappa}(2^n - 1)$.*

Proof. Similar to the proof of the above lemma.

Definition 1. *The linear complexity of a purely periodic sequence is equal to the degree of its minimal polynomial. The minimal polynomial is the characteristic feedback polynomial of the shortest LFSR that can produce the given sequence.*

In the following two lemmas, the minimal polynomials of $(B_{G_A(t)})$ and $(C_{Q_A(t)})$ are considered.

Lemma 3. *If $gcd(2^{W_B} + 1, 2^m - 1) = 1$, then the minimal polynomial of the sequence $(B_{G_A(t)})$ is of the form $I(x)^{\alpha}$ where $2^{\kappa-1} < \alpha \leq 2^{\kappa}$, and $I(x)$ is an irreducible polynomial of degree m. i.e. The linear complexity of $(B_{G_A(t)})$ is L_1 such that: $m2^{\kappa-1} < L_1 \leq m2^{\kappa}$.*

Proof. Recall that if $gcd(2^{W_B} + 1, 2^m - 1) = 1$ then $gcd(G_A(K), M) = 1$.

Upper Bound on L_1: If one starts at location i in the sequence $(B_{G_A(t)})$ for a fixed value of i with $0 \leq i < K$ and chooses every K^{th} element in the sequence $(B_{G_A(t)})$, then this is equivalent to starting at position $t = G_A(i)$ in (B_t) and choosing every $G_A(K)^{th}$ element. Such a sequence is a $G_A(K)$-decimation of (B_t). All the $G_A(K)$-decimation of (B_t) have the same minimal polynomial $I(x)$ whose roots are the $G_A(K)^{th}$ powers of the roots of $g(x)$ [11]. The final sequence $(B_{G_A(t)})$ consists of K such sequences interleaved. [In other words, if $(B_{G_A(t)})$ is written by rows into an array K columns wide, then each column is a sequence produced by $I(x)$]. Hence, the sequence $(B_{G_A(t)})$ may be produced by an LFSR constructed as follows [12].

Take an LFSR with feedback polynomial $I(x)$ and replace each delay by a chain of K delays and only the left most of each such group of K delays is tapped and input to the feedback function with a non-zero feedback coefficient. Thus, $(B_{G_A(t)})$ is produced by an LFSR with the feedback polynomial $I(x^K)$. Hence, the minimal polynomial of $(B_{G_A(t)})$ divides $I(x^K) = I(x^{2^{\kappa}}) = I(x)^{2^{\kappa}}$. Hence, $(B_{G_A(t)})$ has linear complexity L_1 bounded from above by $mK = m2^{\kappa}$.

Furthermore, Chambers [12] has shown that, if $g(x)$ is irreducible, with degree m and exponent M and $gcd(G_A(K), M) = 1$, then the polynomial $I(x)$, like $g(x)$ is irreducible of degree m and exponent M.

Lower Bound on L_1: Let $Q(x)$ denote the minimal polynomial of $(B_{G_A(t)})$. The sequence $(B_{G_A(t)})$ satisfies $I(E)^{2^\kappa}(B_{G_A(t)}) = (0)$ for all t, where (0) is the all-zero sequence and E is the shift operator. Since the polynomial $I(x)$ is irreducible then the polynomial $Q(x)$ must be of the form $I(x)^\alpha$ for $\alpha \leq 2^\kappa$.

Assume $\alpha \leq 2^{\kappa-1}$. Then $Q(x)$ divides $I(x)^{2^{\kappa-1}}$. Since $I(x)$ is an irreducible polynomial of degree m it divides the polynomial $(1 + x^M)$. Therefore, $Q(x)$ divides $(1 + x^M)^{2^{\kappa-1}} = (1 + x^{M2^{\kappa-1}})$, but then the period of $(B_{G_A(t)})$ is at most $M2^{\kappa-1}$ [11] contradicting lemma 1. Therefore $\alpha > 2^{\kappa-1}$ and the lower bound follows.

Lemma 4. *If $gcd(2^{W_C} + 1, 2^n - 1) = 1$, then the minimal polynomial of the sequence $(C_{Q_A(t)})$ is of the form $J(x)^\beta$ where $2^{\kappa-1} < \beta \leq 2^\kappa$, and $J(x)$ is an irreducible polynomial of degree n. i.e. The linear complexity of $(C_{Q_A(t)})$ is L_2 such that: $n2^{\kappa-1} < L_2 \leq n2^\kappa$.*

Proof. Similar to the proof of the above lemma.

Therefore, if $gcd(2^{W_B} + 1, 2^m - 1) = gcd(2^{W_C} + 1, 2^n - 1) = 1$ then the periods of $(B_{G_A(t)})$ and $(C_{Q_A(t)})$ are $P_G = 2^\kappa(2^m - 1)$ and $P_Q = 2^\kappa(2^n - 1)$ respectively and the minimal polynomials of $(B_{G_A(t)})$ and $(C_{Q_A(t)})$ are equal to $I(x)^\alpha$ and $J(x)^\beta$ respectively where $2^{\kappa-1} < \alpha, \beta \leq 2^\kappa$ and $I(x)$, $J(x)$ are irreducible polynomials of degree m and n respectively.

Theorem 1. *If m and n are positive integers greater than 1 satisfying $gcd(m, n) = 1$, and W_B, W_C satisfy $gcd(2^{W_B} + 1, 2^m - 1) = gcd(2^{W_C} + 1, 2^n - 1) = 1$, then the output sequence (Z_t) has period $P_Z = 2^\kappa(2^m - 1)(2^n - 1)$ and linear complexity L such that: $(m + n)2^{\kappa-1} < L \leq (m + n)2^\kappa$.*

Proof. From the above lemmas, the minimal polynomials of $(B_{G_A(t)})$ is $I(x)^\alpha$ and that of $(C_{Q_A(t)})$ is $J(x)^\beta$ where $2^{\kappa-1} < \alpha, \beta \leq 2^\kappa$. Since $I(x)$ and $J(x)$ are irreducible of different degrees then $gcd(I(x), J(x)) = 1$, hence $gcd(I(x)^\alpha, J(x)^\beta) = 1$ [11]. Therefore, the period of (Z_t) is $P_Z = lcm(P_G, P_Q)$ [11, theorem 3.9] and the minimal polynomial of (Z_t) is $I(x)^\alpha J(x)^\beta$ of degree $L = (m\alpha + n\beta)$ [11, theorem 6.57]. Hence, the period of (Z_t) is $P_Z = lcm(2^\kappa(2^m - 1), 2^\kappa(2^n - 1)) = 2^\kappa(2^m - 1)(2^n - 1)/gcd(2^m - 1, 2^n - 1) = 2^\kappa(2^m - 1)(2^n - 1)/(2^{gcd(m,n)} - 1)$ [13, lemma 5.9]. Thus, the period of (Z_t) is $P_Z = 2^\kappa(2^m - 1)(2^n - 1)$ and the linear complexity of (Z_t) is L such that: $(m + n)2^{\kappa-1} < L \leq (m + n)2^\kappa$.

2.2 Statistical Properties

In this section, the number of ones and zeroes in a full period $P_Z = 2^\kappa(2^m - 1)(2^n - 1)$ of the sequence (Z_t) are established. It also shown that when m and n are positive integers greater than 1 satisfying $gcd(m, n) = 1$

and W_B, W_C satisfy $gcd(2^{W_B} + 1, 2^m - 1) = gcd(2^{W_C} + 1, 2^n - 1) = 1$, then any pattern of length $q \leq min(\gamma, \delta)$ where γ and δ are positive integers such that $\gamma = \lfloor (m-1)/2^{W_B} + 1 \rfloor$ and $\delta = \lfloor (n-1)/2^{W_C} + 1 \rfloor$ occurs with probability $2^{-q} + O(1/2^{m-q}) + O(1/2^{n-q})$. [Where $\lfloor \Omega \rfloor$ is the integer part of Ω for any real number Ω.]

Since (B_t) and (C_t) are m-sequences then in a full period $M = (2^m - 1)$ of (B_t) the number of ones and zeroes is $M_1 = 2^{m-1}$ and $M_0 = (2^{m-1} - 1)$ respectively, and in a full period $N = (2^n - 1)$ of (C_t) the number of ones and zeroes is $N_1 = 2^{n-1}$ and $N_0 = (2^{n-1} - 1)$ respectively [1].

If the period of (Z_t) attains its maximum value $P_Z = 2^\kappa (2^m - 1)(2^n - 1)$, then it is obvious that the number of ones and zeroes in a full period of (Z_t) is $2^\kappa[(2^m - 1)2^{n-1} - 2^{m-1}]$ and $2^\kappa[(2^m - 1)2^{n-1} - (2^{m-1} - 1)]$ respectively.

In the following theorem, the distribution of short patterns in the output sequences of the MGCCASG are determined.

Theorem 2. *Let m and n be positive integers greater than 1 satisfying $gcd(m, n) = 1$ and let W_B, W_C satisfy $gcd(2^{W_B} + 1, 2^m - 1) = gcd(2^{W_C} + 1, 2^n - 1) = 1$. Let γ and δ be positive integers such that $\gamma = \lfloor (m-1)/2^{W_B} + 1 \rfloor$ and $\delta = \lfloor (n-1)/2^{W_C} + 1 \rfloor$.*

The probability of occurrences of any pattern $\sigma = (\sigma_0, \sigma_1, ..., \sigma_{q-1}) \in \{0,1\}^q$ of length $q \leq min(\gamma, \delta)$ in the sequence (Z_t) is 2^{-q} up to an error of order $O(1/2^{m-q}) + O(1/2^{n-q})$.

Proof. The proof is given in the appendix.

Experiments have shown that if $gcd(m, n) = 1$, then for any value of W_B and W_C satisfying $gcd(2^{W_B} + 1, 2^m - 1) = 1$ and $gcd(2^{W_C} + 1, 2^n - 1) = 1$ respectively, the output sequences of the MGCCASG have good statistical properties.

Therefore, when m and n are positive integers greater than 1 satisfying $gcd(m, n) = 1$ and W_B, W_C satisfy $gcd(2^{W_B} + 1, 2^m - 1) = gcd(2^{W_C} + 1, 2^n - 1) = 1$, then a MGCCASG with a de Bruijn sequence as the control sequence and m-sequences as the generating sequences generates sequences with period $P_Z = 2^\kappa (2^m - 1)(2^n - 1)$, linear complexity L such that $(m + n)2^{\kappa-1} < L \leq (m + n)2^\kappa$, and these sequences have good statistical properties.

In the following section, some correlation attacks on the MGCCASG are considered.

3 Cryptanalysis

A suitable stream cipher should be resistant against a known-plaintext attack. In a known-plaintext attack the cryptanalyst is given a plaintext and the corresponding cipher-text, and the task is to reproduce the keystream somehow.

Correlation attacks is a very powerfull class of attacks and the most serious threat against the security of LFSR-based stream ciphers. Basically, if a cryptanalyst can in some way detect a correlation between the known output sequence and the output of one individual LFSR, this can be used in a divide and conquer attack on the individual LFSR [14, 15, 16, 17].

The output sequence of the MGCCASG is an addition modulo 2 of its two irregularly decimated generating sequences $(B_{G_A(t)})$ and $(C_{Q_A(t)})$. Thus, one would not expect a strong correlation to be obtained efficiently, especially, if primitive feedback polynomials of high hamming weight are associated with the feedback functions of the registers B and C [16], and the selected W_B and W_C fixed stages $i_0, i_1, ..., i_{W_B-1}$ and $j_0, j_1, ..., j_{W_C-1}$ respectively of the control register that are used to clock the generating registers are considered as part of the key [i.e. $W_B, i_0, i_1, ..., i_{W_B-1}$ and $W_C, j_0, j_1, ..., j_{W_C-1}$ are kept secret].

If the characteristic feedback functions of A, B and C are known then a cryptanalyst can exhaustively search for the initial state of A; each such state can be expanded to a prefix of the control sequence (A_t) using the characteristic feedback function of A. Suppose that one expands the sequence (A_t) until its pth 1 and 0 are produced where $p = max(m, n)$. From this prefix, and from the knowledge of a corresponding p-long prefix of the output sequence of (Z_t), one can derive the value of p non-consecutive bits of the generating sequences (B_t) and (C_t) using the following relation:

$$Z_t \oplus Z_{t+1} = \begin{cases} B_{G_A(t)} \oplus B_{G_A(t+1)} & \text{if } A_t = 1, \\ C_{Q_A(t)} \oplus C_{Q_A(t+1)} & \text{if } A_t = 0. \end{cases} \tag{5}$$

Since the characteristic feedback functions of B and C are known, then the initial states of B and C can be revealed given these non-consecutive p-bits of (B_t) and (C_t) respectively by solving a system of linear equations, but first one has to reveal the values of W_B and W_C in order to determine the locations of these non consecutive p-bits in (B_t) and (C_t). Therefore, the attack takes approximately $O(\Phi\Psi 2^\kappa m^3 n^3)$ steps where:

$$\Phi = \sum_{W_B=1}^{k-1} \frac{(k-1)!}{((k-1)-W_B)!}, \text{ and } \Psi = \sum_{W_C=1}^{k-1} \frac{(k-1)!}{((k-1)-W_C)!} \tag{6}$$

If the number of fixed stages W_B, and W_C are known, but the selected stages $i_0, i_1, ..., i_{W_B-1}$ and $j_0, j_1, ..., j_{W_C-1}$ are kept secret, then

$$\Phi = \frac{(k-1)!}{((k-1) - W_B)!}, \text{ and } \Psi = \frac{(k-1)!}{((k-1) - W_C)!}. \tag{7}$$

For $\kappa \approx 64$, $m \approx 64$, and $n \approx 64$, the MGCCASG appears to be secure against all correlation attacks introduced in [14, 15, 16, 17, 18, 19, 20, 21, 22, 23, 24].

There is also another attack that can be applied to the MGCCASG through the linear complexity, but this attack requires at least $(m+n)2^{\kappa}$ consecutive bits of the output sequence.

For maximum security, the MGCCASG should be used with secret initial states, secret characteristic feedback functions, secret W_B and W_C fixed stages satisfying $gcd(2^{W_B} + 1, 2^m - 1) = gcd(2^{W_C} + 1, 2^n - 1) = 1$, and m, n greater than 1 satisfying $gcd(m, n) = 1$. Subject to these constraints, a MGCCASG with $\kappa \approx 64$, $m \approx 64$, and $n \approx 64$ appears to be secure against all presently known attacks.

4   Related Works

An interesting example of existing FSR-based constructions for comparison with the MGCCASG is the alternating step generator (ASG) [4], and the clock-controlled alternating step generator (CCASG) [5].

The ASG and the CCASG are special cases of the MGCCASG; the first is actually a MGCCASG with $W_B = W_C = 0$; the second is a MGCCASG with $W_B = W_C$. Although the MGCCASG is a slower than both generators, its advantage is that it provides more security. For an ASG and a CCASG with $\kappa \approx l$, $m \approx l$, and $n \approx l$, if the characteristic feedback functions of A, B and C are known, then in order to reveal the initial states of the three registers the attack mentioned in section 3 takes approximately $O(2^l l^6)$ steps for the first generator, and approximately $O(\Phi 2^l l^6)$ steps for the second generator, whereas for the MGCCASG the attack takes approximately $O(\Phi \Psi 2^l l^6)$ steps. Another important advantge of the MGCCASG is that using the same initial states and the same feedback functions, the generator produces a new pseudorandom sequence each time a new selection of W_B, and/or W_C is made.

Conclusion 1. *The paper has presented a new stream cipher generator MGC-CASG for use in stream cipher applications. A complete description of the design of the generator has been given. The basic security requirements such as large period, high linear complexity and good statistical properties have been provided.*

The resistance against some correlation attacks has been investigated. Further-more, using the same key (i.e. same initial states and/or same characteristic feedback functions), the MGCCASG produces a new sequence each time different W_B and/or W_C fixed stages are selected. These characteristics and properties enhance its use as a suitable crypto-generator for stream cipher applications.

References

1. S. W. Golomb, "Shift Register Sequences", Aegean Park Press, 1982.
2. T. Beth and F. Piper, "The Stop and Go Generator", Advances in Cryptology: Proceedings of Eurocrypt 84, Lecture Notes in Computer Science, Berlin: Springer-Verlag 1985, vol. 209, pp. 88-92.
3. D. Gollmann and W. Chambers, "Clock-Controlled Shift Register: A Review", IEEE J. Sel. Ar. Comm. vol. 7, NO. 4, May 1989, pp. 525-533.
4. C. G. Gunther, "Alternating step generators controlled by de Bruijn sequences", Advances in Cryptology: Proceedings of Eurocrypt 87, Lecture Notes in Computer Science, Berlin: Spingler-Verlag, vol. 309, 1988, pp. 5-14.
5. A. Kanso, "Clock-Controlled Alternating Step Generator", Techno-Legal Aspects of Information Society and New Economy: an Overview, A Mendez-Villa, Jose Antonio Mesa Gonzalez Editors, Formatex 2003, pp. 12-18.
6. D. Coppersmith, H. Krawczyk, and Y. Mansour, "The Shrinking Generator", Advances in Cryptology: Proceedings of Crypto 93, Lecture Notes in Computer Science, Springer-Verlag, 1994, pp. 22-39.
7. W. Meier and O. Staffelbach, "The Self-Shrinking Generator", Advances in Cryptology: Proceedings of Eurocrypt 94, Lecture Notes in Computer Science, Springer-Verlag, vol. 950, 1994, pp. 205-214.
8. A. Kanso,"New Self-Shrinking Generator", Proceedings of the Security and Protection of Information Conference 2003, IDET Brno, Czech Republic, pp. 69-74.
9. A. Kanso, "Clock-controlled Shrinking Generator of Feedback Shift Registers", Proceedings of ACISP 2003, Lecture Notes in Computer Science, Berlin: Springer-Verlag, 2003, pp.443-451.
10. Steven A. Tretter, "Properties of PN2 sequences", IEEE Transactions on Information Theory, vol. IT-20, March 1974, pp. 295-297.
11. R. Lidl, H. Niederreiter, " Introduction to Finite Fields and Their Applications", UK: Cambridge University Press, 1986.
12. W. Chambers, "Clock-Controlled Shift Registers In Binary Sequence Generators", IEE Proceedings E., vol. 135, Jan 1988, pp. 17-24.
13. R. Ruppell, "Analysis and Design of Stream Ciphers", Berlin Heidlberg New York: Springer-Verlag, 1986.
14. J. Golic, M. Mihaljevic, "A Generalized Correlation Attack on a Class of Stream Ciphers Based on the Levenstein Distance", Journal of Cryptology, 3, 1991, pp. 201-212.
15. J.Golic, "Towards Fast Correlation Attacks on Irregularly Clocked Shift Registers", Advances in Cryptology: Eurocrypt 95, Lecture Notes in Computer Science, Springer-Verlag, vol. 921, 1995, pp. 248-262.
16. W. Meir, O. Staffelbach, "Fast Correlation Attacks on Certain Stream Ciphers", Journal of Cryptology, 1, 1989, pp. 159-176.
17. T. Siegenthaler, "Correlation-Immunity of Non-linear Combining Functions for Cryptographic Applications", IEEE Trans On Information Theory, 30, 1984, pp.776-780.

18. J. Golic, "On the Security of Shift Register Based Keystream Generators", R. Anderson, Editor, Fast Software Encryption, Cambridge Security Workshop, Lecture Notes in Computer Science, Springer-Verlag, vol. 809, 1994, pp. 90-100.
19. T. Johansson, "Reduced Complexity Correlation Attacks on Two Clock-Controlled Generators", Advances of Cryptology: Asiacrypt 98, Lecture Notes in Computer Science, Springer-Verlag, vol. 1514, 1998, pp. 342-356.
20. M. Mihaljevic, "An Approach to the Initial State Reconstruction of a Clock-Controlled Shift Register Based on a Novel Distance Measure", Advances in Cryptology: Auscrypt 92, Lecture Notes in Computer Science, Springer-Verlag, vol. 178, 1993, pp. 349-356.
21. J. Golic, L. O.Connor, "Embedding Probabilistic Correlation Attacks on Clock-Controlled Shift Registers", Advances in Cryptology: Eurocrypt 94, Lecture Notes in Computer Science, Springer-Verlag, vol. 950, 1995, pp. 230-243.
22. T. Johansson, F.Jonsson, "Improved Fast Correlation Attacks on Certain Stream Ciphers via Convolutional Codes", Advances in Cryptology: Eurocrypt 99, Lecture Notes in Computer Science, Springer-Verlag, vol. 1592, 1999, pp. 347-362.
23. T. Johansson, F.Jonsson, "Fast Correlation Attacks Through Reconstruction of Linear Polynomials", Advances in Cryptology: Crypto 2000, Lecture Notes in Computer Science, Springer-Verlag, vol. 1880, 2000, pp. 300-315.
24. Jovan Dj. Golic, Renato Menicocci, "Edit Distance Correlation Attack on the Alternating Step Generator", Advances in Cryptology, Lecture Notes in Computer Science, Springer-Verlag, 1997, pp. 499-512.

Appendix

Proof of Theorem 7

Since $gcd(m, n) = 1$ and $gcd(2^{W_B} + 1, 2^m - 1) = gcd(2^{W_C} + 1, 2^n - 1) = 1$, then the period of (Z_t) $P_Z = 2^\kappa(2^m - 1)(2^n - 1)$.

Let $t \in \{0, 1, .., P_Z - 1\}$ be represented in the form $t = u + (v + yM)2^\kappa$, $u \in \{0, 1, .., K - 1\}$, $v \in \{0, 1, .., M - 1\}$, $y \in \{0, 1, .., N - 1\}$ and let us first consider the frequency of patterns among subsequences $Z_t, Z_{t+1}, ..., Z_{t+q-1}$ for a fixed $u \in \{0, 1, ..., K - 1\}$.

Let $\rho = \rho(u)$ and $\theta = \theta(u)$ be defined by:

$$\rho_0 = 0 \tag{8}$$
$$\theta_0 = \sigma_0$$
$$\rho_{i+1} = \rho_i \oplus A_{u+i}(\sigma_{i+1} \oplus \sigma_i)$$
$$\theta_{i+1} = \theta_i \oplus (1 \oplus A_{u+i})(\sigma_{i+1} \oplus \sigma_i)$$

for $i \in \{0, 1, ..., q - 2\}$.

Then σ can be written as

$$\sigma_i = \rho_i \oplus \theta_i \tag{9}$$

for $i \in \{0, 1, ..., q - 1\}$.

The matching condition at time t is:

$$Z_{t+i} = \sigma_i \tag{10}$$

for $i \in \{0, 1, ..., q-1\}$.

This is equivalent to:

$$B_{G_A(t+i)} \oplus C_{Q_A(t+i)} = \rho_i \oplus \theta_i \tag{11}$$

for $i \in \{0, 1, ..., q-1\}$.

Using the following relations:

$$G_A(u+i+1) = G_A(u+i) + A_0(i)F_B(\underline{A}_i) \tag{12}$$
$$Q_A(u+i+1) = Q_A(u+i) + (A_0(i) \oplus 1)F_C(\underline{A}_i)$$

the sum of Equation (11) and of the corresponding equation for $(i+1)$ becomes:

$$B_{G_A(t+i+1)} \oplus B_{G_A(t+i)} = \rho_{i+1} \oplus \rho_i \tag{13}$$
$$C_{Q_A(t+i+1)} \oplus C_{Q_A(t+i)} = \theta_{i+1} \oplus \theta_i$$

since, when $A_i = 1$, $\theta_{i+1} \oplus \theta_i = C_{Q_A(t+i+1)} \oplus C_{Q_A(t+i)} = 0$, and when $A_i = 0$, $\rho_{i+1} \oplus \rho_i = B_{G_A(t+i+1)} \oplus B_{G_A(t+i)} = 0$.

This has two solutions:

$$B_{G_A(t+i)} = \rho_i, \, C_{Q_A(t+i)} = \theta_i \tag{14}$$

and

$$B_{G_A(t+i)} = 1 \oplus \rho_i, \, C_{Q_A(t+i)} = 1 \oplus \theta_i \tag{15}$$

for $i \in \{0, 1, ..., q-1\}$.

The number of solutions to this equation is equal to the number of occurrences of the pattern σ in the sequence (Z_t) (where $t = u + (v + yM)2^\kappa$, $v \in \{0, 1, .., M-1\}$, $y \in \{0, 1, .., N-1\}$), i.e., to the quantity we want to determine.

Without restricting ourselves we consider the solution of Equation (14). Making use of the fact that $K = 2^\kappa$ and that $G_A(K) = 2^{\kappa-2}(2^{W_B} + 1)$, $Q_A(K) = 2^{\kappa-2}(2^{W_C} + 1)$, this equation becomes:

$$B_{G_A(u+i)+vG_A(K)} = \rho_i \tag{16}$$

where $i \in \{0, 1, .., q-1\}$. (The term yM is omitted since (B_t) has period M.)

$$C_{Q_A(u+i)+(v+yM)Q_A(K)} = \theta_i \tag{17}$$

Let $\phi(u) = |\{i \mid 0 \leq i \leq (q-2), G_A(u+i+1) \neq G_A(u+i)\}|$ which is less than m since $q \leq \min(\gamma, \delta)$ where $\gamma = \lfloor (m-1)/2^{W_B} + 1 \rfloor$ and

$\delta = \lfloor (n-1)/2^{W_C} + 1 \rfloor$, then the assumptions that (B_t) is an m-sequence imply that Equation (16) has $2^{m-\phi(u)-1}$ solutions if $\rho \neq 0$.

Let $\psi(u) = |\{i \mid 0 \leq i \leq (q-2), Q_A(u+i+1) \neq Q_A(u+i)\}|$, then similarly, (C_t) is an m-sequence and $gcd(m,n) = 1$ imply that Equation (17) has $2^{n-\psi(u)-1}$ solutions if $\theta \neq 0$.

This remains true for $\rho = 0$ and/or $\theta = 0$ if we accept an error at most $O(1/2^{m-q}) + O(1/2^{n-q})$. Note that $\phi(u) + \psi(u) = (q-1)$.

Clearly, the same result also holds for Equation (15).

Hence, the total number of solutions to Equation (10) is:

$$2(2^{m-\phi(u)-1})(2^{n-\psi(u)-1}) = 2^{m+n-q} \qquad (18)$$

which is independent of u.

This finally implies that the frequency of the pattern σ is given by:

$$\frac{2^{m+n-q}}{MN} + O(1/2^{m-q}) + O(1/2^{n-q}) \qquad (19)$$

Therefore, in a full period of (Z_t) any pattern of length $q \leq \min(\gamma, \delta)$ occurs with a probability $(1/2^q) + O(1/2^{m-q}) + O(1/2^{n-q})$.

FDLKH: Fully Decentralized Key Management Scheme on Logical Key Hierarchy

Daisuke Inoue and Masahiro Kuroda

National Institute of Information and Communications Technology,
3-4, Hikarino-oka, Yokosuka, Kanagawa, 239-0847, Japan
{dai, marsh}@nict.go.jp

Abstract. In the next generation mobile environment, which uses 4G cellular and high-speed wireless LANs, novel group communication services among mobile users are expected to grow up. Security technologies for these group type services are challenging research area, especially, decentralization of group key management is important for large users. In this paper, we propose a fully decentralized key management scheme FDLKH that provides a key updating mechanism for dynamic group without any central server. This scheme inherits the key updating mechanism of the Logical Key Hierarchy scheme LKH, which is based on a central server system, and extends the LKH not to expect any central server but to use representative members of a group called captains. On the FDLKH, the total variety of keys in a group is half of that of the LKH. The costs for a member join or leave keep the logarithmic order of the number of members.

1 Introduction

The Internet and wireless communications, such as 3G cellular and wireless LAN, have infiltrated into daily life and next generation mobile environment using 4G cellular and high-speed wireless LANs is expected to come up in the market. In current mobile environment, there are many client-server type secure services, such as mobile e-commerce[1]. These services maintain a central server for secure communications with many users and expect high bandwidth communications for serving users. The next generation mobile environment[2], on the other hand, is said to be flat rated wireless access taking advantage of each wireless communication and novel group communication services among mobile users are expected to grow up in near future. In these group type services, mobile users exchange information securely in a group, where the number of mobile devices is large and many devices have less computational power comparing to computer systems. These services expect dynamic and secure communications because of member changes in a group. Security technologies to satisfy requirements for these services are challenging research area. In particular, decentralization of security management is important for large users. A mechanism for updating a group key, which is shared among all members in a large and dynamic group, is an important issue.

M. Jakobsson, M. Yung, J. Zhou (Eds.): ACNS 2004, LNCS 3089, pp. 339–354, 2004.

The group key should be updated when there is a join or leave in a group not to allow the new member (newcomer hereafter) to access past information and not to allow the left member (seceder hereafter) to access future information in the group, in other words, to provide backward and forward secrecy. There are two types of strategies. One is to update keys in a central system and to redistribute from the system[3]-[11]. The other is to agree a key among all members of a group by means of extended Diffie-Hellman (DH hereafter) key agreement protocols[12]-[16].

The former centralized key management, which targets for large and dynamic groups, concentrates tasks for updating the group key in a central server. There are some issues, such as maintenance cost, service level resilience and key exposure. Since the central server is required high computational resources and bandwidth, the server maintenance costs high. When there is a failure at the central server, services will not be available. When the server is compromised and keys are wrongly distributed to non group members, all the information among the group will be exposed to public. Furthermore, the centralized key management system asks all members to trust the central server; this may allow inspection of the system manager.

The latter extended DH based key management, which aims at relatively small groups, does not need a central server, but imposes computationally intensive modular exponentiations on all members for each join/leave procedure. These expensive computations may not be feasible for a group consisting of mobile devices with less computational power.

In this paper, we propose a fully decentralized key management scheme (FDLKH hereafter) that provides a group key update mechanism for group communications. Our scheme has two design principles: 1) No central server; 2) Some mobile devices having high computation power capable of modular exponentiations. The FDLKH inherits the group key update mechanism of the Logical Key Hierarchy scheme (LKH hereafter), which has been developed as a key management mechanism based on a central server system, and extends the LKH not to expect any central server. The FDLKH proposes to use representative members in a group, called *captains*, instead of a central server, with less network traffics. Only *captains* perform the DH key agreements and each *captain* distributes keys to adequate members. In this scheme, the costs of the DH key agreements and symmetric key encryptions/decryptions keep the logarithmic order of the number of members.

This paper is organized as follows. In Section 2, we describe the centralized key management schemes. We explain the FDLKH scheme in Section 3, and evaluate the scheme in Section 4. Lastly in Section 5, we provide our conclusion and future works.

2   Centralized Key Management Scheme

The centralized key management scheme maintains a group key, a symmetric key, shared among all members of a secure communication group at a server.

When a new member joins or some member leaves the group, the key is updated to provide the backward and forward secrecy. Here we explain two centralized group key management schemes.

2.1 Basic Scheme

The basic scheme to update a group key is that a central server and each group member share an individual key, which is used to encrypt/decrypt the group key. When a newcomer joins a group, the server generates a new group key and encrypts it by two keys, the old group key and an individual key of the newcomer, separately. The server sends the encrypted new group key by using the old group key to the existing members and to the newcomer by using the individual key. When a member leaves the group, the server generates a new group key and encrypts it by using the individual keys of all members except the seceder and sends every encrypted group key to each member. It is obvious that this scheme is not scalable, especially when a member leaves, because the computation at the server for the group key encryption is proportional to the number of remaining members.

2.2 Logical Key Hierarchy Scheme

The Logical Key Hierarchy scheme[5][6] provides a scalable mechanism to update a group key with a central server. The LKH employs a hierarchical tree structure that places each member of a group at each leaf. An intermediate node of the tree is associated with a key that is used to encrypt another key, a key encryption key. A leaf node is also associated with a key, which is an individual key of a member. The key associated with the root node of the tree is the group key. A member has all keys associated with all nodes from the parent node to the root node, called ancestor nodes. Essentially, the LKH divides members into subtrees that are rooted at each intermediate node and contain all descendants of its root node. Members of a subtree share a key associated with the top nodes of the subtree. When a newcomer joins or a seceder leaves a group, the keys associated with the ancestor nodes of the newcomer/seceder are updated. In case of a join, the central server encrypts new keys by using old keys of the ancestor nodes and distributes the encrypted new keys to corresponding subtrees. In case of a leave, the server encrypts new keys by using keys associated with the siblings of the ancestor nodes; especially for sibling members of the seceder, the server uses their individual keys to encrypt the new keys. Thereby encryptions are lumped together for each subtree, as a result, cryptographic rekeying computations becomes $O(\log n)$ instead of $O(n)$, where n is the number of members. Although the LKH provides a way to update the group key, a central server is responsible for the key generation and distribution.

3   FDLKH Scheme

In this section, we describe our scheme FDLKH: fully decentralized key management scheme on a logical key hierarchy. The FDLKH inherits the key hierarchy of the LKH and extends the key management not to expect any central server. The LKH employs a tree with degree d as a hierarchical tree, whereas the FDLKH uses a binary key tree that logically maps symmetric keys into intermediate nodes in the tree and places each member at each leaf. Dissimilarly to members on the LKH, members on the FDLKH have no individual keys, because the FDLKH expects no keys to share with a central server. To allot some portion of tasks of a central server, the FDLKH proposes a *captain* who is one of members in a group that represents a subtree in a binary key tree. When there is a join or a leave in a group, a *captain* is selected for each subtree. Then the *captains* perform key agreements and key distributions. They use the DH key agreement protocol for the key agreements and uses the LKH approach as mentioned in section 2.2 for the key distributions. In other words, the FDLKH combines the DH key agreement with the LKH to establish a rekeying mechanism without a central server.

3.1   Notations

$\langle l, m \rangle$	m-th node at level l in a tree, where $0 \le m \le 2^l - 1$
$M_{\langle l,m \rangle}$	Member who occupies the node $\langle l, m \rangle$
$K_{\langle l,m \rangle}$	Key associated with the node $\langle l, m \rangle$
$K'_{\langle l,m \rangle}$	New key to be associated with the node $\langle l, m \rangle$
$T_{\langle l,m \rangle}$	Subtree rooted at the node $\langle l, m \rangle$
$C_{\langle l,m \rangle}$	Member who represents the $T_{\langle l,m \rangle}$ (i.e., *captain*)
$E(K, X)$	Encryption of data X using a symmetric key K
$A \leftrightarrow B$: K	A and B agree a symmetric key K by the DH key agreement
$A \rightarrow B$: X	A sends data X to B by using multicast or unicast(s)
n	Number of members in a group
i, j, k	Integers $i = 1, \ldots, l,\quad j = 2, \ldots, l,\quad k = 2, \ldots, l - 1$
p	Prime number
g	Generator of Z_p^*

In a binary key tree for the FDLKH, a node is identified by its level l ($l = 0, 1, 2, \ldots$) that the node belongs to and by the position m ($0 \le m \le 2^l - 1$) that is numbered from the leftmost grid in that level. Here a node is described as $\langle l, m \rangle$. The node $\langle 0, 0 \rangle$ is the root of the tree. Members in a group occupy the leaf nodes of the tree. We denote a member who occupies the node $\langle l, m \rangle$ as $M_{\langle l,m \rangle}$. Every intermediate node in the tree, a node unoccupied by a member, is associated with a symmetric key. A key mapped into the node $\langle l, m \rangle$ is $K_{\langle l,m \rangle}$. The key is shared among all members who belong to the subtree rooted at the node $\langle l, m \rangle$. The subtree is described as $T_{\langle l,m \rangle}$. The key $K_{\langle 0,0 \rangle}$, the group key, is shared among all members.

In Fig. 1(a), two members, $M_{\langle 5,8 \rangle}$ and $M_{\langle 5,9 \rangle}$, belong to the subtree $T_{\langle 4,4 \rangle}$ and share the symmetric key $K_{\langle 4,4 \rangle}$. They also belong to subtrees $T_{\langle 3,2 \rangle}$, $T_{\langle 2,1 \rangle}$,

$T_{\langle 1,0 \rangle}$, and $T_{\langle 0,0 \rangle}$. In total, the members have five keys: $K_{\langle 4,4 \rangle}$, $K_{\langle 3,2 \rangle}$, $K_{\langle 2,1 \rangle}$, $K_{\langle 1,0 \rangle}$, and $K_{\langle 0,0 \rangle}$. A member knows all keys associated with its ancestor nodes up to the root node.

When there is a join or a leave in a group, some members are selected as representatives of subtrees to perform key agreements and key distributions. We call the representative member as a *captain*. The *captain* of the subtree $T_{\langle l,m \rangle}$ is denoted as $C_{\langle l,m \rangle}$.

Fig. 1(b) is a generalized binary key tree of the FDLKH, which is illustrated from the viewpoint of the member $M_{\langle l,m \rangle}$. The parent node of $M_{\langle l,m \rangle}$ is described as $\langle l-1, \lfloor \frac{m}{2} \rfloor \rangle$. The sibling member of $M_{\langle l,m \rangle}$ is $M_{\langle l,m+(-1)^m \rangle}$. All ancestor nodes of $M_{\langle l,m \rangle}$ are generalized as $\langle l-i, \lfloor \frac{m}{2^i} \rfloor \rangle$, where $i = 1, \ldots, l$. The subtrees that $M_{\langle l,m \rangle}$ belongs to and the keys that $M_{\langle l,m \rangle}$ has are, therefore, generalized as $T_{\langle l-i, \lfloor \frac{m}{2^i} \rfloor \rangle}$ and $K_{\langle l-i, \lfloor \frac{m}{2^i} \rfloor \rangle}$.

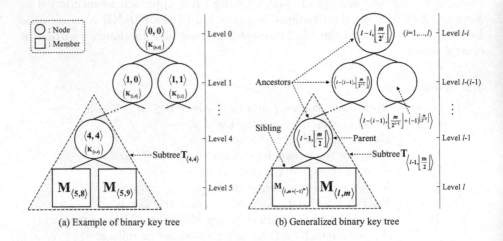

(a) Example of binary key tree   (b) Generalized binary key tree

Fig. 1. Binary key tree

3.2 Flow of Join and Leave Protocol

The operations of the join and leave protocol are as follows:

Join: 1) Tree update, 2) Captain selection, 3) DH key agreement, 4) Key distribution, 5) Key update

Leave: 1) Captain selection, 2) DH key agreement, 3) Key distribution, 4) Key update, 5) Tree update

3.3 Tree Update

When a newcomer joins or a seceder leaves a group, each member independently updates the binary key tree of itself. At the first step of a join, the information of a binary key tree that expresses positions of all members in the tree is sent to the newcomer by a *captain* who represents the subtree rooted at the parent node of the newcomer. The reorganizations of a key tree resulting from a join and a leave of a member are shown in Fig. 2 and Fig. 3.

A newcomer joins in a tree at the shallowest and leftmost leaf. In the case of Fig. 2, a newcomer becomes the member $M_{\langle 3,3 \rangle}$. Owing to this join, $M_{\langle 2,1 \rangle}$ who once occupied the node $\langle 2,1 \rangle$ moves to the deeper level in the tree, thereby becomes the left child of the node $\langle 2,1 \rangle$, namely $M_{\langle 3,2 \rangle}$. In the special case, when the tree has a pyramidal shape, that is, the number of members before a newcomer join is some power of 2, the tree forms a complete binary tree, the root node $\langle 0,0 \rangle$ is changed to $\langle 1,0 \rangle$, the subtree $T_{\langle 0,0 \rangle}$ is moved to $T_{\langle 1,0 \rangle}$, and a new root node is created. After this reorganization, the newcomer becomes the right child of $\langle 0,0 \rangle$, namely $M_{\langle 1,1 \rangle}$.

The join point of a newcomer in a tree is decided unambiguously, however, a seceder leaves a tree at an arbitrary point. In the case of Fig. 3, the member $M_{\langle 3,0 \rangle}$ leaves the tree. The member $M_{\langle 3,1 \rangle}$, who is the sibling of $M_{\langle 3,0 \rangle}$, moves to a shallower level in the tree and becomes $M_{\langle 2,0 \rangle}$. Incidentally, in case where a sibling node of a seceder is unoccupied by a member, the subtree rooted at the sibling node moves to a lower level bodily and updates the name of its nodes and also the name of associated keys. For example, if the member $M_{\langle 2,3 \rangle}$ in Fig. 3 leaves the tree, the subtree $T_{\langle 2,2 \rangle}$ moves up and becomes $T_{\langle 1,1 \rangle}$.

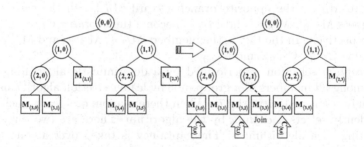

Fig. 2. Member join

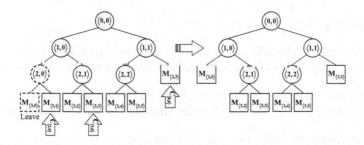

Fig. 3. Member leave

3.4 Rekeying Node

Rekeying nodes, namely nodes having keys to be updated, are all ancestor nodes of a newcomer or those of a seceder. The key generation, the key alternation, and the key destruction are performed on the keys of the rekeying nodes to provide the backward and forward secrecy.

In Fig. 2, the nodes $\langle 2, 1 \rangle$, $\langle 1, 0 \rangle$, and $\langle 0, 0 \rangle$ are the rekeying nodes, so that the key associated with $\langle 2, 1 \rangle$ is newly generated and other keys are altered to new ones. In Fig. 3, the nodes $\langle 2, 0 \rangle$, $\langle 1, 0 \rangle$, and $\langle 0, 0 \rangle$ are the rekeying nodes, so that the key associated with $\langle 2, 0 \rangle$ is destructed and other keys are altered to new ones. In general, when a member $M_{\langle l,m \rangle}$ joins a group, rekeying nodes are denoted as $\langle l - i, \lfloor \frac{m}{2^i} \rfloor \rangle$, where $i = 1, \dots, l$. Similarly, when $M_{\langle l,m \rangle}$ leaves a group, rekeying nodes (excluding a destructed node) are expressed as $\langle l - j, \lfloor \frac{m}{2^j} \rfloor \rangle$, where $j = 2, \dots, l$.

3.5 Captain Selection

In a subtree that is rooted at a rekeying node, one of members of the subtree is selected as a *captain*, a representative member, to perform a DH key agreement and key distribution. In case of $M_{\langle l,m \rangle}$ joining or leaving a group, there are l rekeying nodes; therefore l members who severally belong to the subtrees rooted at the rekeying nodes become their *captains*. From the view of a root node of a subtree, a *captain* of the subtree is selected from under the branch that does not lead to $M_{\langle l,m \rangle}$, the opposite branch toward $M_{\langle l,m \rangle}$. In the case of Fig. 2, the members $M_{\langle 3,0 \rangle}$, $M_{\langle 3,2 \rangle}$, and $M_{\langle 3,4 \rangle}$ become the *captains* $C_{\langle 1,0 \rangle}$, $C_{\langle 2,1 \rangle}$, and $C_{\langle 0,0 \rangle}$, respectively. In the Fig. 3, the members $M_{\langle 3,1 \rangle}$, $M_{\langle 3,3 \rangle}$, and $M_{\langle 2,3 \rangle}$ become the *captains* $C_{\langle 2,0 \rangle}$, $C_{\langle 1,0 \rangle}$, and $C_{\langle 0,0 \rangle}$.

The *captain* selection is performed by a deterministic algorithm, which is shared among all members of a group, not by leader election algorithms expecting strongly connected network[17]. When there is a join or a leave, each member independently selects a *captain* by the algorithm. There are two directions for constructing such algorithm: 1) The captaincy is taken over among all members of a subtree in turn; 2) Some criteria, such as computational power and bandwidth of each member, are used to decide a *captain*. The former is straightforward to make the load of rekeying flat, but the latter is effective when some members are powerful in computation compared to other members.

3.6 DH Key Agreement

A *captain* performs the DH key agreement to create new keys to be associated with the rekeying nodes. There are two strategies for the key agreement:

1. Dedicated Strategy: A single entity takes on the initiator roles of the protocol
2. Distributed Strategy: Several entities share the initiator roles of the protocol

The first strategy dedicates the initiator roles for the key agreements to a newcomer in the join protocol and to a *captain* who represents a subtree rooted at the parent node of a seceder in the leave protocol. This strategy imposes relatively high computations on a single entity. The second strategy allots tasks of the key agreements on a newcomer and *captains* in the join protocol, and also tasks on *captains* in the leave protocol. This strategy is more effective to flatten the computations for the key agreements than the first one; however, it needs additional procedures in the key distribution (Section 3.7). In the following of this section, we explain our key agreement protocols along with the examples in Fig. 2 and Fig. 3. It is important to note that, the following protocols do not include any authentication process. To prevent the man-in-the-middle attack, some authentication process should be combined into the protocols.

DH Protocol on Dedicated Strategy *Join:* In Fig. 2, the newcomer $M_{\langle 3,3\rangle}$ and the *captains* $M_{\langle 3,2\rangle}$, $M_{\langle 3,0\rangle}$, $M_{\langle 3,4\rangle}$ compute the following expression using public parameters p and g, and their random secret $X_{M_{\langle l,m\rangle}} \in Z_{p-1}$:

$$Y_{M_{\langle l,m\rangle}} = g^{X_{M_{\langle l,m\rangle}}} \bmod p \tag{1}$$

$M_{\langle 3,3\rangle}$ sends a resultant value $Y_{M_{\langle 3,3\rangle}}$ to the *captains* via unicast or multicast. The *captains* send resultant values to $M_{\langle 3,3\rangle}$ via unicast or multicast as follows:

$$
\begin{aligned}
M_{\langle 3,3\rangle} &\to \{M_{\langle 3,2\rangle}, M_{\langle 3,0\rangle}, M_{\langle 3,4\rangle}\} : && Y_{M_{\langle 3,3\rangle}} \\
M_{\langle 3,2\rangle} &\to M_{\langle 3,3\rangle} : && Y_{M_{\langle 3,2\rangle}} \\
M_{\langle 3,0\rangle} &\to M_{\langle 3,3\rangle} : && Y_{M_{\langle 3,0\rangle}} \\
M_{\langle 3,4\rangle} &\to M_{\langle 3,3\rangle} : && Y_{M_{\langle 3,4\rangle}}
\end{aligned}
$$

Here the one value $Y_{M_{\langle 3,3\rangle}}$ is used for three agreement procedures. If using the conventional DH protocol, the newcomer computes the expression (1) three times and sends three resultant values to the *captains* severally. Owing to this omission, loads of the newcomer can be reduced. As a result, $M_{\langle 3,3\rangle}$ shares the following new keys with $M_{\langle 3,2\rangle}$, $M_{\langle 3,0\rangle}$, and $M_{\langle 3,4\rangle}$, respectively, where $h()$ is a cryptographically secure hash function for the key derivation:

$$
\begin{aligned}
K'_{\langle 2,1\rangle} &= h(g^{X_{M_{\langle 3,3\rangle}} X_{M_{\langle 3,2\rangle}}} \bmod p) \\
K'_{\langle 1,0\rangle} &= h(g^{X_{M_{\langle 3,3\rangle}} X_{M_{\langle 3,0\rangle}}} \bmod p) \\
K'_{\langle 0,0\rangle} &= h(g^{X_{M_{\langle 3,3\rangle}} X_{M_{\langle 3,4\rangle}}} \bmod p)
\end{aligned}
$$

We denote the above key agreement procedures as follows:

$$
\begin{aligned}
M_{\langle 3,3\rangle} &\leftrightarrow M_{\langle 3,2\rangle} : && K'_{\langle 2,1\rangle} \\
M_{\langle 3,3\rangle} &\leftrightarrow M_{\langle 3,0\rangle} : && K'_{\langle 1,0\rangle} \\
M_{\langle 3,3\rangle} &\leftrightarrow M_{\langle 3,4\rangle} : && K'_{\langle 0,0\rangle}
\end{aligned}
$$

Leave: In Fig. 3, the *captains* compute the equation (1), and then the *captain* $M_{\langle 3,1\rangle}$ sends $Y_{M_{\langle 3,1\rangle}}$ to the other *captains*. The other *captains* send each resultant value to $M_{\langle 3,1\rangle}$ as follows:

$$
\begin{aligned}
M_{\langle 3,1\rangle} &\to \{M_{\langle 3,3\rangle}, M_{\langle 2,3\rangle}\} : && Y_{M_{\langle 3,1\rangle}} \\
M_{\langle 3,3\rangle} &\to M_{\langle 3,1\rangle} : && Y_{M_{\langle 3,3\rangle}} \\
M_{\langle 2,3\rangle} &\to M_{\langle 3,1\rangle} : && Y_{M_{\langle 2,3\rangle}}
\end{aligned}
$$

$M_{\langle 3,1 \rangle}$ shares following new keys between $M_{\langle 3,3 \rangle}$ and $M_{\langle 2,3 \rangle}$, respectively:

$$K'_{\langle 1,0 \rangle} = h(g^{X_{M_{\langle 3,1 \rangle}} X_{M_{\langle 3,3 \rangle}}} \bmod p)$$
$$K'_{\langle 0,0 \rangle} = h(g^{X_{M_{\langle 3,1 \rangle}} X_{M_{\langle 2,3 \rangle}}} \bmod p)$$

We denote the above key agreement procedures as follows:

$$M_{\langle 3,1 \rangle} \leftrightarrow M_{\langle 3,3 \rangle} : K'_{\langle 1,0 \rangle}$$
$$M_{\langle 3,1 \rangle} \leftrightarrow M_{\langle 2,3 \rangle} : K'_{\langle 0,0 \rangle}$$

DH Protocol on Distributed Strategy *Join*: In Fig. 2, the newcomer $M_{\langle 3,3 \rangle}$ and the *captain* $M_{\langle 3,2 \rangle}$ perform the DH key agreement protocol with the key derivation. $M_{\langle 3,2 \rangle}$ also performs it with $M_{\langle 3,0 \rangle}$. Lastly, $M_{\langle 3,0 \rangle}$ performs it with $M_{\langle 3,4 \rangle}$ as follows:

$$M_{\langle 3,3 \rangle} \leftrightarrow M_{\langle 3,2 \rangle} : K'_{\langle 2,1 \rangle}$$
$$M_{\langle 3,2 \rangle} \leftrightarrow M_{\langle 3,0 \rangle} : K'_{\langle 1,0 \rangle}$$
$$M_{\langle 3,0 \rangle} \leftrightarrow M_{\langle 3,4 \rangle} : K'_{\langle 0,0 \rangle}$$

Leave: In Fig. 3, the *captains* $M_{\langle 3,1 \rangle}$ and $M_{\langle 3,3 \rangle}$ perform the DH key agreement protocol with the key derivation. $M_{\langle 3,3 \rangle}$ also performs it with $M_{\langle 2,3 \rangle}$ as follows:

$$M_{\langle 3,1 \rangle} \leftrightarrow M_{\langle 3,3 \rangle} : K'_{\langle 1,0 \rangle}$$
$$M_{\langle 3,3 \rangle} \leftrightarrow M_{\langle 2,3 \rangle} : K'_{\langle 0,0 \rangle}$$

Note that a *captain* who performs the DH protocol twice, such as $M_{\langle 3,2 \rangle}$ and $M_{\langle 3,0 \rangle}$ in Fig. 2 and $M_{\langle 3,3 \rangle}$ in Fig. 3, can merge the two values to be sent into one value using the same idea of the dedicated strategy.

3.7 Key Distribution

A *captain* distributes a new key that is derived from a DH key agreement to the subtree that it belongs to. A new key to be associated with a rekeying node is encrypted with the node's old key in a join protocol and is encrypted by a key associated with a child node of the rekeying node in a leave protocol. The encryptions on the FDLKH, however, are performed by *captains* not by a central server. Our key distribution scheme has slightly different two types of strategies, dedicated and distributed strategy. In the following, we explain our key distribution protocols along with the examples in Fig. 2 and Fig. 3.

Key Distribution on Dedicated Strategy *Join*: In Fig. 2, the *captains* $M_{\langle 3,0 \rangle}$ and $M_{\langle 3,4 \rangle}$ encrypt the new keys $K'_{\langle 1,0 \rangle}$ and $K'_{\langle 0,0 \rangle}$ by using the old keys $K_{\langle 1,0 \rangle}$ and $K_{\langle 0,0 \rangle}$ respectively and then send the encryptions to the subtrees $T_{\langle 1,0 \rangle}$ and $T_{\langle 0,0 \rangle}$ as follows:

$$M_{\langle 3,0 \rangle} \rightarrow T_{\langle 1,0 \rangle} : E(K_{\langle 1,0 \rangle}, K'_{\langle 1,0 \rangle})$$
$$M_{\langle 3,4 \rangle} \rightarrow T_{\langle 0,0 \rangle} : E(K_{\langle 0,0 \rangle}, K'_{\langle 0,0 \rangle})$$

Leave: In Fig. 3, the *captains* $M_{\langle 3,3 \rangle}$ and $M_{\langle 2,3 \rangle}$ encrypt the new keys $K'_{\langle 1,0 \rangle}$ and $K'_{\langle 0,0 \rangle}$ by using the keys $K_{\langle 2,1 \rangle}$ and $K_{\langle 1,1 \rangle}$ respectively and then send the encryptions to the subtrees $T_{\langle 2,1 \rangle}$ and $T_{\langle 1,1 \rangle}$ as follows:

$$M_{\langle 3,3 \rangle} \rightarrow T_{\langle 2,1 \rangle} : \quad E(K_{\langle 2,1 \rangle}, K'_{\langle 1,0 \rangle})$$
$$M_{\langle 2,3 \rangle} \rightarrow T_{\langle 1,1 \rangle} : \quad E(K_{\langle 1,1 \rangle}, K'_{\langle 0,0 \rangle})$$

After that, $M_{\langle 3,1 \rangle}$ who knows all new keys encrypts the new key $K'_{\langle 0,0 \rangle}$ by using the new key $K'_{\langle 1,0 \rangle}$ that was sent on the previous step and performs a supplementary sending to the subtree $T_{\langle 1,0 \rangle}$ as follows:

$$M_{\langle 3,1 \rangle} \rightarrow T_{\langle 1,0 \rangle} : \quad E(K'_{\langle 1,0 \rangle}, K'_{\langle 0,0 \rangle})$$

Key Distribution on Distributed Strategy *Join:* In Fig. 2, the *captains* $M_{\langle 3,0 \rangle}$ and $M_{\langle 3,4 \rangle}$ encrypt the new keys $K'_{\langle 1,0 \rangle}$ and $K'_{\langle 0,0 \rangle}$ by using the old keys $K_{\langle 1,0 \rangle}$ and $K_{\langle 0,0 \rangle}$ respectively and send the encryptions to the subtrees $T_{\langle 1,0 \rangle}$ and $T_{\langle 0,0 \rangle}$ as follows:

$$M_{\langle 3,0 \rangle} \rightarrow T_{\langle 1,0 \rangle} : \quad E(K_{\langle 1,0 \rangle}, K'_{\langle 1,0 \rangle})$$
$$M_{\langle 3,4 \rangle} \rightarrow T_{\langle 0,0 \rangle} : \quad E(K_{\langle 0,0 \rangle}, K'_{\langle 0,0 \rangle})$$

At this moment, the newcomer $M_{\langle 3,3 \rangle}$ only knows the new key $K'_{\langle 2,1 \rangle}$; therefore, $M_{\langle 3,2 \rangle}$ and $M_{\langle 3,0 \rangle}$ encrypt the new keys $K'_{\langle 1,0 \rangle}$ and $K'_{\langle 0,0 \rangle}$ by using $K'_{\langle 2,1 \rangle}$ and $K'_{\langle 1,0 \rangle}$ respectively, and then send the encryptions to $M_{\langle 3,3 \rangle}$ as follows:

$$M_{\langle 3,2 \rangle} \rightarrow M_{\langle 3,3 \rangle} : \quad E(K'_{\langle 2,1 \rangle}, K'_{\langle 1,0 \rangle})$$
$$M_{\langle 3,0 \rangle} \rightarrow M_{\langle 3,3 \rangle} : \quad E(K'_{\langle 1,0 \rangle}, K'_{\langle 0,0 \rangle})$$

Leave: In Fig. 3, the *captains* $M_{\langle 3,3 \rangle}$ and $M_{\langle 2,3 \rangle}$ encrypt the new keys $K'_{\langle 1,0 \rangle}$ and $K'_{\langle 0,0 \rangle}$ by using the keys $K_{\langle 2,1 \rangle}$ and $K_{\langle 1,1 \rangle}$ respectively and send the encryptions to the subtrees $T_{\langle 2,1 \rangle}$ and $T_{\langle 1,1 \rangle}$ as follows:

$$M_{\langle 3,3 \rangle} \rightarrow T_{\langle 2,1 \rangle} : \quad E(K_{\langle 2,1 \rangle}, K'_{\langle 1,0 \rangle})$$
$$M_{\langle 2,3 \rangle} \rightarrow T_{\langle 1,1 \rangle} : \quad E(K_{\langle 1,1 \rangle}, K'_{\langle 0,0 \rangle})$$

After that, $M_{\langle 3,3 \rangle}$ encrypts the new key $K'_{\langle 0,0 \rangle}$ by using the new key $K'_{\langle 1,0 \rangle}$ and performs a supplementary sending to the subtree $T_{\langle 1,0 \rangle}$ as follows:

$$M_{\langle 3,3 \rangle} \rightarrow T_{\langle 1,0 \rangle} : \quad E(K'_{\langle 1,0 \rangle}, K'_{\langle 0,0 \rangle})$$

3.8   Key Update

After the key distributions, each member decrypts and obtains new keys. Finally each member associates the new keys with the rekeying nodes in one's own binary key tree.

The above mentioned join/leave protocols are generalized in the appendix B of this paper.

4   Evaluations

We evaluate the FDLKH from two points of view, number of keys and costs for a join and a leave. To make comparisons, we also apply the same criteria to the two centralized schemes, the basic and the LKH scheme mentioned in Section 2. For simplicity's sake, we assume that the degree of a tree for the LKH is 2 (i.e., a binary tree), the number of members before a leave or after a join is some power of 2, a tree forms a complete binary tree on the LKH and the FDLKH. In the situation, the equation $l = \log_2 n$ is valid when $M_{\langle l,m \rangle}$ joins or leaves a group.

4.1   Number of Keys

Table 1 shows the total variety of keys in a group and the number of keys that a member of a group holds. The number of keys per member on the FDLKH is 1 less than that on the LKH because a member on the LKH has an individual key, whereas a member on the FDLKH does not have it. Owing to the individual keys, the total variety of keys in a group on the FDLKH is approximately half of that on the LKH.

Table 1. Number of keys

	Total	per Member
Basic	$n + 1$	2
LKH	$2n - 1$	$l + 1$
FDLKH	$n - 1$	l

4.2   Cost for a Join

Table 2 describes the costs for a join on the four schemes: basic, LKH, FDLKH on dedicated and distributed strategy. Here the costs mean the number of times of DH key agreement (DH), symmetric key encryption (Enc.) and decryption (Dec.) on each entity. In the table, *Key Server* means a central key management server; *Regular Member* indicates members of a group excepting *captains* and a newcomer. The dedicated strategy needs a newcomer to perform l times of the DH protocol[1], instead of l decryptions with an individual key on the LKH. I.e., the newcomer on the dedicated strategy is required relatively high computational power than the LKH[2]. In contrast, the distributed strategy needs a newcomer to perform the DH protocol only once and $l - 1$ decryptions. On the LKH, the average number of decryptions on a member asymptotically comes close to

---

[1] As mentioned in Section 3.6, the FDLKH can omit a part of the DH protocol. Therefore, in fact, the computational cost of the FDLKH is less than the same times of the conventional two party DH protocol.

[2] Note that a newcomer on the LKH is required additional cost to share an individual key with the central server.

2[6]. The FDLKH inherits this property, therefore, a regular member performs approximately 2 decryptions (this property is also applied to the cost for a leave). The way to derive this average is shown in the appendix A of this paper. The load on the key server on the LKH, i.e., $2l$ encryptions, is distributed to the *captains* on the FDLKH. Fig. 4(a) and Fig. 4(b) illustrate the cost of symmetric key cryptosystem, which is the sum numbers of encryptions and decryptions, for a join on the dedicated/distributed strategy of the FDLKH. The cost on the regular member is derived from the equation (2) in the appendix A.

Table 2. Costs for a join

	Entity	DH	Enc.	Dec.
	Newcomer	-	-	1
Basic	per Member	-	-	1
	Key Server	-	2	-
	Newcomer	-	-	l
LKH	per Member	-	-	2
	Key Server	-	$2l$	-
	Newcomer	l	-	-
FDLKH	per Regular Member	-	-	2
(dedicated)	per Captain	1	1	$\frac{l-1}{2}$
	Newcomer	1	-	$l-1$
FDLKH	per Regular Member	-	-	2
(distributed)	per Captain	$\frac{2l-1}{l}$	$\frac{2l-2}{l}$	$\frac{(l-1)(l-2)}{2l}$

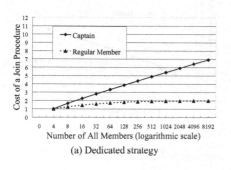

(a) Dedicated strategy

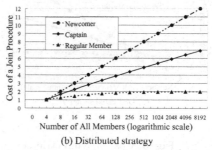

(b) Distributed strategy

Fig. 4. Cost of symmetric key cryptosystem for a join on FDLKH

4.3   Cost for a Leave

Table 3 describes the costs of DH key agreement, symmetric key encryption and decryption for a leave on each scheme. In the table, *Regular Member* indicates members of a group excepting *captains* and a seceder; *Buddy Captain* means a *captain* who represents a subtree rooted at the parent node of a seceder, that is, the neighboring *captain* of the seceder. The dedicated strategy of the FDLKH needs the *Buddy Captain* to conduct many tasks. In contrast, the distributed strategy allots the tasks to all *captains*. Fig. 5(a) and Fig. 5(b) illustrate the cost of symmetric key cryptosystem for a leave on the dedicated/distributed strategy of the FDLKH.

Table 3. Costs for a leave

	Entity	DH	Enc.	Dec.
	Seceder	-	-	-
Basic	per Member	-	-	1
	Key Server	-	$n-1$	-
	Seceder	-	-	-
LKH	per Member	-	-	2
	Key Server	-	$2l$	-
	Seceder	-	-	-
FDLKH	per Regural Member	-	-	2
(dedicated)	per Captain	1	1	$\frac{l-2}{2}$
	Buddy Captain	$l-1$	$l-2$	-
	Seceder	-	-	-
FDLKH	per Regular Member	-	-	2
(distributed)	per Captain	$\frac{2l-2}{l}$	$\frac{2l-3}{l}$	$\frac{(l-1)(l-2)}{2l}$

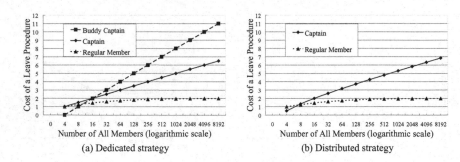

(a) Dedicated strategy   (b) Distributed strategy

Fig. 5. Cost of symmetric key cryptosystem for a leave on FDLKH

5   Conclusion and Future Works

In this paper, we proposed a fully decentralized key management scheme that does not require any central server to update a group key. Our scheme FDLKH is established with the help of *captains* who are ones of members of a group and perform the key agreement and key distribution as the representatives of subgroups in the group, instead of a central server. The FDLKH has two kinds of strategies, that is, the dedicated and distributed strategy. In the former strategy, a single entity dedicates its computational power to the rekeying. In the latter strategy, the computations for the rekeying are further distributed. Whether in the dedicated strategy or in the distributed strategy, each member of the group only knows the keys that it ought to know. We estimated the number of keys on the FDLKH. Since the FDLKH does not need individual keys, the number of keys per member was 1 less than that of the LKH. This reduction cut down the total variety of keys on the FDLKH to approximately half of that of the LKH. We also estimated the cost for a join and leave. Because the FDLKH inherits the efficiency of the rekeying mechanism on the LKH, the cost was kept $O(\log n)$, furthermore, it was highly distributed among the members in the group. The algorithm of the *captain* selection is one of the important components of the FDLKH. We described a couple of directions for designing the algorithm, that is, taking over the captaincy in turn and deciding the *captains* by some criteria (e.g., computational power). We will further discuss detailed algorithms for the *captain* selection that does not need a central server.

References

1. Yoshida, M., Kuroda, M., Kiyomoto, S., Tanaka, T.: A secure service architecture for beyond 3G wireless network. Proc. 6th International Symposium on Wireless Personal Multimedia Communications, Vol. 2 (2003) 579-583
2. Kuroda, M., Inoue, M., Okubo, A., Sakakura, T., Shimizu, K., Adachi, F.: Scalable mobile ethernet and fast vertical handover. Proc. IEEE Wireless Communications and Networking Conference 2004 (2004) A27-3
3. Harney, H., Muckenhirn, C., Rivers, T.: Group key management protocol (GKMP) specification. IETF, RFC 2093 (1997)
4. Harney, H., Muckenhirn, C., Rivers, T.: Group key management protocol (GKMP) architecture. IETF, RFC 2094 (1997)
5. Wallner, D., Harder, E., Agee, R.: Key management for multicast: issues and architectures. IETF, RFC 2627 (1999)
6. Wong, C. K., Gouda, M., Lam, S.: Secure group communication using key graphs. IEEE/ACM Trans. on Networking, Vol. 8, No. 1 (2000) 16-30
7. Canetti, R., Garay, J., Itkis, G., Micciancio, D., Naor, M., Pinkas, B.: Multicast security: a taxonomy and efficient constructions. Proc. IEEE Infocom '99, Vol.2 (1999) 708-716
8. McGrew, D.A., Sherman, A.T.: Key establishment in large dynamic groups using one-way function trees. IEEE Trans. on Software Engineering, Vol. 29, No. 5 (2003) 444-458
9. Perrig, A., Song, D., Tygar, J.D.: ELK: a new protocol for efficient large-group key distribution. Proc. 2001 IEEE Security and Privacy Symposium (2001) 247-262
10. Perrig, A., Szewczyk, R., Wen, V., Culler, D., Tygar, J. D.: SPINS: security protocols for sensor networks. Proc. Mobile Computing and Networking 2001 (2001) 189-199
11. Law, Y. W., Corin, R., Etalle, S., Hartel, P. H.: A formally verified decentralized key management architecture for wireless sensor networks. Proc. Personal Wireless Communications 2003 (2003) 27-39

12. Steer, D. G., Strawczynski, L., Diffie, W., Wiener, M.: A secure audio teleconference system. Proc. Advances in Cryptology-CRYPTO '88 (1988) 520-528
13. Burmester, M., Desmedt, Y.: A secure and efficient conference key distribution system. Proc. Advances in Cryptology-EUROCRYPT '94 (1994) 275-286
14. Steiner, M., Tsudik, G., Waidner, M.: Key agreement in dynamic peer groups. IEEE Trans. on Parallel and Distributed Systems, Vol. 11, No. 8 (2000) 769-780
15. Alves-Foss, J.: An efficient secure authenticated group key exchange algorithm for large and dynamic groups. Proc. 23rd National Information Systems Security Conference (2000) 254-266
16. Kim, Y., Perrig, A., Tsudik, G.: Simple and fault-tolerant key agreement for dynamic collaborative groups. ACM Conference on Computer and Communications Security 2000 (2000) 235-244
17. Lynch, N.: Distributed algorithms. Morgan Kaufmann Publishers (1996)

Appendix A: Number of Decryptions on a Regular Member

Let n be the number of all members in a group, l be the number of *captains*. Since there is a newcomer or a seceder, the number of regular members is $n - l - 1$. Here we assume that n is some power of 2 and a key tree forms a complete binary tree. The regular members in half of the tree, $\frac{n}{2} - 1$ members, perform one decryption; the regular members in further half of the remaining tree, $\frac{n}{2^2} - 1$ members, perform two decryptions. Continuing these calculations, the average number of decryptions on a regular member derives as follows:

$$\frac{\sum_{t=1}^{l-1}(\frac{n}{2^t} - 1)t}{n - l - 1} = \frac{2 - (\frac{l+1}{2^{l-1}} + \frac{l(l-1)}{2})}{1 - \frac{l+1}{n}} \tag{2}$$

$$< \frac{2}{1 - \frac{l+1}{n}} \tag{3}$$

The expression (3) asymptotically comes close to 2 according to increasing n.

Appendix B: Generalized Protocols

In this appendix, we generalize the join and leave protocols of the FDLKH on both the dedicated and distributed strategies. It is assumed that $M_{\langle l,m \rangle}$ is the newcomer/seceder who passed some authentication process of a group and sent a join/leave request to the group. Procedures including integers i, j, k are the repetitive procedures that are repeated according to the integers. Some key distribution procedures marked '*' are performed by a *captain* only when the target subtree, i.e., destination of the key distribution, has one or more members excluding the *captain*.

Join Protocol on the Dedicated Strategy

(1) **if** $(l = 1)$

(2)   **Update** $T_{\langle 0,0 \rangle}$;

(3)   **Select** $C_{\langle 0,0 \rangle}$;

(4) $M_{\langle 1,1 \rangle} \leftrightarrow C_{\langle 0,0 \rangle} : K'_{\langle 0,0 \rangle}$;

(5)* $C_{\langle 0,0 \rangle} \rightarrow T_{\langle 1,0 \rangle} : E(K_{\langle 1,0 \rangle}, K'_{\langle 0,0 \rangle})$;

(6) $K_{\langle 0,0 \rangle} := K'_{\langle 0,0 \rangle}$;

(7) **else if** $(l \geq 2)$

(8)   **Update** $T_{\langle l-1, \lfloor \frac{m}{2} \rfloor \rangle}$;

(9)   **Select** $C_{\langle l-i, \lfloor \frac{m}{2^i} \rfloor \rangle}$;

(10) $M_{\langle l,m \rangle} \leftrightarrow C_{\langle l-i, \lfloor \frac{m}{2^i} \rfloor \rangle} : K'_{\langle l-i, \lfloor \frac{m}{2^i} \rfloor \rangle}$;

(11) $C_{\langle l-j, \lfloor \frac{m}{2^j} \rfloor \rangle} \rightarrow T_{\langle l-j, \lfloor \frac{m}{2^j} \rfloor \rangle} :$
       $E(K_{\langle l-j, \lfloor \frac{m}{2^j} \rfloor \rangle}, K'_{\langle l-j, \lfloor \frac{m}{2^j} \rfloor \rangle})$;

(12)* $C_{\langle l-1, \lfloor \frac{m}{2} \rfloor \rangle} \rightarrow T_{\langle l, m+(-1)^m \rangle} :$
       $E(K_{\langle l,m+(-1)^m \rangle}, K'_{\langle l-1, \lfloor \frac{m}{2} \rfloor \rangle})$;

(13) $K_{\langle l-i, \lfloor \frac{m}{2^i} \rfloor \rangle} := K'_{\langle l-i, \lfloor \frac{m}{2^i} \rfloor \rangle}$;

* if needed

Join Protocol on the Distributed Strategy

(1) **if** $(l = 1)$

(2)-(6) Similar to the join protocol on
         the dedicated strategy

(7) **else if** $(l \geq 2)$

(8)   **Update** $T_{\langle l-1, \lfloor \frac{m}{2} \rfloor \rangle}$;

(9)   **Select** $C_{\langle l-i, \lfloor \frac{m}{2^i} \rfloor \rangle}$;

(10) $M_{\langle l,m \rangle} \leftrightarrow C_{\langle l-1, \lfloor \frac{m}{2} \rfloor \rangle} : K'_{\langle l-1, \lfloor \frac{m}{2} \rfloor \rangle}$;

(11) $C_{\langle l-(j-1), \lfloor \frac{m}{2^{j-1}} \rfloor \rangle} \leftrightarrow C_{\langle l-j, \lfloor \frac{m}{2^j} \rfloor \rangle} :$
       $K'_{\langle l-j, \lfloor \frac{m}{2^j} \rfloor \rangle}$;

(12) $C_{\langle l-j, \lfloor \frac{m}{2^j} \rfloor \rangle} \rightarrow T_{\langle l-j, \lfloor \frac{m}{2^j} \rfloor \rangle} :$
       $E(K_{\langle l-j, \lfloor \frac{m}{2^j} \rfloor \rangle}, K'_{\langle l-j, \lfloor \frac{m}{2^j} \rfloor \rangle})$;

(13)* $C_{\langle l-1, \lfloor \frac{m}{2} \rfloor \rangle} \rightarrow T_{\langle l, m+(-1)^m \rangle} :$
       $E(K_{\langle l,m+(-1)^m \rangle}, K'_{\langle l-1, \lfloor \frac{m}{2} \rfloor \rangle})$;

(14) $C_{\langle l-(j-1), \lfloor \frac{m}{2^{j-1}} \rfloor \rangle} \rightarrow M_{\langle l,m \rangle} :$
       $E(K'_{\langle l-(j-1), \lfloor \frac{m}{2^{j-1}} \rfloor \rangle}, K'_{\langle l-j, \lfloor \frac{m}{2^j} \rfloor \rangle})$;

(15) $K_{\langle l-i, \lfloor \frac{m}{2^i} \rfloor \rangle} := K'_{\langle l-i, \lfloor \frac{m}{2^i} \rfloor \rangle}$;

* if needed

Leave Protocol on the Dedicated Strategy

(1) **if** $(l = 1)$

(2)   **Remove** $\langle 0,0 \rangle$;

(3)   **Update** $T_{\langle 1, m+(-1)^m \rangle}$;

(4) **else if** $(l = 2)$

(5)   **Select** $C_{\langle 1, \lfloor \frac{m}{2} \rfloor \rangle}$ and $C_{\langle 0,0 \rangle}$;

(6) $C_{\langle 1, \lfloor \frac{m}{2} \rfloor \rangle} \leftrightarrow C_{\langle 0,0 \rangle} : K'_{\langle 0,0 \rangle}$;

(7)* $C_{\langle 0,0 \rangle} \rightarrow T_{\langle 1, \lfloor \frac{m}{2} \rfloor + (-1)^{\lfloor \frac{m}{2} \rfloor} \rangle} :$
       $E(K_{\langle 1, \lfloor \frac{m}{2} \rfloor + (-1)^{\lfloor \frac{m}{2} \rfloor} \rangle}, K'_{\langle 0,0 \rangle})$;

(8)* $C_{\langle 1, \lfloor \frac{m}{2} \rfloor \rangle} \rightarrow T_{\langle 2, m+(-1)^m \rangle} :$
       $E(K_{\langle 2, m+(-1)^m \rangle}, K'_{\langle 0,0 \rangle})$;

(9) $K_{\langle 0,0 \rangle} := K'_{\langle 0,0 \rangle}$;

(10)   **Update** $T_{\langle 1, \lfloor \frac{m}{2} \rfloor \rangle}$;

(11) **else if** $(l \geq 3)$

(12)   **Select** $C_{\langle l-i, \lfloor \frac{m}{2^i} \rfloor \rangle}$;

(13) $C_{\langle l-1, \lfloor \frac{m}{2} \rfloor \rangle} \leftrightarrow C_{\langle l-j, \lfloor \frac{m}{2^j} \rfloor \rangle} : K'_{\langle l-j, \lfloor \frac{m}{2^j} \rfloor \rangle}$;

(14)* $C_{\langle l-j, \lfloor \frac{m}{2^j} \rfloor \rangle} \rightarrow T_{\langle l-(j-1), \lfloor \frac{m}{2^{j-1}} \rfloor + (-1)^{\lfloor \frac{m}{2^{j-1}} \rfloor} \rangle} :$
       $E(K_{\langle l-(j-1), \lfloor \frac{m}{2^{j-1}} \rfloor + (-1)^{\lfloor \frac{m}{2^{j-1}} \rfloor} \rangle}, K'_{\langle l-j, \lfloor \frac{m}{2^j} \rfloor \rangle})$;

(15)* $C_{\langle l-1, \lfloor \frac{m}{2} \rfloor \rangle} \rightarrow T_{\langle l, m+(-1)^m \rangle} :$
       $E(K_{\langle l, m+(-1)^m \rangle}, K'_{\langle l-2, \lfloor \frac{m}{2^2} \rfloor \rangle})$;

(16) $C_{\langle l-1, \lfloor \frac{m}{2} \rfloor \rangle} \rightarrow T_{\langle l-k, \lfloor \frac{m}{2^k} \rfloor \rangle} :$
       $E(K'_{\langle l-k, \lfloor \frac{m}{2^k} \rfloor \rangle}, K'_{\langle l-(k+1), \lfloor \frac{m}{2^{k+1}} \rfloor \rangle})$;

(17) $K_{\langle l-j, \lfloor \frac{m}{2^j} \rfloor \rangle} := K'_{\langle l-j, \lfloor \frac{m}{2^j} \rfloor \rangle}$;

(18)   **Update** $T_{\langle l-1, \lfloor \frac{m}{2} \rfloor \rangle}$;

*if needed

Leave Protocol on the Distributed Strategy

(1) **if** $(l = 1)$

(2)-(3) Similar to the leave protocol on
         the dedicated strategy

(4) **else if** $(l = 2)$

(5)-(10) Similar to the leave protocol on
         the dedicated strategy

(11) **else if** $(l \geq 3)$

(12)   **Select** $C_{\langle l-i, \lfloor \frac{m}{2^i} \rfloor \rangle}$;

(13) $C_{\langle l-(j-1), \lfloor \frac{m}{2^{j-1}} \rfloor \rangle} \leftrightarrow C_{\langle l-j, \lfloor \frac{m}{2^j} \rfloor \rangle} : K'_{\langle l-j, \lfloor \frac{m}{2^j} \rfloor \rangle}$;

(14)* $C_{\langle l-j, \lfloor \frac{m}{2^j} \rfloor \rangle} \rightarrow T_{\langle l-(j-1), \lfloor \frac{m}{2^{j-1}} \rfloor + (-1)^{\lfloor \frac{m}{2^{j-1}} \rfloor} \rangle} :$
       $E(K_{\langle l-(j-1), \lfloor \frac{m}{2^{j-1}} \rfloor + (-1)^{\lfloor \frac{m}{2^{j-1}} \rfloor} \rangle}, K'_{\langle l-j, \lfloor \frac{m}{2^j} \rfloor \rangle})$;

(15)* $C_{\langle l-1, \lfloor \frac{m}{2} \rfloor \rangle} \rightarrow T_{\langle l, m+(-1)^m \rangle} :$
       $E(K_{\langle l, m+(-1)^m \rangle}, K'_{\langle l-2, \lfloor \frac{m}{2^2} \rfloor \rangle})$;

(16) $C_{\langle l-k, \lfloor \frac{m}{2^k} \rfloor \rangle} \rightarrow T_{\langle l-k, \lfloor \frac{m}{2^k} \rfloor \rangle} :$
       $E(K'_{\langle l-k, \lfloor \frac{m}{2^k} \rfloor \rangle}, K'_{\langle l-(k+1), \lfloor \frac{m}{2^{k+1}} \rfloor \rangle})$;

(17) $K_{\langle l-j, \lfloor \frac{m}{2^j} \rfloor \rangle} := K'_{\langle l-j, \lfloor \frac{m}{2^j} \rfloor \rangle}$;

(18)   **Update** $T_{\langle l-1, \lfloor \frac{m}{2} \rfloor \rangle}$;

*if needed

Unconditionally Non-interactive Verifiable Secret Sharing Secure against Faulty Majorities in the Commodity Based Model

Anderson C.A. Nascimento[1], Joern Mueller-Quade[2], Akira Otsuka[1], Goichiro Hanaoka[1], and Hideki Imai[1]

[1] Institute of Industrial Science, The University of Tokyo
4-6-1, Komaba, Meguro-ku, Tokyo, 153-8505 Japan
{anderson,otsuka,hanaoka,imai}@imailab.iis.u-tokyo.ac.jp
[2] Universitaet Karlsruhe, Institut fuer Algorithmen und Kognitive Systeme
Am Fasanengarten 5, 76128 Karlsruhe, Germany
muellerq@ira.uka.de

Abstract. This paper presents a non-interactive verifiable secret sharing scheme (VSS) tolerating a dishonest majority based on data predistributed by a trusted authority. As an application of this VSS scheme we present very efficient unconditionally secure multiparty protocols based on predistributed data which generalize two-party computations based on linear predistributed bit commitments. The main results of this paper are a non-interactive VSS where the amount of data which needs to be predistributed to each player depends on the number of tolerable cheaters only, a simplified multiplication protocol for shared values based on predistributed random products, a protocol for fair exchange of secrets based on predistributed data, and non-interactive zero knowledge proofs for arbitrary polynomial relations.

Keywords: Verifiable secret sharing, pre-distributed data, multiparty protocols.

1 Introduction

This paper gives a protocol for information theoretically secure verifiable secret sharing (VSS) in the commodity based model which tolerates a dishonest majority. On the basis of pre-distributed data a dealer can share a secret such that all players are convinced that the shares they hold are valid, i. e., sets of players larger than a threshold t can reconstruct the shared secret. When dealing with an adversary which is able to corrupt a majority of the players, this requirement is slightly relaxed, since corrupted players are always able to abort the protocol.

As an application of this VSS scheme we present very efficient multiparty protocols in the commodity based model which can tolerate up to $t < n$ corrupted parties. If the number t is known the protocols can be chosen to be robust against $n-t$ players trying to abort the calculation. The protocols can be seen as a generalization of [21] to multiparty protocols. But the multiplication procedure

M. Jakobsson, M. Yung, J. Zhou (Eds.): ACNS 2004, LNCS 3089, pp. 355–368, 2004.

used here is much simpler than the one in in [21] and compared to trivial extensions of [21] like pre-distributing two-party computations like oblivious transfer and then applying a general construction like [13] we save data. The amount of data to be pre-distributed to one party depends, for fixed security parameter and fixed size of the field, only on t and not on the total number n of parties. Due to the advantages of the commodity based model we can obtain a non-interactive VSS allowing non-interactive zero knowledge proofs.

VSS. Tompa and Wolf [29] and McEliece and Swarte [20] were the first to study the problem of secret sharing in presence of a corrupted majority. They proposed solutions which work when the dealer is honest and corrupted players may attempt to cheat during the reconstruction of the secret. Later, Chor et al. [7] defined a complete notion of VSS, and gave a solution which was based on some intractability assumptions.

In Ben-Or et al. [4], an information theoretically secure VSS scheme was proposed which worked against any adversary which corrupts up to less than $1/3$ of the players and the dealer. In [4], it was assumed that the players are connected by pairwise secure channels (the so-called secure channels model). As VSS, when implemented without a broadcast channel, implies Byzantine Agreement, the results of [17] show that the solution of [4] is optimal in the secure channels model.

Rabin and Ben-Or [23] were able to show that in a secure channels plus broadcast channel model unconditionally secure VSS is possible against any dishonest minority. In [11], Cramer et al. proposed a VSS scheme secure against an adaptive adversary which can corrupt any dishonest minority by using a linear information checking protocol. The protocols of [11] and [23] are interactive.

While secrecy in the secure channels plus broadcast channel model can easily be maintained even against an adversary which corrupts a majority of players, the same cannot be said of the validity of the shares. Clearly, correct verifiability of the shares in the presence of a faulty majority cannot be achieved in the secure channels plus broadcast channel model without further assumptions [23].

Assuming that the discrete logarithm problem is intractable Feldman proposed a VSS scheme [12] where the verifiability of the shares is information theoretically secure but the secrecy of the secret is only computationally secure. Pedersen [22] proposed a "dual" of Feldman's scheme. Pedersen's scheme protects the secrecy of the secret unconditionally, while verifiability is protected only computationally under the assumption that the discrete logarithm problem is intractable.

In this paper, we introduce a VSS scheme based on pre-distributed data which is information theoretically secure against *dishonest majorities*, that is, both *the secrecy of the secret* and the *verifiability of the shares* are achieved independently of how much computational power is available to an adversary. Moreover, our solution is non-interactive.

Multiparty Computation. As an application of our protocol, we provide a very simple and efficient information theoretically secure multiparty computation protocol based on pre-distributed data which is secure against dishonest majorities. In [1,2,10] protocols for multiparty computations secure against a faulty majority were proposed. In these papers, it was assumed that all the players were connected by oblivious transfer channels and a broadcast channel was available. Due to the use of pre-distributed data instead of oblivious transfer the protocols presented here are more efficient and do not need zero-knowledge proofs based on cut-and-choose arguments which increase the round complexity of protocols. Furthermore our protocol performs computations directly over a field $GF(q)$ and not only over binary fields.

Finally, it should be remarked that, if a protocol is secure against *any* dishonest majority, even a single player should be able to abort the computation as was pointed out in [10]. However, the protocols for secure computation proposed in [1,2,10,13] can be aborted by a single player *even when the number of honest players is known to be much larger than one*. This is not the case with our protocol. Given that there are n players of which at most t are dishonest, then there exists a secure VSS protocol for which $n - t$ players are necessary to abort the execution of this protocol. This property also holds for the application to multyparty protocols.

1.1   Commodity Based Cryptography and Related Work

In [3] the commodity based cryptographic model was introduced on which the protocols presented here are based. In this model players buy cryptographic primitives from "off-line" servers. These primitives can be used later on to implement general cryptographic protocols. The commodity based model was inspired in the internet architecture, which is usually based on the "client-server" paradigm. Once the primitives, or *commodities* as they are called by Beaver, are acquired, no further interaction between the server and the users is required. Therefore, the server need not know any secret values of the players.

In this contribution, we show that the use of off-lines servers provides very efficient and simple protocols for verifiable secret sharing and secure function evaluation over $GF(q)$ in the presence of a faulty majority.

Although this model was formalized just in [3], several independent works share the same flavor. We cite key-pre-distribution schemes [18], unconditionally secure bit commitments [24,6] and unconditionally secure digital signature schemes [16].

The work which comes closest to the application of our VSS scheme to multiparty computations is [21]. There secure protocols for two-party computations in the commodity based model are proposed. Our protocol for multiparty secure computation can be understood as an extension of [21].

1.2   Our Contribution

In this Section we summarize our contribution. Due to the assumption that there is a trusted center which pre-distributes data during a setup phase, we could design a protocol for verifiable secret sharing which has the following interesting features.

- It is the first VSS protocol where the security of the secret and of the verifiability are achieved even against an all-mighty adaptive adversary which can corrupt any majority of the players and the dealer.
- It is non-interactive
- The verifiability of the protocol is not based on any cut-and-choose argument or expensive zero knowledge proofs.
- It is conceptually very simple.

Furthermore for a fixed security parameter k and a fixed field size q the amount of data which has to be pre-distributed depends on t only.

As an application of our VSS, we propose a protocol for secure multiparty computations which also shows very interesting features (which to the best of our knowledge for the first time appear together in a single protocol): It is based on novel verifiable primitives in the commodity based model which allow two players to perform secure multiplication of shares over $GF(q)$; It is information theoretically secure against any adversary which can corrupt any majority of the players; and given that there are n players of which at most t are dishonest, $n-t$ players are necessary to abort an execution of the multy party computation protocols.

2   Model

Here, we present a model for *non-interactive verifiable secret sharing protocol based on pre-distributed data*. Note that we do not give a general definition of a verifiable secret sharing scheme, but rather propose a model we believe is general enough to cover any non-interactive protocol based on pre-distributed data. For a general definition of a verifiable secret sharing scheme, please look at [23]. We work in the commodity based cryptography model as proposed by Beaver in [3]. There are n players $\{P_1, P_2, \ldots, P_n\}$ a dealer D and a trusted center. Also, we assume the existence of an authenticated broadcast channel. Note that this assumptions are only made to simplify the protocol presentation as a broadcast channel can as well be pre-distributed by the trusted center during a setup phase [3]. The trusted center is supposed to act only during a setup phase and no sensitive information concerning the players input is ever transmitted to it. The players are connected to the trusted center by secure channels. Secure channels between the parties are assumed, too, but can be pre-distributed as well.

We assume a central adversary with unbounded computational power who actively corrupts t players, $t < n$.

Notation. For a VSS scheme Π with a trusted center T, a set of dealers $\mathcal{D}$, and a finite set of players $\mathcal{P}$ the protocol consists of $(\mathcal{S}, \mathcal{K}, \mathcal{V}, \text{Commit}, \text{Share}, \text{Verify})$, where

- $\mathcal{S}$ is a finite set of possible secrets,
- $\mathcal{K}$ is a finite set of possible signing-keys,
- $\mathcal{V}$ is a finite set of possible verification-keys,
- $\mathcal{C}$ is a finite set of possible commitments,
- $\mathcal{S}_h$ is a finite set of possible shares,
- $\text{Commit} : \mathcal{S} \times \mathcal{K} \to \mathcal{C}$ is a commitment-algorithm,
- $\text{Share} : \mathcal{C} \times \mathcal{P} \to \mathcal{S}_h$ is a share-generation-algorithm, and
- $\text{Verify} : \mathcal{C} \times \mathcal{S}_h \times \mathcal{V} \to \{\text{accept}, \text{reject}\}$ is a verification-algorithm.
- $\text{Reconstruct} : \mathcal{S}_h^{t+1} \to \mathcal{S}$ is a reconstruction algorithm which regains a secret s from $t + 1$ valid shares.

System Setup by T. For a dealer $D \in \mathcal{D}$, T chooses a signing-key $K \in \mathcal{K}$, and for each player P_i in $\mathcal{P}$, T chooses a verification-key $v_i \in \mathcal{V}$, then transmits the keys via private channels to D and each P_i. Each player keeps the keys secret. After delivering the keys, T never engages in the protocol again.

Share. On input of a secret $s \in \mathcal{S}$, D broadcasts a commitment $c \in \mathcal{C}$ where $c = \text{Commit}(s, K)$ to all players. Then, each player P_i computes his share $s_i \in \mathcal{S}_h$ where $s_i = \text{Share}(c, P_i)$. A verification of the validity of the shares will not be necessary in this stage as this can be guaranteed from the pre-distributed data.

Reconstruct. All the players $\{P_1, P_2, \ldots, P_n\}$ broadcast their shares $\{s_1, s_2, \ldots, s_n\}$. Each player P_i checks if there exits a subset of players $\{P_{i_1}, P_{i_2}, \ldots, P_{i_{t+1}}\}$ with $\text{Verify}(c, s_{i_k}, V_i) = accept$ for all $k = 1, \ldots, t+1$ where $t + 1$ is equal to or greater than the reconstruction threshold. If this is the case, P_i runs $\text{Reconstruct}(s_{i_1}, \ldots, s_{i_{t+1}})$ and outputs s, otherwise it outputs Δ.

The scheme is said to be *secure* if it satisfies the following properties[11]:

1. *Termination*: If the dealer D is honest then all the honest players complete the Share protocol and if honest players decide to run the Reconstruct protocol after a successful run of the Share protocol they should generate output (possibly Δ indicating that no secret could be reconstructed).

2. *Secrecy*: If the dealer is honest and no honest player has started Reconstruct, them the adversary has no information about the secret s unless the reconstruction threshold was chosen to be smaller than the number of players the adversary can corrupt.

3. *Correctness:* Once the uncorrupted players complete the protocol Share, there is a fixed value $r \in \mathcal{S}$, so that the following requirement holds: If at least $t + 1$ players are willing to reconstruct the secret, each uncorrupted player, with high probability, outputs r at the end of Reconstruct. If there are more than $n - t$ Byzantine faults, all honest players output Δ and the protocol terminates. Furthermore if the dealer was uncorrupted $r = s$.

Remark 1. Note that our definition of security is slightly weaker than the definitions of security for VSS protocols with honest majority [11]. In our definition, cheating parties can prevent the completion of the protocol. When dishonest majorities are in question, this situation cannot be avoided. If the protocol is secure against adversaries which corrupt up to t parties, $t > n/2$, always $n - t$ parties will be able to abort the protocol.

3   A VSS Protocol Based on Pre-distributed Data

The protocol Π consists of the following sub-protocols: Setup, Share, Reconstruct, and Verify. In the unconditionally secure protocol below the probability of cheating successfully equals the probability to successfully guess an element from the field over which computations are done. Hence we choose a prime power q and the field $GF(q)$ with q elements depending on the security parameter, e. g., $q = 2^k$.

For simplicity, we assume $\mathcal{S} = \mathcal{C} = GF(q)$, $\mathcal{K} \in GF(q)[x, y]$, $\mathcal{V} = GF(q) \times GF(q)[z]$ as in the following construction.

The basic intuition behind the protocol is simple. The trusted center will share a random value with the players in a way that each player is committed to his share to each other player. When executing the Share algorithm, the dealer changes this random number, to which he is committed by the pre-distributed VSS, into a commitment to his secret.

Setup. A trusted center T randomly chooses bivariate polynomial $f(x, y) \in GF(q)[x, y]$ such that

$$f(x, y) = \sum_{i=0}^{t+1} \sum_{j=0}^{t+1} a_{ij} x^i y^j,$$

where each coefficient a_{ij} is randomly and uniformly chosen from $GF(q)$, and $t + 1$ is the threshold of the secret sharing scheme.

T sends the bivariate polynomial $f(x, y)$ to the dealer D through a private channel. Then T chooses for each player P_i a random verification key (a secret point) $v_i \neq 0$ from $GF(q)$, and sends v_i, $f(v_i, y)$ and $s_i(x) = f(x, i)$ to P_i through a private channel[1]. After delivering these private keys, T does not engage in the rest of the protocol.

For the random "secret" $a = f(0, 0)$ the polynomial $f(v_i, y)$ will later be used by P_i to verify shares of other players and the polynomial $s_i(x)$ is the share of the party P_i for a.

---

[1] The index i which is the "name" of a participant is here interpreted as a value of $GF(q)$. To have enough different names we need $q \geq n$.

Share. In this stage of the protocol the shares of a random secret a as well as the verification polynomials will be changed to shares and verification polynomials for a specific secret s.

Let

$$g(x,y) = \sum_{i=1}^{t+1} \sum_{j=1}^{t+1} b_{ij} x^i y^j$$

denote a publicly known polynomial for which $g(0,0) = 0$. On input s for a secret, the dealer D computes a value c satisfying $c = s - a$, where a is computed as: $a = f(0,0)$

Then, D broadcasts the value c. Next each party P_i calculates the polynomial $g(v_i, y) + c$ and adds it to the polynomial $f(v_i, y)$ which was obtained by P_i in the sharing phase to obtain the new verification function $g(v_i, y) + c + f(v_i, y)$ for the shared secret s. The shares $s'_i(x)$ for the secret s will be computed by adding $g(x, i)$ to $s_i(x) = s(x, i)$ which was obtained by P_i in the setup phase.

For the secret $s = f(0,0) + g(0,0) + c$ the verification functions and the shares computed above have the same distribution as if s would have been equal to the value a used in the setup phase.

As $f(x,y)$ is chosen by the trusted center and $g(x,y)$ is publicly known the validity of the shares computed above is evident and need not be verified at this stage.

Reconstruct. It is enough to show how a shared random secret a is reconstructed. The notation will therefore be as in the setup phase. Each player P_i broadcasts his share $s_i(x)$ over the broadcast channel.

Verify

On receiving a share $s_j(x)$ from the player P_j over the broadcast channel, each player P_i checks the share by checking the following equation:

$$ver_{ji} = \left\{ \begin{array}{c} accept \text{ if } s_j(v_i) = f(v_i, j) \\ reject \text{ otherwise} \end{array} \right\}$$

If $ver_{ji} = reject$, player P_i broadcasts the message $reject(j)$. If more $t + 1$ players broadcast $reject(j)$, the player P_j is disqualified. It is easy to see that (with high probability) all honest players will obtain the same result in the verification procedure.

If $n - t$ or more players are rejected, all the players output Δ and the protocol terminates.

If less than $n - t$ players are rejected, there will be a set of $t + 1$ valid shares $s_{i_1}(x), \ldots, s_{i_t}(x)$ in possession of each honest player P_i. Thus, the secret $a = f(0,0)$ can be reconstructed by Lagrange interpolation from $s_{i_1}(0), \ldots, s_{i_{t+1}}(0)$.

From this construction we will obtain the following result which we state without proof.

Theorem 1. *The above protocol is a secure VSS in the commodity based model.*

Note that in our protocol, for each player P_i the secret "check" information $v_i, 1 \le i \le n$ is never released, so it can be distributed only once for several protocols (even with different dealers). The check information can hence be safely reused within a bigger protocol and reduce communication from the trusted center to the players.

Another interesting fact about this VSS scheme is that, given that each player uses the same verification information v_i in all of its executions, it is linear, that is, the sum of two shares of two secrets becomes a verifiable share of the sum of the secrets. We state the following proposition without proof.

Proposition 1. *Denote by $[s]_i$ the pair of the verification function and the share held by a player P_i for a given secret s. Then for two secrets a, b shared with the above VSS scheme using the same verification information v_i for each player P_i and a value $\lambda \in GF(q)$ it holds that $[a]_i + \lambda[b]_i = [a + \lambda b]_i$.*

Note that the commitment algorithm Commit(s, K) is very related to the idea of check vectors. Pre-distributed commitments are very much similar to Rabin's "check vectors" [23]. The idea of a "check vector" is that a party A provides some correlated secrets to parties B and C, and these secrets let B send an authenticated message to C. This is similar to what we do, except that the typical use of check-vectors in the literature, party A knows the message (whereas in our constructions it does not). Thus, as party A need not know the message when it distributes the check vectors, it can be used in an off-line way.

We note that the trusted center can share a random secret with the players. Moreover, the trusted center can pre-distribute shares to secrets which have a certain relation. This feature will be explicitly used in the next section as well as in the protocols for secure multiparty computations.

4   Proving Polynomial Relations among Shared Secrets

A linear VSS can be seen as a linear commitment to the shared secret. Using techniques from [21] it is possible to very efficiently prove polynomial relations among shared secrets.

We denote by $[a]_i$ the pair of the verification function and the share the player P_i holds from the secret a.

For proving a linear relation among commitments one turns this relation into a set of linear functions which all must equal zero when evaluated on the committed values if and only if the relation holds. Proving that a given linear function evaluates to zero on committed values can be done by means of Proposition 1: using the linearity of the VSS scheme one computes from the given commitments a new commitment which represents the linear function evaluated on the given commitments and this new commitment is then opened to be zero.

To be able to prove arbitrary polynomial relations on committed values we will first restate a protocol from [21] which allows to compute a new commitment which represents the product of two given commitments. This protocol can directly be applied to the linear secret sharing scheme presented here. The protocol is called a *distributed one time multiplication proof (DOTMP)* and consists of two phases: a pre-distribution phase where the trusted center shares additional values among the players and a non interactive proof where the additional shared information is used to compute shares to the product of two shared values without reconstructiong these.

Protocol DOTMP

- Initialization: The trusted center verifiably shares (with the players) three random numbers l, l' and l'', such that $l'' = ll'$. Thus, each player P_i receives $[l]_i, [l']_i$ and $[l'' = ll']_i$
- Multiplication: Each player P_i player now holds shares to three random values l, l' and l'', such that $l'' = ll'$ as well as two shares $[a]_i$ and $[b]_i$ to the values a, b which are to be multiplied, to obtain a share $[ab]_i$ to ab each player P_i computes $[y]_i = [a]_i - [l]_i = [a - l]_i$ and $[y']_i = [b]_i - [l']_i = [b - l']_i$ and together with the other players reconstruct y and y'. Now P_i calculates $[ll']_i + y[l']_i + y'[l]_i + yy'$.

Using this protocol arbitrary polynomial relations can be proven analogously to the linear relations. The polynomial relations are turned into a set of multivariate polynomials which should simultaneously vanish on the committed values. To prove that a polynomial vanishes on given committed values a new commitment representing the polynomial evaluated at the given commitments is computed step by step using the above multiplication protocal as well as addition and scalar multiplication which are granted by the linearity of the VSS scheme. The new commitment is then opened to be zero. Summarizing the above we obtain:

Proposition 2. *For given shared values a, b, c and a constant $\lambda \in GF(q)$ it is possible to calculate shares for the value $ab + \lambda c$ if and only if $t + 1$ players cooperate.*

Especially it is possible to give zero knowledge proofs for arbitrary polynomial relations on shared values.

Proof. The security and correctness are obvious for the linear part and have only to be proven for multiplicative relations, i. e., for the DOTMP protocol:

We now analyze the security and correctness of our protocol for proving multiplicative relations among shares. To show that it is secure, note that the players only learns the values y and y', which give no information on a and b, since l and l' are random numbers.

To show the correctness of our protocol, we note that $[ll'] + y[l'] + y'[l] + yy' = [ll'] + (a-l)[l'] + (b-l')[l] + (a-l)(b-l') = [ll' + al' - ll' + bl - l'l + ab - lb - l'a + ll'] = [ab]$ (due to the linearity of the VSS).

By applying addition of shares and multiplication of shares we can obtain shares for arbitrary polynomial relations among shares. E.g. to prove that $mm' = m''$ the dealer lets the players compute $[mm'] - [m''] = [mm' - m'']$ and shows this to be zero.

For adding two shared values or for multiplication with a constant no-one has to know the shared values which are linearly transformed. Note that in DOTMP, too, no-one has to know the shared values which have to be multiplied in advance as the values y and y' are reconstructed in the protocol. Hence an arbitrary polynomial evaluation on shared values works iff $t+1$ players cooperate. This is optimal as $n-t$ players could abort the VSS scheme anyway. These linear transformations and multiplications on shared values will be the building blocks for the multiparty protocols presented in Section 6. To obtain *fair* protocols we need one more pre-distributed primitive: pre-distributed fair exchange of secrets.

5   Pre-distributed Fair Exchange of Secrets

In this section, we show how to use our VSS protocol so that n parties $P_1, \ldots P_n$, each one holding a secret x_i, can exchange these secrets so that no cheating party can, at the end of the protocol, have substantially more advantage over an honest party. For definitions and more details see [9][13].

The basic idea here is that a trusted center pre-distributes, during a setup phase, verifiable secret sharing (commitments) which can be gradually disclosed. In the following protocols, a cheating party which leaves the protocol before it is terminated achieves an advantage of at most a polynomial fraction of a bit.

Each party P_i holds a secret x_i and each party has shared its secret with all the other players. So, besides his own secret, each player holds shares (including the verification information) of all the other players secrets. Denote the share of the secret x_i in possession of player P_j by $[x_i]_j$. A multiparty fair exchange of secrets in the commodity based model is a protocol where a trusted center pre-distributes some information to a set of players $P_1, \ldots, P_n$ during a setup phase and later on, $P_1, \ldots, P_n$ run a sub-protocol Fair Exchange. At the end of Fair Exchange the following conditions hold:

- If all the parties are honest and follow the protocol, each party will know all the $x_i, 1 \leq i \leq n$.
- A cheating party which leaves the protocol before it is terminated has an extra knowledge over honest parties of at a fraction of a bit which is polynomial in the security parameter k.

The protocol consists of two phases: Setup and Fair Exchange. We assume that the players have already verifiably shared their secrets using the protocol we described above. All computations are done over $GF(q)$.

Setup

- The trusted center sends to each player a random number r_i.
- The trusted center verifiable shares each r_i with all the players.
- Let $r_{i,1}, \ldots, r_{i,p(k)}$ be a string of bits chosen at random such that each prefix $r_{i,1}, \ldots, r_{i,l}$ of this string contains $l/p(k)$ bits of information on the random number $r_i \in GF(q)$. For $1 \leq k \leq p(k)$ and $1 \leq i \leq n$ the trusted center

verifiably shares $r_{i,k}$ with all the players. So, at the end of the setup phase, each player P_i possesses his own secret x_i; shares of all the other players secrets, $[x_j]_i, 1 \leq j \leq n$; a random value r_i and shares for each bit of the above binary string representation of each random number associated to the other players $[r_{i,k}], 1 \leq k \leq \log_2 p$ and $1 \leq i \leq n$. We call these data which is distributed during the setup phase a *one-time distributed fair exchange* (OTDFE).

Fair Exchange

- All the players compute shares to $a_i = x_i - r_i, 1 \leq i \leq n$. Due to the linearity of the VSS, each party $P_j, 1 \leq j \leq n$ only computes $[x_i]_j - [r_i]_j = [x_i - r_i]_j = [a_i]_j$.
- All the players reconstruct $a_i, 1 \leq i \leq n$. Thus, from now on, all the a_i are public values.
- For $k = 1$ to $p(k)$ do:
  - For $i = 1$ to n do:
    * Reconstruct the secret $r_{i,k}$. If $n - t$ or more parties refuse to reconstruct a r_{i_k} the protocol is aborted.
- If all the $r_{i,k}$ were successfully recovered, each party computes $r_i, 1 \leq i \leq n$. Together with the $a_i, 1 \leq i \leq n$ it gives full knowledge of each secret x_i to all the parties.

From the construction it is obvious that we obtain the following result for the above fair exchange protocol:

Proposition 3. *Let $\{P_1, \ldots, P_n\}$ be a set of players holding correct shares of a secret s, then the above fair exchange protocol either terminates with output s for all honest players or any t-subset of players aborting the protocol can only have an advantage of a fraction of a bit which vanishes polynomially in the security parameter k.*

There is a more efficient variant of the above scheme. The bits $r_{i,1}, \ldots, r_{i,m}$ can be shared as elements of a **smaller** field than $GF(q)$. This increases the probability with which a party can successfully present faulty shares, but this does not compromise the asymptotic security. The advantage an aborting party may have over other parties is polinomial in k, whereas the probability of being able to successfully present faulty shares decreases exponentially in the length of the representation of $GF(q)$. Hence there is for a fixed maximal advantage for aborting parties a trade-off between the length of the expansion $r_{i,1} \ldots, r_{i,p(k)}$ chosen for the fair exchange and the size of the field over which the bits are shared. For this modification it is important that correctly guessing one value of the (smaller) field does not allow a party to present many faulty shares. To avoid this one can choose the verification information v_i of a player P_i newly for each shared bit $r_{i,j}$. Of course this implies that the shared bits $r_{i,1} \ldots, r_{i,p(k)}$ do not exhibit any linearity any more, but this is not needed for fair exchange anyway.

6   Secure Multiparty Computations

In this section we will sketch a simple way to obtain multiparty protocols for secure function evaluation from the VSS scheme presented. For details concerning multiparty protocols we refer to the literature, e. g. [1,14,15,13,19].

Intuitively a multiparty computation is a protocol by which n interacting Turing machines can map $n-$tuples of inputs (one input held by each party) into $n-$tuples of outputs (one held by each party). Such a computation will be considered secure if it is private, correct and fair [14], informally these properties are:

Private: No party learns anything more than what can be computed from the own input and the output of the protocol.
Correct: The output received by each party is guaranteed to be the output of the specified function.
Fair: Corrupted parties should receive an output iff honest parties do.

The fairness requirement is usually relaxed in the faulty majority scenario. We assume that the additional information a corrupted party has about the computation's output can be made arbitrarily small in a security parameter k.

The secure multiparty protocols presented here have four stages. A *setup phase* where the trusted center pre-distributes data. An *input phase* where the players receive inputs and commit to these by VSS. A *computation phase* where linear transformations and multiplications are performed on shared values, but no information about the inputs is revealed. And the *opening stage* during which the relaxed notion of fairness described above has to be ensured.

Setup Phase. In this stage, all the players contact the trusted center and receive pre-distributed verifiable secret sharing, DOTMP and OTDFEs. An upper bound on the number of commodities needed must be known in this stage. We call the union of these primitives a *One-Time Distributed Computation*.

Input StagePhase. The players receive inputs from $GF(q)$ and share their inputs with the given commodities for VSS as described in the main part of this paper. As each dealer is a participant of the secure computation as well this party has to compute a share of his own from the pre-distributed data.

Computation Phase. During the computation stage, the players evaluate an arithmetic circuit gate by gate using the linearity of the VSS for linear transformations and the DOTMP protocol for multiplications. Note that computations are necessary on intermediate results as well. Intermediate results are shared among the players, but not known to any player hence it is important that the linearity of the VSS and the DOTMP protocol can be used even if no-one knows the contents of the shared secrets involved.

Opening Phase. All players reconstruct the result of the computation. To ensure fairness the pre-distributed protocols for multiparty fair exchange can be used.

The security of the multiparty protocol can be derived from the security of each sub component of the protocol (VSS, DOTMP, OTDFEs).

References

1. D. Beaver and S. Goldwasser, Multiparty Computation with Faulty Majority, Proc. of FOCS, 1989, pp.468-473.
2. D. Beaver and S. Goldwasser, Multiparty Computation with Faulty Majority, Advances in Cryptology - CRYPTO 89, LNCS 435, 1989, pp.589-590.
3. D. Beaver: "Commodity-Based Cryptography (Extended Abstract)," STOC 1997: 446-455, 1997.
4. M. Ben-Or, S. Goldwasser and A. Wigderson, " Completeness Theorems for Non-Cryptographic Fault-Tolerant Distributed Computation," 20th STOC, pp. 1-10, 1988.
5. G. Blakely, "Safeguarding Cryptographic Keys," Proc. AFIPS, Vol. 48, pp. 313-317, NCC, June 1979.
6. C. Blundo, B. Masucci, D. R. Stinson, R. Wei, "Constructions and Bounds for Unconditionally Secure Non-interactive Commitment Schemes," manuscript, 2001.
7. B. Chor, S. Goldwasser, S. Micali and B. Awerbuch, " Verifiable Secret Sharing and Achieving Simultaneity in the Presence of Faults," 26th IEEE Symp. on Foundations of Computer Science, pages 383–395, 1985.
8. D. Chaum, C. Crepeau, and I. Damgard. Multiparty unconditionally secure protocols (extended abstract). In Proc. 20th ACM Symposium on the Theory of Computing (STOC), pp. 11-19, 1988.
9. R. Cleve: "Controlled Gradual Disclosure Schemes for Random Bits and Their Applications," CRYPTO 1989: 573-588, 1989.
10. C. Crepeau, J. van de Graaf, and A. Tapp, "Committed Oblivious Transfer and Private multiparty Computations," CRYPTO 1995: 110-123, 1995.
11. R. Cramer, I. Damgard, S. Dziembowski, M. Hirt, T. Rabin, "Efficient Multiparty Computations Secure Against an Adaptive Adversary," EUROCRYPT 99, pp. 311-326, 1999.
12. P. Feldman, "A practical scheme for non-interactive verifiable secret sharing," 28th IEEE Symp. on Foundations of Computer Science, 427–437, 1987.
13. S. Goldwasser, L. A. Levin: Fair Computation of General Functions in Presence of Immoral Majority. CRYPTO 1990: 77-93
14. O. Goldreich: Secure multiparty Computation, *lecture notes*, available from http://www.wisdom.weizmann.ac.il/~oded/pp.html
15. O. Goldreich, S. Micali, and A. Wigderson: "How to Play Any Mental Game or a Completeness Theorem for Protocols with Honest Majority," STOC 1987: 218-229, 1987.
16. G. Hanaoka G., J. Shikata, Y. Zheng, Imai H., "Unconditionally Secure Digital Signature Schemes Admitting Transferability," Proc. of Asiacrypt '2000, 130–142, 2000.
17. L. Lamport, R. Shostak, and M. Pease, "The Byzantine generals problem," ACM Trans. on Programming Languages and Systems, 4(3):382– 401, July 1982.

18. T. Matsumoto and H. Imai: "On the Key Pre-distribution Systems: A Practical Solution to the Key Distribution Problem," CRYPTO 1987: 185-193, 1988.
19. S. Micali and P. Rogaway: "Secure Computation (Abstract)," CRYPTO 1991: 392-404, 1991.
20. R. J. McEliece and D. V. Sarwate, "On sharing secrets and Reed-Solomon codes," Communications of the ACM, 24:583–584, 1981.
21. A. Nascimento, J. Mueller-Quade, A. Otsuka, G. Hanaoka, H. Imai, "Unconditionally Secure Homomorphic Pre-distributed Bit Commitment and Secure Two-Party Computations", ISC'03
22. T. Pedersen, "Non-interactive and information-theoretic secure verifiable secret sharing," Advances in cryptology — CRYPTO '91, volume 576 of Lecture Notes in Computer Science, pages 129–140. Springer-Verlag, 1991.
23. T. Rabin and M. Ben-Or, "Verifiable secret sharing and multiparty protocols with honest majority," Proc. ACM STOC '89, pages 73–85, ACM Press, 1989.
24. R.L. Rivest, "Unconditionally secure commitment and oblivious transfer schemes using concealing channels and a trusted initializer," manuscript, 1999.
25. A. Shamir, "How to Share a Secret," Communications of the ACM, 22, pp. 612–613, 1979.
26. J. Shikata, G. Hanaoka, Y. Zheng, H. Imai, "Security Notions for Unconditionally Secure Signature Schemes," EUROCRYPT 2002, pages 434-449, 2002.
27. D. R. Stinson, R. Wei, "Unconditionally Secure Proactive Secret Sharing Scheme with Combinatorial Structures," Selected Areas in Cryptography, pages 200-214, 1999.
28. R. Safavi-Naini and H. Wang, "Multireceiver authentication codes: models, bounds, constructions and extensions," Information and Computation, 151, pp.148-172, 1999.
29. M. Tompa and H. Wolf, "How to share a secret with cheaters," Journal of Cryptology, 1(2):133-138, 1988.

Cryptanalysis of Two Anonymous Buyer-Seller Watermarking Protocols and an Improvement for True Anonymity

Bok-Min Goi[1], Raphael C.-W. Phan[2], Yanjiang Yang[3], Feng Bao[3], Robert H. Deng[3], and M.U. Siddiqi[1]

[1] Multimedia University, 63100 Cyberjaya, Malaysia
{bmgoi,umar}@mmu.edu.my
[2] Information Security Research (iSECURES) Lab,
Swinburne Sarawak Institute of Technology, 93576 Kuching, Malaysia
rphan@swinburne.edu.my
[3] Institute for Infocomm Research,
21 Heng Mui Keng Terrace, Singapore 119613
{yanjiang, baofeng, deng}@i2r.a-star.edu.sg

Abstract. By combining techniques of watermarking and fingerprinting, a sound buyer-seller watermarking protocol can address the issue of copyright protection in e-commerce. In this paper, we analyze the security of two recent anonymous buyer-seller watermarking protocols proposed by Ju *et. al* and Choi *et. al* respectively, and prove that they do not provide the features and security as claimed. In particular, we show that i) the commutative cryptosystem used in Choi *et. al*'s protocol fails to prevent the watermark certification authority (WCA) from discovering the watermark (fingerprint) chosen by the buyer; ii) for both protocols, the seller can discover the watermark chosen by the buyer if he colludes with the WCA. Hence, these protocols cannot guard against conspiracy attacks. We further show that these protocols only provide "partial" anonymity, ie. the buyer's anonymity is guaranteed only if WCA is honest. Our results suggest that the security of these protocols must assume the honesty of WCA, contrary to the designers' original claim. Finally, we propose a new anonymous buyer-seller watermarking protocol which is more secure and efficient, and provides true anonymity.

Keywords: Watermarking, Fingerprinting, Traitor Tracing, Copyright Protection, Anonymity.

1 Introduction

All types of multimedia information can be stored and processed within a computer in digital form. Furthermore, they can be transmitted losslessly over a noisy digital communication networks. However, since the duplication of digital multimedia content results in perfectly identical copies, the copyright protection issue is a main problem that needs to be addressed. *Digital watermarking*

M. Jakobsson, M. Yung, J. Zhou (Eds.): ACNS 2004, LNCS 3089, pp. 369–382, 2004.
© Springer-Verlag Berlin Heidelberg 2004

[SKT98,HK99,VP99,WPD99,CMB02] and *digital fingerprinting* [WNR83,ZK95, PS96,PW97,PS00] are well recognized as two main classes of techniques for the copyright protection over digital data. They constitute two facets of copyright protection in the context of electronic marketplaces. More specifically, water-marking works by imperceptibly embedding a *seller* specific mark, which upon extraction enables provable ownership; fingerprinting embeds a *buyer* specific mark, which upon extraction identifies the buyer who has illegally disseminated the underlying digital data. For more details of the types of watermarking and fingerprinting schemes, the reader is referred to [CSP03]. A *buyer-seller water-marking protocol* [MW01,JKLL02,CC03,CSP03] is one that incorporates tech-niques of watermarking and fingerprinting to protect the rights of both the buyer and the seller.

In this paper, we concentrate on *anonymous* buyer-seller watermarking pro-tocols in the sense that buyers can buy goods anonymously, but nevertheless can be identified by enforcement authorities if they redistribute the goods ille-gally. Anonymity has become one of the main service requirements, especially in e-commerce. The buyer is unwilling to disclose his identity (his public key in particular) when purchasing any content, since this could leak his privacy information, ie. lifestyle, personal interests, and embarrassing details.

A sound anonymous buyer-seller watermarking protocol is expected to fulfill the following requirements [PW97,JKLL02,CSP03]:

1. **Anonymity**: A buyer is able to purchase digital goods anonymously.
2. **Unlinkability**: Given two marked digital items, no one can decide whether or not they were purchased by the same buyer.
3. **Traceability**: The buyer who has illegally distributed digital goods (traitor/copyright violater) can be traced.
4. **No Framing**: An honest buyer should not be falsely accused by a malicious seller or other buyers.
5. **No Repudiation**: The buyer accused of reselling an unauthorized copy should not be able to claim that the copy was created by the seller or a security breach of the seller's system.
6. **Collusion Tolerance**: An attacker should not be able to find, generate, or delete the fingerprint by comparing the marked copies, even if they have access to a large number of copies.

1.1 Previous Work

Pfitzman and Waidner [PW97] are known to be the first to propose the con-cept of anonymous fingerprinting, in correspondence with the needs to achieve personal privacy in the overall context of e-commerce. However, their proposed scheme, based on secure two-party computation, is impractical since the under-lying blocks are too complex to be efficient.

Afterwards, Pfitzman and Sadeghi suggested a method [PS00] without relying on two-party computations, but it is not practical either, because the building block [BS95] uses long codes for embedding.

The first-known buyer-seller watermarking protocol is due to Memon and Wong [MW01], and this was later extended by Ju *et. al* [JKLL02] to provide for anonymity of the buyer. Basically, a buyer-seller watermarking protocol is a combination of digital watermarking and digital fingerprinting. This type of protocol is a good model in the sense that it satisfies virtually all the requirements listed above. However, a problem with such a protocol is that it assumes a trusted *watermark certification authority* and a trusted *judge*. In other words, security of the system is based on the assumption that the seller will not collude with the watermark certification authority nor the judge (no conspiracy attack). Other buyer-seller watermarking protocols are due to Chang and Chung [CC03], and Cheung *et. al* [CLW04] but they do not provide any anonymity.

A recent work by Choi *et. al* [CSP03] claims to overcome this limitation of needing a trusted third party (TTP) by presenting a buyer-seller watermarking protocol secure against conspiracy attacks; but we will show in the next few sections that this is not the case.

1.2   Outline of This Paper

In this paper, we analyze the security of two recent anonymous buyer-seller watermarking protocols due to Ju *et. al* [JKLL02] and Choi *et. al* [CSP03]. We show that they fail to provide the features and security as claimed by their designers. In particular, these protocols cannot combat against the conspiracy attack [CSP03] where a seller colludes with the watermark certificate authority (WCA) in order to discover the watermark chosen by the buyer, and hence recreate the buyer's copy. We also show that even when protocol failures notwithstanding, the underlying commutative cryptosystem used in Choi *et. al*'s protocol still cannot prevent the WCA from discovering the actual watermark chosen by the buyer.

Furthermore, we show that these protocols can only provide "partial" anonymity, namely that the buyer's anonymity is guaranteed only if the WCA is honest. Finally, we propose a *truly* anonymous buyer-seller watermarking protocol without TTP that is more efficient and secure against conspiracy attacks. This protocol provides full anonymity in the sense that its security does not involve any WCA and hence does not have to depend on such parties to be honest. Our approach is that to ensure true anonymity, the buyer should generate his own private watermark, W and so other parties are not able to collude with each other to mount an attack to recreate the watermarked digital content sold to the buyer.

In Section 2, we discuss preliminary concepts and notations used in this paper. We review in Section 3 the protocols due to Ju *et. al* [JKLL02] and Choi *et. al* [CSP03]. We then present an attack on the commutative cryptosystem used in Choi *et. al*'s protocol, as well as conspiracy attacks on both protocols. In Section 4 we present our new protocol. We conclude in Section 5 and also highlight topics for further research.

2   Preliminaries

In this section, we briefly review the preliminary concepts required for an understanding of the rest of this paper.

2.1   Cryptographic Primitives

Since all protocols discussed in this paper use public key cryptography [RSA78, MOV97], we will briefly describe it in this subsection. In public key cryptosystems, each agent, A possesses a public key, pk_A which is easily obtainable from a certification authority center, CA. A also possesses a secret private key, sk_A, which is the inverse of pk_A. For convenience, we stick to $pk_A = g_A^{sk_A} \bmod p$, where p is a large prime (such that $(p-1)/2$ is also a prime) and g_A chosen by A is a generator of the multiplicative group, Z_p^* of order $(p-1)$. Also, unless otherwise specified, all arithmetic operations are performed under Z_p^*. We denote $E_k(m)$ to mean the message, m encrypted with the key, k. Any agent can encrypt a message for A using pk_A, but only A can decrypt this message with sk_A. This ensures *confidentiality*. Furthermore, A can sign a message by encrypting it with sk_A, denoted as $sign_{sk_A}(m)$, so that anybody can verify by using pk_A the identity of A and that the message really originated from A. This provides *authentication* and *non-repudiation*.

All parties – the seller, the buyer and the watermark certification authority (WCA) – have registered with the CA, and have their own pair of keys, which are (pk_A, sk_A), (pk_B, sk_B) and (pk_C, sk_C) respectively.

Definition 1: (Homomorphic Cryptosystem) [CF85,BY87,MW01]. A cryptosystem E^h is said to be homomorphic if it forms a (group) homomorphism. That is, for a certain defined operation, $\otimes$, then given ciphertexts $E^h(x)$ and $E^h(y)$ for some unknown plaintexts x and y, anyone can compute $E^h(x \otimes y)$, or vice-versa, even without the private key. For example, the RSA cryptosystem [RSA78] is homomorphic with respect to the multiplication operation. As in [MW01], we assume that the public-key cryptosystem we are using is a privacy homomorphism with respect to the watermark insertion operation.

Definition 2: (Commutative Cryptosytem) [CSP03]. A cryptosystem E^c is said to be commutative, if for a multiple encrypted (decrypted) message, the same resultant ciphertext (plaintext) will be obtained, irrespective of its order of encryption. That is, $E_{K1}^c(E_{K2}^c(x)) = E_{K2}^c(E_{K1}^c(x))$ and $D_{K2}^c(E_{K1}^c(E_{K2}^c(x))) = E_{K1}^c(x)$ where $D(.) = E^{-1}(.)$.

Since one of our attacks in Section 3 exploits the special properties of the ElGamal-type [ZVM03] commutative cryptosystem chosen by Choi *et. al* [CSP03] for use in their protocol, we will briefly review it here:

ElGamal-type Commutative Cryptosystem [CSP03]. Consider two communicating parties, Alice and Bob, having respectively

$$K_A = \{(p, g_A, x_A, y_A) : y_A = g_A^{x_A} \pmod{p}\}$$
$$K_B = \{(p, g_B, x_B, y_B) : y_B = g_B^{x_B} \pmod{p}\}$$

where x_A and y_A (respectively x_B and y_B) are the private-public key-pair of Alice (respectively Bob). Suppose Alice encrypts first. To encrypt message m, Alice chooses a random number r_A and the obtains the ciphertext C_A consisting of two parts c_{A1} and c_{A2}, ie., $C_A = (c_{A1}, c_{A2})$, where

$$c_{A1} = g_A^{r_A} \bmod p, \quad c_{A2} = m * y_A^{r_A} \bmod p$$

Bob chooses a random number r_B and in turn encrypts Alice's ciphertext. The resulting C_B has two parts c_{B1} and c_{AB}, ie., $C_B = (c_{B1}, c_{AB})$, where

$$c_{B1} = g_B^{r_B} \bmod p, \quad c_{AB} = m * y_A^{r_A} * y_B^{r_B} \bmod p$$

The final ciphertext of the commutative cryptosystem thus consists of *three* parts, $C = (c_{A1}, c_{B1}, c_{AB})$. Note that C_A and C share an element c_{A1}, which will be exploited in one of our attacks in Section 3.2.

Now consider the decryption process. Suppose Alice decrypts first. She computes $c_{AB} * (c_{A1}^{x_A})^{-1} = m * y_B^{r_B} \pmod{p}$ using her private key x_A. Then Bob continues to compute $m * y_B^{r_B} * (c_{B1}^{x_B})^{-1} = m \pmod{p}$ using his private key x_B. Note that the order of decryptions similarly does not affect the final decryption result.

2.2   Notations

For ease of explanation, we use the notations similar to those in [JKLL02,CSP03], as follows:

3   Protocols and Attacks

In this section, we first briefly review the two protocols due to Ju *et. al* [JKLL02] and Choi *et. al* [CSP03], and then proceed with our attacks.

Both protocols comprise three phases, namely *watermark generation, watermark insertion, copyright violator identification*. Aside from the *watermark generation* phase, the two protocols are similar to each other.

For simplicity, we depict the watermark generation phase of the two protocols in Figures 1 and 2 respectively, and the common watermark insertion phase in Figure 3. We omit the copyright violator identification phase since it is irrelevant to our attacks. We refer the interested reader to [JKLL02,CSP03] for details.

Note that in Figure 1, $e = E_{pk_J}(\overline{sk}_B)$ is computed by encrypting with the judge's public key, pk_J. In Ju *et. al*'s protocol, there is a distinction between the

A	Alice, the seller who sells the digital multimedia content
B	Bob, the buyer who can buy contents anonymously
C	Carol, the watermark certification authority (WCA) who can issue watermarks to buyers upon request and certify them
CA	certification authority who can issue the certificate and a pair of keys (pk, sk) for every agent in the public-key infrastructure (PKI)
X	original content with m elements, $x_1, x_2, \ldots, x_m$
W	watermark with n elements, $w_1, w_2, \ldots, w_n$, where $n \leq m$
X', X''	watermarked content
$X \otimes W$	embed W into X with the embedding operation, $\otimes$
σ	random permutation function chosen (only known) by Alice
$cert$	a certificate computed by Bob
$E^h(.)/D^h(.)$	encryption/decryption algorithm of a public-key cryptosystem with homomorphic property
$E^c(.)/D^c(.)$	encryption/decryption algorithm of a commutative cryptosystem

judge, J and the WCA, Carol. This need for a judge as a trusted third party (TTP) was eliminated in Choi *et. al*'s protocol.

Meanwhile in Figure 2, $(\overline{sk}_{B1}, \overline{pk}_B = g^{\overline{sk}_{B1}})$ is an *anonymous key-pair* generated by the buyer, Bob to achieve his anonymity while purchasing. Bob convinces Carol of his possession of $\overline{sk}_{B1}$ via a zero-knowledge proof [C87]. Authenticity of this key-pair is certified by Carol as indicated by s_i, $i = 1 \ldots k$.

Finally, Figure 3 illustrates the common watermark insertion phase which is similar between both protocols, except that ew_j, s_j and W_j are used in Choi *et. al*'s protocol while ew, s and W are used in Ju *et. al*'s protocol. Also, Bob gets in the end a watermarked copy X'' of X that Alice cannot reproduce since she does not know the corresponding private key $\overline{sk}_{B1}$ and W_j even if she colludes with Carol. Plus, since Bob does not know σ, he cannot remove $\sigma(W_j)$ from X'', and neither can he remove V which is unknown to him.

3.1   Attacking the Protocol Due to Ju *et. al*

We first review two previous conspiracy attacks on Ju *et. al*'s protocol, and then further present our attack on it.

Conspiracy Attack I [CSP03]: Collusion of the Seller, the Watermark Certification Authority and the Judge. First, the seller, Alice sends the received $\overline{pk}_B$ and s from the buyer, Bob to the Watermark Certification Authority, Carol. Carol can easily go through her database of stored values and obtain the corresponding $E_{pk_J}(\overline{sk}_B)$ and pass it to the judge. The judge can decrypt it and then returns $\overline{sk}_B$ to Carol and Alice. By knowing $\overline{sk}_B$, w can be decrypted and W will be obtained. Hence, Alice can recreate Bob's watermarked copy, X''.

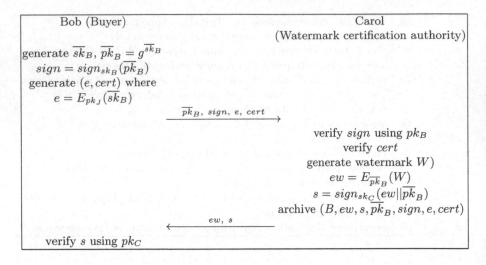

Fig. 1. Watermark Generation due to Ju *et. al* [JKLL02]

Conspiracy Attack II [CSP03]: Collusion of the Seller and the Judge.
Alice can intercept the message communicated from Bob to Carol through an
insecure channel and obtain $E_{pk_J}(\overline{sk}_B)$ and $\overline{pk}_B$. Alice forwards these together
with $E^h_{\overline{pk}_B}(X'')$ to the judge. The judge can easily decrypt $E_{pk_J}(\overline{sk}_B)$ to get
$\overline{sk}_B$ and further use that to decrypt $E^h_{\overline{pk}_B}(X'')$ to obtain X''. Hence, Alice can
receive X'' if he colludes with the judge.

In addition to these two attacks, we present another new conspiracy attack,
as follows:

Conspiracy Attack III [New]: Collusion of the Seller and the Watermark Certification Authority. Carol always knows and can record the
watermark W which is sent to and used by the buyer. Consequently, once Alice
colludes with Carol, she can obtain this and recreate Bob's copy easily since she
has all the information needed, namely X, V, $\overline{pk}_B$ and σ.

By right, Carol should not store the unique watermark used by the buyer,
Bob. However, it is quite hard − in fact, impossible − to prevent Carol from
doing so, because in this protocol, Carol is the one who generates the watermark.
It is this limitation that is the basis behind why a watermarking protocol falls
to conspiracy attacks. We will show in Section 4 how to combat against this by
presenting a new protocol that does not suffer from this and hence is resistant
to conspiracy attacks.

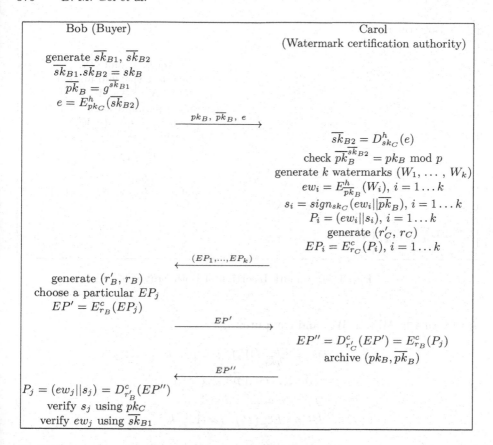

Fig. 2. Watermark Generation due to Choi *et. al* [CSP03]

3.2   Attacking the Protocol Due to Choi *et. al*

In this section, we first show that the commutative cryptosystem used in Choi *et. al*'s protocol fails to prevent the watermark certification authority from knowing the actual mark (fingerprint) chosen by the buyer. Second, we further show that even in the case where a secure commutative cryptosystem is chosen, the protocol itself cannot prevent conspiracy attacks by the seller and the watermark certification authority. In particular, the seller is able to discover the actual mark by colluding with the watermark certification authority and simply exploiting the encrypted watermark presented by the buyer.

Attack on the Commutative Cryptosystem. Recall that to prevent the watermark certification authority, Carol, from colluding with the seller, Alice, the protocol is intended to conceal the actual watermark chosen by the buyer, Bob, from Carol while at the same time enable Carol to certify this watermark. The adopted method as listed in Figure 2 works as follows. Carol first generates

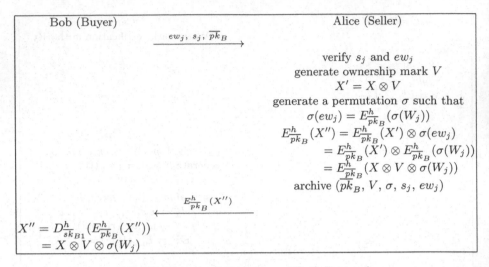

Fig. 3. Watermark Insertion of Both Protocols

k watermarks $(W_1,..., W_k)$ and computes

$$ew_i = E^h_{\overline{pk}_B}(W_i), \ i = 1\dots k$$

$$s_i = sign_{sk_C}(ew_i||\overline{pk}_B), i = 1\dots k$$

$$P_i = (ew_i||s_i), \ i = 1\dots k \tag{1}$$

$$EP_i = E^c_{r_C}(P_i), \ i = 1\dots k$$

where (r'_C, r_C) is respectively Carol's private and public key-pair for the commutative cryptosystem. Carol then sends $(EP_1,...,EP_k)$ to Bob who selects a particular one (EP_j) and encrypts it with his key-pair (r'_B, r_B):

$$EP' = E^c_{r_B}(EP_j). \tag{2}$$

Bob sends EP' to Carol, who then decrypts it yielding EP'' as

$$EP'' = D^c_{r'_C}(EP') = E^c_{r_B}(P_j). \tag{3}$$

Carol sends EP'' to Bob. Bob then decrypts EP'' using r'_B to obtain P_j and in turn W_j. Note that in the interactions, it is anticipated that from EP' and EP'', Carol cannot determine the actual EP_j or P_j chosen by the buyer since Carol does not know r'_B.

The commutative cryptosystem explicitly specified by Choi *et. al* [CSP03] for use in their protocol is an ElGamal-type cryptosystem (See Section 2.1). Therefore, we have $(r'_B, r_B) = (x_B, y_B = g^{x_B}_B \bmod p)$ and $(r'_C, r_C) = (x_C, y_C = g^{x_C}_C \bmod p)$, and EP_i in (1) becomes

$$EP_i = E^c_{r_C}(P_i) = (g^{r_C}_C \bmod p, \ P_i * y^{r_C}_C \bmod p), \ i = 1\dots k. \tag{4}$$

Further, EP' in (2) becomes

$$EP' = E^c_{r_B}(EP_j) = (g^{r_C}_C \bmod p, \ g^{r_B}_B \bmod p, \ P_j * y^{r_C}_C * y^{r_B}_B \bmod p). \quad (5)$$

It is obvious that when Bob sends EP' to Carol, Carol can easily learn the particular EP_j (in turn W_j) chosen by Bob by simply comparing the first elements of EP' and EP_i, $i = 1 \ldots k$. This attack suggests that the commutative cryptosystem chosen by Choi *et. al* actually fails to attain its anticipated objective, ie., to prevent Carol from learning the actual mark chosen by Bob. It is worth noting that the first element ($g^{r_C}_C \bmod p$) must be included in EP' as indicated in (5) since it is needed (See Section 2.1) in the decryption process by Carol.

The most straightforward way to prevent this attack is to replace the ElGamal-type cryptosystem chosen by Choi *et. al* with alternative commutative cryptosystems that do not succumb to this attack.

Further, note that Carol uses the same random number r_C to encrypt all EP_i, $i = 1 \ldots k$ (See [CSP03], Section 4.1). This causes yet another serious problem because at the end of the watermark generation phase, Bob eventually learns the P_j, so by equation (6) he can compute $y^{r_C}_C \bmod p$. With $y^{r_C}_C \bmod p$ in place, Bob can learn via the same equation all the values of the other P_i's, and in turn the corresponding values of W_i, $i = 1 \ldots k$. This might not be desirable in practice.

Conspiracy Attack on the Protocol. We further demonstrate that the protocol itself is vulnerable to a conspiracy attack by Alice and Carol, even if we assume the underlying commutative cryptosystem is secure.

In the watermarking insertion phase (see Figure 3), Bob sends the chosen ew_j, s_j, $\overline{pk}_B$ to Alice for the purpose of watermark insertion. By colluding with Carol, Alice will know the set of possible watermarks $W_1, W_2, \ldots, W_k$ generated for Bob. Then, for $i = 1 \ldots k$, she computes all the values, $ew_i = E^h_{\overline{pk}_B}(W_i)$ and compares them with the ew_j that she received from Bob. The buyer's chosen watermark will then simply be the corresponding W_i.

Alternatively, Alice could forward ew_j and $\overline{pk}_B$ to Carol. By $\overline{pk}_B$, Carol determines the set of ew_i, $i = 1 \ldots k$ that have been produced for Bob. Then Carol compares the received ew_j from Alice with ew_i, $i = 1 \ldots k$. Note that ew_i, $i = 1 \ldots k$, are originally produced by Carol, so she knows the corresponding plaintexts although she cannot decrypt them! It becomes clear that the plaintext of the matching item among ew_i, $i = 1 \ldots k$, is $W_i = W_j$. Upon successfully retrieving W_j, Carol gives it to Alice. In this way, the conspiracy attack by Alice and Carol succeeds. As a matter of fact, to facilitate the process of matching, it suffices for Carol to simply maintain a table for each user as follows:

$ew_i = E^h_{\overline{pk}_B}(W_i)$	W_i
ew_1	W_1
ew_2	W_2
...	...
ew_k	W_k

Once Alice knows the watermark chosen by Bob, many important features of the anonymous buyer-seller watermarking protocol would end up getting compromised. First, traitor tracing does not hold any more since both the seller and the buyer might possibly be the traitor. Second, non-framing fails because an honest buyer may be falsely accused by a dishonest seller. Third, due to the fact both the seller and the buyer can misbehave, non-repudiation obviously no longer holds.

3.3 Failure to Provide True Anonymity

Here, we further remark on the "anonymity" provided by both the protocols proposed by Ju *et. al* [JKLL02] and Choi *et. al* [CSP03]. During the watermark generation phase, for Ju *et. al*'s protocol, Carol uses Bob's public key, pk_B to verify the *sign* from Bob, and so Carol knows Bob's identity. Similarly, in Choi *et. al*'s protocol, Bob sends pk_B along with $\overline{pk}_B$ to Carol. Therefore, Carol would be able to associate $\overline{pk}_B$ to Bob's identity, and so although the anonymous key-pairs appear anonymous to Alice, they are by no means anonymous to Carol. This suggests that buyer anonymity in the protocols is achieved only when the watermark certification authority, Carol, can be trusted, and hence both protocols only achieve "partial anonymity".

4   Our Proposed Protocol

We propose a new truly anonymous buyer-seller watermarking protocol where the buyer is allowed to generate his own secret watermark and hence is the only party who knows it. This is essential to protect the buyer's security from conspiracy attacks, and to ensure his privacy. The watermark generation phase is given in Figure 4, while our watermark insertion phase is identical to Figure 3. Note that only a total of 4 messages are communicated in our protocol (during the entire watermark generation and insertion phases).

The main intuition is that the buyer, Bob enlists the help of a certification authority, CA to certify his chosen anonymous public key, $\overline{pk}_B$. In this way, only CA knows where $\overline{pk}_B$ came from. CA is the one who issues public key certificates containing public and private key-pairs of all agents (including Alice, Bob and Carol) in a public-key infrastructure (PKI) and hence is definitely trustable, otherwise no PKI would be secure and no public and private key-pairs would be binding or confidential. Note that there is no need for a separate watermark certification authority, Carol in this case.

Copyright Violater Identification. When Bob is suspected, the judge will request by law for him to disclose the unique self-generated watermark, W and then compute the deterministic encryption $E^h_{\overline{pk}_B}(W)$. The result is compared with the stored ew in the CA's database, whose integrity can be validated by using s: (i) if they are not the same, B will be guilty because of giving a fraudulent watermark, (ii) if yes, then, the judge will proceed to extract the embedded watermark in multimedia content. Finally, the extracted watermark is compared with $\sigma(W)$. If they match, then B is guilty, otherwise, B is innocent. Alice is not able to recreate X'' because he does not know the unique W. Note that Bob does not need to disclose his identity during the identification process. The interested reader is also referred to [JKLL02] for more details on the identification process.

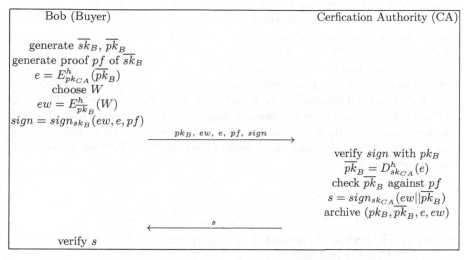

Fig. 4. Watermark Generation of Our Proposed Protocol

5   Conclusions and Open Problems

We have shown that the two recent anonymous buyer-seller watermarking protocols due to Ju *et. al* [JKLL02] and Choi *et. al* [CSP03] are insecure against conspiracy attacks, contradicting their exact security claims. With the success of conspiracy attacks, many important features including traitor tracing and non-repudiation are completely compromised.

We have further shown that protocol failures notwithstanding, the commutative cryptosystem chosen by Choi *et. al* in their protocol makes it insecure in that it cannot prevent the watermark certification authority from discovering the watermark chosen by the buyer.

Though the main claim by Choi *et. al* is that their protocol eliminates the need for a trusted third party, our results have shown that this is not the case at all. On the contrary, the security of their protocol depends entirely on the honesty of the watermark certification authority which is a trusted third party. Further, we have also shown that their protocol does not provide true anonymity since in this case one has to again rely on the honesty of the watermark certification authority.

We further pose some interesting open problems for future work:

- Security analysis of the proposed protocols on their security with different block cipher modes of operation, and underlying cryptographic and watermarking algorithms.
- Design of buyer-seller watermarking protocols for multi-transactions involving multiple copies. There are two issues involved here. First, for a certain content, X, which supposing can only be sold to n different buyers, how do current protocols handle this? In particular, how do we ensure that a seller does not sell more copies of X than what is allowed, or that he does not resell an already-sold copy? Second, on the buyer side, suppose a buyer wishes to buy more than one copy of the same content, X from the same seller. How do current protocols keep track of how many identical copies of X that have been bought by the same buyer from the same seller? One way that we foresee to tackle the second issue is to tag a unique identification number to each content, including identical contents, so that even if two or more contents are identical, they would cause different X values to be input to the protocols.

References

[BS95] D. Boneh, J. Shaw, *Collusion-Secure Fingerprinting for Digital Data*, Crypt'95, LNCS 963, pp.452-465, 1995.
[BY87] E.F. Brickell, Y. Yacobi, *On Privacy Homomorphisms*, Eurocrypt'87, LNCS 304, pp.117-125, 1987.
[CC03] C.C. Chang, C.Y. Chung, *An Enhanced Buyer-Seller Watermarking Protocol*, Proc. ICCT2003, pp. 1779-1783, 2003.
[C87] D. Chaum, *An Improved Protocol for Demonstrating Possession of Discrete Logarithms and some Generalizations*, Eurocrypt'87, LNCS 307, pp. 127-141, 1987.
[CLW04] S.-C. Cheung, H.-F. Leung, C. Wang, *A Commutative Encrypted Protocol for the Privacy Protection of Watermarks in Digital Contents*, Proc. 37th Hawaii International Conference on System Sciences, Hawaii, p. 40094a, 2004.
[CSP03] J.G. Choi, K. Sakurai, J.H. Park, *Does it Need Trusted Third Party? Design of Buyer-Seller Watermarking Protocol without Trusted Third Party*, Proc. Applied Cryptography and Network Security '03, LNCS 2846, pp. 265-279, 2003.
[CF85] J.D. Cohen, M.J. Fischer, *A Robust and Verifiable Cryptographically Secure Election Scheme (extended abstract)*, Proc. IEEE 26th Annu. Symp. Foundations Computer Science, Portland, p. 372-382, 1985.
[CMB02] I.J. Cox, M.L. Miller, J.A. Bloom, *Digital Watermarking*, Morgan Kaufmann, 2002.
[HK99] F. Hartung, M. Kutter, *Multimedia Watermarking Techniques*, Proc. IEEE, vol. 87, pp. 1079-1107, July 1999.
[JKLL02] H.S. Ju, H.J. Kim, D.H. Lee, J.I. Lim, *An Anonymous Buyer-Seller Watermarking Protocol with Anonymity Control*, ICISC'02, LNCS 2587, pp. 421-432, 2002.
[MW01] N. Memon, P.W. Wong, *A Buyer-Seller Watermarking Protocol*, IEEE Transactions on Image Processing, vol. 10, no. 4, pp.643-649, 2001.

[MOV97] A.J. Menezes, P.C. van Oorschot, S.A. Vanstone, *Handbook of Applied Cryptography*, CRC Press, 1997.

[PS00] B. Pfitzman, A.R. Sadeghi, *Coin-Based Anonymous Fingerprinting*, Eurocrypt'99, LNCS 1592, pp.150-163, 2000.

[PS96] B. Pfitzman, M. Schunter, *Asymmetric Fingerprinting*, Eurocrypt'96, LNCS 1070, 1996, pp. 84-95.

[PW97] B. Pfitzman, W. Waidner, *Anonymous Fingerprinting*, Eurocrypt'97, LNCS 1233, pp. 88-102, 1997.

[RSA78] R.L. Rivest, A. Shamir, L. Adleman, *A Method for Obtaining Digital Signatures and Public-Key Cryptosystems*, Communications of the ACM, vol. 21, no. 2, pp.120-126, 1978.

[SKT98] M. Swanson, M. Kobayashi, A. Tewfik, *Multimedia Data Embedding and Watermarking Technologies*, Proc. IEEE, vol. 86, pp. 1064-1087, June 1998.

[VP99] G. Voyatzis and I. Pitas. The Use of Watermarks in the Protection of Digital Multimedia Products. Proc. IEEE, Vol. 87, pp. 1197-1207, July 1999.

[WNR83] N.R. Wagner, *Fingerprinting*, IEEE Symposium on Security and Privacy, pp.18-22, 1983.

[WPD99] R. Wolfang, C. Podilchuk, E. Delp, *Perceptual Watermarks for Digital Images and Video*, Proc. IEEE, vol. 87, pp. 1108-1126, July 1999.

[ZK95] J. Zhao, E. Koch, *Embedding Robust Labels Into Images For Copyright Protection*, International Congress on Intellectual Property Rights for Specialized Information, Knowledge and New Technologies, Vienna, 1995.

[ZVM03] W. Zhao, V. Varadharajan, Y. Mu, *A Secure Mental Poker Protocol Over the Internet*, Australasian Information Security Workshop 2003, Conference in Research and Practice in Information Technology, Vol. 21, Feb. 2003.

Security Analysis of CRT-Based Cryptosystems

Katsuyuki Okeya[1] and Tsuyoshi Takagi[2]

[1] Hitachi, Ltd., Systems Development Laboratory,
292, Yoshida-cho, Totsuka-ku, Yokohama, 244-0817, Japan
ka-okeya@sdl.hitachi.co.jp
[2] Technische Universität Darmstadt, Fachbereich Informatik,
Hochschulstr. 10, D-64283 Darmstadt, Germany
takagi@informatik.tu-darmstadt.de

Abstract. We investigate the security of several cryptosystems based on the Chinese remainder theorem (CRT) against side channel attack (SCA). Novak first proposed a simple power analysis against the CRT part using the difference of message modulo p and modulo q. In this paper we apply Novak's attack to the other CRT-based cryptosystems, namely Multi-Prime RSA, Multi-Exponent RSA, Rabin cryptosystem, and HIME(R) cryptosystem. Novak-type attack is strictly depending how to implement the CRT. We examine the operations related to CRT of these cryptosystems, and show that an extended Novak-type attack is effective on them. Moreover, we present a novel attack called zero-multiplication attack. The attacker tries to guess the secret prime by producing ciphertexts that cause a multiplication with zero during the decryption, which is easily able to be detected by power analysis. We examine the zero-multiplication attack on the above cryptosystems. Finally, we propose countermeasures against these attacks. The proposed countermeasures are based on the ciphertext blinding, but they require no inversion operation. The overhead of the proposed scheme is only about 1% to 5% of the whole decryption.

Keywords: RSA, Multi-Prime RSA, Factoring, Chinese Remainder Theorem, Side Channel Attacks, PKCS #1

1   Introduction

RSA cryptosystem is the most famous public-key cryptosystem in practical use, and it is implemented in plenty of security applications. Especially, security solutions with smart cards have been focused because of its flexibility and high security. However, recent research results point out weakness of RSA implementations on memory constraint devices against side channel attack (SCA) [Koc96, KJJ99,JLQ99,BDL01], etc. Several experimentation ensure practical feasibility of SCA [Nov02,BB03,ABF+02]. These attacks are particularly effective on the implementation using the Chinese remainder theorem (CRT), which accelerates the decryption speed [PKCS]. The attack on RSA-CRT can factor the public modulus, and RSA cryptosystem is completely broken. We have to carefully deal with these attacks.

M. Jakobsson, M. Yung, J. Zhou (Eds.): ACNS 2004, LNCS 3089, pp. 383–397, 2004.

The decryption algorithm of RSA-CRT consists of two parts: (C1) to decrypt m_p, m_q (message modulo p, q) from ciphertext c, (C2) to recover the proper message m from m_p, m_q using CRT, where p, q are secret primes. The most side channel attacks deal with the first part, e.g., a timing attack using the difference of timing between $c < p$ and $c > p$ [Koc96,BB03], the power analysis on the modular multiplication $c^{d_p} \bmod p$ with secret exponent d_p [MDS99,BLW02], the timing attack using the final subtraction of Montgomery multiplication (See, for example, [Sch00]). However, Novak first proposed the attack on the second part [Nov02]. CRT is usually implemented the Garner algorithm [PKCS], and it causes operation $m_q - m_p$. He showed that a characteristic function δ of $m_q - m_p < 0$ can be detected by power analysis, and the modulus can be factored using δ. A standard countermeasure against these attacks is to randomize the ciphertext using the blind signature technique [Koc96,Kal96]. A message is randomized by multiplying r^e and the randomization is removed by multiplying r^{-1} after decryption. A drawback of this method is the computation of the inverse r^{-1}, which is not usually equipped on smartcards designed for RSA cryptosystem.

Incidentally, several cryptosystems based on CRT have been proposed in order to accelerate the decryption speed of RSA-CRT moreover, namely Multi-Prime RSA [PKCS] and Multi-Exponent RSA [Tak98]. Multi-Prime RSA utilizes a public modulus comprised several pair-wise distinct secret primes. Multi-Prime RSA is practically used, e.g., Compaq implemented it for a SSL sever [Com], Sun offers it in the specification of Java Cryptography Architecture [JCA]. Multi-Exponent RSA uses a modulus of form p^2q. The message modulo p^2 is recovered from modulo p using fast Hensel lifting, and the total decryption time of Multi-Exponent RSA is faster than that of Multi-Prime RSA for small exponent e. Other CRT-based cryptosystems are Rabin cryptosystem and HIME(R) cryptosystem [NSS01]. Their advantage over RSA is that they can be proven as secure as factoring problem in the sense of one-wayness or semantic security against chosen ciphertext attack.

1.1 Contribution of This Paper

In this paper, we investigate the security of the above CRT-based cryptosystems against SCA. First, the operations related to CRT of the cryptosystems are examined in the sense of Novak's attack. It is not obvious to construct a Novak-type attack on CRT-based cryptosystems, because the CRT computes with two numbers of different bit-length in these cryptosystems. Note that Novak's attack assume that these numbers are of nearly equal bit-length. In addition, the Novak-type attack is strictly depending how to implement the second CRT. We examine the operations related to CRT of these cryptosystems, and show that extended Novak-type attack is effective on them. Secondly, we present a novel attack called *zero-multiplication attack*. The attacker tries to guess the secret prime by producing ciphertexts that cause a multiplication with zero during the decryption. Note that Goubin [Gou03] proposed a side channel attack using a point with the zero value and an enhancement was proposed by Akishita-Takagi [AT03]. The crucial point of Goubin's attack is that a zero-valued register, which is known for the attacker, appears during the computation. In other words, Goubin's attack is a differential power analysis (DPA) using the *data* zero. On the other hand, the proposed zero-multiplication attack utilizes the *instruction* of the multiplication by zero for revealing the secret. That is, the zero-multiplication attack is a simple power analysis (SPA) using the instruction of zero. In fact, the zero-multiplication appears at CRT with small messages like $m < p \wedge m < q$, namely $m_q - m_p = 0$. We point out that Multi-Exponent RSA and HIME(R) cryptosystem involve additional zero-multiplications arisen from the Hensel lifting. Finally, we propose novel countermeasures against these attacks. The countermeasures are based on the ciphertext blinding technique, but they require no inversion operation. We can randomize ciphertexts and remove the randomization using only modular multiplication. This provides us a practical implication, because no library of computing an inversion is usually equipped on smartcards designed for RSA cryptosystem. The overhead of the proposed scheme is only about 1% to 5% of the whole decryption.

The paper is organized as follows: Section 2 reviews the RSA cryptosystems using RSA-CRT. Section 3 extends Novak's attack to Multi-prime RSA, and proposes zero-multiplication attack on it. Section 4 examines the proposed attacks on the CRT-based cryptosystems. Section 5 proposes countermeasures against these attacks.

2   RSA Cryptosystem with CRT

In this section we review the RSA cryptosystem using the Chinese remainder theorem (RSA-CRT).

Let $n = pq$ be the RSA modulus, where p, q are two secret primes that have the same bit length. Let e, d be the integers such that $ed = 1 \bmod \phi(n)$, where $\phi(n) = (p-1)(q-1)$. The public key and the secret key of the RSA cryptosystem are (e, n) and d, respectively. The message $m \in \mathbb{Z}_n$ is encrypted by computing $c = m^e \bmod n$. The integer c is called ciphertext. The person who knows the secret key d can decrypt the ciphertext by computing $m = c^d \bmod n$.

In order to make the RSA cryptosystem semantic secure against the chosen ciphertext attack, we usually deploy the OAEP padding [PKCS]. We convert the message m to PKCS format $\mu(m)$ before computing encryption. In the decryption, if $c^d \bmod n$ does not satisfy the PKCS format, c is rejected as invalid ciphertext. Note that the attacker is able to choose any ciphertext c as the input for primitive computation $c^d \bmod n$ (the manipulated ciphertexts are eventually rejected at the padding check with overwhelming probability). Although classical chosen ciphertext attacks, e.g. [Dav82] are not feasible, chosen ciphertext attacks using side channel information on the primitive decryption are feasible.

$\downarrow$ side channel information

Ciphertext $c \longrightarrow$ | Primitive Decryption $c^d \bmod n$ | $\longrightarrow$ | Padding Check $\mu(m)$ | $\longrightarrow$ Reject

If we use the Chinese remainder theorem for the decryption of RSA, its speed can be accelerated with additional memory. Let $d_p = d \bmod p - 1$ and $d_q =$

$d \bmod q - 1$. RSA-CRT deciphers $m_p = m \bmod p$ and $m_q = m \bmod q$ instead of computing $m = c^d \bmod n$. Indeed we can obtain them by $m_p = c^{d_p} \bmod p$ and $m_q = c^{d_q} \bmod q$. Then the proper message is recovered by applying the Chinese remainder theorem for m_p and m_q. We describe the standard algorithm of the decryption of the RSA-CRT [PKCS]:

RSA-CRT_Decryption

Input: ciphertext c, secret keys $p, q, d_p, d_q, pInv$

Output: message m

---
1. $m_p \leftarrow c^{d_p} \bmod p$, $m_q \leftarrow c^{d_q} \bmod q$,
2. $h \leftarrow (m_q - m_p) * (pInv) \bmod q$, $m_{pq} \leftarrow m_p + p * h$
3. return(m_{pq})

The Chinese remainder theorem at Step 2 is computed using Garner's algorithm [PKCS]. We pre-compute $pInv = p^{-1} \bmod q$, and Step 2 requires only two multiplications of $\mathbb{Z}_n$. Because the bit-size of p, q is half of n, the running time of computing $c^{d_p} \bmod p$ is about $2^3 = 8$ times faster. The total improvement of the running time is about 4 times.

2.1 Known Attacks

We review several known attacks against the RSA-CRT.

Timing Attack: Kocher proposed a timing attack of computing $c^{d_p} \bmod p$ [Koc96]. If $c < p$ holds, then we do not reduce c modulo p. There is a difference of timing between $c < p$ and $c > p$. The attacker can recover p by the binary search. This attack is called the *timing attack*. Recently Boneh et al. showed an experimental result of this timing attack against the server-client model — several implementation of SSL are vulnerable [BB03].

Fault Attack: If we can manipulate one bit of the register for $m_p = m \bmod p$ (say m', the related fake message), then the modulus can be factored by computing $gcd(m - m', n)$ due to $m' = m \bmod q$ and $m' \neq m \bmod p$ [JLQ99]. This attack is called the *fault attack*. This attack was extended to more sophisticated fault attack [BDL01], etc. Aumüller et al. showed an experimental result of this attack [ABF+02]. They also proposed a countermeasure, which checks every process during the decryption, e.g. $m_p = m \bmod p$, $m^e = c \bmod p$, etc.

SPA/DPA: We can break the secret key by utilizing the side channel information related to the secret key, e.g., the simple power analysis (SPA), the differential power analysis (DPA) [KJJ99]. Messerges et al. showed the modular multiplication $c^d \bmod n$ is vulnerable against SPA/DPA [MDS99]. A DPA against the modular multiplication $c^{d_p} \bmod p$ was demonstrated by den Boer et al. [BLW02]. The ciphertext blinding method resists this type of attacks. The other countermeasure is the *exponent blinding method*, which randomizes the secret exponent by computing $d' = d + \phi(n)r$ for some integer r (or we can use a randomized representation of d, for example, MIST [Wal02]).

Timing Attack against Montgomery Multiplication: Schindler et al. pointed out the weakness of the implementation using the Montgomery multiplication

(See, for example, [Sch00]). The attacker tries to guess the secret key by observing the final subtraction of Montgomery multiplication. A countermeasure is to always perform the final subtraction, and then we choose the proper residue.

Novak Attack: Novak proposed an SPA against Step 2, namely the Chinese remainder theorem [Nov02]. He focused on the following implementation of $m_q - m_p \bmod q$; first compute $y = m_q - m_p$ and then $y = y + q$ if $y = m_q - m_p < 0$ holds. The experimental result shows the side channel information of $y = m_q - m_p < 0$ can be detected by SPA. He developed a binary search algorithm of finding secret key q with about $\log q$ calls. We should note that Novak's attack is effective for $m_q \approx m_p$ only, because y often takes different signs. A countermeasure against SPA is to always compute $y' = y + q$, and then we choose y' if and only if $m_q - m_p < 0$. Note that the exponent blinding method or MIST does not resist Novak attack.

Remark 1. The timing attack and Novak attack are effective on the chosen ciphertext setting. However, they are not feasible to the probabilistic signature, e.g., RSA-PSS [PKCS]. Even if the attacker chooses a message m, it is randomized by padding function ρ such that $\rho(m)$. The attacker cannot control the size of $\rho(m)$. Very recently, Fouque et al. proposed an extension of Novak attack on RSA with the randomly chosen messages, but this attack is restricted to the unbalanced modulus s.t. $p \not\approx q$ [FMP03].

3   Multi-prime RSA

In this section we investigate the security of Multi-Prime RSA against SCA. We assume the chosen ciphertext setting, that is, the attacker can freely choose ciphertexts for revealing the secret.

The public modulus of general Multi-Prime RSA consists of the product of several pair-wisely distinct secret primes [PKCS]. The current practically relevant Multi-Prime RSA modulus is a 1024-bit modulus $n = pqr$ with the same size secret primes p, q, r. In this paper we discuss this modulus, but the attack can be easily extended to other types.

The public-key of Multi-Prime RSA is (n, e), where $n = pqr$. The secret key is $(p, q, r, d_p, d_q, d_r, pInv, pqInv)$, where $d_p = e^{-1} \bmod p-1$, $d_q = e^{-1} \bmod q-1$, $d_r = e^{-1} \bmod r - 1$, $pInv = p^{-1} \bmod q$, and $pqInv = (pq)^{-1} \bmod r$. A message $m \in \mathbb{Z}_n$ is encrypted by $c = m^e \bmod n$, which is equal to the RSA encryption. The ciphertext c is decrypted as follows:

Multi-Prime_RSA_Decryption

Input: ciphertext c, secret key $(p, q, r, d_p, d_q, d_r, pInv, pqInv)$
Output: message m

---

1. $m_p \leftarrow c^{d_p} \bmod p$, $m_q \leftarrow c^{d_q} \bmod q$, $m_r \leftarrow c^{d_r} \bmod r$
2. $h \leftarrow (m_q - m_p) * (pInv) \bmod q$, $m_{pq} \leftarrow m_p + p * h$
3. $h \leftarrow (m_r - m_{pq}) * (pqInv) \bmod r$, $m_{pqr} \leftarrow m_{pq} + (pq) * h$
4. return(m_{pqr})

Each modular multiplication modulo p, q, r is about 27 times faster than $c^d \bmod n$, because we choose these primes have the same size. Thus, the decryption algorithm of Multi-Prime RSA is about 9 times faster than that of RSA for the modulus n with same bit length.

At Step 2, we use the Chinese remainder theorem for p and q. Novak's attack can detect the approximation of prime q and we can factor n into q and pr. In this case, the number field sieve can factor pr much faster than pqr. We consider that the Multi-Prime RSA is broken, since it does not keep the expected security.

At Step 3, we compute CRT for pq and r using pre-computed value $pqInv = (pq)^{-1} \bmod r$. If we can develop a Novak-type algorithm for Step 3, the Multi-Prime RSA is also no longer secure. Note that a straight-forward extension of Novak's attack fails, because $m_{pq} > m_r$ holds in most cases, namely the value $m_{pq} - m_r$ is positive with high probability. In order to construct a Novak-type attack, we need to overcome this problem. In addition, Novak's attack against Step 3 strongly depends on how to implement "$h \leftarrow (m_r - m_{pq}) * (pqInv) \bmod r$". There are several ways to implement it. The possible ways are as follows:

(MP1) $y \leftarrow m_{pq} \bmod r$, $t \leftarrow m_r - y \bmod r$, $h \leftarrow t * pqInv \bmod r$,
(MP2) $y \leftarrow -m_{pq} \bmod r$, $t \leftarrow m_r + y \bmod r$, $h \leftarrow t * pqInv \bmod r$,
(MP3) $y \leftarrow m_r - m_{pq}$, $t \leftarrow y \bmod r$, $h \leftarrow t * pqInv \bmod r$.

The first way is a natural implementation, since we can reuse the modular subtraction module, because we should implement the modular subtraction $m_q - m_p \bmod q$ of Step 2. When we compute $-m_{pq} \bmod r$ in the second algorithm, it is usually computed $y = m_{pq} \bmod r$ and then $r - y$. This procedure avoids treating a signed integer. The third way is a straight-forward implementation.

3.1   Novak-Type Attack on Multi-prime RSA

In the following we investigate Novak's attack against the first implementation (MP1). For m in $\mathbb{Z}_n$, we define the following characteristic function:

$$\delta(m) = \begin{cases} 1 & \text{if } (m \bmod r) - ((m \bmod pq) \bmod r) \geq 0 \\ 0 & \text{otherwise} \end{cases}$$

Because the integer m_{pq} is reduced modulo pq before computing modulo r, it differently behaves from Novak's attack. Indeed, we have the following proposition. In ascending order of m, the sign $\delta(m)$ has the pattern

$$1, .., 1, 0, .., 0, 1, .., 1, 0, .., 0, 1, ..,$$

and it is changed 1 to 0 if and only if $r | m$ holds. In other words, the attacker can factor n into r and pq if he/she detects such m.

Proposition 1. Let $N = P_1 * P_2$, where $\gcd(P_1, P_2) = 1$ and $P_1 > P_2$. For M in $\mathbb{Z}_N$, define $\delta[P_1, P_2](M) = 1$ if $M \bmod P_2 - ((M \bmod P_1) \bmod P_2) \geq 0$, otherwise $\delta[P_1, P_2](M) = 0$. Then we have following properties:

(1) $\delta[P_1, P_2](M) = 1$ holds for all $M < P_1$,
(2) For all $P_1 \le M < N$, we have

$$\delta[P_1, P_2](kP_2) = \dots = \delta[P_1, P_2](kP_2 + l) = 0,$$
$$\delta[P_1, P_2](kP_2 + l + 1) = \dots = \delta[P_1, P_2]((k+1)P_2 - 1) = 1,$$

where k, l are integers with $0 < k < P_1$ and $0 < l < P_2 - 2$.

Proof. Let $N = LP \cup UP$, where $LP = \{0, 1, \dots, P_1 - 1\}$ and $UP = \{P_1, P_1 + 1, \dots, N-1\}$. For successive $M = 0, 1, 2, \dots, N-1$, we evaluate the values $(M \bmod P_1) \bmod P_2$ and $M \bmod P_2$ in the following. If $M \in LP$, then $(M \bmod P_1) \bmod P_2 = M \bmod P_2$ holds due to $M \bmod P_1 = M$. Thus $\delta(M) = 1$ for all $M \in LP$. Next we consider the case of $M \in UP$. Let $f(M) = (M \bmod P_2) - ((M \bmod P_1) \bmod P_2)$. Then $\delta(M) = 1$ iff $f(M) \ge 0$. Note that $M \bmod P_1 \ne M \bmod P_2$ for $M \in UP$ due to $gcd(P_1, P_2) = 1$. Then the value $(M \bmod P_1) \bmod P_2$ is never equal to $(M \bmod P_2)$ for $M \in UP$ because of the Chinese remainder theorem. Therefore, we obtain $f(kP_2) < 0$, namely $\delta(kP_2) = 0$, and $f(kP_2 - 1) = P_2 - 1 - ((kP_2 - 1 \bmod P_1) \bmod P_2) > 0$, namely $\delta(kP_2 - 1) = 1$, where k is a positive integer. Next we consider $f(kP_2 + l)$ for $0 < l \le P_2 - 2$. For $0 < l \le P_2 - 2$, we have two cases:

(i)$M = kP_2 + l$ is not divisible by P_1, (ii)$M = kP_2 + l$ is divisible by P_1.

Let $g(M) = M \bmod P_1$. In the first case, we have $g(M+1) = g(M)+1$ and $g(M)$ is monotonously increasing for $M = kP_2 + l, l = 1, \dots, P_2 - 2$. If we reduce them modulo P_2, then all numbers are pair-wised different due to $P_1 > P_2$. Thus, two sets $(M \bmod P_1) \bmod P_2$ and $M \bmod P_2$ have the following pattern:

$$(M \bmod P_1) \bmod P_2 = \{s, s + 1, \dots, P_2 - 1, 0, 1, \dots, s - 1\},$$
$$M \bmod P_2 = \{0, 1, \dots, P_2 - s - 1, P_2 - s, P_2 - s + 1, \dots, P_2 - 1\},$$

where for some $0 < s < P_2$. $(M \bmod P_1) \bmod P_2$ is the set of s-left-sift of $M \bmod P_2$. Thus the corresponding δ sequence is $\delta[P_1, P_2] = \underbrace{0, .., 0}_{P_2 - s}, \underbrace{1, .., 1}_{s}$. We have obtained the desired sequence. Next we discuss the second case. There is only one integer which is divisible by P_1 in any interval with length P_2. Let t be the number divisible by P_1 in interval $[kP_2, \dots, kP_2 + P_2 - 1]$. The integers $M < t$ have the same pattern above. For $M \ge t$ we always have $f(M) > 0$, namely $\delta[P_1, P_2](M) = 1$. Thus we have the following pattern:

$$(M \bmod P_1) \bmod P_2 = \{P_1 - v, P_1 - v + 1, .., P_1 - 1, 0, 1, \dots, u - 1\},$$
$$M \bmod P_2 = \{0, 1, \dots, v - 1, P_2 - u, P_2 - u + 1, \dots, P_2 - 1\},$$

where $v = t \bmod P_2$ and $u = P_2 - v$. Thus the corresponding δ sequence is $\delta[P_1, P_2] = \underbrace{0, .., 0}_{v}, \underbrace{1, .., 1}_{u}$. Consequently we have proved the proposition. $\square$

If we choose $P_1 = pq$ and $P_2 = r$ we can construct the Novak-type attack from this proposition. The condition $P_1 > P_2$ is satisfied, because the three primes are chosen with same bit length. We describe the Novak-type attack in the following. It is modified from the original Novak attack in order to reduce the number of the oracle calls.

Novak_Type_Attack

INPUT: modulus n, public exponent e, upper bound B of r.
OUTPUT: secret prime r such that $n = pqr$.

---

1. Randomly choose $x_0 \in \mathbb{Z}_n$
    1.1. Compute $\delta(x_0)$ of $c_0 \leftarrow x_0^e \bmod n$ using SPA
    1.2. Set $\delta(x_1) \leftarrow \delta(x_0)$
2. While $\delta(x_1) = \delta(x_0)$
    2.1. If $\delta(x_0) = 1$, randomly choose x_1 s.t. $x_1 > x_0$ and $x_1 - x_0 < B$
        else randomly choose x_1 s.t. $x_1 < x_0$ and $x_0 - x_1 < B$
    2.2. Compute $\delta(x_1)$ of $c_1 \leftarrow x_1^e \bmod n$ using SPA
3. $LB \leftarrow x_0, UB \leftarrow x_1$.
    3.1. If $\delta(x_0) = 0$ then $LB \leftarrow x_1, UB \leftarrow x_0$.
4. While $LB \neq UB$ do:
    4.1. $m \leftarrow \lceil (LB + UB)/2 \rceil$.
    4.2. Compute $\delta(m)$ of $c \leftarrow m^e \bmod n$ using SPA.
    4.3. If $\delta(m) = 1$ then $LB \leftarrow m$; otherwise $UB \leftarrow m$.
5. Compute $r \leftarrow \gcd(n, m)$.
6. Return(r).

At Step 1 we choose an initial integer x_0 randomly from $\mathbb{Z}_n$, and compute $\delta(x_0)$ of $c_0 \leftarrow x_0^e \bmod n$ using SPA. At Step 1 we try to find integer x_1, which satisfies $\delta(x_0) \neq \delta(x_1)$ and $|x_0 - x_1| < B$, where B is the upper bound of secret prime r. At step 3 we assign upper bound UB and lower bound LB of the target whose signs are exactly opposite. Step 4 is the main loop. We find the target based on the binary search of UB and LB. If $UB = LB(= m)$ holds, then we obtain the target. From the above lemma, the secret prime r yields by computing $gcd(m, n) = r$.

We estimate the average oracle calls. At Step 4 we requires at most $\lceil log_2 r \rceil$ oracle calls because $|UB - LB| < B$, where $B = 2^{\lceil log_2 r \rceil}$. We assume that $pq \bmod r$ is randomly distributed in modulo r. Then at Step 2 we can obtain x_1 with a few trials, because the probability of finding x_1 at Step 2 is about $1/2$ on average due to randomness of x_1 and $s = pq \bmod r$. At Step 1 we use only one oracle call. Thus we need about $(\log_2 n)/3$ oracle calls on average.

Remark 2. If we modify the characteristic function δ, the attack described above is basically applicable to implementation (MP2) in the previous section, because the following two conditions are equivalent: $m_r - (m_{pq} \bmod r) \geq 0$ and $m_r + (r - (m_{pq} \bmod r)) \geq r$.

On the other hand, our attack is not applicable to implementation (MP3), because $m_r - m_{pq}$ is negative with high probability. However, we show a different attack on (MP3) in the next section.

3.2 Zero-Multiplication Attack

In this section we deal with the SPA using the multiplication with zero.

In the previous section we discussed that the Novak-type attacks are applicable to the decryption algorithm of Multi-Prime RSA if it deploys a subtraction related to the secret primes, e.g. $m_r - (m_{pq} \bmod r) \bmod r$. However, its practical feasibility causes a controversy, because we can avoid the operation as follows: at first we always compute $t = m_r - (m_{pq} \bmod r)$ and $t' = t + r$, and then "if $t < 0$ then $t = t'$". It is more difficult to detect the last operation using SPA.

However we can mount Novak's attack to the stronger SPA using the multiplication with zero. We call it *zero-multiplication attack* in this paper.

We have the following observation for the Multi-Prime RSA. If we choose $m < r$, then $h(m) = m_r - m_{pq} \bmod r = 0$ holds. Then we compute $0 * pqInv \bmod r$ at Step 3 of the decryption. The chosen ciphertext attack is allowed to generate the ciphertext c with $c = m^e \bmod n$ and $m < r$. Thus the binary search on r is possible using the SPA, and thus the secret prime r can be found. We show an algorithm to find the secret key r in the following. Define $\delta_{ZERO}(x) = 1$ if $h(x) = 0$ otherwise $\delta_{ZERO}(x) = 0$.

Zero_Multiplication_Attack

INPUT: modulus n, public exponent e, bit-length L of r.
OUTPUT: secret prime r such that $n = pqr$.

1. Set $x \leftarrow 0$
2. For $i = L - 1$ down to 0
   2.1. Set $y \leftarrow x + 2^i \bmod n$ and $c \leftarrow y^e \bmod n$
   2.2. Compute $\delta_{ZERO}(y)$ of c using SPA
   2.3. If $\delta_{ZERO}(x) = 1$ holds, then set $x \leftarrow y$
3. Return(x).

This attack is also applicable to the secret prime p at Step 2. If m satisfies both $m < p$ and $m < q$, then we always have $h = m_q - m_p = 0$.

Remark 3. Implementation (MP3) in the previous section is vulnerable against zero-multiplication attack. Because $y \leftarrow m_r - m_{pq}$ is always 0 if $m < r$ satisfies.

4 Application to Other CRT-Based Cryptosystems

There are several cryptosystem based on the Chinese remainder theorem, namely Rabin cryptosystem, Multi-Exponent RSA [Tak98], and HIME(R) cryptosystem [NSS01]. We discuss the effectiveness of the Novak-type attack and the zero-multiplication attack on them. We keep assuming the chosen ciphertext setting in this section.

4.1 Rabin Cryptosystem

We discuss the Novak attack against the Rabin cryptosystem. Let p, q be primes with $p \bmod 4 = q \bmod 4 = 3$. The public-key and secret-key of the Rabin cryptosystem are n and (p, q), respectively. A message $m \in \mathbb{Z}_n$ is encrypted by

$c = m^2 \bmod n$. This encryption function is a $4 : 1$ mapping, and thus there are 4 different solutions for $c = x^2 \bmod n$. The 4 messages are decrypted as follows:

Rabin_Decryption

Input: ciphertext c, secret key $(p, q, d_p, d_q, pInv)$

Output: messages m

---

1. $m_p \leftarrow c^{(p+1)/4} \bmod p, \quad m_q \leftarrow c^{(q+1)/4} \bmod q$
2. $h \leftarrow (m_q - m_p) * (pInv) \bmod q, \quad m \leftarrow m_p + p * h$
3. Compute $\bar{m}$ from Step 1 to Step 2 for $(-m_p, m_q)$
4. Set $m_1 \leftarrow m, \quad m_2 \leftarrow \bar{m}, \quad m_3 \leftarrow n - m, \quad m_4 \leftarrow n - \bar{m}$
5. Find proper m from m_1, m_2, m_3, m_4
6. Return(m_1, m_2, m_3, m_4)

At Step 1 the message modulo p, q are recovered. At Step 2 we compute the original m using the Chinese remainder theorem. The original Novak attack is applicable to Step 2. In order to recover other 3 different solutions for a given ciphertext c, we perform Step 1,2 for messages $(-m_p, m_q)$ and we obtain $\bar{m}$. Then all 4 solutions are $m_1 = m, m_2 = \bar{m}, m_3 = n - m, m_1 = n - \bar{m}$.

Two negative integer $-m_p$ is usually converted to its positive representative class, namely $p - m_p$. There is additionally one more possible oracle:

(R1) if $m_q - (p - m_p) < 0$, then $y = m_q - (p - m_p), h = y + q$.

Using this oracle we can construct a Novak-type attack. If the sign of the oracle changes 1 to 0, then the secret prime p or q appears. Indeed we have the following proposition, which is similarly to Proposition 1.

Proposition 2. *Let $n = pq$ be the RSA modulus. For m in $\mathbb{Z}_N$, define $\delta_{Rabin}(m) = 1$ if $m \bmod q - (p - (m \bmod p)) \geq 0$, otherwise $\delta_{Rabin}(m) = 0$. The sequence of $\delta_{Rabin}(m)$ has the consecutive pattern $\underbrace{0, .., 0}_{a_i}, \underbrace{1, .., 1}_{b_i}$ for succes-*

sive $m = q, q + 1, ..., n - 1$, where $0 < a_i, b_i < \max(p, q)$ and $i = 0, 1, 2, ...$ The integer g that satisfies $\delta_{Rabin}(g - 1) = 1$ and $\delta_{Rabin}(g) = 0$ is divisible by p or q.

Proof. The proof is quite similar to that of Proposition 1. Thus we only describe the sketch of it. There are two cases: $p < q$ and $p > q$. At first we deal with the case of $p > q$. The sequences of $m \bmod q$ and $(p - (m \bmod p))$ are as follows:

$$m \bmod q = 0, 1, ..., q - 2, q - 1,$$

$$p - m \bmod p = s, s - 1, ..., 2, 1, p, p - 1, ..., t + 1, t,$$

where $0 < s, t < p$. Therefore the sequence of δ associated to it has following fixed pattern: $\underbrace{0, .., 0}_{a_1}, \underbrace{1, .., 1}_{b_1}, \underbrace{0, .., 0}_{a_2}, \underbrace{1, .., 1}_{b_2}$ for some $0 < a_1, b_1 < p$ and $0 \leq a_2, b_2 < p$.

The signs are changed at most twice modulo q. If $a_2 \neq 0$ holds, then the integer g such that $\delta(g - 1) = 1$ and $\delta(g) = 0$ always satisfies $p|g$ or $q|g$. Next we deal with the case of $p < q$. The δ sequence is as follows: $\underbrace{0, .., 0}_{a_1}, \underbrace{1, .., 1}_{b_1}, ..., \underbrace{0, .., 0}_{a_i}, \underbrace{1, .., 1}_{b_i}$, where $0 < a_1, b_1, ..., a_{i-1}, b_{i-1} < p$ and $0 \leq a_i, b_i < p$ for some i. The signs are changed at most $\lceil q/p \rceil + 1$ modulo q. The integer g such that $\delta(g - 1) = 1$ and $\delta(g) = 0$ always satisfies $p|g$ for the first $(i - 1)$ changes of the sign and $q|g$ for the last one. Consequently, we proved the proposition. $\qquad\square$

The zero-multiplication attack is also applicable to Step 2, because $m_q - m_p$ is zero if m satisfies both $m < p$ and $m < q$. However, it is not clear to find a zero multiplication for the other three Chinese remainder theorems. For example, without knowledge of p, q we are not able to find the message m that satisfies $p - m_p = m_q$.

4.2 Multi-exponent RSA

We discuss the variant of RSA using modulo p^2q proposed by Takagi [Tak98]. In this paper we call it Multi-Exponent RSA according to [BS02]. The message m is recovered from messages m_{p^2} modulo p^2 and m_q modulo q. The message m_{p^2} is lifted from the message m_p using the Hensel lifting, which requires only quadratic complexity $\mathcal{O}((\log p)^2)$. We present a modified version in the following. The public key is equal to that of the original RSA cryptosystem, namely (e, n) but $n = p^2q$ where p, q have the same bit length. The secret key is $(p, q, d_p, d_q, p^2Inv, eInv)$, where $d_p = e^{-1} \bmod (p - 1), d_q = e^{-1} \bmod (q - 1)$, $p^2Inv = (p^2)^{-1} \bmod q, eInv = e^{-1} \bmod p$. A message $m \in \mathbb{Z}_n$ is encrypted $c = m^e \bmod n$. The ciphertext c is decrypted as follows:

Multi-Exponent_RSA_Decryption

Input: ciphertext c, secret key $(p, q, d_p, d_q, p^2Inv, eInv)$

Output: message m

---
1. $k \leftarrow c^{d_p-1} \bmod p$, $m_p \leftarrow ck \bmod p$, $m_q \leftarrow c^{d_q} \bmod q$
2. $g \leftarrow c - m_p^e \bmod p^2$, $b \leftarrow g * k * eInv \bmod p^2$, $m_{p^2} \leftarrow m_p + b$
3. $h \leftarrow (m_q - m_{p^2}) * (p^2Inv) \bmod q$, $m \leftarrow m_{p^2} + p^2 * h$
4. Return(m)

At Step 1 we decrypt message modulo p, q, and the additional information $k = c^{d_p-1} \bmod p$. At Step 2 we compute message modulo p^2 using the Hensel lifting. Note that m_{p^2} is uniquely represented as $m_{p^2} = m_p + b$, where b is divisible by p and $0 \leq b/p < p$. Thus we have relationship: $c \bmod p^2 = m_{p^2}^e \bmod p^2 = m_p^e + em_p^{e-1}b \bmod p^2$, and thus we obtain $b = g((em_p^{e-1})^{-1} \bmod p) \bmod p^2$, where $g = c - m_p^e \bmod p^2$. Because $(m_p^{e-1})^{-1} \bmod p = c^{d_p-1} \bmod p$, we can correctly decrypt m_{p^2} at Step 2. At Step 3 we compute the Chinese remainder theorem for m_{p^2} and m_q. Thus the Novak-type attack is applicable to Step 3. Note that there is a multiplication with zero at Step 3 if the message is smaller than q. Therefore we can find the secret prime q using the zero-multiplication attack described in Section 3.2.

We discuss the zero-multiplication attack on Step 2. There is the following relation:

(ME1) if $m < p$, then $m_p = m, g = c - m_p^2 \bmod p^2 = 0$.

(ME2) if $m > p$, then $m_p \neq m, g = c - m_p^2 \bmod p^2 \neq 0$ with overwhelming probability over $m \in \mathbb{Z}_n$.

Thus there are two zero-multiplications at Step 3 if $m < p$ holds. The attacker detects whether g is zero or not. Define $\delta_{MERSA}(x) = 1$ if $x < p$ otherwise $\delta_{MERSA}(x) = 0$. Therefore, we can construct a binary search algorithm for p described Section 3.2 using this characteristic function δ_{MERSA}.

4.3   HIME(R) Cryptosystem

We discuss the security of HIME(R) cryptosystem developed [NSS01]. HIME(R) is a provably secure cryptosystem, which is IND-CCA2 under the factoring assumption of modulus $p^2 q$. The decryption algorithm utilizes the Chinese remainder theorem and the Hensel-like lifting, and thus it is faster than RSA-CRT with the same modulus size. We describe the HIME(R) primitive in the following with a modification. Let p, q be primes with $p \bmod 4 = q \bmod 4 = 3$ with the same bit length. Let $pInv = p^{-1} \bmod q$ and $2Inv = 2^{-1} \bmod p$. The public-key and secret key of HIME(R) is n and $p, q, pInv, 2Inv$, respectively. A message is $m \in \mathbb{Z}_n$ is encrypted by $c = m^2 \bmod n$. This encryption function is same as the Rabin encryption ($4 : 1$ mapping). The message c is decrypted as follows:

HIME(R)_Primitive_Decryption

Input: ciphertext c, secret key $(p, q, pInv, 2Inv)$

Output: message m

---
0. Check $c \bmod p$ and $c \bmod q$ are quadratic residue
1. $k \leftarrow c^{(p-3)/4} \bmod p$, $m_p \leftarrow c * k \bmod p$, $m_q \leftarrow c^{(q+1)/4} \bmod q$
2. $h \leftarrow (m_q - m_p) * (pInv) \bmod q$, $m_{pq} \leftarrow m_p + p * h$
3. $g \leftarrow c - m_{pq}^2 \bmod n$, $b \leftarrow g * k * (2Inv) \bmod n$, $m \leftarrow m_{pq} + b$
4. Compute $\bar{m}$ from Step 2 to Step 3 for $(-m_p, m_q)$
5. Set $m_1 \leftarrow m$, $m_2 \leftarrow \bar{m}$, $m_3 \leftarrow n - m$, $m_4 \leftarrow n - \bar{m}$
6. Find proper m from m_1, m_2, m_3, m_4
7. Return(m)

At Step 0 we check the ciphertext c is quadratic residue or not. At Step 1 we compute the message modulo p and q, and additionally $k = c^{(p-3)/4} \bmod p$. At Step 2 the message modulo pq are recovered using the Chinese remainder theorem. Here we can apply the original Novak attack. Note that an integer $m \in \mathbb{Z}_n$ is uniquely represented as $m = m_{pq} + b$, where $m_{pq} = m \bmod pq$, b is divisible by pq and $0 \leq b/pq < p$. At Step 3 we find the unique integer b for given m_{pq} and c. From $c \bmod n - m^2 \bmod n = m_{pq}^2 + 2m_{pq}b \bmod n$, we obtain $b = (c - m_{pq}^2)((2m_p)^{-1} \bmod p) \bmod n$. Here we have $k = m^{(p-3)/2} \bmod p = m^{(p-1)/2-1} \bmod p = \pm m_p^{-1} \bmod p$ due to $m^{(p-1)/2} = \pm 1 \bmod p$. We can correctly recover the message m at Step 3. At Step 4 and 5 we generate other 3 candidates of the proper message. The Novak-type attack described in Section 4.1 is applicable to the message $(-m_p, m_q)$ at Step 4.

There are several operations related to the secret keys p, q. We examine the zero-multiplication attack on Step 3. Recall $c = m^2 \bmod p^2 q$, since c is the ciphertext of m. Then we have following relationship:

(H1) if $m < pq$, then $m_{pq} = m, c - m_{pq}^2 \bmod p^2 q = 0$.
(H2) if $m > pq$, then $m_{pq} \neq m, c - m_{pq}^2 \bmod p^2 q \neq 0$ with overwhelming probability over $m \in \mathbb{Z}_n$.

Thus in Step 3 two zero-multiplications appear if $E(m) = c - m_{pq}^2$ is zero. The attacker detects whether $E(m)$ is zero or not. Define $\delta_{HIME}(x) = 1$ if $E(x) = 0$ otherwise $\delta_{HIME}(x) = 0$. Therefore, we can construct a binary search algorithm for pq described Section 3.2 using this characteristic function δ_{HIME}.

5 New Countermeasures

In this section we discuss how to randomize a ciphertext of RSA cryptosystem.

A standard way is the ciphertext blinding method (see Section 2.1). A drawback of this scheme is the computation of the inverse $r^{-1} \bmod n$. A library that computes an inversion is not usually equipped on smartcards, so that the designer has to additionally develop it. While we can compute $r^{-1} \bmod n$ using the modular exponentiation $r^{\phi(n)-1} \bmod n$, it requires a large overhead.

We present a randomization method, which requires no modular inversion. The proposed algorithm is as follows:

Ciphertext_Blinding_Without_Inversion
Input: public keys n, e, ciphertext c, secret keys p, q
Output: message m s.t. $c = m^e \bmod n$
1. Compute $s \leftarrow r^{e-1} \bmod n$ for random $r \in \mathbb{Z}_n^*$ and $t \leftarrow s * r * c \bmod n$
2. Compute $u \leftarrow t^{d-1} \bmod n$
3. Compute $v \leftarrow u * s \bmod n$ and $m \leftarrow v * c \bmod n$
4. Return(m)

At Step 1 the ciphertext c is blinded by $r^e \bmod n$ such that $t = r^e c \bmod n$, but we store the value $s = r^{e-1} \bmod n$. At Step 2 we decrypt message t using exponent $d - 1$ instead of d, namely $u = t^{d-1} \bmod n$. Note that $u * s \bmod n = (m^e r^e)^{d-1} r^{e-1} \bmod n = m^{1-e} \bmod n$. Thus at Step 3 we can recover message m by $u * s * c \bmod n$. The attacker tries to analyze the computation of Step 4, but ciphertext c is randomized as $r^e c \bmod n$. At Step 2 we can also compute $t^{d-1} \bmod n$ using the Chinese remainder theorem. In that case, we have to modify the secret key d_p and d_q to $d_p = d - 1 \bmod p - 1$ and $d_q = d - 1 \bmod q - 1$, respectively. We also note that public exponent e has to be known, which is not always the case in real-life applications.

This countermeasure is efficient for small encryption exponent. If we choose standard $e = 2^{16} + 1$, then it requires about only 20 multiplications of $\mathbb{Z}_n$. Therefore the overhead is about 5% of the whole decryption computation of RSA with CRT. We require 2 registers of $\mathbb{Z}_n$ for auxiliary paramters (s, u).

In the following we discuss other possible randomization schemes. If we store $(S, T) = (r^e \bmod n, r^{-1} \bmod n)$ in non-volatile memory for a random integer $r \in \mathbb{Z}_n$, then we can randomize a ciphertext c by computing $m = (S^t c)^d T^t \bmod n$, where t is a small random exponent. If we choose 16-bit or 32-bit t, then the overhead of this scheme is about 47 or 98 multiplications of $\mathbb{Z}_n$ (namely about 12% or 26% comparing with RSA-CRT), respectively. We require 2 registers of $\mathbb{Z}_n$ for auxiliary paramters $(S^t c, T^t)$. Consequently, our proposed scheme is more efficient than these schemes.

5.1 Application to Rabin Cryptosystem

The proposed countermeasure is also applicable to Rabin or HIME(R) cryptosystem. The encryption exponent of these schemes is 2, so that this countermeasure is particularly effective. In that case we have to choose quadratic residue r, otherwise the valid ciphertext is not decrypted. Indeed we can construct it as follows:

Rabin_Ciphertext_Blinding_Without_Inversion

Input: public key n, ciphertext c, secret keys p, q
Output: message m s.t. $c = m^2 \bmod n$

---

  1. Compute $s \leftarrow r^2 \bmod n$ for random $r \in \mathbb{Z}_n^*$
  2. Randomize the ciphertext $t \leftarrow s^2 * c \bmod n$
  3. Compute $u_p \leftarrow t^{(p-3)/4} \bmod p$ and $u_q \leftarrow t^{(q-3)/4} \bmod q$
  4. Compute 4 different $w \bmod n$ corresponding to u_p, u_q using CRT
  5. Compute $m \leftarrow w * c * s \bmod n$
  6. Return(m)

At Step 1 we generate a random quadratic residue s. At Step 2 the ciphertext c is randomized by computing $t = s^2 c \bmod n$, so that the attacker cannot manipulate the randomized message $ms \bmod n$. At Step 3 we decrypt the inversion of the randomized message $(ms)^{-1} \bmod p$ and $(ms)^{-1} \bmod q$, respectively. Note that $t^{(p-3)/4} \bmod p = t^{(p+1)/4-1} \bmod p = (\pm ms)t^{-1} \bmod p = \pm(ms)^{-1} \bmod p$. At Step 4 we recover 4 different messages related to $w = (ms)^{-1} \bmod n$. At Step 5 we compute the proper message m by $m = w * c * s \bmod n$.

The overhead of the proposed method is only 5 multiplications of $\mathbb{Z}_n$. It is about 1% of the whole decryption computation.

References

[ABF+02] C. Aumüller, P. Bier, W. Fischer, P. Hofreiter, and J.-P. Seifert, "Fault Attacks on RSA with CRT: Concrete Results and Practical Countermeasures," CHES 2002, LNCS 2523, pp.260-275, 2003.

[AT03] T. Akishita and T. Takagi, "Zero-Value Point Attacks on Elliptic Curve Cryptosystem", ISC 2003, LNCS2851, pp. 218-233, 2003.

[BLW02] B. den Boer, K. Lemke, and G. Wicke, "A DPA Attack against the Modular Reduction within a CRT Implementation of RSA," CHES 2002, LNCS 2523, pp.228-243, 2003.

[BDL01]   D. Boneh, R. DeMillo, R. Lipton, "On the Importance of Eliminating Errors in Cryptographic Computations." J. of Cryptology, 14(2), pp.101-119, 2001.

[BB03]   D. Boneh and D. Brumley, "Remote Timing Attacks are Practical," 12th Usenix Security Symposium, pp.1-14, 2003.

[BS02]   D. Boneh and H. Shacham, "Fast Variants of RSA," CRYPTOBYTES, Vol.5, No.1, pp.1-9, 2002.

[Com]   MultiPrime™, Compaq AXL300 Accelerator.
            http://www.compaq.com/products/servers/security/axl300/

[Dav82]   G. Davida, "Chosen Signature Cryptanalysis of the RSA (MIT) Public Key Cryptosystem," TR-CS-82-2, University of Wisconsin, 1982.

[FMP03]   P.-A. Fouque, G. Martinet, G. Poupard, "Attacking Unbalanced RSA-CRT using SPA," CHES 2003, LNCS 2779, pp.254-268, 2003.

[Gou03]   L. Goubin, "A Refined Power-Analysis Attack on Elliptic Curve Cryptosystems", PKC 2003, LNCS 2567, pp. 199-211, 2003.

[JCA]   Java Cryptography Architecture, http://java.sun.com/products/jdk/1.2/docs/guide/security/CryptoSpec.html

[JLQ99]   M. Joye, A.K. Lenstra, and J.-J. Quisquater, "Chinese Remaindering Based Cryptosystems in the Presence of Faults," Journal of Cryptology 12(4), pp.241-245, 1999.

[Kal96]   B. Kaliski, "Timing Attacks on Cryptosystems," RSA Laboratories Bulletin, No.2, 1996.

[Koc96]   C. Kocher, "Timing attacks on Implementations of Diffie-Hellman, RSA, DSS, and other Systems," CRYPTO '96, LNCS 1109, pp.104-113, 1996.

[KJJ99]   C. Kocher, J. Jaffe, and B. Jun, "Differential Power Analysis," CRYPTO '99, LNCS 1666, pp.388-397, 1999.

[MDS99]   T. Messerges, E. Dabbish, R. Sloan, "Power Analysis Attacks of Modular Exponentiation in Smartcards," CHES'99, LNCS 1717, pp.144-157, 1999.

[NSS01]   M. Nishioka, H. Satoh, and K. Sakurai, "Design and Analysis of Fast Provably Secure Public-Key Cryptosystems Based on a Modular Squaring," ICISC 2001, LNCS 2288, pp.81-102, 2001.

[Nov02]   R. Novak, "SPA-Based Adaptive Chosen-Ciphertext Attack on RSA Implementation," PKC 2002, LNCS 2274, pp.252-262, 2002.

[PKCS]   Public-Key Cryptography Standards, PKCS # 1, Amendment 1: Multi-Prime RSA, RSA Laboratories.

[Sch00]   W. Schindler, "A Timing Attack against RSA with the Chinese Remainder Theorem," CHES 2000, LNCS 1965, pp.109-124, 2000.

[Tak98]   T. Takagi, "Fast RSA-type cryptosystem modulo $p^k q$," CRYPTO '98, LNCS 1462, pp.318-326, 1998.

[Wal02]   C. Walter, "MIST: An Efficient, Randomized Exponentiation Algorithm for Resisting Power Analysis," CT-RSA 2002, LNCS 2271, pp.53-66, 2002.

Cryptanalysis of the Countermeasures Using Randomized Binary Signed Digits

Dong-Guk Han[1]*, Katsuyuki Okeya[2], Tae Hyun Kim[1],
Yoon Sung Hwang[3], Young-Ho Park[4], and Souhwan Jung[5]**

[1] Center for Information and Security Technologies(CIST),
Korea University, Seoul, KOREA
{christa,thkim}@korea.ac.kr
[2] Hitachi, Ltd., Systems Development Laboratory,
292, Yoshida-cho, Totsuka-ku, Yokohama, 244-0817, Japan
ka-okeya@sdl.hitachi.co.jp
[3] Department of Mathematics, Korea University, Seoul, KOREA
yhwang@semi.korea.ac.kr
[4] Dept. of Information Security, Sejong Cyber Univ., Seoul, KOREA
youngho@cybersejong.ac.kr
[5] School of Electronic Engineering, Soongsil University, Seoul, KOREA
souhwanj@ssu.ac.kr

Abstract. Recently, side channel attacks (SCA) have been recognized as menaces to public key cryptosystems. In SCA, an attacker observes side channel information during cryptographic operations, and reveals the secret scalar using the side channel information. On the other hand, elliptic curve cryptosystems (ECC) are suitable for implementing on smartcards. Since a scalar multiplication is a dominant step in ECC, we need to design an algorithm to compute scalar multiplication with the immunity to SCA. For this purpose, several scalar multiplication methods that utilize randomized binary-signed-digit (BSD) representations were proposed. This type of countermeasures includes Ha-Moon's countermeasure, Ebeid-Hasan's one, and Agagliate's one. In this paper we propose a novel general attack against *"all"* the countermeasures of this type. The proposed attack lists the candidates for the secret scalar, however straight-forward approach requires huge memory, thus it is infeasible. The proposed attack divides the table into small tables, which reduces the memory requirement. For example, the computational cost and the memory requirement of the proposed attack for revealing the 163-bit secret key are $O(2^8)$ and $O(2^{23})$, respectively, using 20 observations on the scalar multiplication with Ha-Moon's countermeasure. The computational cost and the memory requirement are $O(2^{21})$ and $O(2^{12})$ for Ebeid-Hasan's one, and $O(2^{40})$ and $O(2^6)$ for Agagliate's one. If 40 observations are used, computational cost for Agagliate's one is reduced to $O(2^{33})$. Whenever we utilize a countermeasure of BSD type, we should

---

* This research was supported by University IT Research Center Project.
** This work was supported by Korea Research Foundation Grant. (KRF-2001-042-E00045)

M. Jakobsson, M. Yung, J. Zhou (Eds.): ACNS 2004, LNCS 3089, pp. 398–413, 2004.
© Springer-Verlag Berlin Heidelberg 2004

beware of the proposed attack. In other words, the security of BSD type is controversial.

Keywords: Elliptic Curve Cryptosystem, Side Channel Attacks, SPA, DPA, BSD Representation, Ha-Moon's Countermeasure, Ebeid-Hasan's Countermeasure, Agagliate's Countermeasure

1   Introduction

Recently, side channel attacks (SCA) have been recognized as menaces to public key cryptosystems. In SCA, an attacker observes side channel information such as computation timing, power consumption, and electro-magnetic radiation while a cryptographic device performs cryptographic operations, and utilizes such side channel information for revealing the secret information stored in the device [KJJ99]. On the other hand, elliptic curve cryptosystems (ECC) are suitable for implementing on a constrained device such as smartcard, since ECC achieves higher security using shorter key size. In ECC, a dominant computation is a scalar multiplication, which computes the scalar multiplied point $kP = \underbrace{P + \cdots + P}_{k \text{ times}}$ from an integer k and a point P. The integer is referred to as scalar, and is often secret. The attacker's goal is to detect the secret scalar during scalar multiplication. Thus constructing an efficient computation method of scalar multiplication which is secure against SCA and analyzing its security are important research topics.

For this purpose, many countermeasures against SCA were proposed. In particular, the countermeasure that utilizes randomized binary-signed-digit (BSD) representations of the secret scalar is a popular countermeasure. This type of countermeasure encodes the secret integer into BSD representation, then computes the scalar multiplied point using the representation. In addition, a different representation is used for each scalar multiplication. This thwarts the attacker's guess. This type of countermeasures is referred to as BSD type and it includes Ha-Moon's countermeasure [HaM02], Ebeid-Hasan's countermeasure [EH03], and the countermeasure of Agagliate et al [AGO03].

Recently, Okeya-Han [OH03] have proposed an attack algorithm to Ha-Moon [HaM02] method. However their analysis technique is ad-hoc in the sense that it tailored specifically to the target countermeasure, and it is not clear how to generalize it to analyze other countermeasures of BSD type. In other words, their attack is not applicable to every countermeasures of BSD type. On the other hand Karlof-Wagner [KW03] proposed the hidden Markov model cryptanalysis, which is a cryptanalytic framework for countermeasures that utilizes a probabilistic finite state machine. In fact, since some countermeasures of BSD type utilize it for encoding the secret scalar k into BSD representation, their attack is applicable. However, if the target countermeasure does not utilize it, the attack is not applicable. Ebeid-Hasan's countermeasure [EH03] is such an example. To sum up, no general attacks that are applicable to every countermeasures of BSD type have been proposed so far.

In this paper, we propose a novel attack against the countermeasures of BSD type. The proposed attack is applicable to *"all"* the countermeasures of BSD type; independent from the encoding method of the secret scalar. The use of several observations of side channel information reduces the search space for the secret scalar, however, this approach increases the memory requirement. The proposed attack reduces the memory requirement using the trick of a division into small tables, which is an analogy of the meet-in-the-middle attack against double DES. If the table is divided into u small tables, the required memory is reduced into the u-th root of the original in general, but this is dependent on the way to divide the table. We experimentally estimated the computational cost and the memory requirement according to the number of AD sequences for standard 163-bit secret scalars. Regarding Ha-Moon's countermeasure [HaM02], the proposed attack revealed the 163-bit secret key with $O(2^8)$ computational cost and $O(2^{23})$ memory requirement using 20 observations of the scalar multiplication. In the case of Ebeid-Hasan's countermeasure [EH03], the computational cost and the memory requirement are respectively $O(2^{21})$ and $O(2^{12})$ using 20 observations. In the case of Agagliate's countermeasure [AGO03], they are $O(2^{40})$ and $O(2^6)$ using 20 observations, and the use of 40 observations reduces the computational cost to $O(2^{33})$ with $O(2^8)$ memory requirement. Therefore, whenever we utilize a countermeasure of BSD type, we should beware of the proposed attack. In other words, the security of BSD type is controversial.

The paper is organized as follows: Section 2 surveys elliptic scalar multiplication and side channel attacks. Section 3 proposes the attack against the countermeasures of BSD type, and shows examples and implementation results for the proposed attack.

2   Elliptic Scalar Multiplication and Side Channel Attacks

In this section, we review elliptic scalar multiplication and side channel attacks. Some countermeasures against side channel attacks utilize randomized binary-signed-digit representations of the secret integer. The main topic of this paper is to construct an attack against such countermeasures. We review the counter-measures of this type in this section.

2.1   Elliptic Scalar Multiplication

Elliptic curve cryptosystem (ECC) is suitable for the implementation on constraint devices such as smart cards due to its short key size. In order to accelerate ECC, we need to optimize elliptic scalar multiplication, since elliptic scalar multiplication is usually a dominant operation in ECC. Note that the elliptic scalar multiplication is the operation that computes the scalar multiplied point kP from an elliptic point P and an integer k, and k is often secret in ECC.

Addition-Subtraction_Method is an efficient method to compute elliptic scalar multiplication, and the algorithm is as follows:

Addition-Subtraction_Method

INPUT A point P, and $k = \sum_{j=0}^{n} k_j 2^j$, $k_j \in \{-1, 0, 1\}$

OUTPUT $Q = kP$

1. $Q \leftarrow \mathcal{O}$
2. for $j = n$ downto 0
  2.1. $Q \leftarrow \text{ECDBL}(Q)$
  2.2. if $k_j = 1$ then $Q \leftarrow \text{ECADD}(Q, P)$
  2.3. if $k_j = -1$ then $Q \leftarrow \text{ECSUB}(Q, P)$
3. Return Q

Here, ECADD, ECDBL, and ECSUB stand for elliptic addition, elliptic doubling, and elliptic subtraction, respectively. $\mathcal{O}$ denotes the identity element of the elliptic addition, namely the point at infinity. Note that the cost of ECSUB is same to that of ECADD, since we can compute the inverse $-P$ from the point P without additional cost.

2.2   Side Channel Attacks

Side channel attacks (SCA) are a serious menace for embedded devices which are running cryptographic applications and leaking critical information through side channels, like power consumptions [KJJ99]. The attack aims at guessing the secret key (or some related information) using the correlation between some side channel information and the secret. For example, SCA retrieves some secret information while Addition-Subtraction_Method performs. The flow calculates ECADD or ECSUB if and only if the j-th bit k_j is non-zero. The standard implementation of ECADD is different from that of ECDBL [CMO98], however, ECADD and ECSUB are very similar, since $\text{ECSUB}(Q, P) = \text{ECADD}(Q, -P)$. Although ECADD and ECSUB are ambiguous in the sense of SCA (e.g. power consumption), the attacker can distinguish these operations from ECDBL. Thus the attacker can recognize whether the bit is zero or not.

2.3   Countermeasures Using Randomized Representations of Binary Signed Digits

Many countermeasures against side channel attacks were proposed. The countermeasure that utilizes randomized binary-signed-digit (BSD) representations of the secret scalar for resisting against side channel attacks is a popular one. This type of the countermeasure is referred to as BSD type. Considering the binary representation of an integer k as one of its BSD representations, different BSD representations for k can be obtained by replacing 01 with $1\bar{1}$ and vice versa and by replacing $0\bar{1}$ with $\bar{1}1$ and vice versa. For example if $k = (13)_{10}$ is represented in 5 bits, i.e., $k = (01101)_2$, the different BSD representations for k are: 01101, $0111\bar{1}$, $10\bar{1}01$, $1\bar{1}101$, and so forth. The countermeasures of BSD type utilizes such different BSD representations for thwarting the attacker's guess. Several examples of BSD type are Ha-Moon's countermeasure [HaM02], Ebeid-Hasan's countermeasure [EH03], and the countermeasure of Agagliate et al. [AGO03]. Ha-Moon [HaM02] proposed the randomized signed scalar multiplication method. Ebeid and Hasan [EH03] proposed a general version of the countermeasure of this type. In addition, Agagliate et al. [AGO03] proposed another countermeasure of this type.

On the other hand, Oswald-Aigner [OA01] proposed the randomized addition-subtraction chains method, which is similar to BSD type. It does not use a BSD representation but a similar one. Note that Oswald's countermeasure directly computes the scalar multiplication without the conversion into another representation of the integer, but it implicitly uses such a representation. Unfortunately, Oswald's countermeasure was broken. Okeya-Sakurai [OS02] proposed an attack against the basic version of Oswald's countermeasure. Later they extends their attack to the advanced version of Oswald's countermeasure [OS03]. Han et al. also proposed the attack against the advanced version [HCJ+03]. Finally Walter [Wal03] broke the generalized version of Oswald's countermeasure.

Recently, Okeya-Han [OH03] have proposed an attack algorithm to Ha-Moon [HaM02] method. However their analysis technique is ad-hoc in the sense that it tailored specifically to the target countermeasure, and it is not clear how to generalize it to analyze other countermeasures of BSD type, for instance, Ebeid-Hasan's countermeasure [EH03] and Agagliate's countermeasure [AGO03]. In other words, their attack is not applicable to every countermeasures of BSD type.

While some countermeasures of BSD type utilize a probabilistic finite state machine for encoding the secret k into BSD representation, Karlof-Wagner [KW03] proposed the hidden Markov model cryptanalysis against such countermeasures. However, if the operational behavior of the target countermeasure does not modeled by a probabilistic finite state machine, their attack does not work. For example, Ebeid-Hasan's countermeasure [EH03] does not utilizes a probabilistic finite state machine, thus the hidden Markov model cryptanalysis is not applicable.

To sum up, no general attacks that are applicable to every countermeasures of BSD type have been proposed so far. In the next section we will propose such a general attack. Hence, the security of BSD type is controversial.

We give some notations which are used in the next section.

Notations: Let $k = \sum_{j=0}^{n-1} k_j 2^j$ with $k_j \in \{0, 1\}$ be the n-bit secret binary value and $d = \sum_{j=0}^{n} d_j 2^j$ with $d_j \in \{-1, 0, 1\}$ be the $(n+1)$-bit random recoded number generated from k by a random recoding method. We obviously have $k = d$. Let the i-th random recoded number of k be denoted as $d^{(i)} := \sum_{j=0}^{n} d_j^{(i)} 2^j$, where $d_j^{(i)} \in \{-1, 0, 1\}$ Let N and N' be the set $\{0, 1, ..., n\}$ and $\{1, 2, ..., n-1\}$, respectively. For $d^{(i)}$, the set of indices $J^{(i)} \subset N$ stands for $\{j \in N | d_j^{(i)} = 0\}$. Define $d^{(i)}(s, t) := \sum_{j=s}^{t} d_j^{(i)} 2^j$. Here, $0 \leq s \leq t \leq n$. $w(d^{(i)})$ denotes the number of non-zero digits in $d^{(i)}$, i.e., hamming weight of $d^{(i)}$. $|d_j^{(i)}|$ denotes the absolute value of $d_j^{(i)}$. For a set A, $\#A$ denotes the number of the elements in A.

3   Proposed Attack

In this section we propose a general side channel attack against the counter-measures with randomized BSD representations, and show the countermeasures are vulnerable to the proposed attack. Namely, the proposed attack algorithm does not depend on the method of randomizing BSD representation.[1] First, we introduce the main idea of the proposed attack, and propose a proposition and a theorem about the relations among BSD representations for the same integer. Then, we describe the attack algorithm with the proposed proposition and theorem, display an example of the proposed attack, and show experimental results.

3.1   Main Idea

We describe the main idea of our proposed attack.

Assumption 1: Assume that an attacker obtained m random recoded number $d^{(i)}$ generated from the secret value k and he knows the positions of zero digit, i.e., he can determine $d_j^{(i)}$ is zero or not. But he does not know whether $d_j^{(i)}$ is 1 or -1 when $d_j^{(i)} \neq 0$. In addition, he knows the plaintext-ciphertext pair (P, kP).

In general, the attacker can find the secret value k from the following ex-haustive search method if his computing power is unlimited. The goal of the attacker is to determine whether $d_j^{(i)}$ is 1 or -1 when $d_j^{(i)} \neq 0$ because he knows the positions of zero digit. Note the non-zero most significant bit (MSB) is 1.

Exhaustive Search Method (ESM).

1. For $i = 1$ to m do
   - Make Table$_i$ which contains $2^{w(d^{(i)})-1}$ integers, which are $n + 1$-bit inte-gers, determined by $d_j^{(i)} \neq 0$ in $d^{(i)}$. The nonzero MSB is 1.

   Here, Table$_i = \{k' \mid k' = \sum_{j \in N - J^{(i)}} d_j^{(i)} 2^j$ with $d_j^{(i)} \in \{1, -1\}\}$.
2. Find the candidates for the secret key k.
   $\cap_{i=1}^{m}$Table$_i$ is the set of all possible keys, and $\#[\cap_{i=1}^{m}$Table$_i] = l > 0$, since $d^{(1)} = \cdots = d^{(m)} = k$.
3. Test l possible keys.
   For any $k' \in \cap_{i=1}^{m}$Table$_i$, compute $k'P$. If $k'P = kP$ then k' is the secret key.
4. Time complexity (TC) of ESM is $O(l)$ scalar multiplications and memory complexity (MC) of ESM is $O(y)$ memory for $n + 1$-bit integers, where $y = \sum_{i=1}^{m} 2^{w(d^{(i)})-1}$.

The goals of this paper can be categorized as follows:

1. Reduce MC of ESM to the reasonable bound.

---

[1] Thus, in this paper, we do not describe the explicit algorithms of these countermea-sures. For comprehensive descriptions, see [HaM02,EH03,AGO03].

2. Accurately determine TC of ESM only with obtained random recoded numbers $d^{(i)}$ without making tables.

The main idea of reducing the memory complexity is very simple. It is similar to meet-in-the-middle attack on double DES. Suppose $d^{(1)}$ and $d^{(2)}$ are $n+1$-bit random recoded numbers from the n-bit secret key k. In Step 1 (in ESM), the required storage is $O(y)$ for $n+1$-bit integers to make Table_1 and Table_2 to find all possible keys, where $y = \sum_{i=1}^{2} 2^{w(d^{(i)})-1}$.

Claim. Suppose that for some t $(1 \leq t \leq n-1)$ the following equations hold:

$$\sum_{j=0}^{t-1} d_j^{(1)} 2^j = \sum_{j=0}^{t-1} d_j^{(2)} 2^j \quad and \quad \sum_{j=t}^{n} d_j^{(1)} 2^j = \sum_{j=t}^{n} d_j^{(2)} 2^j \tag{1}$$

Then required storage is reduced to $O(y')$ with $y' = \sum_{i=1}^{2}(2^{w(d^{(i)}(0,t-1))} + 2^{w(d^{(i)}(t,n))-1})$. In particular, if $w(d^{(1)}) \approx w(d^{(2)})$ and $w(d^{(i)}(0,t-1)) \approx w(d^{(i)}(t,n))$ for $i = 1, 2$, then $O(y') = O(\sqrt{y})$.

In addition, this claim can be enhanced as follows:

Claim. Suppose that for some $t_1, \cdots, t_u$ with $1 \leq t_1 \leq \cdots \leq t_u \leq n-1$ we have

$$\sum_{j=0}^{t_1-1} d_j^{(1)} 2^j = \cdots = \sum_{j=0}^{t_1-1} d_j^{(m)} 2^j, \sum_{j=t_1}^{t_2-1} d_j^{(1)} 2^j = \cdots = \sum_{j=t_1}^{t_2-1} d_j^{(m)} 2^j, \ldots, \sum_{j=t_u}^{n} d_j^{(1)} 2^j = \cdots = \sum_{j=t_u}^{n} d_j^{(m)} 2^j$$

and $w(d^{(1)}) \approx \cdots \approx w(d^{(m)})$, $w(d^{(i)}(0, t_1-1)) \approx \cdots \approx w(d^{(i)}(t_u, n))$ for $1 \leq i \leq m$, then the required storage is reduced to $O(y') = O((u+1) \cdot m \cdot \sqrt[u+1]{2y})$, where $y = \sum_{i=1}^{m} 2^{w(d^{(i)})-1}$. In other words, MC is approximately $(u+1)$-th root of the original.

In the next section, we propose a proposition and a theorem. The proposition shows that when the condition such as (1) is satisfied. Also, the theorem gives a novel formula which indicates the accurate TC of ESM only with obtained random recoded numbers.

3.2   Relations among BSD Representations for the Same Integer

We propose several important relations among BSD representations for the same integer which are used to reduce MC of ESM and to determine accurate TC of ESM. In this section, we keep assuming Assumption 1. Note that $w(d^{(i)}) = n+1 - \#J^{(i)}$.

First, we propose a relation among BSD representations for the same integer, which is used to reduce MC of ESM.

Proposition 1. *Suppose $d^{(1)} = d^{(2)}$. For $t \in N' - (J^{(1)} \cup J^{(2)})$, we have*

$$d^{(1)}(0, t-1) = d^{(2)}(0, t-1) \text{ and } d^{(1)}(t, n) = d^{(2)}(t, n).$$

Proof. $d^{(1)} = d^{(1)}(0, t-1) + d^{(1)}(t, n)$ and $d^{(2)} = d^{(2)}(0, t-1) + d^{(2)}(t, n)$. Without loss of generality (WLOG), assume $d^{(1)}(0, t-1) > d^{(2)}(0, t-1)$. As $d^{(1)} = d^{(2)}$,

$$d^{(1)}(0, t-1) - d^{(2)}(0, t-1) = d^{(2)}(t, n) - d^{(1)}(t, n) \qquad (2)$$

Then the maximum of left hand side (LHS) of (2) is $2^{t+1} - 2$ and 2^{t+1} divides right hand side (RHS) of (2). It's a contradiction. Therefore, $d^{(1)}(0, t-1) = d^{(2)}(0, t-1)$ and $d^{(1)}(t, n) = d^{(2)}(t, n)$.   □

From Proposition 1, the condition (1) described in Section 3.1 is satisfied when $d_t^{(1)}, d_t^{(2)} \neq 0$, i.e., $t \notin J^{(1)} \cup J^{(2)}$. Proposition 1 is generalized to the following Corollary 1.

Corollary 1. *Suppose* $d^{(1)} = \cdots = d^{(m)}$. *For* $t_1, t_2 \in N' - \cup_{i=1}^{m} J^{(i)}$ *with* $t_1 < t_2$, *we have*

$$\begin{aligned} d^{(1)}(0, t_1 - 1) &= \cdots = d^{(m)}(0, t_1 - 1), \\ d^{(1)}(t_1, t_2 - 1) &= \cdots = d^{(m)}(t_1, t_2 - 1), \ and \\ d^{(1)}(t_2, n) &= \cdots = d^{(m)}(t_2, n). \end{aligned}$$

Note that as an integer $d^{(i)}$ can be determined by the non-zero digits, the number of all possible integers generated from $d^{(i)}$ is $2^{n+1-\#J^{(i)}}(= 2^{w(d^{(i)})})$. Namely, we could consider $d^{(i)}$ as a variable which has $2^{n+1-\#J^{(i)}}$ integers.

Now, we estimate the search space l for the secret key when $d^{(1)} = \cdots = d^{(m)}$ are utilized. Note that due to the space limitation we only give the sketch of proof for following theorem which is contained in Appendix A.

Theorem 1. *Suppose* $d^{(i)}$ *is the i-th random recoded number. Then the search space* l *is as follows:*

$$l = \#[\cap_{i=1}^{m} Table_i] = 2^{n+1-\#\{\cup_{i=1}^{m} J^{(i)}\}} = 2^x,$$

where $x = \#\{j \mid d_j^{(1)}, \ldots, d_j^{(m)} \neq 0, \ 0 \leq j \leq n\}$.

3.3   Proposed Generic Attack

In general, ECADD has a different power consumption pattern than ECDBL. Since ECADD and ECSUB only differ slightly, they can be implemented in such a way that they are indistinguishable for an attacker. Thus we assume that the attacker has the following capability:

Assumption 2: *ECADD and ECDBL are distinguishable by a single measurement of power consumption, whereas ECADD and ECSUB are indistinguishable.*

Assumption 3: Scalar multiplication dP is computed by using Addition-Subtraction_Method. Here, d is a random recoded number generated from k by a random recoding method. An attacker has the known plaintext-ciphertext pair (P, kP).

Remark 1. Assumption 1 described in Section 3.1 can be implied from above Assumption 2, 3. In Section 2.2, we described the practicality of Assumption 2, thus Assumption 1 is also practical.

On the other hand, we should note that Addition-Subtraction_Method in Section 2.1 has the following property.

Property 1. Suppose the variable Q is not the point at infinity. Then the recoded digit d_i is not zero if and only if ECADD or ECSUB is performed. That is to say, the recoded digit d_i is zero if and only if ECADD and ECSUB are not performed, only ECDBL is performed.

But we should not overlook the fact that such special cases of ECDBL and ECADD as $Q = 2 * \mathcal{O}$ or $Q = P + \mathcal{O}$ can be avoided in the implementation of scalar multiplication kP. In the ordinary implementation, instead of ECDBL or ECADD operation, the point duplication or assignment can be used.

Property 2. If ECDBL appears firstly in the AD sequence, then the previous bit is one.

For simplicity, ECADD and ECDBL are referred to as **A** and **D**, respectively. **A** and **D** are written with time-increasing from left to right.

Attack Algorithm (Advanced version of ESM). The concrete attack works as follows.

1. **AD sequence collection step:** The attacker inputs an elliptic curve point into a cryptographic device with a random recoding method, for instance Ha-Moon's method [HaM02] or Ebeid-Hasan's method [EH03] and so on, and obtains a sequence of **A** and **D** (AD sequence). He/she repeats this procedure m times and gathers m AD sequences.[2] Let $S^{(i)}$ be the i-th AD sequence $(1 \le i \le m)$.

2. **Data conversion and $J^{(i)}$ determination step:** As **A** and **D** are written with time-increasing from left to right, the attacker converts the obtained AD sequence $S^{(i)}$ into the signed-scalar number $d^{(i)}$ and determines $J^{(i)}$ as follows.

   - For $i = 1$ to m do

   2.1. Split the obtained AD sequence $S^{(i)}$ by symbol | between **D** and **DA** from right to left.
   2.2. Match **D** $\Leftrightarrow$ the random recoded digit $d_j^{(i)} = 0$.
        Add index j in $J^{(i)}$.
   2.3. Match **DA** $\Leftrightarrow$ the random recoded digit $d_j^{(i)} \neq 0$.
   2.4. If the last **D** (or **DA**) appears in the obtained AD sequence then the random recoded digits $d_j^{(i)} = 0$ (or $d_j^{(i)} \neq 0$) and $d_{j+1}^{(i)} = 1$.

---

[2] For some elliptic curve schemes, to gather plural AD sequences may be impossible, like the signature generation of ECDSA. However, some other schemes like ECDH are possible.

3. **All possible keys finding step:** The attacker finds all possible keys using Corollary 1.

   3.1 Find $\cup_{i=1}^{m} J^{(i)}$ $(\subset N)$. Let $\mathcal{A} := N - \cup_{i=1}^{m} J^{(i)}$.

   3.2 By using Corollary 1 split obtained m signed-scalar numbers $(d^{(1)}, \ldots, d^{(m)})$ into a number of sub-signed-scalar numbers, such as $(d^{(1)}(t_v, t_{v+1}), \ldots, d^{(m)}(t_v, t_{v+1}))$.

   Here, (t_v, t_{v+1}) should satisfy following conditions.
   * For any $j \in \{t_v + 1, \ldots, t_{v+1}\}$, $j \notin \mathcal{A}$ and $t_v, t_{v+1}+1 \in \mathcal{A}$.
   * When $t_v = 0$, t_v may not be an element of $\mathcal{A}$.
   * When $t_{v+1} = n$, $t_{v+1} + 1$ need not be considered.

   Note that the sub-signed-scalar numbers $(d^{(1)}(t_v, t_{v+1}), \ldots, d^{(m)}(t_v, t_{v+1}))$ are all same integer, i.e., $d^{(1)}(t_v, t_{v+1}) = \cdots = d^{(m)}(t_v, t_{v+1})$ by Corollary 1.

   3.3 For $i = 1$ to m do
   For any (t_v, t_{v+1}) which satisfies above conditions, make $\text{Table}_i^{(t_v, t_{v+1})}$.

   3.4 For any (t_v, t_{v+1}), find $\cap_{i=1}^{m} \text{Table}_i^{(t_v, t_{v+1})}$.

4. **Key testing step:** Using the known pair of plaintext and ciphertext, the attacker checks all combinations of bit-pattern which are obtained from Step 3.4. Then he/she finds the secret key.

3.4   Example

We will give an example to illustrate the above-mentioned attack against Ebeid-Hasan's method [EH03].

Step 1. AD sequence collection: Assume that the attacker obtains the following AD sequences for a 15-bit secret key k $(= (23862)_{10})$:

$$S^{(1)} = DDADDDDADDDADADDDADDAD$$
$$S^{(2)} = DADDDADDDADDDADDDADDADAD$$
$$S^{(3)} = DADADDADADADADDDADADDDADADAD$$

Step 2. Data conversion and $J^{(i)}$ determination: The attacker converts the obtained AD sequences $S^{(i)}$ into the signed-scalar number $d^{(i)}$ in accordance with Step 2 of the proposed attack algorithm:

$$d^{(1)} = (d_{15}^{(1)}, d_{14}^{(1)}, ..., d_0^{(1)}) = (1, 0, *, 0, 0, 0, *, 0, *, *, 0, 0, *, 0, *, 0),$$
$$d^{(2)} = (d_{14}^{(2)}, d_{13}^{(2)}, ..., d_0^{(2)}) = (1, *, 0, 0, *, 0, *, 0, *, 0, *, 0, *, *, 0),$$
$$d^{(3)} = (d_{15}^{(3)}, d_{14}^{(3)}, ..., d_0^{(3)}) = (1, *, *, 0, *, *, *, 0, *, *, 0, 0, *, *, *, 0),$$

where $*$ denotes a non-zero digit, namely 1 or -1.

$$J^{(1)} = \{0, 2, 4, 5, 8, 10, 11, 12, 14\}, \qquad J^{(2)} = \{0, 3, 5, 7, 9, 11, 12, 15\},$$
$$J^{(3)} = \{0, 4, 5, 8, 12\}.$$

Step 3. All possible keys finding:

- $\cup_{i=1}^{3} J^{(i)} = \{0, 2, 3, 4, 5, 7, 8, 9, 10, 11, 12, 14, 15\}$. Thus $\mathcal{A} = \{1, 6, 13\}$.
- Split obtained 3 signed-scalar numbers $(d^{(1)}, d^{(2)}, d^{(3)})$ into following three sub-signed-scalar numbers:
  ($d^{(1)}(1,5)$, $d^{(2)}(1,5)$, $d^{(3)}(1,5)$), ($d^{(1)}(6,12)$, $d^{(2)}(6,12)$, $d^{(3)}(6,12)$),
  ($d^{(1)}(13,15)$, $d^{(2)}(13,15)$, $d^{(3)}(13,15)$).
  Note that the sub-signed-scalar numbers ($d^{(1)}(0,0)$, $d^{(2)}(0,0)$, $d^{(3)}(0,0)$) is trivially determined as $0 \in \cap_{i=1}^{3} J^{(i)}$, i.e., $d_0^{(1)} = d_0^{(2)} = d_0^{(3)} = 0$.
- Find $\text{Table}_i^{(t_v, t_{v+1})}$. Refer to Table 1.
- $\cap_{i=1}^{3} \text{Table}_i^{(1,4)} = \{10, -10\}$, $\quad \cap_{i=1}^{3} \text{Table}_i^{(6,11)} = \{704, -704\}$,
  $\cap_{i=1}^{3} \text{Table}_i^{(13,15)} = \{24576\}$.

Table 1. $\text{Table}_i^{(t_v, t_{v+1})}$ Note that, for instance, $d^{(1)}(1,4)$ denotes $d_3^{(1)} \cdot 2^3 + d_1^{(1)} \cdot 2^1$ as $d_4^{(1)} = d_2^{(1)} = 0$.

$\text{Table}_1^{(1,4)}$		$\text{Table}_2^{(1,4)}$		$\text{Table}_3^{(1,4)}$	
$(d_3^{(1)}, d_1^{(1)})$	$d^{(1)}(1,4)$	$(d_4^{(2)}, d_2^{(2)}, d_1^{(2)})$	$d^{(2)}(1,4)$	$(d_3^{(3)}, d_2^{(3)}, d_1^{(3)})$	$d^{(3)}(1,4)$
(1,1)	10	(1,-1,-1)	10	(1,1,-1)	10
(-1,-1)	-10	(-1,1,1)	-10	(-1,-1,1)	-10
$\text{Table}_1^{(6,11)}$		$\text{Table}_2^{(6,11)}$		$\text{Table}_3^{(6,11)}$	
$(d_6^{(1)}, d_7^{(1)}, d_9^{(1)})$	$d^{(1)}(6,11)$	$(d_6^{(2)}, d_8^{(2)}, d_{10}^{(2)})$	$d^{(2)}(6,11)$	$(d_6^{(3)}, d_7^{(3)}, d_9^{(3)}, d_{10}^{(3)}, d_{11}^{(3)})$	$d^{(3)}(6,11)$
(1,1,1)	704	(1,-1,-1)	704	(1,-1,-1,1,-1)	704
(-1,-1,-1)	-704	(-1,1,1)	-704	(-1,1,1,-1,-1)	-704
$\text{Table}_1^{(13,15)}$		$\text{Table}_2^{(13,15)}$		$\text{Table}_3^{(13,15)}$	
$d_{13}^{(1)}$	$d^{(1)}(13,15)$	$d_{13}^{(2)}$	$d^{(2)}(13,15)$	$(d_{13}^{(3)}, d_{14}^{(3)})$	$d^{(3)}(13,15)$
-1	24576	1	24576	(-1,1)	24576

Table 2. Implementation results of TC and MC for standard 163-bit keys with m AD sequences (These results do not depend on the elliptic curve and the underlying field.)

# of AD seq. used	Ha-Moon's Algo. [HaM02]		Ebeid-Hasan's Algo. [EH03]		Agagliate's Algo. [AGO03]	
	TC	MC	TC	MC	TC	MC
5	$O(2^{27})$	$O(2^7)$	$O(2^{50})$	$O(2^5)$	$O(2^{54})$	$O(2^2)$
10	$O(2^{15})$	$O(2^{14})$	$O(2^{33})$	$O(2^8)$	$O(2^{50})$	$O(2^3)$
15	$O(2^{10})$	$O(2^{19})$	$O(2^{25})$	$O(2^{10})$	$O(2^{46})$	$O(2^4)$
20	$O(2^8)$	$O(2^{23})$	$O(2^{21})$	$O(2^{12})$	$O(2^{40})$	$O(2^6)$
30	$O(2^6)$	$O(2^{30})$	$O(2^{16})$	$O(2^{15})$	$O(2^{33})$	$O(2^8)$
40	$O(2^4)$	$O(2^{37})$	$O(2^{13})$	$O(2^{17})$	$O(2^{33})$	$O(2^8)$

Step 4. Key testing: There are 4 possible keys $(25290)_{10}$, $(25270)_{10}$, $(23882)_{10}$, and $(23862)_{10}$. Note that, for instance, $(25290)_{10} = (24576)_{10} + (704)_{10} + (10)_{10}$. The true secret key k can be easily checked by using the known pair of plaintext and ciphertext. In fact, the secret key k was $(23862)_{10}$.

Remark 2. As $\#\{j \mid d_j^{(1)}, d_j^{(2)}, d_j^{(3)} \neq 0\} = \#\{1, 6, 13\} = 3$ and MSB is 1, there exists 4 $(= 2^{3-1})$ possible keys by Theorem 1.

Table 3. The average time for detecting 163-bit keys with m AD sequences

	Number of AD sequences used	Performance (sec)
Ha-Moon's Algo. [HaM02]	15	239.52
Ebeid-Hasan's Algo. [EH03]	40	457.12

Remark 3. In this example, the proposed attack algorithm requires only 76 memory for 15-bit integers. However, if ESM is applied to this example, ESM requires $1216 (= 2^6 + 2^7 + 2^{10})$ memory for 15-bit integers.

3.5   Implementation Result

We experimentally estimated the computational cost and the memory requirement according to the number of AD sequences for standard 163-bit secret values. Table 2 shows the time complexity and the memory complexity. Regarding Ha-Moon's countermeasure [HaM02], the proposed attack revealed the 163-bit secret key with $O(2^8)$ computational cost and $O(2^{23})$ memory requirement using 20 observations of the scalar multiplication. In the case of Ebeid-Hasan's countermeasure [EH03], the computational cost and the memory requirement are respectively $O(2^{21})$ and $O(2^{12})$ using 20 observations. In the case of Agagliate's countermeasure [AGO03], they are $O(2^{40})$ and $O(2^6)$ using 20 observations, and the use of 40 observations reduces the computational cost to $O(2^{33})$ with $O(2^8)$ memory requirement. The result of TC and MC depend on m, the number of AD sequences, and the target algorithm. If m is increased, however, TC is always decreasing and MC is always increasing, independent of the target algorithm. So, determining the reasonable m to implement the attack algorithm depends on the target algorithm. From our implementation result, 15 AD sequences are reasonable in Ha-Moon's algorithm [HaM02] and 40 AD sequences in Ebeid-Hasan's one [EH03]. The methods for finding TC and MC are contained in Appendix B.

We have implemented the proposed attack algorithm on typical microprocessors: Pentium IV/2GHz (32-bit μP; Windows 2000, MSVC). Table 3 indicates the average time for detecting a randomly chosen 163-bit keys with 15 AD sequences for Ha-Moon's algorithm [HaM02] and with 40 AD sequences for Ebeid-Hasan's one [EH03]. For instance, the average time for detecting 163-bit keys with 40 AD sequences for Ebeid-Hasan's algorithm was about 457.12 seconds. In the case of Agagliate's one [AGO03], we need to test about 2^{33} possible keys to detect 163-bit keys with 40 AD sequences. It may take approximately 3.8 years. This is not directly implemented result, but it is calculated from (required time per one scalar multiplication)*TC. However, these are quite fast for an attack algorithm because it takes thousands of years to find out a secret value by using a direct-computational attack against the elliptic curve discrete logarithm problem. Thus the results of Table 2, 3 show that essentially all BSD methods are vulnerable to the proposed attack which lies within practical bounds.

References

[AGO03]   Agagliate, S., Guillot, P., Orcière, O., *A Randomized Efficient Algorithm for DPA Secure Implementation of Elliptic Curve Cryptosystems*, in the proceedings of Workshop on Coding and Cryptography 2003 (WCC 2003), (2003), 11-19.

[CMO98]   Cohen, H., Miyaji, A., Ono, T., *Efficient Elliptic Curve Exponentiation Using Mixed Coordinates*, Advances in Cryptology - ASIACRYPT '98, LNCS1514, (1998), 51-65.

[Cor99]   Coron, J.S., *Resistance against Differential Power Analysis for Elliptic Curve Cryptosystems*, Cryptographic Hardware and Embedded Systems (CHES'99), LNCS1717, (1999), 292-302.

[EH03]   Ebeid, N., Hasan, A., *Analysis of DPA Countermeasures Based on Randomizing the Binary Algorithm*, Technical Report of the University of Waterloo, No. CORR 2003-14.
http://www.cacr.math.uwaterloo.ca/techreports/
2003/corr2003-14.ps

[HaM02]   Ha, J., and Moon, S., *Randomized Signed-Scalar Multiplication of ECC to Resist Power Attacks*, Workshop on Cryptographic Hardware and Embedded Systems 2002 (CHES 2002), LNCS 2523, (2002), 551-563.

[HCJ+03]   Han, D.-G., Chang, N.S., Jung, S.W., Park, Y.-H., Kim, C.H., Ryu, H., *Cryptanalysis of the Full version Randomized Addition-Subtraction Chains*, The 8th Australasian Conference in Information Security and Privacy (ACISP 2003), LNCS2727, (2003), 67-78.

[KJJ99]   Kocher, C., Jaffe, J., Jun, B., *Differential Power Analysis*, Advances in Cryptology - CRYPTO '99, LNCS1666, (1999), 388-397.

[KW03]   Karlof, C., Wagner, D., *Hidden Markov Model Cryptanalysis*, Cryptographic Hardware and Embedded Systems (CHES 2003), LNCS2779, (2003), 17-34.

[OA01]   Oswald, E., Aigner, M., *Randomized Addition-Subtraction Chains as a Countermeasure against Power Attacks*, Cryptographic Hardware and Embedded Systems (CHES 2001), LNCS2162, (2001), 39-50.

[OH03]   Okeya, K., Han, D.-G., *Side Channel Attack on Ha-Moon's Countermeasure of Randomized Signed Scalar Multiplication*, INDOCRYPT 2003, LNCS2904, (2003), 334-348.

[OS02]   Okeya, K., Sakurai, K., *On Insecurity of the Side Channel Attack Countermeasure using Addition-Subtraction Chains under Distinguishability between Addition and Doubling*, The 7th Australasian Conference in Information Security and Privacy, (ACISP 2002), LNCS2384, (2002), 420-435.

[OS03]   Okeya, K., Sakurai, K., *A Multiple Power Analysis Breaks the Advanced Version of the Randomized Addition-Subtraction Chains Countermeasure against Side Channel Attacks*, in the proceedings of 2003 IEEE Information Theory Workshop (ITW 2003), (2003), 175-178.

[Wal03]   Walter, C.D., *Security Constraints on the Oswald-Aigner Exponentiation Algorithm*, International Association for Cryptologic Research (IACR), Cryptology ePrint Archive 2003/013, (2003).
http://eprint.iacr.org/2003/013/

Appendix

A   Proof of Theorem 1

Notations: Let S, S_1, and S_2 be the set $\{0, 1, ..., s\}$, $\{0, 1, ..., s-1\}$, and $\{0, 1, ..., s-2\}$, respectively, i.e., $S_2 \subset S_1 \subset S$. Let

$$Table'_i = \{k' \mid k' = \sum_{j \in S - J^{(i)'}} d_j^{(i)'} 2^j \text{ with } d_j^{(i)'} \in \{1, -1\}\},$$

$$Table^*_i = \{k' \mid k' = \sum_{j \in S_1 - J^{(i)^*}} d_j^{(i)^*} 2^j \text{ with } d_j^{(i)^*} \in \{1, -1\}\}.$$

Proof of Theorem 1

Proof. We may assume $\cap_{i=1}^m J^{(i)} = \emptyset$ by Corollary 1. We argue by induction on n. When $n = 1$ is clear. Suppose when $n < s$, the assertion is true.

We must prove the assertion is true when $n = s$. That is, suppose $d^{(i)'}$ is the i-th random recoded number with $s + 1$-bit length and $\cap_{i=1}^m J^{(i)'} = \emptyset$, where $J^{(i)'} \subset S$, for $i = 1, \ldots, m$ then

$$\#[\cap_{i=1}^m Table'_i] = 2^{s+1-\#\{\cup_{i=1}^m J^{(i)'}\}} \cdots (*).$$

1. When $s \notin J^{(i)'}$ for every $1 \leq i \leq m$.
   Since $d_s^{(1)'} \cdot 2^s + d^{(1)'}(0, s-1) = \cdots = d_s^{(m)'} \cdot 2^s + d^{(m)'}(0, s-1)$,

   $$|d_s^{(i)'} - d_s^{(r)'}| \cdot 2^s = |d^{(i)'}(0, s-1) - d^{(r)'}(0, s-1)|$$

   for $1 \leq i \neq r \leq m$. As $d_s^{(i)'} = \pm 1$ for $1 \leq i \leq m$, LHS $= 0$ or 2^{s+1}, and $0 \leq$ RHS $\leq 2^{s+1} - 2$. So, $d_s^{(1)'} = \cdots = d_s^{(m)'} = \pm 1$, and $d^{(1)'}(0, s-1) = \cdots = d^{(m)'}(0, s-1)$. Therefore,

   $$LHS \text{ of } (*) = 2 \cdot \#[\cap_{i=1}^m Table_i'^{(0,s-1)}] = 2 \cdot 2^{s-\#\{\cup_{i=1}^m J^{(i)'}\}} = 2^{s+1-\#\{\cup_{i=1}^m J^{(i)'}\}}.$$
   (By inductive assumption.)

2. When $s \in J^{(i)'}$ for some $1 \leq i \leq m$, by re-indexing if necessary, we assume $d_s^{(i)'} = 0$ if $1 \leq i \leq r(< m)$, and $d_s^{(i)'} \neq 0$ if $r < i \leq m$.
   (1) When $s - 1 \notin J^{(i)'}$ for any $1 \leq i \leq m$, i.e., $d_{s-1}^{(i)'} = \pm 1$.
       Then when $1 \leq i \leq r$, $J^{(i)'} = J^{(i)^*} \cup \{s\}$ for some $J^{(i)^*} \subset S_2$ and when $r + 1 \leq i \leq m$, $J^{(i)'} \subset S_2$. Let $J^{(i)^*} = J^{(i)'}$ for $r + 1 \leq i \leq m$.
       $$LHS \text{ of } (*) = \#[\cap_{i=1}^m Table'_i] = \#[\cap_{i=1}^m Table^*_i]$$
       $$= 2^{s-\#\{(\cup_{i=1}^r J^{(i)^*}) \cup (\cup_{i=r+1}^m J^{(i)'})\}} = 2^{s+1-\#\{\cup_{i=1}^m J^{(i)'}\}}.$$

   (2) When $s - 1 \in J^{(i)'}$ for some $1 \leq i \leq m$.

(2.1) When $s - 1 \in J^{(i)'}$ for some $r < i \leq m$, by re-indexing if necessary, we may assume that $d_{s-1}^{(i)'} = 0$ if $r + 1 \leq i \leq r_1(\leq m)$ for some r_1, and $d_{s-1}^{(i)'} \neq 0$ if $r_1 < i \leq m$. Then when $1 \leq i \leq r$, $J^{(i)'} = J^{(i)^*} \cup \{s\}$ for some $J^{(i)^*} \subset S_2$, when $r + 1 \leq i \leq r_1$, $J^{(i)'} \subset S_1$ with $s - 1 \in J^{(i)'}$, and when $r_1 + 1 \leq i \leq m$, $J^{(i)'} \subset S_2$. Let $J^{(i)^*} = J^{(i)'}$ for $r + 1 \leq i \leq m$.

$$LHS \ of \ (*) = \#[\cap_{i=1}^m \text{Table}_i'] = \#[\cap_{i=1}^m \text{Table}_i^*]$$
$$= 2^{s - \#\{(\cup_{i=1}^r J^{(i)^*}) \cup (\cup_{i=r+1}^m J^{(i)'})\}} = 2^{s+1 - \#\{\cup_{i=1}^m J^{(i)'}\}}.$$

(2.2) When $s - 1 \in J^{(i)'}$ for some $1 \leq i \leq r$, by re-indexing if necessary, we may assume that $d_{s-1}^{(i)'} = 0$ if $1 \leq i \leq r_1(\leq r)$ for some r_1, and $d_{s-1}^{(i)'} \neq 0$ if $r_1 < i \leq r$. Then when $1 \leq i \leq r_1$, $J^{(i)'} = J^{(i)^*} \cup \{s\}$ for some $J^{(i)^*} \subset S_1$ with $s - 1 \in J^{(i)^*}$, when $r_1 + 1 \leq i \leq r$, $J^{(i)'} = J^{(i)^*} \cup \{s\}$ for some $J^{(i)^*} \subset S_2$, and when $r + 1 \leq i \leq m$, $J^{(i)'} \subset S_2$. Let $J^{(i)^*} = J^{(i)'}$ for $r + 1 \leq i \leq m$.

$$LHS \ of \ (*) = \#[\cap_{i=1}^m \text{Table}_i'] = \#[\cap_{i=1}^m \text{Table}_i^*]$$
$$= 2^{s - \#\{(\cup_{i=1}^r J^{(i)^*}) \cup (\cup_{i=r+1}^m J^{(i)'})\}} = 2^{s+1 - \#\{\cup_{i=1}^m J^{(i)'}\}}.$$

$\square$

B   Method for Finding TC and MC in Table 2

For instance, the time complexity and the memory complexity in the case of standard 163-bit key with 40 AD sequences in Table 2 for Ebeid-Hasan algorithm are obtained as follows:

– For $l = 1$ to 100000 do
  • Select a 163-bit string randomly.
  • Obtain 40 AD sequences using another program that outputs characters **A** and **D** depending on the elliptic curve operations it executes while computing a scalar multiplication using the Ebeid-Hasan's randomized addition chains method.
  • Convert AD sequence $S^{(i)}$ into the signed-scalar number $d^{(i)}$ where $1 \leq i \leq 40$.
  • Compute the testing number $TestNum_l$ which is needed to recover the secret key:
  $TestNum_l = 2^{\#\{ j \ | \ d_j^{(i)} \neq 0 \ for \ all \ 1 \leq i \leq 40, \ where \ 0 \leq j \leq 163\} - 1}$.
  • Compute the memory space $MemSpace_l$ which is needed to make $\text{Table}_i^{(t_j, t_{j+1})}$ for $1 \leq i \leq 40$:
  $MemSpace_l = \sum_{i=1}^{40} \sum_{(t_j, t_{j+1})} 2^{w(d^{(i)}(t_j, t_{j+1}))}$.
  Note that t_j, t_{j+1} satisfy the conditions described in sub-step 3.2 in the attack algorithm.

– The average testing number of standard 163-bit key with 40 AD sequences $AveTestNum(163, 40)$ is computed as follows:

$$AveTestNum(163, 40) = \frac{\sum_{l=1}^{100000} TestNum_l}{100000} \approx O(2^{13}).$$

– The average memory space of standard 163-bit key with 40 AD sequences $AveMemSpace(163, 40)$ is computed as follows:

$$AveMemSpace(163, 40) = \frac{\sum_{l=1}^{100000} MemSpace_l}{100000} \approx O(2^{17}).$$

Weaknesses of a Password-Authenticated Key Exchange Protocol between Clients with Different Passwords*

Shuhong Wang, Jie Wang, and Maozhi Xu

School of Mathematical Sciences, Peking University, China
{wshong, wangj, mzxu}@math.pku.edu.cn

Abstract. A password-authenticated key exchange scheme allows two entities, who only share a memorable password, to authenticate each other and to agree on a cryptographic session key. Instead of considering it in the classic *client and server* scenarios, Byun *et al.* recently proposed a password-authenticated key exchange protocol in a cross-realm setting where two clients in different realms obtain a secret session key as well as mutual authentication, with the help of respective servers. In this paper, we first point out that the proposed protocol is not secure, due to the choice of invalid parameters (say, subgroup generator). Furthermore, we show in detail that, even with properly chosen parameters, the protocol has still some secure flaws. We provide three attacks to illustrate the insecurity of the protocol. Finally, counter-measures are also given, which are believed able to withstand our attacks.

Keywords: Password-authenticated key exchange, Cross-realm setting, Security, Dictionary attacks.

1 Introduction

The oldest and probably the most important problem of cryptography is how to provide *private and reliable* communication among parties in a public communication channel. This significant problem is commonly reduced to the problem of generating a secure session-key. Certainly, there are many ways to establish secure session keys with the initial set-up assumption of the existence of Public Key Infrastructure (PKI). In reality, however, it is more convenient and more natural if two parties are allowed to obtain such a strong cryptographic session key without relying on the PKI, but with only a pre-shared memorable password. The solution of the problem in this scenario is known as Password-Authenticated Key Exchange (PAKE).

The concept of PAKE was first introduced by Bellovin and Merritt in 1992 [4] known as Encrypted Key Exchange (EKE) which is improved later in [5]. Since then, a number of PAKE protocols are proposed in the literature [3,11,

---

* Supported by the National Natural Science Foundation of China, NSFC 90104004.

M. Jakobsson, M. Yung, J. Zhou (Eds.): ACNS 2004, LNCS 3089, pp. 414–425, 2004.

12,6,15,21,22,30,31] with different initial assumptions and communication workloads. As far as security is concerned, PAKE protocols are often vulnerable to dictionary attack (brute-force password search) since the possible space of memorable passwords is too small. Some security analyses of these protocols can be found in many literatures, for example, [2,26,19,29]. In practices, most of these proposed PAKE protocols are presented in the context that the two involved entities are client and server respectively and they share a common password [13,22,15]. Although some of them [11,10,28,16,17] are extended to a three-party EKE protocol, in which a trusted server exists to mediate between two communication parties to allow mutual authentication, they are less considered in a cross-realm setting like in kerberos system [27,14].

Recently in *ICICS'02*, based on the scheme in [8], Byun *et al.* designed several password-authenticated key exchange schemes between clients with different passwords, called *Client-to-Client Password-Authenticated Key Exchange* (C2C-PAKE). In these scheme, two clients (could in separate realms) fulfill the authenticated key exchange relying only on their distinct passwords and servers, without any other prior shared secret. Three C2C-PAKE schemes are presented in their paper [7]. One (CR-C2C, hereinafter) is for a cross-realm setting where two clients are in two different Kerberos realms and hence two servers (who are connected with a symmetric key) are involved. The other two are for a single-server setting where two clients are in the same realm: the Single-server Ticket Type (ST-C2C) and the Single-server Non-Ticket Type[1]. They also newly defined the security notions according to their framework for the special settings, and claimed their schemes' security under those definitions.

The goal of this paper is to show some security flaws in [7]. We show that, on the one hand, the security definition in [7] is incomplete for the new framework. That is, in the protocol with a cross-realm setting, that one server can obtain the password of a client in another realm is not considered. On the other hand, the proposed protocols are insecure even under their incomplete security definitions. We illustrate several dictionary attacks for this purpose.

The rest of the paper is arranged as follows. In Sect. 2 we give the security definitions for the PAKE protocols in a cross-realm setting. Section 3 is devoted to review the original CR-C2C protocol, followed by our security analysis in Sect. 4. In Sect. 5, we further discuss the security of the ST-C2C protocol in a single-server setting with kerberos ticket. Finally, we conclude the paper with some counter measures to resist our attacks in Sect. 7 and Sect. 6 respectively.

2 Modes and Security Properties

The definition of formal security [3,6] for PAKE is somewhat technical. It means essentially that the best an active attacker can do is to guess passwords and to

---

[1] The later on which we are not going to discuss much more is similar to usual three-party EKE protocols where both parties (clients) share their passwords with the third trusted server only. (For more details on three-party EKE protocols, readers please refer to references [28,19]).

verify them one-by-one online through communication with an honest party. In particular, this implies that the attacker will not get any information that would allow an off-line dictionary attack. Note that when we say a PAKE protocol is subject to dictionary attack, it does not necessarily mean that the password can be found by brute force. It means that an attacker can get more information than random guess [2].

In [7], two distinct models of password-authenticated key exchange schemes (PAKE) were defined. One is called *Shared Password Authentication Model* (SPA), and the other *Different Password Authentication Model* (DPA). In SPA model, entities involved are a client and a server who share a common password. It is the case for most proposed PAKE protocols. In DPA model, we focus on the cross-realm scenario (CR-DPA, for short) where clients *Alice* and *Bob*, who are in different realms and possess distinct passwords, agree on a session key and authenticate each other with help of key distribution centers KDC_A and KDC_B. Here KDC_A and KDC_B who share a symmetric secrete cryptographic key are servers of (hence in the same realms as) *Alice* and *Bob* respectively. One can easily derives the single server DPA model (SS-DPA, for short) from CR-DPA by replacing KDC_A and KDC_B with one common server KDC. Indeed, SS-DPA is exactly the model of general three-party PAKE.

It is desirable for PAKE protocols (in both SPA and DPA models) to possess the following security attributes:

Known-key security: Each run of the protocol should result in a unique secret session key. The compromise of one session key should not compromise other session keys.

Forward secrecy: If passwords of one or more of the entities are compromised, the secrecy of previously established session keys should not be affected.

Key-compromise impersonation: Compromising passwords of any entities (clients or/and servers) should not enable the adversary to impersonate any other entities.

Unknown key share resilience: Client *Alice* should not be able to coerced into sharing a key with any client *Carol* when in fact she thinks that she is sharing the key with client *Bob*.

Key control: Any entities should not be able to force the session key to a preselected value.

Dictionary attack resilience: All passwords in the protocol must be strongly protected against a dictionary attack, and even if an attacker is given one password, other passwords must be prevented from such a attack.

In addition to above basic properties, more properties should be considered under the environments of DPA model. More precisely, the descriptions of some properties should be modified according to the new framework in DPA, especially in CR-DPA model. At least, we should consider the long-term private keys of entities instead of passwords only:

Forward secrecy - DPA: If long-term private keys (including clients' passwords and servers' cryptographic keys) of one or more of the entities are compromised, the secrecy of previously established session keys should not be affected.

Key-compromise impersonation - DPA: Compromising long-term private keys of any entities (clients or/and servers) should not enable the adversary to impersonate any other entities.

Dictionary attack resilience - DPA: All passwords in the protocol must be strongly protected against a dictionary attack, and even if an attacker is given one password, other passwords must be prevented from such an attack. Further more, the compromise of servers' shared symmetric key should not allow a dictionary attack either. And in the CR-DPA model, it is expected that any entity in one realm should not be able to mount a dictionary attack to other entities belongs to another realm.

3   The Review of the Protocol in a Cross-Realm Setting (CR-C2C)

In this section, we review the CR-C2C protocol in Sect. 4 of [7]. For convenience, we use the same notations and list them in Table 1.

Note that in the original paper of Byun et al., G is chosen as in Table 1. Subsequently g is a generator of a **subgroup** in $\mathbb{Z}_p^*$. However, it is commonly recognized that such a choice is very dangerous. We shall discuss this issue at length in section 4.1. Later, we think this flaw as a type error, and then properly take g as a generator of $G = \mathbb{Z}_p^*$.

3.1   The CR-C2C Protocol

By using notations listed in Table 1, the proposed C2C-PAKE protocol in a cross-realm setting (CR-C2C) can be described as follows (Fig. 1). This is an example of PAKE protocols under the CR-DPA model.

(1) $Alice \rightarrow KDC_A$: $ID(A), ID(B), E_{pwa}(g^x)$
(2) $KDC_A \rightarrow Alice$: $E_R(g^x \oplus g^r, ID(A), ID(B)), E_{pwa}(g^y), Ticket_B$

(3) $Alice \rightarrow Bob$: $Ticket_B, ID(A), L$
(4) $Bob \rightarrow KDC_B$: $Ticket_B, E_{pwb}(g^{x'}), ID(A), ID(B), L$
(5) $KDC_B \rightarrow Bob$: $E_{R'}(g^{pwa \cdot r \cdot r'} \oplus g^{x'}, ID(A), ID(B)), E_{pwb}(g^{y'})$
$\qquad\qquad\qquad E_{H4(g^{pwa \cdot r})}(g^{pwb \cdot r \cdot r'})$

(6) $Bob \rightarrow Alice$: $E_{cs}(g^a), E_{H4(g^{pwa \cdot r})}(g^{pwb \cdot r \cdot r'})$
(7) $Alice \rightarrow Bob$: $E_{sk}(g^a), E_{cs}(g^b)$
(8) $Bob \rightarrow Alice$: $E_{sk}(g^b)$

Fig. 1. The CR-C2C protocol (Cross-realm setting)

Table 1. Parameters and Notations used in C2C-PAKE Protocols.

Notation	Meaning
p, q	two large primes satisfy $q \mid p - 1$
G	a subgroup of $\mathbb{Z}_p^*$ and $|G| = q$
g	a generator of G
$Alice, Bob$	two clients in two different realms
$ID(A), ID(B)$	identities of $Alice$ and Bob
pwa, pwb	passwords memorized by $Alice$ and Bob
KDC_A, KDC_B	two key distribution centers which store password files of $Alice$ and Bob respectively
K	a symmetric key shared between KDC_A and KDC_B
$E_X(\cdot), D_X(\cdot)$	symmetric encryption and decryption under the symmetric key X
H_1, H_2, H_3, H_4, H_5	collision-resistant one-way hash functions (e.g, SHA-1)
x, y, r, b	ephemeral secrets in $\mathbb{Z}_p^*$ randomly chosen by $Alice$ and KDC_A
x', y', r', a	ephemeral secrets in $\mathbb{Z}_p^*$ randomly chosen by Bob's and KDC_B
$R = H_1(g^{xy})$	session key agreed between $Alice$ and KDC_A
$R' = H_2(g^{x'y'})$	session key agreed between Bob and KDC_B
$sk = H_3(g^{ab})$	session key agreed between $Alice$ and Bob
cs	$cs = H_5(g^{pwa \cdot pwb \cdot r \cdot r'})$ computed by both $Alice$ and Bob
$Ticket_B$	the Kerberos ticket issued to $Alice$ for service from Bob, $Ticket_B = E_K(g^{pwa \cdot r}, g^r, ID(A), ID(B), L)$
L	the lifetime of $Ticket_B$, $Ticket_B$ can be reused in L

3.2   Description of the CR-C2C Protocol

1. *Alice* choose $x \in \mathbb{Z}_p^*$ randomly, computes and sends $E_{pwa}(g^x)$ to KDC_A together with $ID(A)$ and $ID(B)$ in (1).

2. KDC_A obtains g^x by decrypting $E_{pwa}(g^x)$, chooses $y, r \in \mathbb{Z}_p^*$ randomly and computes $E_{pwa}(g^y)$ and $g^{pwa \cdot r}$. KDC_A makes $Ticket_B$ and also specifies L, a lifetime of $Ticket_B$. Then KDC_A sends $E_R(g^x \oplus g^r, ID(A), ID(B)), E_{pwa}(g^y)$ and $Ticket_B$ to *Alice*.
   Upon receiving the message from KDC_A, *Alice* computes a session key $R = H_1(g^{xy})$ and decrypts $E_R(g^x \oplus g^r, ID(A), ID(B))$ to find g^r.

3. *Alice* just forwards $Ticket_B, ID(A)$ and L to *Bob*.

4. *Bob* chooses $x' \in \mathbb{Z}_p^*$ randomly and computes $E_{pwb}(g^{x'})$. Then he sends $E_{pwb}(g^{x'}), ID(A)$ and $ID(B)$ to KDC_B together with $Ticket_B$ and L.
   Upon the receipt of $Ticket_B$, KDC_B obtains $g^{pwa \cdot r}$ by decrypting $Ticket_B$. Note that KDC_B also can obtain g^r from this decryption.

5. KDC_B chooses $r' \in Z_p^*$ randomly and computes $(g^{pwa \cdot r \cdot r'})$. KDC_B also selects another random number $y' \in Z_p^*$, and computes $R' = H_2(g^{x' y'})$. Next KDC_B computes $E_{R'}(g^{pwa \cdot r \cdot r'} \oplus g^{x'}, ID(A), ID(B))$ using R', and sends $E_{R'}(g^{pwa \cdot r \cdot r'} \oplus g^{x'}, ID(A), ID(B))$, $E_{pwb}(g^{y'})$ and $E_{H_4(g^{pwa \cdot r})}(g^{pwb \cdot r \cdot r'})$ to Bob.

6. Bob decrypts $E_{pwb}(g^{y'})$ to find $g^{y'}$ and computes $R' = H_2(g^{x' y'})$, and then decrypts $E_{R'}(g^{pwa \cdot r \cdot r'} \oplus g^{x'}, ID(A), ID(B))$ using R' to obtain $g^{pwa \cdot r \cdot r'}$ from $g^{pwa \cdot r \cdot r'} \oplus g^{x'}$. He makes $cs = H_5(g^{pwa \cdot pwb \cdot r \cdot r'})$. Then Bob chooses a random number $a \in Z_p^*$ and computes $E_{cs}(g^a)$. He finally sends $E_{cs}(g^a)$ and $E_{H_4(g^{pwa \cdot r})}(g^{pwb \cdot r \cdot r'})$ to Alice.

7. Alice computes $H_4(g^{pwa \cdot r})$ with her pwa and g^r and uses it to decrypts $g^{pwb \cdot r \cdot r'}$. Alice also can computes $cs = H_5(g^{pwa \cdot pwb \cdot r \cdot r'})$ using $g^{pwb \cdot r \cdot r'}$ and her password. Next, Alice selects $b \in Z_p^*$ randomly, and computes $sk = H_3(g^{ab})$ as well $E_{cs}(g^b)$. Finally she sends $E_{sk}(g^a)$ and $E_{cs}(g^b)$ for session key confirmation.

8. Upon the receipt of $E_{sk}(g^a), E_{cs}(g^b)$, Bob retrieves g^b and computes sk with g^b and a. Then he verifies g^a by decrypting $E_{cs}(g^a)$ with sk. And Bob also sends $E_{sk}(g^b)$ to Alice for session key confirmation. Till now the execution of protocol 1 completes.

4   Attacks on the CR-C2C Protocol

In this section, we analyze the security of the CR-C2C protocol by presenting three dictionary attacks.

First of all, we demonstrate the danger (it is a damage!) to chose generator g in a subgroup of Z_p^* (Attack 1). Then we consider g to be a generator of the whole group Z_p^*, and present other two attacks. Note that Attack 2 is also effective to the case where g is a subgroup generator.

In Attack 2, a malicious key distribution center in one (say, Bob's) realm (KDC_B) can extract the passwords of the users belong to another (Alice's) realm. Note that this attack can be looked as symmetric on the whole system's point of the view, that is to say, if it is Bob who requests the access to Alice's service, then Alice's key distribution center (KDC_A) can extract Bob's password. It is this attack that makes us to extend the concept of security against dictionary attacks for password-authenticated key exchange protocols in cross-realm settings. Obviously, the protocol above does not satisfy the *Dictionary attack resilience - DPA* and *Key-compromise impersonation - DPA* requirements as desired.

The last attack is somehow technical and self-symmetric (i.e, in the same implementation, both Alice and Bob can reduce the passwords space of the opposing entity). Precisely, *Alice* can reduce *Bob*'s password space to half and *Bob* can excludes *Alice*'s passwords too, both succeed with a probability higher than $1-(\frac{3}{4})^t$ after implementing the CR-C2C protocol t times. This attack shows that the C2C-PAKE protocols are insecure under the dictionary attacks.

4.1 Attack 1

Suppose an attacker eavesdrops the implementation of the protocol. He can obtain the exchanged messages $E_{pwa}(g^x)$, $E_{pwa}(g^y)$, $E_{pwb}(g^{x'})$ and $E_{pwb}(g^{y'})$. Then he can mount an off-line dictionary attack to recover pwa and pwb. We only show the process of extracting password pwa as follows. It is the same for password pwb.

1. Decrypts the $E_{pwa}(g^x)$ using a candidate password pwa':
   $\widetilde{g^x} = D_{pwa'}(E_{pwa}(g^x))$.
2. Raises $\widetilde{g^x}$ to power q and checks whether 1 is obtained.
3. If 1 is obtained, excludes pwa' from *Alice*'s password space; Otherwise,
4. Chooses another password and repeats above steps until all the passwords are checked.

If the correct password is not found, one should continue this excluding process by decrypting ciphertext $E_{pwa}(g^y)$ with another candidate password. Note that a candidate password pwa' can not be excluded only if $D_{pwa'}(E_{pwa}(g^x))^q = 1$. We assume that the decryption results randomly in Z_p^* if the pwa' is incorrect. Then it is obvious that the probability of $D_{pwa'}(E_{pwa}(g^x))^q = 1$ is $\frac{q}{p-1}$. Consequently, the valid passwords space of both *Alice* and *Bob* will be reduced by a factor of up to $(\frac{q}{p-1})^2$, on average, through once eavesdropping of session execution. Over a number of sessions the space of valid passwords will be narrowed down to a single password at a logarithm rate.

4.2 Attack 2

As noted above, upon the receipt of $Ticket_B$, KDC_B can obtain $g^{pwa\cdot r}$ as well as g^r by decrypting $Ticket_B$. It is easy to see that a password guessing attack on pwa is available to KDC_B. The start point of the attack is similar to the first one, i.e. an attacker can get enough information to verify the correctness of a guessed password. While there are still some difference: the first attack is probabilistic and this attack is decisional. Since the equality $g^{pwa'\cdot r} = g^{pwa\cdot r}$ if and only if $pwa' = g^{pwa}$.

On the opposite, KDC_A can disclose *Bob*'s correct password when *Bob* requests the service from *Alice*. Therefore, using above CR-C2C protocol, all passwords of the users in one realm may be exposed to a malicious KDC in another realm. This is very dangerous in practice, especially for example, between two realms (corporations) which keeping cooperation as well as competition.

The reason why this attack succeeds is based on the constitution of kerberos ticket $Ticket_B$, in which, both $g^{pwa\cdot r}$ and g^r are included simultaneously, and have nothing to do with the generator g, hence this attack is also effective when g is chosen from the subgroup as in the original paper.

4.3   Attack 3

To reduce the space of *Bob*'s valid passwords, after receiving message (6), *Alice* does the following:

1. Checks whether g is a quadratic residue modulo p, if yes, gives up, otherwise goes on to next step.
2. Computes $H_4(g^{pwa \cdot r})$ with her pwa and g^r and decrypts $g^{pwb \cdot r \cdot r'}$ as she does in the protocol.
3. Checks whether $g^{pwb \cdot r \cdot r'}$ is a quadratic residue modulo p. if not, she claims that pwb is odd and stops. Otherwise, Otherwise,
4. Implements the protocol and repeats above steps again up to t times.
5. If in t times, $g^{pwb \cdot r \cdot r'}$ is always quadratic residue modulo p, then she claim pwb is even and stop.

Now we proceed to the correctness and success probability of this attack. We assume both r and r' are uniformly chosen from Z_p^*.

- For the case pwb is actually an odd number:

  Alice can correctly claim that pwb is odd once $g^{pwb \cdot r \cdot r'}$ is a quadratic non-residue modulo p, this happens if . Under the assumption that r and r' are uniformly chosen, the probability that both r and r' are odd numbers should be $1 - (\frac{3}{4})^t$, i.e, the probability of her success.

- For the case pwb is actually an even number:

  Obviously, $g^{pwb \cdot r \cdot r'}$ is always a quadratic residue modulo p in this case. According to the attack, *Alice* firmly claims pwb even. This claim will be incorrect only if pwb is odd as well as $r \cdot r'$ is even for all the t times. This condition happens with probability $(\frac{3}{4})^t$. So, the probability of her success should be $1 - (\frac{3}{4})^t$.

On all accounts, by this attack, *Alice* correctly judges the parity of pwb with probability $1 - (\frac{3}{4})^t$. Thus she can exclude half of the valid passwords of *Bob* with the same probability by implementing the protocol t times.

To see how *Bob* can reduce *Alice*'s password space, one only need to observe that *Bob* can obtain $g^{pwa \cdot r \cdot r'}$ from message (5): $E_{R'}(g^{pwa \cdot r \cdot r'} \oplus g^{x'}, ID(A), ID(B))$ and that he knows R', his session key shared with KDC_B.

It is valuable to point out that this attack is invalid when g is a subgroup generator, since a subgroup generator is always a quadratic residue modulo p.

5   The Protocol in Single-Server Setting with Ticket (ST-C2C)

5.1   The ST-C2C Protocol

In the original paper, the authors pointed out that the ST-C2C protocol can be easily constructed by modifying the CR-C2C protocol in following way. That is converting the shared key (K) between two *Kerberos* servers into a private key (PK) of the single server KDC and identifying the rest part to those of CR-C2C protocol.

We note that the ticket in the CR-C2C protocol should also be modified to suit the settings of ST-C2C. In detail, the $Ticket_B$ is encrypted by PK and may not be necessarily includes g^r, since g^r is generated by the KDC himself, he can just store it for later use. Hence $Ticket'_B = E_{PK}(g^{pwa \cdot r}, ID(A), ID(B), L)$. As for the other parameters such as R, R', sk and cs are computed in the same way as those in the CR-C2C protocol.

The ST-C2C protocol behaves as follows.

(1) $Alice \rightarrow KDC$: $ID(A), ID(B), E_{pwa}(g^x)$
(2) $KDC \rightarrow Alice$: $E_R(g^x \oplus g^r, ID(A), ID(B)), E_{pwa}(g^y), Ticket'_B$

(3) $Alice \rightarrow Bob$: $Ticket'_B, ID(A), L$
(4) $Bob \rightarrow KDC$: $Ticket'_B, E_{pwb}(g^{x'}), ID(A), ID(B), L$
(5) $KDC \rightarrow Bob$: $E_{R'}(g^{pwa \cdot r \cdot r'} \oplus g^{x'}, ID(A), ID(B)), E_{pwb(g^{y'})}$
$\qquad E_{H_4(g^{pwa \cdot r})}(g^{pwb \cdot r \cdot r' \cdot x})$
(6) $Bob \rightarrow Alice$: $E_{cs}(g^a), E_{H_4(g^{pwa \cdot r})}(g^{pwb \cdot r \cdot r'})$
(7) $Alice \rightarrow Bob$: $E_{sk}(g^a), E_{cs}(g^b)$
(8) $Bob \rightarrow Alice$: $E_{sk}(g^b)$

Fig. 2. The ST-C2C protocol (Single-server with Ticket).

5.2   Analysis of ST-C2C Protocol

It is obviously that above attacks to the CR-C2C protocol can be directly applied to the ST-C2C protocol except for Attack 2, since we change the $ticket_B$ to $Ticket'_B = E_{PK}(g^{pwu \cdot r}, ID(A), ID(B), L)$. This is also because the clients *Alice* and *Bob* are both in the same realm with the unique KDC. While for Attack 1 and 3, the former is due to an eavesdropper and the latter is carried by one client to another. Therefore, they still effective.

6   The Counter Measures

The counter measures to above attacks are very simple. For the subgroup generator attack (Attack 1), we can just select the generator $g \in Z_p^*$.

To resist against Attack 2, we try to unable KDC_B to obtain $g^{pwa \cdot r}$ and g^r simultaneously from the Kerberos ticket $Ticket_B$. Actually, we can set $Ticket_B = E_K(g^{pwa \cdot r}, g^{xr}, ID(A), ID(B), L)$ by involving $Alice$'s contribution x as a mask of g^r. And the followed communication messages should be changed in an obvious way. For example, in step (5), KDC_B will use $H_4(g^{pwa \cdot r})$ to compute and send $E_{H_4(g^{pwa \cdot r})}(g^{pwb \cdot xr \cdot r'})$ instead of $E_{H_4(g^{pwa \cdot r})}(g^{pwb \cdot r \cdot r'})$. After receiving message (6) from Bob, $Alice$ will decrypt $g^{pwb \cdot xr \cdot r'}$, and then compute cs as $H_5(g^{pwa \cdot pwb \cdot r \cdot r'}) = H_5((g^{pwb \cdot xr \cdot r'})^{\frac{1}{x} \cdot pwa})$ using $g^{pwb \cdot xr \cdot r'}, pwa$ and x.

In the last attack, the weakness which an attacker can make use of is when g is a quadratic non-residue modulo p. Therefore, if we simply select g to be a quadratic residue modulo p, Attack 2 would be invalid. In group Z_p^*, there may exist many number of such generators.

The countermeasures for the ST-C2C protocol is the same, one can figure them straightforward from that of CR-C2C protocol.

7   Conclusion

In this paper, we show the insecurity of the C2C-PAKE protocols [7] in both cross-realm setting and single-server setting with ticket, by presenting three effective dictionary attacks. In the original parameters environment, the proposed protocols collapse under the subgroup generator attack. Even configured with the powerful parameters, they are still susceptible to various dictionary attacks in both SPA and DPA/CR-DPA senses. We also provide the corresponding countermeasure against our attacks. At least one lesson can be taken from our attacks, that PAKE protocols in a cross-realm setting are more vulnerable than classic or three-party PAKE protocols because of their intrinsic relationship between different realms. Therefore, more precautions should be taken to prevent various attacks such as compromise of the symmetric key shared between two servers.

References

1. R. Anderson and S. Vaudenay, Minding Your p's and q's, in *Advaces in Cryptology - ASIACRYPT'96*, LNCS 963, pages 236-247, Springer-Verlag, 1995.
2. F. Bao, Security Analysis of a Password Authenticated Key Exchange Protocol, in *Proceedings of ISC'03*, LNCS 2851, pages 208-217, Springer-Verlag, 2003.
3. M. Bellare and P. Rogaway, Entity Authentication and Key Distribution, in *Advances in cryptology - Crypto'93*, pages 232-249, Springer-Verlag, 1993.
4. S. Bellovin and M. Merritt, Encrypted Key Exchange: Password-based Protocols Secure Against Dictionary Attacks, in *Proceedings of IEEE Security and Privacy*, pages 72-84, 1992.

5. S. Bellovin and M. Merritt, Augumented Encrypted Key Exchange: A Password-based Protocol Secure Against Dictionary Attacks and Password File Compromise. *ACM Secrity '93*, pages 244-250.
6. V. Boyko, P. MacKenzie, and S. Patel, Provably-secure Password Anthentiation and Key Exchange Using Diffie-Hellman. in *Advances in cryptology - EURO-CRYPT 2000*, LNCS 1807, pages 156-171, Springer-Verlag, 2000.
7. J. W. Byun, I. R. Jeong, D. H. Lee, and C-S. Park, Password-Authenticated Key Exchange Between Clients with Different Passwords, in *Proceedings of Information and Communications Security - ICICS 2002*, LNCS 2513, pages 134-146, Springer-Verlag, 2002.
8. G. D. Crescenzo, and O. Kornievskaia, Efficient Kerberized multicast in Practical distributed setting, in *Proceedings of ISC'01*, LNCS 2000, pages 27-45, Springer-Verlag, 2001.
9. W. Diffie, P. Van Oorschot and M. Wiener, Authentication and Authenticated Key Exchange, *Designs, Codes and Cryptography*, 2, 1992, pages 107-125.
10. L. Gong, Optimal Authentication Protocols Resistant to Password Guessing Attacks. in *8th IEEE Computer Security Foundations Workshop*, pages 24-29, 1995.
11. L. Gong, M. Lomas, R. Needham, and J. Saltzer, Protecting Poorly Chosen Secrets from Guessing Attacks, *IEEE Journal on Selected Areas in Communications*, 11(5), pages 648-656, 1993.
12. Y. H. Hwang, D. H. Yum, and P. J. Lee, EPA: An Efficient Password-Based Protocol for Authenticated Key Exchange, in *Proceedings of ACISP 2003*, LNCS 2727, Springer-Verlag Berlin Heidelberg 2003, pages 452-463, 2003
13. D. Jablon, Strong Password-Only Authenticated Key Exchange, *ACM Computer Communications Review*, vol.26, no.5, pp. 5-20, October 1996.
14. B. Jaspan, Dual-workfactor Encrypted Key Exchange: Efficiently Preventing Password Chaining and Dictionary Attacks, in *Proceedings of the 6th Annual USENIX Security Conference*, pages 43-50, July, 1996.
15. T. Kwon, Authentication and Key Agreement via Memorable Password, in *Proceedings of the ISOC Symposium - NDSS'01*, 2001.
16. T. Kwon, M. Kang, S. Jung, and J. Song, An Improvment of the Password-Based Authentication Protocol (K1P) on Security against Replay Attacks, *IEICE Trans. Commun.*, E82-B(7), pages 991-997, 1999.
17. T. Kwon, M. Kang, and J. Song, An Adaptable and Reliable Authentication Protocol for Communication Networks, in *Proceedings of IEEE INFOCOM'97*, pages 737-744, 1997.
18. C. H. Lim and P. J. Lee, Several Practical Protocols for Authentication to Threshold Cryptosystems, *Information Processing Letters*, 53, 1995, pages 91-96.
19. C.-L. Lin, Hung-Min Sun and T. Hwang. Three-party Encrypted Key Exchange: Attacks and A Solution. *ACM Operating Systems Review*, 34(4):12-20, 2000.
20. C.-L. Lin, H.-M. Sun and T. Hwang. Three-party Encrypted Key Exchange Without Server Public-Keys. *IEEE Communications Letters*, 5(12):497-499, December 2001.
21. S. Lucks, Open Key Exchange: How to Defeat Dictionary Attacks Without Encrypting Public Keys, in *Proceedings of Security Protocols Workshop*, LNCS 1361, pages 79-90, Springer-Verlag, 1997.
22. P. MacKenzie, S. Patel, and R. Swaminathan, Password-Authenticated Key Exchange Based on RSA, in *Proceedings of AsiaCrypt 2000*, LNCS 1976, pages 599-613, Springer-Verlag, 2000.
23. P. MacKenzie, The PAK suite: Protocols for Password-Authenticated Key Exchange, *Submission to IEEE P1363.2*, April 2002.

24. P. MacKenzie, More Efficient Password-Authenticated Key Exchange, *Progress in Cryptology – CT-RSA 2001*, pages 361-377, 2001.
25. W. Mao and C.H.Lim, Cryptanalysis in Prime Order Subgroups of $\mathbb{Z}_n^*$, in *Advances in cryptology-ASIACRYPT'98*, LNCS 1514, Spinger-Verlag, 1998, pp.214-226.
26. S. Patel, Number Theoretic Attacks on Secure Password Schemes, in in *Proceedings of IEEE Symposium on Research in Security and Privacy*, pages 236-247, 1997.
27. J. G. Steiner, B. C. Newman, and J. I. Schiller, Kerberos: An Authentication Service for Open Network Systems. in *USENIX Conference Proceedings*, pages 191-202, February, 1988.
28. M. Steiner, G. Tsudik and M. Waidner. Refinement and Extension of Encrypted Key Exchange. *ACM SIGOPS Operating Systems Review*, 29(3), pages 22-30, 1995.
29. Z. Wan, and S. Wang, Cryptanalysis of Two Password-Authenticated Key Exchange Protocols, in *Proceedings of ACISP 2004*, LNCS, Springer-Verlage (to appear), 2004.
30. T. Wu, Secure Remote Password Protocol, in *ISOC Network and Distributed System Security Symposium*, 1998.
31. F. Zhu, D. S. Wong, A. H. Chan, and R. Ye, Password authenticated key exchange based on RSA for imbalanced wireless networks, in *Proceedings of ISC 2002*, LNCS 2433, pp. 150-161, Springer-Verlag, 2002.

Advanced Packet Marking Mechanism with Pushback for IP Traceback

Hyung-Woo Lee

Dept. of Software, Hanshin University, Osan, Gyunggi, Korea, 447-791
hwlee@hs.ac.kr
http://netsec.hs.ac.kr

Abstract. Distributed Denial-of-Service(*DDoS*) attack can be done by generating a large volume of traffic through spoofing the IP address of the target system. In response to such attacks, IP traceback technology has been proposed. The method identifies the source of a DDoS attack and restructures the path on the network through which the attacking packet has been transmitted. Existing traceback techniques marked path information on packets or generated separate traceback messages but they increase network load and cannot cope with DDoS attacks actively because they generate traceback information for arbitrary packets without identifying DDoS attacks. Thus this study proposed an improved marking technique that identifies DDoS traffics at routers by applying the pushback function and cope with DDoS attack packets efficiently. According to the result of experiments, the proposed technique reduced network load and improved traceback performance.[1]

1 Introduction

The current TCP/IP system is vulnerable to *DoS (Denial of Service)* attacks such as TCP SYN flooding[1], there have been researches on how to cope with hacking on networks and the Internet[2]. As for techniques to cope with hacking attacks, firewall systems that adopt access control are passive to hacking attacks. IDS(Intrusion Detection System) provides the functions of detecting and blocking abnormal traffic that has reached the victim system, so it is also passive to hacking.

Thus currently available technologies do not provide active functions to cope with hacking such as tracing and confirming the source of DoS hacking attacks. It is because most hacking attacks are carried out by spoofing the IP address of the source system. Thus it is necessary to develop a technology to cope actively with such hacking attacks. Even if the trace-route technique is applied to identify the source address, the technique cannot identify and trace the actual address because the address included in DDoS(Distributed Denial of Service) is spoofed.

Methods of defeating hacking like DDoS attacks are largely divided into passive ones such as vaccines, intrusion detection and tolerance technology, and

---

[1] This work is supported by the University Basic Research Program of IITA and partially supported by University IT Research Center(ITRC) Project.

M. Jakobsson, M. Yung, J. Zhou (Eds.): ACNS 2004, LNCS 3089, pp. 426–438, 2004.
© Springer-Verlag Berlin Heidelberg 2004

active ones such as traceback of the origin of attacks. Active methods are again divided into proactive traceback and reactive traceback according to how to detect the origin of hacking attacks.

When a DDoS hacking attack has happened, methods like ingress filtering filter and drop malicious packets at routers on the network, so they are passive to DDoS attacks. An efficient solution is for the victim system to trace back the spoofed actual address of the origin of the DDoS attack. In traceback methods, routers generate information on the traceback path while transmitting packets on the network, and insert it into the packets or deliver it to the IP address of the target of the packets.

If a victim system is hacked, it identifies the spoofed source of the hacking attacks using the generated and collected traceback path information. PPM (probabilistic packet marking)[5,6] and iTrace(ICMP traceback)[7] are this type of traceback methods. A recently proposed Pushback[3] method provides a identification function for packets when a DDoS attack happens and a transmission control function for packets along the packet transmission path. The method provide a control function for DDoS attack traffic but does not provide the function of trace back the source of the attack. It only provides a transmission control function for packets along the packet transmission path, so enhances the overall network performance.

Thus this study proposes a technique to trace back the source IP of spoofed DDoS packets by combining the existing pushback method, which provide a control function against DDoS attacks, with a traceback function. A router performs the functions of identifying/controlling traffic using the pushback technique, and when a DDoS attack happens it sends a pushback message to its upper router and transmits traceback information by marking it on the header of the corresponding packet. Compared to existing traceback techniques, the proposed technique reduced management system / network load and improved traceback performance.

Chapter II reviewed the weaknesses of existing technologies for tracing back the source of hacking attacks and directions for improvement, and Chapter III reviewed the weaknesses of existing pushback techniques. Chapter IV and V proposed a new packet marking technique that adopted a pushback technology to trace back the source of DDoS attacks, and Chapter VI compared and evaluated the performance of the proposed technique.

2 Related Works

2.1 Taceback Mechanisms

The rapidly spreading DDoS attacks generate a number of servers and a lot of subordinate servers (clients), connects to the master server, and carry out DDoS attacks to one or several IP addresses. In that case, *Trinoo* Master communicates with subordinate servers in order to attack one or several IP addresses during a specific period.

Because an attacker can carry out fatal DDoS attacks to victim systems by controlling a large number of servers where attacking tools are installed, such a method can be abused by hackers who mean to disturb the Internet. Up to now, when hacking attacks occur in the Internet, they have been defeated passively using firewall, IDS, scanning and trusted OS-based system security, etc. In particular, existing methods cannot restrict or prevent an attempt at hacking itself, so they are often useless and powerless against attacks paralyzing the Internet. To solve such a problem, active hacking prevention methods were proposed.

Traceback: *an essential technology to cope with hacking and virus actively. Traceback technology traces back the source of hacking attacks real-time and resultantly suppresses hacking attacks fundamentally.*

2.2   Discussion on Existing IP Source Traceback Technologies

Existing IP Traceback methods can be categorized as proactive or reactive tracing. Proactive tracing (such as packet marking and messaging) prepares information for tracing when packets are in transit. Reactive tracing starts tracing after an attack is detected.

Proactive methods sample and transmit packets at a probability of p, and there can be several variations. If a router generating PPM or iTrace messages can adjust probability actively according to the characteristics of entire network traffic rather than sampling at a fixed probability of p, the method may be superior to existing ones in network load, memory, traceback function, etc. In addition, an advanced method can be provided by integrating a traceback module with traditional security structure in order to prevent hackers from restructuring error paths.

PPM Methods[5,6]. In PPM mechanism, a router, an important component of a network, inserts information on packets transmitted through the router into IP packets in order to find the packet transmission route for spoofed packets.

That is, for packets transmitted through the Internet, a router routes them by checking packet header information centering on the IP layer. At that time, the router inserts information on the router address into a writable field of the IP header and sends the packet to the adjacent router.

Information inserted at each router is transmitted to the next router and finally to the target victim system. If a hacking attack occurs later, router information recorded in the packet corresponding to the hacking attack is reconstructed and generates the actual packet transmission path. *However, because all packets are marked with information at each router, transmission rate throughout the entire network will be lowered.* According to how to compose information marked at routers, there are methods such as *node sampling, edge sampling and improved packet marking.*

2.3   Weaknesses and Improvement of Existing PPM Technologies

With PPM technology, a router samples packet information at a probability of p, and marks the message header with its IP address and sends it to the target of the packet. A router samples packets at a probability of p and sends them, but a large number of marked packets are necessary to restructure the path to the source of DDoS attacks. If packets are transmitted without the edge or node information of a specific router, it is impossible to restructure the complete path using marked information. In addition, in order to mark the information of a node or an edge, the algorithm has to select and mark at least eight packets, so the overall efficiency is low.

What is more, existing PPM techniques may not mark hacking traffic in sampling and transmitting packets if the probability of p is satisfied. Because, in such a case, traceback path information is marked on general packets, the spoofed source of the attack cannot be restructured when hacking attacks such as DDoS happen. Thus if a router can adjust the probability rather than fixing it in sampling, the PPM method will have improved performance in network load, memory use and traceback compared to existing methods.

3   Pushback Mechanism

3.1   Pushback Based DDoS Traffic Identification/Control Mechanism

From the viewpoint of a router composing the network, *a hacking attack on the Internet is a kind of congestion.* Thus coping with hacking attacks may be approached from *congestion control* between end systems and relevant technologies. A DDoS attack transmits a large volume of traffic from one or more source hosts to a target host, there should be researches on how to identify and block DDoS traffic in order to cope with hacking attacks on the Internet.

A technology to control DDoS traffic at routers is *ACC (aggregate-based congestion control)* and pushback. Because hacking attacks are extremely diverse, it evaluates traffic based on *congestion signature*, which is corresponding to the congestion characteristic traffic.

ACC: *If traffic shows congestion exceeding a specific bandwidth based on the characteristic of DDoS attack nework traffic, the ACC module judges based on congestion signature that a hacking attack has happened and, working with a filtering module, provides a function to block the transmission of traffic corresponding to the DDoS attack.*

The Fig. 1 shows the structure of *ACC-based identification/control* when a router is congested. As in the figure, the process of identification/control is integrated with a pushback module. The pushback module confirms a DDoS attack and sends a pushback message to its adjacent previous router on the network path. In the figure below, if traffic explodes at link L_0, router R_0 detects (identifies) a high bandwidth. ACC module at R_0 blocks traffic to link L_0 and send a pushback message to router R_2 and R_3, upper routers on the transmission path. R_2 delivers the pushback message just for congestion control to its upper router R_4, and R_3 to R_7. *However, it cannot trace back the final origin of the attack when a hacking attack occurs.*

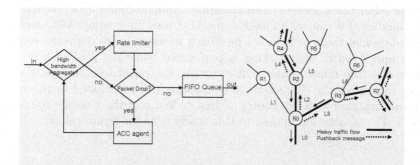

Fig. 1. ACC-based traffic identification/control and pushback mechanism.

3.2   Weaknesses and Improvement of Existing Pushback Technique

A network is defined as a graph $G = (V, E)$ composed of a set of nodes V and a set of edges E. The node set V is again divided into end systems and routers corresponding to internal nodes. Edges are physical connections among nodes in set V. Here, $S \subset V$ is defined as an attacker and $t \in V/S$ as a victim system.

$|S| = 1$ means an attack by a single attacker, and attack path information $P = (s, v_1, v_2, ..., v_d, t)$ means an attack path through which an attacking system s attacked a victim system t using routers on the path d. Let's say the number of packets transmitted is N. If there is a field in packets to mark with router link information $(v, v') \in E$, routers sample the packets at a probability of p. Routers can sample packets at a fixed probability of p and transmit information on edges and distances between routers by including it in the packets.

In existing methods, routers sample packets at a certain static probability of p and transmit router information by marking it on the packets. Probability α_i that a packet is marked at node v_i on the network and not remarked at other routers is computed as follows.

$$\alpha_i = Pr(x_d = (v_{i-1}, v_i)) = p(1-p)^{d-1}(i = 1, 2, ..., d)$$

Thus α_i means a probability that an attack packet is delivered to the victim system without being remarked by other routers. After all, p should be large in order to heighten α_i, which, however, means that routers have to perform marking frequently and consequently the network performance is degraded.

The existing pushback method sends a message to upper routers for the source of attack, however, it cannot trace back the final origin of the attack when a hacking attack occurs. That is, an additional process is necessary for a hacking victim system to trace back the path to the origin of the attack.

4   Packet Marking Based Traceback of DDoS Attacks

4.1   Traceback Structure Using Pushback

The method proposed in this study does not sample and mark at a fixed probability of p but mark packets when abnormal traffic is found by a pushback-based
ACC module. Of course, unlike the method used in existing ACC techniques,
when abnormal traffic is found, a pushback message is not delivered recursively
to the upper router but marking is performed while the pushback message is
delivered to the upper router. On receiving the pushback message, the upper
router recognizes the characteristic of hacking traffic included in the message,
performs marking with two router addresses and sent the message to the target
system. The structure proposed in this study is as the figure below.

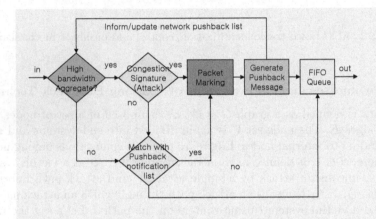

Fig. 2. Proposed Marking-based DDoS source traceback structure.

In the proposed structure, a router checks the traffic bandwidth of a received
packet and if the bandwidth exceeds a certain level the router judges whether it
is a congestion signature corresponding to an attack pattern. If the traffic bandwidth corresponds to an attack pattern, the router marks the packet, generates a
pushback message for the packet and sends it the next router through the output
queue of the router. If the traffic does not meet the bandwidth condition, the
router check whether there is information coming through a pushback message
from neighboring routers and if there is, it marks the packet. If the packet meets
none of conditions above, the router regards it as a normal packet and delivers
it to the next router.

4.2   Traceback Marking Method Using Pushback

(1) Packet Header Marking Field M_x. Let's say A_x is the IP address of
R_x, P_x is IP packet arrived at R_x, and M_x is 24 bits on the header of P_x in

which marking information can be stored. In packet P_x, M_x is composed of 8-bit *TOS(type of service)* field, and 16-bit *ID field*. TOS field has been defined is not used currently. Thus the use of TOS field does not affect the entire network. In TOS field, the first 3 bits are priority bits, and next three bits are minimum delay, maximum performance and reliability fields but not used currently.

Recently, however, TOS field is redefined as Differentiated Service field(DS field) according to *RFC2474*, in which only the first 6 bits are used. Thus this study defines the unused 2 bits out of TOS field as *PF(pushback flag)* and *CF(congestion flag)*. Particularly for CF, RFC2474 defines it as 1 if the network is congested.

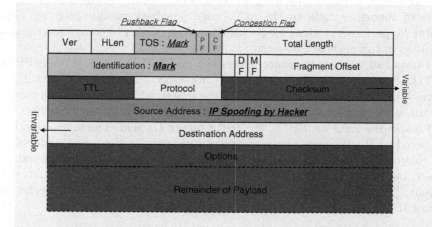

Fig. 3. Packet marking field in the proposed method.

(2) Marking Structure using TTL Information. the IP address A_x of router R_x is marked on 24-bit M_x through the following process. When abnormal traffic happens in the course of pushback for the writable 24 bits of a packet, router R_x marks A_x, which is its own IP address, and A_y, which is the IP address of the next router R_y. To mark the two router addresses within the 24 bits, the router uses address values based on the hash values of the routers, which also provide an authentication function.

TTL(time to live) in all packets is an 8-bit field, which is set at 255 in ordinary packets. The value of TTL field is decreased by 1 at each router until the packet reaches the target.

Currently TTL value is used to secure bandwidth in transmitting packets on the network and to control packets that have failed to reach the target. In previous researches, TTL value was not used but a separate hop counter field was used to calculate the distance that the packet has travelled. This study, however, uses part of TTL value in packets arrived at router R_x for packet marking.

Specifically because the maximum network hop count is 32 in general, the distance of packet transmission can be calculated only with the lower 6 bits out of the 8 bits of TTL field in packet P_x arrived at router R_x. That is, the router extracts information of the lower 6 bits from the TTL field of packet P_x, names it T_x and stores it in TOS 6-bit field P_x^{TF} of the packet.

$$T_x = TTLofP_x \land 00111111$$

T_x value indicates the distance of the packet from the attack system. If the packet with the value is delivered to target system V, it is possible to calculate the distance from router R_x to target system V using the value V and T_v obtained in V in the same way.

(3) Traceback Path Marking at Routers. When informed of the occurrence of abnormal traffic by the ACC-based pushback module proposed above, router R_x performs marking for packet P_x corresponding to congestion signature included in the pushback message.

First of all, because the router received a pushback message, it resets PF field in TOS field as 1. Then it calculates T_x for 8-bit TTL field of packet P_x and stores it in the 6 bits of TOS field. Then the router calculates 8-bit hash value for A_x the address of router R_x and T_x calculated earlier using hash function $H(\cdot)$, and marks the value on P_x^{MF1}, the first 8 bits of ID field. The marked packet is delivered to R_y, the next router on the routing path to the target address.

Now when router R_y checks P_x^{PF} the value of PF field in the packet and finds it is 1, the router applies the hash function to the value obtained by subtracting 1 from P_x^{PF}, which is corresponding to the 6 bits of TOS field in the packet, and router IP address A_x and marks the resulting value on P_x^{MF2}.

$$P_x^{MF1} = H(T_x|A_x), P_x^{MF2} = H(P_x^{TF} - 1|A_y)$$

After marking, the router set CF at 1 and sends the packet to the next router. The next router, finding PF and CF are set at 1, does not perform marking because the packet has been marked by the previous router.

5   Structuring Packet Traceback Path

5.1   DDoS Attack Packet Traceback

For a packet transmitted through the network, victim system V restructures the DDoS attack path. As in the figure below, let's assume that DDoS attacks have been made against S_1, S_2, S_3. For the attack packet, router R_x, R_y and R_z marked 24 bits in the packet header with its own IP information and the information of 6-bit TTL field of the packet. When the DDoS attack occurred, the victim systems perform traceback as follows for packets arrived.

First of all, let's say P_v is a set of packets arrived at victim system V. P_v is a set of packets corresponding to DDoS attacking, and M_v is a set of packets within P_v, which were marked by routers.

To distinguish M_v from packet set P_v, the system selects packets in which PF field P_x^{PF} and CF field P_x^{CF} have been set at 1 as below.

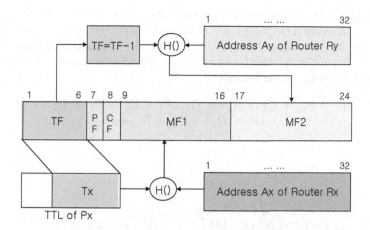

Fig. 4. Packet marking structure in the proposed method

$$M_v = \{P_x | P_x^{PF} == 1 \wedge P_x^{CF} == 1, x \in v\}$$

That is, for packet M_i belonging to packet set M_v in a victim system, its 8-bit TTL value can be defined as $TTLofM_i$. The value is compared with T_{M_i} marked on TOS field, and the network hop count $D(M_i)$, which is the distance since packet M_i was marked, is calculated as follows.

$$D(M_i) = M_i^{TF} - (TTLofM_i \wedge 00111111)$$

If $D(M_i) == 1$, it indicates that the packet was marked at the router just in front of the victim system. The method proposed in this study, however, adopts a pushback technique, it can restructure a traceback path using a packet with $D(M_i) == 2$.

5.2   DDoS Attack Path Reconstruction

Packet M_i satisfying $D(M_i) == 2$ means that the packet was marked by router R_y and R_x two hops apart from the end router in front of the victim system. That is, $D(M_i)$ for packet M_i is 2 because the packet was marked by router R_x, which is 2 hops apart from the router directly connected to the victim system. Thus R_x, 2 hops apart from packet M_i can be identified in the following way.

$$M_i^{MF1} == H(M_i^{TF} | R_x), (R_x \in D(M_i) == 2) and$$
$$M_i^{MF1} == H((TTLofM_i \wedge 00111111) + 2 | R_x), (R_x \in D(M_i) == 2)$$

Of course, packet M_i can prove in the following way that a packet was marked by router R_y 1 hop apart from the victim system.

$$M_i^{MF2} == H(M_i^{TF} - 1 | R_y), (R_y \in D(M_i) == 1) and$$
$$M_i^{MF2} == H((TTLofM_i \wedge 00111111) + 1 | R_y), (R_y \in D(M_i) == 1)$$

Now the victim system can restructure the actual attack path through which packets in DDoS attack packet set P_v were transmitted by repeating the same process for M_j satisfying $D(M_j) == n, (n \geq 3)$. When the proposed method is applied to a network structured as below, DDoS attack path AP to a victim system can be obtained as follows.

$$AP_1 = R_y \rightarrow R_x \rightarrow R_z \rightarrow S1, AP_2 = R_y \rightarrow R_3 \rightarrow R_7 \rightarrow S2,$$
$$AP_3 = R_y \rightarrow R_3 \rightarrow R_7 \rightarrow S3$$

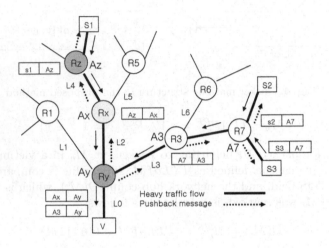

Fig. 5. Attack path traceback using the proposed method.

Through the process, routers could perform not only a monitoring/identification function on network traffic using an ACC module but also a network control function using modified pushback technology. What is more, the proposed method could restructure the source of attackers by providing the function of tracing back spoofed packets adopting improved packet marking technology in order to trace back DDoS hacking paths. Furthermore, it provided a structure for verifying information marked by attackers using a hash technique.

6 Performance Analysis for the Proposed Method

6.1 Experiment Results

In order to evaluate the performance of the proposed method, the author analyzed the performance using ns-2 Simulator in Linux. A network was composed as shown in the figure below and DDoS attacks were simulated against node 0, 1 and 2.

According to the results of the experiment, in existing packet marking methods each router samples and marks at a probability of p to cope with DDoS attacks. Thus the number of marked packets has increased in proportion to DDoS traffic. In the method proposed in this study, a pushback technique is adopted in marking DDoS traffic and as a result the number of marked packets has decreased by 25.4%.

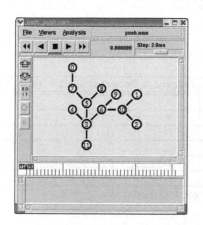 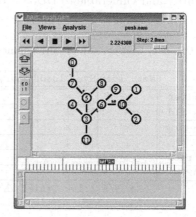

Fig. 6. Attack Architecture and Its Simulation on ns-2.

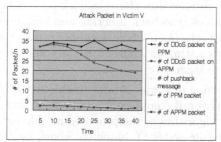 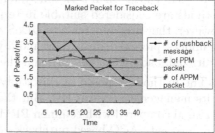

Fig. 7. Traffic Simulation Results by the Proposed Method .

We can control the DDoS traffic by issuing Pushback message to upper router and marking router's own address in IP packet. So, proposed mechanism can identify/control DDoS traffic by using existing Pushback module and trace back its spoofed real origin address with fewer marking packet compared with previous PPM mechanism.

6.2   Analysis and Discussions

[Table 1] shows the comparison of the performance of the proposed method with that of existing IP traceback-related technologies. Filtering, which provides an access control function at routers, does not reduce the load of the entire system and the victim system but inspect packets at routers like SYN flooding. Thus the method does not need additional memory, but it cannot provide a traceback function nor security and cannot cope with DDoS attacks. The method that manages the log of packet information at routers requires a large volume of memory at routers. Although it provide a partial traceback function it is poor in security and vulnerable to DDoS attacks.

Table 1. Comparison of performance with existing IP traceback methods.

	Net. load	Sys. load	Memory	Traceback	Security	DDoS	# of packet
Filter	×	×	×	×	×	×	×
SYN fld.	×	↓	×	×	×	×	×
Logging	×	×	↑	▽	◇	▽	1
PPM	↓	↑	↑	△	◇	▽	↑
iTrace	↓	↑	↑	△	◇	▽	↑
APPM	↓	↓	↑	△	◇	△	n

×:N/A ↓:low ↑:high △:good ◇:moderate ▽:bad

Existing packet marking methods and iTrace methods based on node and edge sampling cause low load on the management system and the network but create heavy load when a victim system restructures the traceback path. These methods are considered suitable in terms of traceback function and scalability. However, they are vulnerable to DDoS attacks. As a whole, most of IP traceback techniques proposed up to now modify existing established routers and cause additional load on the network and the system.

The method proposed in this study runs in a way similar to existing PPM, so its management load is low. But the overall computational overhead will be increased compared with common PPM algorithm as the proposed mechanism is combined with ACC-based pushback module and TTL based traceback module. But, we can ignore these overhead because it provide better traceback functionality. Furthermore, because it applies identification/control functions to packets at routers it reduces load on the entire network when hacking such as DDoS attacks occurs. What is more, while existing PPM methods mark packets by sampling them at an arbitrary probability of p, the method proposed in this study uses an ACC-based congestion control function and marks path information using the value of TTL field, which reduces the number of packets necessary for restructuring a traceback path to the victim system.

Thus the method improves the bandwidth of the entire network and can restructure the path to the source of DDoS attacks with a small number of marking packets. In the method, the path to the source of attack can be restructured only with n traceback messages if the packet has been transmitted via n routers on the network. As a disadvantage, the method requires additional memory at routers for the DDoS-related identification function performed by the ACC-based pushback module. Proposed method requires about 18.8% of additional memory for pushback function compared with common traceback mechanism.

7   Conclusions

As a technology to cope with rapidly increasing hacking and viruses on the Internet, this study proposed a method for a victim system to trace back the actual IP address of the attacker for spoofed traffic when a DDoS attack happens. Reviewing the structure, current state and problems of existing traceback technologies, the author proposed a new marking technique that provides the functions of identifying/controlling DDoS hacking attacks on the network and at the same time enables victim systems to trace back the spoofed source of hacking attacks.

The proposed method is superior to existing ones in load, performance, stability and traceback function. Recently mobile networks and ad-hoc-based networks are found to have vulnerable points to DDoS attacks. Thus it is necessary to study how to provide filtering for packets and trace back the source of attacks in mobile environment. Furthermore, traceback functions should be considered in IPSec-based environment, which provides security protocol at the IP layer, and in ordinary IP layers. Lastly, it is necessary to inquire into methods that provide safety to the entire network including routers, which has been performed by firewall and IDS, and at the same time provide an improved traceback function for packets.

References

1. Computer Emergency Response Team, "TCP SYN flooding and IP Spoofing attacks", CERT Advisory CA-1996-21, Sept, 1996.
2. L. Garber, "Denial-of-Service attacks trip the Internet", Computer, pages 12, Apr. 2000.
3. S. Floyd, S. Bellovin, J. Ioannidis, K. Kompella, R. Mahajan, V. Paxson, "Pushback Message for Controlling Aggregates in the Network," Internet Draft, 2001.
4. P. Ferguson and D. Senie, "Network ingress Filtering: Defeating denial of service attacks which employ IP source address spoofing", May 2000. RFC 2827.
5. K. Park and H. Lee, "On the effectiveness of probabilistic packet marking for IP traceback under denial of service attack", In Proc. IEEE INFOCOM '01, pages 338-347, 2001.
6. D. X. Song, A. Perrig, "Advanced and Authenticated Marking Scheme for IP Traceback", Proc, Infocom, vol. 2, pp. 878-886, 2001.
7. Steve Bellovin, Tom Taylor, "ICMP Traceback Messages", RFC 2026, Internet Engineering Task Force, February 2003.
8. Tatsuya Baba, Shigeyuki Matsuda, "Tracing Network Attacks to Their Sources," IEEE Internet Computing, pp. 20-26, March, 2002.
9. Deering, S. and R. Hinden, "Internet Protocol, Version 6, (IPv6) Specification", RFC 2460, December 1998.
10. Andrey Belenky, Nirwan Ansari, "On IP Traceback," IEEE Communication Magazine, pp.142-153, July, 2003.

A Parallel Intrusion Detection System for High-Speed Networks

Haiguang Lai[1], Shengwen Cai[1], Hao Huang[1], Junyuan Xie[1], and Hui Li[2]

[1] Nanjing University, Nanjing, China,
lite@263.net,
[2] PLA University of Science and Technology

Abstract. The process speed of network-based intrusion detection systems (NIDSs) is still low compared with the speed of networks. As a result, few NIDS is applicable in a high-speed network. A parallel NIDS for high-speed networks is presented in this paper. By dividing the overall traffic into small slices, several sensors can analyze the traffic concurrently and significantly increase the process speed. For most attacks, our partition algorithm ensures that a single slice contains all the evidence necessary to detect a specific attack, making sensor-to-sensor interaction unnecessary. Meanwhile, by making use of the character of the network traffic, the algorithm can also dynamically balance all sensors' loads. To keep the system as simple as possible, a specific sensor is used to detect the scan and the DoS attack. Although only one sensor is used for this kind of attacks, we argue that our system can still provide high process ability. ...

1   Introduction

NIDSs detect attacks by sniffing and analyzing network packets [1,2]. Because of the dramatic increase of the network speed, there is an urgent need for higher process ability of NIDSs. Currently, most NIDSs can cope with the network traffic at a speed up to 100-200 Mbps [3]. There is no problem when they are used in a 100 Mbps shared network. However, It is easy to observe gigabit traffic on the mirror port of the switch in a 100 Mbps switched network. The NIDSs' weak process ability is mainly because that the analysis of network packets needs much computing. So it seems that the problem could be resolved if the processors' speed is increased. Unfortunately, the speed of networks increases faster than the speed of processors. It's impossible to keep up with the speed of networks by just increase the CPU's speed of NIDSs.

To resolve the problem, several sensors could be used to process the traffic concurrently. Since each sensor only processes one part of the traffic, the whole system can process the traffic at higher speed. The key of such system is how to split the network traffic into slices as equally as possible and not loss any evidence necessary for attack detection. A simple, effective parallel intrusion detection system for high-speed network is presented in the paper. The system's partition algorithm provides good splitting equality and makes sensor-to-sensor interaction completely unnecessary.

M. Jakobsson, M. Yung, J. Zhou (Eds.): ACNS 2004, LNCS 3089, pp. 439–451, 2004.

2   Related Work

Christopher Kruegel et al design a high-speed NIDS, in which the traffic is divided into slices and each slice is processed by one or more sensors [4]. The partitioning is done so that a single slice contains all the evidence necessary to detect a specific attack. The architecture of the system is showed in Fig. 1.

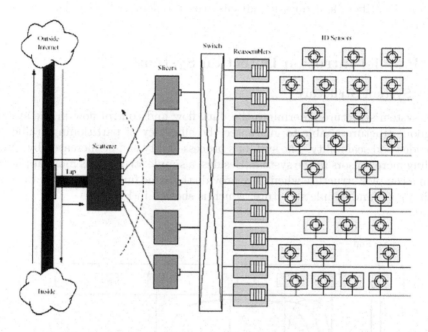

Fig. 1. Architecture of the high-speed intrusion detection

The scatterer only scatters frames in a round-robin fashion to guarantee high speed. The task of the slicers is to route the frames they receive to the sensors that may need them to detect an attack. The reassemblers are responsible to reassemble the possibly disordered frames. The system's throughput nearly reaches 200 Mbps in their experiment.

The paper mainly discusses how to divide the network traffic to avoid losing the evidence for intrusion detection. But the author does not present a feasible method to equally divide the traffic although he shows that the load balancing can be done by dynamically change the slices' filters. In the experiment, the traffic is statically divided according to the address range. Besides, the system is also complex, which needs many devices and has to reassemble the disordered frames. All of these limit its application in the real world.

The traffic splitter is the key of the parallel intrusion detection system. Charitakis et al examine a splitter's architecture in their paper [5]. Two methods are used to improve the system's performance. The first is the use of early filtering where a portion of the packets is processed on the splitter instead of the sensors. The second is the use of locality buffering, where the splitter reorders packets in a way that improves memory access locality on the sensors. The experiment shows that these methods do improve the performance. However, since early filtering and locality buffering may cause some packets been dropped or reordered, it is impossible for the sensors to do state analysis which is important to improve the detection accuracy. In addition, the author splits the traffic by simply hashing on flow identifiers and does not discuss the problem of load balancing in the paper.

3   Parallel Intrusion Detection System

3.1   System Structure

The system structure determines the data flow and control flow in the system. A good structure is able to guarantee the efficiency of partitioning traffic and provide good scalability. The system's process ability can be increased by simply adding more sensors in the system. Besides, a simple structure is more applicable than a complex structure when they provide the same functions. We try to design such a good and simple structure, which is showed in Fig. 2.

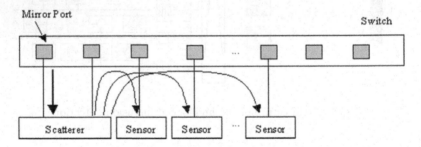

Fig. 2. Structure of the parallel intrusion detection

The scatterer is equipped with two network cards. One card is used to receive network packets from the switch's mirror port and the other one is used to send out the packets. Whenever a packet is received, the scatterer decides which sensor is responsible to process it according to the partition algorithm. Then the packet is sent out after changing its destination MAC address to the sensor's MAC address. The switch's mirror port mirrors all ports' traffic except the ports to which the scatterer and the sensors connect. The pairs of the sensors' MACs and the ports to which they connect are stored in the switch's "MAC-Port" table as static entries so that the broadcasting process of establishing the table is avoided.

This is a very simple structure since only a few devices are needed. To increase the system's process ability, all that we need to do is to add more sensors and configure the switch. Our preliminary experiment has proved that the system is effective, scalable and efficient.

3.2 Partition Algorithm

The partition algorithm is the core of the system. An ideal partition algorithm should satisfy these requirements:

1. The algorithm divides the whole traffic into slices with equal sizes.
2. Each slice contains all the evidence necessary to detect a specific attack.
3. The algorithm is simple and efficient.

The first requirement is the key to guarantee the system's performance. If one slice is much larger than others are, the sensor that processes the slice will become the bottleneck of the system and waste other sensors' process abilities. The second requirement assures that each sensor can detect attacks without any interaction so that the system's complexity is greatly reduced. The third requirement is also for the performance. It is obvious that a simple and efficient algorithm is easy to archive a high throughput. Unfortunately, in practice, it is very hard to satisfy all of these requirements. For example, the round-robin partition algorithm, which sends the packets to the sensors in turn, completely satisfies requirement 1 and requirement 3. However, because the algorithm does not consider any character of the packets, it is very possible that several packets relevant to the same attack are sent to different sensors. As a result, no sensor has enough information to detect the attack. The round-robin algorithm does not satisfy requirement 2. On the other hand, to satisfy requirement 2, it is difficult to partition the traffic equally and keep the algorithm simple. After studying the network attacks, we design a simple algorithm that satisfies requirement 2 and guarantee that the slices have the nearly same sizes.

There are two kinds of network attacks. The attacks in the first category are those that can be detected after inspecting all the packets belonging to one TCP/UDP connection (Although there is no connection using UDP, we call it connection for convenience). Most attacks fall into this category, such as the attacks making use of the bugs of the programs. On the contrary, several connections have to be inspected to detect the attacks in the second category. Scan and DoS fall into this category.

For the first kind of attacks, the sensor would be able to detect the possible attacks without other information if all packets belonging to the same TCP/UDP connection are sent to it. So, no sensor-to-sensor interaction would be needed if partitioning according to TCP/UDP connections.

One TCP/UDP connection is identified by source IP address, source port, destination IP address, and destination port. Here, they are expressed respectively as src_ip, src_port, dst_ip, and dst_port. The TCP/UDP connection is defined as $conn(src\_ip, src\_port, dst\_ip, dst\_port)$. U denotes the aggregation of the packets belonging to the same partition. The constraint of the partition to satisfy requirement 2 is:

Constraint. *For any packets p_i, p_j, $p_i \in conn$, $p_i \in U$, $p_j \in conn'$, $p_j \in U'$, if $conn = conn'$ then $U = U'$.*

It is easy to prove that partitioning with any function of the source address, source port, destination address, and destination port is the sufficient condition of the constraint.

$f(src\_ip, src\_port, dst\_ip, dst\_port)$ denotes the function of the source address, source port, destination address, and destination port. Partitioning with the function means that:

Proof. For any packets p_i, p_j, $p_i \in conn$, $p_i \in U$, $p_j \in conn'$, $p_j \in U'$, if $f(p_i.src\_ip, p_i.src\_port, p_i.dst\_ip, p_i.dst\_port) = f(p_j.src\_ip, p_j.src\_port, pj.dst\_ip, pj.dst\_port)$ then $U = U'$.

Now, if $conn = conn'$ then $p_i.src\_ip = p_j.src\_ip$, $p_i.src\_port = p_j.src\_port$, $p_i.dst\_ip = p_j.dst\_ip$, $p_i.dst\_port = p_j.dst\_port$. So, $f(p_i.src\_ip, p_i.src\_port, p_i.dst\_ip, p_i.dst\_port) = f(p_j.src\_ip, p_j.src\_port, p_j.dst\_ip, p_j.dst\_port)$, then $U = U'$, the constraint is satisfied.

Since partitioning with the function of the source address, source port, destination address, and destination port guarantees detecting attacks without sensor-to-sensor interaction, a natural partition algorithm is to split the traffic with one or combination of these parameters. For instance, the address space of the protected network can be divided into several parts according to the destination address. One sensor is responsible for one part. Whenever the scatterer receives a packet, the scatterer checks the destination of the packet and forwards it to the sensor responsible for this address. However, although the interaction between sensors is avoided, it is hard to balance the loads of the sensors for the algorithm. Because the network traffic is dynamic, the static partition is unable to keep all parts equal. The dynamic adjustment of the partition is necessary to balance the loads of the sensors. This can be achieved by using an analyzer to collect and analyze the loads of the sensors. When finding one sensor's load is too high, the analyzer tells the scatterer to adjust the partition of the traffic so that the sensors' loads can be balanced. The resolution sounds good. However, to guarantee no evidence of the attacks is lost because of the load balancing, a sensor has to keep and exchange with other sensors the information of the connections currently processed. This is resource consuming and complex. Besides, the interaction of the analyzer and the sensors also increase the complexity of the system. In order to keep the system as simple as possible, no additional device is added in our design and the load balance is achieved by a special partition algorithm.

In the real networks, especially the large networks providing services, such as WWW and FTP, plenty of TCP/UDP connections are established and terminated all the time. Because the connections is established and terminated by the computers individually, the appearance of new connections is statistically random. As a result, there are always new connections during a short period. It is seldom that no new connection appears in a very long period. Therefore, the scatterer will frequently receive the packets belonging to the new connections in a real network. For a new connection, all sensors are available to process its packets. The dynamic load balance is archived by choosing the sensor with the lightest load to process the new connection's packets. To measure the load of the sensor, the packets sent to every sensor are counted. The load is considered in direct proportion to the value of counting. The partition algorithm is described in details as following:

Algorithm 1. There are two tables on the scatterer. One is the table S that maps $src\_ip\|src\_port\|dst\_ip\|dst\_port$'s hash value k to the sensor's index ("$\|$" denotes concatenation). The other is the table C that maps the index of the sensor to the count of packets. C is used to record the number of the packets each sensor has processed. Initially, S is empty and the count is zero for every sensor in C. When the scatterer receives a packet, the packet is processed as following:

1. Calculate $src\_ip\|src\_port\|dst\_ip\|dst\_port$'s hash value k.
2. Search in S for the sensor to which k maps. If it is found, the packet is forwarded to that sensor and the sensor's count is increased by one in C. If it is not found, the packet is forwarded to the sensor with the lowest count. Meanwhile, an entry that maps k to the sensor is inserted to S and the sensor's count is creased by one in C.

In this algorithm, TCP/UDP connection is represented by the hash value k. The traffic is partitioned with k. As we have proved, partitioning with any function of the source address, source port, destination address, and destination port is the sufficient condition of the constraint. Therefore, partitioning with k satisfies the constraint. Using the hash value k instead of $src\_ip\|src\_port\|dst\_ip\|dst\_port$ is because that $src\_ip\|src\_port\|dst\_ip\|dst\_port$ needs 96 bits in total. If it were used as the index of the table S, there would be 2^{96} entries in S. It is impossible in practice to implement a table with such huge size.

Algorithm 1 guarantees that the packets belonging to the same connection are processed by the same sensor so that the attacks in the first category will not be missed after partitioning. For the attacks in the second category, the packets relevant to one attack appear in different connections. Using algorithm 1, they may be sent to several sensors so that no sensor will have adequate evidence to detect the attack.

There is usually no significant signature for intrusion detection in a single packet belonging to the attack in the second category. Normal connection establishing or finishing packets can be used to probe whether some services are provided in the target host. Although some DoS attacks' packets do have certain signatures, it is usually not sufficient to make a conclusion that a specific attack occurs when a packet with the signature is detected. However, the attack's packets share some common characters. All packets of a scanning have the same source addresses while the destination addresses of the packets of a DoS attack are completely same. It is obvious that no scan and DoS attacks will be missed if all packets with the same source addresses are processed by the same sensor and all packets with the same destination addresses are processed by the same sensor.

Algorithm 1 is modified to ensure that the packets with the same source addresses are sent to the same sensor and the packets with the same destination addresses are sent to the same sensor. Obviously, no attack in the first category will be missed because the packets belonging to the same connection must have the same source or destination addresses. The following is the modified algorithm:

Algorithm 2. Three tables are used on the scatterer. S is the table used to map the source address to the index of the sensor. Table D is to map the destination address to the index of the sensor. Table C is used to record the number of the packets each sensor has processed. At first, S and D are empty and the counts in C are all zero. Whenever a packet is received, the following steps are executed:

1. Get the packet's source IP address src_ip and destination IP address dst_ip.
2. Search in S for the sensor to which src_ip maps.
3. If it (called A) is found, the packet is forwarded to A and the count of the sensor A is increased by one in C. Search in D for the sensor to which dst_ip maps. If it (called B) is found, the packet is forwarded to B and the count of B is increase by one in C. If B is not found, an entry that maps dst_ip to A is inserted to D.
4. If A is not found, Search in D for the sensor to which dst_ip maps. If it (called B) is found, the packet is forwarded to B and the count of B is increased by one. Meanwhile, an entry that maps src_ip to B is inserted to S. If B is not found, the packet is forwarded to the sensor with the lowest count. At the same time, an entry that maps src_ip to the sensor is inserted t to S and an entry that maps dst_ip to the sensor is inserted to D. The count of the sensor in C is increased by one too.

Algorithm 2 ensures that no evidence of the attacks will be missed after partitioning the traffic. Nevertheless, it brings new problems. First, the performance of the system is reduced because one packet may be sent to two sensors. Moreover, in the real networks, many connections may have the same destination address, a server's address for example. If algorithm 2 were used, all packets belonging to these connections would be sent to the same sensor and make its load too heavy. After some experiments, we find that algorithm 2 is completely unpractical.

Because of the attacks in the second category, it is difficult to keep the loads of the sensors balanced without the sensor-to-sensor interaction. To resolve the problem, we decide to modify the structure of the system. A single dedicated sensor is added to detect the attacks in the second category. Algorithm 1 is still used as the partition algorithm on the scatterer. The structure of the new system is showed in Fig. 3.

The sensors of type A are only responsible to detect the attacks in the first category. Sensor B is only used to detect the attacks in the second category. Like the scatterer, sensor B is connected to the mirror port of the switch. Therefore, it can receive all the packets of the network. No attacks in the second category will be missed as long as sensor B's speed is fast enough. In fact, it is not very difficult. For the attacks in the first category, the sensor has to reassemble the

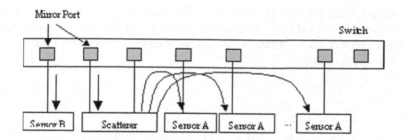

Fig. 3. Structure of the modified system

TCP streams and even the HTTP, FTP sessions. Then, the signatures of the attacks are searched in the payloads [6]. The whole process, especially the step of signature matching is time consuming. Therefore, the speed of intrusion detection is hard to keep up with the speed of the networks. However, to detect the attacks in the second category, the process is much simpler. Only the heads of the packets need to be checked. Since the flags of the packets' heads are limited, it is easy to detect the attacks at a high speed. R. Sekar designs a method to detect the attacks in the second category [7]. The method guarantees a high detection speed by translating the attacks' patterns into finite-state automata. Their system participated in an intrusion detection evaluation organized by MIT Lincoln Labs, where their system worked well at 500 Mbps. Therefore, the system structure showed in Fig. 3 is feasible. At least, the structure is still effective at 500 Mbps if Sekar's method is used in sensor B.

4   Experiment

In our prototype, the scatterer is a PC (Pentium4 1.8 G 512 M) equipped with two Intel8254GC Gigabit network cards, running Linux 2.4.18-13 (Redhat 7.3). The switch is Intel NetStructure4701T. The sensor for the detection of the attacks in the second category is not implemented in the prototype. The major purpose is to evaluate our partition algorithm.

To improve the performance of scattering, we implement the forwarding of the packets in the Linux kernel [8]. In more detail, the entries of the network protocols' process functions are stored in the array `packet_ptype_base`. First, we use function `dev_remove_pack()` to remove all protocols' functions for the array. Second, Our process function is inserted to `packet_ptype_base` by `dev_add_pack()` so that the packets will be processed by our function immediately after it is processed by the network card driver. According to the partition algorithm, the destination MAC addresses of the packets are changed and the packets are sent out by `dev_queue_xmit()`. Since the sensors process only IP packets, all packets except IP packets are dropped by the scatterer to further increase the scattering speed. The hash function used in the scatterer is the FNV hash, which is fast while maintaining a low collision rate [9].The last 24 bits of the hash value k is used as the index of table S. As a result, the size of table S is 16 M bytes. The experiment consists of two parts. The effectiveness and the performance are evaluated respectively.

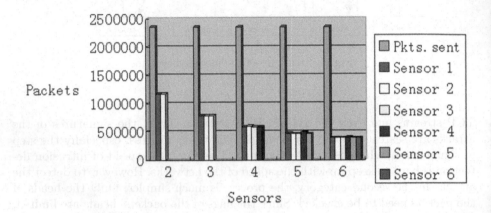

Fig. 4. Counts of scattered packets

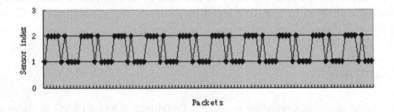

Fig. 5. Scatter packets to two sensors

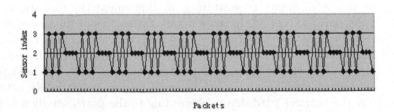

Fig. 6. Scatter packets to three sensors

4.1   Effectiveness

The evaluation of the effectiveness is to examine whether the traffic could be divided into slices with nearly the same size by the partition algorithm. We use tcpreplay to replay the traffic produced by MIT Lincoln Labs as part of the DARPA 1999 IDS evaluation [10]. The scatterer is configured to scatter packets to 2~6 sensors. The number of the packets sent to the sensors is counted in the scatterer. Figure 4 and table 1 show the result.

Table 1. Counts of scattered packets

	2 sensors	3 sensors	4 sensors	5 sensors	6 sensors
Pkts. sent	2356503	2356503	2356503	2356503	2356503
Sensor 1	1169906	779103	581735	468647	388624
Sensor 2	1169900	779101	595170	459843	388649
Sensor 3		781553	581710	459841	388625
Sensor 4			581708	490155	393249
Sensor 5				461229	390935
Sensor 6					389588

As the result shows, the packets are almost equally scattered to all sensors. However, the result only demonstrates that the total numbers of the packets received by the sensors are nearly the same. It is also important that the instantaneous speed of the traffics scattered to the sensors are nearly equal, which means that the packets scattered to one sensor are nearly as many as those scattered to other sensors in a short period. Figure 5~Fig. 9 show the process that the scatterer scatters packets. As the figures demonstrate, the packets are sent to different sensors in turn. It is not observed that all packets are sent to one sensor during a long period.

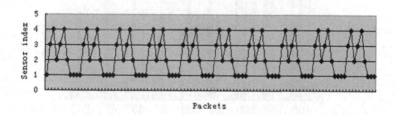

Fig. 7. Scatter packets to four sensors

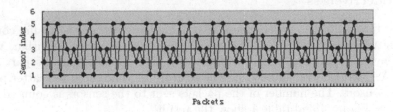

Fig. 8. Scatter packets to five sensors

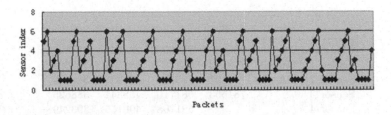

Fig. 9. Scatter packets to six sensors

4.2   Performance

Because the maximum amount of the traffic tcpreplay can generate is 160 Mbps,
A SmartBits 600, which can generates faster traffic, is used to evaluate the performance. The percentage of the packets processed by the scatterer is recorded
when the packets are sent out by the SmartBits with different size. The result
is showed in Fig. 10 and table 2.

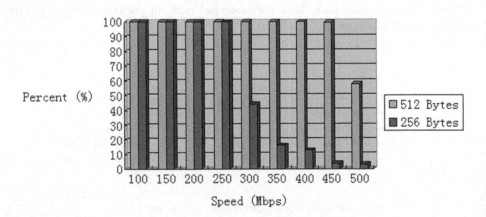

Fig. 10. Percentage of the packets processed

Table 2. Percentage of the packets processed

Speed (Mbps)	100	150	200	250	300	350	400	450	500
512 Bytes	100%	100%	100%	100%	100%	99.977%	99.848%	99.588%	58.132%
256 Bytes	100%	100%	99.968%	99.708%	44.341%	16.251%	12.969%	3.921%	3.533%

5 Conclusion and Future Work

A parallel intrusion detection system for high-speed networks is presented in the paper. The high-speed traffic is divided into several low-speed traffics, which are processed respectively by many sensors. Because of the parallel process, the system's performance is much better than the performance of one sensor. For all attacks except the scan and the DoS, the partition algorithm guarantees that the packets sent to each sensor contain all evidence necessary to detect a specific attack, making the complex sensor-to-sensor interaction unnecessary. Meanwhile, the algorithm provides the ability of dynamically balance the loads of the sensors. In more detail, the algorithm always chooses the idlest sensor to process the packets belonging to a new connection. In addition, the algorithm is very simple and efficient. For the scan and DoS attacks, it is difficult to keep the sensors' loads balanced while making sensor-to-sensor interaction unnecessary. Therefore, we use a specialized sensor to detect them and explain that the system's performance can still keep high despite only one dedicated sensor is used. Our preliminary experiment proves that the parallel intrusion detection system is of high performance and scalability. Our approach also has some shortages. The scatterer is the bottleneck of the system and the partition algorithm consumes much memory. Future work will include implementing the partition algorithm in hardware and the research on parallel detecting the scan and DoS attacks.

References

1. Rebecca Bace, Peter Mell: Intrusion Detection Systems. NIST Special Publication on Intrusion Detection Systems. (2001)
2. G. Vigna, R. Kemmerer: NetSTAT: A Network based Intrusion Detection Approach. Computer Security Applications Conference. (1998)
3. Bob Walder: Gigabit IDS.
   http://www.westcoast.com/artframe_report.html. (2003)
4. Christopher Kruegel, Fredrik Valeur, Giovanni Vigna, Richard Kemmerer: Stateful Intrusion Detection for High-Speed Networks. IEEE Symposium on Security and Privacy. (2002)
5. I. Charitakis, K. Anagnostakis, E. Markatos: An Active Traffic Splitter Architecture for Intrusion Detection. 11th IEEE/ACM International Symposium on Modeling, Analysis and Simulation of Computer Telecommunications Systems. (2003)
6. V. Paxson: Bro: A System for Detecting Network Intruders in Real-Time. The 7th USENIX Security Symposium. (1998)

7. Sekar, R., Guang, Y., Verma, S., Shanbag, T.: A High-Performance Network Intrusion Detection System. ACM Symposium on Computer and Communication Security. (1999)
8. kossak: Building Into The Linux Network Layer. Phrack Magazine. **9**(1999)
9. Glenn Fowler, Phong Vo., Landon Curt Noll: Fowler / Noll / Vo (FNV) Hash. http://www.isthe.com/chongo/tech/comp/fnv/.
10. MIT Lincoln Laboratory: DARPA Intrusion Detection Evaluation. http://www.ll.mit.edu/IST/ideval/. (1999)

A Novel Framework for Alert Correlation and Understanding

Dong Yu[1,2] and Deborah Frincke[1]

[1] Center for Secure and Dependable Software, University of Idaho, USA
dongyu@csds.uidaho.edu
[2] Microsoft Research / Redmond, USA, frincke@cs.uidaho.edu

Abstract. We propose a novel framework named Hidden Colored Petri-Net for Alert Correlation and Understanding (HCPN-ACU) in intrusion detection system. This model is based upon the premise that intrusion detection may be viewed as an inference problem – in other words, we seek to show that system misusers are carrying out a sequence of steps to violate system security policies in some way, with earlier steps preparing for the later ones. In contrast with prior arts, we separate actions from observations and assume that the attacker's actions themselves are unknown, but the attacker's behavior may result in alerts. These alerts are then used to infer the attacker's actions. We evaluate the model with DARPA evaluation database. We conclude that HCPN-ACU can conduct alert fusion and intention recognition at the same time, reduce false positives and negatives, and provide better understanding of the intrusion progress by introducing confidence scores.

1 Introduction

Intrusion detection system (IDS) is originated as a mechanism for managing the detection of system misuse through the analysis of activity [3]. A typical state-of-the-art IDS detects intrusions by analyzing audit data from various sources (hosts and networks) and alert users or defense systems automatically when possible intrusive behaviors are observed. A key factor in determining an effective IDS is its ability to properly correlate information drawn from appropriately placed IDS sensors due to the following three reasons. First, IDS sensors can generate massive amount of alerts [17], if they have a high sensitivity to potential misuse; examining these alerts is costly and not all of this information leads to good decisions. Second, the false positive rate is one of the most serious problems with current IDSs [2,4]. Third, false negatives are another problem – those intrusions missed by the IDS may later result in damage to the system. Given these, intelligent analysis of activity is critical to the overall success of the IDS. Alert Correlation and Understanding (ACU) can improve the effectiveness of the IDS by examining how the outputs of IDS sensors (the alerts) may be used to better identify misuse and develop response plans.

Current approaches in ACU can be classified into two primary categories: alert fusion and intention recognition. *Alert fusion*, also known as aggregation,

M. Jakobsson, M. Yung, J. Zhou (Eds.): ACNS 2004, LNCS 3089, pp. 452–466, 2004.

or clustering, is to aggregate similar alerts from multi-sensors into so called meta-alerts (or hyper-alerts) based on feature similarities, with the hope to enhance the quality of the resulting information [35,33,9,10,20,6,17,29]. The fusion process usually involves the merging of the features of the two alerts. For example, alerts from the same sensor and belong to the same attack (identified by the same source and target IP address) are considered similar alerts [33]. In alert fusion, alerts are first classified into alert clusters that correspond to the same occurrence of an attack based on similarity. Each cluster is then merged and a new, global alert is generated to represent the whole cluster [9,29]. The main purpose of the alert fusion is to reduce the number of alerts to be provided to the administrators and reduce the false positives to some extent [10].

In contrast, *intention recognition* (or attack plan recognition) [16,32,13,12,7, 8,26,27] seeks to recognize an attacker's intention from the alerts. The emphasis here is to give administrators and active reactors better understanding of on-going activities so that they can make appropriate responses. The importance of intention recognition is not so much in the "average" generic attack on a system, but for instances where it is important to more fully identify complex, multi-stage scenarios. Detecting an attacker's plan at an early stage would make it easier to prevent the attacker from achieving his/her goal. Intention recognition is also aimed to reduce some false positives during correlation; further, it should be possible to increase true positives (therefore reducing false negatives) by inferring the existence of attacks during correlation.

Some of these technologies have already been implemented in Commercial Off The Shelf (COTS) intrusion detection tools from companies such as Net-forensics, Q1, Object neworks, and Arcsight, to name a few. However, current ACU approaches have several limitations:

- Alert fusion and intention recognition are usually two separate steps. Inten-tion recognition approaches are applied on the result of alert fusion [9].
- Uncertainty information is usually not used in the ACU process. For exam-ple, the rate of false positives and false negatives would provide some hint on whether a conclusion that an attacker did take some action can be drawn reliably when an alert was observed. Other sources of uncertainties include trustworthiness of alerts gathered from different sensors.
- No confidence score is associated with the ACU's outputs.

In this paper, we propose a novel framework named Hidden Colored Petri-Net for Alert Correlation and Understanding (HCPN-ACU). This model is based upon the premise that intrusion detection may be viewed as an inference problem – in other words, we seek to show that system misusers are carrying out a se-quence of steps to violate system security policies in some way, with earlier steps preparing for the later ones. We assume that the attacker's actions themselves are unknown, but the attacker's behavior may result in alerts. These alerts are then used to infer the attacker's actions. In this paper, we discuss how HCPN can model the attacker's behaviors, intrusion's prerequisites and consequences, security policies, and the alerts. We argue that HCPN-ACU can conduct alert fusion and intention recognition at the same time, reduce false positives and negatives, and provide better understanding of the intrusion progress.

The remainder of the paper is organized as follows. In section 2, we introduce the background and motivation of this research. Specifically, we discuss the task of ACU and the limitations in current ACU approaches. In section 3, we propose the HCPN- framework to model the ACU inference process, present basic theories related to the inference process, and describe how HCPN-ACU works. We introduce the inference and learning algorithms in section 4, and evaluate our system with the DARPA intrusion detection evaluation database in section 5. In section 6, we conclude this paper.

2   Background and Motivation

ACU is increasingly gaining attention as an area of research due to the following two reasons: the potential to improve efficiency by reducing the number of alerts that an IDS would generate to more manageable levels while still retaining strong detection capacities, and the potential to improve IDS correctness by reducing the false positives and negatives in the alerts generated by the IDS sensors and/or low level heterogeneous IDSs.

Fig. 1 depicts the architecture of an IDS that contains the ACU component. In this architecture, audit data are first analyzed and alerts are generated. These alerts are then fed as the observations into the ACU component. We can consider ACU as a second level analyzer or booster that uses the first level analyzers' results as inputs.

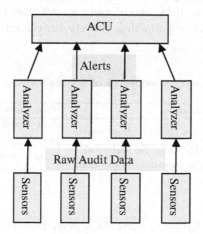

Fig. 1. The Architecture of an IDS that contains ACU

Three tasks are associated with ACU: aggregating alerts to reduce the total number of alerts presenting to the administrators and active reactors; reducing false positives and negatives; and understanding the attacker's intrusion behavior and plan.

ACU is usually conducted as two steps: First, similar alerts from multi-sensors are aggregated into so called meta-alerts (or hyper-alerts) based on feature similarities. These meta-alerts are then correlated based on the prerequisite-consequence relationships [7,8,26,27].

Let's examine how current approaches work using the Distributed Denial of Service (DDoS) attack as an example. Assume that an intruder needs to conduct the following five steps to launch a DDoS attack:

1. IPsweep the hosts from a remote site;
2. Probe (SadmindPing) live IPs to look for the sadmind daemon running on Solaris hosts;
3. Break into some of the hosts via the sadmind vulnerability (SadmindBOF);
4. Install the Trojan mstream DDoS software on some of the hosts;
5. Launch the DDoS.

To correlate alerts with current ACU approaches, security experts build a set of rules that describe each action's prerequisites and consequences. In other words, each action is associated with a set of prerequisites that must be met before the attacker can take the action, and a set of consequences that the action would lead to. Table 1 lists the prerequisites and consequences of the Sadmind-Ping action and the sadmindBOF action. From the table, we can see that the intruder can conduct the SadmindPing action only if he/she already knows that the host exists. As a result of probing, the attacker would know whether the sadmind daemon is running on the host. Similarly, an intruder usually launches the sadmind attack only if he/she already knows that the sadmind daemon is running on the host. After launching the attack, the intruder compromises the host.

Table 1. Prerequisites and consequences of actions SadmindPing and sadmindBOF

Action	Prerequisites	Consequences
SadmindPing	Knowledge that the host exists	Knowledge that the sadmind daemon is running on the host
SadmindBOF	Knowledge that the sadmind daemon is running on the host	The host is compromised

Let us consider the following three ACU scenarios. To make discussion easier, we assume that SadmindPing's prerequisites are always met and no other action other than SadmindPing would provide the prerequisites for SadmindBOF.

Scenario 1: alert_SadmindPing and alert_SadmindBOF are both issued by the low level analyzers. A typical ACU component will correlate these two alerts since the set of consequences of SadmindPing contains all the prerequisites of SadmindBOF.

Scenario 2: alert_SadmindBOF is issued by the low level analyzers but alert_SadmindPing is not. A typical ACU component will consider alert_Sadmind-BOF as a false positive since the prerequisites of SadmindBOF are not met.

Scenario 3: alert_SadmindBOF is issued by the low level analyzers ten times but alert_SadmindPing is not issued. A typical ACU component will first aggregate the ten alert_SadmindBOF into one hyper alert_SadmindBOF and then correlate the hyper alert_SadmindBOF with other alerts. Since the prerequisites of SadmindBOF are not met, alert_SadmindBOF is considered a false positive.

From these scenarios, we can observe three issues in current ACU approaches:

First, in current approaches, IDS's observations (alerts) are not distinguished from an attacker's real actions. This can be easily noticed when we examine the correlation process – **alerts** are correlated based on **actions**' prerequisites and consequences directly. An action is assumed to have happened iff the corresponding alert is issued and the prerequisites of the action are met.

However, alerts and actions are not one to one mapped. Due to false positives, the low level analyzers may issue alert_SadmindBOF while no Sadmind-BOF action is actually conducted. This suggests that the co-occurrence of alert_Sadmind-Ping and alert_SadmindBOF in scenario 1 does not necessarily mean that SadmindBOF is really carried out by the intruder. Similarly, due to false negatives, SadmindPing might be missed by the low level analyzers and no alert is issued. This suggests that issuing alert_SadmindBOF alone, as what happened in scenario 2, does not necessarily mean that SadmindBOF is not taken by the attacker. Table 2 summarizes these two error conditions.

Table 2. Conditions in which the current ACU approaches may generate errors

Scenario	Alerts Issued	ACU Result	Failure Condition
Scenario 1	alert_SadmindPing, alert_SadmindBOF	Both SadmindPing and SadmindBOF have happened	When alert_SadmindBOF is a false positive
Scenario 2	alert_SadmindBOF	SadmindBOF did not happen	When alert_SadmindPing is a false negative

Note that the reason ACU errors occur here is that alerts are treated the same as actions during the correlation process. Information such as false negative rate and false positive rate of that action is not used in the correlation process.

Second, the number of the occurrence of the same alert is not used in the correlation process due to the two-step strategy in current ACU approaches. The drawback of this limitation can be observed when comparing scenario 3 with scenario 2. We would guess that the action SadmindBOF very likely has happened in scenario 3 since the alert_SadmindBOF is issued ten times; while it less likely has happened in scenario 2, where alert_SadmindBOF is issued only once. However, as we already discovered, current ACU approaches typically generate exactly the same result in both scenarios. The number of the occurrence of alert_SadmindBOF does not affect the correlation result.

Third, no confidence scores are provided in the current ACU approaches. Alerts are either correlated and should be delivered to the administrators, or not correlated, considered as false positives, and discarded. Using scenarios 2 and 3 as examples, confidence scores would aid administrators and active reactors to better understand the whole attack picture.

3   The Hidden Colored Petri-Net Framework

In this section, we propose a novel framework named Hidden Colored Petri-Net for Alert Correlation and Understanding (HCPN-ACU). HCPN is our extension to Colored Petri-Net (CPN) [19]. CPN has been used in modeling Discrete Event Dynamic Systems (DEDS) such as "communication protocols, operating systems, hardware designs, embedded systems, software system designs, and business process re-engineering" [21]. It has also been introduced to model the intruder's misuse behaviors [11,22,23].

An *HCPN-ACU* is an 11-tuple $HCPN = (\Sigma, Q, D, A, O, G, E, \Pi_0, \Delta, \Gamma, \Theta)$, where:

1. Σ (*color set*) is a non-empty finite set of *agents*;
2. Q (*place set*) is a finite set of *resources*;
3. D (*transition set*) is a finite set of *actions* agents might take;
4. A (*arc set*) is a finite set that $A = A_1 \cup A_2$, where $A_1 \subseteq (Q \times D)$, and $A_2 \subseteq (D \times Q)$;
5. O (*observation set*) is a set of *observations*. It can be alerts or raw audit and traffic data;
6. G (*guard function set*) is a set of *guard functions* associated with arcs A_1, such that $G = \{g : A_1 \to S_{M(\Sigma)}\}$. Guard functions represent the conditions to be met before an action can be conducted by the agents.
7. E (*effect function set*) is a set of *effect functions* associated with arcs A_2, such that $E = \{e : A_2 \to S_{M(\Sigma)}\}$. Effect functions represent the agent-resource relationship change due to an action.
8. Π_0 (initial marking distribution) is the initial agent-resource ownership probability distribution $\Pi_0 = P_0\left(Q, S_{M(\Sigma)}\right) = \left\{\pi : \left(Q, S_{M(\Sigma)}\right) \to [0,1]\right\}$.
9. Δ (transition probability) is the probability that actions might be conducted next: $\Delta = P(D \text{ will be fired next}|D \text{ is enabled}) = \{\delta : D \to [0,1]\}$
10. Γ (observation probability) is the probability that O is observed given action D and is defined as $\Gamma = P(O|D) = \{\gamma : (D, O) \to [0,1]\}$.
11. Θ (*tolerance*) is the tolerance function used to determine whether two states are indistinguishable.

In HCPN-ACU, a *token element* (q, c) stands for the fact that the agent c has access to resource q. An *enabled transition* means that the prerequisites of the corresponding actions are met. The *marking distribution* Π represents the agent-resource ownership probability. The *progress of intrusion* is represented by the change of marking distribution along time.

The HCPN-ACU can be further simplified with the following default settings due to the nature of the IDS:

1. Use a transition named *normal* to absorb the false positives.
2. The number of token elements (q, c) does not affect the agent-resource ownership. For this reason, we need to consider only the probability $\{(q, c)\} \leq M$ and don't distinguish between one single token element and multiple ones.
3. All guard functions need only to care about the probability $\{(q, c)\} \leq M$ with the same reason.
4. We may add in the model an arc from the transition to each input places to indicate that the carrying out of the action would also affect the input. With these additional arcs, the system will be able to automatically infer that the input places have been compromised if the action is determined to have been taken. Thus, the model has potential to infer missing alerts from other alerts to reduce false negatives.

Let us use the local-to-root (L2R) attack from [16,11] as an example. The attack involves four actions: copy, chmod, touch, and mail. Each action would grant the access of one resource to the attacker. Fig. 2 depicts the HCPN-ACU model of this L2R attack. There are five transitions in the graph. Transitions are used to model the actions copy, chmod, touch, and mail; a special transition named "normal" is used to model the unintrusive actions. Six places are used in the figure to represent resources involved. The place q1 is a special place to model the resource that would be accessible to all agents. Arcs in the figure describe the prerequisites and consequences of actions. For example, an attacker needs to hold both q4 and q5 to be able to conduct the mail action. After the mail command is issued, the attacker would be able to hold q6. Each attacker is assigned a color. For instance, user1 might be represented as red. If q3 is dyed with red, q3 is compromised by user1.

Although the HCPN-ACU also describes the prerequisites and consequences of actions, there are several differences between HCPN-ACU and the ACU approaches discussed earlier in this paper.

First, instead of assuming a one-to-one mapping between alerts and actions, we assume that the low level analyzers may observe each action as different alerts with different probabilities (named observation probabilities). These probabilities are induced from the false positive rate and false negative rate of each action. For example, the copy action might be observed as alert_copy, alert_touch, or normal (simply missed). For this reason, the correlation results in HCPN-ACU are determined by alerts, the observation probabilities, and the number of each kind of alerts.

Second, HCPN-ACU presents the compromised resources instead of alerts to the administrators and active reactors. Since the number of compromised resources is usually much smaller than the number of alerts, this can effectively reduce the amount of data passed to the administrators and active reactors.

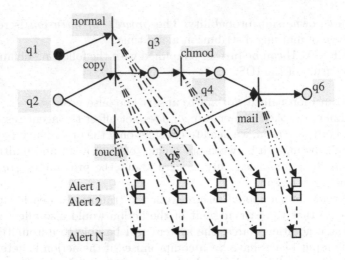

Fig. 2. An Example HCPN-ACU Model for the L2R Attack

Presenting compromised resources also helps administrators and active reactors to pick up a wise reaction.

Third, HCPN-ACU not only presents the compromised resources but also indicates the probability that a specified resource has been compromised by a specific intruder.

Three assumptions are made in HCPN-ACU:

First, the action prerequisites and effects are known as domain knowledge. This assumption is reasonable since the prerequisites and consequences of the alerts are usually known when the alerts are defined in an IDS,. All intention (or plan) recognition approaches are based on this assumption and they usually include this knowledge as rules in a database [7].

Second, the initial probability of resources owned by the agent can be determined by the system through such ways as policy and logon credentials. To deal with the situation where information is incomplete, we can assign a small probability to all agent/resource pairs using smoothing technology [31] to indicate that each resource may be accessible by an agent through unknown approaches.

Third, agents do not cooperate with each other. With this assumption, we can represent agents (identified as different source IPs and user IDs) with different colors and consider them separately. This assumption is valid for many intrusion cases because many attacks happened today are launched by isolated, script-based intrusion such as worms[1]. However, this assumption is not valid for sophisticated intrusions where a skilled attacker controls several agents and attacks the same system at the same time. To handle attacks launched by coop-

---

[1] We perceive that future worms may act as cooperative agents and would thus be more dangerous.

erating agents, an improved model is needed to correlate cooperating agents as "one" agent. We consider this as our future work.

4   Inference and Learning Algorithms

In this section, we briefly introduce the algorithm to infer an attacker's most probable action sequence given the model and the observations, as well as the algorithm to learn the model's parameters based on intrusion logs.

4.1   Basic Operations

In HCPN-ACU, a transition (action) is enabled iff all input places (prerequisites) satisfy the guards. In other words, given a marking distribution Π_t, the probability that a transition $d \in D$ is enabled can be determined by the following calculation:

$$P\left(E\left(d\right)|\Pi_t\right) = P\left(d \text{ is enabled}|\Pi_t\right) = P\left(\bigwedge_{q\in I(d)}\left(\Pi_t\left(q\right) \geq G\left(a = (q,d)\right)\right)\right)$$

$$= \prod_{q\in I(d)} P\left(\Pi_t\left(q\right) \geq G\left(a = (q,d)\right)\right) = \prod_{q\in I(d)} \pi_t\left(q\right) . \tag{1}$$

Similarly, a place q will be compromised by the color c iff it's compromised by c or at least one of the transitions (of which q is an output place) is enabled. Given a state $S_t = (\Pi_t, \Delta_t)$, the probability that a transition $d \in D$ will be fired next without knowing the observation can be determined by this calculation:

$$\delta_t'\left(d\right) = P\left(D = d|\Pi_t\right) = \delta\left(d\right) P\left(E\left(d\right)|\Pi_t\right) = \delta\left(d\right) \prod_{q\in I(d)} \pi_t\left(q\right) . \tag{2}$$

$$\delta_t\left(d\right) = \frac{\delta_t'\left(d\right)}{\sum_{d'}\delta_t'\left(d'\right)} . \tag{3}$$

Given the state $S_{t-1} = (\Pi_{t-1}, \Delta_{t-1})$ and an observation O_t, the probability that the action d is taken is denoted as $P\left(D_t = d|S_{t-1}, O_t\right)$ and can be determined by the following calculation

$$P\left(D_t = d|S_{t-1}, O_t\right) = \frac{P\left(D_t = d, O_t|S_{t-1}\right)}{P\left(O_t|S_{t-1}\right)}$$

$$= \frac{P\left(D_t = d|S_{t-1}\right) P\left(O_t|D_t = d, S_{t-1}\right)}{P\left(O_t|S_{t-1}\right)} . \tag{4}$$

Because $P\left(D_t = d|S_{t-1}\right)$ is equal to $\delta_{t-1}\left(d\right)$ and O_t is independent of S_{t-1} given D_t, the above equation becomes:

$$= \frac{\delta_{t-1}\left(d\right) P\left(O_t|D_t = d\right)}{P\left(O_t|S_{t-1}\right)} = \frac{\delta_{t-1}\left(d\right) \gamma\left(O_t|d\right)}{\sum_{d'\in D}\delta_{t-1}\left(d'\right) \gamma\left(O_t|d'\right)} . \tag{5}$$

4.2 Inference Problem

The inference problem (the correlation process) can be stated as follows: Given observations $O_1, O_2, \cdots, O_t$, and the model parameter λ, which action sequence, represented by $D_1, D_2, \cdots, D_t$, is most likely to have produced O from λ? That's to say, which sequence of state transitions is most likely to have led to this sequence of observations? In other words, we want to optimize the following criteria:

$$\arg \max_D \left[P\left(D|O, \lambda\right) \right] = \arg \max_D \left[\frac{P\left(O|D, \lambda\right) P\left(D|\lambda\right)}{P\left(O|\lambda\right)} \right] . \tag{6}$$

Since the term $P\left(O|\lambda\right)$ is not related to D, we can discard it when selecting paths. So we need to only optimize:

$$\arg \max_D \left[P\left(O|D, \lambda\right) P\left(D|\lambda\right) \right] = \arg \max_D P\left(O, D|\lambda\right) . \tag{7}$$

This problem can be solved with dynamic programming (DP) by defining $\omega_t\left(j\right)$ as the maximum score of a length t state sequence ending in action j and producing the first t observations from O, as shown in the following equation:

$$\omega_t\left(j\right) = \max_{D_1\cdots, D_{t-1}} P\left(O_1, \cdots, O_t, D_1, \cdots, D_{t-1}, D_t = j|\lambda\right) . \tag{8}$$

where $\delta_{t-1}^i\left(j\right) \approx P\left(D_t = j|S'_{t-1}, \lambda\right)$ and S'_{t-1} is the state corresponding to $\omega_{t-1}\left(i\right)$.

4.3 Model Parameter Estimation Problem

The model parameter estimation problem can be stated as: Given observations $O_1, O_2, \cdots, O_t$, the model structure, and associated attacks, how can we estimate the model parameters so that the model best explains the known data.

We solve this problem with Expectation Maximum (EM) algorithm [25]. The EM algorithm consists of two major steps: an expectation step (E-Step), followed by a maximization step (M-Step). In the E-Step, the unobserved data (transitions in HCPN) is estimated based on the current model parameters λ_k. In the M-Step, Maximum Likelihood (ML) estimation is used to estimate model parameters λ_{k+1} using estimated data. This process is iterated until the segmentation is fixed. In our current system, we assume that the initial probabilities are determined based on the security policies. We need to estimate the observation probabilities and transition probabilities. Likelihood of observations given the observation probability $\theta = \gamma\left(o|d\right)$ is defined as:

$$L\left(\gamma, d\right) = \sum_i \ln\left(P\left(O_i|\gamma, d\right)\right) = \sum_{O_i = o} \ln \gamma + \sum_{O_i \neq o} \ln\left(1 - \gamma\right)$$
$$= N \ln \gamma + L \ln\left(1 - \gamma\right) . \tag{9}$$

where N is the number of instances that O is observed when transition d is taken and L is the number of instances that O is NOT observed when transition d is taken. Observation probability is chosen to maximize the above likelihood as shown in the following equation:

$$\frac{\partial L(\theta, d)}{\partial \theta} = \frac{N}{\theta} - \frac{L}{1 - \theta} = 0 \Rightarrow (N + L)\theta = N \Rightarrow \theta = \frac{N}{(N + L)} . \qquad (10)$$

Transition probabilities can be estimated similarly.

5   Experiments on DARPA Dataset

We have developed an off-line alert correlation system based on our HCPN-ACU framework and performed several experiments using the two DARPA 2000 intrusion detection evaluation datasets [24]. Each dataset includes the network traffic data collected from both the DMZ and the inside part of the evaluation network. In the datasets, attackers probe, break-in, install the DDoS daemon, and launch DDoS attacks.

Instead of running our low level analyzers to generate alerts, we used alerts generated by RealSecure Network Sensor 6.0 as what Ning et. al. [28] did: "In all the experiments, the Network Sensor was configured to use the *Maximum Coverage* policy with a slight change, which forced the Network Sensor to save all the reported alerts." We choose to use RealSecure Network Sensors because attack signatures used in RealSecure Network Sensor 6.0 are well documented, and Ning et. al. already have a set of rules to describe action's prerequisites and consequences.

In the experiments, we used the second dataset and one set of data (associated with one host) from the first dataset as the training set. We do this because the second dataset is lack of representative data. We used the first dataset as the testing set. We performed two sets of tests, one on the DMZ traffic and one on the inside network traffic.

The HCPN-ACU model used in the experiments consists of 20 places (resources), 29 transitions (actions), and 28 alerts. The actions used in the experiments have the same names as the alerts. However, each action might be observed by the sensors as different alerts. We used 0.02 as the initial probability for all resources other than the resource known to all users - SystemExisits. The training takes less than 20 seconds and the inference takes less than 5 seconds for about 900 alerts on a Celeron 1.0GHz PC.

As mentioned in section 3, our HCPN-ACU system outputs resources compromised instead of alerts themselves. Table 3 lists the correlation result for the inside network traffic. From the table we can see that the attacker has installed daemons on hosts 172.016.112.010, 172.016.112.050, and 172.016.115.020, and ready to launch the DDoS attack. Note, however, our system does not report that it's ready to launch DDoS attack on host 172.016.115.020 due to false negatives.

Table 3. Correlation results for the inside traffic

Host	Place Name	Probability
172.016.112.010	SystemCompromised	1.00
	VulnerableSadmind	0.66
	DaemonInstalled	0.55
	ReadyToLaunchDDOSAttack	0.95
172.016.112.050	SystemCompromised	1.00
	VulnerableSadmind	0.66
	DaemonInstalled	0.55
	ReadyToLaunchDDOSAttack	0.95
172.016.115.020	SystemCompromised	1.00
	VulnerableSadmind	0.66
	DaemonInstalled	0.80
131.084.001.031	DDoSHappened	0.90

Table 4 shows the detection and false alert rates for RealSecure Network Sensor 6.0. Table 5 shows the experiment results of our approach. We separated them into two tables because our approach presents different information.

Table 4. Detection Rate (DR) and False Alert Rates (FAR) for RealSecure Network Sensor 6.0: AD = Attacks Detected; RA = Real Attacks

Dataset	# of Attacks	# of Alerts	# of AD	DR	# of RA	FAR
DMZ	89	891	51	57.30%	57	93.60%
Inside	60	922	37	61.67%	44	95.23%

Table 5. Detection and False Positive Rates (FPR) for HCPN-ACU: CR = Compromised Resources; T = True; D = Detected

Dataset	# of CR	# of CR Shown	# of D CR	Detect Rate	# of T CR	FPR
DMZ	12	15	12	100.00%	12	20%
Inside	13	12	12	92.31%	12	0%

We counted the numbers in Table 4 the same way as what Ning et. al. did [28]. When counting the compromised resources in Table 5, we noticed that the attacker tried Sadmind_Amslverify_Overflow towards the targets 172.016.114.010, 172.016.114.020, and 172.016.114.030. No additional attacks were carried out against these hosts. This suggests that the Sadmind_Amslverify_Overflow attacks were failed. However, since our rules indicate that the consequence of the Sadmind_Amslverify_Overflow attack is SystemCompromised, our HCPN-ACU would report that these hosts are compromised. In our calculation, we considered these reports as false positives. These false positives might be eliminated by using the system configuration information in the prerequisites.

From Table 4 and 5, we can clearly observe that HCPN-ACU can reduce the number of "alerts" presented to the administrators and active reactors, improve the detect rate, and reduce the false positive rate.

6   Conclusions and Future Work

In this paper, we described a novel framework named HCPN-ACU for the alert correlation and understanding task. We showed that HCPN-ACU has the following features:

- It combines alert fusion and intention recognition in one system.
- It presents resources compromised to show the progress of an attack instead of alerts themselves. Since the number of resources compromised are much smaller than the number of alerts generated, HCPN-ACU can reduce the number of alerts shown to the administrators and active reactors.
- It can reduce false positives with a special transition named "normal action". In the inference process, false positives are automatically associated with this transition.
- It can reduce the false negatives because later alerts would increase the probability that a missing action has happened.
- It provides confidence scores to the detection result by assigning probabilities to each mark indicating how likely an attacker has compromised a resource.
- The inference process is very efficient and the HCPN can be organized in layers to scale up. This makes it applicable in real world systems.

We perceive three weaknesses of HCPN-ACU. First, it requires the knowledge of the alerts and the system to be protected. For large networks, complete system information may not be easily available. Second, it requires training data to learn the system parameters. Training data might be difficult to get in real system. Third, a careful intruder may fool the system by carrying out specially designed steps.

Our system can be improved in the following two areas:

- **Experiments on alerts from multiple sources**: Our current experiments are carried out on DMZ and inside network traffics separately. It would be interesting to see the results using the information from both sources.
- **Detection of coordinated attacks**: One of the major assumptions in the current framework (and all other intention recognition based approaches) is that no attacks are cooperative. This may not be true when sophisticated attacks happen. To eliminate this assumption, we plan to integrate attacker correlation into the HCPN.

References

1. D. Armstrong, S. Carter, G. Frazier, T. Frazier: A Controller-Based Autonomic Defense System. Proc. of DARPA Information Survivability Conference and Exposition (DISCEX), 2003
2. J. Allen, A. Christie, W. Fithen, J. McHugh, J. Pickel, and E. Stoner: State of the Practice of Intrusion Detection Technologies. Technical Report CMU/SEI-99-TR-028, 1999
3. J.P Anderson: Computer Security Threat Monitoring and Surveillance. Technical report, James P Anderson Co., Fort Washington, Pennsylvania, April 1980
4. S. Axelsson: The base-rate fallacy and its implications for the difficulty of intrusion detection. In 6th ACM Conference on computer and communications security, pp 1-7, November 1999
5. D. Barbara, S. Jajodia: Applications of Data Mining in Computer Security. Kluwer Academic Pub, June 2002
6. R. C. de Boer: A Generic Architecture for Fusion-Based Intrusion Detection Systems. Master Thesis, Erasmus University Rotterdam, October 2002
7. F. Cuppens, F. Autrel, A. Miège and S. Benferhat: Correlation in an intrusion detection process. Internet Security Communication Workshop (SECI'02), Septembre 2002
8. F. Cuppens, A. Miège: Alert Correlation in a Cooperative Intrusion Detection Framework. IEEE Symposium on Security and Privacy, May 2002
9. F. Cuppens: Managing Alerts in a Multi-Intrusion Detection Environment. In 17th Annual Computer Security Applications Conference, New-Orleans, USA, December 2001
10. H. Debar and A. Wespi: Aggregation and Correlation of Intrusion-Detection Alerts. In Proceedings of the 4th International Symposium on Recent Advances in Intrusion detection (RAID), 2001.
11. D. Frincke, D. Tobin, and Y. Ho: Planning, Petri Nets, and Intrusion Detection. In Proceedings of the 21st National Information Systems Security Conference (NISSC'98), 1998
12. C. Geib and R. Goldman: Plan Recognition in Intrusion Detection Systems. In DARPA Information Survivability Conference and Exposition (DISCEX), June 2001
13. R. P. Goldman, W. Heimerdinger, S. Harp, C. W. Geib, V. Thomas, and R. Carter: Information Modeling for Intrusion Report Aggregation. In Proceedings of the DARPA Information Survivability Conference and Exposition (DISCEX), June 2001
14. J. Haines, D. K. Ryder, L. Tinnel, S. Taylor: Validation of Sensor Alert Correlators. IEEE Security and Privacy, January-February 2003 (Vol. 1, No. 1) pp. 46-56
15. M.-Y. Huang, and T. M. Wicks: A Large-scale Distributed Intrusion Detection Framework Based on Attack Strategy Analysis. Web proceedings of the First International Workshop on Recent Advances in Intrusion Detection (RAID'98), 1998
16. K. Ilgun, R. Kemmerer, and P. Porras: State Transition Analysis: A Rule-Based Intrusion Detection System. IEEE Transactions on Software Engineering, 21(3), Mar. 1995
17. K. Julisch and M. Dacier: Mining intrusion detection alarms for actionable knowledge. In Proceedings of the 8th ACM International Conference on Knowledge Discovery and Data Mining, pp 366-375, July 2002

18. K. Jensen: An Introduction to the Theoretical Aspects of Coloured Petri Nets. In J.W. de Bakker, W.-P. de Roever, G. Rozenberg (eds.): A Decade of Concurrency, Lecture Notes in Computer Science vol. 803, Springer-Verlag 1994, pp230-272
19. K. Jensen: Colored Petri-Nets–Basic Concepts, Analysis Methods, and Practical Use, 2nd ed. New York: Springer-Verlag, 1996, vol. 1.
20. K. Julisch: Mining Alarm Clusters to Improve Alarm Handling Efficiency. In Proceedings of the 17th ACSAC, New Orleans, December 2001
21. L. M. Kristensen, S. Christensen, K. Jensen: The practitioner's guide to coloured Petri nets. Int. Journal on Software Tools for Technology Transfer, 2 (1998), Springer-Verlag, pp98-132
22. S. Kumar and E.H. Spafford: A Pattern-Matching Model for Intrusion Detection. Proceedings of the National Computer Security Conference, 1994
23. S. Kumar and E. Spafford: A Pattern Matching Model for Misuse Intrusion Detection. In 17th National Computer Security Conference, 1994
24. Lincoln Lab, MIT. DARPA 2000 intrusion detection evaluation datasets. http://ideval.ll.mit.edu/2000 index.html, 2000.
25. T. Moon: The Expectation-Maximization algorithm. IEEE Signal Processing Magazine, pp. 47–60, Nov. 1996
26. P. Ning, Y. Cui, D. S. Reeves: Analyzing Intensive Intrusion Alerts Via Correlation. In Proceedings of the 5th International Symposium on Recent Advances in Intrusion Detection (RAID 2002), LNCS 2516, pp 74-94, October 2002
27. P. Ning, Y. Cui, D. S. Reeves: Constructing Attack Scenarios through Correlation of Intrusion Alerts. In Proceedings of the 9th ACM Conference on Computer & Communications Security, pp 245-254, November 2002
28. P. Ning, D. S. Reeves, Y. Cui: Correlating Alerts Using Prerequisites of Intrusions. Technical Report, TR-2001-13, North Carolina State University, Department of Computer Science, December 2001
29. P. A. Porras,M. W. Fong, and A. Valdes: A Mission-Impact-Based Approach to INFOSEC Alarm Correlation. Proceedings Recent Advances in Intrusion Detection. October, 2002. Pp 95-114
30. P. A. Porras and P. G. Neumann: EMERALD: Event Monitoring Enabling Responses to Anomalous Live Disturbances. 1997 National Information Systems Security Conference, October, 1997
31. J. S. Simonoff: Smoothing Methods in Statistics. Springer-Verlag, 1998
32. S. J. Templeton, K. Levitt: A requires/provides model for computer attacks. Proceedings of the 2000 workshop on New security paradigms, Pp 31-38, 2001
33. A. Valdes and K. Skinner: Probabilistic Alert Correlation. In Proceedings of the 4th International Symposium on Recent Advances in Intrusion Detection (RAID) 2001
34. N. Ye, X. Li, Q. Chen, S. M. Emran, and M. Xu: Probabilistic techniques for intrusion detection based on computer audit data. IEEE Transactions on Systems, Man, and Cybernetics, Vol. 31, No. 4, 2001, pp. 266-274
35. N. Ye, J. Giordano, J. Feldman, and Q. Zhong: Information Fusion Techniques for Network Intrusion Detection. 1998 IEEE InformationTechnology Conference, Information Environment for the Future, 1998.

An Improved Algorithm for $uP + vQ$ Using $\mathrm{JSF}_3^{1\star}$

BaiJie Kuang, YueFei Zhu, and YaJuan Zhang

Network Engineering Department Information Engineering University,
Zhengzhou, 450002, P.R.China
{kbj123,zyf0136,springzyj}@sina.com

Abstract. Techniques for fast exponentiation (multiplication) in various groups have been extensively studied for use in cryptographic primitives. Specifically the joint expression of two exponents (multipliers) plays an important role in the performances of the algorithms used. The crucial optimization relies in general on minimizing the joint Hamming weight of the exponents (multipliers).

J.A.Solinas suggested an optimal signed binary representation for pairs of integers, which is called a Joint Sparse Form (JSF) [25]. JSF is at most one bit longer than the binary expansion of the larger of the two integers, and the average joint Hamming density among Joint Sparse Form representations is $1/2$.

This paper extends the Joint Sparse Form by using a window method, namely, presents a new representation for pairs of integers, which is called Width-3 Joint Sparse Form (JSF$_3$), and proves that the representation is at most one bit longer than the binary expansion of the larger of the two integers and its average joint Hamming density is 37.1% via the method of stochastic process. So, Computing the form of $uP + vQ$ by using JSF$_3$ is almost 8.6% faster than that by using JSF.

1 Introduction

Known to all, the design of the Public Key Cryptosystem mostly depends on the particular algebra construction. The basic public-key operation in a finite field F_q is to compute g^a for a given element $g \in F_q$ and a positive integer a. This is typically accomplished by the the binary method [6], based on the binary expansion of a. The method requires $\sim l/2$ general multiplications and $\sim l$ squarings (on average). ($l = \lceil \log_2 q \rceil$).

More generally, it is needed to evaluate expressions of the form $g^a h^b$. In particular, most common digital signatures (RSA,ECDSA) are verified by evaluating an expression of the above. This is typically accomplished by the Straus' Methods [5,6,2]. The method requires $\sim l$ general multiplications and $\sim l$ squarings (on average). After then, numerous methods of speeding up scalar multiplication have been discussed in the literature; for a survey, see [8].

$\star$ This work was supported by NSF(No.90204015), Found 973(No.G1999035804), and Elitist Youth Foundation of HeNan Province(No.021201400) in China.

M. Jakobsson, M. Yung, J. Zhou (Eds.): ACNS 2004, LNCS 3089, pp. 467–478, 2004.

While on general Elliptic Curve $E(F_q), P = (x, y) \in E(F_q)$, then $-P = (x, -y)$. Thus point subtraction is as efficient as addition. This property motivates using a signed binary expansion (allowing coefficients 0 and ± 1). A particularly useful signed digit representation is the non–adjacent form (NAF) [3,24]. By using a window method, one processes some other signed digit representation, called the width–w nonadjacent form (NAF_w) [1,3,8,24]. (when w=2, NAF_w is equivalent to NAF). There is a simply and efficient algorithm for presenting NAF_w of any integer. When computing kP, the method requires $\sim l/(w + 1)$ general point additions and $\sim l$ doubles.

Furthermore, many Elliptic Curve Cryptosystems require the computation of the form $uP+vQ$, where P, Q are points on an elliptic curve and u, v are integers, such as verification schemes of ECDSA [10]. In the following, we will call this form multi scalar multiplications. So the efficiency of implementation depends mostly on the efficiency of evaluation of multi scalar multiplications. Thus, fast multi scalar multiplications is essential for Elliptic Curve Cryptosystems. There are lots of research papers on the problem of speeding up $uP + vQ$ in the recent years [1,2,3,7,8,12,16,21,25,26].

Computing the form $uP + vQ$, J.A.Solinas [25] suggested an optimal signed binary representation for pairs of integers, called Joint Sparse Form (JSF). There is an algorithm to product JSF for pairs of integers. And it is at most one bit longer than the binary expansion of the larger of the two integers, and the average joint Hamming density among Joint Sparse Form representations is 1/2.

In [25], Solinas remarks that a generalization would allow coefficients other than ± 1. Avanzi [1] presents an analogue of JSF with windows, whose average joint Hamming density is 3/8.

This paper also extends the JSF by using some other signed digit representation of integers and presents the concept of the form representation of integers, and brings forward Width–3 Joint Sparse Form (JSF_3). At last it also proves the average joint Hamming density (AJHD) is 37.1% via the method of stochastic process. So, this improvement can speed the computation of the form $uP + vQ$ by up to 8.6%, compared to compute that by using JSF. Computing $uP + vQ$ by using JSF_3 wins that by using the other previous forms.

The rest of the paper is organized as follows. In Section 2, we briefly review elliptic curves and give some preparation knowledge on the representation of integers. Section 3 first gives the definition of JSF_3 for pairs of positive integers u_1, u_2, then proves its existence, i.e. presents an algorithm for producing it, and last shows AJHD of that is 37.1% via stochastic process. Section 4 gives the application of the technique and discusses avenues for further work.

2   Preparation Knowledge

2.1   Elliptic Curves

Up to a birational equivalence, an *elliptic curve* over a field **K** is a plane nonsingular cubic curve with a **K**–rational point [22]. Elliptic curves are often expressed

in terms of Weierstraß equations:
$$E/\mathbf{K} : y^2 + a_1xy + a_3y = x^3 + a_2x^2 + a_4x + a_6.$$
where $a_1, \cdots, a_6 \in \mathbf{K}$. If characteristic Char $(\mathbf{K}) \neq 2, 3$, the equation may be simplified to $y^2 = x^3 + a_4x + a_6$, and if Char$(\mathbf{K})=2$ the equation (for a non-supersingular curve) may be simplified to $y^2 + xy = x^3 + a_2x^2 + a_6$.

Together with an extra point $\mathcal{O}$, the points on an elliptic curve form an Abelian group. We use the additive notation. The scalar multiplication is the form:

$$kP = \underbrace{P + P + \cdots + P}_{k \ times}.$$

And multi scalar multiplications is the form $uP + vQ$. The crucial optimization relies in general on minimizing the joint Hamming weight of the two multipliers.

2.2   Expansion of Integer

A given nonegative integer n has a common binary expansion
$$n = (a_{l-1}, \cdots, a_1, a_0) = \sum_{i=0}^{l-1} a_i2^i, \quad a_i = 0, 1.$$
and integer n has another binary expansion
$$n = (b_{t-1}, \cdots, b_1, b_0) = \sum_{i=0}^{t-1} b_i2^i, \quad b_i \in \{0, \pm1, \pm3, \cdots, \pm(2^{w-1} - 1)\}, (w > 0).$$

We call it the width–w generalized (binary) expansion form of n (GF$_w$). Obviously, there are many such expansions. We say that GF$_w$ is *reduced* if the expansion has the property that the product of any w consecutive terms is nonegative. More, the reduced GF$_w$ is width–w non adjacent form (NAF$_w$) if the expansion has the property that there is at most a nonzero term of any w consecutive terms. We know, every integer has unique NAF$_w$ [3,24]. There is also a simple and efficient algorithm for computing the NAF$_w$ of a given integer. The NAF$_w$ of a positive integer is at most one bit longer than its binary expansion, and the NAF$_w$ has the minimal Hamming weight among GF$_w$s of n. Namely, The average Hamming density among NAF$_w$ is $1/(w + 1)$ [3,24].

Let n be a positive integer, the notation "$n \ mods8$" denotes that the modular reduction 8 is to return the smallest residue in absolute value. Correspondingly for Width–3 generalized expansion of $n, n = (a_{l-1}, \cdots, a_1, a_0)$, obviously, $a_0 = 0$ if n is an even number; and if n is an odd number, then
$$a_0 \in \{ n \ mods8, \ (n + 4) \ mods8, \ -(n \ mods8), \ -((n + 4) \ mods8) \}.$$
So, we may call a_0

Fetching-Original-Value of n (FOV(n)), if $a_0 = n \ mods8$;
Fetching-Anti-Value of n (FAV(n)),   if $a_0 = (n + 4) \ mods8$;
Fetching-Sign-Value of n (FSV(n)),   if $a_0 = -(n \ mods8)$;
Fetching-Number-Value of n (FNV(n)), if $a_0 = -((n + 4) \ mods8)$.

Example 1: For an integer $n=13$, $n = (a_{l-1}, \cdots, a_0)$.
   If $a_0 = n \ mods8$, namely, $a_0 = -3$, then $n=(1,0,0,0,-3)$, a_0=FOV(n).
   If $a_0 = (n + 4) \ mods8$, namely, $a_0 = 1$, then $n=(1,0,-1,0,1)$, a_0=FAV(n).

If $a_0 = -(n \bmod 8)$, namely, $a_0 = 3$, then $n=(1,0,1,3)$, $a_0=\text{FSV}(n)$.
If $a_0 = -((n+4) \bmod 8)$, namely, $a_0 = -1$, then $n=(1,0,3,-1)$, $a_0=\text{FNV}(n)$.

From the example above, we can draw that:

Lemma 1. For an integer n, $n = (a_{l-1}, \cdots, a_0)$, we can have that:

If $a_0=\text{FOV}(n)$, then $a_1 = 0, a_2 = 0$.
If $a_0=\text{FAV}(n)$, then $a_1 = 0, a_2 \neq 0$.
If $a_0=\text{FSV}(n)$ or $a_0=\text{FNV}(n)$, then $a_1 \neq 0$.

Definition 1. (joint Hamming weight (JHW)) [26] Let n_0, n_1 be two l–bit elements of N. Considering the $2 \times l$ array whose rows are the signed expansions of the elements, we say that the joint Hamming weight (JHW) of n_0 and n_1 with the expansions form is the number of nonzero columns of the array and denote JHW of n_0, n_1 by $\text{JHW}(n_0, n_1)$ (JHW for short). The average joint Hamming density (AJHD) is the ratio of $\text{JHW}(n_0, n_1)$ to its length, where n_0, n_1 run over l–bit elements N.

2.3   JSF for Pairs of Integers

Computing the form $uP + vQ$, J.A.Solinas [25] suggested an optimal signed binary representation for pairs of integers, called Joint Sparse Form (JSF). The expansion takes on the following properties:

(JSF–1.) Among three consecutive columns at least one is a double zero.
(JSF–2.) It is never the case that $u_{i,j+1} \cdot u_{i,j} \neq -1$.
(JSF–3.) If $u_{i,j+1} \cdot u_{i,j} \neq 0$, then $u_{1-i,j} = 0, u_{1-i,j+1} \neq 0$.

There is an algorithm to product JSF for arbitrary pairs of integers. JSF is at most one bit longer than the binary expansion of the larger of the two integers, and the average joint Hamming density among Joint Sparse Form representations is $1/2$.

3   JSF. for Pairs of Integers

We call the joint width–3 generalized expansions for integers n_0, n_1 the width 3–joint generalized expansion form of n_0, n_1 (JGF$_3$). More, we call it the reduced width–3 generalized expansion form of n_0, n_1 (JRF$_3$) if both are reduced. Analogically, call it the joint NAF$_3$ (JNF$_3$). It isn't difficult to see that JHW of JNF$_3$ is quite smaller, but it is not the smallest among all JGF$_3$s. Thereinafter, we give the expansion that is quite small among JGF$_3$s, whose AJHD is 37.1%, while that of JNF$_3$ is 43.8%.

Definition 2. The joint width–3 generalized expansion for integers n_0, n_1,
$$n_0 = (u_{0,m-1}, \cdots, u_{0,1}, u_{0,0}).$$
$$n_1 = (u_{1,m-1}, \cdots, u_{1,1}, u_{1,0}).$$

is called Width–3 Joint Sparse Form ($JSF_3(n_0, n_1)$), shortly noted by JSF_3, if the expansion satisfies the following conditions:

(**JSF_3–1.**) Of any three consecutive columns, at least one is zero,and of any five consecutive columns, at least two are zeros.

(**JSF_3–2.**) For every row, the product of adjacent terms is not -1.

(**JSF_3–3.**) If $\exists i \in \{0, 1\}$ satisfies $u_{i,j} \neq 0$, $u_{i,j+1} \neq 0$,then, $u_{1-i,j+1} \neq 0$, and $u_{1-i,j} = 0$.

(**JSF_3–4.**) If $\exists i \in \{0, 1\}$ satisfies $u_{i,j} \neq 0$, $u_{i,j+2} \neq 0$, then $u_{1-i,j+2} \neq 0$.

Example 2. For two integers $n_0 = 2365$ and $n_1 = 2921$, we have the JSF_3 shown below:

$$n_0 = (\ 1, 0, 0, 0, 1, 3, 0, 0, 0, 0, 0,\text{-}3).$$
$$n_1 = (\ 1, 1, 0, 0,\text{-}1, 0, 0, 0,\text{-}3, 0, 0, 1).$$

3.1   The Existence of JSF_3 for Pairs of Integers

Algorithm 1. (JSF_3)

Input: Nonnegative integers n_0, n_1, not both zero.

Output: JSF_3 for integers n_0, n_1

$$n_0 = (u_{0,m-1}, \cdots, u_{0,1}, u_{0,0})$$
$$n_1 = (u_{1,m-1}, \cdots, u_{1,1}, u_{1,0}), u_{i,j} \in \{0, \pm 1, \pm 3\}, i = 0, 1, 0 \leq j < m.$$

Set $k_0 \leftarrow n_0$, $k_1 \leftarrow k_1$
Set $j \leftarrow 0$
While $k_0 > 0$ or $k_1 > 0$ do
  For i from 0 to 1 do
    If k_i is even, then $u \leftarrow 0$
    Else
       $u \leftarrow \text{FOV}(k_i)$
      If k_{1-i} is even, then
        If $k_{1-i} \bmod 8 = 4$, then $u \leftarrow \text{FAV}(k_i)$
        If $k_{1-i} \bmod 4 = 2$ and $k_i \bmod 32 = \pm 1, \pm 3$,   then $u \leftarrow \text{FNV}(k_i)$
        If $k_{1-i} \bmod 4 = 2$ and $k_i \bmod 32 = \pm 5, \pm 11$,   then $u \leftarrow \text{FSV}(k_i)$
        If $k_{1-i} \bmod 4 = 2$ and $k_i \bmod 32 = \pm 13, \pm 15$, then $u \leftarrow \text{FSV}(k_i)$
        If $k_{1-i} \bmod 32 = \pm 2, \pm 6$ and $k_i \bmod 32 = \pm 7$, then $u \leftarrow \text{FSV}(k_i)$
        If $k_{1-i} \bmod 32 = \pm 2, \pm 6$ and $k_i \bmod 32 = \pm 9$, then $u \leftarrow \text{FNV}(k_i)$
        If $k_{1-i} \bmod 32 = \pm 10, \pm 14$ and $k_i \bmod 32 = \pm 7$, then $u \leftarrow \text{FNV}(k_i)$
        If $k_{1-i} \bmod 32 = \pm 10, \pm 14$ and $k_i \bmod 32 = \pm 9$, then $u \leftarrow \text{FSV}(k_i)$
      Else
        If $k_i \bmod 32 = \pm 13, \pm 15$ and $k_{1-i} \bmod 16 = \pm 5, \pm 7$,
        then $u \leftarrow \text{FAV}(k_i)$
        End If
      If $k_i \bmod 16 = \pm 5, \pm 7$ and $k_{1-i} \bmod 32 = \pm 13, \pm 15$,
      then $u \leftarrow \text{FAV}(k_i)$

     End If
    End If
   End If
   Set $u_{i,j} \leftarrow u$
  Next i
  Set $k_0 \leftarrow (k_0 - u_{0,j})/2, k_1 \leftarrow (k_1 - u_{1,j})/2$
  Set $j \leftarrow j + 1$
EndWhile

In order to prove the desired properties of JSF$_3$, it is necessary to generalize Alg.1 by allowing as inputs JRF$_3$ for pairs of e_0, e_1.

Algorithm 2. (JSF$_3$)

Input: JRF$_3$ for integers e_0, e_1, not both zero.
  $e_0 = (e_{0,m-1}, \cdots, e_{0,1}, e_{0,0})$
  $e_1 = (e_{1,m-1}, \cdots, e_{1,1}, e_{1,0}), e_{i,j} \in \{0, \pm 1, \pm 3\}. i = 0, 1, 0 \le j < m.$
Output: JSF$_3$ for integers e_0, e_1

 Set $j \leftarrow 0$
 Set $d_0 \leftarrow 0, d_1 \leftarrow 0$
 Set $u_{0,-2} \leftarrow 0, u_{0,-1} \leftarrow 0, u_{1,-2} \leftarrow 0, u_{1,-1} \leftarrow 0$
 Set $a_0 \leftarrow e_{0,0}, b_0 \leftarrow e_{0,1}, x_0 \leftarrow e_{0,2}, y_0 \leftarrow e_{0,3}, z_0 \leftarrow e_{0,4}$
 Set $a_1 \leftarrow e_{1,0}, b_1 \leftarrow e_{1,1}, x_1 \leftarrow e_{1,2}, y_1 \leftarrow e_{1,3}, z_1 \leftarrow e_{1,4}$
 Set $k_0 \leftarrow a_0 + 2b_0 + 4x_0 + 8y_0 + 16z_0$
 Set $k_1 \leftarrow a_1 + 2b_1 + 4x_1 + 8y_1 + 16z_1$

 While $k_0 > 0$ or $k_1 > 0$ do
  For i from 0 to 1 do
   If k_i is even then $u \leftarrow 0$
   Else {SIMILAR TO Alg.1}
   End If
   Set $u_{i,j} \leftarrow u$
   Set $\beta_{i,j} \leftarrow (u_{i,j-2}, u_{i,j-1}, d_i, e_{i,j}, e_{i,j+1}, e_{i,j+2}, e_{i,j+3}, e_{i,j+4})$
  Next i
  Set $S_j \leftarrow (\beta_{0,j}, \beta_{1,j})$
  Set $d_0 \leftarrow (d_0 + a_0 - u_{0,j})/2, d_1 \leftarrow (d_1 + a_1 - u_{1,j})/2$
  Set $a_0 \leftarrow b_0, b_0 \leftarrow x_0, x_0 \leftarrow y_0, y_0 \leftarrow z_0, z_0 \leftarrow e_{0,j+5}$
  Set $a_1 \leftarrow b_1, b_1 \leftarrow x_1, x_1 \leftarrow y_1, y_1 \leftarrow z_1, z_1 \leftarrow e_{1,j+5}$
  Set $j \leftarrow j + 1$(if $j > m$, let $e_{i,j} = 0$)
  Set $k_0 \leftarrow d_0 + a_0 + 2b_0 + 4x_0 + 8y_0 + 16z_0$
  Set $k_1 \leftarrow d_1 + a_1 + 2b_1 + 4x_1 + 8y_1 + 16z_1$
 EndWhile

The most straightforward way to prove the existence of JSF$_3$ for every pair of positive integers n_0, n_1 is to present an algorithm to produce it.

It is easy to check that, in the special case in which the $e'_{i,j}$s are "ordinary" unsigned bits, $Alg.2$ is equivalent to $Alg.1$. So the correctness of the $Alg.2$ insures that of the $Alg.1$.

We call the vectors S_j the states of the algorithm, The output vector $(u_{0,j}, u_{1,j})$ is a function of the state S_j. Thus we may describe the action of $Alg.2$ as follows: that j^{th} iteration of the Do loop inputs the state S_{j-1}, outputs $(u_{0,j-1}, u_{1,j-1})$ and changes the state to S_j, namely,

$$S_{j-1} \xrightarrow{(u_{0,j-1}, u_{1,j-1})} S_j.$$

Let $t_{i,j} = d_i + e_{i,j} + 2e_{i,j+1} + 4e_{i,j+2} + 8e_{i,j+3} + 16e_{i,j+4}$.

We next enumerate the possible values for the state and all the states are divided into below 12 cases based on the difference of S_j.

Table 1. State-Table

S_j	$\beta_{i,j}$	$\beta_{1-i,j}$
B_0	$t_{i,j} \equiv 0 \bmod 16$	$t_{1-i,j} \equiv 0 \bmod 16$
B_1	$t_{i,j} \equiv 8 \bmod 16$	$t_{1-i,j} \equiv 0 \bmod 8$
B_2	$t_{i,j} \equiv 4 \bmod 8$	$t_{1-i,j} \equiv 0 \bmod 8$
B_3	$t_{i,j} \equiv 4 \bmod 8$	$t_{1-i,j} \equiv 4 \bmod 8$
B_4	$t_{i,j} \equiv 2 \bmod 4$	$t_{1-i,j} \equiv 0 \bmod 4$
B_5	$t_{i,j} \equiv 2 \bmod 4$	$t_{1-i,j} \equiv 2 \bmod 4$
B_6	$t_{i,j} \equiv 1 \bmod 2$	$t_{1-i,j} \equiv 0 \bmod 2$
B_7	$t_{i,j} \equiv \pm13, \pm15 \bmod 32$	$t_{1-i,j} \equiv \pm5 \bmod 16$
B_8	$t_{i,j} \equiv \pm13, \pm15 \bmod 32$	$t_{1-i,j} \equiv \pm1, \pm3 \bmod 16$
B_9	$t_{i,j} \equiv \pm1, \pm3 \bmod 32$	$t_{1-i,j} \equiv \pm1, \pm3 \bmod 32$
B_{10}	$t_{i,j} \equiv \pm1, \pm3 \bmod 32$	$t_{1-i,j} \equiv \pm5, \pm7 \bmod 16$
B_{11}	$t_{i,j} \equiv \pm5, \pm7 \bmod 16$	$t_{1-i,j} \equiv \pm5, \pm7 \bmod 16$

Table 2. State-Following-Table

S_j	S_{j+1}	S_j	S_{j+1}
B_0	B_0, B_1	B_6	$B_j, j \neq 4, j \neq 6$
B_1	B_2, B_3	B_7	B_5
B_2	B_4	B_8	B_1
B_3	B_5	B_9	B_0
B_4	B_6	B_{10}	B_2
B_5	$B_j, j = 7, \cdots, 11,$	B_{11}	B_3

It is easy to verify the following by checking all the cases. As a result, we have the following values for S_{j+1} for each S_j. All following states are shown in Table 2.

Theorem 1. *Alg*.1 always outputs the Width–3 Joint Sparse Form for its inputs. *Proof.* It is straightforward to verify that the expansion produced by the *Alg*.2 is in fact JGF for n_0, n_1. It remains to prove that this expansion satisfies terms of **Definition 2**. The process is similar to that [25]. And the proof appears in the Appendix A of the paper.

3.2 Efficiency of JSF$_3$ for Pairs of Integers

Now, Our primary task is to prove the AJHD of JSF$_3$ is 37.1%.

It is easy to see that GF$_3$ is at most one bit longer than the ordinary binary expansion. As a result, JSF$_3$ is at most one bit longer than the binary expansion of the larger of the two integers.

Theorem 2. The average joint Hamming density among Joint 3–Sparse Form representations is 37.1%.

Proof. Let state space
$$\Gamma = \{G_i | i = 0, 1, \cdots, 10, 11\}, \text{ where } G_i = B_i, \ i = 0, 1, \cdots, 10, 11.$$

We can prove that a stochastic process $\{S_n | n \geq 0\}$ output by *Alg*.2 takes values in a countable set Γ and is a homogeneous Markov Chain in terms of Γ [see definition in page 252 [9]]. So, let $p_{i,j}$ denote the *transition probabilities* $p_{i,j}(n)$, where $p_{i,j}(n) = P\{S_{n+1} \in G_j | S_n \in G_i\}$. $\{p_{i,j}\}$ forms the following transition matrix P.

$$
P = \begin{bmatrix}
\frac{1}{4} & 0 & \frac{3}{4} & 0 & 0 & 0 & 0 & 0 & 0 & 0 & 0 & 0 \\
0 & 0 & \frac{2}{3} & \frac{1}{3} & 0 & 0 & 0 & 0 & 0 & 0 & 0 & 0 \\
0 & 0 & 0 & 0 & 1 & 0 & 0 & 0 & 0 & 0 & 0 & 0 \\
0 & 0 & 0 & 0 & 0 & 1 & 0 & 0 & 0 & 0 & 0 & 0 \\
0 & 0 & 0 & 0 & 0 & 0 & 1 & 0 & 0 & 0 & 0 & 0 \\
0 & 0 & 0 & 0 & 0 & 0 & 0 & 0 & \frac{1}{4} & \frac{3}{16} & \frac{1}{4} & \frac{1}{4} \\
\frac{1}{64} & \frac{3}{64} & \frac{1}{8} & \frac{1}{16} & 0 & \frac{1}{4} & 0 & \frac{3}{32} & \frac{15}{128} & \frac{5}{32} & \frac{3}{32} & \frac{5}{32} \\
0 & 0 & 0 & 0 & 0 & 1 & 0 & 0 & 0 & 0 & 0 & 0 \\
0 & 1 & 0 & 0 & 0 & 0 & 0 & 0 & 0 & 0 & 0 & 0 \\
1 & 0 & 0 & 0 & 0 & 0 & 0 & 0 & 0 & 0 & 0 & 0 \\
0 & 0 & 1 & 0 & 0 & 0 & 0 & 0 & 0 & 0 & 0 & 0 \\
0 & 0 & 0 & 1 & 0 & 0 & 0 & 0 & 0 & 0 & 0 & 0
\end{bmatrix}
$$

From transition matrix P, for any two states $G_i, G_j \in \Gamma$, the state G_i is equivalent to G_j, so $\{S_n | n \geq 0\}$ is irreducible, and for any G_j, it is nonrecurrent. Therefore, the chain exists *stationary distrubution* $\{\pi_j, G_j \in \Gamma\}$, and $\lim_{m \to \infty}(\frac{1}{m} \sum_{n=1}^{m} p_{i,j}^{(n)}) = \pi_j$, where $p_{i,j}^{(n)} = P\{S_{(m+n)} \in G_j | S_m \in G_i\}, (G_i, G_j \in \Gamma, m \geq 0, n \geq 1)$.

From the equations below, which $\pi_j (j = 0, 1, \cdots, 11)$ satisfies [9],

$$(\pi_0, \pi_1, \cdots, \pi_{11}, 1) = (\pi_0, \pi_1, \cdots, \pi_{11})(P, g^{\perp}).$$

where $g = (1,1,1,1,1,1,1,1,1,1,1,1)$, and the symbol $\perp$ denotes matrix transposition.

We get the solution

$$\left(\frac{4}{163}, \frac{12}{163}, \frac{20}{163}, \frac{16}{163}, \frac{20}{163}, \frac{61}{326}, \frac{20}{163}, \frac{19}{326}, \frac{129}{2608}, \frac{43}{2608}, \frac{19}{326}, \frac{43}{652}\right).$$

Let its absorbing probabilities $p_j(n) = p\{S_n \in G_j\}, j = 0,1,\cdots,11$, and initial distribution probabilities $p_j = p\{S_0 \in G_j\}, j = 0,1,\cdots,11$ of the chain, then the vector of $(u_{0,j}, u_{1,j}) = (0,0)$ is output by $G_j, j = 0,1,\cdots,5$. So AJHD is given by

$$
\begin{aligned}
\Sigma &= \sum_{j=6}^{11} \lim_{m\to\infty} \frac{1}{m} \sum_{n=1}^{m} p_j(n) &&= \sum_{j=6}^{11} \lim_{m\to\infty} \left(\frac{1}{m} \sum_{n=1}^{m} \sum_{G_i \in \Gamma} p_{i,j}^{(n)} p_i\right) \\
&= \sum_{j=6}^{11} \sum_{G_i} p_i \left(\lim_{m\to\infty}\left(\frac{1}{m}\sum_{n=1}^{m} p_{i,j}^{(n)}\right)\right) &&= \sum_{j=6}^{11} \lim_{m\to\infty}\left(\frac{1}{m}\sum_{n=1}^{m} p_{i,j}^{(n)}\right) \\
&= \sum_{j=6}^{11} \pi_j.
\end{aligned}
$$

Therefore $\Sigma = 121/326$. The AJHD of JSF_3 is 37.1% approximately.

4   Applications to ECC

The execution time of ECC schemes such as the ECDSA are typically dominated by point multiplications, In ECDSA, there are two types of point multiplications kP, where P is fixed (signature generation), and $uP + vQ$, where P is fixed and Q is not known a priori (signature verification). Using the above algorithm technique, the latter type can be sped by precomputation some data for points,such as $2P, 2Q, 3P, 3Q, P \pm Q, P \pm 3Q, 3P \pm Q, 3P \pm 3Q$, and storing some data for points such as $P, Q, 3P, 3Q, P \pm Q, P \pm 3Q, 3P \pm Q, 3P \pm 3Q$. Adapting the fast Straus' Method by using JSF_3 yields a technique which requires $\sim l$ doublings and $\sim (0.37)l$ general additions (on average). In other words, that sometimes works almost 8.6% faster than that by using the Joint Sparse Form.

The front type can also be sped. The following is a simplest approach. Suppose that the order r of the private key space is less than l. Let $Q = 2^{(\lfloor l/2\rfloor+1)}P$, then $k = a + b2^{(\lfloor l/2\rfloor+1)}P$, thus compute $k = aP + bQ$, one applies **Alg.1** to generate JSF_3 for integers a, b. This technique of computing it using JSF_3 requires $\sim l$ doublings and $\sim (0.19l)$ additions, which wins over that using JSF.

If the Elliptic Curves are particular curves, as Koblitz Curves, there may be the form with width–3, analogous to JSF_3. So, it would be of interest to construct the forms which apply to Koblitz Curves.

References

1. R. Avanzi. On Multi-exponentiation in Cryptography. 2003, manuscript, Available at http://citeseer.nj.nec.com/545130.html.
2. D. J. Bernstein. Pippenger'2 exponentiation algorithm. Available at: http://cr.rp.to/papers.html,2002.
3. M. Brown, D. Hankerson, J. Lopez and A. Menezes. Software Implementation of NIST Elliptic Curves Over Prime Fields. CACR Technical Reports. CORR 2000-56, University of Waterloo, 2000.
4. R. Crandall. Method and Apparatus for Public Key Exchange in a Cryptographic System. U.S. Patent # 5, 159, 632, Oct 27.1992.
5. H. Cohen. *A Course in Computational Algebraic Number Theory*, Volume 138 of Graduate Texts in Mathematics, Springer, 1996.
6. T. ElGamal. A Public-Key Cryptosystem and a Signature Scheme Based on Discrete logarithms. *IEEE Trans. on Information Theory* IT-31 (1985), pp. 469-472.
7. R. Gallant, R. Lambert and S. Vanstone. Faster Point Multiplication On Elliptic Curves with Efficient Endomorphisms. *Advances in Cryptology – Crypto 2001*, *LNCS*, Volume 2139, Springer-Verlag, pages 190-200, 2001.
8. D.M. Gordon. A Survey of Fast Exponentiation Methods. *Journal of Algorithms*, 27(1):129-146,1998.
9. KaiLai Chung. *Elementary Probability Theory with Stochastic Processes*. Springer-Verlag Berlin Heidelberg New York Toppan Company (S)Pte Ltd. Singapore 1978.
10. IEEEP 1363-2000,(2000). *IEEE standard Specifications for Public-Key Cryptography*. IEEE Computer Society, August 29,2000.
11. D.E. Knuth. *The Art of Computer Programming*. Vol 2: Semi numerical Algorithms 2nd ed., Addison-Wesley,1981.
12. Mathieu Ciet, Tanja Lange. Franceso Sica, and Jean-Jacques Quisquater. Improved Algorithms for Efficient Arithmetic on Elliptic Curves using Fast Endomorphisms. *Advances in Cryptology – Eurocrypt 2003, LNCS*, Volume 2656, Springer-Verlag, pages 388-400, 2003.
13. Neal Koblitz. Elliptic curve cryptosystems. *Mathematics of Computation*, 48(1987), 203-209.
14. Neal Koblitz. CM-Curves with Good Cryptographic Properties. *Advances in Cryptology – Crypto 91, LNCS*, Volume 576, Springer-Verlag, pages 279-287, 1992.
15. V.Miller. Uses of elliptic curves in cryptography. *Advances in Cryptology – Crypto 85, LNCS*, Volume 218, Springer-Verlag, pages 417-426, 1986.
16. F.Morain and J.Olivos. Speeding Up the Computations on an Elliptic Curve Using Addition-Subtraction Chains. *Inform.Theor. Appl.*, Volume 24, pages 531-543, 1990.
17. Willi Meier, Othmar Staffelbach. Efficient Multiplication on Certain Nonsupersingular Elliptic Curves. *Advances in Cryptology – Crypto 92, LNCS*, Volume 740, Springer-Verlag, pages 333-344, 1993.
18. V.Muller. Fast Multiplication on Elliptic Curves over Small Fields of Characteristic Two. *Journal of Cryptology*, 11(4):219-234, 1998.
19. V.Muller. Efficient Point Multiplication for Elliptic Curves over Special Optimal Extension Fields. In Walter de Gruyter, Editor, *Public-Key Cryptography and Computational Number Theory*, pages 197-207, Warschau, Poland, September 11-15, 2000(2001).
20. National Institute of Standards and Technology. *FIPS – 186-2: Digital Signature Standard (DSS)*, January 2000. Available at http://csrc.nist.gov/publications/fips.

21. Y-H. Park, S. Jeong, C. Kim, and J. Lim. An Alternate Decomposition of an Integer for Faster Point Multiplication on Certain Elliptic Curves. *Advances in Crytpology – PKC 2002, LNCS*, Volume 2274, Springer-Verlag, pages 323-334, 2002.

22. J.H. Silverman. *The Arithmetic of Elliptic Curves*, GTM 106, Springer-Verlag, 1986.

23. J. Solinas. An Improved Algorithm for Arithmetic on a Family of Elliptic Curves. *Advances in Cryptology – Crypto 1997, LNCS*, Volume 1294, Springer-Verlag, pages 357-371, 1997.

24. J. Solinas. Efficient Arithmetic on Koblitz Curves. *Designs, Codes and Cryptography*, 19:195-249, 2000.

25. J. Solinas. Low-Weight Binary Representations for Pairs of Integers. CACR Technical Reports, CORR 2001-41 University of Waterloo, 2001, Available at: www.cacr.math.uwaterloo.ca/techreports/2001/corr2001-41.ps, 2001.

26. Yasuyuki Sakai and Kouichi Sakurai. Algorithms for Efficient Simultaneous Elliptic Scalar Multiplication with Reduced Joint Hamming Weight Representation of Scalars, *5th International Conference, ISC 2002, LNCS*, Volume 2443, Springer-Verlag, pages 484-499, 2002.

27. N.P. Smart. Elliptic Curve Cryptosystems over Small Fields of Odd Characteristic. *Journal of Cryptology*, 12(2):141-151, 1999.

Appendix A: The Proof of Theorem 1

Theorem 1. $Alg.1$ always produces the width–3 joint sparse form expression of its inputs.

$Proof$: It is straightforward to verify that the expansion produced by the $Alg.2$ is in fact JGF for n_0, n_1. It remains to prove that this expansion satisfies properties (JSF$_3$–1.), (JSF$_3$–2.), (JSF$_3$–3.), (JSF$_3$–4). From the **Table 1** and **Table 2**, The process that proves the conclusions follows as:

(JSF$_3$–1.): This condition is equivalent to the assertion that, for every j, at least one of S_j, S_{j+1}, S_{j+2} is in one of states B_i, $i = 0, \cdots, 5$, and at least two of $S_j, S_{j+1}, S_{j+2}, S_{j+3}, S_{j+4}$ are in the states B_i, $i = 0, \cdots, 5$. Firstly, we prove that for every j, at least one of S_j, S_{j+1}, S_{j+2} is in one of states B_i, $i = 0, \cdots, 5$. Suppose that S_j isn't in any $B_i, i = 0, \cdots, 5$, then S_j is in states $B_i, i = 6, \cdots, 11$. If S_j is in states B_6, then S_{j+1} or S_{j+2} is in one of states B_i, $i = 0, \cdots, 5$; if S_j is in one of states $B_i, i = 7, \cdots, 11$, then S_{j+1} is in one of states $B_i, i = 1, \cdots, 5$. So S_{j+2} or S_{j+3} is in one of states B_i, $i = 0, \cdots, 5$. Secondly, the process that proves at least two of $S_j, S_{j+1}, S_{j+2}, S_{j+3}, S_{j+4}$ are in the states B_i, $i = 0, \cdots, 5$ is similar to the above.

(JSF$_3$–3.): Might as well, suppose that $u_{0,j} \neq 0, u_{0,j+1} \neq 0$, then it follows from the Table 2 that S_j is in the states B_6 and S_{j+1} is in one of states $B_i, i = 7, \cdots, 11$. It is straightforward to compute and to verify that $u_{1,j+1} \neq 0$, $u_{1,j} = 0$.

(JSF$_3$–4.): Might as well, suppose that $u_{0,j} \neq 0, u_{0,j+2} \neq 0$, then S_j is in one of states B_6, B_7, and S_{j+1} is in the state B_5, and S_{j+2} is in the state $B_i, i = 7, \cdots, 11$. It is straightforward to compute and to verify that $u_{1,j+2} \neq 0$.

(JSF$_3$–2.): Might as well, suppose that $u_{0,j} \neq 0, u_{0,j+1} \neq 0$, then S_j is in the states B_6 and S_{j+1} is in one of states $B_i, i = 7, \cdots, 11$. Suppose $u_{0,j} \cdot u_{0,j+1} = -1$, then $u_{0,j} = 1, u_{0,j+1} = -1$, or $u_{0,j} = -1, u_{0,j+1} = 1$, $t_{0,j}$ mod 8=± 1. So $u_{0,j}$ only fetches FSV ($t_{0,j}$), and $t_{0,j} = \pm 1, \pm 7, \pm 9, \pm 15$ mod 32. Thus, according to the **Alg.1** the conditions that may be satisfies $u_{0,j} \cdot u_{0,j+1} = -1$ shown as following,

(1.) $t_{0,j} = \pm 7$ mod 32 and $t_{1,j} = \pm 2, \pm 6$ mod 32.

(2.) $t_{0,j} = \pm 9$ mod 32 and $t_{1,j} = \pm 10, \pm 14$ mod 32.

(3.) $t_{0,j} = \pm 15$ mod 32 and $t_{1,j} = \pm 2, \pm 6$ mod 16.

If $t_{0,j} = \pm 7$ mod 32 and $t_{1,j} = \pm 2, \pm 6$ mod 32, then $u_{0,j} = \pm 1, u_{0,j+1} = \pm 3$, so it is not correct.

Similarly, if $t_{0,j} = \pm 9$ mod 32 and $t_{1,j} = \pm 10, \pm 14$ mod 32, then $u_{0,j} = \pm 1, u_{0,j+1} = \pm 3$, so it is not correct.

Similarly, if $t_{0,j} = \pm 15$ mod 32 and $t_{1,j} = \pm 2, \pm 6$ mod 16, then $u_{0,j} = \pm 1, u_{0,j+1} = \pm 3$, so it is also not correct.

Therefore, there is not the condition which satisfies the $u_{0,j} \cdot u_{0,j+1} = -1$. Namely, $u_{0,j} \cdot u_{0,j+1} \neq -1$.

New Table Look-Up Methods for Faster Frobenius Map Based Scalar Multiplication over $GF(p^n)$

Palash Sarkar, Pradeep Kumar Mishra, and Rana Barua

Cryptology Research Group,
Indian Statistical Institute, 203 B T Road,
Kolkata-700108, INDIA

Abstract. We describe a new scalar multiplication algorithm for elliptic and hyperelliptic curve cryptosystems. The algorithm is obtained by combining Koblitz's idea of using Frobenius automorphism along with a very special kind of look-up table. In the case where the base point is unknown, we present an efficient algorithm to compute the look-up table online. Our algorithm applies to prime power fields $GF(p^n)$. One important subclass of such fields are Optimal Extension Fields (OEF's) which are believed to be ideal for efficient implementation of cryptographic primitives. Over prime power fields, our algorithm compares favourably to other known algorithms for scalar multiplication.

Keywords: Scalar multiplication, Frobenius map, elliptic curves, hyperelliptic curves, window methods, look-up table, normal basis.

1 Introduction

Elliptic and hyperelliptic curves provide a rich source of cyclic groups over which the discrete logarithm problem is believed to be hard. Hence these groups are suitable for defining public key cryptosystems. The dominant operation in any such cryptosystem is the so called *scalar multiplication*, which is the operation of computing mX, where m is an integer and X is either a point of an elliptic curve or a reduced divisor in the Jacobian of a hyperelliptic curve.

The efficiency of an elliptic or hyperelliptic curve cryptosystem is crucially dependent on the speed of scalar multiplication. Not surprisingly, this has led to a tremendous research in algorithms for fast scalar multiplication. These algorithms fall naturally into two classes.

- General algorithms which work for any cyclic group.
- Algorithms which exploit the algebraic properties of elliptic and hyperelliptic curves.

One of the most important technique of the second kind is the use of endomorphisms to speed up scalar multiplication. This was first proposed by Koblitz [13] and has also been studied by later authors (for example see [4,5,7,10,14,23,24]).

M. Jakobsson, M. Yung, J. Zhou (Eds.): ACNS 2004, LNCS 3089, pp. 479–493, 2004.

The most natural endomorphism is the Frobenius automorphism and was initially proposed by Koblitz [13]. A series of research papers have resulted in the applicability of the Frobenius map technique to elliptic and hyperelliptic curves over any finite field. See [14] for a more detailed description of the development of this technique.

Let F_q be the underlying field. The Frobenius map technique (and hence our algorithm) really applies when the q is a prime power (rather than a prime). The case $p = 2$ has been explored extensively by the researcher community. Our algorithms apply to the case $p > 2$, for example, for Optimal Extension Fields. Optimal Extension Fields (OEF's) are finite fields of the form $GF(p^m)$, $p > 2$, where p and m are chosen to match the underlying hardware. OEF's, optimally utilising the underlying hardware offer considerable advantage in software implementations of elliptic curve cryptosystems. In prime power fields, of which OEF's are special cases, our algorithm provides a substantial reduction in the number of point arithmetic (addition/doubling) operations as compared to other existing algorithms.

In this work, we concentrate on developing a new scalar multiplication algorithm based on the Frobenius map. The basic idea of the algorithm is known and has been described for both elliptic curves [10,24,23] and hyperelliptic curves [4, 14]. The principle innovation that we introduce is a very special kind of look-up table. Given a point X, we define a look-up table Tab_X in the following manner: The table stores 3^h points and for $(a_0, \ldots, a_{h-1}) \in \{0, \pm1\}^h$, we define $\mathsf{Tab}_X[a_0, \ldots, a_{h-1}]$ to be the point

$$\mathsf{Tab}_X[a_0, \ldots, a_{h-1}] = a_0 X + a_1 \phi(X) + \cdots + a_{h-1}\phi^{h-1}(X) \qquad (1)$$

where ϕ is the Frobenius map. This is a simple idea. Aoki et al [1] have worked on similar lines for elliptic curves. A proper utilization of this idea provides a substantial reduction in the number of point arithmetic operations.We also extend the idea to the situation when $\{a_0, \ldots, a_{h-1}\} \in \{0, \pm1, \pm2, \ldots, \pm2^w\}^h$ for some $w > 0$. The table can be precomputed and stored when the point X is known in advance. However, there are applications where the point X is not known in advance. We present an algorithm to compute Tab_X in such a situation. It turns out that by using a simple trick, it is possible to reduce the number of point additions needed to compute Tab_X.

The size of the look-up table is determined by the number of points to be stored. In the case, where the underlying field is represented using normal basis, the number of points required to be stored is quite small. However, if polynomial basis representation of the field elements are used, then the storage requirement increases. Thus our algorithm is most useful when the underlying field is represented using normal basis.

The plan of the paper is as follows. In Section 2, we present the necessary preliminaries. Section 3 describes the basic idea of the table look-up algorithm. This is developed into a general look-up table based algorithm to compute scalar multiplication in Section 4. In Section 5, we describe algorithms to compute the look-up tables online. Section 6presents a detailed discussion on the results obtained and compares the performance of the algorithm to other scalar multiplication algorithms. Finally, Section 7 concludes the paper.

2 Preliminaries

Let K be a field and $\overline{K}$ be the algebraic closure of K. A *hyperelliptic curve* C of genus g over K is an equation of the form $C : v^2 + h(u)v = f(u)$ where $h(u)$ in $K[u]$ is a polynomial of degree at most g, $f(u)$ in $K[u]$ is a monic polynomial of degree $2g + 1$, and there are no solutions (u, v) in $\overline{K} \times \overline{K}$, which simultaneously satisfy the equations

$$\left. \begin{array}{l} v^2 + h(u)v \quad = f(u); \\ 2v + h(u) \quad\quad = 0; \\ h'(u)v - f'(u) = 0. \end{array} \right\} \tag{2}$$

Elliptic curves are hyperelliptic curves of genus 1. If L is any extension field of K, then the set of all L-rational points of C is the set $\{(x, y) \in L \times L : y^2 + h(x)y = f(x)\} \bigcup \{\infty\}$ where ∞ is a special point called the point at infinity. The set of L-rational points of an elliptic curve form a group under a suitably defined addition operation. On the other hand, for $g > 1$, the set of points on a hyperelliptic curve does not form a group. Instead it is customary to consider the free abelian group generated by the set of points. Elements of this group are called divisors. The set of certain special kinds of divisors called *reduced divisors* form an additive group.

The additive group of the set of points of an elliptic curve has been used to obtain ElGamal type cryptosystems. Similarly, the group of reduced divisors of hyperelliptic curves has also been proposed for such types of cryptosystems [11]. One of the most important structures for practical applications is the binary Koblitz curves, which are elliptic curves over the binary field.

In the rest of the paper by a *point* we will mean either a point on an elliptic curve or a reduced divisor of an hyperelliptic curve. The main operation for realizing elliptic and hyperelliptic curve cryptosystems is mX, where m is an integer and X is a point. This operation is called *scalar multiplication*. Our focus in this paper will be to obtain efficient algorithms for scalar multiplication.For details of elliptic and hyperelliptic curve cryptosystems we refer the reader to [11, 17,3].

2.1 Prime Power Fields

For cryptographic applications, binary fields $GF(2^n)$ and prime fields $GF(p)$ were considered most attractive for software implementations. Later Optimal Extension Fields (OEF's) [2], a special class of finite fields of the form $GF(p^m)$ were proposed, where p and m were chosen suitably to exploit the underlying hardware optimally for performance gain. An OEF is a finite field of the form $GF(p^n)$, where (i) p is a pseudo-Mersenne prime and (ii) an irreducible binomial $P(x) = x^n - \omega$ exists over $GF(p)$. The prime p is generally chosen to be very close to the word size of the processor, so that each machine word can accomodate one element of the subfield $GF(p)$ and each element of the OEF $GF(p^n)$, can be accomodated in n words, with minimum wastage of memory. Also, OEF's allow efficient modular reduction for arithmetic in the extension field. The algorithms proposed in this work are suitable for the prime power fields of type $GF(p^n)$, which contains the OEF's as a subclass of it.

2.2   Normal Basis

Let q be a prime power. A field F_{q^n} is said to have a normal basis if it has a basis (over F_q) of the form $\{\alpha, \alpha^q, \cdots, \alpha^{q^{n-1}}\}$. Any element of the field can be represented as $x = \sum_{j=0}^{n-1} a_j \alpha^{q^j}$ or briefly as an ordered n-tuple $x = (a_0, \cdots, a_{n-1})$. In the field F_{q^n}, we have, $x^q = (\sum_{j=0}^{n-1} a_j \alpha^{q^j})^q = (\sum_{j=0}^{n-1} a_j \alpha^{q^{j+1}})$. Thus if x is represented by the tuple $(a_0, \cdots, a_{n-1})$ then x^q is represented by $(a_{n-1}, a_0, \cdots, a_{n-2})$, as $\alpha^{q^n} = 1$. With a normal basis representation of elements, x^q can be computed from x by a circular shift operation only. See [16] for more details on normal basis.

2.3   Frobenius Map

Let F_q be a finite field. The Frobenius map $\phi : F_{q^n} \to F_{q^n}$ is an automorphism of F_{q^n} and is defined as $\phi(x) = x^q$. The map is extended to points of an elliptic or hyperelliptic curve over F_{q^n} in the following manner: A point of an elliptic curve is represented using a pair of elements of F_{q^n}; similarly a reduced divisor of a hyperelliptic curve is represented using a tuple of elements of F_{q^n}. An application of the Frobenius map to a point is to actually apply the map individually to the field elements which represent the point. We note that ϕ^n is the identity map on F_{q^n}. If the field F_{q^n} is represented using a normal basis, then the computation of $\phi(x)$ is "for free". Further, as observed in [24,23], in the case $q = 2$, the Frobenius map is $\phi(x) = x^2$ and hence can be computed using a field squaring which is a relatively cheap operation even if polynomial basis representation of elements is used.

2.4   Scalar Multiplication Using Frobenius Map

In [13], Koblitz had suggested the use of Frobenius map to speed up scalar multiplication algorithm. This idea has later been developed by several authors [5,7, 10,18,22,23]. For hyperelliptic curves, it has been shown [14,4] that the Frobenius map based method can be used over any field of finite characteristic.

Let q be a prime power, F_q be the finite field of order q and F_{q^n} an extension field of F_q. Let C be the curve of genus g to be used for the cryptosystem and we consider the F_{q^n}-rational points of C. Let ϕ be the Frobenius map from F_{q^n} to F_{q^n}. Let m be an integer, X a point (either a point of an elliptic curve or a reduced divisor of a hyperelliptic curve) and we wish to compute mX. The base-ϕ expansion of m is $\sum_{i=0}^{n-1} u_i \phi^i$, where under reasonable assumptions each u_i is an integer in the range $[-q^g, q^g]$. It is possible to obtain the base-ϕ expansion of m. Next we define some additional parameters which will be required in the rest of the paper.

1. $A = \max\lfloor \log_2(|u_i|) \rfloor$.
2. For $i \in \{0, \ldots, n-1\}$ write $|u_i| = \sum_{j=0}^{A} u'_{i,j} 2^i$, where $u'_{i,j} \in \{0, 1\}$.
3. $u_{i,j} = \mathsf{sgn}(u_i) u'_{i,j}$, where $\mathsf{sgn}(u_i)$ is the sign of u_i.
4. For $0 \le i \le n-1$, define $X_0 = X$ and $X_i = \phi^i(X_0) = \phi^i(X)$.
5. Parameters h and w are respectively the column and row window sizes.
6. Parameters s and r are defined by the equation:
   $n = s \times h + r$, where r is a unique integer in the set $\{1, \ldots, h\}$.
6. Parameter $k = \lceil (A+1)/w \rceil$.

The expression mX can be written as

$$\left. \begin{aligned} mX &= u_0 X_0 + u_1 X_1 + \cdots + u_{n-1} X_{n-1} \\ &= (u_{0,0} + u_{0,1} 2 + \cdots + u_{0,A} 2^A) X_0 \\ &\quad + (u_{1,0} + u_{1,1} 2 + \cdots + u_{1,A} 2^A) X_1 \\ &\quad + \cdots \\ &\quad + (u_{n-1,0} + u_{n-1,1} 2 + \cdots + u_{n-1,A} 2^A) X_{n-1} \end{aligned} \right\} \tag{3}$$

We consider the above expression to be an $n \times (A+1)$ matrix. Let $\tau = q^n$. Then depending on the nature of the underlying field F_τ, there are several cases.

1. Case $n = 1$ and $\tau = q$ is a prime: In this case, (3) reduces to a single row. In this situation, the Frobenius map based technique does not really apply. Hence we will not consider this kind of fields in this paper.
2. Case $n > 1$: In this situation (3) will have more than one rows and the Frobenius map technique can be applied. It will be convenient to divide this into two subcases.
   - Subcase $q = 2$: The field is F_{2^n} and the curves are the binary Koblitz curves. In this case each $u_i \in \{0, \pm 1\}$ and hence (3) is actually a single column. This is the other extreme to Case 1 above. In [24,23], equation (3) is called the ϕ-adic expansion of m.
   - Subcase $q > 2$: In this situation, (3) has a more square shape and again our algorithm offers improvements over existing algorithms.

The following simple algorithm can be used to compute mX from (3) (see [4,10, 14,23,24]).

Algorithm 1.
Input : integer $m = \sum_{i=0}^{n-1} u_i \phi^i$ and point X .
Output : mX.
    1. For $0 \le i \le n-1$ and $0 \le j \le A$, compute X_i and $u_{i,j}$;
    2. Set $Y = \sum_{i=0}^{n-1} u_{i,A} X_i$;
    3. For $j = A - 1$ down to 0
    4. $Y = 2Y; Y = Y + \sum_{i=0}^{n-1} u_{i,j} X_i$
    5. return Y.

Proposition 1. *In the above algorithm, the average numbers of additions and doublings needed to compute mX are $n(A+1)/2$ and A respectively.*

3   Basic Table Look-Up Methods

We describe a new table look-up method to compute mX from (3). We observe that the right hand side of (3) has the structure of a matrix. Algorithm 1 performs a column by column computation. Our first observation is the fact that the number of rows in (3) is equal to n (the extension degree of F_{q^n} over F_q) and is independent of both m and X. Given a point X, we define a table Tab_X in the following manner: There are 3^n entries in Tab_X which are indexed by the elements of $\{0, \pm 1\}^n$. For any $(b_0, \ldots, b_{n-1}) \in \{0, \pm 1\}^n$, we define

$$\mathsf{Tab}_X[b_0, \ldots, b_{n-1}] = b_0 X_0 + \cdots + b_{n-1} X_{n-1} \qquad (4)$$
$$= b_0 X + b_1 \phi(X) + \cdots + b_{n-1} \phi^{n-1}(X).$$

Hence the look-up table Tab_X stores 3^n points. If this table is available, then computing mX becomes quite easy and is described by the following algorithm.

Algorithm 2.
Input : $m = \sum_{i=0}^{n-1} u_i \phi^i$ and point X .
Output : mX.
    1. Set $Y = \mathsf{Tab}_X[u_{0,A}, \ldots, u_{n-1,A}]$
    2. For $j = A - 1$ down to 0
    3. $Y = 2Y$;
    4. $Y = Y + \mathsf{Tab}_X[u_{0,j}, \ldots, u_{n-1,j}]$;
    5. return Y.

Proposition 2. *Algorithm 2 computes mX using A additions and A doublings. The table Tab_X stores 3^n points.*

3.1   Using Smaller Look-Up Tables

In Algorithm 2 we use a table of 3^n points, where n is the extension degree of F_{q^n} over F_q. If n is relatively small (≤ 4), then the table is of moderate size. However, if n is larger, then the required storage space may be prohibitively high. In this section, we show how to tackle this problem.

Let h ($1 \leq h \leq n$) be a small positive integer which is the column window size. Write $n = s \times h + r$, where r is a unique integer from $\{1, \ldots, h\}$. Then for $(a_0, \ldots, a_{n-1}) \in \{0, \pm 1\}^n$ we can write

$$a_0 X_0 + a_1 X_1 + \cdots + a_{n-1} X_{n-1} = a_0 X_0 + a_1 X_1 + \cdots + a_{h-1} X_{h-1}$$
$$+ a_h X_h + a_{h+1} X_{h+1} + \cdots + a_{2h-1} X_{2h-1}$$
$$\vdots$$
$$+ a_{(s-1)h} X_{(s-1)h} + \cdots + a_{sh-1} X_{sh-1}$$
$$+ a_{sh} X_{sh} + \cdots + a_{sh+r-1} X_{sh+r-1}.$$

For $0 \leq i \leq s$, we define a set of tables $\mathsf{Tab}_X^{(i)}$ in the following manner: Define $\rho = (s+1)h$ and set $X_n = \cdots = X_{\rho-1} = 0$. Each table $\mathsf{Tab}_X^{(i)}$ stores 3^h points indexed by elements of $\{0, \pm 1\}^h$. For $(b_0, \ldots, b_{h-1}) \in \{0, \pm 1\}^h$, define

$$\mathsf{Tab}_X^{(i)}(b_0, \ldots, b_{h-1}) = b_0 X_{hi} + b_1 X_{hi+1} + \cdots + b_{h-1} X_{hi+h-1}. \tag{5}$$

Note that $X_n = \cdots = X_{\rho-1} = 0$ and hence $\mathsf{Tab}_X^{(s)}$ stores only 3^r points. The following algorithm can now be used to compute mX.

Algorithm 3.

Input : $m = \sum_{i=0}^{n-1} u_i \phi^i$, $n = s \times h + r$ and point X.
Output : mX.

1. Set $Y = \mathsf{Tab}_X^{(s)}[u_{sh,A}, u_{sh+1,A}, \ldots, u_{sh+r-1,A}, 0, \cdots, 0]$;
2. For $i = s - 1$ down to 0 set $Y = Y + \mathsf{Tab}_X^{(i)}[u_{ih,A}, u_{ih+1,A}, \ldots, u_{(i+1)h-1,A}]$;
3. For $j = A - 1$ down to 0
4. $Y = 2Y$;
5. $Y = Y + \mathsf{Tab}_X^{(s)}[u_{sh,j}, u_{sh+1,j}, \ldots, u_{sh+r-1,j}, 0, \cdots, 0]$;
6.   For $i = s - 1$ down to 0 set $Y = Y + \mathsf{Tab}_X^{(i)}[u_{ih,j}, u_{ih+1,j}, \ldots, u_{(i+1)h-1,j}]$;
7. End for;
8. return Y.

Proposition 3. *Algorithm 3 correctly computes mX using $(s + 1)A$ additions and A doublings. For $0 \leq i \leq s - 1$, table $\mathsf{Tab}_X^{(i)}$ stores 3^h points and $\mathsf{Tab}_X^{(s)}$ stores 3^r points. Thus the total number of points stored is $s \times 3^h + 3^r$.*

The storage requirement decreases from $3^n = 3^{sh+r}$ points to $s3^h + 3^r$ points. The trade-off is an increase in the number of additions. In the situation where the field F_{q^n} is represented using a normal basis, the storage requirement can be further reduced. This is based on the following observation.

Proposition 4. *For any $(b_0, \ldots, b_{h-1}) \in \{0, \pm 1\}^h$ and $i > 0$ we have,*

$$\mathsf{Tab}_X^{(i)}[b_0, \ldots, b_{h-1}] = \phi^{hi}(\mathsf{Tab}_X^{(0)}[b_0, \ldots, b_{h-1}]).$$

Proof: We compute

$$\begin{aligned}
\mathsf{Tab}_X^{(i)}[b_0, \ldots, b_{h-1}] &= b_0 X_{hi} + b_1 X_{hi+1} + \cdots + b_{h-1} X_{hi+h-1} \\
&= b_0 \phi^{hi}(X) + b_1 \phi^{hi+1}(X) + \cdots + \phi^{hi+h-1}(X) \\
&= \phi^{hi}(b_0 X + b_1 \phi(X) + \cdots + b_{h-1} \phi^{h-1}(X)) \\
&= \phi^{hi}(\mathsf{Tab}_X^{(0)}[b_0, b_1, \ldots, b_{h-1}]).
\end{aligned}$$

This completes the proof. □

Since the field is represented using a normal basis, the map ϕ can be computed simply by a circular shift (see Section 2.3). Thus instead of storing the $(s + 1)$ tables $\mathsf{Tab}_X^{(0)}, \ldots, \mathsf{Tab}_X^{(s)}$ we simply store the table $\mathsf{Tab}_X^{(0)}$ and for $i > 0$ we use Proposition 4 to compute any entry of $\mathsf{Tab}_X^{(i)}$ as and when required. Using this idea we obtain the following improvement.

Proposition 5. *Suppose the field F_{q^n} is represented using a normal basis. Then Algorithm 3 requires to store 3^h points. The numbers of additions and doublings remain the same as Proposition 3.*

4   General Table Look-Up Methods

In this section, we present our general table look-up algorithm. Let w $(1 \leq w \leq A+1)$ be a positive integer which is the row window size and set $k = \lceil (A+1)/w \rceil$. We express all u_i occurring in the base-ϕ expansion of m in the base 2^w. In such an expansion we will use the elements of the set $\Omega_w = \{0, \pm 1, \pm 2, \cdots, \pm 2^{w-1}\}$ as digits. Note that since $\{0, \pm 1, \pm 2, \ldots, \pm(2^{w-1}-1), 2^{w-1}\}$ is a complete system of residues modulo 2^w, any integer m can be represented uniquely in base 2^w using these numbers as digits. The set Ω_w has one extra digit which ensures that the set is closed under negation. Thus, if $u = \sum_{i=0}^{t} a_i 2^{wi}$ then a representation of $-m$ over Ω_w can be obtained by simply negating all the a_i's. For $0 \leq i \leq n-1$, write

$$u_i = c_{i,0} + c_{i,1}2^w + \cdots + c_{i,k}2^{wk}, \tag{6}$$

where $c_{i,j} \in \Omega_w$. Then

$$\left.\begin{aligned}
u_0 X_0 &= (c_{0,0} + c_{0,1}2^w + ... + c_{0,k}2^{wk})X_0 \\
u_1 X_1 &= (c_{1,0} + c_{1,1}2^w + ... + c_{1,k}2^{wk})X_1 \\
&\vdots \qquad \vdots \\
u_{n-1} X_{n-1} &= (c_{n-1,0} + c_{n-1,1}2^w + ... + c_{n-1,k}2^{wk})X_{n-1}.
\end{aligned}\right\} \tag{7}$$

We have to compute $mX = u_0 X_0 + \cdots + u_{n-1}X_{n-1}$. Let h $(1 \leq h \leq n)$ be a small integer (which is the column window size) and write $n = s \times h + r$ where r is a unique integer in the set $\{1, \ldots, h\}$. We define $(s+1)$ tables $\mathsf{Tab}_X^{(0)}, \ldots, \mathsf{Tab}_X^{(s)}$, where each $\mathsf{Tab}_X^{(i)}$ stores $(2^w + 1)^h$ points. The entries of $\mathsf{Tab}_X^{(i)}$ are indexed by elements of $\Omega_w^h = \underbrace{\Omega_w \times \cdots \times \Omega_w}_{h}$. For $(a_0, \ldots, a_{h-1}) \in \Omega_w^h$ we define

$$\mathsf{Tab}_X^{(i)}[a_0, \ldots, a_{h-1}] = a_0 X_{ih} + a_1 X_{ih+1} + \cdots + a_{h-1}X_{(i+1)h-1}. \tag{8}$$

Let $\kappa = (s+1)h$ and set $X_n = \cdots = X_{\kappa-1} = 0$. Hence $\mathsf{Tab}_X^{(s)}$ stores only $(2^w + 1)^r$ points. With this set of tables at our disposal we can compute mX using Algorithm 4.

Algorithm 4.
Input : $m = \sum_{i=0}^{n-1} u_i \phi^i$ and point X .
Output : mX.

    1. Set $Y = \mathsf{Tab}_X^{(s)}[c_{sh,k}, c_{sh+1,k}, \ldots, c_{n-1,k}, 0, \ldots, 0]$;
    2. For $i = s-1$ down to 0
    3. $Y = Y + \mathsf{Tab}_X^{(i)}[c_{ih,k}, c_{ih+1,k}, \ldots, c_{(i+1)h-1,k}]$;
    4. For $j = k-1$ down to 0
    5. $Y = 2^w Y$;
    6. $Y = Y + \mathsf{Tab}_X^{(s)}[c_{sh,j}, c_{sh+1,j}, \ldots, c_{n-1,j}, 0, \ldots, 0]$;
    7.   For $i = s-1$ down to 0
    8. $Y = Y + \mathsf{Tab}_X^{(i)}[c_{ih,j}, c_{ih+1,j}, \ldots, c_{(i+1)h-1,j}]$;
    9. return Y.

Proposition 6. *Algorithm 4 correctly computes mX using $(k-1)+ks$ additions and $(k-1)w$ doublings. For $0 \le i \le s-1$, table $\mathsf{Tab}_X^{(i)}$ stores $(2^w+1)^h$ points and table $\mathsf{Tab}_X^{(s)}$ stores $(2^w+1)^r$ points. Thus a total of $s(2^w+1)^h + (2^w+1)^r$ points are required to be stored.*

As in Section 3.1, the storage requirement can be further reduced if the field F_{q^n} is represented using a normal basis. This is based on the following observation.

Proposition 7. *For any $(a_0, \ldots, a_{h-1}) \in \Omega_w^h$, and $i > 0$, we have*

$$\mathsf{Tab}_X^{(i)}[a_0, \ldots, a_{h-1}] = \phi^{hi}(\mathsf{Tab}_X^{(0)}[a_0, \ldots, a_{h-1}]).$$

Since the field is represented using a normal basis, the map ϕ is easy to compute online. Hence it is sufficient to store only $\mathsf{Tab}_X^{(0)}$ and compute the required entry of $\mathsf{Tab}_X^{(i)}$ as and when required. This gives us the following result.

Proposition 8. *If F_{q^n} is represented using a normal basis, then Algorithm 5 requires to store only $(2^w+1)^h$ points. The numbers of additions and doublings remain the same as in Proposition 6.*

5   Unknown Point

The algorithms described so far use one or more look-up tables. These tables are parametrized by a point X. If the point X is known in advance (as in signature generation for ElGamal algorithms), then the tables can be precomputed and stored. However, there are applications where the point is not known in advance (for example in variants of Diffie-Hellman key agreement protocols). In such a situation, the look-up tables have to be computed online. In this section, we describe algorithms for this task.

We start by describing an algorithm to compute the tables used in Algorithm 3. For this it is sufficient to describe an algorithm to compute $\mathsf{Tab}_X^{(0)}$. The Frobenius map can be used to compute the other tables from $\mathsf{Tab}_X^{(0)}$. Let X be a point and we wish to compute the table $\mathsf{Tab}_X^{(0)}$ having 3^h entries and indexed by the elements of the set $\{0, \pm 1\}^h$. For any vector $\alpha \in \{0, \pm 1\}^l$, we define $-\alpha$ to be the vector obtained from α by negating all the components of α. The following algorithm computes $\mathsf{Tab}_X^{(0)}$.

Algorithm 5.
input : X.
output : $\mathsf{Tab}_X^{(0)}$ used in Algorithm 3.

1. Compute $X_0, \ldots, X_{h-1}$.
2. $\mathsf{Tab}_X^{(0)}[0, 0, \ldots, 0] = 0$; $\mathsf{Tab}_X^{(0)}[1, 0, \ldots, 0] = X$; $\mathsf{Tab}_X^{(0)}[-1, 0, \ldots, 0] = -X$;
3. For $l = 1$ to $h - 2$
4.   For $\alpha \in \{0, \pm 1\}^l$ set $\mathsf{Tab}_X^{(0)}[\alpha, 1, \ldots, 0] = X_{l+1} + \mathsf{Tab}_X[\alpha, 0, \ldots, 0]$;
5.   For $\alpha \in \{0, \pm 1\}^l$ set $\mathsf{Tab}_X^{(0)}[\alpha, -1, \ldots, 0] = -\mathsf{Tab}_X[-\alpha, 1, \ldots, 0]$;
6. End.

Proposition 9. *Algorithm 5 correctly computes* $\mathsf{Tab}_X^{(0)}$ *used in Algorithm 3 using* $\frac{1}{2}(3^h - 3)$ *point additions and* $(h-1)$ *Frobenius map computations. The tables* $\mathsf{Tab}_X^{(1)}, \ldots, \mathsf{Tab}_X^{(s)}$ *used in Algorithm 3 can be computed from* $\mathsf{Tab}_X^{(0)}$ *using* $sh3^h$ *Frobenius map computations.*

Proof: First we prove the correctness. Let $\beta \in \{0, \pm1\}$. If $\beta = (0, \ldots, 0)$, then clearly Algorithm 5 computes $\mathsf{Tab}_X^{(0)}[\beta] = 0$. So assume that $\beta \neq (0, \ldots, 0)$ and write $\beta = (\alpha, b, 0, \ldots, 0)$, where $b \neq 0$ and $\alpha \in \{0, \pm1\}^l$ for some $l \geq 0$. We show that $\mathsf{Tab}_X^{(0)}[\beta]$ is computed correctly. If $b = 1$, we have by definition $\mathsf{Tab}_X^{(0)}[\beta] = \langle \alpha, (X_0, \ldots, X_l) \rangle + X_{l+1} = \mathsf{Tab}_X^{(0)}[\alpha, 0, \ldots, 0] + X_{l+1}$, where $\langle \rangle$ denotes the usual inner product. On the other hand, if $b = -1$, then

$$
\begin{aligned}
\mathsf{Tab}_X^{(0)}[\beta] &= \langle \alpha, (X_0, \ldots, X_l) \rangle - X_{l+1} \\
&= -(-\langle \alpha, (X_0, \ldots, X_l) \rangle + X_{l+1}) \\
&= -(\langle -\alpha, (X_0, \ldots, X_l) \rangle + X_{l+1}) \\
&= -(\mathsf{Tab}_X^{(0)}[-\alpha, 0, \ldots, 0] + X_{l+1}) \\
&= -\mathsf{Tab}_X^{(0)}[-\alpha, 1, \ldots, 0].
\end{aligned}
$$

This completes the proof of correctness. Since $X_i = \phi^i(X)$, Step 1 of Algorithm 5 requires $h - 1$ applications of the Frobenius map. The number of point additions is clearly $3 + 3^2 + \cdots + 3^{h-1} = \frac{1}{2}(3^h - 3)$.

Note that for any $\beta \in \{0, \pm1\}^h$, and $i \geq 0$, we have $\mathsf{Tab}_X^{(i+1)}[\beta] = \phi^h(\mathsf{Tab}_X^{(i)}[\beta])$. To compute $\mathsf{Tab}_X^{(i+1)}$ from $\mathsf{Tab}_X^{(i)}$ we need $h3^h$ computations of the Frobenius map. Since s tables have to be computed, a total of $sh3^h$ computations of the Frobenius map is required.   □

Note that if the field F_{q^n} is represented using normal basis, then for $i > 0$ the tables $\mathsf{Tab}_X^{(i)}$ need not be stored. Also the Frobenius map computation is essentially "for free".

Now we turn to the problem of computing the set of tables used in Algorithm 4. For $0 \leq i \leq h - 1$ and $j \in \Omega_w$, we use the variable $Z_{i,j}$ to store the value of jX_i.

Algorithm 6
input : X;
output : $\mathsf{Tab}_X^{(0)}$ used in Algorithm 4.

1. For $i = 0$ to $h - 1$, set $Z_{i,0} = 0$; $Z_{0,1} = X$;
2. For $j = 2$ to $2^w - 1$
3. $Z_{0,j} = Z_{0,j-1} + X$; $Z_{0,-j} = -Z_{0,j}$;
4. End for,
5. For $i = 1$ to $h - 1$
6.   For $j = 1$ to $2^w - 1$
7. $Z_{i,j} = \phi(Z_{i-1,j})$; $Z_{i,-j} = -Z_{i,j}$;
8.   End for;
9. End For;
10. For $j \in \Omega_w$, set $\mathsf{Tab}_X^{(0)}[j, 0, \ldots, 0] = Z_{0,j}$;

11. For $l = 1$ to $h - 1$
12.   For $\alpha \in \Omega_w^l$
13.   For $j = 1$ to $2^w - 1$ set $\mathsf{Tab}_X^{(0)}[\alpha, j, 0, \ldots, 0] = Z_{l+1, j} + \mathsf{Tab}_X^{(0)}[\alpha, 0, \ldots, 0]$;
14.   For $j = 1$ to $2^w - 1$ set $\mathsf{Tab}_X^{(0)}[\alpha, -j, 0, \ldots, 0] = -\mathsf{Tab}_X^{(0)}[-\alpha, j, 0, \ldots, 0]$;
15.   End for;
16. End for;
17. End.

The following result whose proof is similar to that of Proposition 9 states the correctness and complexity of Algorithm 6.

Proposition 10. *Algorithm 6 correctly computes* $\mathsf{Tab}_X^{(0)}$ *used in Algorithm 4 using*

$$\left((2^w - 2) + \frac{2^{2w} - 1}{2^w}((2^w + 1)^{h-1} - 1) \right)$$

point additions and $(h - 1)(2^w - 1)$ *computations of the Frobenius map. Further, the tables* $\mathsf{Tab}_X^{(1)}, \ldots, \mathsf{Tab}_X^{(s)}$ *used in Algorithm 4 can be computed using an additional* $sh(2^w + 1)^h$ *computations of the Frobenius map.*

6   Results and Comparison

In this section, we present detailed results and also compare our algorithm with known scalar multiplication algorithms. At the outset, we would like to point out that the Frobenius map based method (and hence our algorithm) is really useful in the situation where the underlying field is a prime power field (rather than a prime field). Hence all our comparisons are to algorithms which work over prime power fields, in particular Optimial Extension Fields.

We recall the parameters of the algorithms (see Section 2.4): n is the field extension degree; h and w are respectively the column and row window sizes; $k = \lceil (A + 1)/w \rceil$ and s, r are defined by the equation $n = s \times h + r$, where r is a unique integer from the set $\{1, \ldots, h\}$. Table 1 summarizes the results for scalar multiplication using Algorithm 4. Algorithm 3 is obtained from Algorithm 4 by putting $w = 1$. Further, Algorithm 2 is obtained from Algorithm 4 by putting $w = 1$ and $h = n$.

Table 1. Summary of Algorithm 4.

Additions	Doublings	Normal basis	Standard basis
$(k - 1) + ks$	$(k - 1)w$	$(2^w + 1)^h$	$s(2^w + 1)^h + (2^w + 1)^r$

The first two columns of Table 1 gives the numbers of additions and doublings required. The third column gives the number of points required to be stored when normal basis is used and the fourth column gives the number of points required

Table 2. Summary of Algorithm 6.

$\mathsf{Tab}_X^{(0)}$		$\mathsf{Tab}_X^{(1)}, \ldots, \mathsf{Tab}_X^{(s)}$
Additions	*Frobenius map*	*Frobenius map*
$(2^w - 2) + \frac{(2^{2w}-1)}{2^w}\left((2^w + 1)^{h-1} - 1\right)$	$(h - 1)(2^w - 1)$	$sh(2^w + 1)^h$

Table 3. Comparison with other algorithms.

Algorithm	*additions*	*doublings*
Binary	max $(t - 1)$; avg $(t/2)$	t
ω-NAF [6]	$t/(\omega + 1)$	t
Algorithm 1	max $(t - 1)$; avg $(t/2)$	A
Algorithm 4	$t/(wh)$	A

to be stored when standard (or polynomial) basis is used. Table 2 summarizes the result for Algorithm 6. The first half of Table 2 gives the numbers of additions and Frobenius map computations required to prepare the table $\mathsf{Tab}_X^{(0)}$ and the second half gives the additional number of Frobenius map computations required to prepare the tables $\mathsf{Tab}_X^{(1)}, \ldots, \mathsf{Tab}_X^{(s)}$. Note that Algorithm 5 can be obtained from Algorithm 6 by setting $w = 1$. Let us denote the numbers of point additions and point doublings by $\mathbf{A}$ and $\mathbf{D}$ respectively. From Table 1, $\mathbf{A} = (k - 1) + ks$ and $\mathbf{D} = (k - 1)w$. Using the fact that $k = \lceil (A + 1)/w \rceil$ and $s \simeq \lfloor n/h \rfloor$ we have the $\mathbf{A} \simeq (n(A+1))/wh$ and $\mathbf{D} \simeq A$. The parameters w and h are respectively the row and column window sizes and hence wh is the size of the $w \times h$ submatrix window.

Define $t = n(A + 1)$. Then the total number of bits required to represent the integer m in binary is $\simeq t$. The usual binary add-and-double algorithm requires t point doublings and on an average $(t/2)$ add point additions. A more efficient algorithm uses a non adjacent form (NAF) representation of m [23]. A window method using NAF and look-up table requires $t/(\omega + 1)$ additions and t doublings while storing $2^{\omega-2}$ points, where ω is the window size (see [6]). The basic Frobenius map based algorithm (Algorithm 1) requires A doublings and $t/2$ additions. These results are summarized in Table 3 which clearly show the superiority of Algorithm 4 over the other algorithms. Algorithm 4 achieves the speed-up by using a look-up table. This look-up table can either be precomputed or can be computed online. Further, depending on the basis representation of the underlying field, the amount of storage space can vary.

In Table 4, we present results of storage and computational requirements under various conditions. The values in Table 4 clearly shows that the storage and computational requirements of the look-up tables can vary. For example, in the situation $n = 4$, $h = 2$ and $w = 1$, it is sufficient to work with total storage space for 18 points (9 if normal basis is used). Only 3 point additions and 19 Frobenius map computations are required to compute the tables. The number of additions required for scalar multiplications is approximately $(t/wh) = t/2$ and the number of doublings is approximately A. This is better than the binary method. On the other hand, for $n = 12$, $h = 2$ and $w = 4$, using normal basis representation and storage for 289 points, the number of additions in the scalar multiplication can be brought down to $t/(wh) = t/8$. A total of 269 point additions are required to compute the tables in this situation. Thus Algorithm 4 provides a wide choice of trade-offs between storage space and efficiency of scalar multiplication.

Table 4. Storage and computation requirements of the look-up tables.

Parameters			storage requirements		computational requirements		
n	h	w	normal basis	standard basis	$\text{Tab}_X^{(0)}$		$\text{Tab}_X^{(i)}$ for $i > 0$
					Additions	Frob	Frob
4	4	1	81	81	39	3	0
		2	625	625	467	9	0
	2	1	9	18	3	1	18
		2	25	50	17	3	50
		3	81	162	69	7	162
8	4	1	81	162	39	3	324
		2	625	1250	467	9	2500
	2	1	9	36	3	1	54
		2	25	100	17	3	150
		3	81	324	69	7	486
12	4	1	81	243	39	3	648
		2	625	1875	467	9	5000
	2	1	9	54	3	1	90
		2	25	150	17	3	250
		3	81	486	69	7	810
		4	289	1734	269	15	2890

7   Conclusion and Further Research

We have described a new table look-up algorithm for performing Frobenius map based scalar multiplication for elliptic and hyperelliptic curve cryptosystems over prime power fields. The algorithm compares favourably with previous Frobenius map based algorithms and other scalar multiplication algorithms. Note that, we have not used NAF representation of the multiplier in our algorithm. Using NAF will further increase the efficiency of the proposed algorithm. Also, recently in [15], [19] more general techniques have been proposed for utilising the Frobenius map. It is an interesting work to see how the algorithm proposed in this work can be modified to suit the generalisation and how much of performance enhancement can be achieved. In conclusion, it can be said that our algorithm (or a version modified to suit the general scenario) is a serious contender for implementing scalar multiplication for elliptic and hyperelliptic curve cryptosystems.

References

1. K. Aoiki, F. Hoshino, T. Kobayashi A Cyclic Window Algorithm for ECC Defined over Extension Fields *ICICS 2001*, LNCS 2229, pp 62–73, Springer Verlag 2001.
2. D. V. Bailey and C. Paar. Efficient Arithmetic in Finite Field Extensions with Application in Elliptic Curve Cryptography In *J. Cryptology 14*, pages 153–176, 2001.
3. D. G. Cantor. Computing in the Jacobian of a Hyperelliptic curve. In *Mathematics of Computation*,volume 48, pages 95–101, 1987.
4. Y. J. Choie and J. W. Lee. Speeding up the scalar multiplication in the Jacobian of hyperelliptic curves using Frobenius map. *Indocrypt 2002*, LNCS 2551, Springer Verlag 2002, pp 285–295.
5. M. Ciet, T. Lange, F. Sica and J.-J. Quisquater. Improved algorithms for efficient arithmetic on elliptic curves using fast endomorphisms. *Eurocrypt 2003*.
6. K. Fong, D. Hankerson, J. Lopez and A. Menezes. Field inversion and point halving revisited. *Preprint*.
7. R. P. Gallant, R. J. Lambert and S. A. Vanstone. Faster point multiplication on elliptic curves using efficient endomorphisms. *Crypto 2001*, LNCS 2139, pp. 190–200, 2001.
8. C. Gunther, T. Lange and A. Stein. Speeding Up the Arithmetic on Koblitz Curves of Genus Two, *Selected Areas in Cryptography, SAC 2001*, LNCS, pp. 106–117, 2001.
9. E. Knudsen. Elliptic scalar multiplication using point halving. *Proceedings of Asiacrypt 1999*, LNCS 1716, pp 135-149, 1999.
10. T. Kobayashi, H. Morita, K. Kobayashi and F. Hoshino. Fast elliptic curve algorithm combining Frobenius map and table reference to adapt to higher characteristic. *Eurocrypt 1999*, LNCS 1592, pp 176–189, 1999.
11. N. Koblitz. Hyperelliptic Cryptosystems. *Journal of Cryptology*, 1(3), pp 139–150, 1989.
12. N. Koblitz. *Algebraic Aspects of Cryptology*. Algorithm and Computation in Mathematics. Springer Verlag, 1998.
13. N. Koblitz. CM Curves with Good Cryptographic Properties. *Advances in Cryptology - Crypo'91*, LNCS 576, pp. 279–287,Springer Verlag 1992.
14. T. Lange. *Efficient Arithmetic on Hyperelliptic Koblitz Curve*. PhD thesis, University of Essen, 2001.
15. T. Park, E. Kim, K. Park, M. Lee. *A General Expansion Method Using Efficient Endomorphism*. In *Proceedings of ICISC, 2003*, LNCS, Springer-Verlag 2003.
16. R. Lidl and H. Niederreiter. *Introduction to finite fields and their applications*. Cambridge University Press, revised edition, 1994.
17. A. Menezes, Y. Wu and R. Zuccherato. An Elementary Introduction to Hyperelliptic Curve. Technical Report CORR 96–19, University of Waterloo (1996), Canada. Available at http://www.cacr.math.uwaterloo.ca
18. V. Müller. Fast multiplication on elliptic curves over small fields of characteristic two. *Journal of Cryptology*, 11(4):219–234, 1998.
19. T. Park, K. Park, M. Lee. *Efficient Scalar Multiplication in Hyperelliptic Curves using a new Frobenius Expansion*. In *Proceedings of ICISC, 2003*, LNCS, Springer-Verlag 2003.
20. R. Schroeppel. Elliptic curve point halving wins big. *Proceedings of 2nd Midwest Arithmetical Geometry in Cryptography Workshop*. Urbana, Illinois, November 2000.

21. F. Sica, M. Ciet and J.-J. Quisquater. Analysis of the Gallant-Lambert-Vanstone method based on efficient endomorphisms: elliptic and hyperelliptic curves. *Selected areas in cryptography.*, LNCS, 2002, to appear.
22. N. P. Smart. Elliptic curve cryptosystems over small fields of odd characteristic. *Journal of Cryptology*, 12(2):141-151, 1999.
23. J. Solinas. Efficient Arithmetic on Koblitz Curves. *Designs, Codes and Cryptography*, 19:195–249, 2000.
24. J. Solinas. An improved Algorithm on a Family of Elliptic Curves. In *Advances in Cryptology - Crpto'97*, LNCS 1294, pp.357–371, Springer-Verlag.

Batch Verification for Equality of Discrete Logarithms and Threshold Decryptions

Riza Aditya[1], Kun Peng[1], Colin Boyd[1], Ed Dawson[1], and Byoungcheon Lee[1,2]

[1] Information Security Research Centre,
Queensland University of Technology,
GPO BOX 2434, Brisbane, QLD, 4001, Australia
{r.aditya, k.peng, c.boyd, e.dawson, b6.lee}@qut.edu.au
[2] Joongbu University,
101 Daebak-Ro, Chuboo-Meon, Kumsan-Gun, Chungnam, 312-702, Korea
sultan@joongbu.ac.kr

Abstract. A general technique of batch verification for equality of discrete logarithms is proposed. Examples of batching threshold decryption schemes are presented based on threshold versions of ElGamal and RSA cryptosystems. Our technique offers large computational savings when employed in schemes with a large number of ciphertexts to be decrypted, such as in e-voting or e-auction schemes using threshold decryption. The resulting effect is beneficial for producing more efficient schemes.

Keywords: Batch verification, Proof of equality of discrete logarithms (**PEQDL**), Threshold decryption, Threshold ElGamal, Threshold RSA

1 Introduction

Threshold decryption [14,18,11] is essential in fault-tolerant schemes, whether it is e-commerce (e.g: e-auction) or e-government (e.g: e-voting). In a threshold decryption protocol, the public (encryption) key is published, while the corresponding private (decryption) key is shared among n participants. A threshold $t < n$ is set, such that more than t participants are required to cooperate to decrypt a ciphertext while the cooperation of no more than t participants will find no information about the decryption key. In e-auction, these participants are auctioneers sharing the power to open the bids. In e-voting, the participants are counting authorities sharing the power to tally the votes.

To ensure correctness, it is necessary to guarantee that the shared decryption is performed correctly through some public verification functions, without revealing the encrypted message, the private key, and its shares. In many popular cryptosystems, the verification process is implemented by using zero-knowledge proof of equality of discrete logarithms (**PEQDL**) [6].

M. Jakobsson, M. Yung, J. Zhou (Eds.): ACNS 2004, LNCS 3089, pp. 494–508, 2004.

1.1 Performance Issue

Consider a secure e-auction [1,16] or e-voting scheme [2,4,8,11], where the submitted bids or ballots are required to be anonymous. After the encrypted bids or ballots are made anonymous through the use of an anonymous channel (e.g: mix network), they are decrypted by the decryption authorities. Each decryption share requires a proof of correct decryption. The proof is required to verify and identify correct decryption shares to reconstruct the original bid or vote. Verification of many instances of such proofs leads to costly computation which can further develop into a bottleneck affecting the performance of the scheme.

Batching is a useful technique to decrease computational cost in processing the proofs of correct decryption together. Bellare *et al.* [3] proposed three batch verification techniques - RS (random subset) test, SE (small exponent) test, and Bucket test. However, their scheme is not applicable to our threshold decryptions verification problem for two reasons. Firstly, their techniques batch the verification of common base exponentiations, not the verification of PEQDLs (i.e: common exponent). Secondly, Boyd and Pavlovski [5] demonstrated that although the theorems in [3] are correct, their application in the paper is inappropriate since the assumptions on the group structure are not strong enough. Hoshino *et al.* [12] later fixed and extended Bellare's work to batch verify exponentiations in multiple bases. However, this is also irrelevant to our problem of batch verifying PEQDLs with a common exponent.

1.2 Main Contributions

The following summarises our main contribution presented in the paper:

1. We fix the problem presented by Boyd and Pavlovski in SE test, and also extend the test to batch verify PEQDLs.
2. We present and formally prove theorems on the extended test.
3. We present applications of the theorems to verify valid decryption shares in threshold versions of two popular cryptosystems - threshold ElGamal, and threshold RSA.

Our result improves computational efficiency of verifying valid decryption shares in threshold decryption. As threshold decryption is fundamental in various applications (e.g: e-auction, e-voting, e-cash) to provide robustness, our result offers improvement in efficiency, performance and practicality when integrated with many schemes.

The remainder of this paper is structured as follows. Section 2 offers an introduction to threshold decryption. Section 3 presents two theorems and their corresponding proofs essential to our result. In section 4, the theorems are applied to threshold versions of the two popular cryptosystems. Sections 5 and 6 analyse the security and efficiency of our applied batch verification. Section 7 is a conclusion.

2   Background

In this section we recall decryption of a single ciphertext in threshold decryption schemes for simplicity. Note that many schemes require decryption of many ciphertexts in threshold decryption.

2.1   Threshold Decryption

In a threshold decryption scheme, a secret s is encrypted using some public-key encryption algorithm as $c = E(s)$. The private decryption key d is shared by using Shamir's (t, n) secret sharing scheme [17] among n participants (decrypting authorities) P_i, for $i \in \{1, \ldots, n\}$. Each P_i holds a d_i, a share of d. The ciphertext c is partially decrypted by each P_i as $z_i = D_{d_i}(c)$, and later reconstructed using the decryption shares from the set S containing at least $t+1$ honest participants by Lagrange interpolation.

A verification function $V(c, z_i, v_i)$ is used to determine honest participants. Normally the verification key v_i of participant P_i contains a commitment to d_i.

Threshold decryption is often employed in many crypto-based applications. The two most commonly used are threshold versions of ElGamal and RSA algorithms. E-auction and e-voting schemes employing them include [11,2,4,8,1, 16].

2.2   Threshold ElGamal

Pedersen [14] presented a threshold ElGamal signature scheme. It is straightforward to adjust the scheme into a threshold decryption protocol. We recall the protocol as follows:

1. Key generation and sharing:
   Randomly select a large prime q, such that $p = 2q + 1$ is also a prime. G is a cyclic subgroup in $\mathbb{Z}_p^*$ of order q with a generator g. The private decryption key is $d \in \mathbb{Z}_q$, while g and $e = g^d$ is the public encryption key. Using Shamir's secret sharing scheme, let $f(x) = \sum_{r=0}^{t} a_r x^r$, where $a_0 = d$, and the rest of a_r are random values. For $i \in \{1, \ldots, n\}$, distribute the secret share $d_i = f(i)$ to n participants $\{P_i\}$, and each P_i computes the verification key $v_i = g^{d_i}$. The parameters p, q, g, c and v_i are made public, while d and d_i are kept secret for $i \in \{1, \ldots, n\}$.
2. Encryption:
   Select a random $r \in \mathbb{Z}_q$ and encrypt a secret message $s \in \mathbb{Z}_p^*$ as a pair (α, β), where $\alpha = g^r$ and $\beta = se^r$.
3. Shared decryption:
   Each participant P_i computes the decryption share $z_i = \alpha^{d_i}$ and proves the knowledge of the secret share d_i using non-interactive zero-knowledge that:

$$\log_g(v_i) = \log_\alpha(z_i) \tag{1}$$

Since q is public, g and α can be publicly verified to be generators of G.

4. Shares combining:
Correct decryption share z_i of P_i is verified as P_i proves the knowledge of d_i shown in the previous step. S is the set of more than $t + 1$ participants providing correct shares. The original message is reconstructed by computing $s = \frac{\beta}{\prod_{i \in S} z_i^{\mu_i}}$, where $\mu_i = \prod_{i' \in S, i' \neq i} \frac{i'}{i' - i}$.

2.3   Threshold RSA

Shoup [18] presented a threshold version of RSA signature scheme, which can be adjusted to a threshold decryption scheme as shown by Fouque *et al.* [11]. We recall the scheme as follows:

1. Key generation and sharing:
Randomly select primes p' and q', such that $p = 2p' + 1$ and $q = 2q' + 1$ are strong primes. Set $N = pq$ and $M = p'q'$. Select a prime $e > n$ and compute d, such that $ed = 1 \bmod N$. The public encryption key is $PK = (N, e)$, while d is the private decryption key. Using Shamir's secret sharing scheme, let $f(x) = \sum_{r=0}^{t} a_r x^r \bmod M$, where $a_0 = d$ and random values for rest of $a_r \in \{0, \ldots, N * M - 1\}$. For $i \in \{1, \ldots, n\}$, distribute the secret share $d_i = f(i)$ to n participants P_i. Randomly select a verification base v in the cyclic group of squares in $\mathbb{Z}_N^*$. Each participant P_i then computes the verification key $v_i = v^{d_i} \bmod N$. The parameters N, e, v and v_i are made public, while M, p, q, p', q', d and d_i are kept secret, for $i \in \{1, \ldots, n\}$.
2. Encryption:
Encrypt a secret message s as $c = s^e \bmod N$.
3. Shared decryption:
Each participant P_i computes the decryption share $z_i = c^{2\Delta d_i}$, where $\Delta = n!$ and proves the knowledge of the secret share d_i using non-interactive zero-knowledge that:

$$\log_v(v_i) = \log_{c^{4\Delta}}(z_i^2) \tag{2}$$

Notice that as v and $c^{4\Delta}$ are squares, Shoup argues that they are of order M with a large probability (accurately: $1 - \frac{p' + q' - 1}{pq}$). Thus, the proof is assumed to be PEQDL in a group with a known order.
4. Shares combining:
Correct decryption share z_i of P_i is verified as P_i proves the knowledge of d_i shown in the previous step. S is the set of more than $t + 1$ participants providing correct shares. The original message is obtained by first calculating $s^{4\Delta^2} = \prod_{i \in S} z_i^{2\Delta \mu_i} \bmod N$, where $\mu_i = \prod_{i' \in S, i' \neq i} \frac{i'}{i' - i}$. Since $e > n$ is relatively prime to $4\Delta^2$, extended Euclidean algorithm can be applied to obtain a and b, such that $a \times 4\Delta^2 + b \times e = 1$. Therefore, s is reconstructed as $s = s^{a 4\Delta^2} s^{be} = (s^{4\Delta^2})^a c^b \bmod N$.

As in the original scheme [18,11], parameters in the key generation and sharing stage are generated by a trusted dealer. The random verification base v is trusted to be in the cyclic subgroup of squares in $\mathbb{Z}_N^*$. Therefore, v and v_i are squares in the group of $\mathbb{Z}_{N^2}^*$. As a result, when verification of Equation 2 is performed to check the validity of the decryption share, it is guaranteed to be PEQDL in the same cyclic group with a large probability.

3   Batch Verification for Equality of Logarithms

In many cryptographic applications as mentioned in the previous sections, normally there are many ciphertexts (c_j) to be processed in threshold decryption. This is illustrated in Figure 1. For m encrypted messages to be decrypted by n authorities, one requires $m \times n$ instances of PEQDL verifications of decryption share $z_{i,j}$ (participant i's decryption share from ciphertext c_j). Verification of correct shared decryption for every share $z_{i,j}$ is the greatest factor contributing to computational cost in a threshold decryption scheme.

$$
\begin{array}{ccccccc}
 & P_1 & P_2 & & P_i & & P_n \\
c_1 \longrightarrow & z_{1,1} & z_{2,1} & \cdots & z_{i,1} & \cdots & z_{n,1} \longrightarrow s_1 \\
c_2 \longrightarrow & z_{1,2} & z_{2,2} & \cdots & z_{i,2} & \cdots & z_{n,2} \longrightarrow s_2 \\
\vdots & \vdots & \vdots & & \vdots & & \vdots & \vdots \\
c_j \longrightarrow & z_{1,j} & z_{2,j} & \cdots & z_{i,j} & \cdots & z_{n,j} \longrightarrow s_j \\
\vdots & \vdots & \vdots & & \vdots & & \vdots & \vdots \\
c_m \longrightarrow & z_{1,m} & z_{2,m} & \cdots & z_{i,m} & \cdots & z_{n,m} \longrightarrow s_m \\
\end{array}
$$

Fig. 1. Threshold decryption of n participants $\{P_i\}$, m ciphertexts $\{c_j\}$, mn decryption shares $\{z_{i,j}\}$, recovering m secret messages $\{s_j\}$

Techniques presented in [3], [5] and [12] only address batch verification for modular exponentiation. However, tests in [3] can be modified and extended to batch verify PEQDL. Hence, the efficiency of the threshold decryption scheme, as discussed in the previous paragraph, can be greatly improved.

This section presents two theorems on the modified SE test to batch verify PEQDL, i.e: verifying common exponent. Batching verification of common base is also briefly discussed. In Section 4, the theorems are used as a foundation to the applications proposed.

RS test randomly selects subsets of the instances to be verified in avoiding "bad pairs". This test is not sufficiently efficient, and thus is not discussed in this paper. SE test introduces random small exponents on the instances, such that an attacker needs to guess the random values to produce an accepted incorrect batch. This test is more suitable for our purpose and we modify this test on batch verification for PEQDL. Bucket test forms groups of the instances to be batched, and performs random SE tests on them. Our SE test can be extended naturally to Bucket test for batch verifying PEQDL. However, the extension of SE test to Bucket test for batch verifying PEQDL is omitted for simplicity. In the theorems below, we batch the verification of j instances of PEQDL on one participant ($i = 1$), and omit the subscript i.

3.1 Batching PEQDL within the Same Cyclic Group

Theorem 1 provides the foundation for batching PEQDL within the same cyclic group.

Theorem 1. *For $j \in \{1, \ldots, m\}$, G is a cyclic group with q as the smallest factor of $ord(G)$, generators g and c_j, and a security parameter l, where $2^l < q$. The small exponents t_j are random l-bit strings, and $y, z_j \in G$. If $\exists k \in \{1, \ldots, m\} \wedge \log_g y \neq \log_{c_k} z_k$, then $\log_g y \neq \log_{\prod_{j=1}^m c_j^{t_j}} \prod_{j=1}^m z_j^{t_j}$ with a probability (taken over choice of t_j) of no less than $1 - 2^{-l}$.*

To prove Theorem 1, we first prove the following lemma:

Lemma 1. *If $\exists k \in \{1, \ldots, m\} \wedge \log_g y \neq log_{c_k} z_k$, given a definite set $S = \{t_j | t_j < 2^l \wedge j \in \{1, \ldots, k-1, k+1, \ldots, m\}\}$, then there is only at most one t_k satisfying $\log_g y = \log_{\prod_{j=1}^m c_j^{t_j}} \prod_{j=1}^m z_j^{t_j}$, where $j \in \{1, \ldots, m\}$.*

Proof (Lemma 1). If the lemma is incorrect, the following two equations are satisfied simultaneously where $\log_g y \neq \log_{c_k} z_k$ and $t_k \neq t'_k$.

$$\log_g y = \log_{\prod_{j=1}^m c_j^{t_j}} \prod_{j=1}^m z_j^{t_j}$$

$$\log_g y = \log_{(\prod_{j=1}^{k-1} c_j^{t_j})(c_k^{t'_k})(\prod_{j=k+1}^m c_j^{t_j})} (\prod_{j=1}^{k-1} z_j^{t_j})(z_k^{t'_k})(\prod_{j=k+1}^m z_j^{t_j})$$

Suppose $y = g^x$, we re-write the two previous equations as:

$$(\prod_{j=1}^m c_j^{t_j})^x = \prod_{j=1}^m z_j^{t_j}$$

$$((\prod_{j=1}^{k-1} c_j^{t_j})(c_k^{t'_k})(\prod_{j=k+1}^m c_j^{t_j}))^x = (\prod_{j=1}^{k-1} z_j^{t_j})(z_k^{t'_k})(\prod_{j=k+1}^m z_j^{t_j})$$

Without losing generality, suppose $t'_k > t_k$, we can simplify the previous two equations to be $c_k^{x(t'_k - t_k)} = z_k^{t'_k - t_k}$, or $(\frac{c_k^x}{z_k})^{t'_k - t_k} = 1$. As $\frac{c_k^x}{z_k} \in G$, $t'_k - t_k$ is a factor of $ord(G)$ if $\frac{c_k^x}{z_k} \neq 1$. Since $0 < t'_k - t_k < q$, therefore, $\frac{c_k^x}{z_k} = 1$ or $c_k^x = z_k$. This is contradictory to the assumption of $\log_g y \neq \log_{c_k} z_k$. $\square$

Proof (Theorem 1). Lemma 1 means that among the $(2^l)^m$ possible combinations of t_j for $j \in \{1, \ldots, m\}$, at most $(2^l)^{m-1}$ of them can satisfy $\log_g y = \log_{\prod_{j=1}^m c_j^{t_j}} \prod_{j=1}^m z_j^{t_j}$ when $\log_g y \neq \log_{c_j} z_j$. Therefore, given a random t_j for $j \in \{1, \ldots, m\}$, if $\log_g y \neq \log_{c_j} z_j$, then $\log_g y = \log_{\prod_{j=1}^m c_j^{t_j}} \prod_{j=1}^m z_j^{t_j}$ is accepted with a probability of no more than 2^{-l}. $\square$

3.2   Batching PEQDL in Different Cyclic Subgroup of $\mathbb{Z}_p^*$

In Theorem 1, there is a condition that $g, y, c_j, z_j \in G$ for $j \in \{1, \ldots, m\}$. However, in some applications there is uncertainty of satisfaction on this condition, and additional computation is often required to verify the condition. This is a problem ignored by Bellare *et al.* [3]. In reality, this extra computation is too expensive so that in many cases it prevents the applicability of Theorem 1.

To overcome this problem, Theorem 2 is proposed. This theorem does not require the pre-condition that the LHS and RHS of the batching equation be in the same cyclic subgroup of $\mathbb{Z}_p^*$.

Theorem 2. *Suppose p and q are large primes, such that $p = 2q+1$. G, of order q and generator g, is a cyclic multiplicative subgroup in $\mathbb{Z}_p^*$. For $j = 1, \ldots, m$ and $x \in_R \mathbb{Z}_q^*$, $y = g^x, z_j \in \mathbb{Z}_p^*$, l is a security parameter satisfying $2^l < q$ and $t_j \in_R \{1, \ldots, 2^l\}$. If $\exists k \in \{1, \ldots, m\} \wedge \log_g y \neq \log_{c_k} \pm z_k \bmod p$, then $\log_g y \neq \log_{\prod_{j=1}^m c_j^{t_j}} \prod_{j=1}^m z_j^{t_j}$ with a probability of no less than $1 - 2^{-l}$.*

Due to space restrictions and similarity of Theorem 2 and Theorem 1, we defer the proof for Theorem 2 to the full version of the paper.

3.3   Screening

For m ciphertexts processed in threshold decryption, the previous two theorems are suited to batch each verification of valid decryption shares produced by one participant P_i. Thus, if the batch verification fails, we can identify that particular participant to be dishonest. This is examined in detail in Section 4 and Section 5.

In this subsection, we briefly explain another type of batch verifying valid decryption shares using a common base (same ciphertexts, different participants). If there is only one message in the threshold decryption process ($m = 1$), we can slightly modify the two theorems above to verify valid decryption shares produced by all the participants $\{P_i\}$ together as:

$$\log_g(\prod_{i=1}^n y_i^{t_i}) \stackrel{?}{=} \log_c(\prod_{i=1}^n z_i^{t_i})$$

We call this technique 'screening' because it can only detect invalid decryption share(s), but is unable to identify the dishonest participant(s). However, divide and conquer, cut and choose, or binary search method [13] can be applied for identifying the bad decryption share(s), thus identifying the dishonest participant(s). Note that this technique only offers considerable performance increase if used in identifying dishonest participants in a large group (i.e: n is large).

4   Applications in Threshold Decryption

In this section, we present the application of our batching theorems (Section 3) to batch verify threshold versions of two popular cryptosystems - threshold El-Gamal and RSA. We apply Theorem 2 to batch verify threshold ElGamal, and

Theorem 1 to batch verify threshold RSA. The protocols presented in this section are based on Chaum-Pedersen [6] with a slight modification where the verifier randomly selects the small exponents on the first step.

4.1 Batch Verification in ElGamal

Theorem 2 is suitable to batch verify threshold ElGamal as:

1. For threshold version of ElGamal, the group G is the subgroup of $\mathbb{Z}_p^*$ with an order q.
2. For $i \in \{1, \ldots, n\}$ and $j \in \{1, \ldots, m\}$, $v_i \in \mathbb{Z}_p^*$ and $z_{i,j} \in \mathbb{Z}_p^*$ can easily be checked by testing whether $0 < v_i, z_{i,j} < p$.
3. The values $g \in G$ and $\alpha_j \in G$ are publicly verifiable by testing $\left(\frac{g}{p}\right) = 1$ and $\left(\frac{\alpha_j}{p}\right) = 1$ (using the Legendre symbol as in [12]). This proves g and α_j to be generators of G, if $g \neq 1$.
4. For $i \in \{1, \ldots, n\}$ and $j \in \{1, \ldots, m\}$, $t_{i,j}$ can be chosen randomly while still satisfying $t_{i,j} < 2^l < q$.

According to Theorem 2, verification of PEQDL in threshold ElGamal (Equation 1) can be batched using SE test as:

$$\log_g(v_i) = \log_{\prod_{j=1}^m \alpha_j^{t_{i,j}}}\left(\prod_{j=1}^m z_{i,j}^{t_{i,j}}\right) \tag{3}$$

To verify: $\log_g(v_i) = \log_{\alpha_j}(z_{i,j})$, for $i \in \{1, \ldots, n\}$ and $j \in \{1, \ldots, m\}$.

P_i		Verifier
		$t_{i,j} \in_R \{1, \ldots, 2^l\}$
	$\xleftarrow{\quad t_{i,j} \quad}$	
$r_i \in_R \mathbb{Z}_q$		
$\gamma_{i,1} = g^{r_i} \bmod p$		
$\gamma_{i,2} = (\prod_{j=1}^m \alpha_j^{t_{i,j}})^{r_i} \bmod p$		
	$\xrightarrow{\quad \gamma_{i,1},\gamma_{i,2} \quad}$	
		$u_i \in_R \mathbb{Z}_q$
	$\xleftarrow{\quad u_i \quad}$	
$w_i = r_i - u_i d_i \bmod q$		
	$\xrightarrow{\quad w_i \quad}$	
		$\gamma_{i,1} = g^{w_i} v_i^{u_i} \bmod p$
		$\gamma_{i,2} = (\prod_{j=1}^m \alpha_j^{t_{i,j}})^{w_i}$
		$(\prod_{j=1}^m (z_{i,j})^{t_{i,j}})^{u_i} \bmod p$

Fig. 2. Batch verification of valid decryption shares for threshold version of ElGamal cryptosystem.

Interactive batch verification protocol for threshold version of ElGamal is shown in Figure 2. Using a hash function and employing the well-known Fiat-Shamir heuristic [10], the protocol can be made non-interactive by producing the challenge u_i using a collision-resistant hash function H, where $H : (0,1)^* \to \mathbb{Z}_q$ and $j \in \{1, \ldots, m\}$, as follows:

$$u_i = H(\gamma_{i,1}, \gamma_{i,2}, g, v_i, \alpha_j, z_{i,j})$$

Producing the small exponents non-interactively requires a different scenario further explained in Section 5.2. We slightly extend the coin-flipping protocol for the participants to provide a shared source of randomness. This is required in order to prevent a prover from cheating by trying multiple $z_{i,j}$ values until a suitable $t_{i,j}$ value is found. The random values provided are then used to compute the small exponents using a collision-resistant hash function. These are conducted during the shared decryption stage. The protocol to produce the small exponents is shown in Figure 3 and is detailed as below.

1. Each participant (prover) P_i selects a random value τ_i, commits to it using a suitable commitment function, e.g: a hash function as $H(\tau_i)$, and publishes the commitment.
2. Each participant P_i then produces and publishes their decryption share as $z_{i,j} = \alpha_j^{d_i}$.
3. The random value τ_i selected in the first step is then revealed by publishing it.
4. The random small exponents are then calculated using a collision-resistant hash function as: $t_j = H(\tau_i, \alpha_j, j)$, where $i = \{1, \ldots, n\}$ and $j \in \{1, \ldots, m\}$.

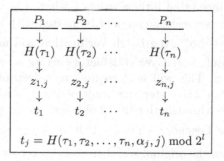

Fig. 3. Producing the small exponents non-interactively

Note that the use of digital signature on the published values is required to authenticate them. Non-interactively, each prover uses the same small exponents t_j as opposed to using different $t_{i,j}$ values provided by the verifier for each prover in the interactive version.

The prover then publishes $(\gamma_{i,1}, \gamma_{i,2}, w_i)$ for public verification. The verification process can be conducted publicly by calculating the small exponents and challenge as above, and checking:

$$\text{To verify: } \log_v(v_i) = \log_{c_j^{4\Delta}}(z_{i,j}^2), \text{ for } i \in \{1,\ldots,n\} \text{ and } j \in \{1,\ldots,m\}.$$

P_i	Verifier
	$t_{i,j} \in_R \{1,\ldots,2^l\}$

$$\xleftarrow{\quad t_{i,j} \quad}$$

$r_i \in_R \mathbb{Z}_N$
$\gamma_{i,1} = v^{r_i} \bmod N$
$\gamma_{i,2} = (\prod_{j=1}^m (c_j^{4\Delta})^{t_{i,j}})^{r_i} \bmod N$

$$\xrightarrow{\quad \gamma_{i,1},\gamma_{i,2} \quad}$$
$$u_i \in_R [0,A)$$
$$\xleftarrow{\quad u_i \quad}$$

$w_i = r_i - u_i d_i$

$$\xrightarrow{\quad w_i \quad}$$
$$\gamma_{i,1} = v^{w_i} v_i^{u_i} \bmod N$$
$$\gamma_{i,2} = (\prod_{j=1}^m (c_j^{4\Delta})^{t_{i,j}})^{w_i}$$
$$(\prod_{j=1}^m (z_{i,j}^2)^{t_{i,j}})^{u_i} \bmod N$$

Fig. 4. Batch verification of valid decryption shares for threshold version of RSA cryptosystem.

$$\gamma_{i,1} = g^{w_i} v_i^{u_i} \bmod N$$
$$\gamma_{i,2} = (\prod_{j=1}^m (\alpha^{t_j})^{w_i}(\prod_{j=1}^m (z_{i,j})^{t_j})^{u_i} \bmod N$$

If all these are satisfied, the verification is accepted. Otherwise, it fails.

We are only convinced that if there exists k where $1 \leq k \leq m$ and $\log_g(v_i^2) = \log_{\alpha_j}(z_{i,j}^2)$, the batch verification can only be passed with negligible probability. Namely, unless $z_{i,j} = \pm\alpha_j^{d_i}$, the batch verification will always fail. Thus, our batch verification result is not yet satisfactory as $s_j = -\alpha_j^{d_i}$ may also satisfy our batch verification. This will lead to incorrect decryption. To fix this, the decryption requires one extra step, i.e: multiplying s_j with (-1) when $s_j \notin G$. After s_j is recovered through the threshold decryption procedure, we test if $\left(\frac{s_j}{p}\right) = 1$ (using the Legendre symbol). If it is accepted, $s_j \in G$. Otherwise, $s_j = -s_j \bmod p$. Then the original secret message is recovered as $\frac{\beta_j}{s_j} \bmod p$. The additional cost is only one exponentiation.

4.2 Batch Verification in RSA

Theorem 1 is applicable to batch the verification of RSA threshold decryption shares as:

1. For threshold version of RSA cryptosystem, G is the cyclic group containing all the squares in $\mathbb{Z}_N^*$ with order $M = p'q'$, the smallest factor of which is $min(p', q')$.

2. The value v is trusted to be a generator of squares in $\mathbb{Z}_N^*$. As v_i is produced using v, and $z_{i,j}^2$ are squares that can be generated by the verifier, thus $v_i, z_{i,j}^2 \in G$ (cyclic subgroup of squares in $\mathbb{Z}_N^*$).

3. The value of $c_j^{4\Delta}$ is a square, and v is trusted to be squares in $\mathbb{Z}_N^*$ chosen by the trusted dealer. Therefore, both $c_j^{4\Delta}, v \in G$. Thus, $c_j^{4\Delta}$ and v are generators of G (see [18]) with a very large probability $(1 - \frac{p'+q'-1}{p'q'})$.

4. For $i \in \{1, \ldots, n\}$ and $j \in \{1, \ldots, m\}$, $t_{i,j}$ can be chosen randomly while still satisfying $t_{i,j} < 2^l < min(p', q')$.

According to Theorem 1, SE test can be implemented as the following:

$$\log_v(v_i) = \log_{\prod_{j=1}^m (c_j^{4\Delta})^{t_{i,j}}} \left(\prod_{j=1}^m (z_{i,j}^2)^{t_{i,j}} \right) \tag{4}$$

Interactive batch verification for threshold version of RSA is shown in Figure 4. Where $A \times ord(G)$ is much smaller than N, the challenge u_i must be chosen in $[0, A)$ such that the shared secret key d_i is statistically hidden in the response w_i as in [15,2]. Analysis in [15] suggests the minimum size of the challenge $|A|$ to be 80 bits, and 128 bits for more secure applications.

Using a hash function and employing the well-known Fiat-Shamir heuristic, the protocol is made non-interactive similar to the previous section. The prover produces the small exponents as shown in the previous section (Figure 3), and produces the challenge u_i using a collision-resistant hash function H, where $H : (0, 1)^* \mapsto \mathbb{Z}_M$ and $j \in \{1, \ldots, m\}$, similar to the previous section as follows:

$$t_j = H(t_1, t_2, \ldots, t_n, \alpha_j, j) \bmod 2^l$$
$$u_i = H(\gamma_{i,1}, \gamma_{i,2}, v, v_i, c_j^{4\Delta}, z_{i,j}^2)$$

The prover then publishes $(\gamma_{i,1}, \gamma_{i,2}, w_i)$ for public verification. The verification process can be conducted publicly by calculating the small exponents and challenge as above, and checking:

$$\gamma_{i,1} = v^{w_i} v_i^{u_i} \bmod N$$
$$\gamma_{i,2} = \left(\prod_{j=1}^m (c_j^{4\Delta})^{t_j} \right)^{w_i} \left(\prod_{j=1}^m (z_{i,j}^2)^{t_j} \right)^{u_i} \bmod N$$

If all these are satisfied, the verification is accepted. Otherwise, it fails.

Unlike in threshold ElGamal, extra verification to ensure that decryption shares passing the batch verification are not $-z_{i,j}$ is not necessary. This is because decryption shares $z_{i,j}$ are explicitly squared in the share combining phase to reconstruct the secret message.

5   Security Analysis

5.1   Completeness

Completeness of each of the two protocols in Section 4 is straight-forward. This is because if the batch verification equations in the two protocols are correct, they output positive results.

5.2   Soundness

The two protocols in Section 4 are very similar. They are based on Chaum-Pedersen's protocol. We slightly modify the protocol where the verifier randomly selects the small exponents at the beginning of the protocol run. The proof of soundness for the protocols follows from Chaum-Pedersen's scheme as they are essentially the same. The small exponents $t_{i,j}$ are chosen randomly in a very similar manner $(t_{i,j} < 2^l)$ to choosing the random challenge.

Given the same random small exponents and commitments, no matter which challenge is chosen, the prover reveals no other information than the fact that the discrete logarithms of the verification key to the base of verification base equals the discrete logarithms of the product of the decryption shares to the base of the product of the ciphertexts (Equation 3 and 4).

In the interactive version, the probability for a prover to cheat is negligible. It is not feasible to forge the decryption shares where the verification is accepted without the knowledge of the share decryption key. Also, where the prover indeed holds the decryption key share, the probability of producing bad decryption shares where the verification is accepted is also negligible. This is because the small exponents and challenge are chosen randomly by the verifier. For example, in batching the verification of correct ElGamal decryption shares, the probability of a prover guessing a correct random small exponent and challenge, and the verification is accepted is $2^{-l}q^{-1}$.

In the non-interactive version, we also follow Chaum-Pedersen's protocol with a slight addition in choosing the random small exponents (Figure 3) based on the coin-flipping protocol. We avoid the use of a hash function with the input (the decryption share $z_{i,j}$) chosen by a single prover to compute the small exponents. This is because it might be possible for a dishonest participant to try fixing the decryption share(s) and produce the small exponents, such that the verification is accepted and the share combining fails. A distributed source of randomness (based on the coin-flipping protocol) is required as the small exponents are only of length l, where l is small.

The probability of a prover forging his decryption share and fixing the small exponent share is negligible. This is because the prover is required to commit to the random share first before publishing his decryption share, and the small exponents are produced by hashing the combined random shares (common reference string) of all the participants. As a collision-resistant hash function is used to produce the small exponents, a prover can only attempt to forge his decryption share if all the participants collude.

The rest of the protocol is a Σ-protocol [7], and thus has a special soundness property as proven in [7]. The proof of soundness for the batching operation has been proven in Section 3.1 and Section 3.2.

5.3   Error Probability

In any of the two batch verification protocols presented, the probability that a dishonest participant is discovered is overwhelmingly large as the following:

- As indicated by Theorem 1, the probability that the batch verification equation is satisfied given incorrect share decryption(s) is 2^{-l}.
- As the prover has to guess the challenge u_i at random, the probability that the batch verification test is accepted where the batch verification equation is not satisfied is $\frac{1}{q}$.
- Therefore, the probability that the batch verification is not accepted given incorrect share decryption is $(1 - 2^l)(1 - q^{-1})$

As q^{-1} is very small, e.g: 2^{-1024}, the probability that a dishonest participant being undetected given incorrect share decryption(s) is approximately 2^{-l}.

6   Efficiency Analysis

Most schemes employing threshold decryption take the decryption process for granted. For example, in the mixnet scheme by Boneh and Golle [4], they focus on improving the efficiency of correct mixing operation and only mention the use of threshold decryption. Using our result, the overall performance of the mixnet scheme can be greatly improved.

We follow Bellare *et al.* in measuring the cost of our algorithms, where $ExpCost^m(l)$ denotes the time to compute m exponentiations in a common base with different exponents of the same length l. The computational cost comparison of naive verification against interactive batch verification for threshold versions of two popular cryptosystems - ElGamal and RSA - is summarised in Table 1 in terms of the number of modular multiplications required.

Suppose $ExpCost(x) = 1.5x$ and $ExpCost^y(x) = y + 0.5xy$. Table 1 also illustrates an example of verifying valid decryption shares from 50 ($m = 50$) ciphertexts for 10 participants ($n = 10$, $\log_2 \Delta \approx 22$), where the length of the integers involved is 1024 bits and the acceptable error is 2^{-20} ($l = 20$). Implemented in the mixnet of Boneh and Golle, our result offers a great reduction of the computational cost in the threshold decryption phase of the shuffled ciphertexts to be decrypted in the final phase of mixnet.

The performance increase in Table 1 is calculated based on the difference of modular multiplication required in the naive and batch version. According to Table 1, it is estimated that performance increase when batch verification is employed would be about 97%.

Our results offer better proving and verification performance, while the probability of an invalid decryption share being accepted is no more than 2^{-l}. When m increases, the computational verification cost saved by using our scheme also increases.

7   Conclusion

The SE test by Bellare *et al.* is originally designed to batch verify modular exponentiations in the context of signature verification. We modified and extended the scheme to batch verify PEQDL in the context of threshold decryption.

Table 1. Performance (number of modular multiplications required) comparison on interactive batch verification of valid decryption shares for threshold versions of two popular cryptosystems, with 10 participants (decrypting authorities, $n = 10$), 50 secret messages to process ($m = 50$), and 2^{-20} acceptable error ($l = 20$).

		Naive	Batch
ElGamal	Each prover	$m(2ExpCost(\log_2 q) + 1)$ $= 153650$	$ExpCost^m(\log_2 l)$ $+2ExpCost(\log_2 q) + 1$ $= 3623$ (97.64% more efficient)
	Verifier	$2nmExpCost^2(\log_2 q)$ $= 1026000$	$n(2ExpCost^m(\log_2 l)$ $+2ExpCost^2(\log_2 q))$ $= 31520$ (96.93% more efficient)
RSA	Each prover	$m(2ExpCost(\log_2 M) + 1)$ $= 153650$	$ExpCost^m(\log_2 \Delta + \log_2 l + 2)$ $+2ExpCost(\log_2 M) + m + 2$ $= 4274$ (97.22% more efficient)
	Verifier	$2nmExpCost^2(\log_2 M)$ $= 1026000$	$n(2ExpCost^m(\log_2 \Delta + \log_2 l + 2)$ $+2ExpCost^2(\log_2 M))$ $= 43520$ (95.76% more efficient)

The scheme presented in this paper greatly improves the efficiency of identifying correct decryption shares (honest participants) with an overwhelmingly high probability when a large number of ciphertexts are involved. The bucket test by Bellare *et al.* (a variant of SE test) can similarly be modified and extended to achieve better efficiency.

It is quite straight-forward to apply the scheme to batch verify decryption shares in threshold version of Paillier cryptosystem [9], similar to that of threshold version of RSA. Due to space constraints, we provide the application in the full version of this paper.

Our scheme can easily be implemented in cryptographic applications employing threshold decryption in lowering their computational cost. This offers great performance benefit to various applications requiring verification of many PEQDLs, such as in secure e-auction or e-voting schemes.

Acknowledgements. We acknowledge the support of the Australian government through ARC Discovery 2002, Grant No: DP0211390; ARC Discovery 2003, Grant No: DP0345458; and ARC Linkage International fellowship 2003, Grant No: LX0346868.

References

1. Masayuki Abe and Koutarou Suzuki. M+1-st price auction using homomorphic encryption. In *Public Key Cryptography—PKC 02*, pages 115–124, 2002.
2. Olivier Baudron, Pierre-Alain Fouque, David Pointcheval, Jacques Stern, and Guillaume Poupard. Practical multi-candidate election system. In *Twentieth Annual ACM Symposium on Principles of Distributed Computing*, pages 274–283, 2001.

3. Mihir Bellare, Juan A. Garay, and Tal Rabin. Fast batch verification for modular exponentiation and digital signatures. In *Advances in Cryptology—EUROCRYPT 98*, pages 236–250, 1998.
4. Dan Boneh and Philipe Golle. Almost entirely correct mixing with applications to voting. In *ACM Conference on Computer and Communications Security—CCS 02*, pages 68–77, 2002.
5. Colin Boyd and Chris Pavlovski. Attacking and repairing batch verification schemes. In *Advances in Cryptology—ASIACRYPT 00*, pages 58–71, 2000.
6. David Chaum and Torben Pryds Pedersen. Wallet databases with observers. In *Advances in Cryptology—CRYPTO 92*, pages 89–105, 1993.
7. Ronald Cramer and Ivan Damgård. Secure signature schemes based on interactive protocols. In *Advances in Cryptology—CRYPTO 95*, pages 297–310, 1995.
8. Ronald Cramer, Rosario Gennaro, and Berry Schoenmakers. A secure and optimally efficient multi-authority election scheme. In *Advances in Cryptology—EUROCRYPT 97*, pages 103–118, 1997.
9. Ivan Damgård and Mats Jurik. A generalisation, a simplification and some applications of paillier's probabilistic public-key system. In *Public Key Cryptography—PKC 01*, pages 119–136, 2001.
10. Amos Fiat and Adi Shamir. How to prove yourself: Practical solutions to identification and signature problems. In *Advances in Cryptology—CRYPTO 86*, pages 186–194, 1986.
11. Pierre-Alain Fouque, Guillaume Poupard, and Jacques Stern. Sharing decryption in the context of voting or lotteries. In *Financial Cryptology—FC 00*, pages 90–104, 2000.
12. Fumitaka Hoshino, Masayuki Abe, and Tetsutaro Kobayashi. Lenient/strict batch verification in several groups. In *Information Security, 4th International Conference, ISC 01*, pages 81–94, 2001.
13. Jaroslaw Pastuszak, Dariusz Michatek, Josef Pieprzyk, and Jennifer Seberry. Identification of bad signatures in batches. In *Public Key Cryptography—PKC 00*, pages 28–45, 2000.
14. Torben P. Pedersen. Non-interactive and information-theoretic secure verifiable secret sharing. In *Advances in Cryptology—CRYPTO 91*, pages 129–140, 1992.
15. Guillaume Poupard and Jacques Stern. On the fly signatures based on factoring. In *ACM Conference on Computer and Communications Security—CCS 99*, pages 37–45, 1999.
16. Kazue Sako. An auction protocol which hides bids of losers. In *Public Key Cryptography—PKC 00*, pages 422–432, 2000.
17. Adi Shamir. How to share a secret. *Communications of the ACM*, 22(11):612–613, November 1979.
18. Victor Shoup. Practical threshold signatures. In *Advances in Cryptology—EUROCRYPT 00*, pages 207–220, 2000.

Author Index